Forever and Two Days More

Our 50-Year Journey

A Memoir by

Cadance & Catherine Anderson

ISBN: 979-8-9896769-1-0

Library of Congress Control Number: 2024932443

info@4everand2daysmore.com

https://www.4everand2daysmore.com

Cadance & Catherine Anderson, Publishers

Tukwila, Washington

Dedication

This book is dedicated to all the lifelong couples who abide through transition. And to our sons, Casey and Corin, who supported us during ours.

Table of Contents

Introduction

This book is set up with parallel, mostly alternating paragraphs covering both Cady and Cathy's same-time experiences. These paragraphs are interposed with other people and experiences. At times, Cady's pronoun use will flow back and forth as she slowly comes to terms with who she truly is. In any event, Cady has always been Cady regardless of other misplaced monikers assigned to her. Cady will not be deadnamed it serves no good purpose, instead. C---- will be used when the need arises.

The book takes place in the time of the Covid plague and recalls the story of Cathy and Cady's meeting each other, becoming a couple, and marriage. Its conclusion is announced as "So closes the autumn of 1974 and part one of our book."

Part two is an interlude of what happened after the wedding, birth of children, and middle age. This comes to an end with the sharing portion of Cady's personal journal started in August 2005.

Cady's personal journal takes over at this point to chronicle all of the events leading to and completing transition. These are the words she wrote day by day as the whirlwind of dysphoria carried the couple from lightning strike to a slow and at times unsteady transition.

The spark that set off this book was the uncovering of forgotten love letters from the summer of 1973… They lay doubled-boxed in a dark corner of our basement, hidden and forgotten under piles of stuff that had accumulated from years of living in our home. It was just by chance in October of 2020, while we were rummaging in the basement, that we came across a very thick cardboard box sealed with all kinds of tape. We had no clue what was inside so imagine our surprise when we opened up the dusty box and there inside were smaller boxes of our old love letters! By the time the Summer of 1973 had waned toward autumn, our love for each had grown to us both adding "Forever and Two Days More" at the close of each letter. It became our code for our vow to trust and love endlessly. We realized the gift we our past selves had sent us. Here, coupled with my journal, was the story of us, waiting to be written for some great-grandchild or other family in need of it...

Cady and Cathy
Forever and two days more
Love everlasting

Timeline Highlights by Year

2005: Starting Therapy with Sandy Fosshage

2006: Starting Laser

2007: Starting Electrolysis and HRT; Coming out to Dr. Marsden

2008: Coming out to Marsha; What My Faith Is

2009: First Solo Grandbabies Sitting

2010: The Dam Is Gone

2011: What I Think About; Effexor Withdrawal

2012: Goodbye J.P. Patches

2013: Being Distracted

2014: Rejection by Doctors

2015: Tracheal Shave; Gender Odyssey; Coming out to Corin

2016: Trail Ride

2017: Esprit Gala; Coming out to Casey

2018: Last Sandy F Appointment; Real Life Cruise; Surgery

2019: Coming out to Family on Our 45th Anniversary

2020: Coming out to Extended Family; So Many Surgeries

2021: Vaginoplasty vs. Vulvoplasty

2022: FFS; Vulvoplasty; Surgeries Complete

Part 1: How We Began

We had all the 2020 Covid 19 barriers to overcome to get into the exam room. I had helped Cathy get into the crinkly paper gown and there she now sits in the exam chair. Here I sit in the visitor chair in the corner. I remind myself that this is her show and she is the star, it is my place to be the alert supporting wife. Still, I think of the times she sat in the visitor corner, five surgeries so far to quiet my gender discord, so it is good for me to be here in her corner now. As long as I have known Cathy she hasn't been fond of her breasts nor was I of mine. If the time was right back then and we could have traded, we most certainly would have. It has always been an amazement how God brought the two of us together, two outcasts in our own way but meshing together to fill each other's voids. Looking back, I wonder how our union, our story, started really?

***

Most stories start at the beginning if you can find it, but what was our beginning? Did it have a singular place and exact time? Was it at our wedding day, proposal day, or some day earlier? Perhaps it was when two high school girls, both in their junior year, schemed to surprise with a birthday cake two senior members of the 'early-morning-before-anyone-gets-here-school-group.' Whose membership was by default limited to totally-under-the-radar-loner-types. Or maybe it was one year earlier when one of the girls, who herself was lost and out-of-place, tried during Piñata making in Spanish class to explain how to properly use dull scissors effectively to an all-but-invisible shy girl standing before her. Or even three years earlier, when a well-meaning middle school English teacher shared a remarkable

4

journal page with that same all-but-invisible shy girl that just happened to be written by that same lonely, lost, out-of-place girl.

***

Whatever the beginning moment, that all-but-invisible shy girl and the lonely out-of-place girl each separately found themselves continually being drawn closer together. Over four years, each would be shaped by life experiences in and out of high school, to become the complement of the other. Their lives would touch and cross, in small vignette encounters year by year, without full recognition of each other's personal journey. The all-but-invisible-girl, in her senior year of high school, battered by bullying and seeing only a foreign male image in the broken bathroom mirror each morning in place of her own, had no future to go to. All that was left to her now was sitting in the cafeteria each morning two hours before the start of school, desperately hoping that the few friends she did have might come sit and talk. Soon, so very soon, they would all be lost to her. No one had ever seen her or heard her truth; no one had ever been her friend. Those few who had come close enough befriended a male image, a construct, not the girl underneath.

It was impossible to have a friend of her own gender because of that male image standing in the way, but one day something happened, something wonderful, something in reality that save her life. Two bright giddy girls walked over to the one lone table set up in the cafeteria early before school. One carried a chocolate frosted chocolate cake and on the cake in white letters was 'Happy Birthday'... You see, the all-but-invisible girl's male image had been befriended, over the years, by a male classmate who was as outrageous and off the wall as any outsider could be. This seemed to make him a bit of a chick magnet to a very small but unique group of girls. His birthday was two days after the all-but-invisible girl's birthday; today was the day that filled the space between them. So here is where the two meet, the lonely out-of-place girl with a crush on the best friend of the male-imaged all-but-invisible girl. The scene is set, all of the crossings, the intersections, of their two separate lives lay in wait at

5

this tipping point, to propel the two of them together for life. Two sizable problems seemed to be an irritant to fate though. First, the lonely out-of-place girl had a crush on the wrong senior. Second, there behind the male image that sat at that table was a broken all-but-invisible girl. She was a product of hiding, hurt, and denial. There was no way to rectify the ongoing identity conflict between mind and body for her. She knew of no real person like her anywhere and learned six years ago to never ask anyone about her brokenness. She denied being female to herself daily but couldn't resolve the feelings of mind-body conflict she had each and every day either. In her view the end of high school was the end of life. All the fragile support structure that held her male image together would have to be rebuilt and it was just too much to bear, better to slip away from life altogether…

***

Cathy was truly out of place starting her 8th grade year at Showalter Middle School and truly lonely. Most of the student body of the South Central School District #406 had been together since early elementary school. They were brothers and sisters following after each other through a cloistered system that had also seen their parents and grandparents as kids. For the most part everyone knew each other and they had the whole school system in common; anyone new was at best a curiosity at worst an outsider. This made it very difficult to establish oneself into the group if you happen to be the new girl from a different school district, especially that being the much bigger Highline School District #401. South Central School district was small. It had a single high school, Foster High School where as Highline had five high schools. The curriculum Cathy was following in her old school was for the most part well ahead of curriculum here. This quickly became apparent in classes, creating an instant stumbling block to inclusion. She was very private even somewhat uncomfortable about her body and this brought bullying in gym that extended into other classes. Her choice in clothes and the colors she enjoyed wearing also added fuel to her bullies. As did her mysterious summer long disappearances to her grandparents' orchard in Eastern

Washington. Since Cathy had been taught that you couldn't do anything but ignore bullies, she chose escape. Cathy escaped into the school library and the cafeteria by volunteering to help, the benefit being these were controlled safe places. The library of course, held nonjudgmental sanctuary in all of its stacks. Cathy's fate seemed now to be fixed to one of loneliness and being continually out of place. There would be little victories, she would befriend a new girl Emily, who herself was an outrageous, introspective loner. Together they would expand each other's world-view and become each other's support in many ways.

***

Cady was an all-but-invisible girl. Anyone who was looking at her saw a fat clumsy boy lumbering around. She came to the South Central School District #406 at the beginning of the eighth grade (just as Cathy did one year later) and found a tightly formed neighborhood of families who had always lived here. Many of the children had the underappreciated richness of living in family generational space. She was ill equipped to fit in anywhere even in the most welcoming neighborhood imaginable. All that was left to her was her imagination. It had helped hold her together during the last two years, in even a more tightly formed place than here. She had lived on a historic 200-acre cattle ranch currently belonging to her grandparents in Eastern Washington. In a little private cemetery in one of the ranch fields stood two stone monuments for the original settlers of the Kittitas Valley F. M. Thorp, Margaret Thorp, Dulcena Splawn, and Violet Splawn. The ranch was located outside of the little proudly unincorporated town of Thorp (population well under 500 people). Thorp had a little two bay firehouse, a poorly lit squeaky floored little Post Office run by the nice lady who lived next to it, a public phone booth, a two-pump gas station, an old country store, the T&E Tavern, a Baptist Church, and a box factory. If you drove west from Thorp you passed an old, abandoned waterwheel powered flour mill on the edge of town and if you continued driving up the Taneum Creek you would reach Cady's grandparents' ranch. Here Cady lived with her grandparents, her mother, and younger brother David although they all knew her by C---- her assigned-at-birth male name. Her grandparents had rescued the three castaways when, after the divorce, her mother couldn't make the mortgage payment and the homeowners insurance was canceled because, well, mom was a single female parent (yes it was a weird ugly time then). A 1960s style divorce had stigmatized the three of them, leaving the little broken family to be shunned in the little suburban community they lived in north of Seattle. Losing the house made them castaways they needed rescuing. Cady had been so happy there before the divorce, she had friends all around her, each summer day was full of play and the ever growing mind/body discord was just an odd feeling she didn't fully understand.

With the remarrying of Cady's estranged dad to her mom a reformed family moved back to Western Washington, this time south of Seattle. Cady always wondered what drove her father to abandon them and what drove her father back to reclaim them. Cady started at the middle school and her younger brother David at one of the elementary schools. Cady had been traumatized during her time in the little school in very rural Thorp. There was a certain amount of physical violence directed at her, but this was considered normal behavior for boys in a country setting. The problem that shook her to the core was P. E. she could not force herself to go into the boys' locker room. She had no idea what was going on! Yes the mind/body conflict was greater now and yes in her dreams she was female, but she had never had an attack such as this. As she came to the doorway leading to the boys' locker room something in her mind screamed that this was wrong and she couldn't go any farther. Cady in panic turned and ran down the hallway to a seldom-used bathroom and hid. She cowered in self-imprisonment with the darkest of personal demons pointing and laughing at her for an hour a day. This was a very old sleepy country school that rested in a pocket of an older time, some of the desks had spaces for inkwells to drop into; the aged wood trim all around was dark amber and the floors ancient from generations of footsteps squeaked. It had been the only school building for time out of mind until a more modern utility looking high school building was built next to it. The only other staff aside from the teachers themselves was a single custodian and two lunch ladies. Yet there among the strict black and white of a country school was a kind of gentle grey area. That gentle grey area was granted to Cady; for the six months of winter P. E. (which required a change into indoor P. E. clothes) she hid in that bathroom listening for anyone who might come near and returned to class with the rest of the boys after P.E. was over. No one said a thing about her absence or came looking for her, she was even given credit for the P.E. class… No one looked for her before class each morning cither. The old tinny school bus got Cady and her brother to school forty minutes before the start of class each morning. The door to Mr. Taylor's split fifth/sixth grade classroom would be locked until just before class; fortunately for her brother Mrs. Ozanich's lower grade classroom opened up early. The gloomy hallway was not a good place to wait it teamed with juvenile judgment. Cady had found a dark room with an unlocked door to hide out in. It was the elementary school's mostly unused library. Here she read book after book of science fiction (including *The Universe Between* by Alan E. Nourse who happened to live in seclusion up the Taneum Creek Canyon near the ranch) sitting under a table in the shadows until the minute before class was to start. It was a painful escape as for some reason she had to reread each page several times over before understanding the words; years later as an adult she would come to understand she was dyslexic. Cady was left with the inescapable fact that something was wrong in her brain; she turned into herself looking for answers and found none during her two year career here.

She has now been delivered to a new school in a sudden paradigm shift, it's 8th grade, and she has totally isolated herself to hide the terrible truth that she is a fraud. She is hiding a secret that despite her outfacing male image something was wrong in her brain she felt female.

***

Cathy added to her isolation in this new school by getting 4.0 grades. She had the same gentle hearted scholastically minded English teacher as Cady had the year before. Mrs. Kate Ostrom believed in and required daily journals. You could write about anything, Cathy would write about her life, her split time each year between Western and Eastern Washington the urban and the rural. Cathy's grandparent's orchard was five miles outside of the little town of Quincy, which is 50 miles further east from Cady's grandparent's ranch outside of Thorp. The orchard was 188 acres planted with apples, five acres of cherries and 20 acres shared between other fruits and vegetables. Cathy also wrote about the ponies at the orchard and how she rode one particular pony each summer day to go get the mail. She journaled about evenings sitting along the irrigation canals watching the water flowing dreamily by and what it was like to walk bare-footed in the thick dust covering the tree lanes. Cathy touched on being out of step and not belonging since her family had sold their first house to move to this current home. She fondly remembered Sunnydale Elementary School from her old home and neighborhood in Burien. She even continued to go to the Camp Fire group from her old neighborhood because of the acceptance she felt there. Cathy didn't fully find the acceptance she yearned for in this new place and the summers of isolation in Eastern Washington changed her. She was introspective, her own best company, and lonely. Cathy's younger brothers and sister all seem to fit into their new schools while she was adrift. She had found two friends Emily and Sandy both new to the district and therefore outsiders; this gave her some balance and a form of default acceptance. Emily would also lead Cathy in adventures when high school came around for the two of them.

***

This middle school accepts Cady as a loner who disappears whenever possible. She doesn't join in any activities before or after school, is quiet and awkwardly shy. She seems to always be looking over her shoulder, is clumsy because of her weight, and ill clothed. Cady is bullied by a small group of boys. One in particular that hurts her immeasurably almost seems to know the secret she keeps deep inside. Her tormentor pokes daily insults liking her to an ugly girl among other things. These taunts land too close to her hidden truth and she yearns for the only true escape in life that of death itself. Cady disappears each summer to help on her grandparent's ranch. This further isolates her from the neighborhood she lives in during the school year just as it does with Cathy who spends her summers at the orchard. So, each school day is hell but even within hell there are a few small victories. Best friend to be Michael Deraitus befriended the male-imaged Cady as she stood outside the middle school side door during lunch one day. She was hiding from everyone as she always did, when Michael came outside to ask a sullen Cady for her vote for ASB Vice President. They talked for a few minutes as Michael explained the qualities he would bring to the office of ASB. He was shorter than Cady, had short dark hair and wore thick black-framed glasses fastened in the back with an elastic band. Secretly she felt she now had a friend. Together as the school year played out they would expand each other's world-view and become each other's support.

***

Cathy's sophomore year brought her to acquaintance standing with several other girls. Not quite friends but a feeling of oasis in the desert of isolation. This was also the greatest year of bullying for her to endure. The greatest bullying occurred in classes where she was doing better than anyone else in that subject and of course in P.E. In fact, had Cady known the level of bullying that could happen in the female side of P.E., she would have added it to her growing list she kept of why being female is too hard. Cathy was a hold-your-head-up, ignore it, and don't react person. She was strong but there are limits, something had to give or this was going to be a crash and burn year for her. Cathy was open for such a thing to come along; she was also missing her church family from the old neighborhood. She enjoyed Sunday school there and being a part of the church congregation. Her family had dropped going to church after the move and her mom never got around to starting again. Cathy saw a post on the school entrance bulletin board announcing a Young Life Ministries meeting after school in the Home-Ec room. She checked a box in her mind to stay late after school tomorrow and ride the second bus home. Next day she walked into the Home-Ec room and became the acquaintance of Debbie, Vickie, and Jan. The girls casually chatted together after an opening prayer. The little meeting was closed by an announcement that there was to be a Halloween haunted house in the parsonage at Church By the Side of the Road (CBSR). That church was currently without a pastor so the parsonage was vacant and could host such an event. Cathy was excited by the prospect of the haunted house, here was a path to fit in again or come as close as she dared hope for. Cathy's mom wasn't as excited; CBSR was a full gospel church and she didn't know much about that denomination. They had been Presbyterian but in the end she did give her permission. Cathy is under 16 at this time so her dad drove her over with admonishment for Cathy to call him if she couldn't get a ride home. The party had food, games, a little sermon and lots of noisy chatter after. It ended with call to come to church at CBSR this Sunday. An older boy with a car was offering rides home for all interested, Cathy and four other girls accept his invitation. She called her dad and told him she had a ride home and would be home soon. Cathy opened her front door that night with the resolve to go to CBSR on Sunday.

***

Cady was heartsick from the spot-on bullying but there was nothing to be done about it. The only thing for it was to get away from the bullies. This was impossible during shared classes and in the common hallways, but there were a few classes without the beasts hounding her. Cady used two tactics to avoid trouble in the form of bullying; she never ate lunch at school and she never used the restrooms at school. Her house was nearby (this was a true gift from God) and she just left and went home when the need arose. Yes it was a closed campus, but she just did it and just as with hiding in the bathroom in Thorp, no one said a thing about it. The bullying has also set up a denial response in Cady's mind about the whole mind/body conflict; she can be a boy there is no other path she just hoped that life would be short. Cady also found a path to tolerating the boys' locker room, stay in a corner, just look down, dress quickly, and never shower. Bullying was not tolerated in gym class, but on the other hand it wasn't needed, the class itself was a sort of bully. Cady was tall, fat, clumsy, slow, and weak. All she had was mass and it was hard to move mass around, it was amazing how fast the few muscles she had developed from summer ranch work faded away in the fall. Of course, this was because she was completely sedentary hiding at home. Then there was food (anything sweet) her one great escape drug. Cady loved English class and loved to write especially in a required daily journal. She had anxieties with spelling and math that stood in the way of her love of writing and science. She could never tackle study problems directly but always had to find a way around being so very poor in both.

***

Cathy had found her home church in CBSR, all the girls she had met in the Young Life Haunted House party also went to this church. She attended Sunday school at 10:00am but would be at the sanctuary by 9:30 to socialize with the other girls before the start. Next came the main service, which ran from 11:00 to 12:30 then of course more socializing afterward and back home at 1:00. Cathy also attended evening service from 6:00 to 7:30pm. After service she would go out with a group for ice cream at Farrell's Ice Cream Parlor and be home again by 9:30pm. In addition, she joined Youth Group these meetings were on Tuesday for outings to Zenith nursing home. In theory, Cathy had regained the inclusion she had lost with the move from her old neighborhood. In reality, school and her place in it remained the same as it was before and now new pressures have come to invade her new church space. Single teens in Youth Group had a tendency to pressure each other into forming couples. This naturally happened, but single late-teenaged boys especially one who had left his teen years behind him, was frowned upon. The place at that age should be the Young Adult Group to find your mate. Cathy was fifteen, unattached, and he fancied her even though their age difference was over five years. Enough to say there was pressure to be a couple it brought status to Cathy and a place at the female table of respect. It was a mistake, a questionable union at best that would take her over a year to free herself of leaving a path open to be happily single again.

***

Cady's senior year of 1973 brought release in many forms. She had become surprising good in electronics class to the point that a separate advance self-study class was formed just for her, for the first time in her life she beamed with pride. All the bullying had faded especially after sophomore year was over. She took all the sciences the school offered leaving the general classes and her bullies behind. The heartache that P.E. always had been to her was over as now it was no longer a required class. Each morning she escaped from home very early to sit in the near empty school cafeteria with her best friend Michael. Some mornings she even caught up with him as he walked by her home. They had grown up together through their shared time in and around high school. They learned the art of the Northwest form of humor each morning before school at Cady's house by watching a kids' show starring a clown named J. P. Patches. This had become a tradition over the years and often included a second friend. Michael came along to Friday night drive-in movies with Cady's dad Merrill and brother David. He played pool on a table in Cady's basement. Cady knew many of her friend's secrets but he had no clue of hers. She had gone on adventures led by Michael; they had walked the streets all around her home well after midnight and well before dawn. That time when nerves are stretched tight and the adolescence mind is wide-eyed. They had slept in the same bedroom at Cady's house but still he had no clue what lay in her deep still waters. Again, Cady knew much about his deep waters, his hopes, his yearning to experience the raw world of Alaska, his rebellious act in learning to play guitar despite his parents' objection. Time with Michael was now precious; soon he would be gone to Pullman to University leaving her alone to face the end of her life…

***

Cathy's junior year brought a break-up with her first and only boyfriend. He was five years her senior and she expected her parents breathed a sigh of relief at her news. She was free emotionally or at least thought she was, but to what end? She was still the same outcast girl who had been bullied in the most cruel way; the way that seemed to hit right at some dark internal fear she had. She had become more self-reliant after the break up, she now understood how domineering he had been, how abusive, and that feeling of dread she had when she was with him was now gone. Cathy felt like a great weight was lifted off her shoulders, new possibilities were now within sight. She had been in a one-sided broken relationship and wondered what it would be like to be in a truly equal one. It was an odd thought really, male and female wise, you would need to find a totally under the radar type of guy. He would have to be kind of outrageous and fly outside of the given gender norms sort of guy. Perhaps, kind of like her friend Emily did from time to time; Emily called Cathy 'Cat' and she liked that. So, with this vaguely exact idea she took notice of Michael. Michael was well outside of everyone and everything to the contrary point that he looked like he comfortably belonged in all of the social groups in our High School, everything from the druggies to the intellectuals. Yes Michael was very intriguing…

***

Senior year moved too quickly from fall to early spring for Cady. It wasn't without turmoil; summers at the ranch had given her the strangest experience, she had crossdressed for the first time there. The experience was disturbingly alluring; to see herself as herself for the first time in a full-length mirror was the most freeing and troubling experience she ever had. There was no role model to turn to for understanding, no book to read for guidance, just she herself alone in an impossible place to try to come to terms with an impossible truth. The ranch was isolated she was often alone and each time she crossdressed she grew a little more into her true self. Even after some sort of climax it wasn't over; she wanted to be herself, the girl she saw in the mirror always, she lingered as long as possible until fear of discovery drove her away. She had seen herself in that mirror and her life would never be the same from that moment on. The feeling of guilt and shame that came afterwards was terrible. Then the fear that like her mother she had some sort of mental illness also fed her silence in carrying her secret. Her grandmother had died in her junior year she was the only person to have known about Cady's crossdressing the only one she trusted. Cady now wrapped herself in a cloak of hopeless steel with a sad outward facing male image for protection.

***

We had overcome the 2020 Covid 19 barriers once again and were allowed into the reception office of the plastic surgeon. After which, we are again in the same exam room where Cathy had her consult for breast reduction four weeks ago. My place again is in the chair in the corner while Cathy is center stage in the exam chair. Dr. Megan Dreveskracht had gained Cathy's confidence with steady direct answers to all of her questions. Confidence enough for Cathy to book her surgery with a deposit on that first visit. Here we are at her pre-op appointment. I am trying to be a good supporting wife by remembering all the pre-op instructions coming at her. Unfortunately, at sixty-six my memory is as old as I am making it an arduous task. Our youngest son suggested just recording the whole thing on my phone clandestinely. I thought about it only fleetingly before dismissing it. Jasmine another medical assistant, is filling us both in on all that will happen next week on surgery day. She is also asking her own set of questions of Cathy. Cathy is very prepared she has a copy of the Mammogram finding and the clearance for surgery from her Primary Care Doctor just in case they didn't get to the office by mail. Yes, they both were needed, for some reason the two reports didn't get delivered to the office. Score Cathy! I offer my name to Jasmine and Cathy offers my relation as wife for Jasmine to record in Cathy's chart. It is dawning on Cathy that this surgery is really going to happen and now the excitement is beginning to really build up. I know this feeling well now, having a problem for like always, then suddenly, there is this physical correction available and it's going to happen right now! Cathy stops at the reception desk to pay for the surgery in full before we leave. Cathy is on cloud nine but we will be back tomorrow for my consult with Dr. Megan. I had this idea that it would be a good to have Dr. Megan's advice on my FFS (facial feminization surgery) list of surgeons too. I would have all of Cathy's coming experience with her to give me confidence and Cathy would get one more chance to chat with Dr. Megan in person since she would be with me tomorrow.

***

Cady felt her world spinning into darkness all around the bright spot of the last few months of her senior year of 1973. Her brother David had fallen deeper and deeper into drug abuse. The younger brother she knew seemed to melt away more each day into a total stranger seemly bent on self-destruction. She tried with words; she tried with force, both to keep him safe but in the end both failed terribly. David was a drift from school and had abandoned all his friends except the few who like himself never wanted to come down from a perpetual high. Her parents in a downward spiral were drifting apart once again. Cady's mother, as loving as her heart was, also battled mental illness the symptoms of which were increasing day by day. The pressure of her son David's troubles, added to the recent loss of her own mother, to be then followed by her father quickly remarrying only added volatile fuel to her mental fire. Cady's father, who was ever seeking a more spirit filled church, moved often from one church to another, and in doing so tended to adopt troubled youth; often her home had strangers hanging around. Cady's father Merrill from his boyhood was in a constant searching rigor, day after day, year after year looking for someplace for his restless spirit to find peace in. He was forever burdened to find a spiritual answer to a very troubling and intensely personal internal question. So, Cady's escaping to the high school each morning was just that; an escape into a world she finally felt she had a handle on. She knew this world was so very short lived, but after eighteen years of turmoil it's peaceful consistency was a daily blessing. Even so, an odd new facet had formed out of that consistency, one that seemed to swoop right into the nest Cady had become used to occupying with her friend Michael each school morning. The routine was she and Michael would meet well before school began each morning at the only unfolded table in the corner of the sleepy cafeteria then sit and chat. The more bizarrely funny their conversation was with each other the better. As the morning oozed along several other acquaintances would stop by for a few minutes of comic chatter. It became a show of sorts for the pair to perform; once a friend Dennis stopped by just to take down the patter on paper. When asked what he was doing by Cady, Dennis replied he had a 'Theater of the Absurd' assignment in English due that morning. Dennis was all smiles the next day from the grade he got on that paper. Throughout high school a protective chrysalis bubble had always held the relationship of Cady to Michael separating it from the outside forces of family, friends, and adolescence. Summers would separate them, but as soon as fall came, Cady would meet up with Michael and slip right back into that chrysalis just as if their separate life experiences hadn't touched either one. Their relationship was the center of the storm, always unchanged while the rage of the storm continued all around it. So, it was for Cady anyway, she continually stood in the rage of her personal storm, but within that relationship with Michael the quiet of the storm prevailed. To anyone viewing this relationship, these were two male buddies thoroughly enjoying each other's company with joke after joke. Cady didn't understand yet who or what she was, but the structure of the relationship gave her a place to be her male image with minimum conflict. Over the years, there had never been any girls within their company of friends, just other boys drifting in and out. Conversations very rarely had any hint of gender at all, instead they would speak of the drama of the natural world, of the quiet places they had each experienced away from the urban noise. Humor would be ever-present, breaking right into the poetry of the woods along with how funny J.P. Patches was this morning. Cady was always curious about Michael's life, living vicariously was something she couldn't escape. It was the temporary glue she used to hold her fracturing mind/body together. Both Cady and Michael never spoke

18

of being anything but single, in fact, Michael's mantra was to live the hermit life supreme. This had been the way of it until this last year of high school at Foster, but not anymore. The change came in the guise of a new facet to their relationships' dynamic, that being the inclusion of girls, or we should say the invasion of. Because it happen as such with Cathy and Lydia showing up with a birthday cake one morning creating a new paradigm from a broken chrysalis. It was comical in a tragic way (which was appropriate really considering the love of any form of comedy Cady and Michael had), as two special girls swept in targeting Michael but also including Cady.

**

Cathy had never had many friends mostly because finding shared common experiences to work toward didn't present themselves with any regularity. She had a circle of friends, some more some less, at the Church's youth group when she had a boyfriend there. They were a couple then. The other girls respected this and gave her a place at the table of female fellowship, even though some questioned her choice of the boyfriend. Now she was free, but the moniker of 'couple' was lost to her and she slid back from that table of female fellowship. Cathy was single, but at a high price the eventual loss of her church family. Cathy's ex-boyfriend continued to go to the church. The breakup had been more of an escape from him and now he continued to pursue her at church. It had been a very hard life lesson for her and she swore she would never go back to him or those like him. A modicum of respect remained as she had accomplished the 'couple' state once so could do it again, even if she could no longer go to CBSR.

Cathy's brother Phil her junior by seventeen months was one class behind her. He was attracting the attention of girls his age and was dating Celia one half of a set of twins. Her sister Lydia occasionally made an appearance at Cathy's home and they had traded conversation. The Dixon home was full of the comings and goings of Cathy, her two brothers Phil and Mark, and sister Linda. One early morning before school Cathy and Lydia wandered into the cafeteria separately, but with the same destination in mind the lone table in the corner. About that table, each night to clean the cafeteria floor all the tables were folded up and wheeled away to a storage area under the stage at one end of the cafeteria. School custodians are indeed a very special breed; working amongst a sea of young people they too are subject to the ebb and flow of adolescent life. The difference is custodians have life experience and therefore wisdom. The head custodian arrives well before he has to each morning and unlocks the cafeteria. He rolls out one table, unfolds it, and leaves it sitting in the far corner. He has seen the need over many years for this seed of placement to the adolescent day. He leaves to unlock the many doors around the school knowing that some young person will be sitting at that table before he is through; it has never failed in all his years. At that table Cady, whose birthday it is, and Michael are holding a court of sorts and as local friends drift in the chatter rolls on. This morning Cathy is grateful to have gotten up early to be here and when she sees Lydia she has a slight flash of annoyance. Lydia is bouncy and breezes right to the table and sits on the bench on Michael's side. Michael cranes his neck in his best imitation of a mischievous puppy looking sideways. Cathy has moved to sit across from her, the side Cady is on. Michael flies away from that moment of recognition of Lydia and delves into chatter with everyone at the table. Lydia has a little bit of a past with Michael, they were at the same school camp together one year. Cathy found herself intrigued with Michael she played with her perceptions of him, his curly dark hair, his boisterous matter full of mini explosions of mirth, he played guitar, and always seemed to be in motion toward some exciting life destination. Lydia was busy flirting in her own distinct style; perhaps style wasn't the right word, a more descriptive word like chaos that's the one coming into Cathy's mind. The morning bell was near to ringing and Michael and Cady both got up to leave. Cathy watched the pair amble away toward the far door. They were both a mystery and she liked mysteries. Michael lurched forward in spurts making changes in direction with each step while Cady seemed to make allowance for these changes without misstep almost like a couple. Of the two Cady was the greater mystery there was something uniquely hidden about this person. Lost in thought until Lydia blurted, "Tomorrow is the day they share between their birthdays. It would be so cool to do a birthday cake, it will drive them crazy!" Cathy was more than up for the challenge, "I can drive us to Lucky's Grocery to get what we need to do the cake." Cathy thought, "Today was Cady's birthday and it didn't seem like anything was being done to celebrate it." Cathy was becoming excited with the anticipation of rectifying this offence.

Cathy asked to use the family car and explained her plan. Her mom gave permission in the parental matter of okay, but be careful. Her mom was happy to see Cathy was indeed over her ex-boyfriend and interested in someone more near her age. Cathy drove to Lydia's home to find her partner in crime overflowing with excitement of pulling off the coup of the year. They exchanged small talk, as Cathy drove to South Center Mall where Lucky's Grocery sells the food of life. Parking was easy, Cathy found a pull through so she didn't have to back up going out. There was giggling going on, neither girl could help it and neither wanted to. It was the coolest thing to do. They got the cake mix and a container of chocolate frosting at Lucky's but had to go to Pay 'n Save to find the candles and birthday cards. Lydia announced, "I'm going to buy a card for Michael." Cathy had studied Michael and the other girls that also drifted over to sit at the table in the corner. Janice was such a girl. Cathy had seen the way Janice had looked and acted around Michael. There was a familiar interplay developing between them. Cathy had chatted with Janice enough to know she was getting a card for Michael too. A sudden realization formed into a certainty. Cathy told Lydia, "I'm going to buy a card for Cady." At that moment Cathy felt a common bond with Cady. Cathy had been hurt many times by being left out, to be one sitting on the sidelines while others stand in the spotlight. It wasn't fair and she wasn't going to let it happen to Cady! Cathy and Lydia walked back to the car to find that the headlights were still on. Cathy thought, "I'll have to call Dad," it was the last thing she wanted to do. She tried the key in the ignition and the car started right up! Lydia decided to let Cathy make the cake and waved as Cathy pulled away from Lydia's home. As Cathy mixed the cake batter she thought of the kind thing she was doing for Cady. That thought reshaped itself into not a simple act of kindness, but one she wanted to do with all her heart. She started to put together all the little pieces of what she had come to know about the mystery that was Cady; they began to form the frame of a picture that she mentally gazed at and smiled about tomorrow.

***

Cady drifted through her 19th birthday as if it was just any other day at school, it was all very low key as all of her birthdays had always been. She enjoyed the freedom she had been given by independent study in electronics and being lab assistant to the lower electronic class gave her a sense of respect she hadn't ever had before. After school she walked home alone; Michael only had half a day at school this year, the other half he spent at the rocky beach of Seahurst Park. The Occupational Skills-Marine Technology Center located at the very far end of the park is shared by several high schools. Its charter is to teach the biology of the ocean and the art of seamanship. Michael loved this place; he was coming into his own emancipation here with a set of common friends from Foster at his side. Together they let the male rowdiness flow and boy it sure did. This wasn't Cady's world; despite her minimal math skills she took all the traditional sciences Foster had to offer, but in only one did she shine that was Electronics (A+ the only one Mr. Rapp had ever given). Still, she did have her mornings with Michael to look forward to sitting at the lone table over in the corner of the cafeteria.

The one great advantage to the little two bedroom house Cady and her family lived in was its daylight basement. Cady's dad had bought a Sears seven-foot pool table that just fit into the finished part of the basement. Cady and David's basement instantly became an after school hangout. Cady being older garnered most of the time with her friends here. One day Lydia knocked on the downstairs basement door, Cady was there alone poking at the pool balls hoping someone might show up. Cady opened the door to be surprised and perplexed by Lydia who waltzed right in. "Hi, you are looking for someone?"

Cady questioned. "Just thought Michael might be here," Lydia responded. She moved close to Cady and Cady backed uncomfortably away. Lydia giggled, "Can we play pool?" Cady replied, "Sure, I guess so." Male-imaged Cady hoped that someone would show up soon; she didn't care to be alone with Lydia for some reason. Lydia had discovered the power of her beauty and art of flirting that naturally followed this discovery. Cady understood that Lydia was flirting now and she didn't like it at all, for some reason it was playing havoc with her mind/body conflict. Lydia leaned over to shoot the cue ball and smiling looked up at Cady. The same panic feeling that had happened at the door to the boy's locker room years ago was screaming now in Cady's mind. She mumbled, "I have to do stuff, you should go." Lydia teased, "What if I don't want to go?" Cady was helpless and being cornered by a girl two-thirds her height. Cady all but pleaded, "Lydia please go." Lydia giggled moving so close she almost touch Cady's chest. Cady looked into her eyes and saw them seeming to search side to side rapidly, Cady looked down and noticed Lydia's shoes. They were too big for her feet so she had stuffed Kleenex in the backs of the heels. Cady turned away pleadingly, "Please Lydia it's time for you to go." Lydia stepped back teasingly and walked out the door. Cady was relieved, but deeply troubled by how she felt inside and though she didn't know it at the time, she had just been labeled as 'gay' by Lydia. Male-imaged Cady had never had a girlfriend in her nineteen-year life, she had never been kissed by a girl or desired to kiss a girl. She had internally longed to be female and all that it entailed. Since that was just plain sick, it said so right in the Bible, and is impossible physically, she gave no thought to sexuality whatsoever; it was a dead thing to her. It all didn't matter anyway; everything was either coming to an end or crashing down around her very soon. She climbed the outside stairs to the front door of her house and closed it behind her as she entered. It was her birthday as simple as it would be. She and David shared a bedroom, she didn't know if he would be there or not. Mom would be home soon and Dad, well maybe. Tomorrow morning will be here soon and she could escape once more to the school cafeteria.

***

Cathy was excited! The birthday cake sat on the front seat between her and her brother Phil. Cathy had been driving to school in the family car more and more. Her dad had a little red Datsun pickup truck he used to drive to Boeing and her mother as a student rode the city bus to Highline College daily. This left the station wagon free for Cathy's use to and from school. Of course, there were restrictions, she had to bus whatever brother or her sister to whatever place they needed to be. Today though it was just Phil catching a ride and not caring what she was up to. Parking was easy in the student lot this time of morning so no trouble being close to the cafeteria. The parking lot itself was a paved hillside and many a shabby student car was compression started by rolling from the top of the slope to the bottom. Again, Cathy was excited, her heart was fully vested into how cool this surprise was going to be for Cady and for Michael, but especially for Cady. Cathy waited just outside of the cafeteria door for Lydia to show up. Cathy pondered as she waited; excitement was driving her emotions all morning, but her sensible side checked off just what she wanted to convey to Cady, "Please be impressed with the caring I am showing to you Cady, you are special today and I would like to get to know you." Yes, that sensible side of Cathy was now satisfied and if Lydia would just get here the excited emotional side would also be.

Lydia came up to Cathy in little quick steps, "Let me see the cake. Where did I put that card?" Cathy waited until the whirlwind that was Lydia calmed down and together they marched into the cafeteria to that lone table in the corner and its unsuspecting occupants. Before even reaching the table Lydia was squealing, "Happy Birthdays!" Michael, who always sat with his back to the wall saw the pair coming toward them. Cady always sat across from Michael and had to turn around. This is it, thought Cathy and put the cake down right in the middle of the table. She told Cady directly, "It's for you both." Lydia had already moved to sit next to Michael. Cathy stood next to Cady administrating the cake cutting. She handed Cady the birthday card and said, "Along with this!" Cady was dead silent for a moment then a blush flowed across her face. It was like a locked away joyful emotional storm was trying to get out, but there was no way it could. A faint smile of being loved spread on Cady's face and in an instant Cathy was never so gratified by anything she had done before for anyone.

"Thank you, oh thank you!" came from Cady. Michael was deeply surprised and touched also, but kept his comic face on. Michael was also taken aback by his friend Cady's reaction. He had never glimpsed this odd side of her in all of their comings and goings. The drama continued in a new direction when Janice came slide-stepping (a sort of skating without skates) into the cafeteria right over to the under-the-radar-types' table. She paused behind Lydia sizing up the distance between Michael and Lydia. In a single graceful movement, she wedged herself between Michael and Lydia on the bench seat. Lydia was scooted over and Janice gained purchase right next to Michael. Michael tried to keep a straight face, but couldn't contain the hilarity from bursting out all over. He made noises and made faces and loved the whole attention getting thing. Unseated, Lydia still gave Michael a hug much to his chagrin and to annoy Janice. Cathy and Cady were now the audience only as the focus switched to this new drama across from them.

The party broke up at first bell; Cathy headed to her locker then off to English Class with Mr. Escame. She felt warm all over from this morning's drama. In some ways the reaction she felt her kindness had gotten from the boys wasn't as great as it could have been. There weren't any hugs or big fireworks and then the drama Janice brought into the group took some of her attention away. Yet, there was this deep feeling of gratification she felt from the self-muted reaction Cady had given her. Cathy satisfied herself with, "At least now I am part of a group, even if it is a group of castaways." Cathy thought about the mystery Cady was to her, after the aggression of her only other boyfriend, the idea of peeling back whatever shell Cady seemed to have could be a very worthwhile.

***

25

Michael had been his jovial self that morning on their day between their birthdays. The cafeteria was in its quiet sleepy state before the herds of adolescent charm would migrate through the place toward various cells of learning. This is the one day that Cady would gain two years of age past Michael, tomorrow it would return to only one year separating the two of them. Ray Bradbury's book *Something Wicked This Way Comes* has two central characters Jim Nightshade and William Halloway. These two were separated by two minutes at birth; William born one minute before midnight Oct. 30 and Jim one minute after midnight Oct. 31. Cady loved to think of her and Michael on this day 'between' as akin to William and Jim of that book. In some ways they had the opposing traits of those two characters. At length Michael and Cady would walk side by side. Given the slightest provocation Michael would rush into the dark to explore, while Cady would hold back even though she would eventually follow on her own terms. Michael was freeing himself more and more of the bonds that had hindered him from childhood. His stepfather, the only man he had ever known as Dad, had held a tight rein on him as childhood marched by. Even granting the intention of this action was supposed to be for his own good; Michael chaffed at this rein stubbornly, he crafted plans, and acted upon them. Cady many times was simply pulled along by the vortex created by Michael speeding past her. No one was reining in Cady there was no need to. Life itself held a tighter rein on her than any parent ever could. In theory, she could do or go almost anywhere, this greatly impressed Michael, but in fact she was highly self-restricted, this at times baffled Michael. Michael craved the sense of wild abandon or at least the image of it. He viewed Cady as an equal in this craving, but would overlook her hesitancy on account of their friendship. Cady had fearful secrets to bear, to keep hidden both from herself and anyone coming near. The resulting cost was the loss of her self-worth. In her mind everything about her physical self was grotesquely mismatched. Above all she had to keep this awful truth from coming out. She had to constantly guard against any slip of a word or an action that might give her away. This kept her tightly in check, her love of having a soul friend in Michael allowed her to stretch her boundaries. Cady's back was to the cafeteria itself she faced her friend who kept his back to a wall. He always sought out a commanding view of what was coming toward him. Cady verbally fenced with Michael as he tossed out comic phrase after phrase as thrusts for her to parry. Michael's attention was drawn somewhere over Cady's shoulder. Cady turned to see Cathy and Lydia coming toward them. Cathy was carrying something with her two hands and Lydia was just being a little too bubbly for this time of morning. Lydia walked right past Cady over to Michael's side of the table and with a flourish sat down. Cathy came to stand at the end of the table next to Cady. Lydia was bubbling, "Happy Birthday" all over Michael. And Cathy looked right into Cady eyes saying, "This is for you both on your special day between." Cady was dumbfounded, this was the second girl in her lifetime to look her directly in the eyes. They being the windows to your soul, the ones she kept carefully curtained. Unlike the feeling Lydia's eyes gave of trying to take something from her the feeling from Cathy's was one of giving. Cady's face grew warm with the idea of being singled out by a caring person. An instant later, alarms screamed loudly in her brain just as a feminine urge to jump up and hug Cathy for her kindness swelled up. A dual conversation raged in that short time, "You can't it's not right, but there is this joy where there has been none for so long; you aren't good enough remember what you are." The conversation ended with Cady clumsily saying to Cathy "Thank you" twice. There had just been a battle within Cady and with any battle there was collateral damage. The damage was to the chrysalis wall she had built around herself even extending it to around Michael. Cady had a crack in that chrysalis now that could not be repaired; even so she would always remember the look she saw in Cathy's eyes. The battle within Cady hadn't settled, but was distracted by the comic drama of Janice determining just who was to be with Michael. Janice's act of supplanting Lydia was priceless and led to the first bell…

***

27

Cathy sat expectantly in Mr. Escame's first period English class. The tables were arranged down either side of the room and across the back to form a squared U shape. At the open end of the U stood a single table with an overhead projector sporting a spooled roll of clear film for use with a grease pencil. The projector's screen was mounted high above the chalkboards at the ceiling wall intersection. Mr. Escame's style of center-stage teaching was a darkened room, a bright screen, and sharp wit. Mr. Escame performed as he lectured in front of a participating audience to the edification of his students. And edified they would be, even if he had to bang out the rhythm of iambic pentameter with a wood pointer until it broke! As always, "all the world's a stage" and in his case the stage included the script flowing from his grease pencil onto the transparency projector's illuminated surface. Cathy, along with her classmates, was expected to write everything down he put up on that screen. She wondered secretly if one of his baby toys had been a grease pencil. Cathy loves grammar, she is comforted by how it brings bounds to language and Mr. Escame is a grammarian; the class is never a burden to her. Period two is Homemaking with Mrs. Copeland, Cathy likes the teacher but the sewing machines were ancient. Period three (first semester) Typing with Mr. Booker is as dreadful as with homemaking's sewing machines since the typewriters are just as ancient. Period three (second semester) Girls Crafts with Mr. McInnis. Cathy loved this class and to this day is a diehard crafter of many media. Lunch volunteer Cathy never sees Cady in the cafeteria during lunch. Period four is U.S. History with Mr. Wieland, she liked the teacher but don't expect to get past the Civil War. Period five is Biology Lab Assistant with Mr. Linde. This becomes interesting; Cathy spends most of her time in the little prep-room that is shared between the biology classroom and the other sciences room. Cady is in this shared sciences room for her Electronics and Physics classes. Cathy, seeing Cady busily helping students in the Electronics lab, takes note of her demeanor as she moves from station to station answering student questions. She is at home with this subject just as much as the teacher Mr. Rapp is! Cathy ponders, this is a completely different side of Cady that you would not

28

guess she had. Cathy is momentarily distracted from filling test tubes for a biology lab and starts to plot out a plan of action in Cady shell peeling. Period six Cathy has a study hall that she spends mostly in the prep-room not studying. Cady on the other hand now has a Physics class that alternates between Mr. Rapp lecturing and team lab work. Cathy invites herself into the Physics lab whenever Cady is at a workstation with her teammate Dale. Dale and Cady are quite the pair Cady is tall and heavy where Dale is short and thin. "This is perfect," Cathy thought, "Dale and I had become friends on a biology field trip so visiting with him and getting to know Cady will fit together nicely." Cathy wandered over to station one and asked innocently, "What are you doing?" Cady would reply with a little grin, "Making waves." An apparatus pushed water in little waves that were contained in a glass tank, a light source shown through the transparent tank projecting shadows of the waves onto a piece of paper. Cady made measurements with a ruler and Dale copied the data down and did the math. Cathy teased the two of them trying to get the hang of flirting. The result that came from Cady was a friendly and relaxed one. No tension, no expectation just three pals enjoying each other among the waves. Not exactly the one Cathy had hoped for but for now it's a start, she has a few more puzzle pieces for the picture of the mystery that is Cady. The final bell rings but this brings no change in what Cady is doing. In fact, Cathy will learn that Cady will hang around this wing of school as long as Mr. Rapp does, she will leave only as Mr. Rapp locks up to go home. Cathy's day is over at the bell since she has to catch the bus home.

***

Cady tried to dismiss the weekend, but it persisted in her thoughts. David has completely dropped out of school now. He gets high with his friends and Cady does everything she can to keep him safe even to the point of pulling their mom's car out into the road to block David and current company from driving while high. They both just grin stupidly at her and pass a small gas-can one to the other taking turns breathing in the contents of whatever was in the can. Mom comes out and tells her to just to let them go as other cars honk wanting to get by. It is just another defeat. Cady never knew David to use alcohol and wonder if this was an outcome of mom's drinking. Odd that Mom's addiction would have a deterrent facet reflecting onto David's seeming addiction. Mom and Cady worry about David when he doesn't show up for days and again when he does. It is a hopeless spiral downward causing the household to despair. Cady's dad is staying away more and more at work. Cady finds herself mirroring her dad's behavior by going to school earlier and staying later. School was a prison for her for years now it has become her second home. Cady has come across a few stories of males changing their gender and dreams hopeful dreams. In the light of day though this is so unattainable, so abstract and the fact is she is just too broken for any redemption of this kind. Cady decides that she must have a further shield against her mind/body conflict and starts to grow a beard. She speaks to herself, "This will put a stop to it as I am reminded each time I look into the mirror that I am a man." In an unconscious act she lets her hair grow long not because of the fashion of the day but because it is feminine. Cady is now gone to war with herself. The broken-in-half mirror in the bathroom is now her battleground. During high school Cady has never come across any actual examples of anyone who was outside the gender divider of straight male and female. None that she understood from her point of view anyway and sexuality wasn't apparent except to hear some guys talk about a Fag haircut. Shag haircuts were starting to make their way into the tightly closed world around her. The guy's response to any male getting one was, "Different shags for different fags." Cady didn't have that kind of haircut and gave little thought as to what being gay was. She only saw the students around her as friendly or not to each other no matter what gender.

***

Cathy is coming to the realization that her church family is no more. Yes she has not been denied access here but the place that was hers has dwindled to a synthetic construct. Cathy's family's philosophy as typified by her father's life is to never look back, always keep your eyes on what is to come and never have regrets. He lived his whole life in this context and Cathy is her father's daughter. Her first couple relationship hurt her and that hurt shaped her but it is gone now. Cady is becoming more fascinating as each day goes by. The problem is establishing a relationship with someone who doesn't seem to understand their part in it. Cady is so different from any guy in this. Cathy's experience is the guy constantly craves her attention; he pursues, gains, and then controls her. Always using increased body contact with her to push her down a path of his choosing. This path leads to the fulfillment of his ultimate desire to fully control her in all ways. This is not Cady in anyway and it is a real relief. Cathy does create opportunities to talk with Cady by being around her at school and the more conversations they have the more Cathy falls for her. Cathy's plan is for Cady to become curious enough to take an interest in her and it follows true female fashion by Cathy asking questions about her. The problem is time, graduation is only a few days away and there is the very real possibly that Cady will be lost to Cathy completely unless there is some movement on Cady's part. So little time left for so much to happen, Cathy begins to pray each night to let Cady be hers.

***

This morning like so many others Cady could escape to school. Michael hadn't come by her house this morning, but that didn't mean he wasn't already there in the cafeteria at the corner table. Cady walked up hill through the calm of early morning past Showalter Middle School, Foster Stadium, and across the parking lot to Foster High School. Cathy was taking her place in the circle of friends Cady had, but Michael remained at the center of that circle. Cady walked into the cafeteria finding the table empty. This was her worst fear and it was coming right at her. There was just one month left before graduation, just a handful of days, and her world would be forever empty just like now. It was a coming horror but not here yet. Perhaps Michael is just around someplace it would be just like him. There wasn't a dark corner anywhere in the High School that Michael hadn't investigated. She thought of the stage and climbed the three stairs to look behind the heavy weighted stage curtains. There in the darkness lay Michael in a lump taking a nap on some stacked choir risers. Her heart leaped with relief. Cady said a quiet, "Hi." A few words came in response. Michael still lying in a lump closed his eyes again ending any further conversation. In the dim light Cady sat down a few feet away from him just waiting and hoping for conversation to return to still her panic of what lay ahead of her. From the other side of the curtain she could hear footsteps breaking the silence.

Suddenly Lydia finding the cafeteria empty and thinking to look backstage popped around the heavy dark maroon curtain. She stood there staring at the two figures then said something about, "Not wanting to interrupt the two of you," and ducked out.

Michael was up in a flash bolting after her. Wow did he move! Cady called out, "What's wrong!" Michael said, "I just don't want her to get the wrong impression of what was going on." Shocked, Cady realized what Michael meant and that Lydia probably had labeled her gay from the rejection she had gotten in the basement the other day. Sudden clarity came; Cady realized that she did have a form of love for Michael and had she been a true girl in both mind and body she would have done anything to have him like her. Just anything. Cady rubbed her very thin beard she was beginning to grow as a shield and thought, "I'm not a true girl in body and I am not gay as a guy, Michael will always be a soul friend, and me just a broken being looking for relief from my suffering. It seems like there was only one true path to relief for broken beings in life and that is unspeakable; if there was only a pill I could take to reach it." Cady gathered herself up and walked alone to class with the knowledge that the days of her and Michael are fading away for good. Cady's working philosophy was the past was a pain that flowed into present and the future was to be avoided at any cost...

***

Cathy was strong-willed yet kindhearted. She had been hurt but she wanted release from that hurt. Conversations with Cady began to ease Cathy's hurting. She started to open up about her world and in doing so they both became aware of common backgrounds. Cady was hurting from the probable loss of the relationship she had had for five years with Michael; a friendship would remain but the innocence was lost for her. Cady was in need of a friend and Cathy was right there. Cathy was peeling Cady's shell away little by little trying to understand the puzzling parts but loving the caring parts. One of the puzzlements was Cady seemed to have no sense of time after graduation. When questioned all Cathy got were vague guarded responses about the coming summer at the ranch. On the other hand, there was gentleness to Cady that was in total contrast to her body image. She is empathetic, insightful, made fun only of herself, and had the most beautiful spirit. Cady never moved to touch Cathy, but instead listened intensely to her as Cathy found herself talking more and more about herself. Cady seem to relate more to the words coming from Cathy's mouth than Cathy's overall body image. Cathy told Cady nothing about her relationship with her ex-boyfriend. This was just as well because Cady didn't at the moment even have the concept of anything past a simple friendship. Cady was a totally clean slate in this way and that was just what Cathy needed. In truth, Cathy had been hurt very deeply by that first relationship and oddly enough Cady seemed to sense this. This was another shared background that would come out much later. It would be many years into the future for both Cathy and Cady to come to terms with their individual demons. For now, the onus was on Cathy to lay the groundwork of saving them both. She had to find a way to give Cady the opportunity to see her as a close friend. From there it was up to Cady to look past friendship and see a future with her. Cathy knew only one week stood between holding onto Cady and losing her. The plan was to give Cady everything Cathy could think of in terms of being visible to her.

***

Cady knew she would lose Michael after graduation; it was a forgone conclusion, it was cast in stone, it was so sad, and yes it was heartbreaking. Michael had several thousand dollars from his birth father's estate to use for college. Washington State University at the very east border in Pullman was his choice and he was going to take it by storm. Hell and high water all the way. Although he wouldn't begin until fall Cady wouldn't be around, the ranch called her as it always did all summer long. In her heart she would always hold on to the years where the two of them were best friends, even partners in crime, it was more than a gift it was an anchor in her storm. There was nothing sexual about it; they were kindred spirits, plain and simple. Cady lived vicariously holding on to parts of other people's life stories as a way to bury her own. She understood Michael like no one else did at this time and because of that she knew his truth. Michael from here on in life would never be still. He would be pursuing the biggest, loudest, and toughest experiences in the wildest places he could find in Alaska. In these wild places he would strive to find his lost self-worth through experience; he had to, because that tight well-meaning rein his stepfather had used on him drained it all away. They say women love a bad boy or redeemable rogue thus enter Michael. Cady without thinking about it was looking around for a bridge friendship to the end of the year. The science wing was her afterschool hangout and she struck up a casual but consistent dialog with another male student of her class. He provided good conversation and Cady wanted the mental closeness of another human being. Michael was leaving a heck of a hole and it hurt. She had no idea a little circle of fellow classmates had already decided she was gay and that this was the start of a new gay couple. Michael was indeed right in running after Lydia that day; rumors do and did start so quickly. That respite with the male fellow student only lasted a week but it got Cady to graduation week. Cathy picked up from there by keeping time with Cady and she used her new friend as a life-ring. Cathy was there at Cady's Baccalaureate that is held at CBSR the Sunday before graduation. This year's crop of graduates sat together in the main sanctuary to listen to a sermon by Pastor Forseth on this big step in life. Cady looked around and there was Cathy sitting nearby looking back. After the sermon was over and folks gathered in foyer to chat Cathy came to Cady's elbow. Cady was very much pleased for this; it was a new feeling for her. As the crowd ebbed and flowed around each other Cathy gracefully maintained her place with Cady. Together it was Cady and Cathy as a couple chatting with the other soon-to-be-graduates. It was nice, a weight was being lifted suddenly from Cady's heart; she wasn't alone anymore. Cady spent the rest of that Sunday wrestling with her lack of self-worth; if Michael felt he was short of that stuff she was completely empty. From the moment she came to the understanding of being broken, to the seemingly endless cycle of crossdressing followed by self-loathing then crossdressing again, her self-worth was the target of damage. There were so many things in her life going more than wrong. The idea that someone could like her, especially when she so very badly needed someone to care, was so completely overwhelming to her. It flooded over her empty places and filled the dry pools, she prayed, "Oh please God guide me and don't take her away." Cady the next morning walked to school early but the cafeteria was no longer a haven, the occupants that made it one had moved on. Michael had surrendered to coupledom with the most down to earth and vivacious girl that Cady had ever encountered (other than Cathy of course) her name was Janice. Janice was a pleasantly proportioned ponytailed whirlwind, always smiling about a pleasant thought dancing in her mind. Her brown eyes shone brightly through her glasses and she was forever in well-worn blue jeans and sleeveless tops. Michael would never find a mate in life better suited to him or one that would love him more. In a thought secret to herself, Cady was happy to lose her spot with Michael to Janice. The school was transforming itself; the gym was continuously open, and risers were being assembled on the tarp-covered floor to form a stage. Soon chairs would be in place and the bleachers would be pulled out in preparation for the coming graduation ceremony in just three days. And there was Cathy wandering toward her. Cady's heart lifted as they chatted, Cathy had finals this week where Cady's were all finished, they parted with a plan to see each other in the science wing at sixth period. There is no pressure for a senior this week except what they put on themselves. Cady hung out in the science wing helping Mr. Rapp as needed. Sixth period came and so did Cathy, and for the first time Cady looked at Cathy's image. Cathy was pretty, just a little bit shorter than Janice (some folks thought the two were sisters) proportionally trim but not too thin. She had waist long brown hair parted in the middle flowing equally down each shoulder, deep blue eyes that twinkled through brown rimmed glasses, she wore a pleasant collared polo top, jeans, waffle stompers and came up to Cady's chin in height. Cathy was no stranger to dresses and she generally carried shoulder length bags in solid colors or patchwork. If Cathy had been drop dead beautiful Cady could not have tolerated her. Once a very beautiful young woman with perfect make-up in place had come to their home to deliver a rosebud vase that Cady's dad had purchased from her. Cady stared speechless and then hid in her room until the young woman left. Hard to explain, but that beauty drove a stake into the heart of her hidden identity it made her feel terribly ugly. Cathy had a bright easy smile, beautiful blue eyes and a remarkably intelligent mind. Cady tentatively surrendered to her it was a natural and involuntary action. Somehow word spread quickly that they were now a couple.

***

Cathy had anxiously hoped Cady would show up at Baccalaureate after church. Cathy wore a nice dress to be ready just in case. She had prayed that Cady would be here and that Cady would like seeing her. Cathy even went so far as to ask her mother for any advice on how to get a boy to like you. It proved just to be more embarrassing and not much help. Mom's advice was just to be nice to him, that's all it takes. Cathy thought, "You've never met Cady he isn't just any boy." Cathy thought about that, she had been comparing Cady with other boys she knew and there was definitely something else going on. It didn't matter though; she was falling more and more for him each day. Something about him seemed to mesh with something about her. Cathy drove to church giving a ride to her sister Linda; they were the only two from the household that attended CBSR (Church By the Side

36

of the Road). Actually, Cathy had invited Linda to start going to church with her just after Cathy had broken up with her now ex-boyfriend. This gave Cathy a sort of buffer from him. Church went slowly by, the sanctuary emptied, and would reopen in an hour. Being with Linda worked every time Cathy needed to get out of a conversation about her breakup. Cathy would use looking for Linda as an excuse to walk away. The soon to be graduates or pre-grad as it were began to show up. Cathy kept an eye out and finally Cady walked up to the door with several others. Cathy waved to Cady and other church members noticed when it was Cady waving back. The pre-grads all sat together pastor gave a nice sermon and the sanctuary emptied out. Cathy came right up to Cady and she beamed. Cathy noticed for the first time Cady had hazel green eyes. Cathy was at Cady's elbow and felt right at home there, it was good to be a couple again even if it wasn't official. They circulated together in the crowd chatting with girls in Cady's class that had come. Cathy felt so right to be there next to Cady she wanted so much to be with Cady all the time. Cathy's heart was just singing away and it showed on her face for anyone to see. Unfortunately anyone did see and several youth group members were watching along with her ex-boyfriend. Cathy counted this encounter with Cady as a complete answer to prayer, but it would cost her a place in this church in the end. The cold-shouldering that would eventually drive her away started the very next Sunday, but for now Cathy had everything she could hope for.

***

Cady drifted through the school day toward her sixth period time with Cathy. Cady was already in the science wing when Becky a fellow classmate walked in and sidled over to her saying, "Hi Cady! Would you march with me at graduation? I already checked with Cathy and she says she is fine with it." Cady hadn't given any thought to this mostly because Cathy wasn't eligible to march since she wasn't a senior. She answered, "Yes and thanks for asking me, see you at rehearsal!" Cady pondered the concept of one girl going to another girl for permission to borrow a boyfriend and then questioned, "I'm

Cathy's boyfriend?" This spring here at school was full of couples forming all around her. Cady herself was far removed from the concept; she didn't feel like she could be either side of a couple. Even as a nineteen year old she didn't have any sexuality per se, only a conflict that left her impaled on that thin line between male and female. Cady knew what love was as an emotion; it was a binding force between two people that kept them together for a lifetime. Love for things was different from love for people. Cady's mom and dad didn't have a complete love for each other especially the second time around. She was certain of her mom's parental love for her and her brother, even though it was full of mental health holes. The love of her father for her was a mixture of parental obligation, guilt, and a personal hopelessness. Make no mistake, her father was the strongest of all of them, he was gregarious, generous, handsome, and goodhearted. Where mom's mental health problems were in full view of Cady and David, Dad's all too real personal demon was closeted totally out of sight. (It would be fifty years before Cady, the one remaining member of that family of four, would know the truth about her father's tormentor). Right now in this place and time there is a battle raging within Cady, the only visible evidence of it was the new thin beard growing on her face. She answered her thought, "So yes, I am Cathy's boyfriend." Still the idea was wobbly in her head. Cathy comes into the science wing and floats over to Cady. They sit at a workstation in the far corner of the lab chatting and laughing together. Cathy is feeling that warm comfortable place form around the two of them as a couple. Cady tells her about marching with Becky and Cathy is delighted it is going to happen. Cathy tells Cady that she will sit as close as she can to the stage and wave. Cady is vicariously curious about Cathy as a person, and soon Cathy is explaining her summers at the apple orchard in Eastern Washington near Quincy. Cady chimes in that she knows that area because she spends her summers at the ranch in Thorp! What would become an amazing common background starts to reveal itself to the two. Cady is doing what she always does with someone she is coming to care deeply about. She is taking in their life structure, to Cady it is who and how they are. Each little piece given

38

her will be preciously stored within Cady's heart and as time passes, be pieced together as the image of that special life of a very special person to her. Cathy has no idea that her life is now becoming part of Cady shared experience. Cathy tells about her family, she is the oldest then Phil, Mark, and Linda. Cady is the oldest in her little family of four with little brother David. Cathy's mom is Joyce and dad Ainsley. Cady's parents are Dorothy and Merrill. The afternoon flows gently on until Mr. Rapp tells them it's time to lock up. Mr. Rapp is a gentle soul. He has been Cady's teacher in General science, Chemistry, Physics, and Electronics. It was Mr. Rapp who put together a self-study Advance Electronic course for Cady when he saw her potential. He also gave Cady his only lab assistant position. Cady walks toward home alone knowing that tomorrow it all comes to an end. Cady's mom tells her as she walked into the little two-bedroom single bathroom house, "Tomorrow after the graduation ceremony we are having a party for you right here! All of the Anderson family have been invited!" Cady's mom was clearly happy to be able to give this gift. Cady is happy but also stunned. The Anderson family count is nine aunts, four uncles and a whole bunch of cousins. The total floor square footage of the little house is 625 square feet without furniture. Most of the aunts and uncles are married, which increases the number. The house wouldn't hold them all even if only a third show up! The party was all Cady's mom and dad could afford to give her. The party was basically snacks and pop; Andersons could be counted on to bring snack stuff along with them to a party. Cady retired to her bedroom; brother David was out someplace. There in her little shared bedroom Cady continued to fight her war with impending abandonment of her friends, family, and life in general. Crossdressing had opened a forbidden window into an impossible world, but it hadn't just been the act physically. No, it was the constant discord of identity, the feeling of being female in the face of fact that froze her in place and took away her future. Her friends were flying away into the future and her family would be dissolved by it. Cady needed not to be alone; she needed this desperately, for without it she was going to be cast into the abyss. More importantly, she needed both to care for and be cared for by someone. There was Cathy. Cathy had glided right into her life in these final weeks of it. The one thought that crystallized in Cady mind that night was the resolve to ask Cathy into the chaos that her graduation party would surely be. In bed that night Cady along with her normal prayers prayed to God to guide her with Cathy that they might become the best of friends. Cady had always prayed each night asking God for things she felt she needed, but she had always left room for God not to grant them, tonight she felt she had no room left…

***

Cathy stepped off the bus onto the sidewalk in front of her family's home of five years. The grass was trim, the flowerbeds neat, and the awnings over the living room windows were lowered her dad was expecting a sunny tomorrow. She latch-keyed the left side of the front double doors, thoughtfully stepped on each of six stairs down to the basement and her bedroom. The basement bedroom was the most private of all of the five that house had to offer. Her bedroom was unique in that all of the others were upstairs. When the time came each of her siblings would claim that room as rite of passage. The daylight basement also had a half bath, rec room with fireplace, workroom and a double garage. The home supplied 2400 square feet of living space for the family of six, more if you consider the back deck off of the kitchen. Cathy dumped her books on the desktop, if the top was showing, if not on whatever had come to rest there before. The dress she wore so that Cady might notice it was replaced with jeans and a t-shirt. Relief flowed through her being, school was just days from ending for the year, and God willing, she and Cady would be a lasting couple tomorrow. Down deep in her being where she stored hopes and dreams a cloud still covered this one. Tomorrow if Cady doesn't move toward her, doesn't hold her hand, or doesn't affirm her in anyway, that is it; she has lost her. Cathy needed to care for, and be cared for by, Cady. "The two of us belonged together Cady loves horses; she would love the orchard as much as I would love the ranch." Cathy's super power is that she is forward looking. There is still time left to make room for things to happen. She shook off the cloud that had drifted over her hope and planned what she would wear tomorrow at graduation. Dinner that night at the kitchen table with Phil and Cathy on one side and Linda and Mark on the other with parents on either end. Cathy announces that she wants to go to graduation tomorrow night. She asks if her dad would give her a ride. Dad's response included a question, "Sure how do you expect to get back home afterward?" Cathy responded. "I'll get a ride with someone, I have lots of friends in that class." It's Cathy's night to put the dishes in the dishwasher. The evening news plays on the television in the living room with at least two of the household watching it. She took the garbage downstairs to drop it off on the way to her bedroom. Cathy in her room, digs out her camera for tomorrow and tries to escape into a book, it works only in spurts until bedtime. Her prayer was a simple heartfelt one; "Please Lord if it be your will for Cady and me to be together please, oh please, let it happen tomorrow."

***

Cady wakes up to see David asleep across from her in his own bed. David had been back living at the ranch with their grandpa most of this winter. It was a failed attempt to get him out of the decaying cycle that was claiming him both mentally and physically. For now everything was up for grabs in David's future. Cady still has reasons to get up, school has one last escape left for her. Today will be full of graduation preparations and reflections (annual signing). Cady was photography editor for 1973 addition of the *Klahowyah* the school's annual. The theme this year was *We've Only Just Begun*. Next to Electronics classes, the Annual class had the most effect on Cady's social growth. She could hide behind the camera and enter places she would never have the nerve to as just herself. She was allowed to approach teachers as peers. She was challenged to learn film printing in the school darkroom on her own. There was even a power struggle over who was to be Editor of the Annual. This occurred half way through the class term as one girl usurped the other by assuming the position. The girl who lost just disappeared from the Annual class altogether. All these were learning experiences that strained her identity image to the breaking point then released it again. Graduating high school was a big achievement in the Anderson family; Cady was part of the first generation to do so. Neither her mother nor father had made it through classic high school. Despite Cady's parents' financial problems they equipped their graduating child with a little pile of grad gear. She had a cap and gown, class ring, printed announcements, and a senior portrait print for each announcement.

So Cady escaped to the school for one last time. All the seniors were giddy they learned the hesitation step during rehearsal so they could march carefully with the solemn music. The girls had white gowns and the boys purple; Cady was a little wistful but only for a moment. Cady would just remind herself to imagine being a girl in the situation she was in right now at home and in life. She kept a mental list of reasons not to be a girl in life and reviewed them very often as the need arose. Rehearsal would not be over until everyone got it right or nearly right. The whole affair was taking a surreal feeling of gain, of loss, of new, of old, of being swept away. Cady had fun trying to get marching right with Becky; they both laughed it was sad, too. Becky was just going to be someone she never knew. School was still going on for the rest of the school body. Cathy was busy more or less with classes but sixth period was still coming and Cady would be there. After rehearsal a good number of seniors headed out to party together somewhere. Cady roamed the halls down to the science wing to wait for Cathy. If you happened to have seen Cady lately with Cathy then on a moment's notice try to guess what was going on in Cady's mind; a very good guess would be she is getting up the nerve to ask a special girl a big question. The truth was she was trying to get the nerve to ask herself to be someone she wasn't. The prize was the 'pearl of great price,' that pearl being a relationship with Cathy.

Cathy freed herself from what was left of her classes to walk down to the science wing; the two met in their quiet corner. The senior recognition assembly had come and gone. Cady's resolve wasn't complete; hope and despair were trying to balance on a scale in the windstorm of internal truth vs. external image reality. Cady seemed in a jocular mood one funny after another funny. Cathy giggled at the right places and hoped that it would lead somewhere. It did but it wasn't obvious to Cathy. Within Cady something snapped and Cady blurted out, "Will you be at graduation, will you come find me?" "Yes and yes," Cathy responded. It wasn't a direct answer to Cathy's prayers but it kind of was. There was more silliness on Cady's part now' this is what she always uses to shield herself. Truth be told both Michael and Cady use the trick of self-debasing comedy to hide their vulnerabilities, self-worth being but one. Cathy turned the conversation in a new direction and they were off in another common experience about Eastern Washington. The two separated with the excuse to go home to get ready for graduation night. Cady had to be back at the school at six o'clock. Once home it was find food and ride with Mom and Dad to pick up Grandma Ida Anderson at her little home in Burien. Cady had two very dear grandmothers, Hazel who had two grandsons and Ida with many grandchildren; she was loved by both and in return loved them. One had known about her (Hazel) and the other did not (Ida). Cady's four tickets went to her mom, dad, brother, and grandmother Ida Anderson. Back home to get dressed, be ready, and perhaps have some food. The clock took Cady away, it was up to Mom, and Dad, with David and Grandma Anderson to be there an hour later. At school it was one last rehearsal march. Afterward the grads all stood outside the gym in the hallway waiting for the music to start.

***

Cathy had dressed carefully making sure everything was just right. Cathy bounded up the stairs all the way up to the living room. She looked at her father who said with a wry smile, "Where are you going all dressed up?" "Dad!" Cathy flushed, "You know very well where I'm going down to graduation!" Cathy was in on his favorite game, "Get up and let's go!" Her dad slowly arose with mock straining, "Give me a minute will you I'm old." Cathy loved her dad so much, but tonight she was nervous, it was a very important night, maybe the most important night she would have. Father and daughter drove together down to the high school crowded with cars dropping off people. Her dad teased, "What a mess wonder what is going on?" Cathy let it pass, she wanted out she had already seen Janice standing in the crowd. "Let me out here please." Her dad did so and waved as he left. Cathy was at Janice's elbow asking her how she looked. "You look great!" came Janice's exuberant answer, "How about me?" "You're going to knock him dead JJ!" Cathy returned in kind, "Let's get in there to find a place to sit. It will have to up in the bleachers if we are going to see anything and wave like crazy." Janice quips, "I'm going to be real loud so hold your ears!" Cathy and Janice wiggle through the crowd, climbing up into the bleachers. They couldn't gain the top-level seats that back up against the wall; instead they settled at two-thirds the way up and about ten feet in from the end. "So how's it going with Michael? I'm so happy you two got together!" Cathy teased. "Yeah, he's zany but I love him anyway; they both kinda are really," Janice observed. "Cady is fun but so reserved I'd be happy if she would even hold my hand," Cathy remarked. Janice popped up with, "Wow! Sorry Cathy, I finally had to make something happen with Michael. As zany as he is, he is slow on the uptake; it's like he never had a girlfriend before." Cathy quietly confided, "I'm praying for something from Cady soon; she asked if I would be here tonight." Janice exploded, "There you go girl prayer will do it!" Pomp & Circumstance droned from the band and the crowd quieted looking expectantly at the far doorway. First to appear was the single line of the top ten graduates rhythmically hesitation stepping toward the stage. The rest of the graduates then came in pairs. The whole procession was painfully and traditionally slow but this was the solemn expectation. As the marchers reached the stage each stood before an empty chair and all would sit together on command. Photos were taken as they passed proud family members and a shouted catcall or two punctuated the march. The marchers did a pretty good job staying in step until almost at the very end of the line when it became impossible to hold onto that mind-numbing step to that dreadful rhythm any longer. The crowd applauded when the last two just walked the rest of the way. There were speeches and awards then as

44

each graduate's name was called, they walk to the podium for a handshake and an envelope. True to her promise, JJ whistled when Michael's name was called and to be fair to her friend Cathy, she did it again when Cady's name was called. The graduates moved their tassels from the right to left, de-hatted, and cheered then filed out each receiving a rose as they exited to the outside the building. As soon as the last graduate cleared the door Cathy and Janice were wiggling through the crowd. Outside it was bedlam, graduates in tears, cheers, and hugs everywhere. At 80 degrees it was the warmest June 6th anyone could remember for a graduation evening. Families holding still for pictures that would last a lifetime suddenly embraced the nearest grad. Cady's family had already left with Grandma Ida Anderson to get the house open for the party. Cady was all smiles and for this moment in time all troubles were lifted from her, she stood in the middle of a world in emotional climax wanting it to be this way forever. She also wanted Cathy and saw her coming toward her along with Michael and Janice. As Cathy reached Cady's elbow Cady asked if Cathy would like to have her rose. Cathy's heart soared, "I would love it" and she hugged Cady for the first time. The world became the brightest place for Cady with Cathy at its center, now the question, "Cathy would you come to my graduation party, it is just family and will be pretty crowded." And the perfect answer from Cathy, "I would love to! Let me call my dad and tell him I don't need a ride I got invited over to a friend's." Her dad said, "Fine have fun but don't be too late it's still school tomorrow." Cathy loves her dad she surely does. Michael and Janice joined Cady and Cathy for the walk down to Cady's house. Cathy put her hand in Cady's and Cady held it gently as they walk hand in hand for the first time in their lives together. The two couples walked down that same sidewalk Cady and Michael had traveled since they were in the ninth grade twice each school day together. This time the two best friends, these two kindred spirits, had each had a new life added to their own. Only one couple would continue to walk hand in hand for the rest of their lives…

***

45

Cady, clad in her purple gown with a mortar board precariously covering her head waited in the cafeteria with all the other members of the class of 1973. The setting wasn't lost on her, as she stood there in line next to Becky. Becky was aglow with excited energy where Cady was experiencing such a wave of contrasting emotions that she was numb. For a year this corner of the cafeteria that they were now standing in was her escape place. She savored what time she had left with Michael here and she was safe from turmoil of home here. It was hot even with the double doors open and loud as chatter filled the heated air. The music Pomp & Circumstance that they all had been rehearsing that dreadful hesitation step to now trundled in from the gym at the end of the hallway. The single line of the cream of the crop, the top ten graduates of the class of 1973, stepped in carefully spaced single file out through the double doorway into the hall. This was it; the numbness faded from Cady's mind, all that remained was concentrating on her marching in step with Becky. The line moved steadily the cafeteria was lost to her as they entered the hallway Cady felt that loss as this bit of her life was torn away. They turned left marching past the school trophy case. Cady glanced at the triumph trinkets of past lives of other classes. The music is louder now the open double doors of the gym close by. The line pauses here Cady and Becky are standing next to the girls' restroom just before the main door to the gym. Cady has the oddest thought, she as a student had never seen the inside of any of the restrooms in the school, especially this one, and had now missed the experience for good. Becky reached up to Cady's head to straighten out her mortar board. Cady thanked her profusely, this had been her greatest fear of the cap falling off at the most embarrassing moment possible. Cady made up her mind there at the doorway to the gym to ask Cathy to the party at her house, more than just that, she would open herself to accepting the role of couple maybe even more. In her mind there was the strange bitter sweetness of acquiescence mixed with a growing sense of being a fraud. She mentally chafed against this last part. She wasn't a fraud she was a male, that declaration hurt something inside of her but she resolved then and there to do what was needed. There was some laughter inside

46

the gym something had happened but now the line resumed marching. They entered the gym in the corner nearest the main school building. Cady's mind picked up every detail of the structure of this school as in some vain effort to keep from the final separation that was coming. The school itself was built in what was called California Style as a radiating campus centered from administration offices and cafeteria connected by a long trunk hallway lined with lockers. Branching from either side of the trunk hallway were open breezeways making up the wings of classrooms. The gym building stood isolated with an enclosed breezeway connecting it to the trunk hallway near the offices and cafeteria. On the floor of the gym was row upon row of uncomfortable metal chairs in two groups forming a center aisle from the front of the gym to the temporary stage at the back of the gym. The bleachers were fully extended out from either wall to give the most seating possible; even with this, the place was completely packed to standing room. Cady and Becky marched into the gym turning right at the end of the nearby bleacher from here it was a straight march down the aisle with fully extended bleachers on the right and folding chairs on the left for the length of the gym. At the end of the rows of chairs Becky turned the two of them to the left, now they passed the chair backs making for the central aisle. Reaching the homestretch, the center aisle, they marched straight towards the temporary stage. Cady turned her head slightly to find her parents seating near the central aisle. There they were all smiles and waves; Cady let go of all thoughts except the experience she was currently having, it would be a once in a lifetime one for her. Mom, Dad, Grandma Ida, and Brother David she didn't know it, but this would be the last time they would be together as a family. Cady scanned the crowd as best as she could without upsetting her cap. She didn't see Cathy yet… Becky and Cady separated at the center of the stage to walk to the ends and climb onto the stage. Now standing Cady could see better, there was JJ standing and waving like crazy and next to her was Cathy. Cady alternated glances between Cathy and Cady's family with "I still have a few more minutes of this life that is all that is important right now," running through her mind. Pomp & Circumstance came to an end and they all breathed a sigh of relief, especially the band. Cady located Michael in the second row his normally scruffy out of control hair remarkably tame at the moment. Michael turned and caught Cady's glaze and smirked. "Thanks Michael I needed that," Cady thought. There were speeches, awards, applause, and photoflashes. Each graduate's name in turn was called, hand shook, and folder handed them all in one motion. There was a loud whistle as Michaels name was called and again as Cady's name was called. The grads stood up changed their tassels from right to left and were presented to the applauding crowd. JJ sure can whistle! The graduates filed out into the lawn outside of the gym and joyful chaos reigned supremely in every face of every graduate. Michael and Cady found each other then lost each other again. Cady found her family got hugs and kisses before they slipped away to go open the house for the party. Cady moved in through the celebrating mass of movement, hugging and smiling as the need be, she was looking for Cathy. Trying to form a plan she looked up and there was Cathy along with Michael and Janice coming over to her. Cady was filled with the best of feelings at that moment; she was recognized and had a place with someone. There was no more questioning conflict she knew where and with whom she want to be with. Cathy came over to her and looked her in the eyes Cady remembered to offer her the rose. And that hug she got in return for a mere flower went on and on in her mind, the closeness and simple sincerity lives in memory to this day. Cady then asked Cathy if she would come to her family's graduation party and when she accepted with, "I just have to get to a payphone to call my dad," Cady's heart soared. Cady had cut herself off from the world to protect herself, she had built a shell around her to be safe but it worked both ways, she was shielded from caring human contact from the love of another. Cady at nineteen was totally innocent of the hurt love can bring and the joy. The couples turned to walk to Cady's house she and Michael knew the way and Cathy and Janice were eager to learn it. As they walked Cady simply and naturally held her hand out to Cathy and Cathy in the same way took that hand to be hers. Cady felt the touch of Cathy's hand in hers, the warmth, the completeness of human touch.

Cady swore to herself that she would hold this hand as much and as long as possible.

***

Cathy was floating on air as she walked with her Cady. At the driveway to Cady's little house they said their goodbyes to Michael and Janice. Cathy hugged her friend Janice; prayers had been answered. Janice whispered, "See I told you." Michael and Janice would continue the long walk down the hill toward Michael's family's home and whatever the evening would bring them. Cathy was now part of a couple again and her expectations for a long caring relationship danced in her mind. Cathy could see that Cady was different in some internal way from even yesterday. Cady led her up the front stairs of the little house. The front door was standing open, the driveway blocked with cars, and the sound of loud conversation boomed toward them. Cady turned to Cathy and teased, "Last chance to bail." "No thank you," she grinned, "I wouldn't miss it!" The front single door was narrow and the little living room alive with people stuffed in every inch of space. It was loud and cigarette smoke hung in the air. As soon as the two of them entered they were greeted by a chaos of congratulations coming from every square inch of the room. Cady faltered for a moment then recouped to acknowledge each person's greeting. Cathy followed right behind Cady into the center of the room. Cady introduced Cathy over and over; Cathy smiled waved and held Cady's hand. She did love it. Cathy saw Cady's mom waving them into the kitchen and tugged Cady in that direction. Dorothy needed a picture of them with the cake! Once that was done Cady introduced Cathy to Dorothy. Cathy got the nicest hug from her as a welcome. Merrill, Cady's dad, was nearby and got both an introduction to her and a hug. Cathy was impressed by the happiness that all the people had brought into this small space. Cady tried to get to David but there just wasn't any clear path to get into the bedroom that several cousins were occupying with him. Cathy had never seen so many people crowded into such a small space. Cathy followed Cady over to the chair Grandma Ida was sitting in for an introduction.

Seeing the gentle thin white hair gracing Ida's head Cathy thought of her grandmother and made a mental note of it. Cady had been full of energy making the rounds, but now faltered. Cathy spoke up in her ear saying, "Is it time to go?" Cady made the announcement to the room and asked to borrow the car from her dad. The compact crowd cheered them as they left through the front door and down the stairs to the car. Cady ditched her cap and gown, opened the passenger door of the big four door green sedan and Cathy slid onto the passenger seat. Cady looked down at the middle of the bench seat and then back at Cathy saying, "You know there is a seat here with a seatbelt and everything." Cathy's eyes danced as she happily slid over. "Where are we going," Cathy gently asked. "I don't really know," came Cady's answer just as gently in return. "Sounds good as long as I can go there with you," Cathy quipped. Cathy felt comfortable next to her. Cady backed the car out of the carport, made a choice and turned right up the street.

***

Cady was bold, she was nervous, she was brave, she was fearful, and the loop repeated over and over. Mostly she was grateful for the young woman walking next to her. In the oddest way Cady felt like she had always belonged to Cathy and vice versa. It was a dance they were doing following each other's cues and she was just learning it. Everything was happening so fast as they squeezed between parked cars to get into the walkway of her home. The yard had little cousins that Cady could never remember the names of. It didn't matter, they were unaffected by the couple walking across the little yard to the little house. As Cathy looked up the few stairs to the front door Cady joked that there was still time to bail on the party. Humor served as a shield for Cady and was always popping up as needed. Cady didn't want to leave, it wasn't the right thing to do; but there was that humor thing she sometimes couldn't help. Cathy just grinned, "No thank you I wouldn't miss it for anything!" Cady took a deep breath there at the bottom of the squeaky steps; at the top of those five steps was a chaotic world that would lay bare where she came from and to an extent who she is. This world was at its peak, it was never going to be any better, any sounder than on this occasion, and soon it would decay away. The joke Cady made wasn't for Cathy's sake it was for Cady's sake. If they go in Cathy will know things about the family and Cady will forever be another person. The risk is loss of self but the gain is tremendous, the gain is Cathy. Cady led and Cathy followed into the little house so very full of loud happy people. They were happy to be together over at Merrill's; there had never been a family party here. They were happy that another Anderson child had made it through high school, these were the first generation to do so and they were happy that their children were growing up. Every one of the twelve offspring of Ida Anderson had clawed their way up working instead of finishing High School. They didn't get along; there was always an interfamily feud going but parties were truce times. As soon as Cady set foot into the room she stopped. There was nowhere she could go, it was wall-to-wall family, there had never been so many people here ever! This changed as everyone shouted greetings and congratulation! Uncles and Aunts would put an envelope into her hand and roar approval as Cady introduced Cathy. Cathy was perfect, she smiled and waved and fitted herself right into the family. Cady was relieved and amazed; she saw Cathy in a new light. She also had a twinge of envy but beat it down. Cady knew her job, move the two of them around as best as possible to introduce and accept complements. Cady really hadn't imagined what she would be facing after graduation. She was so into her own head about the end of all things that she had not planned for anything that might be born anew. Mom, Dad, David, and Grandma Ida all needed to meet Cathy. Cathy was just amazing, she was patient, she was sweet. Cady was falling in love more and more with this person. The air in the little house was heavy with cigarette smoke, it was the early 70s everyone smoked all the time, except Cady and Cathy. David just wasn't reachable in his bedroom filled with cousins. It was so loud that Cady had to shout at times to be heard. After making the rounds as it were Cady realized that she and Cathy had no place at this party, it wasn't a party for her but a celebration of a family graduation, a coming of age of the product of the marriage of Merrill and Dorothy. Cathy came to her rescue by asking if it was time to go.

The whole room was in agreement with their leaving; there were funny grins and one-eyed winks. All of this went right over the head of Cady. Cady and Cathy made their exit outside and down the stairs to the family car. Another moment Cady hadn't planned for; where to go from here? Cathy was gentle with Cady that shell was all falling away fast it was lovable to see her in her innocence and Cathy considered this relationship could last a long time with God's help…

***

Cathy and Cady flowed through the dark streets leading toward Seattle. There were two hours before the couple needed to be back to Cathy's home. The couple sat close together on the bench seat of the car as Cady drove without a clue in mind as to a place to stop. It seemed like the right thing just to listen to the car noises and be together. They found themselves at the Seattle Center, parked on the street, and got out to wander into the Center House. This park had been the sight of the 1962 World Fair and remained the jewel of the urban park system of Seattle. They walked together in the evening light, beginning the process that would go on and on. Cady who encouraged, then listened to, the life expression of who she cared for now was turned around as Cathy encouraged her to speak about her life. Cathy who had been charged with taking care of a partner's emotional needs now had someone who only saw her needs to be ministered to. They looked in the window of a little shop in the Center House that did glass blowing. Cathy loved the little figurines; she collected them and now loved sharing this with Cady. Cady was filling herself with the experience of a life being shared with her. Cathy carried the long stem rose in her free hand, it was a nice one and Cady had chosen her to give it to. Time was short they returned to the car and settled in on the bench seat near each other. They drove back along the waterfront toward their two houses. Chatting back and forth, reversing each other's roles in conversation, and unbeknownst to them finding foothold after foothold in building a unique relationship. Cathy directed the way to her family's house and Cady parked in the driveway. Cathy had the door part way open on the passenger side as

Cady came around to help. The door was heavy and the driveway sloped up. The two walked up the stairs to the front door and paused in the dim light. There was small talk, as Cady flustered not knowing what to do now, there was action as Cathy made a decision and then the ensuing kiss of a lifetime.

***

Cathy took her place in the middle of the bench seat as they left the Seattle Center. It had been a perfect evening; one that she'd hope would be repeated multiple times. The aimless drive seemed to be timeless until they found themselves at the Center House. Now the drive passed by all too quickly and Cathy found herself directing Cady down her street to her house. She had promised to be home by 11:00 and it was just after that now. Cady came around to her side of the car and together they walked up to the front double doors. Cathy was on the doorstep, Cady one step down and both staring at each other. Cathy's mind was serene, it truly was a perfect evening. She needed to tell Cady this and tried, "I had fun tonight," was all what came out. Cathy really wanted to tell Cady just how wonderful this evening had been and how warmly serene she felt right now. She also wanted Cady to have felt as happy as she did about their evening together; she looked into Cady eyes searchingly. Then the porch light came on the universal signal to end the date and come in. Cady was flustered maybe being shy thought Cathy, "The time was now if is to be its got to come from me." Cathy saw an answer in Cady's hazel eyes tilted her head slightly and leaned close to Cady and whispered, "Kiss me Cady." Cady hugged her gently and kissed Cathy on her lips. It was a tentative kiss, soft and sweet, not one full of passion, but one that held definite promise of more to come. It was exactly the kiss that Cathy had hoped for and with that she turned and opened the door saying good night. Cathy came in and started to go down the stairs to her room when her dad called out teasingly, "I wondered how long it was going to take you to come in?" Cathy walked up the stairs gave her dad a smile and said, "Good night." Cathy changed into a nightgown her bedroom floor was cold even though it was carpeted. The heat came in from the ceiling and at this time of night her dad had turned the furnace down to 55 degrees. She was happy all that she had wanted from the evening came to flower out. Cady was sweet and gentle, there was a rose in the little vase on the bookshelf. She sat on her day bed and played Yahtzee until her eyes grew sleepy. She and Cady would have time to see each other before they both had to go to Eastern Washington for the summer. And who knows what will come even over there. Cathy's prayers included thanks for Cady, she felt warm air coming from the ceiling one last time for the night.

***

Cady shut the door to the passenger side of the car and walked around to the driver's side. Cathy was already in place in the middle of the bench seat waiting. It was an amazing experience to have a girlfriend to sit next to, to be cared for and to care for. She didn't think of Cathy as a girlfriend exactly, even now she thought of Cathy as the best lasting friend that there could ever be. Cathy would be the one friend that Cady would empty herself for; she would push out all her fears, anxieties, and insecurities leaving room only for Cathy. Cady had loved the drive to and the walk through the Seattle Center, as yearbook photo editor she had used the place to stage a bunch of photographs of classmates. Tonight the lighting was soft and dreamy with a few other couples walking hand in hand. Cady felt peaceful with Cathy's hand in hers, Cady loved that Cathy seemed to want to be with her. This last feeling brought a return feeling on her part of submission to Cathy. Cady had never given any thought of what it meant to have a girlfriend or what was required to make one happy, on the contrary she had dismissed the concept completely. For now she let her feelings guide her, be kind, be gentle, learn all you can about her, be honest, and listen to her. Cady actively thought of how she would have loved to be treated in Cathy's place, this could be a good guide. Cady wanted nothing from Cathy except not to be lonely. The little glass figurines Cathy loved fascinated Cady too she loved little things, but by nature of her male-imaged body you wouldn't know it. Time turned around to flowing faster and faster as they walked back the car. Cady thought with panic rising, "There will be an end to this date thing, what will I do then at the end? Will Cathy just walk out of my life?" Calm came to her again, "There is still time, she seems happy, and I have never been here before." In a blink Cathy was pointing out her house and driveway. In a misty mind fog Cady got out and came around the passenger side door Cathy already had the door open a little. Cathy slid out gracefully smoothing her dress. She led Cady up the front steps to the front double door. It was dark; a glow from the curtained living room showed someone was still up. Cathy stepped up one step to the door level and Cady remained one step lower. At this level Cathy's head was even with Cady's. Cathy told Cady, "I had a wonderful night and thanks again for the rose." Cady flustered; the battle that had been won a day ago that allowed her to be where she stood at this moment rose again then subsided. Her feelings were trying to guide her, in fact, they were shouting at her. Cady avoided Cathy's face while reaching inside for some funny thing to say as a shield. Cathy quietly tilted her head slightly to one side and Cady looked directly into her eyes. Cady found her eyes searching back and forth. Cathy eyes smiled and Cady's eyes found rest in them. Cathy whispered, "Kiss me Cady." Cady surrendered, her eyes closed, her lips gently touched Cathy's and the porch light came on. They both giggled, Cathy turned and latch-keyed the door and turned back, "Call me tomorrow, goodnight."

Cathy was through the door and Cady stood a moment on the steps. Cady floated back to the car, started it and backed out of the driveway, then it hit her. Cady had never had a full-blown orgasm before except maybe once. She was crossed-dressed and looking in the full-length mirror seeing the reflection of her true female image while her cheeks burned like crazy. This was different, it came in waves each bigger than the first, inside the car driving down the hill she shouted and giggled over and over. Her whole body tingled there was no center to it. Her mind raced with the joy of being freed from all chains and anchors. By the time she pulled into the carport at home all that was left was the most pleasant feeling of peace she had ever had. Cady turned the key to the off position and sat there considering all that had happened today all that had changed for her. This didn't work, the peaceful feeling wouldn't tolerate the invasion of such deep soul searching, so instead she climbed the outside steps up to the front door to use the bathroom before going to bed. The house gave full credit to the celebration of the evening. The television was on with her parents watching the news. Cady got a nice welcome-back from her parents and gave a quick report of her evening then goodnight to all. There was no heat in her new bedroom in the basement aside from a small portable heater. Cady dialed the heater to the on position most of her stuff hadn't yet made it downstairs from her old bedroom. It was the first private bedroom she had ever had and now both of the Anderson boys each had their own room. Boys, she may look the part but didn't feel the part. Although tonight there was an amazing reward for being a boy, there was Cathy. Cady pondered, "There has to be a way of maintaining myself, of holding this conflict at some fixed level or even getting rid of it entirely." Cady promised herself that she would not be dishonest with Cathy about anything especially this. Cady's mother's alcohol and mental health problems had been hidden from Cady's dad before marriage. There were signs right after marriage of strange behavior on the part of her mother that Dad noticed apart from her drinking. Pregnancy came and after both boys' births a slow and very steady return of these problems made themselves shockingly known. When Merrill had asked his mother-in-law about her daughter's behaviors her glib answer was that she had always had them... Dad was hurt and never forgave his in-laws for hiding this from him before the marriage.

"No secrets from Cathy," Cady resolved, "But am I sure just what my hidden truth is? I have never had a girlfriend before it would be a very male thing, perhaps it changes you inside, gives you completeness of mind and body. It's barely summer, Cathy and I both have time to learn about ourselves as well as each other. Stop thinking and go to sleep Cady you have lots to dream about tonight and remember you are no longer alone..."

***

Cathy woke up. Cady woke up. It was Thursday, these were the last two days of school and the house was noisy with clumping feet upstairs. Cathy got ready and headed out to the bus stop just outside of her home. Cady escaped and walked the short distance to school. Two half-days at school Cathy wondered if she would see Cady there at all. Cady entered the cafeteria. "This place abides year after year," she thought and took her place at the empty table in the corner with a single expectation. The graduates were completely through now except to stop by the office to pick up their actual diploma, all that they got last night was an empty envelope. In reality for the rest of the remaining classes, all that these two days held were socializing and annual signing. In theory, if you had some important piece of homework you missed you still had time to get it in. Cathy wandered into the cafeteria and there was Cady over in the corner alone. Cathy's heart skipped a beat; Cady's heart skipped a beat as they sat together until the morning bell. Cady dropped Cathy off at her classroom door and walked the main hall to the office. At the reception desk Cady stood in a short line for her turn at the reception desk. It was like signing out of a hotel you had stayed in for four years, your place and time here was over. Cady signed her assigned-at-birth name to the list of graduates picking up their diplomas. She had a new status now the jump from student to past student to adult had befallen her. In addition to her diploma, she also was given a pocket-sized copy of it to carry in her wallet. The office staff was all proud smiles; Cady now understood that she was the product of their labor. This is what the school did; it produced finished grads year after year. Cady had no place here anymore, but was granted space in deference of her new standing these last few days of the year. Cady was free to roam the halls and visit until her heart was content. The science wing was now in the period when Cady would normally be there, so there is where she went. Cathy had study hall in that same period so the two used the time to chat as they had done during the year. They also helped Mr. Rapp clear the lab space of loose equipment by storing it for the next year's classes. Cathy was still floating on air but a dark cloud stood only two days away. Cady told her, "I have to go to Thorp this weekend for the summer." Cathy returned, "I have to go to Quincy next weekend for the summer." Cathy's mind pointed out to her how it was just so ironic that she had prayed for something to happen graduation night, it did, and now they only had two days together. In that short time Cathy and Cady walked and talked. Cady had even stopped by Cathy's house to meet her parents before she left on her way to the ranch. The very last action was Cady's; she pressed a Thank You note into Cathy's hand. It read simply, "Thank you for the graduation gift (a New Testament) please write!!! Here is my phone number and address at the ranch, Love Cady." Cady had already planned to write to Cathy continuously no matter what happened...

***

We had all the Covid 19 barriers to overcome to get into the exam room (the same one Cathy had been in the day before) and a nice medical assistant named Grace helped us to straighten out the paperwork since there were two of us now. She asked about face or breast being a priority and then said she would bring in the sizing stuff either way. Cathy is sitting in the corner chair as the alert supporting wife and I am in the center-stage exam-chair waiting for Dr. Megan Dreveskracht. My plan was to explore lots of FFS (facial feminization surgery) questions and then maybe ask about breast enhancement information. Hormone replacement had changed the shape of my face leaving me with lots of loose skin in addition to giving me a huge craving for dark chocolate. When I smile the wrinkles start at my mouth causing waves all the way to my ears. The chocolate thing is just spooky although I expect it's better than craving pickles. Anyway, if Cathy needed to ask a question or two about her upcoming surgery she could do this also. Dr. Megan Dreveskracht pops in suddenly with, "Good to see you and how are you two doing?" She is thin and athletic and aside from plastic surgery running is her passion. There is a pile of breast forms in a plastic crate staring at me from the counter. Cathy had already poked at one of them just before the doctor came in, hard to resist not to. I tell Dr. Megan, "I am interested in FFS (Facial

58

Feminization Surgery) stuff and perhaps breast enhancement." She confides, "I don't do face procedures, that is left to my partner Dr. Tony Mangubat. So you can come see him on another day." Trying to hide my disappointment (I have never met him and had such confidence in her) I tell her, "Cool, I am so into getting information on breast implants with you!" At this point, something in my brain sort of stutters to a stop leaving me on autopilot. Dr. Megan tells me to stand and slip off my shirt, so she can measure me. I comply then ask my bra also, yes that too. I am standing bare-chested with a female doctor judging my insignificant little breasts, for as tall as I am I feel very small. It is traumatic I haven't had to face anyone bare-chested for many years. Never has my whole transitioning identity, as female, been stripped naked to be judged. She tells me I already have quite a good amount of breast tissue right near a C cup, more than she is used to seeing. I focus on the affirming comment it gives me an anchor to hold onto as she makes her measurement from each nipple to the crease below my neck. She helps me into a tight front closing surgical bra she uses to size different breast forms and has me slip my t-shirt back on. She chats idly with us for a few minutes and I am pretty sure it is to let me calm my nerves. Breast form sizing is kind of like what the eye doctor does as she asks which lens is clearer to look through 1 or 2, A or B. Dr Megan hands me a breast form to slip into the bra and quickly learns that I am not very good at centering the sticky forms on my nipple. To my relief she steps up to center them herself; I am tall and she is beautifully short so I bent my knees to help. She starts with smaller forms asking me what I thought of each from looking in the mirror. Dr. Megan grabs the back of my t-shirt to pull it tight so I can really see my curves. I am lost really with the realization of this huge step I find myself taking. The only person to have ever seen me with this many breast curves has been Cathy. Thankfully both Dr. Megan and Cathy offer to help me. Cathy doesn't think the first forms at 375cc fill out my chest width and Dr. M agrees. She tells me, "To get the width you need, we should use a medium profile form and since you are so tall you could easily carry 475 to 500cc under the muscle." She works those two forms between my breast tissue and the bra, the forms stick to my skin so it is a chore to center each of them. My left breast is smaller than my right and using a 500cc on it and a 475cc in the other evens them out. As Dr. Megan says, they are sisters but not twins. I have been looking in the mirror without my glasses and ask Cathy for them. This does no good as they just steam up as soon as I put them on from my mask and me being so nervous. When I do look at my reflection in the mirror, I see someone else looking back and I really like what she looks like. Cathy seems to approve also. This is a milestone in my transition, one that I never thought I would reach. The whole time, in these last fifteen years with my therapist Sandy Fosshage, I have always approached the idea of transition in tiny steps. In my mind, I held onto the concept that I could hop back any number of those steps at any time and stand still. During my life I had constructed a world full of reasons to do just this; someone's failure in their transition could be found if I looked long enough. What I wouldn't fully face, as I moved along, was even though I held on to that concept of reversal, I didn't actually possess the option to use it. That concept is still with me, as broken as it is, as I find surprise in a mirror that my continuing transition is marching along leaving the male world behind me. The idea of having permanent breast curves, which pretty much completely locks me out of men's spaces, doesn't hold as much fear as that reversal concept demands. On the contrary, those curves complete Cadance; they open a world up to her the only problem is recognizing the extent of needing such things. I have my face to do now also my bust, and even lower. All that I ask of myself is to finish it within the coming year and not be afraid anymore… Cathy has even pointed out with faces being masked perhaps I should move breast enchantment higher up in priority it would give a better clue as to my gender.

***

The Anderson household packed up their oldest child and began the drive east to the ranch near Thorp; it was Saturday June 9,1973. No one understood the true significance of this particular trip, leastwise Cady. In her lifetime I-90 was an old acquaintance sometimes fair and sometimes foul, but always leading to and from the ranch. Today it was just numbing. Along with Cady there was Mother Dorothy and brother David; Father Merrill didn't care to make the trip. For the three in the car traveling along the freeway, it was just a trip to a place that had been home for two years and a summer home since fifth grade. This time will be the longest stay for Cady apart from the two years the little family of three lived there year around. Cady had started her life in the little house next to the big ranch house, so had Merrill and Dorothy started their married life there. Merrill had worked in a gas station in the city of Ellensburg. The couple would move to Coulee City just before the birth of Cady's brother David, although there would be a mad dash to drive back to Ellensburg for the actual birth of her brother. Cady had seen letters talking about her mom Dorothy's need to be farther away from her mother Hazel. Dad Merrill found a job at a gas station in Coulee City one hundred miles away. The culture of the ranch for Dorothy had moved from Hazel and Charley her parents' place, to Joyce and Charley her father's place.

The summer of 1972 had been an amazing summer for Cady and David at the ranch. Beloved Grandma Hazel had done the inconceivable, she had died in the fall of 1971 leaving behind a grieving family especially Grandpa Charley. Cady had watched her grandfather at the November funeral service in Ellensburg. The service was at its end, everyone stood and embraced nearby weeping loved ones. Charley, this tall strong man stood alone in a room full of friends looking desperately for but not finding comfort, so very sad to see. Cady resolved from here on in to help her grandpa find comfort once again. She didn't know if it had been her idea for her mother to remain a week there with Grandpa while the rest of the family had to return home for school and work. Later someone had the idea for the Andersons all to go back over to the ranch for Thanksgiving to surprise Grandpa. Cady and her entire family arrived at the ranch late the night before Thanksgiving, waking Grandpa up from his night's sleep. Cady had never seen him so shocked or pleased. Anyway let's just say Cady was in full agreement when the idea came up to spend the summer of

1972 along with her brother David helping her grandfather on his ranch. The three worked and lived together. Cady found she could do many things like keeping the house along with outside ranch work, and she found she couldn't do many things like keeping the account books and arc-welding. David and Cady both grew from the experience, and male-imaged Cady also became a friend to her grandfather as least she felt like she had. The summer of 1972 came to an end and Cady and David returned home leaving Grandpa alone once again. During the gray Autumn months that followed in the Kittitas Valley Grandpa had several single widow ladies come visit him; friends were doing their part to cure his aloneness and perhaps theirs too. Joyce had sold her and her husband Ray's farm after his death two years earlier then moved into Ellensburg to semi-retire. She was childless and happily living alone at least for the first year there. Grandpa had met her before Grandma Hazel's death when he leased a ranch right across the street from theirs and had also custom baled hay for them. Cady had worked the sled pulled behind the baler that summer and had dinner at Ray and Joyce's table. Now it was Joyce inviting Grandpa to supper at her home in town and as Grandpa put it about Joyce, "We both looked at each other and decided there was no reason either of us should be lonely…"

Cady's mother was trying very hard to get along with her new stepmother Joyce. Charley had married Joyce just a few months ago and Dorothy was determined not to lose access to her father. It is an odd concept for a kid to conceive of her mother as an adult now having a stepmother. Cady never considered this at the time and it would have been helpful in understanding her mom's desperate actions if she had. Joyce viewed the three as invaders into her new home space, they had no claim or place here. Joyce had never had kids of her own and was fiercely independent, which just added to the initial animus she had for Dorothy, Cady, and David.

***

The three Andersons parked outside the ornate little front gate. Cady gave the car keys back to her mom and gathered up her stuff.

The ranch just felt like home, after all, it had been theirs for a while. The towering wind-swept pine tree in the front yard stood silently at the moment and the still air full of familiar scents. They knocked at the front door, a very strange thing to do considering the years past when you just walked right in. Grandpa opened the door; Mom gave him a big hug and everyone filed in. Cady and family had met Joyce before in short bursts. Cady dropped her life-pile of possessions on the floor at the bottom step of the stairs leading up to the second floor. The trip was just to drop Cady off no overnight stays anymore. It was all so disjoint, being kind of like a familiar stranger in a familiar strange land. Folks sat down to talk before Mom and David would return home. At some point David walked through the kitchen to the bathroom. On his way back he checked out the kitchen cabinet, just like he had done a hundred times before. It was a habit formed from living there; sort of like looking in the refrigerator every time you passed by. This time Joyce took great offence to someone being in her kitchen let alone opening a cabinet! She was loud and harsh causing David to slink away. Mom was visibly shaken but kept it in. Joyce would tightly explain to Cady later after they left that this is her place now. Okay fine. Grandpa put gas in our car, Mom hugged Cady one last time, and then Dorothy and David were gone...

**

In order to stay here Cady would have to carve out a place in this house to be her own. It was an easy decision where in the ranch house to stay. The upstairs held four bedrooms, two of which belonged to Cady and David and their mom for the two years they lived here full time. Cady chose the bedroom his mom had used it was plenty roomy. Joyce had no clue that the upstairs had served as home for the three invaders for two years. Everyone was happy with Cady upstairs and Charley and Joyce downstairs. Mom's old folding dining room table was already in that bedroom. It would make a good desk, just had to find a chair and everything was set except for the bedroom door. That bedroom door had never closed all the way while this was Cady's mom's bedroom. Something deep inside Cady was demanding this to be fixed so she would have a barrier to her past. Cady spent two hours unhinging the door and shaving the bottom until the door would swing smoothly shut.

Next day Grandpa had a surprise for Cady, a new horse, he was a light brown bay with a dark black mane and beautiful dark eyes. He was just old enough to begin breaking for riding. Cady named him Rocky for the rocky Taneum Creek that ran through the ranch. The summer was new and the irrigation season was full on. Grandpa had their work all laid out, rubber boot cowboys and fence builders.

Cady needed letter writing supplies so she asked Joyce if they had any she could spare and she did, cool. A swarm of bees had made a temporary home on a lower branch of one of the two cherry trees just outside of the back screen-door. Cady clears her mind of the tension of the drop off here of the drama that happened. She considers, "The bees are free to make a new home wherever the queen decides." The bees as a mass suddenly undulate at the end of the branch momentarily distracting her thought, "This is just a temporary place for them, but if the queen is satisfied a home will be built all around her." Cady is free from the turmoil of home, at the start of her nineteenth year of life, and there are no expectations put upon her except the ones she puts upon herself. "This is all so foolhardy in reality, but after suffering so much for so long even four months looks like a brave new world to you," Cady thinks to herself, "I also have a chance to be free from loneliness forever, there is Cathy. I am going to be the best boyfriend ever for Cathy. Starting tomorrow I am going to gather my thoughts each day and share them with Cathy regularly via mail."

Joyce is slowly becoming more comfortable with Cady being around. Cady has to be respectful of space not allotted to her in the ranch house. Of course, this boundary is ever expanding as male-imaged Cady is asked to do things around the house. Joyce does like to make cookies, one kind in particular she calls ranger cookies. It is a take on a chocolate chip type but instead of using the oven she uses the waffle maker. Cady enjoys them whenever she gets the chance. Friends of Joyce's are staying for a week, she and Grandpa go out with them in the evenings leaving Cady alone in her room. Cady is nothing to them except as Joyce's male-imaged step-grandson so Cady simply disappears for the day after a morning glass of milk to work the ranch. During the workday Grandpa continues to visit with company so Cady is working alone this week. Joyce always has a fresh pickle of some sort available on the main dining table. Breakfast for Cady is a glass of milk to everyone's chagrin; they insist it isn't enough to work on. It seems to be okay for her though. Dinner is a country style big meal and supper something light and yes Cady does eat. The hours she keeps are up by 6:00am out by 7:00am, the day will be parceled out as needed with the exception of dinner hour and ended at the supper hour around 6:00pm, bedtime is targeted at 8:30. Cady spends as little time in the evening with her grandpa and Joyce as she has to, Cady would rather be upstairs writing letters to Cathy. So, it is 'good night' by 7:00pm and upstairs to be with Cathy via a letter. It slowly dawns on them that Cady is writing to her honey each night and this fact makes up for the lack of time spent with Grandpa. Truth is Cady is physically worn out from the ranch work each day but on the other hand she revels in it too. Overcoming the battle Cady fought on graduation day allowed her to be a 'he', to be male, to have a girlfriend, and to put the discord deep into the darkness never to see the light of day again; it took much out of her too. In a conversation with herself male-imaged Cady dwells, "I'm a guy alone doing manly work bending things toward the way I want them to go. It makes you feel powerful and in control of mind and body; even if you aren't really." Cady's horse would temper this bravado quite a bit over the next month too. Cady thinking to herself, "Okay, even as a 'he' there was still room in my mind to love the little things I see each day; I need to share them with Cathy especially all the places and feelings I love."

***

Cady alone in her room on Wednesday June 13 begins a nightly letter writing ritual. (We will allow Cady to be 'he' at this moment forward in honor of all he has come through so far in the quest to not be alone in life.) He writes to Cathy with the idea the letter will reach

65

her when she arrives at the Orchard in Quincy, the timing is tricky but she will be there soon. Cady is sitting at the ancient oak dining room table that had traveled to the ranch along with Dorothy and her two kids after their rescue. Only a few of their family possessions made the journey. It's folded into its narrowest form and pushed against the wall opposite of the doorway to serve as a desk. Two dormer windows on either side both are open to the evening air. Right in the middle of the room a rough brick chimney rises up from the floor and exits through the roof. This chimney services the freestanding oil furnace in the living room below and is the main heat source for the house; even with this utility it is still an intruder in the bedroom. The continual streaming travel hum from I-90 flows in through the front facing window set on the south side. The lone tall pine tree moves in the evening breeze enough to be heard above this din. 'Dear Cathy.' Cady writes of his feeling at the moment in missing Cathy and the deep desire to simply have her with him to talk quietly soul to soul. He has begun to read the New Testament she gave him on graduation. Then the impressions of the day fill the middle of the page, the swarm of bees, and a joke about petting the swarm, leaky rubber boots, and the changing colors of the sky during the day. Cady has been on foot walking the length and width of the ranch tending irrigation water (he refers to this as playing in the water) because the horses need new shoes that they will get tomorrow. He ends with love and a blessing. The letter is sealed, addressed, and stamped. Sleep comes quickly to a tired body while the music of the I-90 freeway plays in the background throughout the night. A balance has been created at the ranch; Cady is his grandpa's right hand but this time he is being treated as a young adult. The lifetime border from childhood to adult was crossed and his grandpa takes delight in knowing Cady is the most perfectly experienced hired man he could ever have. It is the delight a father might have in taking his son into the family business. For now, it is a great gift for both Cady and his grandpa to share for this time will pass all too soon and the experiences of these days will pass with it.

***

Cathy had yet to travel to the orchard near Quincy; she would reach her summer home on Saturday June 16th a week after Cady's arrival at the ranch. Her letter writing ritual had begun on June 11th ahead of Cady's but her first letter would arrive after Cady's. Her letter details a two-day stay at Mr. Linde's cabin retreat with several other classmates include Michael and his electric guitar. In a very similar fashion to Cady's letter, she details the sounds and feelings of Hood Canal making a verbal pictures to share. Classmates out in boats, clamming on the beach, and the loneliness that comes from not being part of the group these are what Cathy conveyed. Cathy includes in the letter pressed flowers that she has found and dates and time markers. Ending it with missing you and love. Cathy seals her letter with a wax seal this time she uses a four-leaf clover. Her final act is to light the wick of a stick of sealing wax with a match. Tip the stick so the wax drips down dropping through the air onto the closed envelope forming a puddle right at the center of the closed envelope flap. Quickly she presses a metal seal down on the wax puddle as it hardens. Without sharing a letter yet they both had kindred spirits in what they valued to share with each other. Cathy wasn't sure just how often or what Cady would write about. It would be at least four weeks before they both would be back in Seattle over the fourth of July holiday. Where she had floated on air before she now had heartache, coloring all she experienced daily. Cathy had a growing empty space in her heart; she thought to herself, "Why had I been so slow to approach Cady? We could have had so many more days with each other if I had acted at Cady's birthday." Cathy decides to start a continuous letter to Cady, one she will write in each day and then give to him when they see each other. Again the two have each decided on their own, to write each day.

***

Cathy back home after the Hood Canal trip is in her inner sanctum her basement bedroom, she is writing in her continuous letter to Cady. Her best guess she writes is that she will be driven to the orchard in three days. Her ride will be with her grandparents, who are in Seattle because of the release of her grandmother from the hospital after a six-month stay from a nervous breakdown. It will be the weekend but until then a sort of sad boredom has settled itself upon her. She attends her friend Sue's wedding and has a great time with a group of giggling girls decorating the happy couple's car. This was a welcome diversion from loneliness creeping up in her thoughts. Cathy spends time packing, planning, and praying. Cathy misses Cady and the more she thinks about him the more she misses him. A struggle is taking place within her heart she had admitted love for a guy once before, he was twenty and she fifteen. It was wonderful then awful. He hurt her over and over again until she freed herself from him. Cady was so different, gentle, and undemanding, so opposite of him. There was something else about Cady that made Cathy want to run to him but not yet... Friday night comes, her grandparents arrive and in doing so supplant Cathy from her bedroom for the night. Tonight it will be bedtime in the rec room for her.

***

The Tuttle family of two packs up their oldest Dixon granddaughter Cathy and drive east toward Quincy. The drive on I-90 is well known to Cathy, up over Snoqualmie Pass and down the other side. She like Cady has known this trip even before I-90 was a freeway that now by-passes towns like North Bend, Cle Elum, and Ellensburg. It was a single lane road then flowing through the main streets of those towns, following the railroad path up into the Cascade Mountains and making a crossing at Snoqualmie Pass. Here I-90 had continued to climb up to and go over the pass while the railroad had tunneled through the mountain instead of climbing it. The hazard in the long climb for cars was getting behind a slow heavily loaded semi-truck, with no passing lane it was frustratingly slow and her dad would get grumpy. The old I-90 had lots of forced stops at towns it wandered through, Cathy enjoyed stopping in Ellensburg and eating at the Hi-Way Grille with her grandparents it was something only they did. She would always order the same thing fish and chips with extra lemon and mustard for dipping. On the road again to the modern I-90 that is a two-lane freeway unimpeded by traffic lights and full of cars and trucks flowing continuously rushing to be somewhere else as fast as they dare.

The Tuttle family car, a 1965 Ford Falcon, turns onto their long dirt driveway coming to a dusty stop at a little green oasis compound surrounded by a sea of dusty agriculture. The oasis is bounded between two houses, one small old and barely adequate in its day, the other big modern with many bedrooms but not quite complete and a nearby workshop that has always abided in its location. Now at the orchard Cathy had frustrations to add to her heartache. Cathy's grandmother had been incapacitated with mental health problems for the last six months, so the house, which Cathy is now in charge of, needs lots of cleaning. Cathy walks into a kitchen the deep sink is full of dirty dishes needing to be hand washed and a thick layer of dust is on every surface in the house. The dust is just part of the agriculture of the Columbia Basin. In the orchard a super fine layer of satin feeling dust covers the dirt. When the wind blows it collects everywhere and adheres to everything. Cathy also was hoping to stay in the little house trailer permanently parked near the big house this would have given her the most freedom and privacy as she could come and go without notice. Cathy loved to go out into the orchard at night when the heat of the day had gone. She instead had to settle for a room near her grandparent's bedroom in the big house forcing her to have go past their door in all her comings and goings.

The orchard started off as raw desert land purchased before the irrigation waters from the Grand Coulee Dam project began to flow. The main point of the Grand Coulee Dam was to bring water to the desert for agriculture. Cathy's grandfather with his engineering background from his time with the Army Corp of Engineers built upon the near-empty land little by little. The vision he formed came from years of planning a retirement to an orchard of his own construction. During his career he had been part of big construction projects from the very start to the finish such as the dams controlling floodwaters of the Green River and White River in Enumclaw, Washington. He had been the Head Engineer of both the Howard Hanson and Mud Mountain Dams. So yes he had his plan, his vision for his orchard. He was its chief architect, builder, and laborer. The land at time of purchase had one original small shanty house and shed shortly followed by him building another smaller house nearby. As time would go by the original shanty house would yield to being enlarged to a more substantial two-bedroom home. Following this was the construction of much bigger modern style home just across the yard from the little two-bedroom home. It had three times the bedrooms and built-in air conditioning but still lingered being completely done construction-wise. Still in concept of one main house and a little adjunct house nearby. Not unlike the concept of Cady's grandparents' place having two houses, one big main home with nearby shed and a smaller adjunct home close by. These two little houses stand as a similarity between Cady and Cathy. Cady's first year of life was spent with his parents at the little house at the ranch so too was Cathy's first summer of life at the orchard in that small house with her parents. Both of these houses were near moving water, Cady's the Taneum Creek and Cathy's the West Canal of the Columbia Basin Reclamation Project. Just another similarity among many the two would soon come to know.

***

Cathy spent the day cleaning the big house before her mother, brothers, and sister arrive. The Dixon family is reunited minus Cathy's dad when a dusty cloud following a Ford station wagon brings Cathy's mother and sibling to the big house. Cathy and her mother spent the next near hour unloading the vehicle of groceries and housewares. The kitchen was fully restocked and ready for many meals to come. Cathy takes the opportunely to carve out her place at the orchard by buttonholing her mother about moving into the trailer. Cathy had thought this through; if her mom simply says 'no' Cathy has a quick backup plan of what about the empty bedroom in the little original house. The trailer was the most private but you had to go outside to use the bathroom at the pool. The little original house was almost as private and had its own bathroom. As Cathy had predicted the negotiations landed her in one of the original house's bedrooms. She was happy it was so much better than where she is now. Cathy lightheartedly moved her stuff over to the little house with its screened porch, kitchen, freezer room, bathroom, and two bedrooms (one of which had stuff stored in it). The bedroom she chose had a nice vanity dresser, a double bed and a closet. Cathy unpacked into the space; she placed the picture Cady had given her as a gift on the dresser so she could easily look at it. She sat at the dresser and opened the first of two letters from Cady. These had been waiting for her when she arrived at the orchard. The letters are written in a tightly formed flowing script sometimes so tightly formed that it takes time to make out the words. As Cathy makes her way through the letters a curtain was being lifted, this was Cady in a letter. This was exactly how he talks it was as if he was there with her. She felt a warm feeling of happiness hugging her. Cady wrote of loneliness for her and deep desire to talk to her face to face, there was news of the ranch, a bee swarm, fence building, tending water, horses getting new horseshoes, and reading the New Testament she had given him. Most important was of loneliness for a girl named Cathy, how lucky he had been in finding her and the four slow weeks until they would see each other. Cathy reread the letters and gazed at Cady's picture. She thought to herself, "I was so foolish to have waited so long to get to know him." Cathy understood she was falling in love with Cady and four weeks was just too long to wait to see him. Cathy needed a plan, perhaps a phone call to the ranch just to hear Cady's voice would help. She realized also what it meant to say, "I love you" to Cady, the use of those words came with pain she still held from someone else. It was turning out that Cathy hadn't freed herself completely from the emotional pain her last boyfriend had inflicted upon her. She still owned that pain and it wasn't hers to own she didn't cause it. Cathy was simply being who she is, the pain was from being pushed to be someone else. The only way to be free to be with Cady was to tell him about what happened. She so didn't want to do this; the risk in her mind was losing Cady. That was unthinkable, but still somehow Cady was the one person she could trust, the one person she needed.

A balance is now being created with Cathy's mother acting as farm labor manager. Cathy and brother Phil will both have standard orchard jobs, the younger ones miscellaneous tasks. Cathy's grandpa had already had it in his mind that Cathy would thin apples for the next three weeks leaving her pretty much on her own every day. Phil would pick cherries as part of the larger picking crew of fifteen. Grandpa's was the lion's share of managing all the daily mechanics of the working orchard. The rhythm was now set as each summer day bloomed forth then faded into night. Cathy would aim to be out in the new orchard to pick then drop little apples from young trees to the ground until the summer heat drove her to shelter. She did at least six hours each day, eight at the start but as the heat increased the hours had to give as her skin turned angry red. Hot, tired, and sore Cathy writes to Cady extending an invitation for him to come to the orchard this coming weekend and spend an afternoon with her. She encloses a pressed flower that had gotten her attention, a foxglove, and her orchard phone number in the letter. Cathy puts a bridle on Blondie the Shetland pony and rides her down the long dusty driveway to the mailbox. Blondie had been her favorite horse for years and had also been her confidant over many a summer. Today Cathy explains to the horse, as she plods slowly along, how much she is looking forward to seeing Cady and just how much she needs to see Cady, "It will be so wonderful I will show him every special place I love here and we will talk and talk. Blondie I think I love him." Blondie knew from experience the best return answer was to continue to plod along.

***

Cady gently hung up the telephone; it had been just before 10pm when he heard the ringing. His eyes had not fully yielded to sleep so at the sound he was up and running downstairs to answer the phone. It had been Cathy, her voice so familiar so happy that he was uplifted just hearing it. Grandpa came out of their bedroom, saw that Cady had the phone and chuckled to himself as he returned to their bedroom.

Cathy had been so eager to see him that she couldn't wait for a letter to come with the answer to her invitation. Cady fell in love with her at that very moment. Cathy hadn't actually said, "I love you" but Cady instantly discerned the unspoken words in his heart. Such a powerful thing to have someone love you, it is disarming in a way that frees you to love them in return. Cady's isolative shell was partially disarmed by burying the disabling thoughts of his mind/body gender conflict and the instant he heard Cathy's voice that night Cady was freed to love her. There were still barriers he would have to overcome, pain that he owned but wasn't his to own, because he didn't cause it. His trust in Cathy was boundless in this moment. He had never trusted anyone in this way before he couldn't explain it just knew it. Cady and Cathy talked for only a few minutes as long-distant per-minute charges were expensive over the telephone wire, but the feelings flowed on and on afterward. Cady's day was spent tending irrigation water across the ranch and keeping the cattle in whatever field they had been moved to. He had put the ditching plow on the tractor's three-point hitch. Cady loved the Ford 8N wheel tractor, he knew every nut and bolt of the thing. His love came from the utility of the machine; Cady would spent hours either driving around each field pulling some implement or at the shop changing one implement for another. With the cattle in a field where the irrigation water was currently turned off, Cady would tractor over to the field the cattle just left to repair the damaged irrigation ditches before turning the water on there. The ditch plow implement was just the best friend he had for this. It would clear irrigation ditches in nothing flat and where it couldn't be used, well, Cady with a shovel was the answer. Setting and moving water from one set to another was another story in itself, one that involved spending the day on horseback with a shovel on Cady's shoulder. On this particular day Cady was alone on the ranch, the dinner at noon was a very simple one, a sandwich he made from left over roast and a glass of milk. The custom set by his grandpa was to nap after eating until one-thirty in deference of the heat of the day. Cady used that time today to walk among the scanty Moth Mullein growing in the sandy gravel along the creek behind the house. Here he could rest his mind looking for agates and experiencing the life of the slow moving water world. Little thin fish hovering under and water skippers on the surface, both made unique shadows on the bottom of the now shallow creek. Over the years the ranch had grown in area as a new parcel across the street was added. With more land cleared it was as if to keep pace with Cady's growth from childhood to adult the two akin to each other. Over this time Cady had passed through the milepost of childhood identity, the ranch had passed through the milepost of identity of its own from wheat, sheep, goats, and finally yearling cattle. The ranch would remain a cattle ranch its true identity. Cady had great love of place here on the ranch, he had walked every inch as a boy and now as a young man followed every ditch and cow path to where it led. A railroad had crossed this land once; little bits of it were still visible at the base of the hills to the north of the ranch house. One or two old telegraph poles still stood along the grassy wide path that the rail-bed had become and if you dug down just a little you would find the railroad ties were still intact. The history of ranch house itself called to Cady with every creak and moan of its over hundred-year lifetime. Little bits of pottery from the original log cabin of the first settlers (Thorps and Splawns) could be found while weeding the garden next to the house and arrowheads in the orchard. Part of the love of this place for Cady was he could always count on this two hundred acre micro-world as a safe unchanging place. There were times in childhood during the time they lived there when all the adults especially his mom, had abandoned him and his brother by falling into a drunken stupor, but the ranch outside always gave sanctuary. So as long as he was here he was safe and protected even if it was only an illusion. If you want to understand Cady you needed to walk the ranch, know where all the old, long-gone structures as barns, corrals, cabins, dry creek beds, and the railroad bed were and the magic they had that still lay in those places. Cady was a prose writer, these came from a steady stream of conscience he renewed each day from the ranch itself. Cady was very much a solitary being keeping himself company even more so since the time he was nine years old and discovered gender. More to the point that a male body didn't align with a female soul, from that moment on Cady was both set apart and gathered within self. It had happened during a visit to the ranch and a solo stay with Grandma Hazel. Cady, with all the curiosity of a nine-year-old plus some, had been exploring the old mysterious ranch house coming across a hidden closet under the stairs. It was completely full of Grandma's old dresses and Grandpa's old western boots and hats. A new and odd curiosity filled Cady about all this stuff. He pulled on one of Grandma's dresses up over his head and looked at himself in the nearby full-length mirror hanging on the wall of the hall. Up to that point Cady didn't have much of an image of himself in his mind, he just looked out of his eyes each day never thinking what he looked like or was. It didn't matter he just was, but the image Cady saw in the mirror on that day aligned with something in his brain with a complete assurance of being. The experience froze him in place there at the mirror while his mind cleared away the fog. Cady danced around, spun, and stared at 'herself' again; she was that girl in the mirror! Cady's grandma Hazel had spied this little drama going on and grinned at Cady. Cady stopped and experienced another new feeling, embarrassment. It was now set in his mind he had done something wrong, to rectify he pulled off the dress and tried on Grandpa's boots and hat just to balance things out. Grandma Hazel giggled, Cady on the other hand did notice the very solemn difference, he now knew he was 'her' the girl in the mirror. The dress had felt so right it was in step with what she was inside, but for some reason Grandpa's hats and boots was what he had to wear for the world to see. Later Cady overheard Grandma Hazel telling Grandpa Charley that little Cady had tried on Grandpa's hat and boots, she didn't tell him that little Cady had also tried on Grandma Hazel's dress. Cady was grateful for this and always felt 'she' and Grandma shared a secret. Cady was looking for agates along the creek that he might share with Cathy this weekend but wasn't finding any. The old dry creek-bed upstream from here was a better place to look for agates, but it was heavily over-grown with transitional saplings making walking hard and didn't serve as the proper place for what Cady was really doing. Cady was fighting a battle once again, the one he thought he had put an end to. It wasn't much of a battle, but the idea that the mind/body gender conflict wasn't gone altogether was disturbing. He was walking the ranch to calm it and to look for an answer. The ranch always abides it remained steady even if he wasn't, the beard did help push the thoughts of being female down but not completely, what else could he do? Cady had let his hair grow long and was teased for it here even though it was within the accepted style these days. With the suddenness of most bad ideas it came to Cady to get a very conservative and very male haircut. He could do this in Ellensburg before heading to the orchard. It would help him to impress Cathy's grandfather a very important thing to do and punish his brain for female thoughts. After all, he was a boyfriend now and wasn't going to lose Cathy for anything.

***

Cathy thinned apples on established trees today in the upper and older part of the orchard nearest the canal, the idea was to prevent the overcrowding of young apples. By dropping the little inch in diameter apples onto the ground from a cluster of several bigger apples gave the biggest the chance to be even bigger. Cathy rhythm was to pinch the stem between her forefinger and thumb then snap the stem by bending it sharply from the branch without damaging the branch by breaking the little spur because that's where next year's apple will come from. Her mind was steadily busy building expectations for Sunday's visit with Cady. Cathy made a game when she finished a tree to take one of the little apples by its stem and give it one full turn while pulling. If the stem popped out in one turn it was an 'A' for Anderson if it popped out on the third turn it was a 'C' for Cady. Cathy made sure the stems mostly popped on either one or three turns avoiding other letters of the alphabet. Those expectations for future joy also brought the ever-growing lonely feeling of missing Cady at the moment. Cathy had so many places throughout the breadth and width of the orchard to share with Cady. She loved how Cady wrote about the ranch forming image by image and wanted him to know the images she saw each day of the orchard so that he might also come to love them. Cathy had begun to see the orchard through Cady's eyes, the changing sky the hums of the day then the drone of the evening giving way to nightfall. Cathy's dad was now at the orchard for a long weekend so her family was complete for a few days. Cathy had asked her mom if it was all right for Cady to come on Sunday for a visit and getting the answer of, "Fine but not for dinner, only for the afternoon Grandma Tuttle wasn't well enough to handle anything more." Cathy sighed thinking, "Grandma seemed pretty good to me." She took a chance and asked first her mother and later her father on their opinion of Cady. Both had similar answers from the short visit Cady had with them before he headed to the ranch a very Dixon answer of, "Liked him better than the last one." To Cathy it was music to her ears. Cathy already knew that her grandfather must like Cady because he liked to tease her about all the letters she got from him, a very good sign. Cathy completed a row of trees and moved to the next row, she counted by rows and not trees, a row held something like fifteen to twenty-five trees again she went by rows not trees. The number of trees in a row varied on the age of that part of the orchard. An established area had fewer trees because over the years the trees themselves were thinned. In young areas the trees were closer together so rows held many more trees. The heat of the day was in full blast, Cathy's lunch in the shade helped cool her down but back out in the orchard it was clear she would need to stop soon. She finished the tree and moved the ladder to a new tree it was almost 2:00 and she decided to call it a day. There were shade trees near the ponies' corral and after a break under them Cathy wandered over to the corral for a talk with a group of four very good listeners. Cathy almost had the feeling the ponies understood her daily talks with them about how much Cady meant to her. Blondie a dapple-gray was the oldest and the ringleader. Cathy had grown up with her. She was trained to the pony cart as well as saddle or bareback riding the others not so much so. Goldie was next she was a palomino and a loner her mother was Blondie. Coco or Coco-Loco as Cathy called her was a chestnut brown she was the shyest and hardest to approach. The last and smallest was Little Ivory Bar of Soap she was a light dapple-gray and a clown. There would always be something she was doing that could give Cathy a laugh. Like the time she casually walked out of the corral while

Cathy's little sister Linda whose back was turned at the time was busy putting Blondie in. Ivory was Blondie's granddaughter. All of these ponies came to the orchard in 1967 from their home near Enumclaw where Cathy's grandfather and grandmother had made their home. Herman and Freda Tuttle raised their children here during Herman's 25 plus year career in the Army Corps of Engineers as Chief Engineer during the construction and the operation of the two flood control dams, the Mud Mountain Dam and the Howard Hanson Dam. The orchard had been built to be the retirement home for Cathy's Grandparents, Herman and Freda Tuttle. Herman was the most amazing man, he was a career engineer in the Army Corp of Engineers his lifelong dream was to retire to and run his own commercial apple orchard. He had painstakingly planned it over the years by purchasing property, some 320 acres near Quincy, Washington, in the early 1940s. After the original purchase the previous owner Henry Weber farmed the property for two or three years in dry land wheat. In the late 1940's Cathy's grandfather built his own small structure house. Irrigation water became available late in 1951 and officially available in 1952 from the Columbia River to turn the desert to irrigated farmland. Another small structure house was built and subsequently enlarged in the mid 1950's and across from it the big dream house (along with a pool) for Cathy's grandmother was built in the 1970's. In Cathy's lifetime the orchard grew as she did, rows of trees would be planted in smaller sized lots, other parts of the land would be farmed in different crops until the time was right to plant more trees. The ultimate goal was to have almost all the land in apples and some other tree fruits. Cathy felt part of the orchard, it was family it was her grandparents but the trouble that came with her grandmother's mental state had shaken this world. Still the orchard was the same it abided and this gave her a sense of peace. Cathy didn't sleep soundly that night before the day of Cady's visit, she had all kinds of expectations dancing through her brain and a trepidation or two poked its nose in just to make the party crazier.

***

Cady had completed Sunday's light schedule of work consisting mostly of checking water sets in the fields actively under irrigation. It was another hot day, they had had several one hundred degree days this summer something very unusual but not unheard of. Cady was nervous about driving to the orchard it was located outside of Quincy in the wilds of Grant County, which had few natural landmarks for the navigationally challenged. Cathy had been very patient with him in going over the directions, first take I-90 to George, Washington, get off onto State Route 281 toward Quincy, watch for the house with the airplane parked behind it; that should be 7 NW turn left, drive until you get to S NW and turn right, drive to 7.5 NW and turn to the right follow the dirt road to the house. No problem, what Cathy didn't know was how easily Cady gets lost especially when he is out-of-his-mind nervous. Cady had the use of his grandpa's well-worn sun-faded blue Ford F100 pickup, it was a work truck dented and scratched even so Cady had washed it with care. Cady was focused, Cathy was fifty miles away from him at the moment about an hours' drive, he needed a short male haircut and something beside himself to bring to Cathy. The only barber Cady knew of in town was the one his grandfather had used after Grandma Hazel passed away. Grandma Hazel cut everyone's hair; whenever Cady and family came to visit the first order of business were haircuts for the kids. Hazel and Cady talked for hours on every visit, mostly in the kitchen while work was being done there. Cady thought of his grandma Hazel being just as much a best friend as a grandmother. Hazel painted in oils, her easel stood in one corner of the living room always with a work in progress. The walls of the ranch house were covered in framed paintings she had completed; even if, as she told Cady, they are never done you just come to a stopping point. The palette board she used was thick with layer upon layer of dried paint in every detectable color. Hazel also did ceramics and dabbled in fabric arts. Her true love was panning for gold along the creek. Hazel was a daughter of the dust bowl years; living in Kansas she learned every skill a farmer/rancher's wife should know. Hazel, two summers ago, was determined that Cady learn these arts even though Grandpa had other work for Cady to do. So it was

Cady standing at the easel under the direction of Grandma Hazel for hours on end that wonderful summer. Mixing titanium white with other colors, how to use a palette knife, and what each brush is for. Oh, and she taught Cady to cut hair also, a skill he would greatly appreciate later.

Cady drove to Ellensburg and found the barbershop open, the gray-haired barber was happy to have a customer. Cady, even though very conflicted, sat himself down in the barber chair and watched long strands of dark brown hair slide down the cape unto the floor. After paying the barber Cady resolved not to think about what he had just done. The next stop was Zittings department store the shirt Cady had on was okay but his jeans were full of rips from barbed wire. Cady had never shopped for clothes completely by himself, he had lost weight, and now his go-to size didn't feel right. At the end of the guys' department shelf just before the shelf was taken over with ladies clothes was a pair of brushed light blue denim pants. They had pockets front and back although the back pockets were some shade of pastel pink. Something inside of Cady loved these they fit great were soft and the next thing he knew a decision had been made to buy them. While wandering back and forth in the store looking for something that felt right to give Cathy he came to a display of flowering plants and a gloxinia with purple blooms shouted at him. Cady made his purchases, changed into his new pants in the pickup, and drove to the entrance ramp of I-90 eastbound. Cady would wonder later how it was he would get a punishingly short male haircut and then buy soft pants with pink pockets. It was hot and air conditioning was still rare in cars and non-existent in farm trucks. Cady knew I-90 from Seattle to Ellensburg by heart, east of town was unknown to him. The miles blew noisily by as the truck's tires howled, Cady climbed out of the Kittitas Valley then down to the Columbia River and across up to the Columbia Basin. The exit to George and Quincy comes up and Cady exits onto State Route 281. Now being in a strange place alone making the most important trip of his life stretches his nerves taught. Road signs are in numbers and letters not names. Cady passes a house and glimpses a small two-seat airplane parked behind it. He turned around in joy! Cathy had saved him by giving him this landmark. Cady crosses a little bridge and wonders if the canal under it is the one that goes through the orchard somewhere nearby. A right turn then another onto a dust covered dirt road brings Cady to a little green oasis with apple trees in neat rows all around. Cady parks near what looks like a workshop, turns off the truck, whispers a prayer, and gets out.

***

Cathy had been waiting and thinking what would the appropriate place for Cady to find her when he drove up. Cathy thought, "Stretched out in the hammock would be cool, kind of not too eager, kind of flirty, and it's comfortable for me." The downside was she couldn't be still and she was eager. Time was just dragging; there was no way to know just when Cady would arrive just sometime between noon and two. A dusty old truck pulled to a stop at 1:00, Cathy jumped up from the chair near the hammock and all but skipped over to the figure getting out shouting, "You're here!" She stopped short and stared, something wasn't right about the way Cady looked.

Cady's heart rose to his mouth as Cathy stared at him, he asks, "What's wrong???"

"You got your hair cut!!!" Cathy blurted this out in a tone of 'how-could-you.' She tilted her head to one side and stood for a long moment looking at Cady. Her expectations of seeing the exact-image of Cady she had last time they were together was all she had dreamed of every day since they had been apart. That image was the picture she had on her dresser of him the one she whispered, "I love you" to at bedtime. A tear nearly came to her eye then she saw the pants with the pink pockets, this was so Cady, joy took over and the tear receded. Cathy of course couldn't know then that Cady had sacrificed his hair for her, to become a man for her, and to love just her.

"It will take a while to get used to is all," Cathy smile was unrestrained and her blue eyes sparkled. Disappointment melted away it had no place in her this day. She was with her love and there just isn't any better place to be than next to him.

81

Cady felt Cathy's disappointment, he looked inside himself and thought, "I've hurt her, it's the haircut I bet I've made myself look like her ex-boyfriend" Any confidence Cady had slid away, but Cathy came to his side and took his hand in hers, and Cady was composed once more.

"I have something for you," Cady reached inside the cap of the pickup and brought out the gloxinia, "Hope you like purple."

Cathy squealed, "I love it! How did you know?" The super power Cathy has of regrouping from a disappointment and not looking back is a very useful power to have, "Let me show you my room, I have just the place for it there!"

Cathy and Cady side-by-side, well Cathy was a little in front leading the way, began the grand tour of the Tuttle Orchard starting at the little house. Cathy had this all planned out she introduced her Cady to each family member they came upon. Most of her siblings (two brothers and little sister) simply acknowledged Cady's place as belonging to Cathy. Her parents chatted small talk but her grandpa was the most welcoming in conversation with Cady. Cady noticed that Cathy's dad used Granddad when referring to Cathy's grandfather while she used Grandpa as Cady did with his grandpa. They came upon Cathy's grandpa sitting on the patio of the big house reading the *Wall Street Journal*. He put the paper down onto the table as they approached and Cathy made introductions. "So you're the one that has been writing to my granddaughter," he said with a twinkle in his eye. Her grandpa was interested in Cady's grandpa's ranch. Cady explained the operation of the place and Cady asked good questions about the orchard. In fact, it surprised Cathy how Cady could lead someone into conversation about themselves. Cathy's grandpa went on about his passion for investing and seemed to really enjoy describing it to Cady. Because it was Sunday, there was no fruit-picking going on so the non-family fruit-picking crew was not at the orchard at all. Together they walked around the pool, Cathy explained that the pool was just a big empty hole for the longest time until her grandma, tired of waiting, took it upon herself four years ago to drive to Spokane and buy the big fiberglass shell. Cathy introduced her Cady to the ponies and to trees she was currently thinning apples from. They walked the orchard hand in hand with its rows of trees that seemed endless, they stood on the canal bank watching the deep water silently flowing by and poked their heads into the two houses to see places Cathy called home. Cathy was so filled with joy she was floating as they walked swinging clasped hands, she would pull back suddenly and turn her head to kiss Cady first on the cheek and then a sudden peck on the lips. This was great fun for Cady and he was happily content with the world as long as Cathy was in it with him. Cady had promised his grandpa he would leave Cathy by 5:00 and while time had dragged for Cathy in the wait for her Cady, now it flew by in the possession of all she had hoped for from that arrival, now all too quickly coming to the stopping point, as Grandma Hazel said of her paintings. Although Hazel was gone before Cathy could have met her Cady would assure Cathy that his grandma would have loved everything about his Cathy. Cathy and Cady tarried by the blue Ford pickup, they had held hands in the sweetness of the day and now they had to let go in the sourness of the twilight.

"I don't want to go, I want to stay here with you and have this day go on and on," Cady said sadly. The feelings came in waves of joy and sorrow, of being complete then torn in two. It was actually physically hard to move into the truck. Cady had fallen deeply in love with Cathy, his first and only love. There was no doubt in his mind at all about what person he would spend his life with, only his inadequacy as a person. Now in this place and time even that didn't stand in the way.

***

Cathy loved every bittersweet second of their good-bye, she never felt so cherished or so valued. Each little good-bye kiss was so sweet and the hug that went with them went on forever, but it had to stop even if painfully. Cady climbed into the cab, started the truck, and turn it around waving at his life's love as he drove away. Cathy waved until the blue truck disappeared in a cloud of dust. She didn't stand, she floated on air there near the chair, near the hammock where she had

83

waited for Cady to come to her just a little while ago… "It had been only a little while ago hadn't it?" Her thought confirmed that time had stood still. Cathy lay in the hammock eyes closed floating dreamily in a daydream of the last hug Cady had given her. It was so peaceful there in that dream nothing mattered all was good and sweet. She sighed to herself, "So this is what being in love is." An hour passed by, she swung her feet out of the hammock to the reality that Cady was probably back at the ranch now. Still the warm feeling lingered, it made her feel grateful for everything and everyone around her, her family, friends, the ponies, the orchard, the hammock, the swimming pool, and especially for that one beautiful person who loves her. Cathy's feet still hadn't touched the ground as she wandered into the kitchen of the big house to find something to nibble on. Everything all around her was so bright and beautiful even the leftover pork chop she had for dinner. Evening continued on to bring twilight and Cathy retired to her room to write to Cady. Cathy reread some of Cady's letters and fawned over being called 'Cat' by Cady. She had a very special friend call her Cat all the time in high school and kind of loved it. Cathy had given that friend sanctuary one night when she had been forced to run away from abuse at home. Cathy hid her friend downstairs to keep her safe but the police were called and well, it was out of Cathy's hands, but not her prayers. Cathy writes to her Cady and the letter takes on her feeling of the moment the rise and fall of the emotional waves of young love. She dutifully seals the letter with wax and presses the four leaf clover stamp onto the warm wax, each leaf a miniature heart to send to her love.

***

Cady is a half hour late getting back to the ranch and gets teased for it. Grandpa had taken care of checking the evening water set for Cady as well and he just laughed about it. The feeling Cady experienced all the way back was that same euphoria he felt graduation night. This time what was added to that euphoria was a sense of accomplishment, he had done most things right except for the haircut and that stung his heart. What Cady feared most was hurting

Cathy in any way, his greatest joy was being with her and in turn receiving her love. Cady had promised Cathy to come back to see her again next Sunday for a longer visit, which meant starting earlier in the day. For now it was bedtime after a short letter to his love and yes it was full of I love you, miss you, and had the most wonderful time with you, all true. This next week was full of work; Cady had water running in all the fields except the one currently holding 180 head of cattle all with nice dry hooves. These days were the heaviest time for irrigation of the summer, any dry spots and the grass would quickly wilt reducing the hay harvest dramatically. Cady rode Sandy the buckskin; he was the oldest of the horses, next oldest was Taneum Red the Appaloosa, and the youngest Cady's horse Rocky the bay. Rocky was being trained by Cady to be a saddle horse or perhaps Rocky was training Cady to be a much better horse trainer. Either way if a lot of work needed to be done without horse/rider conflict Sandy the buckskin was the horse for it not Rocky the bay.

Cady was now a lovesick rubber boot cowboy and what do you do with such a critter? You put them to work on horseback with a shovel on their shoulder! Every horse on the ranch had been trained by his grandpa. Grandma Hazel would tell Cady that Grandpa Charley loved riding horses so much that he would walk two miles to catch a horse to ride a mile somewhere. It was true, Grandpa had a way with horses and they responded in-kind, this was unmatchable in Cady's eyes. Cady fed Sandy some oats then brushed his coat with a currycomb while Sandy finished his treat. Sandy solemnly and steadily ground the oats in his mouth while looking side to side. Cady had a favorite western saddle out of the three in the barn, it had a low cantle, comfortable pommel, and slick aged leather that makes a creaking sound as he rides along. Sandy was stalling now the feedbox was clearly oatless despite his busy lips rooting over every inch of it. One of the reasons Cady liked this saddle was because it was much lighter to pick up and throw across the horse's back than the others. Grandpa's saddle was custom made in 1968 at 'Mills Saddle and Togs' in Ellensburg by saddle maker C.H.C. Allison. It had been

Grandma Hazel loving present to her husband of 46 years on their wedding anniversary. She would pass away from cancer in 1971, seven months short of their 50th anniversary with all of her family gathered around her at a hospital in Seattle. The saddle Hazel gave her husband was his exclusively and his most prized possession. The day after Grandma Hazel gave it to him, he brought it back to the saddle maker, so that it could be fitted to his body, Cady was with him that day in 1968. The saddle was heavily made to resist anything you roped that in turn would pull against the saddle horn and the wide leather cinch strap. Grandpa wanted some of the padding removed from the high cantle seat he said, "I don't want to bounce as I ride." Where Grandma Hazel had insisted Cady learn her arts both of the home and oil painting so did Grandpa Charley insist that Cady learn his arts of horsemanship and cattle ranching. Cady got Sandy's bridle and bit off the hook it was kept on with several others and brought to Sandy's head holding the bit up near his mouth so that the bit just touched his soft lips. Sandy was good about taking the bit into his mouth, if he hesitated, Cady would have to put his fingers in past those soft lips to the space behind the back teeth. It was a very good idea to stay clear of those wide molars that could grind down tough hard grain. He had seen Grandpa use his fingers to deftly tickle the mouth open but those teeth were to be respected at all cost. However Cady had never had to do this since as soon as Sandy felt the bit touch his front teeth he open up and took the bit without any problem. The bridle gets looped on the head behind the ears this bridle had only one ear loop. As soon as the bridle and bit with its long leather reins were in place Sandy set to chomping on the bit. Grandpa had one bit on a bridle hanging on the hook that had a little metal ring that was free to spin in the middle of the bit. This was so a nervous horse could play with the thing using its tongue. The reins are looped over a hitching rail while Cady rubbed his gloved hand over Sandy's back feeling for anything that might irritate from pressure against the saddle. Next came a saddle blanket (this one was actually a Navaho rug from a time out of mind). Once the blanket was all centered Cady held the saddle by its horn with one hand and the slack reins with the other then threw the saddle up over and onto Sandy's back. The buckles from the cinch strap and the flank straps had to be controlled so that they didn't hit anything especially the horse in the process of getting the saddle in place. It was sort of a game with Sandy, after Cady reached underneath Sandy's chest to grab the other side of the cinch and bring it to the cinch strap for tightening Sandy would inhale. This would swell his chest as Cady tightened the cinch making it seem as though the saddle was secure. If you went and tried to mount the saddle Sandy would exhale and you find yourself back on the ground and the saddle on one side of your horse. Not again; once was enough. Cady waited, Sandy could only hold his breath so long and as soon as he exhaled Cady finished tightening the cinch properly. The flank strap was buckled loosely and Sandy was ready. Cady had learn much of Grandpa's art, Cady could open and close fence gates while still on horseback, he could grab a shovel and shoulder it without dismounting. He knew what to ask of a horse, what not to ask of a horse, and he knew what odd things Sandy loved to do. One such thing was when they worked cattle in an open corral Grandpa always left Sandy free to walk around without a rider. Sandy would station himself near the exit of the cattle chute and as each steer came out one by one Sandy would cut him into one of two groups, one on the left and one to the right. If a steer resisted and tried to get around him Sandy would have none of it and run the steer down cutting it in the proper group. Grandpa told Cady that Sandy was a cutting horse and this was like candy to him. Today Cady and Sandy would cover lots of irrigated ground setting water, water came in to a field at one point and then could be diverted from there into many ditches one at a time as each portion of the field was soaked. A set was closing one ditch and opening another also fixing leaking or collapsed ditches. Cady rode to the field that backed against I-90 freeway it was his favorite place to work because cars often slowed down to see the sight of a working cowboy on a horse. Cady would ride up to a diversion ditch then throw his shovel down in a fashion that it stuck in the upright position, then step off the horse dropping the reins to the ground. Sandy was trained to stay at the point the reins hit the ground and he was very good to graze nearby while Cady shoveled muddy earth. People traveling the freeway would wave and stare as they sped past the lone horse and nearby rider. Cady loved the idea that he was playing a scene from a forgotten time for some little kid to see. Today wasn't so pleasant to be on horseback the wind challenged Cady while on the ground to stand straight up, it tore at his jacket and stung his eyes. Sandy stood with his hindquarters to the wind but his mane and tail were just playthings for the wild gusts. So the day went by with damp leaky rubber boots and a shouting wind. Cady thought to himself, "The wind was sure in a hurry to get somewhere," then he realized it was heading east toward Quincy and shouted into a gust, "I Love You Cathy!" His version of putting a note in a bottle and tossing it out into the waves of the ocean hoping it would find his true love. Cady turned to find he had been clearing a ditch for quite some distance and Sandy had properly stayed put so Cady had a little walk to get back to the horse. Cady pushed the shovel blade into the ground so that it stuck there handle upright. He held the reins and turned the stirrup half around and with his left foot in the stirrup he swung up and into the saddle. Sandy neck-reined that is if he felt pressure on the right side of his neck from the rein he would go left and vice versa. Cady reined the horse over to the shovel and as they passed it Cady reached down grabbed the handle and in one motion brought it up and over his right shoulder. He hoped that someone had just seen the show of a lone rubber boot cowboy neatly retrieving his tool of labor.

Between tending morning and night water sets remaining working hours were focused on fence mending. One lone steer had figured out how to break through the fence and it was becoming a real problem. Steers were getting out onto the country roadway usually in a group of three with a lone ringleader and chief fence buster at the lead. The fences around the ranch's fields were made up of four tight parallel runs of mean barbed wire. The ringleader was a white-faced Holstein steer who had discovered how to put his head between two of the runs then just keep pushing. He evidently tolerated the barbs until the wire broke. His reward was achieving freedom to discover just how tasty roadside grass was! The only answer at hand to quell this behavior was to strengthen the fence by putting in more posts between the existing ones and even adding another new parallel run of barbed wire to the four to help out. Cady had a pile of thirty-five green and white steel fence posts (T studded posts) in the back of the sun-faded blue Ford pickup parked next to the fence. These needed to be added to the fences today between water sets. Each post had to be hand driven 20 inches into the ground with a post driver tool. This muscle-building or muscle-breaking tool, depending on how you look at it, was made of a heavy galvanized pipe with a diameter a little bigger than the diameter of a steel post itself, allowing free movement over the post. The pipe was closed on one end by a welded plug. Raising the heavy driver up and slamming it down against the top of the steel post over and over until it was driven deep into the earth completed the job. It was one of those famous homemade tools that worked so much better than a sledgehammer so Cady had no complaint about the tool per se. It was just that the thing was so darn heavy and there were thirty-five posts to drive. Couldn't we just turn the ringleader steer into hamburger and be done with it? Guess not. By the thirty-fifth steel post Cady's arms were like rubber but he kept banging away. The last post was deep enough but Cady decided to give the driver one more whack just to be sure. The welded end-plug went sailing up into the air and the pipe crashed down onto the ground at the bottom of the post. Cady looked at the piece of now useless pipe and thought, "I wonder what kind of day Cathy is having?" On the plus side all the posts are driven in with the minus side being no more driver until it gets fixed. For as long as Cady had been working with his grandpa each season had always brought one breakdown after another in equipment or a tool. Cady couldn't lift his arms up very high anymore so attaching the wire to these new posts would have to wait until tomorrow. Cady got into the pickup and sat awhile wondering if he could actually turn the steering wheel to drive, he also realized his neck hurt. Looking at his neck in the mirror he saw the sides were cherry red, OUCH! That big tough male hair cut had left pale unprotected skin now turning angry red. There are times when you can't move your arms and you offended your girlfriend by cutting your hair so it is good to reconsider just how smart you aren't. How am I going to write a letter tonight? Rather shakily, I guess…

Friday morning came Cady's arms were sore but still worked and his neck was hot to the touch. Cady had slept restlessly because of the sunburn and muscle aches. For some reason Cady's mind took this morning to remind him that, no, the gender conflict wasn't put to rest forever. Cady had lived in this house, had come to discover his internal gender here, and the conflict it would bring to him. He had beat it, smashed it down, but Cady wondered that morning if his little stash of clothes were still in the place he put them for safekeeping years ago. Cady, David, and mother Dorothy all packed up to start a new life on the other side of the mountains with their reconciled father and husband. Cady had simply walked away from the little drawer in an old unused dresser that held his crossdressing shame. This was an act of purging himself of it, if anyone found the few female garments among the other old clothes it was no big deal and didn't point towards Cady. This morning Cady was alone and couldn't shake the curiosity to see if anything was still in that drawer. Cady had his milk and left the house to walk to the barn to feed the horses. He chatted with Sandy and Red told them about the broken steel post driver and assured both horses that he had things well in hand. Cady walked back to the house to use the bathroom and once the screen door slammed behind him, he knew he had to check that drawer. He opened the door to the far bedroom and pulled out the bottom drawer as he had done so many times before. It was empty. Joyce of course when she moved in cleaned house of anything Hazel had for clothes. She would check in the dressers around the house, it was a natural thing for her to do.

Cady stared at the empty drawer thinking, "One thing living on a ranch does teach you, are the differences between male and female, in temperament, in function, in desire, and in worldview at least as it pertains to animals." Hate swelled up in Cady for himself followed by a profound sadness, what would he have done if that drawer hadn't been empty. There was no denying what had happened once at the downstairs closet when he was small and then there was three summers ago. That was the experience that he couldn't shake out of his mind. That memory just burns away, "It was just Grandma Hazel and me at the ranch for a week while Grandpa was in California. Grandma had to go grocery shopping in town leaving me to begin my workday. Before heading out to the barn I was poking around the dresser in the downstairs guest room I was sleeping in that summer. Pulling open the bottom drawer I found a huge collection foundation garments. Grandma must have kept these for years; it is that Kansas not-ever-throwing-anything-away philosophy again. Looking through collection in the bottom drawer there are girdles, panty girdles, corsets, bras, nylons, and one-piece shapers. I didn't think at all I acted. I stripped off my clothes and put on the one-piece and it did re-shape my fatty body into a familiar female form, I was breathless, I stuffed the top and made straight for the closet under the stairs. I pulled on one of the dressed and zipped it up then turned to the mirror. There are no words that rightly describe the experience when you see yourself truly for the first time. This time the walls around me didn't melt, they disappeared completely. I saw a correctly shaped young woman in a dress that conformed to her curves in that mirror looking back at me she was me and I her. I felt so right, complete and at peace. I even felt while standing there I was truly part of the world after all. I wanted this so much to be true, despite my talk with myself. Tears came to my eyes in realization any suffering is well worth it. What am I and what am I going to do? I heard a car turn onto the driveway gravel and I quickly undressed and returned to my regular clothes. It actually hurt to put them on again. This was my first real crossdressing experience. I walked out to the garage to help Grandma bring in the groceries feeling a strange lingering happiness covering my body lightly. I never told anyone about it not even Grandma simply because I didn't know if what had happed was right and I sure didn't want any disapproval from anyone especially from her. I also wondered if my current state had anything to do with my mom's mental problem falling on me as her offspring."

It didn't matter the drawer was empty and relief pushed away the hate and the old memory. Cathy keeps writing that she has to tell me something about herself that she fears would break our relationship. It couldn't be anything compared to what I have to tell her. The thought of losing Cathy brought on a wave of despair that almost smothered Cady. From this came a new resolve to overcome this battle and afterward he will tell Cathy all about it before ever asking her to be his love forever.

***

Cathy was out early in the orchard to beat the heat, it was 5:00am. The air between the rows of trees is country morning still with many of the trees standing in deep shadow. Cathy's mind is drifting toward that shadowy corner where she holds things that she would like to forget or even better would dream to purge herself of. This morning she will be thinning the Red King Delicious apple trees. It isn't disagreeable work in the world of apple thinning. The trees are young so they aren't tall enough to have to use a ladder. You don't have to decide what apple to drop and what apple to leave, you simply strip each tree clean. The Red King Delicious apple is a mutation first found in the very little town of Riverside Washington on a Starking Delicious apple tree, that mutation being a weirdly huge fruit on one of the tree's limbs. This year these trees are simply too young and too weak to support the developing fruit. Although the apple is huge it makes up for that amazing size by being pretty tasteless. Cathy wasn't impressed, she prides herself on being a connoisseur of the distinct flavors of apple varieties. Tuttle orchard as viewed from above is a lone patch of standing trees surrounded by miles and miles of flat fields full of low crops such as beets and potatoes. In true oasis fashion it was a bird magnet and this morning the sound of birds greeting the sunrise was deafening. It was standing orders to shoo birds out of the trees, it was kind of a comical serious ongoing task being there were more birds than people in the orchard. Cathy just by being among the trees deterred the birds, mostly Starlings from perching. Cathy found a distracting joy by thinking about Cady's visit; Cathy would go over their time together step by step. The rhythm of her work intertwines with her thoughts to form a stream of consciousness chant, "Pinch twist drop. He loves me. Pinch twist drop. He loves me not. Pinch twist drop." Then there is that dark corner at the edge of her mind working away. Will he love me if I tell him? Drop goes the green apple to the ground, "Cathy so pretty. Cathy so fair. Attracting an innocent boy with long dark hair. Except that he cut it. Twist pinch drop. I wonder how do I tell him? Twist pinch drop. What do I say? Twist pinch drop. If I tell what's wrong? Twist pinch drop. Will he run away? Twist pinch drop. Woe to me. Twist pinch drop. The things I've done. Twist pinch drop. I'd like to undo. Twist pinch drop. To earn this boy. Twist pinch drop. Whose love is so true. Twist pinch drop. Twist pinch drop." Cathy stops to retie her triangle scarf and now there is a sadness creeping across her face. She returns to her natural cadence of motion of thinning apples from the trees. Pinch twist drop. Her mind is battling that dark corner looking for just the right way to purge the darkness that stands between her and the love that is so close she can almost touch it. Tree by tree a resolve makes itself clear to her, she must tell him there is no question about it. Little does she know while she is in her personal battle, it is not the only one being fought this day; her love is similarly occupied with a similar resolve. Noon and Cathy's arms are hot and pink it is time for lunch and her seven-hour shift to be over. There is work going on in unseen places of the orchard. As Cathy walks toward the big house, she hears voices some speaking Spanish, they are invisible up on three legged ladders set deep into a cherry trees picking Bing, Lambert, Sam, Van, and the new Rainer varieties of cherries. Her brother Phil and his friend Dale are up on one of those ladders in one of those trees somewhere. Cathy and her brother cross paths occasionally at breakfast in the kitchen of the little house. There was this odd interplay of being solitary with people all around you. Someone is singing inaudibly in the near distance of the forest of orchard trees while you stand there all alone thinking of lunch. In the kitchen Cathy pours lemonade into a tall glass, it was her reward for both making the stuff every morning for everyone else to enjoy and for completing her shift before noon. There was ham in the refrigerator Cathy sliced enough for an ample sandwich of white bread and yellow mustard. She sat at the kitchen table and ate quietly. In her mind she plotted out the rest of her day, visit the ponies, meditate at poolside dandling her legs in the water, read in her room and collect her thoughts on what to say to her love this weekend. Dinnertime was at 5:30 it was family style and Cathy would eat with her grandmother, grandfather, mom, dad, and siblings. Family conversations interspaced with Grandpa questioning how far Cathy had gotten in the thinning or how the cherry picking was going for Phil. The adults would gab about the ins and outs of their days and set their sights on what to do tomorrow. Grandma wanted to cook a turkey in her new combination microwave/conventional Sears Kenmore range this weekend since Aunt Gladys Pearson was being brought over for a visit. She is Grandpa's sister and alone since her husband Uncle Walt had passed away four years ago. Walt and Gladys were on their farm just outside of Quincy before Grandpa established the orchard. Cathy announced she and Cady were going on a picnic this weekend so they wouldn't be at dinner that day. Cathy had crafted her plan to find someplace to enjoy a nice picnic with Cady and perhaps find a time to do some heart-to-heart talking. After dinner Cathy walked along the canal ditches in the twilight of early evening listing to frogs call to each other. The orchard was as quiet as it could be, thousands upon thousands of leaves lay still as the light fades. Cathy was trying to think of a place for a picnic that she might suggest to Cady and Crescent Bar drifted into her mind. It was right down at the bottom of the Columbia Riverbank, she hadn't been there before but the turn off wasn't too far from the orchard. She wondered if Cady knew about the place. "At least it is a place we can start looking from," Cathy mused, "We are a couple, Cathy and Cady, it's so nice to think about being a couple doing things together." Water flowing into the irrigation siphon pipes sometimes draws air with a gulping sound as if gasping for breath before refilling with water again. The change in background sound breaks Cathy's daydream thought. Cathy has wandered down to where Grandpa had set irrigation into the lower orchard today. She stood there listening and thinking about walking just behind her grandpa while he set siphon pipes. He tried to show her how to start a siphon pipe siphoning water from the feed ditch. A siphon pipe was a light aluminum pipe perhaps three to four feet long. It is shaped into a stretched-out 'n' shape basically the shape of one side of a ditch. In theory you fill the pipe with water by submerging it in the water filled feed ditch. Cover one end with your hand then bring that end up and over the side of the feed ditch careful to keep the other open end under the water of the feed ditch. Remove your hand and siphon action starts pulling water over the ditch bank and down into the field ditch without washing away the ditch bank in the process. There are many little field ditches, one for each tree row usual around 50 to 60 per field. Grandpa had a trick of putting the feed ditch end of the siphon pipe into the water while holding the row end. He would jerk the pipe right to left then quickly cover the siphon end of the pipe as he felt water on his hand at the siphon end. Grandpa would lower the siphon end and release his hand then moves on to the next field ditch and repeat the action. Sometimes he was successful after just one time using this motion, more often it took two to three jerks through the water of the feed ditch to catch the siphon into action. Cathy couldn't get the timing of the motion right she would release the siphon too soon only to have the water stop after just a trickle. Her only hope was to suck the water with her mouth to start the siphon and the taste was awful so that was a definite a no-go. Her grandpa while respecting her for trying had to tease about the failure. She would stick to thinning, picking, housework, and overseeing you-pickers. She continued to walk behind her grandpa as he marched along setting siphons. The dirt covered in dust turned to a thick sticky brown mud quickly as the water oozed down the dry field ditch. A field of tree rows would be completely muddy in as little as four hours. This was the main indicator of irrigation being complete in that field; to go longer was a waste of water. Cathy wore rubbery flip-flops in the wet areas and tennis shoes in the dry areas. She walked in the muddy mess with her flip-flops slapping up mud onto the back of her legs and bottom. The mud refusing to let go of her flip-flops on each step made walking an adventure. Her cadence of walking was slap-slap-ooze, slap-slap-ooze. Sometimes a single flip-flop stuck so stubbornly that she would step and it would remain in the arms of the mud monster. Cathy would have to un-stick it while standing on one foot, it pays to be graceful in a muddy field. Grandpa wore ankle high work boots that became thick and heavy with mud; he would stomp his feet and wipe his boots on any greenery they came to. Cathy had a bone to pick with her grandpa about muddy boots getting into the house on floors she had just mopped and Grandpa was getting better about no boots in the house. Cathy avoided the dark muddy ground and returned to the little house where her bedroom was waiting for her. Inside sitting at the vanity where Cathy did her letter writing, she pondered all she had to report of her day to Cady. Cathy had two letters to write, one would be mailed in the morning and the other was a daily continuous letter she added to each night and would share with her Cady when they next met face to face. Outside her window darkness filled the living orchard and the sky revealed a vista of stars hidden by the light of day. Cathy had her day experiences all ordered out in her mind and ready for letter writing so when she sat down pencil in hand the sentences flowed out continuously onto her single day letter, "As each day comes to me I realize just how much you mean to me and how I am beginning to love you more and more. This brings on the realization that if I don't tell you something very important soon, it's going to eat me up inside, and yet if I do you tell you I am afraid that you will not want anything to do with me." In her continuous letter she writes of all the little things she has carefully and completely filed away in reporting, "Today I made $12 thinning apples and I miss you and love you. I will move on to thinning Winter Banana and Golden Delicious apples tomorrow, I have to use a three-leg ladder to do them ugh. I visited the ponies, Blondie says Hi! My legs were so pink from the sun that I sat at the poolside with my legs in the water. I think a picnic would be fun this weekend. How about Crescent Bar?"

In the morning Cathy's alarm woke her at 4:30, it was always a struggle between hitting snooze for another 30 minutes and working later into the day, or jumping up and avoiding sunburn. It wasn't as if

Cathy didn't use lots of Coppertone on her arms and legs, it simply didn't do anything to stop the sunburn from all the hours in the sun. One afternoon during her visit with the ponies she would confide to them, "I am so quick to burn and so slow to tan that even if I took a bath in Coppertone it wouldn't help." Cathy didn't hit the snooze button instead pulled herself up to meet the new day. She had a surprise this morning her brother Phil was in the kitchen and he greeted her with, "Hey would you like to have some oatmeal I made extra!" Cathy answered back happily, "Sure thank you!" The hot oatmeal was a treat, she put milk and brown sugar in her bowl just the thing to start the day off right! Cathy walked into the orchard finding her way to the rows of Winter Banana and Golden Delicious apple trees. Grandpa had left a three-leg orchard ladder for her at the start of the first row, it was up to her to move the ladder as she progressed, something Cathy didn't look forward to doing. Cathy had brought along a thermos jug full of ice water and a little cup. She put the thermos in the forming shade of the first tree and set the ladder deep into its limbs. There was magic in the single leg of a three-leg ladder that offset how heavy it was to move; it easily poked right into the thickest bunch of branches. The magic was revealed in that it formed a stairway right into the center of a tree. You could even sit on the top step comfortably or turn around and sit on each step as you worked your way down or up the tree. Cathy's philosophy was to do all she could while standing on the ground before beginning with the ladder and working her way up. Cathy started her rhythm of pinch twist drop, but now another step was added to the sequence now it was select pinch twist drop. She had to make a snap judgment on which apples to keep so they would get larger and which to drop to make room for the remaining apples. The Winter Banana Apple trees were used for cross-pollination with the Golden Delicious trees. Golden Delicious trees were not self-pollinating and in order to produce apples had to have another apple variety tree near them. The Winter Banana apple on its own is a gorgeous apple it's yellowish with a pink blush, it showed up on a farm in Indiana around 1876. The down side is it doesn't taste good but it is useful in cooking. In the orchard there were only two rows of this tree group, some 120 trees total. The fruit from the 100 Golden Delicious trees was sold while the fruit from the 20 Winter Banana trees were not, but would find a place in a batch of applesauce. So the pollination occurrence of the trees in a row would be one Winter Banana apple tree followed by four or five Golden Delicious trees in series repeating down each row. Cathy moved the three-leg ladder to the final tree of her day judging by the sun; she was hot, tired, and her thermos was empty. She looked at her watch, it was just after noon, it had been over seven hours since she had started this morning. She was making a mental note to finish this tree first thing tomorrow, but then it dawned on her tomorrow was Cady's visit, and wasn't a workday! Her mood lifted several notches; she grabbed the empty thermos, and headed back to the big house for some lunch. A lemonade and potato chips power lunch; there was a little patch of shade from a birch tree near the pool to relax in. The pool was so nice now with the cement deck all around it and a little shower house with two completely separate showers and bathrooms, one for guys and one for gals near the deep end of pool. Grandpa with Grandma's help had built the orchard from empty land, a labor of the last 33 years. Her grandparents' differed as to the priority of what and when in that building cycle. Grandpa's grand vision was the orchard itself with all of the support buildings included. Grandma's grand vision all came down to home and family. It was a place for her son and two daughters to bring their families to enjoy, after all, they all helped to build the place too. It really came down to the term 'support buildings.' In Grandpa's view a support building supported the orchard such as packing shed, machine shop, hay shed, and the like. In Grandma's view a support building supported family those living on and those visiting the orchard. These structures were the big house itself, patio, outdoor kitchen, pool, pool house with its showers and changing rooms. There were areas of agreement, both agreed that houses supported the orchard because you needed a place to eat and sleep while working in the orchard. It was the quality of the comfort of the living that was the issue. As an example, indoor plumbing wasn't finished until the late 1960's in the houses and that only happened after a demand by Grandma and her daughters. She was also promised the house of her dreams and Grandpa, true to his promise worked steadily with the help of his son and sons-in-law to slowly make progress on it. Cathy had really never known the orchard as a completed work, each visit held some marker of progress toward that never fully reachable goal. She along with her siblings were elated when Grandma forced the issue of installing the pool, but it was years before the pool deck would be poured. Also for several summers the new pool was just a place for frogs and algae to live in. Now the clear water soothed the memory of that time with its permanent promise of an oasis from the summer heat. Grandma wanted a place for their adult children and her grandchildren to come to and truthfully so did Grandpa, just they had different paths in doing it. Cathy re-read Cady's last letter there by the pool and thought about purging herself of anything hidden to Cady. It was afternoon when she in her bedroom sealed a letter to Cady with wax and walked out to the ponies to see if Blonde would mind giving her a ride down to the mailbox.

***

Cady had taken off the sway-bar of the Ford tractor's lifting arms, these being the bottom part of the tractor's three point hitch system. He backed the tractor up to a posthole auger that stood propped up against a fence. The posthole auger had its own connection points to the lifting arms but it was a heavy thing to wrestle into place. Better to bring the tractor to the connection points than the other way around, even if it took several attempts. Cady was nervous today, he was to be seeing Cathy over at the orchard but there was a good three hours of ranch work to do first. This morning the foreman of Stuart Anderson's Black Angus Cattle Ranch, a neighbor to the east of the ranch wanted Grandpa to fix the common boundary fence, and Grandpa was willing to do it now. Cady called it Uncle Stu's place but Stuart Anderson was no relation to his Anderson family. Cady had gotten the tractor close enough to hook the lifting arms to the built in connection points of the auger and nudged the tractor forward to bring the top bar in line with the top hitch point of the tractor. He would now use the hydraulic lift arms of the tractor's hitch to lift up the posthole auger and drive forward back to the shop to complete the attachment. Cady was kind of enamored with the thing, it dug perfect post holes all on its own. Cady had earned his manual PHD 'post hole digger' many summers ago. It was a clamshell like hand tool that was similar to two shovels hinged together. You drove it into the earth just like you would a shovel using muscle power then push the two handles away from each other and pull up. With luck it removed a plug of earth with each action, this beats using a single shovel all to pieces. It had been Cady favorite posthole digging tool until the tractor-driven implement was acquired at some farm sale. Farm sales/auctions were bittersweet affairs as much needed used farming equipment could be had at good prices, but at the great human cost of a family farm being sold out, many times because of a death of a family member... At the shop Cady removed the cover of the rear power take-off shaft of the tractor and fitted the drive shaft with its splined universal joint from the auger onto the rear power take-off shaft. A clevis and locking clevis pin secured the universal joint to the tractor. So with great glee Cady raised the posthole auger up off the ground then engaged the power take-off; the big auger turned like a giant drill bit. Had Cady lowered the lift he could have drilled a big hole right in the gavel driveway, but it was enough to shut the tractor down and grease the fittings on the machine instead. He was to drive the tractor up the road to the driveway of Uncle Stu's place where the fence needed resetting while Grandpa followed in the Ford pickup. At tractor speeds it was a ten-minute trip. Two men making up the Black Angus contribution to the shared boundary fence-fixing project were already there. The one was the foreman of the place, he was a well-weathered guy very near sixty, and the other a younger laborer; both with dusty cowboy hats pulled down forehead tight. Cady's grandpa was never without his dusty Stetson work hat and pointed toed cowboy boots while Cady was kind of an embarrassment outfit-wise. Cady was off times bareheaded and wore tennis shoes while on horseback. Although while tending irrigation water both Cady and Grandpa wore rubber boots on or off horseback. Suffice to say Cady stood out in the area that was well used to western ways. Cady had no idea just how many laborers worked for Black Angus, it was after all a huge place. Before Stuart Anderson came around the area it was two separate farms with the Taneum Creek running through them. The Harold family owned the one that bordered the ranch they were nice neighbors, the other farm bordering the Harold farm reached down to the Yakima River. Stuart Anderson bought both and formed them into one monster sized holding. They didn't know much about cattle ranching and were continually over at Grandpa's place asking for help or advice. Cady with a chill remembered the day a big black limousine pulled into the driveway of the ranch five years ago; Grandpa walked out to see what they wanted and turned out it was Stuart Anderson himself. Grandpa chatted through the window of the limousine for a long time. When he returned back to the house again he was in a jolly mood. He told us that Stuart Anderson had asked to buy his place and he told him no. Cady was actually afraid the ranch might be taken away forever that day. The area to reset the boundary fence was the corner of Grandpa's field and where the driveway for Black Angus met the country road. Grandpa had left that area unfenced because it was a rocky hill at the edge of his flat field so he instead fenced the little hill off. So now we are moving the fence to include our little hill. Incidentally, the little hill had been a Native American campsite from time out of mind. Cady backed the posthole auger up to an agreed upon spot and started it running then lowered the lift arm so that the big bit could bite into the rocky soil. Some big square wooden fence posts had been piled up for use nearby, normally the wood fence posts around the ranch are made by splitting a round log into three long wedge or triangle shape posts. Steel posts were fence repair material. Since this was going to be the structural corner of a long fence it had to be very strong to pull the barbed steel fence wire taught from. The structure was three heavy wood post set in the ground six feet apart forming a corner. Two more heavy posts would be affixed horizontally two feet down from the top of the vertical post to act as single cross ties making the structure stronger. Finally, several strands of fence wire would be looped around the posts running along the crossties and twisted super tight.

For now though it was Cady and the auger up to bat to dig the postholes pretty darn quick. There was lots of standing around by the older gents leaning on their shoves gabbing with each other while the auger spun away. Grandpa started the verbal ball rolling telling the other men that Cady was off to make time with his girlfriend after this so they better hurry up and get this done. That started the teasing with the three older men loving every second of it. It was all in fun and Cady didn't mind, in fact, it made him feel like one of the guys. Although, there was an uneasiness in his mind that little gender kernel refusing to fall in line with all this male stuff. Still he had status with these men, a place at their male table by having a girlfriend. Time passed and the auger was making no headway against the hard rocky soil the only pressure pushing it down was the weight of the auger itself. Cady shut off the tractor and hopped off. After everyone pondered the problem, an idea came. They would use one of the long heavy post as a leaver arm anchored on top of the auger's drill casing while all three of the guys put their combined weight on the far end of the arm. Cady started the tractor back up and sure enough the auger gained a few inches. Time was flying and grandpa and the guys had all day but Cady didn't. Grandpa checked his watch and made an announcement to the group as to what they thought Cady should be doing at this very minute? All three of the men pointed to the Ford pickup and Cady was on his way to town to get something for Cathy...

Cady drove into Ellensburg right to Zittings the department store where he had found the gloxinia last weekend. He hurried into the store then stopped short looking over the many departments. Cathy liked the plant but nothing looked just right over in the flower corner. Cady begins to walk down each aisle desperately searching for the perfect themed gift. Nothing came from it no idea or even a spark of an idea. A whole store full of stuff and nothing there to buy what was he going to do? There wasn't any place else to try, after all this is small town Ellensburg. Near the sundries section Cady spied a candle, it was set in a clear tall drink glass looking like a wax orange sherbet Sunday with a wax bright red cherry on top. That's it!!! The lady checker at the cash register asked Cady, "Who's the candle was for?" When Cady said, "My girlfriend." She smiled saying, "I'll find you a box." Now with a pretty good gift in hand, Cady started the pickup down the road to the freeway entrance eastward. He had the pickup's wind-wing windows wide open blowing air into the cab to cool it. The temperatures were in the very upper 90s a very typical Columbia Plateau day. Time flowed and so did the miles, the pickup climbed up the east slope of the Kittitas Valley to the little pass at Ryegrass. A swift drive along the steep downslope brings the Vantage Bridge that spans the swollen Columbia River backed up here by the Wanapum Dam. Once across the bridge, Cady bears left towards Quincy climbing up to the Columbia Plateau. He exits I-90 at George taking SR 281 toward Quincy. Now the problems start, Cady off times reverses numbers and letters so navigation is mostly by landmarks. What is left in his mind is the image of a Piper Cub airplane parked behind a house on the left side of the highway. This image marks the place to turn left onto the country road leading to the orchard, all of the letters and numbers are lost just when he needed them. The image has more details, such as a lawn in front of the house, and two out buildings, but if that plane has been moved he is totally lost without hope of help. There are few people around, only miles of planted fields some marked with little signs as what is growing in the field, it's kinda cool really. Even as his nerves climb and climb toward panic he adds to the place-image of this highway and tries desperately to remember the number letter combination leading to his love. Nothing comes and as the Quincy town limit sign comes into view he disparages his mental shortcoming knowing he has gone too far. Turning around in the driveway of a very impressive fire station Cady retraces his route. Got-to-find-that-plane plays over and over in his very worried mind. Road numbers begin to go back down in value, coming this way his turn would be on the right, 7 pops into his mind as 8 passes by and sure enough from this side of the road the plane is clearly visible behind the house at road 7. A sudden slow down to make the turn onto little road, a huge feeling of relief brings him to understand just how sweaty his face is. Cady slows the pickup down and fully opens the window to really blow air right at him. A new image is pulled up into his mental navigator, a house with a big driveway just before a little bridge then turn right onto a lettered road. The odds are still against him, but now the image is more certain. Cady comes to the house and goes across the bridge and turns right at S. The orchard is in view and now it sinks in, he is going on a for-real picnic date with his Cathy! A little smile comes to his face and a little prayer in his heart. Driving slowly down the dusty lane so he will arrive not in a big cloud of dust but a classy gentle mist of dust. Cady parked the pickup in the same place as before, but now there was also another car nearby. He opened up the squeaky truck door and there was Cathy hands on her hips…

***

Cathy had trouble sleeping last night after her prayers, she was thankful that God had brought Cady into her life. Even though she prayed fervently for guidance with choosing the right words for her talk with Cady sleep was slow to come afterward. Cady would be here soon even though soon was like three hours away. The orchard sometimes called the farm by Aunt Gladys was busy with family today. Aunt Gladys was visiting; she was here for an early turkey dinner that Grandma was making with the help of Cathy's mom. Cathy was careful to stay out of the chaos of the kitchen of the big house. Her plan was to go out and pick some nice ripe cherries for the picnic right after a bite of breakfast. Aunt Gladys had taken up residence in the screen porch of the little house where Cathy's bedroom was located. It was a pleasant porch shaded by a vine growing up along the side of screen door and was the coolest place to be on a hot day. Although there was the promise of air conditioning coming to the big house soon it remained on the to-do list for Grandpa. Aunt Gladys as Grandpa's older sister intimidated Cathy for the most part; she always had a judgmental stare in Cathy's direction. Cathy wondered if her mom or even her grandma ever felt that intimidating stare on them by Aunt Gladys. With relief Cathy left the little house to walk to the cherry tree rows nearby, no matter whether the trees were already picked through, there was always fruit that was missed on the lower

104

limbs. Cathy was floating along again as she found the nicest Bing cherries, she was at the very start of a wonderful bright experience to come today. With the greatest care and scrutiny, she selected her little pile of fruit it all had to be just right. She wandered around to see if any other super nice fruit was ripe, there could be early apricots, but didn't find any acceptable. Cathy put the cherries in a paper bag in the refrigerator of the little house. She heard a truck and saw the dust rising up from the driveway and hurried out to see a dusty blue Ford pickup slowly driving up the lane.

Cathy with her hands on her hips stood waiting, her stance was part of a plan to give Cady a little teasing upon his arrival. The quickness of her heartbeat would have given the act away, but she was confident of her cool outward appearance.

"Hi Cady I am so glad you're here I thought maybe you got lost or something! I've been so very patiently waiting. I've got part of our lunch ready just need to make the sandwiches, you should see the nice cherries, but first we have to say 'hi' and 'bye' to everyone." Cady stood there trying to catch up with the words coming at him then saw the bright gleam in Cathy's blue eyes and held out the box with, "I've got something for you to keep you cool in all this heat!" Cathy was thrilled that Cady had thought of her once more. When she opened up the box and held the candle it contained in her hand her heart soared, "I love it! It is so gorgeous I love it so much. I am going to put it next the gloxinia and every hot night I'll look at it and feel cool relief, oh it's so perfect!" Cathy gave Cady a hug and a kiss not even caring if any siblings were around to see her doing it. Cady had been so lovingly thoughtful with his gifts to her, no boy had even come close to doing this before. It was almost the kind of thoughtfulness you expect from a close girlfriend; with boyfriends it would be candy or cut flowers. Cathy was so in love with Cady and the feeling just got stronger and stronger by the moment. She took Cady by the hand and they walked together with Cathy just a little ahead of Cady over to the little house. Cathy introduced Cady as her boyfriend to her Aunt Gladys and left him with her as she put the candle into her bedroom. Returning there was Cady chatting with intimidating Aunt Gladys or rather listening to her. Aunt Gladys didn't talk very much but Cady was very good at drawing people out, he would ask a small question and get a long personal answer. Cathy steered Cady back to herself in the kitchen as she cut thick pieces of ham for sandwiches, she asked Cady what he would like on his sandwich and the answer was music to her ears, "Just mustard." A 'just mustard' person after her own heart! Cady was duly impressed with the cherries, potato chips, sodas, sandwiches, and especially Cathy. Cady stood by Cathy in the kitchen while she made cherry juice from the frozen Bing cherry concentrate to refill the pitcher in the refrigerator for dinner that they would not be around for. Cathy with Cady in tow made the round of parents to say goodbye before leaving. She left Cady standing outside of the big house while she checked to see if her parents were around. Cady was standing on the patio when Cathy's grandma Freda came out holding a big heavy turkey on a platter. She saw Cady standing there and reached into her memory for a name that wasn't there all that came was Cathy's ex-boyfriend's name. She was stressed trying to find someone to take the heavy roasted bird off her hands and beckoned to Cady calling him the old name. She knew this wasn't the person but there was no other name available to her. Cady puzzled hesitated just long enough for Cathy's mom to pop out of the house looking for her mother. Cathy's mom rescued Cady and Grandma Freda too. Cady had been introduced to Cathy's grandma a week ago, but her hesitancy in reaching for his name and that lost look in her eyes was a clue he had seen before in someone he loved. He was sorry for not instantly coming to her to reintroducing himself and helping with her burden. Cady at that moment came to the understanding he was in Cathy's ex-boyfriend's shadow here. Cady had never had a girlfriend before or ever been a boyfriend to a girl. So he viewed his relationship with Cathy as a completely new and wondrous virgin experience, he had nothing to compare it to. On the other hand, Cathy had an empty loveless experience to compare this new relationship with. Cady began to worry for Cathy and to look at his own inadequacies. Truth was, Cady's need to be loved was so great it pretty much blinded him to anything that might spill over into this relationship with Cathy from her last relationship with her ex. Cady also felt but didn't admit to himself, the relationship he was bringing to Cathy was going to be very unorthodox if it survived. For now Cady was completely sure he would be with Cathy forever, he would be the best boyfriend and husband to her that there ever was. They would love each other and be each other's best friends. Cady would not do the hurtful things his father had done in abandonment only the good things before that and Cady would love as his mother had before her nightmarish mental illness. Cathy came out of the big house smiling telling Cady, "All set let's go!" Cady helped Cathy into the passenger side of the Ford pickup, he walked around to the drivers' side and slid behind the wheel. Cathy scooted over to be as close as she could to him considering the gear shift in the center of the cab. Cady turned the truck around and drove back down the lane but stopped dead at the end. Cady was clearly waiting for instructions he needed the help of a life partner. While he was fully ready to drive wherever Cathy directed, Cady clearly wasn't a 'sit still I've got his handled' kind of guy. "Do you know how to get to Crescent Bar? I'm completely lost in this area," Cady asked shyly. In reality, the last part of this question was kind of a hidden metaphor for Cady in his blossoming relationship with Cathy he really was lost. Cathy had escaped one very serious boyfriend who knew exactly where he wanted to go and what he wanted her to do when they got there. Cady was a breath of fresh air, the kind that saves you from the dark, dank, gloomy place she was being dragged to and trapped in. Cathy had a general notion of where the Crescent Bar turn off from SR 281 was since years ago her family that driven down in the general area property hunting. "Head back towards George the reverse of how you came here and we should find it somewhere along the way," Cathy smile was beaming next to her Cady. In her mind she had been given a second chance at happiness and escape from something crushing. The old pickup had a well-worn bench seat with cracked upholstery that squeaks on every bump, it was noisy, hot, didn't have air-conditioning, but to Cathy it was a dream come true machine. She sat next to her love nothing else mattered they were on the road together with the whole day to spend. Even though this joy seemed unbounded there is always clawing icy fingers from the past demanding its end. This was true for both Cathy and Cady they shared a common burden that needed to be swept away without destroying the frail seed of their promising relationship. A sign pointed to a spur road leading down the high basalt cliffs to a bar of land in the shape of a crescent extending into the Columbia River. This road led to an entrance gate of a camping resort, Cady stopped and the man asked, "What's your pleasure." "To have a picnic lunch," was the short answer from both Cady and Cathy at once. "Just to have lunch no camping or anything else," the gatekeeper questioned then returned, "Well, I hate it but I have to charge you $5 for day-use, it used to free but not today." The guy was very apologetic and really seemed embarrassed by the whole thing. Something else caught Cady's eye, the man's manner to him seemed as to one guy to another. An unsaid guy-to-guy understanding, "I'm sorry I know you have a girl and how it is when you have plans, still there's nothing I can do." Cathy looked disappointed she hadn't planned on any barriers to her plans. Cady feeling inadequately male to all of this returned, "Five dollars is okay where do we park?" The gate guy seemed relieved, "Anywhere in the camping lot that's empty." The place was pretty full but Cathy spotted an empty spot over in a corner and Cady pulled in to it. They got out and walk around near the river. This weekend was the limited hydroplane races out on the river. The modest crowd wasn't a problem but the noise from the little boats echoed loudly within the river canyon walls. The best bet to escape the noise was to lunch back at the pickup, Cathy set out their picnic on an old blanket on the tailgate of the pickup. They sat with food between them chatting and chewing. The cherries were wonderful, the sandwiches filling, and the company divine. Conversation flowed back and forth bracketed by laughter and the occasional thunder from a passing boat. Cathy was becoming visibly nervous and uneasy there was a tug-of-war going on between her heart and mind. The sandwiches, which were her last distraction, were gone now along with the cherries. Cady who is by nature very intuitive wasn't yet fully in tune with the full spectrum of

Cathy's emotions, he didn't know her unique body language of trepidation. How could he given their short time together? But he caught the sudden change in her voice. Cady had in a sense been forewarned that this moment was coming by little glimpses in Cathy's letters to him, but decoding her written passage of, "I sincerely doubted I could ever love or even like another guy again," into human trauma was a fearful event that poked at his inadequacies. Cathy pulled herself up internally and externally. "I need to tell you something," she looked straight at Cady's eyes at that moment as if she wanted to freeze them in her memory. Cady was quiet, internally he was thinking there was nothing Cathy could tell him that would make any difference to the fact that he loved her. Although seeing the pain this was bringing to Cathy demanded he understand more than just words alone. Cathy abruptly looked down at her hands, "This has to do with things that happened between my ex-boyfriend and me." Cathy glanced up at Cady's face and seeing only empathy continued. Cathy purged herself of that near disastrous relationship by disclosing guilt she was carrying and keeping hidden out of fear. She looked to Cady to acknowledge her pain in doing this and to forgive her. Cady's mind raced to understand what Cathy had painfully and fearfully told him, on the surface; it didn't seem to merit such deep guilt on her part, in fact, the guilt wasn't hers it belonged to someone else. Furthermore none of what Cathy told him made any difference he loved her and couldn't conceive of being with anyone else ever. So Cady gave Cathy what he understood she needed, he acknowledged her pain with empathy. When she asked if Cady could forgive her for her part in that relationship he said, "With all my heart." A chill ran up Cady's spine in a flash of sudden realization. Who was he but someone full of guilt of unspeakable actions he could confess to no one, but that was in the past, he was different now he wouldn't be that person anymore. Cady felt dirty but the change in Cathy pushed his darkness away for the time being. Cathy moved over to her Cady who had the sense to embrace her. Her eyes were teary red, but the weight that had just been removed from her soul lifted her up. Cady could feel this happening as he hugged her close. All Cady cared about was the love he was feeling for her, it would take 46 more years before more of Cathy's story would come to the surface but this start is enough for now. Cathy was ready to move on and Cady agreed, it had been a serious time for them it would be good to just leave all that behind and introduced themselves to each other anew. The pickup climbed the windy road back up to the top of the basalt cliffs that lined the Columbia River. Once back at I-90 Cady turned westward toward an overlook just off the freeway, here he parked the pickup and they sat close together taking in the river canyon. Cathy's relief was electric it touched every part of her mind and body. She was free to be with Cady to build a relationship without fear of it being taken away by anyone. The fear of this had hovered over her like a cloud of gnats that she couldn't escape from day or night no matter how she twisted or turned and now it was all swept away, "Thank you dear God, thank you dear Cady." She snuggled close to Cady there in the near 100-degree heat feeling not heat but pure bliss. Cady was in the arms of relief also, down below the river flowed in contrast to the desert on its banks. All the desert-years of his self-imposed solitude and the loneliness that resulted from it was melting away. Time slowed down to the pace of the slow moving water below. Cathy got the idea to try to find a rock shop she remembers from years ago on the road into Wenatchee; it would be so much fun to show it to Cady. There was no map in the old pickup's catchall, but Cathy had the general direction in her mind and they had all day. The sun-faded blue pickup that was more at home out in a cow pasture than flying down the highway was their magic carpet. Cathy figured that there would be signs to Wenatchee once they returned to Quincy so they just needed to get to Quincy. Cady felt powerful with Cathy sitting close to him something he had never felt before, this was totally new and rarified every minute he shared with Cathy was a unique experience. He was completely in the moment no past or future. Cathy was moving forward going down the road with the joy of travel, she was completely free; her only attachment was that of being loved. Quincy gave them a sign pointing to Wenatchee on highway 28. The pickup was noisy but not so much that Cathy couldn't chat with Cady. Cady listened to Cathy's story of driving down this stretch of road with her grandma in a big truck full of freshly picked cherries. Cathy said, "It was just about this spot where the truck started to overheat. Steam started to pour out from under the hood and Grandma just kept going. I wasn't so sure what might happen. We finally came to the fruit packer and they helped us put water into the super hot radiator; after that it gave us no trouble." Cady returned, "Wow!" He then noticed that the pickup's temperature gauge had just pegged over at H, "No way at the same exact spot!" Sure enough steam was venting out from under the pickup's hood. Cathy looked alarmed then they both laughed, what are the odds. That powerful feeling Cady had drained away in a cloud of steam. Fortunately they had reached the outskirts of Wenatchee and Cady rolled into the first gas station he came to and stopped. Cady got out and opened the hood and the attendant came over eyed the engine then pointed to the heater hose that was leaking. There was that male camaraderie thing again. He saw Cathy in the truck then said, "I got a hose in the shop and can fix it for ten bucks just take a few minutes to do." Cady returned, "Sounds good." Two service guys busied themselves while Cady sat with Cathy in the cab. All fixed and gassed up, Cady was left with five of the thirty dollars he started with. He thought to himself, "If the pickup was going to mimic the old big truck of Cathy's adventure we should have no problems from here on." Even with the universe's assurance that the pickup was going to behave per the old truck tale Cady and Cathy abandoned the search for the rock shop and heading back toward Quincy. The day was waning and early evening coming so very quickly as they parked the pickup at the orchard. It was 5:45 and they were still sitting in the pickup cab next to each other. Cathy didn't want to yield to their date being over and getting out was final. Cady didn't want to lose the touch of her next to him and that was all it was just being with her. It was silly of course but very real. They hadn't physically done as many couples would have on a date. Cathy did know as much as she would have liked for this day to go on forever it was time so she slid over to her side of the pickup. Cady got out and opened the door for her, they hugged good-bye and Cathy kissed Cady's cheek. Then they still stood together until Cady was over an hour past time to go. Cady got back into the pickup and started the engine put it into reverse and backed up into the car parked behind him. Being lovesick causes all sorts of bad things to happen. It was just a fender-to-fender bang and plenty mortifying to Cady. The pickup just yawned about the whole thing; after all it had done all it could to give the two star-crossed lovers a special date, so one more thing to give a definite stopping point to the date was within reason. Cathy watched Cady's dust settle as the truck sped down the drive; she thought, "He is so beautiful, I'm so lucky."

Cady was in trouble; he was two hours late, it was dark, and there was nothing he could do but drive as fast as possible. He should have called his grandpa to explain, but long-distance charges would mean a big phone bill. And he wasn't thinking very clearly at the time. He did arrive safely back at the ranch to a worried Grandpa and could only apologize over and over. Cathy floated back into the big house; her parents asked if she had fun. Cathy answered that she did and explained about the pickup overheating as to why she was late. Her brother snickered as if to say, "Sure it did." Cathy would have loved to have shared with her grandma, "The pickup overheated at the same place as the big truck did when you were driving with me to Wenatchee to deliver cherries. Wasn't that the oddest thing?" She would then have asked if Grandma remembered that day, but no she wouldn't remember; Grandma wasn't mentally up to remembering. Cathy sighed and batted it away and asked instead about what she thought about Cady. Grandma returned with, "The next time he comes have him bring a change of clothes for swimming." Cathy chatted with her parents who both voiced that they really liked Cady much better than the other guy. The way they said it and the tone of their voices while they said it took Cathy aback for a minute. She didn't realize until that moment that her parents had actively felt disapproval and concern about her ex-boyfriend. She had never felt moved to ask them either, it truly was a 'don't ask don't tell' stalemate but with Cady it was different, he was different and she truly loved Cady. Cathy said her goodnights and walked over to the old house and into her bedroom.

She sat down to write a letter to Cady thanking him for the day and to say 'I love you' one more time tonight.

***

Cady sits at his makeshift desk in the upstairs bedroom his mother used to sleep in for the two years they lived with Grandma Hazel and Grandpa Charley. That was five years ago, so much has changed since then now it's Charley and Joyce and he is hired help in a place that was his home. Tonight Cady is dreamily blissful from yesterday with Cathy. His senses are also keenly enamored with the physical place he is in; the ranch itself. It is a moving experience flowing into the spiritual and Cady deeply mourns not being able to share it with Cathy but there is pen and paper.

Cady writes to her:

"The night wind is moving outside my window, slowly, surely, and sleepily. In sleep the wind moves its great body in response to the world it touches, sometimes in recoil sometimes in caress. The trees are whispering of the happenings of the day. Now the night sings the song it has sung since the third day and will continue to sing until days are no more. I reach out, touch it become part of it, but then a part is gone from me. It was by my choice and I will regain that part whenever I touch your hand. So this is love, a filling of an empty place near the heart. It is a shared second of silence near sunset, a whisper of movement in a still lonely night. It is a parting with only one thought, that of the reuniting of spirits after time, the ever-moving thing that brings together and takes away. It is the night that will lay tears upon the leaves for the sun in love to dry for her."

Cady paused then went on to list the things he had done today. *"I changed irrigation sets and got my tennis shoes wet. I stretched new barbed wire on a fence and did fence repair. I missed Cathy and missed Cathy and missed Cathy."* To end the letter on a light note Cady recounted one task that sent sparks flying. *"I was replacing a light fixture in the bathroom and had a little audience of two watching over my shoulder. I undid the wire nuts and then asked if the power was turned off. The answer was yes, but I thought just to be doubly sure I lightly tapped the two wires together sort of quickly. Wow! Sparks flew and my audience left. "* Cady signed the letter with 'I love you' and carefully folded it to fit the envelope. He addressed it to Cathy; her address at the orchard was Rt. 1 Box 155 Quincy, WA 98848. Cady's in true little village fashion was simply Rt. 1 Thorp WA 98946. Rural routes stretched for miles and miles of country road, no house addresses just names of the sparse people. Everyone in the little post office knew of the love letters coming to and going from Cady out at the Lawler ranch heading over to Cathy in Quincy. If Cady happened to be out at the mailbox when a car pulled up he expected to be good-naturedly teased by the lady who did his route. She knew his grandparents, his mother, and her two sons over the years and always waved as she drove past. Cady put the letter in his outgoing box for in the morning. He sat back from the desk listening to the far away noise of the interstate freeway I-90. A stray thought came to his mind, "The little bedroom's only window faced away from the freeway so you couldn't hear it..."

A sudden chill passed through his mind as if some far off memory had physically walked into his room and stood next to him placing a cold hand on his shoulder. The bedroom he was in had indeed been his mother's bedroom five years ago, his and David's little bedroom was right next to it. Cady had a strong unconscious aversion to that little bedroom, so much so, he refused to go into it. He didn't try to overcome this feeling any more than you would try to overcome the feeling of not jumping off a high cliff. That time in his life had been lost to his mind or better to say it was pushed as far away from it as possible. Here after writing a lovely letter about a lovely experience with Cathy yesterday comes this dark memory to blot out the joy. He thought about the little bedroom next to his and closed his bedroom door in response. He couldn't shut out the memories that night as they tumbled into his conscience mind bringing with them the pain and hopelessness of those two years where he called the little bedroom home from age 12 to 14. Those winters were terribly isolating, his grandparents would be gone to California from November through

February. It was their custom to do this and that didn't change because of the little family now living upstairs. Cady alone with his mother and brother in that big empty house had lain awake late at night listening to his mother crying in her room. It was a mournful and hopeless crying that went on and on. He got up and crept into her room asking, "Can I do could anything to help?" She would just say to him, "No honey, no one can, just go back to bed it's okay, I love you." Cady returned to his bed in despair still listening to the crying in his mother's room. He watched his brother quietly sleeping in the bed across from him and Cady silently prayed that David might not be awakened by the noise. Cady wouldn't have any words to give to David as comfort because he had none. How do you comfort someone when you yourself are completely overcome with hopelessness? Cady would nod off only to awaken again after an hour with the crying still drifted through the paper-thin walls separating the two rooms, thankfully David continued to sleep quietly. There was no one for Cady to turn to he was totally alone. Yes, Cady did know the reason why his mother cried. She shared it one night with him, this was 1966 before they came to the ranch to live it was when he was 11 years old. There had been drinking on his mother's part and in that cloudy state out came words loosened by alcohol that frightened him, words that would soon end his childhood altogether. Those words haunted him again this night because of what they described and what Cady feared he might also fall prey to being her son. Cady's mother was mentally ill. Her reality was a constant mental agony, which was fully controlled by an unseen tormentor, a very real being to her with outside control of her brain. He would sometimes raise the torment level to the point where she would wither and lay crying for hours. Other times he would bring people or circumstances to her life to hurt her. She could never escape him. He had no name except those she would give to him. Her tormentor could bring physical pain or drown her with the memories of every nightmarish hurt or loved one's death she had struggled through during her life. Alcohol was her means of escape; she must have felt it gave her some level of control over him, but in end the tormentor just followed right along deeper into her drunk. Cady at 11 only had fear and hopelessness in the face of a remote unseen being. Cady thought at one time it was the alcohol bringing out this dark delusion his mother had, but he came to understand it was there even when his mother was her normal loving sober self. This was the time just after his father had left them and Cady left his childhood behind, he had to find a way to help his mother to keep her safe. Cady's fear for himself began at this time also. His mother was this wonderful sweet loving person that he always felt love for and from. She worked at some awful jobs to earn enough money to keep her and her sons going. Everyone in the big Anderson family loved her dearly as the one woman who got along with all the Anderson sisters. Cady's fear for himself was as his mother's son he was developing his own mental illness with its own tormentor. Was this gender conflict the start of what his mother had? Cady didn't have any notion of a separate being having influence over his life other than God. God was not a tormentor in any way, shape, or form. His mother viewed her tormentor as a separate physical being not the devil or God but a mean-spirited human like being without a name.

This question haunted him in 1973 just before his high school graduation. Cady at 19 years old decided he would do something his mother couldn't do he would overcome this gender discord and even if it still remained in some way, he would not let it drive his life. He had one chance for happiness; one glimpse of a possible future, and it all depended on burying this feeling so deep that it would never surface again.

Cady was physically tired from the workday but now his mind was troubled. Still he had become confident in sleeping here in this room, he was resolved that things were different now, this was his safe bedroom and sleep did find him.

The next morning Cady was awakened by sunlight coming in through his open windows. He dressed and headed downstairs for his morning glass of milk. Store bought milk was a treat on the ranch. There had always been a milk cow when they lived here years ago and it had always been Cady's job to milk it twice each day. Cady

116

preferred whole milk from a carton to the raw watery cow's milk directly from an udder. All of the cream had been skimmed off for making butter leaving something behind that tasted less than 1% did. On the other hand, years ago Cady had formed a friendly relationship with the butterscotch and white Guernsey cow he named Susan. She had the most beautiful long eyelashes and was a good listener. Cady sat on the one legged milking stool milking away twice a day before school and after school. Cady had told Susan all of his secrets and fears during their time together. He sang all the songs he knew to her to keep her calm while she stood there crunching oats. It was true that they did have disagreements from time to time; as occasionally she was prone to picking up her hind hoof and putting it down again right into the milk pail with a splash! Her timing in this act of nonverbal communication was perfectly planned to occur just before Cady had finished the milking. Cady learned to finish milking as expeditiously as possible and to move the pail quickly on detecting any mischievous cow movement. There on balance, were many more good times than bad, especially went you included the barn cats into the equation. Build a barn and soon it will be populated with a clowder of elusive cats who permit you to feed them. An old tin plate was used to spill a little milk out for the cats. They expected this each morning and would gather in wait. Cady had the most outlandish idea one morning. Normally you squirt the milk straight down into the milk pail, this time Cady on purpose squirted some toward one of the cats. To his surprise the cat soon figured out how to use its paws to help direct the milk into its mouth! In no time Cady had several very willing cats all lined up to get squirted. All fun had to be tempered with reason and Cady was careful to do so. He also pondered the difference of male and female temperaments from his time with Susan the cow; she was a patient teacher in many ways. It all came to a sudden end while Cady, David, and their mom were away for a week to visit the Anderson family over the mountains during that year. Here they had visited Grandma Ida Anderson and two of her daughter's households, the Smiths and the Hansons. It was an odd time since the estrangement from his dad clouded the family relationship with Aunts and Grandmother. When

117

they returned to the ranch Cady was greeted with the news that Susan was dead. She had been feeding on a bale of hay that was still left in the discharge chute of the baler machine parked near the barn. As the bale was consumed she had to reach further into the chute, at some point she got her neck caught and strangled to death. Cady was heartbroken, the trip to Seattle had trauma enough visiting Aunts and Uncles of a family he felt a stranger to and now his normal here was shattered. That was then and this is now. And the now was Cady had received a welcomed letter from his mother last night filled with general news from home she wrote:

***

"Dearest Cady. We were glad to receive your nice letter. I got my first unemployment check Thursday the $46 will help. Merrill, David, and Rollin went fishing out on Lake Washington in Rollin's boat but they didn't catch anything. Marg and Olie flew to Minn for a week's visit Mother didn't go I think she's a little tired. Orval is up from Calif but we haven's seen him yet. We take Dave to the UW dentistry tomorrow to see if they can help him. Dad's on vacation he's taking two weeks now. So far he's been mostly resting. We finally got the color T.V. back 'good'. Have you seen Birtie lately? We haven't seen Michael lately. Depending on Dave's appointment we should be over on the 3rd. Love Mom, Dad, and Dave."

***

Cady had to smile because as a poor speller himself he could make out what his mother wrote. She always took a stab at words she couldn't spell with the idea people could still figure them out. 'Marg' and 'Olie' were Dad's sister Margaret and her husband Jerole 'Ole' Hanson, Rollin and Orval were two of Dad's brothers. Dad actually lived during the separation years with Uncle Rollin who normally lived by himself. Mother was Grandma Ida and of course 'Calif' was California, 'Minn' was Minnesota Dad's early boyhood home. 'Birtie' was the nickname Bertie Remkie a nice lady that had fancied Grandpa before Joyce came along. What was disjoint was her switch from David to Dave. Cady had only heard his brother being called Davy and later David. So strange, David had two other friends one was a Dave P. and the other was David D. Cady wondered what had been going on to change this, was home not how he left it? What changes would he be returning to?

Anyway, on with the day, his parents were coming to bring him home today they would stay the night to visit and leave the next day. Cady finished his glass of milk quickly, there were things to be done to get ready for his eleven-day absence from the ranch over the fourth of July weekend. He and Grandpa both on horseback checked the irrigation sets across the ranch so that Grandpa would know the state of all the fields. Cady admonished his grandpa to do a good job with the irrigation in his absence, his grandpa just laughed. After putting away the horses, Cady mowed the lawns of both houses and wandered down to the creek. He walked along the rocky creek behind the ranch house alone just as he had year after year hunting agates. Ellensburg is famous for a blue agate called properly the Ellensburg Blue it is a semiprecious agate that facets well. Cady had never found one but always found common agates along the creek. His mother and grandma Hazel had started this tradition of rock hunting in time out of mind for Cady and David. Some of the best times Cady had with his mother and brother happened during rock hunting together. What joy to bring a found agate to his mom and have her make a fuss over it! Grandma Hazel's great passion was gold prospecting fully equaling Grandpa Charley's passion for horses. There was no gold in Taneum Creek Grandma had verified this with gold pan in hand! It was near noon as Cady hopped from rock to rock along the creek; he was pondering the troubling memories of last night. His brain skipped back to the day his dad directed the packing up of that little bedroom four years ago. Cady and David were moving what little furniture there was out of their shared bedroom. The beds were stripped and the mattresses lay bare on their wood bed frames. Cady pulled up a mattress to take it downstairs and under it was a pair of panties. Seeing this his dad hit the ceiling shouting, "I'll put a stop to this right now we're not going to have any of this kind of behavior!" Cady was at a loss about how

119

the panties got there but that was the risk of closeted crossdressing you forget where you hide things. The vehement reaction of his father's rage at finding these more than frighten Cady, it drove a psychological nail into his coffin. He remembered that rage from before when he was small, the yelling and cursing while he could only stand there as each word hit him with the force of a physical blow to his face. Cady knew then that the dark thing he was could never be told to anyone. His mom had intervened with his dad that day and everything did calmed down but the damage was done. In the oddest way, Cady would come to understand more about his father's journey much later in life, but for now his life looked hopeless once more. Cady's mind shook itself back to the understandings of today, he was a 'he' and was going to be the very best boyfriend to Cathy, she had trusted him with her love and he would trust her with his. Cady misstepped and almost fell into the creek, the rock he had trusted as a foothold turned out to be loose. Cady was a 'he' but still there was the need to tell Cathy something about his conflict. He wouldn't be free to be with her until he did, the conundrum is he didn't know just what to tell her. Cady had backslid since graduation night by convincing himself it was all about female clothes, in a damning act of denial he had shut the door on the impossible problem of being female. Cady left the creek behind his parents would soon be here and it was dinnertime. He walked up the west field to its gate by the county road to let himself out. The Anderson family car was parked just off the country road near the front gate to the house. It couldn't have been there more than ten minutes. He hurried into the house to find his mom and dad sans David chatting civilly with Grandpa Charley and Joyce. There were hugs with his mom and dinner to share together. Cady's mom tried so very hard to navigate the treacherous path of not offending Joyce while still clinging to her father. Cady's dad just stayed out of Joyce's way altogether. He was gregarious by nature but there was the strike of divorce against him so Dad didn't even try. Joyce was hard-nosed, this came from being on her own in life, and she was never one to be moved to tears, which would show weakness. Grandpa was an alpha male and would never be anything but this, he didn't bend, so Joyce

120

despite herself was being tempered. Her last husband Ray was very malleable and easily dominated, but he had one unchangeable trait that set him apart from anyone else in the entire valley. He never drove any faster than 25 miles per hour on any of the county roads or 35 miles per hour on the freeway. Three years ago, Cady had once caught a ride with Ray thinking he could be back to the ranch an hour ahead of his grandfather who was driving the tractor back from Ray's farm. Grandpa Charley laughed at Cady's plan knowing Ray was driving. It was the longest most boring trip Cady had ever had in a pickup. Grandpa and the tractor beat Ray in the pickup by 30 minutes.

After dinner Cady had irrigation sets to check while everyone else was busy socially getting along. The afternoon hurried unto early evening and suppertime. Cady used the time after to pack his things for the trip home and to write to Cathy. He shared with Cathy the events of the day and closed with the joyful fact that soon not only would they see each other face to face, but also they could talk to each other on the telephone for hours! Long distance charges had kept telephone calls down to being a very rare thing. Cady also felt the strain his mother was under, not only was Hazel her mother gone, but also Joyce now stood as a barrier between daughter and father Charley. Joyce had no skin in the game, but Cady's mother had only her father left in life and the love of a daughter for her father is a powerful thing. It is also a very distressing thing to sleep in the downstairs' guest bedroom next to your father and his new wife. Cady pondered his mother's plight as he lay there in bed this night, soon the familiar touch of hopelessness stroked his forehead just as sleep claimed his mind. A last dreamy thought lingered before the blackness completely descend, "This is just like the time dad came over to move us back to Seattle."

Wednesday morning came and with it the clamor of people discarding sleep and preparing for the day. After a civil breakfast with only careful civil conversation had come to a neutral end, Cady announced he was headed out to feed the horses. His dad joined him in the walk down to the big barn. Cady's dad cracked the joke that Charley would make a lady out of Joyce. It was a guy-to-guy joke in the custom of the time. Cady was never comfortable around this stuff and considering the male world he was part of was filled to the brim of dirty jokes, his defense was to become numb to them. Although his father did have a point in as much as Joyce had no empathy and Grandpa certainly was providing a path where empathy as a seed could grow. Cady drove the family car westward, his dad was always willing to let someone else do the driving. It was odd paradigm shift going back to being a son in his mom and dad's house from being a hired hand over at the ranch. Today was the Fourth of July and Cady could hardly wait to get home to spend it with Cathy.

***

Cathy rode in the family Ford station wagon with her dad heading home from the orchard. I-90 melted mile by mile behind them, just now on the passenger side of the car Cathy caught sight of the Black Angus sign standing in a field. She was excited it had become a welcome landmark, because next to come was a little fenced cemetery standing in a field all by itself, this was the pioneer cemetery where Mortimer Thorp rested. Cathy strained to see the tall wind-shaped pine tree some distance in a little valley behind the cemetery. The tree stood in front of a white plantation style house and within that house was her Cady. Cathy sighed loud enough for her dad to take notice; Cathy pointed out the house telling her dad, "That's Cady's grandfather's ranch way over there. He should be heading to his home sometime today too." Sudden expectations of seeing Cady again arrived in her brain along with the continuing commonality of both their journeys, "Here we are on the same day leaving Eastern Washington to return to our homes it's just like a story in a book except I'm actually living it." Cathy blissfully listed all the things she would tell Cady as soon as she saw him. She began to keep track of the land passing by, her father suggested they stop in Cle Elum at McKean's burger place to eat and use the restroom. Her dad loved this burger place on the east outskirt of Cle Elum it was a pleasant place to stop and catch your breath. McKean's was locally famous for its Frenchie Burger made using a French bread baguette. This was her dad's favorite treat here and he loved to sit at their picnic tables scattered around their green lawn taking his time enjoying his burger and vanilla milk shake. Cathy ordered a fishwich this was her treat along with a caramel milk shake. She would work as a server in the high school cafeteria and her payment was to fix a fishwich in the special way she loved. Cathy was done with her food and anxious to get going again but her father was immune to being rushed until completely fulfilled with his food experience. Cathy with a mixed sense of frustration marveled at her father, he was never rushed in life, he never voiced a regret at any action he had taken, and he was always looking forward into the coming future. They resumed the trip up and over the Cascade Mountains at Snoqualmie Pass down to North Bend and Issaquah. Issaquah was a fun place to drive by, there was a little grass airstrip right along the freeway and every weekend skydivers floated the skies coming to rest around the grassy airstrip. Today being the Fourth of July, the place was all but quiet. Issaquah passed by and I-90 time was done, Cathy's dad exited unto I-405 south bound. Tukwila exit, then unloading the car in their driveway, and Cathy's orchard time was done for this summer. It was an unusual year, normally she would find herself back at the orchard or the farm, as her dad would sometimes call it, over the fourth of July. Traditionally she and her family would be in the little town of George with its big iconic 'Martha Inn Cafe' sign to watch a fireworks show set off over a dry field near the edge of town. Without miss every year the show would set the field on fire and the fire truck handily standing by would be applauded as the fire was put out. George had a tradition of baking the world's largest Cherry Pie something like ten feet square in a custom built oven someone local got the idea to construct. It was all very colloquial and very country. This year she was going to miss it due to family circumstances, but on the other hand, being home gave her time to spend with Cady and to prepare for Summer Camp at Camp Sealth. This was going to be her third summer attending camp. After her two weeks of camp, it would be toward mid-August and this year Cathy's August was empty of Eastern Washington. Cathy repopulated her basement bedroom with her stuff from the orchard, especially her gifts from Cady. The gloxinia found a home on her windowsill although she dithered on whether or not it would get enough sunlight in that location as the sundeck above greatly reducing the sunlight to her room. The orange ice cream candle looked nice sitting on her little bookcase. Now, all she had to do was wait for a phone call from Cady announcing he was back home too. Cady called within 30 minutes asking if Cathy would like to go see fireworks with him at Moshier Field in Burien. Cady had borrowed his family's car and arrived at Cathy's front door minutes later. Moshier Park was sort of the center of Burien it had play fields, assorted event buildings, and a long tradition of fireworks displays on the Fourth of July. Cathy sat close to Cady on the aluminum bench seats of the softball bleachers. Little kids danced all around the field holding sparkers until it became dark enough for the main show to begin. There was serene contentment in Cathy's heart just to be sitting next to Cady in the dusk of a summer evening. Add the excitement of exploding fireworks overhead and you have the setting of a beautiful memory to treasure into the future. There was the traditional traffic jam in the parking lot after the show, followed by a slow meandering drive back to Cathy's house. In the following eleven days Cady and Cathy became closer and closer day by day. Cathy found herself pouring out her childhood memories to Cady, he treasured her experiences and Cathy found joy in reliving them. She reveled in the secret places around her old house that meant so much to her and the adventures that came with them. Cady by listening looked through Cathy's eyes at a girl's childhood and silently compared it to his own. They talked about what their dream homes and their dream lives would look like. Adopting a son and a daughter, the house wouldn't be too big just comfortable sized, it would have a large covered carport that easily transformed into a rainy day play area with its own outdoor chalk board. Both of them decided to be well away from the now all-to-near cities like Seattle or even Burien. Cathy and Cady agreed that the school district they are in now would not be the best for any child in the future. Michael and Janice have become a steady couple now with Janice doing her best in guiding Michael in the art of coupledom. She has her work cut out for herself for this is the summer of release from the bonds of restraint for Michael and he explodes existentially in every direction. Michael has a thirsty intellect drinking books dry as he voraciously devours them. He craves every physical experience to be the most outrageous in expanding both mind and body. Janice matches this in her own way, while fire doesn't burn in her veins she is drawn to the fire burning in Michael's. Cathy and JJ are friends they both attend a weekly bible study at Dave M's house and now have the added bond of Cady and Michael. In the girls' eyes, Cady and Michael had been what amounted to an inseparable couple. Cathy and JJ acknowledge the budding love they have for the guys and actively compared notes on how their relationships with them are going. It is a natural occurrence that the two couples would get together for some activity. One night they did, how it worked was Janice invited Cathy to stay the night at her parent's house, of course it was just a ruse, the real idea was to meet up with Michael and Cady later. It was a warm night Cathy and JJ were going to sleep outside on the screen porch or they let it be known to the household that this was their intention. The two girls talked the dusk hours away confiding in each other on the ups and downs of their relationships with Michael and Cady. "There is a labor in being Michael's girlfriend," JJ explained to Cathy, "But it is an exciting labor! He is so untouched by not ever having a girlfriend before; he's both sweet and clueless, leaving it up to me to steer. He's zany, everything he's involved with has to be the biggest, brightest, and loudest around. It is just the wildest ride you could have, also the saddest, after all the loud music and bright lights he is hurt somehow, it has something to do with his dad." Cathy pondered this, but before she had her turn in conversation an odd noise caught Janice's attention. "That's Michael's call, it's time to go grab your jacket!" Janice commanded. Cathy followed Janice as she deftly cut through a neighbor's backyard to the alley on the other side. The night was cooling now but Cathy didn't feel it, all she felt was the excitement of doing something daring something akin to breaking the barriers of adolescence to be with her true love. To Janice this was old hat, she craved the fire burning in her love's veins, the excitement he generated around him, this was simply payment to how

Michael rolls. In the alley waiting by Cady's car for the night the two guys welcomed their counterparts. Michael was dressed in black; he also owned a black cape for extreme mood enhancement during night constitutionals he was prone to take. Such was Michael. Cady on the other hand was wearing a white undershirt under a light colored short sleeve shirt and blue jeans. Cathy smiled when she saw Cady and also thought he always seems so uncomfortable in his clothes while Michael's clothes screamed who he is. Cathy sat next to Cady in the front while Janice and Michael cuddled in the back. Sitting there next to her love Cathy felt that life had brought her to the one true place she would be forever. Cady did as he always did with Michael, let him take the lead to adventure and right now Michael wanted food. "Off we go to Jack in the Box for Breakfast Jacks," came the reply from Michael. The drive-thru guys over at Jack in the Box burger place knew Michael and those like him. He in particular was famous for driving up to the clown head late at night or very early in the morning with a load of wild and crazy cohorts, all ordering ten Breakfast Jack sandwiches each. The fry cook would roll his eyes and start cracking eggs like crazy. The ham, egg, cheese, on a bun sandwich had only been around in the area for like two years and to Michael they were Manna from Heaven. He consumed them in great quantities. Cathy was along for the ride wherever it led and right now it was in line to fuel up with ten Breakfast Jacks for the four of them. Cathy enjoyed the zany comic banter between the two guys, Cady would kept pace with each sharp comment Michael made while Michael would return an even more outrageous one upping the ante. It was a verbal tennis match with one gracious player vs. one unhinged player. Most of the time Cady was the gracious one but on occasion the roles would briefly reverse. Cathy and Janice had fun spiking the verbal tennis ball in mid-volley with their own verbal antics. It was left up to Cady to drive somewhere so Cady chose the route he was most familiar with I-90 up to Snoqualmie Pass. He knew they needed a place to picnic at night and there was a little day-use place up there. It was an hour drive up the pass and a few minutes longer to Crystal Springs Campground. He had never seen people at the place and tonight was no different.

Cathy pointed out a parking spot and Cady pulled in and everyone tumbled out. The summer night was twilight from the moon and city lights over the mountaintops. They all sat at a heavy log picnic table spreading the slightly warm sandwiches out to admire. They prayed one lead by Cady and the other by Michael. Cady had told Cathy how Michael became a believer in Christ. She asked Michael while he was finishing his third sandwich about it, he paused to explain, "Cady and I would go to the El Rancho drive-in theater with his father to see horror movies on Fridays. The flick we were watching one night had to do with the power of the occult and centered in on Satan worship. I can't remember the name of the flick, but it all happened when I said something about the pentagram symbol they were using and the demon they would bring up with it. Merrill Cady's dad blew a gasket! He asked me how I knew about this subject? I answered that I had been studying the occult by reading books on it. Then he asked me what I knew about Jesus Christ. I answered just the basic stuff. He schooled me right then and there about the spiritual danger of this study without understanding Biblical principles; in short, I had better get right with Jesus before fooling around with the devil. I turned to Cady sort of dumfounded by his father's stern admonishment asking is this what you believe too and Cady nodded saying he did believe in Jesus being the Son of God. It was Cady's agreement that actually started me on the road to knowing Jesus." Michael asked Cady, "So why had you not ever nailed me on this before that movie?" Michael had returned to his sandwich as Cady spoke, "It was like this Michael, I am very close to you and I simply didn't know how to tell you. I kept worrying and praying as you dove deeper and deeper into reading all about the satanic occult symbols; you were so impressed with the power they claimed. I needed a path and a defense, but also I had a fear you would walk away from me because of my inadequacies in persuasion. The pure black candles you asked me to make I sabotaged with white wax in the center of each hoping they would fail you in your use of them in some ceremony or other." Janice and Cathy glanced at each other with that knowing glance, which held understanding that these two guys shared a very deep bond and now they are also part of it with them. The moment was over one sandwich was left and by mutual agreement it was awarded to Michael for being spiritually courageous. It was becoming cold now as the night moved on, so they all tumbled back into the car and were on their way west to Snoqualmie Pass itself. Cady parked near the rest stop at the pass and they all made good use of the facilities. Afterward the two couples walked across the street to the bare ski slopes. Michael and Janice were in the lead up an access road winding its way to the top of the slope. In theory Cathy's jacket kept her warm, but in fact it was Cady's hand in hers that really did the trick. Half way up the slope they all stopped and sat on a fallen log chatting aimlessly in a symphony of random emotions of place and time. There was never any thought of making out in either Michael's or Cady's mind. No passionate caressing with their loves under the stars, it was all about being in the moment on a mountain trail with each other. Cathy didn't miss this physical form of expression, in a real way she had just escaped from a trap it was leading her into. Janice knew Michael; she was patient and fulfilled all at the same time. She knew whatever Michael would do in the near future the ride would be fraught with enormous emotional twists and turns, all she could do was to hold on and be true to her mantra of, "Neato-Nifty-Jet, followed by Icky-Bad-Wicked."

***

Cady had a twinge of jealousy involving Janice pop up on that early morning drive back from Snoqualmie Pass. The two couples had stayed until the small hours of the morning, that time before dawn when there is just a detectable glow to the west. Michael and Janice were quiet in the back seat and Cathy leaned against Cady's shoulder eyes half closed. Cady was playing back the drama up on the mountain, the part when Michael had shed his coat in defiance of the falling temperature. He had left it lying on the log where they all had been sitting at the turning point of the hike. Cady had picked it up as they gathered together to walk back down the mountain slope. Cathy was next to him as Cady made the joke, "What has it got in its pocketses," this being a reference to a line Gollum says in *The Hobbit*.

Of course it was a mistake to think it was a funny thing to do, it's the kind of thing that when done brings out something that was best left private. This time was exactly that kind of time, Cady pulled out a nearly empty baggie of pot. The baggie had been open in his pocket and had remnants crusting the inside. Cady was livid, to him this was a breach of trust. It also frightens him this was 1973 if a policeman for any reason stopped them, then in random search found this in the car that was entrusted to Cady there would be hell to pay. The trust issue was in two pieces. The first piece: Cady had always trusted Michael not to put him in jeopardy, even though Michael had never agreed to this Cady just assumed he wouldn't. The second piece: Cady was a child of an untreated alcoholic, he was hypervigilant of any hidden substance, and finding one was a sure sign of danger to him. Cady also had a fear of policemen even though he had never had an encountered with one, it was the natural fear someone builds from hiding something forbidden about themselves. Michael had made light of it when confronted; he emptied what was left in the baggie onto the ground saying, "Maybe something interesting will grow here next year!" Michael was engaging in all of life's hidden pockets, in all the places and physical experiences that he had been kept from by the tight hand of his stepdad. Cady wouldn't and couldn't begrudge him this, but Cady's insecurities lay painfully bare at times. The friends reunited and the drive home was a quiet one with passengers nodding off to sleep. The first stop was to drop off Michael the second was Janice and Cathy. It was early dawn as Cady drove toward Michael's house; several chickens were on the edge of the road. Janice suddenly perked up and warned Cady not to hit them because they were beautiful. Michael added, "She is always seeing beauty in the smallest of living things around us." Cady had a sudden twinge of jealousy, Michael had over the years given him credit for such a view of life and now that credit belonged to Janice in Michael's eyes. The ember of jealousy suddenly flared to hot flame then burned completely out; a spontaneous gender battle had come and gone. Cady remembered just who was dozing next to him on the front seat; Cathy who had come to be with just him and no one else. Michael took leave of JJ in a very

129

robust and definitely comical way leaving Cady to clandestinely deposit Cathy and Janice back to where they were rumored to be. Cady parked in the alley back of Janice's parents' home.

Cathy was fully awake getting out of the car her brain sharp with the tingle of the night's adventure having but one more dangerous angle to overcome before their secret was safe. Cathy melted into the hug from Cady while Janice impatiently stood on the other side of the car. She rebuked, "Okay enough already next time get a room, we gotta go now!" Cathy again followed Janice's cat like movements through the neighbor's backyard. JJ suddenly stopped and Cathy nearly bumped into her. A figure in shadow had just rounded the corner of Janice's house and had stopped as suddenly as Janice had. Janice brightly greeted her younger brother Mark who had just snuck out an orifice of the home other than the front door, "Leaving?" Mark smirked in retort, "Coming back?" Janice continued past her brother toward the house's screen porch with Cathy right at her heels. Once fully inside they climbed into their sleeping bags and Cathy heartbeat started to return to normal. Cathy whispered to Janice, "Will Mark say anything?" Janice with a start replied, "What and spoil the fun, that would be zany! It's like the nuclear missile thing on a sister/brother level." Cathy stumbled for minute with this turn of conversation. Janice seeing this in her friend explained, "You know it's a mutual assured destruction standoff and it couldn't be anymore loving family-wise." Janice sighed, "Wow we can get almost two hours of sleep before everyone's up." Cathy suddenly sleepy agreed.

Cady was in bed an hour before the household awoke. If he needed the car he would have to drive his dad to work but today he was going to sleep late. It had been an adventure last night complete with drama. Tomorrow he would be on the road with his dad to return to the ranch and would not be home again for four weeks.

**

Cathy had hugged Cady as her eyes filled of the coming tears from their parting; it was Friday the 13th of July. So much had happened since the end of school and so much was continuing to happen as each

130

summer day came and went. She had made sure to have a letter waiting for Cady as soon as he entered his room at the ranch. It was back to letter writing for now and Cathy found joy in the thought of it. To have someone to share all the intimate experiences of each day with, no matter how small they might be, was just the greatest feeling. He loved her and she loved that he did; with every pencil movement across each line of her letters to him she felt him at her side patiently listening to her. Not only did he listen to understand her, as she read his letters he spoke lovingly about all his daily life as if she was there next to him. It would be hard these next four weeks until August when they would once again be together. For now she had her cousin staying with her. Her cousin is the same age as Cathy so it is assumed by family that the two cousins would keep great company with each other. And for the most part this was true, but Cathy needed private time for letter writing, which was difficult to carve out. Especially, when you have a cousin sleeping in the same room with you.

Cathy resumed going to youth group at church; she was grateful to have Cady and since this was God's house she felt it was the right thing to do in gratitude. Still there was an ever-growing social tension here but Cathy was numb to it as of yet anyway. She would be gone herself in a week to attend Camp Sealth on Vashon Island. She is a Horizon Club girl in Camp Fire and a returning camper. Camp starts with the boat trip from Golden Gardens Park aboard an Argosy boat chartered by Camp Fire for this purpose. The special memory of a ten-year-old Cathy arriving at Camp Sealth for the first time on the wooden steamboat Virginia V lives forever in Cathy; the modern Argosy boats are nice but the Virginia V was special. Her camp stay this summer was in two parts. The first week was training to be a resident camp aide, which amounts to being a counselor to younger campers but still under the direction of a senior counselor. The second week was to actually work with a particular group of younger girls adding to their weeklong camp experience. Cathy was diligently writing each day but in installments over length of each day. She would find spaces of time she could steal away as the day progressed to chronicle the morning, midday, and night. So not only did she begin to carry her active letter along with her during the day it also became a companion to her experiences. Cathy writes, "This morning, in about 10 minutes, I have to go down for a first aid class. Later we will have tool school. Tomorrow morning is pajama breakfast. It is now after lunch during rest hour. This afternoon we are going on a snipe hunt with some second and third graders. Tonight will be folk dancing in the orchard with the other Horizon girls and then make ice cream. It's going to be fun." As the day's time passes her writing continues, the magic of chatting with her new found companion, who by the way, solemnly promises to relay all she has experienced this day to her true love far away in Thorp, deepens her appreciation of place she is in. Her companion challenges her to do better than simple lists and new dimension of sharing graces her heart. Cathy writes, *"I have moved from my cabin to an area just about the beach and below the road. They were playing two competing radios and I didn't want to listen to the cacophony. The wind is blowing telling its story to the leaves and grass. The waves of the rising tide gently cover the beach with a song of her own voyage."* Then later at night she writes, *"The night looked so beautiful after the sun had gone down. The sun reflected off the distant clouds showing a myriad of shapes and lights on the far-off shore reach out touching the banks of Sealth through the waters of Puget Sound."* Cathy closed her letter by adding a clover flower she picked. She used a little sealing wax to hold it right at the top of the letter where Cady would see it. Cathy added a note next to the little flower saying, *"A part of Sealth from me to you, love Cat."* Cathy had come to camp alone where most of the other Horizon Club campers had come with friends making the group an odd number. So when paring up came she was often left out, but this year it didn't matter Cady was here in her heart with her sharing all the laughter and love put into these two weeks. Cathy got to teach the craft of Swedish huck weaving to a happy giggling group of six graders and it was great. They caught her writing to her Cady during a break and had the grandest time teasing her. Cathy didn't mind after all what happens at camp is always joyful to behold. On the return boat trip there was the exchanging of phone numbers and addresses with girls she most likely would not hear from again. This time there was something else she was leaving behind, her girlhood. The steam powered Virginia V had given way to the modern Argosy boat that now was steadily making its way towards a coming adult time with her Cady. Today was August 3rd and Cady would be home in two days and Cathy couldn't wait.

***

Cady and his dad are on I-90 eastbound heading toward the ranch on this Saturday morning the 14th of July. This was the last day of Merrill's two-week vacation and it was being spent together just the two of them. It should have been a time to talk father-to-son and vice versa, but of course nothing happened. The perfect time really for a dad to be giving advice to a son about serious relationships with women, and for a son to be asking for said advice, but again nothing came of it. Instead, the roar of hot air blowing in through the open wind-wings pointed directly at the occupants of the front seat of the 1968 model car, forbade any conversation. The further east they traveled the hotter the outside temperature became and at the moment it was still climbing past the mid-90s. By the time they reached the ranch the thermometer was over 100 degrees. Cady stood by the car and stretched, the familiar scents and sounds of his home-away-from-home filled his body and mind. The scent of the tall lone pine in the front yard, the dry grass at the front gate, and the old house. His dad wasn't staying there was nothing to stay for, the sad feeling of loss hung in the hot dry familiar air. Grandma Hazel was gone and Joyce was now in her place, Cady had an adopted place here as hired help, but Merrill was just a casual semi-welcome visitor now. For the first time in a long time Cady wondered about how his dad must feel about the ranch now. Cady hugged his dad goodbye, but something about the embrace felt different, even a little foreboding it sent a shiver up his spine. Cady's relationship with his dad was a myopic puzzle at best. During Cady's early childhood his dad was seldom home until late at night, well after his sons were in bed, and gone again before breakfast time. If it wasn't a second job it was a church function or some other odd thing even on weekends. Cady saw more of his dad around the house during the two years right before the divorce. But even then there was a disconnect; such as when they all went to church as a family Dad would disappear into the crowd leaving them to fend for themselves. If you had asked Cady to describe his dad during this time he would say, "My dad loves to go do things with other people and he loves to sing." They had one amazing vacation during that time driving back to Minnesota to see family. It was just the little Anderson family of four, on the road traveling across country together, and Cady thought it was the best time ever. After Cady's mom and dad reunited after the divorce Cady greatly appreciated his dad taking over the responsibility of the care of his mother and brother. All of the time they were alone at the ranch Cady had failed at keeping his mother sober and safe, he had failed to keep himself safe and sane from his gender conflict. Failing these things brought a constant state of worry to him about his brother. His mom's drinking pretty much stopped for three years after the remarriage but her delusion of a mental tormentor continued. It was in Cady's middle adolescence where he came to know the person that his father was. Cady's early adolescence came during the separation time, it brought a crash course in the person that his mother was, but his father was an unknown to him except by title. Cady in a sense, became enamored with his father being the one to bring stability into his life and lift the crushing responsibility off his shoulders of his mom's paranoid schizophrenic condition. That relief was so great that Cady had forgiven the abandonment his dad had done to them without a second thought; it had been just an extended time away from family as had occurred over and over again. He had come to learn from his dad's sisters that even as a little boy Merrill would wander away and join up with some other family. Cady didn't understand the root of his dad's behavior neither did he understand the root of his mom's behavior. The normalizing role of a father who was predictable and fun, as he loved to play family card games with his sisters, and Grandma Ida weekly, was priceless to Cady. It gave Cady and David four precious years to have a stable family experience, but now there was that odd foreboding feeling at the end of the hug from his dad. An old trust issue Cady had with his dad blinked to life again, this issue had been pushed away as a concession to the relief his dad offered five years ago. As the car drove back west Cady turned away and shook off the parting. His mind switched to other things when he saw that the lawn was half mowed and half over grown. He walked up to the front door and knocked before entering. He was welcomed back by his grandpa and told of the tails of a broken tractor which needed parts installed right away, they were going to need to move cattle tomorrow, and one steer in particular needs doctoring. In short, get to the lawn and then start on the tractor. The lawn was straightforward but the day was very hot, Cady had to take it in smaller steps. By midafternoon Cady called a truce with the lawn mower to switch to getting the tractor back together. It was parked in full sun near the shop all in pieces with tools scattered around. Cady quickly learned that 100-degree tools are too hot to hold barehanded! By suppertime the tractor was back together, the lawn all shorted, and Cady's neck was hot pink. It was too hot to eat much but true to form the wind made its daily evening appearance to cool things off although at the moment it wasn't doing a very good job of it. Cady had a letter waiting up in his room and it was just the thing to turn the day around. He carefully slit the letter open leaving the wax seal that held his prize closed intact, the seal imprint was in the form of double pierced hearts. Unfolding the letter Cady was greeted by a clover flower pressed on the paper with a note that read, "A part of Sealth from me to you, love Cat." The warm wind tumbled in one open window of his room and pushed itself out the other taking with it a few unwanted degrees of heat. Cady immersed himself in Cathy's story thinking what it must be like to be at camp, how wondrous it would be to be brave like her, and to do things like this. Cady was lightheaded from the strain of being out in the heat of the day; this along with the physical exhaustion of work provided a combination that was disarming to his disjoint thoughts. He thought to himself, "Cathy and I will be together, I'll get to share all of her experiences, and know what it's like to be her." Cady rubbed his aching head, "What an odd thing to think." Honesty comes to disarmed brains in such times, but Cady shook it off he had to write a short letter to Cathy before falling into bed. Morning brought air that was all wrong for mornings to have, it was still hot but despite this the sounds outside were proper. The rain-bird sprinkler sourced by the well was busy making chck-chck-chck sounds turning its head in a circle to bring water to the thirsty lawn. Birds chattered and bees buzzed totally indifferent to the rising temperature. The bees searched out little puddles; ones made on the concrete stepping-stones by the busy sprinkler, even bees get thirsty. Cady stopped outside the screen door and inhaled the mist from the sprinkler; it was not going to be pleasant to move cattle today. On the other hand, the yard around the ranch house was an oasis, it was good to pause and reflect on the relief it would bring at the end of the day. The walk to the barn by landmark: first cross the yard to the little bridge built by Cady's great grandfather Bill Booth before Cady was born. Cady had played on this little three foot long bridge as a small child watching the clear irrigation water flow under it, now a grown Cady took the three steps over it without pausing. Second is the white painted and metal roofed freestanding two-car garage and shop. The shop had three doors two for vehicles and the one for people that had its own little bridge over the irrigation ditch. When the shop was built they use a window unit on one wall in the same style as found on the ranch house giving the shop a nice view of the vegetable garden. Cady entered the shop to collect a claw hammer from the pile of tools on the bench. There wasn't any machine of any size, shape, or description on the ranch that couldn't be repaired with stuff from the shop. The sheets of aluminum on the roof were already moaning and creaking from the morning heat, air did not flow freely through the shop despite having one big door open; soon it would turn into an oven as the day passed. Third came the main gate to the barn complex. Main gates are a point of pride on ranches and totally reflect the philosophy of the ranch itself. Whenever Cady visited a ranch he always studied its main gate as it tells a lot about the people living there, the good and the bad. Cady's grandpa had built the main gate board-by-board interlocking straight boards with diagonals to support the gate's full twenty-foot length. He had used two 20-foot railroad ties one as the hinge-post and the other a fixed-post both buried deep into the ground leaving 14 feet above ground. The gate's heavy hinges bolted onto the hinge post. The fixed post stood at the opposite side of the gateway giving a place to receive the gate when shut. Even with the massive hinge-post the gate would have been too heavy to open. Grandpa attached a steel cable to the top of the gate's opening end. The cable was then strung to a free-swinging pivot point he had attached to the center of the top of the hinge-post. The cable was tightened to support the entire weight of the gate so it now could be opened or closed easily without dragging on the ground. Grandpa attached a steel horseshoe to a block with the ends pointing up. He dug a little hole at the foot of the fixed post and attached the block to it and covered the block with dirt. This left the horseshoe pointed up out of the ground so that the gate's bottom when closed could rest shackled within the two sides of the horseshoe. Grandpa from horseback could lift that end of the gate to unshackle it and do the reverse to close it again. The philosophy comes from Grandpa in three parts: the strength of the massive uprights standing in defiance of time, the ease of opening gives gratification for daily labor, and the heart which comes from the half-buried horseshoe is Grandpa's love of horses. Strength, labor brings gratification, and heart, this place will always have a love of horses. Finally the barn complex, which is made up of the enclosed barn with hay storage and three feed stalls, an International TD6 diesel crawler tractor with dozer blade installed is currently parked in one of the stalls. The equipment shed (a favorite playground for Cady and David growing up) stands next to the barn; it's closed on two sides and is currently home to the International 55W baler, an old International 1940s flatbed truck, and a hydraulic lift attachment for the tractor. An old granary whose roof leaked far more than it shed leaned against the equipment shed's wall. The horses were already standing in the feed stall waiting for their morning's oats. Cady hammered down a nail poking up into the feed trough and laid the hammer down next to all the tack hanging on the stall wall. An old coffee can used to dish out the feed was kept in a 50-pound sack of feed oats located on the hay storage side of the barn. Each horse got half a can in the feed trough. It was no surprise to either Red or Sandy as Cady slipped a loose rope around their necks. Rocky was left free he was not being ridden today. Cady curried each horse while they crunched away on the oats in their trough. A saddle blanket then the saddle itself was put up on the horse's back. Cady was careful not to let the cinch slap Sandy's underside as he threw the saddle up and onto Sandy's back. Both Sandy and Red were very tolerant of being saddled as long as Cady was thoughtful. He reached underneath Sandy and caught the cinch and threaded the cinch strap loosely through its loop and back to the front rigging D on the left side of the saddle. There was no point to tightening the cinch strap as long as the horses were eating. Cady went ahead and set the flank-strap, as it was never tightened anyway. The oats were long gone now; Cady brought bit and bridle to each horse and they accepted such taking it gracefully. Cady's grandpa walked into the feed stall and inspected Cady's work. Grandpa tightened the cinch on Red and then moved to Sandy to do the same. A little game ensued between Sandy and Grandpa as it always did until Grandpa won and the cinch was secure. Cady and Grandpa Charley rode back up to the ranch house; there they tied the reins of the horses to the decorative fence around the yard. You could ride into the front yard by going around the fence at the far end but expect Grandma Hazel's fiery rebuke if she saw you riding a horse in her yard. Grandpa from time to time would do just this to tease Grandma Hazel but he was always quick to retreat afterward. Since Grandma Hazel's passing Cady had never seen him do it again. In the country, ranchers trade favors and Grandpa had helped the guys at the Black Angus Cattle Ranch innumerable times, this day would be a little payback on the help-debt, the one ranch hand with a horse was coming to give a hand to Charley. It would be three of us to move 180 head of cattle from the field directly south of the ranch house to the corral east of the barn. There were two more very indispensable ranch hands to add to our ranks these being Queenie and Stripe the ranch's cattle dogs. Grandpa was amazing in working with horses he too was very good in training dogs. The dogs were a collie/shepherd mix and lived to herd livestock. With this in hand we pretty much had the cattle outnumbered. Still, this was going to be tricky since the county road separated that field from the field we needed the cattle to move to. In the ranch house we gathered meds to doctor the one steer and grandpa called to let the horseman know it was time to come. Cady untied Sandy and rode back down the lane to the barn towards the corral. The idea was to set all the gates either open or shut to force the cattle to move in the direction leading into the corral. Cady had already shut the main gate behind him, next he had to dismount to shut the gate next to the granary closing off the barn complex. The corral gate was opened and the gates to the North backfields closed. Cady started across the remaining field toward the country road at a quick clip as he could see two horsemen waiting for him at the road crossing. There is a rush you feel as your horse gallops, but at a trot it is all about being bounced up and down. Cady prefers a good steady walk and if needed a gallop, but not the in-between gait. It is so hot today it would have been smart for Cady to have his western hat on, the one currently in the pickup, but Cady had never mastered the art of keeping it on his head while moving cattle. So it's fingers crossed on sunburns. Cattle are curious by nature so as soon as three horsemen make their way into the field all bovine eyes are on them. The three riders two of which knew exactly what to do and how to make their steeds comply into doing it and one that was a good space holder took action to mindfully circle the cattle together. No one needs to be galloping about in the heat the trick is to keep things nice and calm. Cady figured it was all about pushing the cattle in a direction, once started they tended to move together. A big plus with this field is its lack of tall brush and trees. You never know when one steer will take it into his head to break away and run toward a bramble for cover. The cattle were docile because of the heat today and soon with the help of the dogs the herd was bunched near the closed gate that opens unto the county road. The gate on the opposite side of the road stood open to the field leading toward the corral. Cady quietly urged Sandy through the herd and over to the gate, Cady leaned over to unlatch the gate and pulled it open as he rode Sandy up onto the road. Cady kept an eye for coming cars but this was normally a very untraveled road. Once across the road Cady rode into the field and took a position to turn the cattle as they wandered in directing them toward the empty corral located in the far corner of this field. Grandpa gave some verbal signals to the dogs and the whole herd wandered across the road to the new field. Cady tried to kept the line of cattle turned and for the most part there wasn't any resistance. As the other riders pushed the last of the cattle over the road and shut the gate they could join in pushing the whole herd toward the next open gate in the corner. Just on the other side of that gate a little brook separated them from the open corral. It was very hot today and the beckoning cool water brought the herd right to it. Except for one steer that for some reason bolted before leaving the field right past Cady. This was an embarrassment to both Sandy and Cady and called for a gallop to regain some sense of decorum for the pair. Sandy bolted after the steer and Cady tried to match his body movements to Sandy's. Pressure down on the stirrups and toes pointed outward puts the rider deeper into the saddle. Sandy turned sharply at Cady's direction and Cady followed by shifting his body's weight with the force of the turn. The steer stopped sort of holding his ground until Sandy started toward him. This steer that had been the one to push through fences on a whim causing Cady hours of fence repair; he decided it was a better idea to join the herd at the brook than to face the horse. Sandy triumphantly walked back head held high. Pushing the cattle into the corral was only complicated by having to try to find the one steer in the herd that had an ulcerated eye; a condition known as pink eye to the ranchers. He was spotted and the corral gate closed while Cady walked back up to the barn; he had been forced to use his knees to hold onto the turning horse and they were pretty sore now. Partly his fault of wearing tennis shoes instead of western boots; tennis shoes were fine most of the time, but not having the high heel to lock with the stirrup during cattle chasing causes pressure on the knees. Cady reached the pickup that held his much needed hat and the meds for the steer and drove it back to the corral. Grandpa and his helper from the next ranch over already had the hurt steer in the cattle chute. Cady climbed the heavy corral fence boards and pushed his way through the cattle to the mechanical cattle squeeze. Cady's job was to work the cattle squeeze; it was device to hold an animal tight so as to give access for branding, castrating, dehorning, or doctoring. Timing the squeeze's operation was critical, if properly timed the animal was safe and the operator was safe. Cady had become very skilled at doing this, it was his promise to himself to minimize the pain of each steer. There was no reciprocation of that promise by the steers and there had been several incidents before that skill was mastered and each brought with it the lesson of being alert and careful. The rear gate of the squeeze was open the steer bolted ahead and Cady dropped the gate closed then squeezed the hinged sides tight and trapped the steer's head all in one motion. Cady had great sympathy for cattle suffering from pink eye, their eyes become opaque with a raised blue ulcer where the lens had been beautifully clear; it was awful to look at. There was salve to put under the eyelid and a blue powder to apply to the lens ulcer. On the other hand, Cady had seen steer's eyes completely heal given time after doctoring. Releasing the steer from the squeeze was just as much an art as catching him in one. The hinge side pressure was released just a few seconds before the head restraint was let loose. If done right the steer is suddenly free before he knows it and will just walk safely out instead of bolt out. The cattle are now going to be let loose out of the gate leading into the north field. This is the most demanding part for Cady; it is his job to count the cattle going out of the corral. Cady has the hardest time keeping track as they either run through or tumble through the gate opening in threes or fours. Today his count is one extra better one extra than two few is the philosophy as at the end of the season the number that head off to the feedlots is generally the same as come in spring. The horses are unsaddled and put away, the cattle are knee deep in good feed and shade and it is dinnertime. As is the custom our friend from the ranch next door will join us for the noontime meal. His horse is left in the barnyard to rest while Sandy, Red, and Rocky get to enjoy the orchard. Joyce is a good cook and the conversation is centered on Grandpa telling jokes to the neighbor, but the feeling at the kitchen table isn't the same as when Grandma Hazel's fried chicken was the star here. Cady mourns within and thinks about his Cathy, his grandmother would have loved her so much... Cady also mourns the times gone by that it was both he and his brother David on horseback working cattle with grandpa. David rode a perky Shetland pony he named Judy. A dark shadow of loss brought on a deep sigh to Cady, so much has passed away with Grandma Hazel. The afternoon is light work done slowly in the heat; Cady drives the pickup to the now empty south field to close the gates and check that the field is truly empty. Tomorrow he will set irrigation water to flowing there. Parking the pickup in front of the shop Cady sits for a while pondering his life here. He has in his lifetime at this place with his grandpa as instructor he has learned to maintain, repair, and operate wheel tractors, crawler track tractors, balers, cars, trucks, hay elevators, and all sort of small engine implements right down to lawn mowers. On the animal side, how to take care of cattle, horses (including shoeing them and there had been ten horses over the years), sheep, goats, chickens, ducks, bees, cats, and dogs (there had been five dogs over the years). He had learned how to plant crops and tend them along with the entire infrastructure of the ranch. He had learned the world of his grandparents' arts and crafts. All this and he was completely lost, his grandmother was gone, his grandfather was becoming a shadow of what he was, his mother was failing again, his brother teetering in life's struggle, and there was this odd foreboding feeling from his dad's hug. Finally, what is he going to do about his unspeakable problem it wasn't going away, he sighed deeply with only the pickup to hear him. He opened the door and felt a new cooling breeze, this time coming from the west gently touching his sun burnt skin as he walked toward the house. Cady was an empty entity that lived vicariously because of the denial of self. Cady knew the people that his parents, grandparents, close friends, and favorite teachers where, as he had a constant drive to learn these things. Cady was too frightened to know the true person he was, the person who in Deuteronomy 22:5 was abhorrent to God, instead he had become a construct made from the people around him. They gave him a way to be without dipping into his true self, a way to hide in plain sight from himself. After being sociable with Grandpa and Joyce, Cady climbed the stairs to his room quickly passing the door to the little bedroom on his way to his safe space. Cady had an old swamp cooler that could only function as a fan running in his room, but that cooling breeze in and of itself was of more relief this evening. That new breeze snaked its way into the south-facing window blessing the entire room and exited out the east-facing window taking with it many degrees of discomfort. Cady wrote to his Cathy of the news of the day, what it was, and how it felt. He chronicled each action and climax, giving birth to the depth of the experiences through his senses and heart. There was red blood mingled with white foam from the horse's mouth. This was the neighbor's horse the one who was helping with the cattle. Cady was horrified at the sight; it turned out the bridle bit the man was using was an evil one, it cut into the roof of the horse's mouth. It was a mean and sad thing to use. There was a thick dust stirred up with each hoof-fall in the corral; the smell of it replayed every experience through the years that Cady had had there. It was the smell of dry blood, burnt hair, and mother earth. There had been horror in that corral as well as life. Cady stopped his letter writing and drifted into a cold memory of when he lived here year round. Cady had then walked through a mist of cool blood squirting from the steer's heads after the horns had been dismembered from them. The blood stream splattered every direction the steer turned its head; every surface of the corral had wild designs drawn in dried blood. Cady had been 'doc' at the time his only thought was, "Get it over fast keep the pain short." He was using a coagulation powder to stop the bleeding after a hot iron was used to initially cauterize the wound left by the ugly dehorning tool. Cady had kept the branding irons hot and the large sized hypodermic syringes full of antibiotics to combat infections from dehorning and castration. As Grandpa's strength failed it was Cady who had to help squeeze the handles of the ugly giant cutter together to clip the horns off; the crunching sound was nauseated. The trauma never left him completely, it smoldered in some dark corner of his mind. He had seen people, out of curiosity, come and sit on the top board of the corral fence to watch the spectacle of the spring cattle being worked, most would get sick and turn away from the reality of it. He couldn't turn away standing there in the dust, he had to persist because he had nowhere to go, it was his world and his responsibility now, it was old fashion 1950s style ranching in all its rawness.

None of this estranged thought made it into the letter he was writing to Cathy it just hung mockingly in his memory a product of his mental turmoil triggered by being down at the corral today. He shook his head and massaged his temples, he wished with all his heart to have never gone through what he did in the corral working spring calves those years. The cold fact was if he had been outwardly female he wouldn't have had to, as he wouldn't have been judged strong enough. Cady returned to writing to his Cathy sharing with her through word pictures the many nuances of the day. *"The heat hung in the air like a thin curtain that you had to physically part to move through; it baked the dust on your face guaranteeing a bath tonight."* There was yin and yang as he wrote, *"The cattle joyfully splash through the brook as they moved into the corral and after being released found the most beautifully peaceful shade in glens of the creek fields."* Cady had explored here on his many walks. Cady was troubled, it showed in his letter writing as other more dark thoughts tried to push their way onto his paper. What he wanted to write about couldn't be put on paper or even at this moment spoken out loud. Cathy had shared her heart's trouble on their picnic with him; a truly beautiful and feminine act, she must have thought about the great risk of doing this. The risk of forever staining her image in the eyes of another, so that, whenever he looked at her from then on, assuming they stayed together afterward, the stain would persist far into the future in coloring whatever perception about her was being made at the moment. She must have looked at the depth of this then accepted the risk then decided exactly what she needed to rid herself of to go forward with a new honest relationship free of the specter of the past. An honest unfettered relationship leading to an unfettered love. This was the key, the reward that was worth the great risk. This is what Cady must ask of himself to do. There in his safe room, the one his mother had cried herself to sleep in, Cady struggled and as the western breeze put the cooling hand of God on his shoulder for support Cady tried to know the person 'she' was…

***

Dorothy was taking care of son David and nephew Tony; she misses Cady greatly. It is a typical Seattle area July day cloudy and warm. She is grateful for the task of making breakfast for the two boys but wishes it had been three. Dorothy giggled to herself at the thought, "Tony has never had a sunny-side up egg before, what fun to get to be the one to introduce them to him." Even David seems mellow with Tony around. David, her baby, is near 17 he reminds Dorothy of herself in many ways, one of which was heartbreaking to her. David was born with a cleft palate just as she had been.

This was chief of the many buried memories of childhood pain Dorothy carried along with her into adulthood.

In the decade she was born into very little could be done to fix this malady, especially for a little girl born many miles from any cities. Her parents were poor farmers in rural Kansas and the nearest local doctor tried in vain to stitch her palate closed but there was nothing to work with. The little girl Dorothy was in constant pain from this failed attempt, because as she grew the stitches cut more and more into what little was left of her palate. She couldn't eat or talk properly all that was left to her to do was cry hopelessly. She stayed with family while her parents looked for work and the crying never stopped as the pain never stopped. She was shut up in a dark closet for hours to, as they say, "Cry it out." Even this was finally given up on because little Dorothy's crying never ceased. Dorothy didn't know what she had done or why this was being done to her, she just knew the constant pain. The result was a faceless parasitic tormentor that took on corporeal form in her mind to take responsibility of all pain inducement. That tormentor never left but matured along with her as she grew into womanhood. She and her nomadic parents came to the Seattle area to live. It would be here that Dorothy would get a more successful surgery that made way for an appliance she could wear that spanned the opening in her palate. At 21 she had to again learn to talk, swallow, and accept that she would never be without what she called her 'arm-trainer' appliance. After giving birth to her first child the first thing Dorothy did was put her finger in Cady's mouth and felt for a palate, it was there and she rejoiced. When David was born Dorothy again felt in the little mouth and cried out in agony with her heart breaking, it was her faceless tormentor at work hurting both her and her newborn baby. David's surgery to correct this condition came just after birth and was successful although he did have a very noticeable under bite. Dorothy today, was occupied with her two house-fillers; normally they awoke and rolled out of the bedroom they shared around 8:30 totally missing Merrill who had gone off to work earlier. She was up to get breakfast for Merrill and then the kids had their turn. Dorothy loved the idea that David had in his 13-year-old cousin a sort of 'little brother' to pal-around with. The two of them got along pretty well and after breakfast they would tromp down the outside stairs to the rec room in the basement for the day. She wouldn't see them again except at mealtime. David would make his daily rounds of the neighborhood and Tony would tag along. There were interesting things going on that David clued Tony in on and that Dorothy didn't know about. David was growing a Marijuana plant in his bedroom closet; he had lined the closet with aluminum foil and added a grow light and had started another plant outside in an unvisited corner of the yard. What Tony remembered 40 some years later about his time with David was, "David didn't care what the hell anyone else thought and he was a super cool rebel!" Dorothy's day after the kids left fell flat, she had little things to do but the feeling of loss was creeping in all around her. Cady was over at the ranch, he was all grown now and had a girlfriend of his own, but he was taking care of her daddy for her and this comforted her. She loved her daddy so much, he was her first love and then along came Merrill to whisk her away, but Merrill was drifting away from her again. "He never stayed he always strayed," she giggled to herself, "He would have made a good tumbleweed. He was never happy being still he would always return to drifting, looking for something somewhere else." She knew she wasn't helping things by not working but she had put in applications everywhere that would take them. At least there was unemployment for a while. She had always done little things like working as a motel maid, working at Howard's Delicatessen/Ice Creamery, or cleaning houses for nice people. She never thought about the time Merrill had left them all alone or the drinking that she was subject to. No one understood; she only drank when she needed it, they couldn't understand that she could be free for a time from the 'old technician' as she called her tormentor now, by drinking. He'd go to sleep or she just couldn't hear him anymore. Her Cady always tried so hard to help even as a little boy. She knew he would always love her no matter what happened, but she was so very tired of hurting him too. She so loved her two sons and they were almost grown, her grandpa Bill and mother Hazel were gone, her daddy now belonged to Joyce and was moving out of her reach. Smoking had always helped and now she had the gift of family buzzing in and out. Cady would be home soon too and it is summertime. Dorothy giggled to herself, "I just have to learn something new like Cady has so I can find a job, I used to type I think it's time to dig the machine out again. Cathy is so cute and Cady is so silly in love with her." The days pass with the routine of David and Tony filling Dorothy's to-do list each day. Tony is in Washington State visiting all of the family in the same way that Dorothy, Cady, and David did during the separation time. In Tony case it's for the summer, his mother had died last fall and his father needed someplace for his kids to be while he worked things out, after all what else is family for but to help. Tony will stay off and on with Merrill and Dorothy during July and will spend time over the other months of summer with the other Anderson Aunts and Uncles later. The next week Dorothy was facing a week all to herself; not only had Tony gone to visit the Smiths for a few days but also David was tent camping with his friend David D. She was alone with herself not a good thing, but it would be the end for Merrill to come home to find her in shambles from drinking.

Of course it wasn't the end and what happened that week is unknown because Cady never heard anything about it. Whatever had happened it wasn't by her choice since she really wasn't alone; that faceless tormentor was with her always. A change did take place in the way Dorothy signed her letters to Cady after David had also left on his camping trip for a week twice. She no longer signed David's name at the end of the letters only love 'Mom' and 'Dad' and by the end of July it was 'Dad' and 'Mom'. Dorothy was viewing her world as autumn leaves falling to the ground, David was making it clear his time at home was for sleep only and Cady was in love with someone else now. She had only Merrill and by the end of July something had happened to make her emphasize 'Dad' then 'Mom'. Perhaps both Cady and Dorothy had noticed the recurrence of an old awaking change in Merrill.

**

David had been sick of his brother's hovering this last year, but despite this he still loved him. He knew that Cady didn't fully understand this and wouldn't for a long time. There were times in the last seven years when David couldn't find the words to express how grateful he was that his brother was there for him when no one else was. When mom was drunk and out of her mind there was always Cady to pick up the pieces. David was angry from fear when he figured Cady was up to something with woman's clothes. It happened at the ranch during the summer; it was just Grandpa and his two grandsons, he never told anyone or held it up in Cady's face. David kept his brother's secret even from his brother. Cady had no clue David knew. When David returned from a night hangout with friends at the gravel pit in Thorp all covered in orange paint it was his brother that scrubbed it off his back in the bathtub without any questions. During these last two years though, David kept running into his brother's shadow at school and at home, he wasn't his brother and he was failing in school. He didn't see any point in staying in a place where you didn't have a chance to do anything other than fail, but he did find a group of like-minded party rebels to hang with so he continued. Where Cady was fat David was thin the opposite of his brother, where Cady was afraid to do something wrong David wasn't afraid to take the chance, but there was no escaping the fact that they were still brothers forever down deep. They shared the common bonds of the trauma of the childhood they had lived through. David was the teaser of his older brother when they were both very small it was fun because Cady was so easily teased. David melted into the fabric of the ranch shirtlessly embracing the wild country, unlike his brother who was never without a top on. David loved to fish, to shoot, to roam, a day away not caring where he was going. Even with all of this David in his own way was now lost as much as his brother was. He didn't need or want Cady to lead him along and even if he did his brother couldn't really help anymore. David saw this in his brother but not in himself, ironically this was the same for Cady. If some third party had come along they would have commented on the common state of the Anderson brothers. In Cady's mind he was trying desperately to come up with answers that would save his brother, even though he currently had no answers to apply to himself. It didn't matter anyway, David had found a party path, all you needed was a little money and it was easy to get a hook up. David had looked at himself and decided this was the person he was for better or worse; he didn't need to live vicariously as his brother did. He had tried the girlfriend thing but the attraction wasn't right. Cady was gone to the ranch for the summer and David was no longer welcome there, it hurt like fire and David was envious of his brother's ability to escape. The person David knew he was did not yearn for the ranch as Cady did; David was now beyond that point. David did yearn to mindlessly fly above his limits but not conquer them. He was part of a trio of friends, David Anderson, David D, and David P. David P was the oldest and his get-high friend, whereas David D who was the youngest was a buddy for life. David P and David D didn't run in the same circles. David and David D hatched a plan to go tent camping for a week even though neither had experience camping on their own. David talked to his dad about it and to his surprise Dad fully agreed to it. Dad was even eager for David to have the experience of being out on his own. He took the Davids shopping for groceries and offered them our Coleman camp stove, ice chest, fishing poles, sleeping bags, and other miscellaneous supplies. David

D had a well-worn two-man tent that leaked just a little to complete their kit. David and David D dug worms for bait because they would live off the land and decided Lost Lake up near Snoqualmie Pass was the place to go. Dorothy wasn't so sure about the whole adventure, the boys would be out of contact for five days, they could in theory hike four miles to I-90 and flag down some passing car if an emergency came up. In hindsight it was kind of scary, not something his brother would do, but the person David knew himself to be wasn't afraid to take the chance.

In another piece of irony Grandpa Charley would try to coerce Cady into riding his horse Rocky by himself up into the mountains for a weekend. Grandpa said to Cady, "It would do you both good, your horse will learn a lot and you will too. I remember the first time I lit out from home on my own and the first night I slept out alone with my horse. In the middle of the night something moved and I was a feared but in the morning I could see that it was just a little old skunk. And from then on I was never scared to sleep outside alone again."

David and David D loaded the Anderson family car with their entire kit and mom Dorothy would drive them up to Lost Lake. Both Davids were excited and trepidatious at the same time, it was David driving the whole plan and David D trusting his friend. Dorothy was just at home driving eastbound on I-90 as Cady was although she hadn't driven it as many times in her life, she had out of necessity learned to drive just six years ago. After stopping at the Pass to use the public restrooms they continued to exit 62 at Crystal Springs and started slowly down the gravel road turning onto FR-54 (Forest Road) it narrows to one lane for the four miles to Lost Lake. David had been eyeing the area as they drove along and had his mom stop the car as the lake came into view. Dorothy parked and marveled at the beauty of the lake. She was also glad to see that there was one other camper nearby so they wouldn't be completely alone. David on the other hand was hoping to be completely alone but one neighbor was okay.

The two Davids unloaded the car quickly and picked a nice place for the tent. Mom Dorothy stayed until the tent was set up and at

150

David's insistence turned the car around and waved goodbye. It must have been a long solemn drive for her going home to an empty house also knowing that Merrill never came straight home after work. Still she was excited for David to have this thing he wanted so much. He hadn't focused on anything for a long time with anything like the positive intensity he was showing for this. Any loving mother gladly sets herself aside to have her child climb out of the pit he was in. Dorothy ran into traffic as she passed Issaquah nearing the old Bellevue Air Field. She smoked as she drove in the slow, closely-packed freeway. She used the little Smokey the Bear cigarette snuffer glued on the dashboard, it had been a present from her sons to keep her driving safe. On I-405 going south down through the S-curves the traffic crawled along at a snail's pace. She didn't care; slower was better as far as she was concerned. She daydreamed about the fun the boys were going to have and then began to miss her Davy intensely.

David was the leader and David D was the thoughtful follower it had always been that way. They set up camp in more or less orderly fashion and vowed to each other to make the most of their newfound freedom. The other campers at the lake were an older couple they were perfectly happy to keep to themselves holding on to every square foot of privacy they could while acknowledging the boys would want their own. Team David and David D hiked all over, caught seven fish in the cool lake, rationed groceries along with cooking fish, and stared at the stars together at night. There was no way to know just what else happened during that trip but it was a good guess that both boys grew to know more about the person each was. It was more than a guess, it was a profound hope that they without the bounds of convention for that time could savor their freedom to the fullest, because for one of them there wasn't much future left...

Dorothy had made a roaster full of spaghetti complete with a top layer of Banquet Fried Chicken then tied the lid down with a kitchen towel and put it in a cardboard box. She got into the car with Merrill and the two of them started out to retrieve their youngest son and his buddy David D from the camping trip of a lifetime. It had been so many years since it was just the two of them going somewhere together. It was both melancholy and adventurous; it harked back to a time long ago full of the joy of expectation and touched on a time coming full of change. The trip was smooth and traffic light. Soon Merrill was turning on exit 62 making the comment that it had been a while since they were here. They found the boys in camp and when Dorothy brought out the roaster full of spaghetti she was greeted with shouts of joy. Merrill and Dorothy spent the day with their youngest son David and his friend. It was creating a blessed memory to be fully appreciated in a little more than a year from then. Dorothy tended the campfire while the men were out and about she even visited with an older couple camping nearby. She was in Heaven, this was an experience from her days as a young woman with her mother and daddy. Here she was with her husband and her son David in a beautiful place. Dorothy also considered just how dirty David and David D looked she thought about what the bathtub would look like in a few hours and would it ever come clean again! David had a swagger in his voice and the movements of someone who had considerably matured in a short time, his mom took this into her heart to hold and keep. Merrill looked like he was thoroughly enjoying himself, he looked like a weight had been lifted from him and he was as energetic as the boys were. Dorothy took this into her heart also. At the end of the day with the car all packed up the two Davids were soon asleep in the backseat; they had clearly been through a lot together. Merrill stopped at the iconic Boehm's Candy shop just east of Issaquah. He was in a very good mood and it was time to get a treat for his family especially the conquering hero of the day his son David. David loved their chocolate covered Sea Foam and today he deserved to have a large piece. The trip home was soon over and David D was dropped off at his house and the little family of three was peacefully home again.

Tony was back again from visiting with more Anderson families, Aunt Dorothy was glad of it and David was happy to have time with him. The two of them had formed a bond of loss. Tony's mother had died last fall and Richard M a next-door friend to David had also died near the same time. David had a rebel's swagger now and this impressed Tony even more than before. Their daily ritual trip through the neighborhood was the same, but with a little more intensity and vigor. David was happily planning another week camping trip with David D for next week. Dad had already gotten a bigger and better tent after lessons the two Davids had earned from the little two-man-tent. They would be better equipped food-wise this time too. David was very eager to be with David D again for a week at Lost Lake. David had grown, there was a sense of time and place being very important and a limited commodity to him. The next weeklong camping trip was joyful as the last, but you always remember the first time as being best. This would be the last time the two Davids would do such a thing together. It would become a lifetime memory for both of them, a time of coming of age.

***

Merrill had made a very hard decision five years ago in 1968, it was a gut wrenching one and only he knew the full personal implication of it. He had decided to ask Dorothy to remarry him and reform their family after their divorce and ensuing two-year separation. He knew full well the person Dorothy was; better than anyone else really, after all how could he not? At the time he had originally proposed to her in 1952 he had no knowledge of the person that was Dorothy. There was no hint of the mental illness, the alcoholism, the Jekyll and Hyde nature of his bride. He had held a grudge against his mother-in-law Hazel for not sharing this dark side of her daughter with him before the wedding. When he confronted Hazel about it, her response was, "We thought her getting married and having kids would fix the problems she had." "It did for them," thought Merrill. Merrill did as best as he could and as time progressed so did the Merrill Anderson family, they had two sons. His work improved from gas station attendant into the world of concrete and masonry sales. They owned their own home, a small two-bedroom place moving later to two very nice four-bedroom homes one after the other. Merrill loved the Lord and knew Christ as his Savior, he loved singing in the church choir, being with other people, especially women, you could always find him in the church kitchen chatting with them, and he loved his job. He loved his sons and wife but in a dark corner of his mind he felt like he was incarcerated in a personal prison because of them.

Merrill as a very little boy in rural North Dakota knew something wasn't right, he didn't belong in the family around him or even as who he appeared to be in the mirror. A very subtle little seed of discord formed, the kind that life gives you leading to a continual conflict in your immature sense-of-self. This was troubling and pushed him to act in a peculiar searching matter. He would leave his family each Sunday as they all sat together there in church getting ready for the service to start. He would stand up walk himself over to another family and sit down with them, not only did he sit with a different family, he joined that family, he nestled in with them. He did this over and over with several different families all of which were black. At the end of church he would get up to leave with the family he had chosen only to be lovingly redirected back to his own family. Here was this sweet little boy with a big family of his own doing this curious action each Sunday. He did have his own family that included three brothers, eight sisters, a deeply loving God-fearing German mother Ida and a strict and severe English father Amer. His siblings teased him about this, he was an embarrassment to them, he stood out in an odd way, and he did it in church of all places. At home he was much more interested in doing housework, he was industrious at it, this in itself seemed to calm his conflict of sense-of-self. Here within the traditional female domain appeared to be his proper place and gave him a deep feeling of purpose and accomplishment. Anything else on the farm outside of the home was disjoint to his sense-of-self. As he aged, hearth and home became even more important, he craved this domain, it was somehow bringing him to understanding the person he was, but it didn't bode well within the family. Able-bodied boys could be hired out as day labor for cash and Merrill's father Amer only saw his brood as a potential income source. He was routinely abusive to his wife and children, especially to his daughters. In stark contrast Amer had a beautiful voice and loved to sing in church. Some said, "Little Merrill was the spitting image of his father." As an aside, all of his children in their adulthood remember Amer as just plain mean and abusive. One day, young Merrill was working away in the family home when his father came in, looked at him, and flew into a rage. His father loudly made accusations as to his son being a 'Faggot' and drew a knife to dispatch this abomination from his family right then and there. This slur wasn't Merrill but he now fought with his father for his life because of it. It was a deadly and clumsy wrestling match and the noise of it brought Mother Ida into the room. She stared wide-eyed in horror then let out a loud scream and fell to the floor in a dead faint. The fight was stopped and Merrill slipped outside while his father in a panic at the thought of losing a valuable wife came to her side. Merrill kept a low profile for a week and afterward his father seemed not to remember the whole affair. Of the damage done to young Merrill's body it was just a few very sore muscles but to his sense-of-self, that was cut to shreds.

Merrill at the age of 14 was living in the Burien area South of Seattle with his parents, brothers, and sisters. Still searching Merrill was trying to put the pieces of his identity together while at the same time denying the picture those pieces might show. It was fall and Halloween party time; Merrill's fancy was to go as a little girl holding a large lollipop. It was easy to get all the things for his costume as he had lots of sisters' things to borrow from. Just before the party he dressed carefully, combed his hair forward and curled it for bangs, dawned a cute hat, and looked in the mirror at his reflection. He saw a perfect little girl quizzically looking back at him. It was a breath-taking moment of self-recognition that would haunt him all of the rest of his life. Standing there in the mid 1940's it wasn't anything more than a strange experience because anything more was unthinkably impossible for him to comprehend. Still, Merrill had the best time of his life that night so did the little girl, and no one ever figured out who she was. Merrill never told anyone for many years afterwards until he shared it with his oldest son one odd night. Merrill at 17 along with his family received a morbid gift; his father died, and most in the family breathed a sigh of relief. Everyone in the Anderson family loved music they all loved to sing together including Amer. Merrill's voice was his pride and joy. What he longed for was someone to accompany him and along came Dorothy. She was five years older than he was and could play fair piano and steel guitar. She was sweet and easy to entertain and have fun with. Merrill's sisters loved her, she fit in well to the family, and her father owned a little grocery store so she seemed well off too. Merrill couldn't resist that Dorothy so openly loved him. Merrill and Dorothy were married and for 14 years, even with their personal demons clawing at their relationship they still made do. Merrill tried to drink along with his wife at parties but the tactic failed because there couldn't ever be enough to satisfy her craving for it. On Dorothy's side she spent hours alone waiting for Merrill to come home after work even as he was continually driven to be away from home. Their home was now Dorothy's domain and this irritated Merrill's restless self-image conflict even more. There was a painful irony to this since it was Merrill who had to teach Dorothy all the basics of being a housewife. Dorothy didn't have a clue about cooking, doing laundry, cleaning, sewing, and even the most basic skills of the home. Again Merrill confronted Hazel about this after all she was very skilled in all the skills of the home and then some, she replied, "Dorothy was just too hard to teach, it was just easier to do the work myself then to try to teach Dorothy anything." Just as Dorothy's demon couldn't be quieted Merrill couldn't stop his 'searching out and joining families he was not related to' demon. Always searching always seeking vicariously throughout adulthood even to his death. He would never be whole until this puzzle was solved. He had to find the person that he was inside and where that person belonged, in short he had to find his identity. Adding to the dilemma, gender was now an unacceptable part of it through the shadow of a little girl looking quizzically at him in the mirror. Merrill had to be free to attach to other people's lives, especially people of color who loved Full Gospel music in Church. Merrill felt spiritually fulfilled there but not on a gender level, he related to the women of the church but not on an attraction level. It was very confusing for him and since he was married with children he was held in a prison of his own making of being a father, husband, and straight male. He couldn't contain his spiritual/Biblical conflict over gender and attraction anymore, as far as he could see no one else in the whole world had this unspeakable problem. There was nowhere to turn it was an impossible predicament. One that had been building for his whole life and there was no path for resolution within Biblical guidelines and even prayer seemed to fall short. He needed to put the fire out by living vicariously through women who had it all together in life; they had the answer somehow, but the problem was he wasn't married to such a woman. He was married to someone who not only didn't demand anything sexually from him she didn't respond to him sexually either. She came with ever increasing requirements of mental health care and non-treated alcoholism that left him totally empty in the face of his own battle of self. There were the two boys to take care of and as they now approach adolescence there would be the unavoidable sexual awakening turmoil. He felt he had no resource to spare them as he continued to fight through his own turmoil. Merrill loved God through Jesus Christ, but it was man that gave no Biblical path through this fire pit he was in. He made the acquaintance of wives of his friends and employers who took him by the hand and pointed him toward divorce. Some of these were themselves happily divorced. Desperation colored what divorce looked like making it appear falsely as an easy path to freedom. Dorothy and the kids had a completely reliable safety net in her parents if anything went wrong at all and what could? They all would be safe and cared for while Merrill could make his way through the minefield that was his identity and finally understand just who he is. After all, his father had nearly killed him years ago because of this unspeakable conflict it was time to bring an end to it. Life will be better for everyone and he would find the happiness that eluded him for so long.

It didn't work exactly this way; ironically Merrill would do to his first-born son Cady exactly what was done to him by his mother-in-law Hazel after the wedding. That being dropping young innocent Cady right in the middle of his mother's alcoholism and mental health ailments with no adult to turn to for help. Yes, Charley and Hazel would be there most of the year but the during the long winter Cady would be alone and vulnerable. The cost of divorce was way more than anyone could afford. Dorothy and her two boys were ostracized by the church they had attended as gossip started making its way around that she was the one who had asked for the divorce. Then Dorothy's homeowners insurance was canceled for some odd reason that was never explained, but a new high risk policy could be had at a ten-fold payment increase that she couldn't afford, this started a domino chain of collapse. A few weeks later after the lapse of her insurance she found herself in foreclosure on the house the court had awarded her six months before. Dorothy had lost the house completely and had to sell most of its contents to meet bills leaving Dorothy and her sons to drop penniless head first into the safety net that her parents represented. Hazel and Charley came over one weekend and packed up what was left of the bedroom furniture and spirited Dorothy and the boys away. Dorothy would pay rent for them to live in the rooms upstairs at her parent's house. Free now, Merrill was exclusively introspective, he would deny himself nothing over the next two years; he sought out every experience possible to feed the monster his self-image conflict had become in hope of mollifying it. He accumulated male toys and experiences to flood and drown any semblance of female feelings he had. He bought a cabin cruiser to fish and learn to scuba dive from, a motorcycle as a crotch rocket, he drove a used convertible, learned to ski, he kept his own hours and company. He made guy friends to do guy stuff with. He moved in with his bachelor brother Rollin to keep costs down and he felt free to make friends who were women. If you hadn't known about the unspeakable gender component to this crisis Merrill was going through and you were a learned and concerned person, you would have labeled those two years as an understandable mid-life-crisis. Hey, all guys go through this right? You would advise your friend and/or client Merrill to look at

158

what he had lost in these two years, beg forgiveness of God and his estranged family then rise up to try again with them.

Merrill called Dorothy in late summer of 1968 and asked if he could come visit her and the boys at the ranch. He said he had some important things to talk with her about. Merrill drove his Ford convertible eastbound on I-90 he had the top down so the speed of the car and the rush of the headwind melted together giving the powerful feeling of flying at ground level. He rested his left elbow on the windowsill of the driver's side door and his right hand at the two o'clock position of the steering wheel. He was the master of this powerful vehicle slicing its way through the wind at 75 miles per hour just as he was master of himself. He loved the looks he got as he passed car after car by the slightest increase of the accelerator. Looks of envy from the young men who had yet to take the first few steps into manhood, from the young women who wished to be seen as a possession of and there by possessing the power that came with the image he transmitted. Merrill had come to terms with his mid-life-crisis. It was a common thing for men his age and all the rage on television of late. It was something very trendy there was no shame in it anymore. He was relieved really, life in these last two years had been empty in many ways, he had watched friends come and go some of which were in the same divorce boat as he had been in; he was going to fix that now. Divorce had lost its luster more importantly it hadn't solved anything, but the male mid-life-crisis title had given him something to hold onto. It was like a get-out-of-jail-free card. Friends and clergy would get behind him in his plan to rebuild his family it was the right thing to do and this was the right time to do it. He also missed being loved by his sons and wife he missed being a dad and husband. He could turn this all around on this trip to the ranch. Merrill was pretty sure Dorothy would jump at the chance to be free of her parents again, but strangely it was Cady and David that might be tricky, especially Cady. He didn't worry about Hazel and Charley they had been relieved to have had Dorothy married off 16 years ago and he expected they would be relieved again to have her back with him.

He figured it had been a lot of work on Hazel's part taking care of her daughter again, along with her grandsons, he fully expected to be welcomed by her. Merrill parked his car near the front yard gate in the waning shade from the tall pine tree. The smell from that pine along with the dry grass and sunbaked earth all touched off his memory of the start of his life with Dorothy in this place 16 years ago. His sons had always known this place its sounds and smells, but before they had taken their first breath of life he had known the sound of the wind in that lone pine tree and smell of dry grass. Merrill was accepted as he came through the front door, but as a visitor. He didn't mind, he had the bravado of sanctification there wasn't any decisions to be made by Dorothy and the kids; it was already a done deal. He would give space for them to voice their feelings but no space to criticize or question these last two years. Cady and David delighted in showing Merrill around the ranch house, all the special places they had come to know, and Merrill obliged them with comments of, "I think I remember that too." He acted the part of honored visitor to his sons and regaled them with stories of his own adventures such as scuba diving from his cabin cruiser or riding his motorcycle. Cady and David were enthralled by his stories they lusted to have a father even one they didn't remember very well. It was like finding your birth father after living in an adopted family and he turned out to be rich royalty.

The repetitive daily rhythm of the ranch day was completely broken, all chores were lifted from the boy's schedule. Cady and David had spent every precious spare summer moment playing in the creek or in the main irrigation canal that ran through the ranch. Since bathing was normally only once a week a good swim every day was a treat that knocked the dust off. There were even special times when some odd visitor from the neighborhood they used to live in would find his way over for a day visit. The ranch had water rights to Taneum Creek and most of all the water except for stock water was diverted east of the ranch into the main irrigation canal giving life to the fields. Cady and David had a stock of old inner tubes they used to float down short deep sections of the canal. The canal itself looked very much like a brook flowing naturally along through the property with manual gates here and there that opened onto the fields. Cady had longed to use the diving mask and snorkel he had purchased with his earnings but the canal was too shallow. Each time they had driven to Ellensburg Cady would see the little lakes along I-90 and sigh. They would have been perfect to swim in, but there was never a chance it would ever happen. Cady even spied an access road that may be useful to get to them. Merrill asked if the boys would like to go somewhere away from the ranch for a play-day near some water. Cady's heart leaped and he couldn't describe his dream place fast enough. Swim gear on the ranch consisted of cutoff jeans for both and a t-shirt for Cady and none for David. Today was so unusual already, now they and their mother were leaving with their estranged father, who the boys did not quite remember, to play at lake that Cady had only dreamed about. Merrill changed into a low cut set of bikini swim trunks showing off his male prowess, an open shirt showing off his hairy chest, and his ever-present classic sunglasses showing off his attitude. He was in good physical shape; he combed his full head of dark hair directly back over his head. Dorothy had changed into a one-piece beige swimsuit that Cady had never seen her wear before. Merrill loaded his euphoric boys into the back seat of his convertible with he and Dorothy intimately installed in the front. Cady directed the drive down I-90 by shouting over the wind noise until they passed the little lake and he pointed out the access road. Merrill found a little used gravel road leading to a roughly shaped parking area. The family climbed out and gathered up their kit consisting of towels, old inner tubes, and a blanket to sit on. Merrill led the walk under the freeway to the little lake on the other side. Cady was following his dad and wondered why anyone would wear a swimsuit that didn't cover his entire bottom. As soon as they could Cady and David were joyfully in the water. Merrill and Dorothy hung out in a shady spot up on the lake bank. The party was all in Merrill's hands now; he had talked briefly with Dorothy earlier in the day describing how he had been swept up by the power of a mid-life-crisis. It was over, so how did she feel about getting back together again? Sitting together while their sons splashed in the lake below he again brought up the subject. Merrill was right Dorothy was malleable towards being together once again and agreed to it. She agreed just as she had when he explained to her that he wanted her to be the one to file for the divorce, because it would be less complicated to get it. She agreed just as she had after a short time when he couldn't afford to make child support payments anymore and completely stopped them, she said, "Sure I understand." She had loved Merrill even then and continued loving him now; she would always do what he asked. In truth, Dorothy didn't have any real options in the life she currently had with her parents; it was just about making do for her sons day by day anything would be better and Merrill had been better once. Surprisingly to Merrill Dorothy did hesitate when it came to Cady. Dorothy did the unthinkable, she told Merrill that it was up to what Cady thought. She couldn't come back with him if Cady wouldn't come too. Merrill was taken aback with the uncharacteristic severity of Dorothy's comment. He was the man here, he had been treated as a child way more severely by his father and this change was at a great cost to him. How did a 14-year-old boy figure into such a deciding position? Of course, he thought, "Dorothy loves her son just as his mother loved him." But what Merrill didn't know was what had passed between mother and son in these last two years. Merrill didn't know that all he had endured as husband from Dorothy's mental health malady and alcoholism had also fallen directly upon his young son's shoulders. Cady had lived through the darkest times and had been changed because of it. Dorothy loved her children and had a mother's guilt for her actions that she couldn't control. It was Cady who was pushed into a role of an adult during her spells and without his agreement Dorothy couldn't escape with Merrill from her parents once again. This didn't faze Merrill after all as Cady's dad he was in authority here; he would simply tell Cady what was going to happen and that was that. He had also been advised by friends that the right thing to do was to seek the feelings of his sons on this matter and he guessed this was the time to do it. Merrill thought about Cady; he hadn't been around for these last two years and Cady was kind of a stranger to him. Cady was as tall as he was and at times seemed almost a peer to talk to and then would revert back to being a kid again. Back from the swim, Merrill found Cady downstairs on the guest bed enjoying the coolness the room had to offer during the heat of the afternoon.

Cady was staring at the ceiling contemplatively weaving all the threads of the day's meaning into some form of sensible image in his mind. Why was his dad really here, why was he being so nice to them now? It was especially disconcerting seeing his dad physically playing up to his mom. Cady had noticed the short whisper-quiet conversations between his grandparents and his mother, a mean tightness hung in the air around the adults. Now was the best time of the year here, school was still a month away, the bloody gore of working spring cattle was long gone, the sickness he had from baling hay was finally over, and mom is fully shut down from drinking; it doesn't get any better than right now. Cady had been through hell to get to this one short time of year, he even sort of had a clue on how to survive living here this next year. He had a sinking feeling that whatever motive his dad had brought along with him on this visit, it was going to totally derail Cady's hold on life here.

Merrill hadn't thought long about what to say to Cady; it was enough he was going to talk to him at all. His father Amer would have done his talking with a club. "So what do you think about all of us getting back together again as a family?" Merrill asked this quietly in a tone that clearly inferred, "Kid you better take this chance it's the best you'll ever get." Merrill decided to use the guest bathroom while Cady pondered his reply they could just talk through the door.

Cady rolled over and stood up from the guest bed, it was strange that his father's words didn't surprise him. Cady didn't say what he thought about this for himself, instead his words in reply were, "I think it would be a good thing for David." In Cady's mind it was simply a sentence of doom for him as he couldn't see how it could possibility work. Down deep Cady had lost all trust in his father and mother and was afraid to ever trust them again. He loved them as a child does his parents and blindly trusted, but as it turned out in his life, love and trust were separate from one another. You can love someone but not trust them and the reverse is also true, at least for Cady it is now.

Merrill came out of the bathroom satisfied with Cady's response. It was the kind of thing he would have said in Cady's place. There was no welcome back reconciliation embrace between father and son. Cady didn't know all that Merrill was going to give up in swooping in to rescue his kids and their mother. Merrill didn't have a clue in all Cady was losing by being rescued.

It was truly sad that the vastly remote chance for personal relief was lost in that place and time for the two of them. If somehow and someway these two troubled souls had honestly spoken their inner truths to each other, well, that didn't happen and because of this, courses in their lives were set to be at odds with each other. They would suffer in a like matter but with very different outcomes. Merrill felt he had set his life back to moving forward once again, it wasn't going to be easy, but many times in the last two years had been far worse for him. He had found out so many things about the person he felt himself to be that in the end really weren't part of him at all. In dismay he was constantly comparing his pursuits of living out his true self with where he was at before the divorce and coming up empty; something still wasn't right. Their little 1968 wedding at the Baptist Church in Thorp had been quick and clean.

Merrill had Dorothy and the boys staying with him over the next week in the Burien area south of Seattle to look for a place to call home. They were staying in the little two-bedroom house that he and Uncle Rollin rented using it as their base camp for house hunting. Grandma Ida, her daughters Aunt Sally, Aunt Margaret, Aunt Luella, Aunt Deloris, and their families all live in this area. Merrill had plenty of family support here and his work was nearby just inside the Seattle City limits. He could either rent or purchase a home but because time was short as was money renting seem to be the solution. Another problem was they had no furniture excepting bedroom pieces. Even in the face of such difficulties Merrill was upbeat and Dorothy was too; the only dour member of the little family was Cady. All during the week they inspected one broken down house after another and Cady had trouble seeing any bright spots looking through the dirty broken glass windows. The more Merrill looked at what he could afford to pay in house rent the less he found to choose from. Finally, a small run down two-bedroom single bathroom house built in 1938 was their only option; it did have a partial daylight basement that added a little more living space. The owner had moved out six months ago and was more than willing to rent it out on the spot for $165 a month. Done deal! Merrill had a place to move his family to and it couldn't have happened soon enough for him. He didn't like the feeling of being mentally judged by his in-laws while at the ranch; it gave him a sense of failure and he couldn't stand that feeling. Merrill always refused to apologize for anything he had done; he equated apologizing to admitting to a failure. The divorce had begun to feel like a failure to him. It hadn't given him what he was looking for so it had to be rubbed out without apologies or explanation. Merrill was a gregarious man full of the joy of food, singing, laughter, and the church, but he had the Anderson trait of a quick temper and holding a grudge. There was always a mean feud within the family Anderson that no one remembered the start of. Merrill drove his brood back to the ranch in his convertible to gather up their meager positions. He would borrow Charley's pickup for the move and probably have to make two trips.

Hazel was quiet about the ruckus of Dorothy's things being packed downstairs and put into the pickup. She suddenly felt very lonely as if life itself was being sucked away from her; the same feeling she felt right after she and Charley's initial move to the ranch years ago. They had then left their newly married daughter Dorothy behind in Burien with her husband. Hazel had fixed this; she had lobbied to have the newly married couple come live in the separate two-bedroom house next to the big ranch house. This time the loneliness was deeper, her grandsons were leaving and Merrill was being cocky about it.

Merrill was directing the emptying of Cady and David's bedroom when a pair of female panties turned up under a bed in their room.

Merrill blew up, it was classic Merrill; he was loudly shouting directly into the face of his youngest son who was locked in place by the full force of the tirade. He never struck his children he berated and belittled them; in some ways this was worse than a physical blow. Merrill who couldn't stand any perceived shame of being wrong in himself hated it in his children. The attack was put into full white-hot verbal force; he would berate that weakness out of his children so they too would hate it. He would obliterate that abomination of perverted gender right then and there. In an unknowing act of incredible irony, he acted very much like what his father Amer was going to do years ago when he attacked his son Merrill with a knife. Merrill at that time was about the same age Cady was at this moment. Just as Merrill's mother Ida had interceded in that intense attack by breaking the moment so did Dorothy intercede now breaking the moment with words where Ida had done so by fainting dead away. What Cady couldn't perceive standing next to his brother that day was the intense motivation behind Merrill's berating attack on both of his sons. Fourteen year old Merrill years ago couldn't perceive the reason for his father's attack on him either... The packing resumed until the pickup truck was full and the two-vehicle caravan returned westward on the I-90 magic carpet to a new old home.

Merrill backed the pickup up to the rickety stairs of the front porch of the little house. Cady got out and with sad critical eyes looked up at the forlorn structure. The moss-covered roof sagged noticeably from the weight of too many layers of rotten shingles. Cady slipped inside to use the bathroom and he was greeted by a filthy brown threadbare carpet in the living room, tattered curtains on a few of the windows, and a strong mildew smell coming mostly from the bathroom. The whole house, which was heated by electricity using large glass infrared heaters on each wall, was clammy cold and the walls were sticky, best not to touch them. The house had been a long time all shut up with no heat. The clamminess was pervasive into every corner of every room. In a bedroom Cady opened the closet door to peek inside and immediately slammed it shut again. The mildew smell was overwhelming complete with a black dust floating inside. The kitchen contained a cast-off old shaky table, two wobble chairs, an electric stove with a broken oven door, the walls sported a thick greasy brown film, on the ancient linoleum floor were lumps of black sticky stuff, and the ceiling was covered in places by black mildew. There was an empty greasy dirty spot in one corner where the refrigerator had been. Merrill called for Cady to come help as the convertible had just pulled into the driveway. They untied the ropes that held the load onto the bed of the pickup truck. The three bed frames were moved into the two bedrooms both of which had cold ancient linoleum floors. Mattresses were wrestled onto the bed frames and the beds were made up with sheets and blankets. It was important to get this done as it gave a place to sit. There were two chest-of-drawers (packed full of clothes) one for each bedroom, Mom's hope chest, and old vanity less the mirror that had fallen off the truck onto the side of freeway on the trip over. The vanity looking incomplete along with mom's hope chest helped fill her and Merrill's bedroom. The bedrooms looked almost real as they now had beds in them. The living room looked unreal. The only furniture it had was an old aluminum outdoor lounge that Dorothy had grabbed at the last minute from the ranch house front yard; this had been hers from before the move to the ranch along with an old portable black and white television set. Merrill had no furniture of his own, the house he had been sharing with his brother Rollin was filled with stuff Rollin owned including the bed in the spare room that Merrill sub-rented from him. Dorothy had very few dishes, eating utensils, or cookware aside from a couple of pans that came from Rollin's place to put in her kitchen. Merrill did have two aquariums that would travel over from Rollin's house at some point, he still had his boat for the time being and car, but that was it for his possessions.

Cady lay in his bed that night between the uncomfortably clammy sheets trying to get warm enough to sleep, the air didn't circulate throughout the house instead it lay stale around him. Cady pondered the choice-less fate he was at the mercy of, it had put him in this vulnerable place of fear of what tomorrow would bring. This house was just one house down from the imposing Middle School that he would be starting at in just one week. What would happen to him there? Would anyone care about him? Would he and his secret be safe? He missed being at the ranch and the security that his grandparents gave. Cady, after saying his prayers, cried very quietly into his already damp pillow.

David listened to his brother's congested breathing he wasn't bothered so much as Cady seemed to be. Mom and Dad would take care of them, if they didn't Cady would help him. David turned onto his side to face the wall; he heard little indiscernible noises coming from Cady's bed and found in them the comfort of having someone nearby, soon a gentle sleep found its home in David.

Merrill slept with Dorothy for the first time in two years that night. It was both familiar and foreign for them both. The thought never entered Dorothy's mind that Merrill might have slept with someone else in these last two years. In Dorothy's mind Merrill had just been away, he was like that, she just picked up from where they left off. Merrill knew that it was inconceivable for Dorothy to have slept with anyone, she had been his and he knew exactly how she felt about things...

***

Cady had settled in for the evening it was the last week of July 1973. He reflected how Grandpa had him doing what he thought of as a nuisance job of picking up large rocks by hand from a rocky field and moving them to fill in eroded ditches in another field. There was no glamour in this and frankly not much to be gained by the task. No dent was being made in either field rock-wise, no matter how many loads were moved. Cady also didn't like to physically change anything about the ranch he loved it just as it was, in fact, he needed it to be immutable. This summer was but a stark shadow of all the other ones Cady had spent here. There wasn't a summer he could remember when he didn't feel the flow of water from the creek or canal cover his body on a hot day or had the time to spend under a tree contemplating the movement of birds. These things had been lost to him this summer.

The ranch was here just as he was, but it was serving only as a reminder of past times. He quieted his mind and opened a letter written in Cathy's perfect cursive script that he loved so much to read. She could spell, he could not, her cursive script was beautiful, his was jerking and malformed, Cathy was all he had longed to be; right there in what had been a peaceful moment gender dysphoria had crept up on him. Cady shook it away and read the following letter dated July 28th and written in light pencil from camp Sealth:

Dear Cady,

I love you!!!!! I wish you were here tonight to see the sunset! There were a few clouds on the horizon and the sun reflecting off of them of them gave off the most beautiful reds and pinks and oranges. And the water reflected the same hues. It was so very beautiful. It's one of the many memories I will always have of Sealth.

The girls have figured out my real name now. I had your picture in my New Testament which I keep in my magic ring notebook and that I had with me tonight. Anyway I was showing it to a couple of the girls and they grabbed it from me and read the back and now they know my name is Cathy and not Dixie. Oh well, that's life.

I'll write more latter since we're going to go and sing for a while...

I love you, Cady. And I miss you terribly. I'll sure be glad to see you again in a few days.

Love,

Cathy.

Cady finished the letter and looked around for a much needed distraction from the bothersome flash of gender conflict. He had another letter to read tonight this one was from his mom dated July 31st she writes in blue pen with her own cursive script one that is much more flowing than Cady's but with malformed letters in an attempt to cover her spelling trouble. She shares:

Dearest Cady,

How are you doing? We havn't [sp haven't] heaid [sp heard] from you lately. Sunday we took Dave & Dave up to Lait [sp Lost] Lake to camp another week this time they have better groceries and a bigger tent they seem to really enjoy this. Tony is gone for a couple of days, he was sure nice to have around. I kept the car today to go grocery shooing [sp shopping] & do a little looking for a job oh yes they are to pick up the boys at the lake Sat. We wanted to know when you wanted us to pick you up and that we can any day but Sat because the boys have so much camping gear to come back.

Lots of love,

Dad and Mom

Cady wrote back to his mom:

Dearest Mom,

Thanks so much for your letter! Sorry I haven't writing for a while, but I do miss you all. Grandpa keeps me pretty busy everyday. Grandpa is doing well and the cattle all seem to be growing more each day. I'm glad David got to go and do all this camping this summer. I bet he loved it! And it is nice too that you weren't so lonely with Tony staying at our house. Sunday August 5th is a very good day to be picked up for the welcome trip home.

See you soon!

Love,

Cady

***

It would be five more days until he and Cathy would get to see each other. Cady would be home until August 29th when he had to return to the ranch for the last leg of the cattle season. Somewhere in that 25-day stretch at home, Cady had to answer every unanswerable life question that plagued his heart and soul. Every one of them, there was no half in or half out. Months ago on graduation night he had made a stab toward what was the heart of the hornet's nest that being his identity conflict, but missed it completely leaving only the partial band-aid of denial. Denial doesn't shut off the conflict just numbs it, but in Cady's case it was long enough with God's help for him to find the one true love of his life. It all came down to the perceived simplicity of mapping out who and what he was. Cady knew who he loved and would live with for the rest of his life and beyond. But he couldn't complete this mapping equation though without presenting his true self to Cathy for her inspection and hopeful acceptance. Simplicity is a reluctant next-door neighbor to impossibly complex. Cady didn't even know the terms enumerating his conflict; the definitions of words used to explain when someone is not as they see themselves. He knew how his biological sex functioned and what gay or straight was as a vague concept, but that was all.

Cady was lost and afraid, he had surrounded himself with a shell of protection that the immutable ranch provided, that was why he was here this summer. But it wasn't immutable it was just an illusion of a safe harbor that couldn't rise up and keep him from harm emotionally, spiritually, and physically. Cady had wished his life to be at an end hundreds of times in his 19-year lifetime. He thought everyone did this, it was just a natural state of being. Each time the despair of what he was or what was happening to him overwhelmed him, it settled in on his heart to bring his life to a merciful end. In that dark place and time, he kept one single hidden thought as a safety valve; the harm to others his death would bring. Cady was hurting and there seemed only one way out, but he couldn't trade pushing pain onto someone else to gain peace for himself. One time during the winter months when the little family of three had been left alone at the ranch, 14 year old Cady held a very sharp knife blade to his left wrist warning his mother if she didn't stop drinking right now he would take his life. He had read about steel being cold as a deadly description and now the crazy sharp knife blade really was a cold ugly thing biting lightly into his skin. Dorothy had simply and sadly said, "I would just hope that you wouldn't." Those words shook Cady to the core and defeated him, he had expected some pledge that she would at least try to quit drinking right now if he pledged not to cut himself, but her pledge didn't come. His loving, kind, gentle mother wasn't going to stop drinking that night no matter what. From this came a stark, dark, and ugly reality, Cady now understood she couldn't ever stop. Totally defeated he put the knife away; he couldn't have done it anyway. What would happen to David or to Mom? In his absence, who would be there to help when no one else was? It had been a stupid act spurred on by the desperation of the start of a coming drunk that was, as always, unstoppable. Yes mom got very drunk that night and yes Cady could hear her sobbing away until he finally fell asleep. Cady had read a column earlier today in the local Ellensburg paper *The Daily Record* that had arrived just after dinnertime. It was a letter to *Dear Abby* and her response to the letter had touched the very raw nerve of Cady's mind/body identity conflict. In the letter the writer asked Abby what she thought about a man who truly felt he was a woman and was seeking gender reassignment surgery, "Was this an abomination or was the person just mentally sick and needed to be put away?" Cady stared at the column as if his hidden secret was suddenly printed on his forehead for all to see. Cady looked around the room to see if anyone was looking at him reading the paper. There had never been anything like this that Cady had seen in print, he thought he was the only person to feel like this. Abby's answer was a carefully crafted one ending with, "It is God that gives us skilled surgeons who can cure these ills." Cady felt like God had brought this to his attention; who else could have? How in a rural conservative place could something like this come to him to read? No one else in the house paid any attention to *Dear Abby* except for Cady so there wasn't any open discussion about it. The serious discussion that was going on was within Cady's persona. He had not escaped doubt by simply deciding that he could denounce the conflict and become a true-blue male by acting as one. He had cut his hair short, he had immersed himself in the company of other men, he continuously admonished himself each time his body/mind mismatch brought some envious thought into his head after seeing a nearby

172

woman living out her daily life. He was suddenly very tired and broken. Aside from many things he had done during past summers here at the ranch, which he didn't do this summer, crossdressing stood out. Not that he simply stopped; now it wasn't even possible, as he didn't have any clothes here. Even so in his mind the female experience that he felt when crossdressing was still present. He realized the need to crossdress wasn't going away and promised himself two things: he would resist it and he would confess that it was a real thing needing to be truthfully shared with Cathy. He would not hide it from her as this would just lead to disaster at some point in the future and would become a 'Sword of Damocles' hanging over his head. All in all, better to have the disaster now. That had been two months ago and now the time of reckoning was here. Cady was opening the door to the person he/she truly was; this was the beginning of understanding. It was also the beginning of the risk assessment of being honest with Cathy weighing against the reward of an honest relationship that would be unfettered by hidden guilt/shame. Cady had learned the mechanic of this act from Cathy's confession of the guilt/shame she had felt she needed to free herself of during their picnic at the beginning of summer. Cady pondered the amazing coincidence of Cathy's act laying the structure for him to do the same this time with her. Cady really did believe along with Cathy that God was leading all this along to build their unique relationship. Cady would find out soon enough just how far God would go to weld the two of them together as one. Cady looked at the act of crossdressing and made the mistake of minimizing it in his/her case. There was no deep symbolism in the act just a surface oddity kind of thing. He had the beginning of understanding but not the depth of it. Cady decided he would confess to having enjoyed crossdressing from time to time that is to look and act female. Cady loved Cathy so much and this would let them be together forever if Cathy could accept this part of him.

The risk was great, this was no small thing Cady was confessing to Cathy, she might very well just turn away and leave him. The risk was attenuated because he wasn't the person in the *Dear Abby* letter, that wasn't him, it just couldn't be him. Cady hadn't seen any great risk that Cathy had in her confession to him about the dynamic of her previous relationship. The guilt belonged to her boyfriend not her; she had taken steps to stop it. Cady's problem was the guilt/shame was totally his; there was no second party to own it or lessen it, no place to turn except to look in the mirror. The fear of losing Cathy was too great in this case, so without realizing it Cady denied the person he/she truly was. It was a huge mistake at that moment; Cady didn't fully trust Cathy or God even in the face of seeing the mechanic at work for Cathy with him. Cathy didn't have to water down her confession as God brought clarification of it to Cady's mind as soon as he heard it from Cathy. God would have done so with Cady's confession had Cady only trusted God. It would take Cady 40 more years to fully see the true person she was but stay tuned, he/she did make some current progress, God is still in control after all. Cady had come to a balance of sorts in several areas. He accepted he had a strong female self-image so strong that it overshadowed his male body. He accepted that to be female in presentation was the most affirming thing he had ever experienced and sex wasn't such a big thing. This last part was just something that naturally settled between the two of them. Cathy and Cady held hands continuously, they cuddled close to each other whenever possible, hugged in passing, and kissed occasionally. That was the physicality of their dates no more no less. Cady packed up clothes enough to last him for three weeks and came downstairs to say goodbye to grandpa Charley and Joyce. The magic carpet of I-90 would fly him home with his dad at the wheel.

***

Cathy and Cady were back together and inseparable, each day Cady would keep the family car and they would explore someplace close by. Cady visited Cathy at her house and they read comic books together in her room. Cady had quite a collection of comic books that ranged from *Donald Duck* to *Archie* to the *Space Family Robinson*. They would play pool in the rec room next to her bedroom. Cathy took

Cady bowling at Lewis and Clark bowling lanes, she had a great time teaching Cady to bowl; in one game he even broke 100. Cathy's family had a tradition of bowling after church until she was 13; the family that plays together etc. There were three Anderson family birthdays in August David, Dorothy, and Merrill all to be celebrated. Tony visited again at the Anderson's house and Cathy joined the family on a picnic up at Lake Keechelus for him. Cathy played with Cady's family dog and did game night with Grandma Ida's at her house. Then one Saturday Cady invited Cathy to come and bake chocolate chip cookies with him. The house was open to the warm August air, the days were becoming shorter now. Cady loved to both bake and eat chocolate cookies and there were always all the ingredients in the kitchen cupboards of their house to make them. Deep yellow colored butter, eggs, flour, salt, baking soda, Nestle Tollhouse Chocolate Chips, no nuts, all put together in a big yellow Pyrex bowl then metered out and baked at 375 degrees on an old slightly warped cookie sheet. Cady and Cathy nibbled on raw cookie dough while each batch was baking. The mood was wonderfully open they were by themselves, all the other Andersons were gone with the winds except Dorothy who was working a night shift at Howard's Ice Creamery up on Pac Highway. Cady suggested they sit outside on the front steps in the cool of the evening. They cuddled together with barely a breath between them watching cars roar up the hill toward Pac Highway. Cady did the most remarkable thing of his lifetime between batches of cookies timed to 12 minutes each, he proposed marriage to Cathy. Cady told Cathy he had something to ask her, Cathy held her breath. Cady quietly told her he wanted to be with her forever, but there is something he needed to tell her about himself first. Cathy leveled her eyes into Cady's in an attentive and open manner. She had longed for this moment, she had prayed for this person to be with, no other time would ever be as important in her life as here and now. Cathy quietly focused all of the mental energy she could muster toward her Cady that he might feel strong for her. Cady paused, he was doing something so beyond his limits it was becoming surreal to him, he became detached to the sound of his own voice, the one that was speaking such important words. Sitting on the top step next to Cathy he took her hand and looked intensely at her delicate fingers and amazingly competent thumbs. Cathy giggled. Cady at a loss to find a starting sentence began with, "Cathy I have a secret, there is something about me that absolutely no one knows and you should know. I will understand if you can't accept it or if it is too strange, because sometimes it is very hard for me to accept it. I have a need to crossdress to appear female sometimes." Cathy was still and shocked since her ex-boyfriend the one she was determined to be free of at all costs had something like this too, what was God doing? God had given her Cady who was nothing like her ex in anyway, how could they both have this in common? Still, Cady was everything to her and he was so very different there must be more to this so her response was simply, "That's okay my other boyfriend was kind of like that too." Cady was gobsmacked or better to say God-smacked, he had denied the truth about himself by watering it down to attenuate the risk of losing Cathy, now in her sight he was her ex-boyfriend remade. Cady didn't know what was up with Cathy's ex it didn't matter. What did matter was to do as Cathy had done, disclose what was in your heart then trust in God. Cady had made a terrible mistake he had held back, why had he not fully trusted? Cady to be free before God and Cathy knew the three of them needed to hear the full truth from Cady's mouth no matter what happened after this. Cady stood up and walked to the bottom of the stairs so his eyes were again level with Cathy's.

Cady for the first time in her life confessed out loud the truth about the person she is, "You don't understand; it isn't about the clothes themselves it is about how I feel inside when I wear the clothes it's affirming to me. I know it is strange but I feel female; I am female all of the time, when you see me you see a male image, but I am not that image to myself I'm a girl." Cady heard it with her own ears and she completely trusted Cathy to know it. In her mind, Cathy reached for a fixed point to hold onto and one came to her. Cady was truly nothing like her ex even in the vague similarly about clothes the difference was huge. She felt it in every movement Cady made with her and in every word Cady shared with her. Something clicked inside of Cathy this is how she had seen Cady all this time without fully knowing it. Cathy tilted her head slightly to the right looking directly at this person who seemed so vulnerable and so sincere, her heart filled as she thought, "I will be with him or her forever and I will love and be loved." Cathy in her most happy and reassuring voice said, "Yes I will be with you forever! Don't worry we will work it all out no matter however long it takes, we will figure it out together." The timer on the oven rang out that the cookies were done. Cady shook her head as if to get it going again and Cathy got up walked down to where she stood and kissed her. Cady said, "Oh it will take time for me to figure out how to support us too." Cathy grinned, "Cady I love that you are you. We'll figure all of it out. I smell cookies!"

***

We had all the 2020 Covid 19 barriers to overcome to get into the exam room. We have been taken to a now familiar exam room by medical assistance Grace; she chats with us while making notes of Cathy's post-op experiences. Grace leaves as the doctor comes in. Dr. Megan Dreveskracht is very pleased with how everything is healing and is genuinely happy for Cathy. She removes one layer of tape from all the suture lines then tells us the remaining tape is made up of steri-strips and will come off by themselves. Cathy's nipples look like they have been through a lot; there is tape all around the circumference of each of them. Cathy tells me that she still has feeling in her nipples, a very good thing.

I sit in the support chair in the corner listening to the conversation between Dr. Megan and Cathy and watch as the tape was gently but firmly removed from Cathy's much-reduced breasts. I hold the slightly blood stained surgical bra in my lap that the doctor had just helped Cathy to take off. Right now, in this moment, I am in intimate female space and I don't feel completely worthy of being in this space. Cathy is a natural female having her natural breast reduced by a woman doctor who can relate completely woman-to-woman with her. What kind of unnatural construct am I in this space thinking to have

177

my small breast artificially increased in the future by this same doctor? Will she relate to me in the same way or even more pointedly can she? I am only female here because of their consent that I am, as my body doesn't reveal my mind. In a flash I realize this is what being triggered is like. I am female in a female space, but I also have to grow into that space in steps. The same steps each developing human takes into their gender space. I calm down, I do have a natural place here albeit one that requires faith and strength to grow into... The only unnatural construct was the one I formed of me as a male.

Dr. Megan takes after pictures and answers Cathy's questions (Cathy has a list she made). Here are the answers: "You can shower now no restrictions, I removed 300 grams on the left and 625 grams on the right for a total of 2 pounds, yes I do tummy tucks, but let's get you through this first, the bra size is 38, no pressure on the breast, half side sleep only, nothing went to pathology the tissue looked fine." Dr. Megan had instructions, "You will be swollen for up to two months use ice and meds, the swelling is mostly on the top of the breast as it really has no were else to go, wear the bra 24 hours a day." Dr. Megan had a warning, "Cathy everything is going great with your recovery, couldn't be better, the big trouble with this is it will give you a false sense of security and you will overdo, don't overdo! You have lots of sutures deep in your breasts don't do anything to strain them. If you do you will come back to a very angry Dr. Megan!" We leave in good spirits and stop at the front desk to make Cathy's next appointment (Oct 8th) the ladies there are super friendly and complement us on our matching tie-dye. What a difference being on the other side of self-paid surgery, when we were just here for a free consulting they were so cold to us...

So I realized two big things. Two years ago I had bottom surgery (orchiectomy) and now Cathy has had top surgery of sorts, kind of unique for a couple in the transgender world. I had been fitted for breast implants, the total of my implants is in the 900 grams range, this is the same amount Cathy just had removed from her breasts. So I could have the exact amount added to my breasts as Cathy had removed from hers, fulfilling her longstanding offer to trade breast lines; pretty much the ultimate in intimate physical sharing between the two of us. (Well okay we do share many other things too but I mean; Wow!)

***

Cady had stayed up late floating on an impossible cloud of happiness, he was in a place that he would never know or so he had thought, all this after dropping Cathy off at her home. Cady was so in love so happy that it was almost indescribable this feeling even over shadowed the fear of all that was involved in actually getting married. Being with Cathy would just fix everything, because now there were no secrets between them and Cady could still be a 'he' to everyone else and a 'she' only to her. To be your true self even to one other person lifted such a weight off of Cady's soul. Cathy knew the truth and that was enough for now and maybe that would be enough forever. Cady could share Cathy's femininity and live vicariously through her.

And so, we will again honor or perhaps condemn Cady to a 'he' as the little shell around the two of them is the only space for 'her' to exist in the world of her time. Cady had made the choice to choose sides. When we first met Cady in school she is a male-imaged all-but-invisible-girl she is who she is nothing more or less. Male pronouns are thrown at her and she responds by acknowledgment. Within her heart, her soul, her inner being, she is female but necessity bends us, it twists us into schemes of survival of making do. In Cady's mind she has been given the world in Cathy so adjustments are more than fair. It will be a long while before we use the proper pronoun for her; Cady has to grow, to learn, and to come into crisis. Until then, Cady holds on by knowing secretly that Cathy understands who she is and still loves her. Only with Cathy's support can this be possible, without it there is no future. Cady will be a 'he' until her true self demands otherwise but Cady will always be Cady and not dead-named.

After their traditional goodnight phone call Cady slept so very peacefully all night long. Next day, Cady had gotten up early to keep the family car by driving his dad to work at Pratto Sales. Merrill was

179

a one man shipping and receiving department at Pratto Sales. The small family business sold service station equipment such as gasoline pumps and shop fixtures. Cady and David had spent many weekends over these last several years helping their dad move the big heavy boxes labeled Tokheim or Gilbarco and containing gasoline dispensing pumps around in the warehouse. They would help with boxing part orders to be shipped on the next standard workday. There were no wages, it was just fun to help their dad and get the chance to drive the forklift truck. There was even a big steel door hiding a freight elevator to ride on! Cady was very proud of his dad, it impressed him how his dad could juggle so many responsibilities of shipping, packaging, receiving, inventory, cleaning, and even repairing used equipment for resale. The entire warehouse was his entire domain and here he was king. The big downside to his kingdom was one person within a five-day workweek couldn't complete the required work and his salary was set for a five-day workweek. So, weekend work was for free, but it was cool to be doing it with Dad who would rather be here than anywhere else on a weekend. Cady and David were taught what seemed to be an Anderson-thing that you worked because it needed doing; the concept of getting a wage was an abstract in their minds.

After dropping his dad off at work Cady had the car back at home in plenty time to give Cathy a ride to school. This was the first day of Cathy's senior year, she was waiting as Cady drove up and with a big smile she scurried over to the car and climbed in. This would be the most bittersweet little drive the two of them would take together. Cady drove Cathy to his house and parked the car in the driveway. The young couple walked together to Foster High School along with the steady stream of students on the sidewalk along 144th. The only difference was these two sweethearts were floating on air as they walked along hand in hand where the others merely trudged. They had decided not to announce their engagement until after Cathy's graduation no other path had even entered into their minds. It would be a secret between them and no one else. Cathy would have a wonderful senior year experience just as she deserved, then they would figure out what to do and when to do it afterwards. Cady had never been so happy in his whole life, he suddenly had a future, he had never had one before, it was a sweet wonderful thing he could hardly contain himself. And yet he had to leave his true love this very day… Before they stepped onto school grounds they hugged each other, kissed lightly, and brushed away tears. Then they walked towards the school cafeteria with the mob and parted company just inside with a fleeting glance at the lone cafeteria table in the corner. The head custodian had made sure it was again in place to be used by a new group of early rising totally-under-the-radar-loner-types. Cady held fast to Cathy's warm hand until the last minute, then turned to walk away teary eyed toward home. As he retraced his steps back to the sidewalk along 144th he spied his friend Michael striding in a cadence reeking of he-who-is-free of all childhood encumbrances. Cady quickened to catch up with him. Michael was on his way home from seeing Janice and in a jovial mood. The two friends walked spouting comic banter back and forth to Cady's house where Michael stopped in to say hello to Cady's mom. Cady offered to drive his friend home, Michael who then assured Cady that he didn't need his arm twisted to accept the invitation. Cady enjoyed seeing Michael it would be the last time for a long time as Cady was heading back to the ranch today. Michael would be leaving to start his freshman year at Washington State University in Pullman at the far eastern border of Washington State well before Cady would be back. Cady had a momentary thought about telling Michael about the big news but let the idea go dry. Instead the two talked about a plan for Cady to bring Cathy along with Janice for a visit with Michael when he was well established over at WSU in October. Michael's sentimentality was bound up inside a comic chainmail coat he wore all the time and everywhere. He was always safe from the sadness of goodbyes by sprouting a stream of almost funny one-liners. Cady would hold the moment in his heart while groaning at the last batch of Michael being Michael. Cady drove home and packed his clothes he had said his goodbyes to his dad this morning. Cady would drive the I-90 magic carpet over to the ranch with his mom and she would return home alone after dinnertime.

Again in the isolated cocoon the ranch offered, Cady picked up the rhythm of daily work right where he had left off. Cady resumed the irrigation tasks along with washing and waxing the car and pickup just to fill in a day. The more he did the better it kept his mind off of being away from Cathy. Every minute needed filling. Cady spent much time riding his horse Rocky a serious task, because without constant reminding Rocky would assume he wasn't a saddle horse anymore, and take offence to returning to such a low station in life. Rocky would shy and buck until the horse/rider relationship was established once again. It was work for both horse and rider. Cady was thrown off once as Rocky reared up when they came upon a friend during a training ride, the fellow was just walking along. Rocky's head came up so quickly that Cady didn't have time to lean forward and touch the top of Rocky's head canceling the action; instead he fell off over the horse's hindquarters. The breath was knocked out of Cady's lungs as he hit the hard earth and it was a struggle to even stand up, but he did and followed the rule of getting right back up into the saddle again. Cady had only fallen from horseback a hand full of times and two of those times he had jumped off. When he was a little inexperienced Cady he rode once with a group of kids at Aqua Barn Ranch located in the outskirts of Renton. He was asked if he had ever ridden a horse before and had answered yes, of course this was a mistake. He was assigned a lively little horse that bolted halfway around the field they were circling, the horse galloped straight across the field heading toward the barn. Cady pulled at the reins to no avail, then he gave up figuring all was lost, and in a panic he stood up in the stirrups at full gallop. People were watching as Cady pulled his right foot up and over the saddle so he was now standing on only one stirrup on the left side of the saddle. Cady watched the ground zooming along under him and his maniacal steed hoping for a soft spot to jump to before the coming crash at the fence. The fence grew closer; Cady let go of the saddle horn and pushed away from the horse and in doing so flew through the air and slammed onto the turf. Cady figured he was dead lying there on the ground, the horse stopped well short of the fence. After a few minutes Cady came to the understanding he was not in heaven, but still earthbound and with no grace stood up. He saw the wrangler of the ride galloping toward him and he fought back tears thinking he was in big trouble. The man pulled his big tall horse up to a stop and dismounted, he stood with Cady and pushed his own cowboy hat back so you could see his pink forehead and said, "That was quite a trick; you okay little guy?" Cady humbly nodded. The wrangler went on to say, "Here you take my horse he has a gentle gait sort of like rockin' in an old rocking chair. I'll go get your horse and have a word with him." He helped Cady get up onto the very tall horse that to Cady's great relief didn't care much for anything but slowly walking along.

***

Even with filling his day with as many busy tasks as he could Cady was desperately lonely. He wrote to Cathy that night,

"A funny thing happened to me last Monday at home when I went shopping with my mom. We were at the Wigwam store along Pac Highway and as I wandered in the store I kept automatically putting my left hand out and slightly back of me hopping you would take hold of it and be there walking with me. I miss you Cathy, of course you already know that, but I'm going to say it over and over and over along with I love you…

Love,

Cady"

***

Cady had been studying to take the FCC radiotelephone test and get his first class license. There were three books to study from; he had just completed the first book and was waiting for the second to arrive in the mail. The first book was mostly rules to follow while on the air; the next two were electronic theory. Cady's fingers were crossed in hopes he could come to terms with all the math. Cady, who usually studied after all letter writing and reading was finding it difficult to study at all. Cathy was always present in his mind and the loneliness distracted both his heart and mind until all that was left was to close his eyes in sleep.

183

***

Cathy was faced with a senior year that would be difficult. She too was lonely for her Cady, but this would be remedied in three weeks. What wouldn't be remedied was the loss of two steadfast teachers who over the years had become a tradition for the senior class to reckon with. Mr. Rule an iconic teacher who provided an unforgettable rite of passage for senior students would be forced by cancer into retirement early in the year. He was loved by so many generations of seniors from Foster; they all would remember his stern serious countenance that at times was outrageously humorous and mentally stretching for his students. Cady and Cathy would visit with him on the telephone while he lay in the hospital during his last days. Mr. Ziolkowski had started his career at Foster at the same time Cady and Cathy began their high school journey. He was affable, idealistic, and passionate about teaching and quickly became a favorite teacher who Cathy had looked forward to having in senior history. After the first semester he decided to leave teaching altogether. Other teachers juggled around to cover for senior English and senior History classes, but it wasn't the same experience and the stress level was high.

***

Cathy writes to Cady on September 5th:

Dearest Cady,

Hi! I love you and I miss you greatly!! I survived again today at school. Although when I awoke this morning, I wasn't so sure. Oh well, only 178 more days to go (less really since I'm a senior). I mentioned the trip to WSU Pullman to my parents and they seemed to go along with it. Yay!!! I bought my ASB card and Annual today. No pictures on all of the ASB cards this year. My Aunt just called a few minutes ago. They took my grandmother back to the hospital tonight. I don't know how long she's going to have to be there. Not too long, I hope.

I'm so lonely, even though you just left yesterday I have so many things that I want to tell you and yet when it comes to writing them down, I've forgotten it. I love you so very, very much and whenever

184

you're away from me, I feel part of me is missing. I sure will be glad when you come back to this side of the mountains.

How's it going for you over there? How is Rocky and Sandy? Say "Hi" to your grandparents for me. Lots and lots of hugs and kisses!!

I'll love you forever (and then two days more).

Love,

Cathy

***

Cathy had been a lonely, lost, out-of-place girl all of her young life. This had made her a singularly introspective girl and out of that introspection she taken action. She had sought out social environments such as Camp Fire Girls, school clubs and camps, church groups and camps, all to find a place where she would feel in step with her peers giving that valued feeling of acceptance she had never had. The end of childhood is a fuzzy boundary, it at times is both a well-defined sharp line drawn in the sand by sudden events or a broad plain with the distant foothills of adulthood barely visible. One can, without notice, be forcibly thrown across a sharp line or labor a lifetime in a slow off-timed fettered journey across an endless plain. You always cross as a singular person with or without introspection, but those who seek support are most apt to find it. Cathy subconsciously pondered the school year she was beginning. Yes, she was lonely for her love, but the feel of Foster High School wasn't right. The base feelings of being out-of-place that she had always had seemed to be now squeezing the life out of her emotions. Cathy had no classes with her friend Janice who was one graduating class after hers. They did meet up on occasion at lunch or before school and commiserated by giving hugs to each other, there was great feminine comfort to be had in this. Other than these few times Cathy took her lunch outside away from everyone and when she was allowed to she volunteered to help in the cafeteria. Cathy was in her own way laboring to both understand the person she is, especially in the light of this new relationship with Cady, and the new life process her labor is laying the foundation for. Cathy sat at the desk nearest the door in Advanced Algebra Class. This class was one of a group of classes generally required for college-bound students. This particular spot in the room let her entertain the notion she could, at any time, be out the door in the blink of an eye. Generally seniors had this class completed by their junior year; Cathy had let it slide until her senior year. She had other class choices that had always conflicted; they were more interesting than this subject taught by this teacher. This trick worked until Cathy's senior year, it was now or never. It wasn't that she had trouble with math in-and-of-itself. In fact, math in all of its dimensional constructs was her favorite subject, but there was the irritation of this particular teacher and her brother Phil who was also in the same class. Cathy was stuck here so during lectures she writes letters to Cady instead of taking notes; it was her own private rebellion (yes she completed the classwork and tests). The new life process working away was reshaping timid Cathy into a more forceful persona; she would at times finish her work early and leave abruptly before Algebra class was through seeking neither permission nor forgiveness. Her brother Phil never passed along this fact to their parents just as Cathy didn't pass along anything about her brother. Cady had a window into Cathy's school day since many of the letters she wrote came from spare moments during that day (sometimes other students passing by seeing Cathy writing away would add a note of their own onto her current letter to Cady). The change in Cathy was subtle and her understanding of it came one day as she read a letter from Cady where he pointed out that Rocky was now her horse too. Clarity comes to Cathy's thought, "I'm going to be Mrs. C---- Anderson! I'm a woman engaged to a man. His home will be my home. His worries will be my worries, and mine his. I'm no longer alone or out of place. I have a place and a soon to be husband." From that moment on high school was just a juvenile shadow of what it had been to her. Cathy had returned to going to church and the youth group activities it offered. One such was a ballgame with another youth group from an affiliated church up north of Seattle. The Saturday afternoon ballgame leads to a prayer meeting afterward and wound up at 9:00 pm. The church van had everyone back by 10:00 pm. Cathy tumbled out of the van and goodbyes were passed around as people hurried off to the waiting cars. Cathy called from the church office for a ride home only to be told that Mom and Dad were out at a bridge game. Cathy and three other girls seemed to be stranded when her ex offered to give everyone a ride home. His offer came with, "It will be okay there are four of you." Cathy accepted thinking, "After all, what is over is over and there are three other girls in the car." When it becomes apparent by the sudden change of direction her ex is going, his plan is to leave Cathy to the very last drop off isolating her with him. Cathy saw the direction they were traveling and suddenly told her ex, "Stop right here! Right here at Cady's parent's house I'll get out here, they're expecting me." Cathy announced this to the entire carload. Her ex reluctantly stopped Cathy got out and said, "Thanks for the ride," and waved goodbye to the three other girls. Before the car was out of sight Cathy breathed a sigh of relief; she had just avoided making a very big mistake. She had become more forceful in her person.

Cathy had seen that the lights were on in Cady's parents' house and even at 10:30 at night she knew she had a place here. She knocked on the front door, Dorothy opened the door and seeing Cathy standing there gave a big smile in welcome. Cathy settled herself in and chatted with Merrill and Dorothy while they watched television. When the news came on at 11:00 Merrill happily drove her home.

Cathy would see her betrothed in two weeks for a two-day weekend visit. He had been baling hay for Black Angus Cattle Company and there was the chance that the baling would have to stop for the weekend. Cathy felt a power over her life that she hadn't before, a veil was lifted with a new goal to be a great wife to Cady one that he could always count on and turn to. This traditional view of husband and wife was set with them, it was comfortable in its familiarity, but their own nature told of a different union that they were destined to achieve. Cathy was also determined to be malleable based on the unfolding needs of her betrothed although she had no idea as to what that would entail. This matched perfectly for Cady as he also had no idea what this would entail either.

***

Cady's grandpa had made a deal with ranch manager at the Black Angus Cattle Company to custom bale a portion of several large fields of hay. The fields were already laid to windrows by a machine called a swather. A neat machine that with the single pass cut the hay and rolled it into windrows for a baler to come along and make into bales. Grandpa had an inside track he was located right next to the fields and he owned a two-wire International 55W baler circa 1954 all ready to go. This baler made two wire bales about four feet long weighing between 80 to 100 pounds each. All Cady would have to do was pull the baler back and forth across the fields and let the baler do its work in leaving a steady stream of single bales of hay on the ground to be picked up by someone else. Cady would get 25 cents for each bale the machine dropped. Sweet deal except Cady was deathly allergic to all grasses.

During the ranch's short haying season, you would find Cady glassy eyed and wheezing for breath and this was after using the allergy medicines of the time. His normal place in the process of baling hay was to ride on a sled pulled behind the baler while his grandpa pulls the baler with a tractor. As each bale was pumped out of the balers' discharge-chute Cady would latch on to it with two nine-inch hay-hooks then swing the bale onto a growing stack at the back of the sled. The stack was complete with four tiers of three bales to a tier giving at total of 12 bales on the sled. At this time Cady rammed a five-foot long steel bar into the ground through a channel in the center of the sled's floor, the sled continued forward while the now stationary bar did not. The bar would make connection with the stack of bales and push it off the sled. Cady would retrieve the bar as soon as the stack was completely off the sled. If he pulled the bar up while the bales were half off the sled the stack would be pulled apart. The neat stacks of 12 bales each would be trucked into the barn later. This work was made worse by the hay dust and dirt thrown up into the air by the baler's feed hopper right into Cady's face. He would be sick for weeks afterward.

But this time the job didn't use a sled and Cady would be in front of the baler driving the tractor. With luck, a cross-field wind would keep down the dust and the sickness would be short. Cady began each day early so he would be in the field by 7:00am; the idea was to complete the job as soon as possible as weather was always a factor. He would stop for dinner at the ranch house then right back to it until darkness drove him home again. There were breakdowns and mishaps as there always is with farm equipment, as his grandpa always said, "You could set you watch by it happening." At one point Cady tired and slightly ill sidestepped into a moving feed belt that cut into his side. Cady never thought about just how dangerous ranch work is, you just do it, and it is what it is. Cady finished the job on the third day as the bale counter read 1100 bales. Cady happily pulled the tired baler back to the equipment shed and backed it in for the winter. Cady had survived another haying season and was free to recoup his health but there was an odd feeling of finality to the whole experience.

There was such joy to look forward to in just five days; Cathy was coming with his mom to the ranch on Saturday! So wonderful and to top this off Cady was returning home with them! Cady had much to do to get the ranch ready for winter this week, as he wouldn't be back this year. This idea began to really gnaw at him, but for now there was equipment that had to be winterized and much work to do. The Ford wheel tractor had to have its snow removal implement installed and then parked in the shop next to the car where Grandpa could easily get at it. The pickup would be in the big barn and well protected in its winter home. All of the outside faucets needed to be covered, firewood split and stacked away in the wood house. Finally there was a livestock auction tomorrow in Ellensburg that Grandpa and he needed to monitor. The most important thing to be done was to convince his grandpa that Cady really was not staying the winter with him. Cady had to find the right time and right place to do this.

***

Cady and his grandpa sat second row back from the cable fence barrier of the livestock sale arena in Ellensburg. The arena floor was

189

a mixture of sawdust, straw, and manure, some of which would fly up into the air from time to time. Livestock entered by the gate on the right, an auctioneer would verbally push in high hopes for the highest price per pound. When the gate on the left was opened, the livestock exited onto a fenced scale platform and now price per pound was the new owner's problem. Seven some months ago they were in the same seats with the idea of buying some 180 head of spring calves, today it is all about the price yearling steers are currently going for. As they entered the sale yard Grandpa was warmly greeted by his cronies with, "How ya doin' Charley!" "You keepin' ahead of it?" He was a long-time member of cattle ranching community most of which were now weathered men with gray hair and leathery skin. They all shared a common bond of being at the mercy of a heartless numbers game of fluctuating cattle prices. The game was never about who won just about how well you survived from year to year. How Grandpa made his living was to buy spring calves around March, then hold them on his ranch until early fall and sell his now feeder steers to a cattle buyer working for a feedlot. It was all price-per-pound and how much weight his steers had gained during the summer. Grandpa had been worried, the prices had been falling very close to the point where he wouldn't make any profit at all perhaps even to losing money. Cady watched the little group of professional cattle buyers feign interest in the sale arena as 50 yearling steers tromped in completely filling the space. The buyers knew each other and Cady always found it fascinating how at one moment they pat each other on the back as old friends, then suddenly turn hostile to one another when the bidding started. Cady listened carefully to the auctioneer begin his chanting plea to come bid, the buyers didn't flinch at all for the most pregnant of pauses then without warning an intensely subtle bidding war took on a life of its own between two of the buyers. The current need of the feedlots to resupply with fall cattle was still in place to Grandpa's relief. Cady followed the bid price until 'sold' was announced and took note of the final price-per-pound; if these prices held for a few more weeks Grandpa would show a profit, although not a banner year in any way, but still a profit. Cady shared his grandpa's relief and added some of his own. Cady didn't want to hurt his grandpa Charley in any way and leaving was going to do this. Cady wanted Grandpa to look back at this summer out of all the summers they had had together and see personal success both with his grandson and financially.

***

It was a quiet early fall day, the fields lay empty the cattle now belonging to someone else were gone off to feedlots. The irrigation water was completely shut down and every field ditch dry all that was left was constant trickle flow of stock water in the main canal. Taneum Creek was again in full charge of whatever water made its way down the Taneum Canyon and through the ranch toward the Yakima River. Cady pondered, "This time of year is so eerie so foreboding, all that was green and growing is wilting down to the inevitable fact of the coming winter." Cady sat in the snug chair by the oil furnace, his grandpa sat half reclined in his chair with his slippers loosely on his feet. Grandpa Charley's leather Acme cowboy boots were on the back porch standing right next to the boot-jack he always used to remove them before entering the house. The tan colored recliner chair he sat in was a gift from his daughter Dorothy. Cady remembered how excited his mother was to give it to her daddy on his birthday years ago. Cady thought how strange it is to be quietly sitting here in the house during the day that odd sense of finality scratched its way to the surface of his mind again. The chair he sat in was his favorite place to sit and get warmed up each morning when he lived here; the whole house would be chilled except around the freestanding oil furnace. The furnace made a roaring noise that raised and fell as the flame consumed the fuel oil fed into the open pan burner. 'Spark' the furnace had a glass window on its front-side so you could see the fire burning within; the glass had a chrome frame surrounded with the word Spark at the bottom. Cady as a little boy had slept on the couch near the furnace when visiting before the divorce, he had watched the fire glow in defiance of the darkness of a long night. "So long ago," thought Cady, "And now I'm going to give it all away to be with Cathy; to let it all slip away through my fingers like the cold irrigation waters on a hot day." Cady had pieced together an understanding out of all of the little bits of conversation he had had with his grandpa during this last month. Grandpa had planned for Cady to be here all winter and repeat the next summer cycle after cycle. Cady hadn't responded to it then because he was too frightened to. He had never planned for life to continue for himself; soon everything was to come an end including Cady. Cady's only plan had been to escape to the ranch and wait until his existence collapsed in on itself, he didn't know how long that would take but it wouldn't be long. Everything that made up Cady's universe his mother, father, brother, grandfather and Cady would all collapse he didn't see any way that it wouldn't. There was no plan B. Cady had measured himself against his father as he watched Merrill at work and found himself incompetent at being Merrill. Cady had measured himself against his grandfather Charley during their time together in these last five years and again Cady found himself incompetent at being Charley. He had pictured himself doing their tasks with the verve they both had at their command and he failed over and over. He couldn't fully mimic these men especially Charley, they had a natural respect from other men they interacted with daily that Cady couldn't navigate. Cady could and did master the mechanics of the ranch from beginning to end, he was thoroughly practiced in every way, but his self-image got in the way when dealing from one male to another male. Cady didn't see the root cause of male interaction being self-image exactly, but felt the effect nonetheless. He could rely on association with Charley for some mutual respect from known males near the ranch, but a time was coming when his grandpa would be gone. All in all, Cady was going to abandoned the one place he felt in step with, the one place where he wasn't lonely, the one place where he wasn't lost, the one place he truly had a place in and could trust. It was going to be very hard; any leap of faith usually is.

Cady got his grandpa's attention and made his little speech, "Grandpa I've got to go back home and be with Cathy. I have to find a job somewhere there. I've just got to do it. I'll come back weekends whenever you need me." His grandpa's somewhat lighthearted response surprised him, "Okay you do what you have to do." Everything had fallen into place, but Cady had expected Grandpa to make some appeal, in reality his simple reply was just the best Cady could have hoped for. They both returned to idle conversation of ranch life and the coming year. Cady would write in his letter to Cathy that night that he had told his grandpa he was heading back to be with Cathy and Grandpa said, "He couldn't top that in any way." Cady was fearless in his love for Cathy, but other than this he was on shaky ground. In a leap of faith he was heading back to the place he had escaped from based on an absolute faith in his love for her. The ranch would abide, but his place in it would be gone…

***

Cathy asked her brother Phil if she could get a ride with him and he responded begrudgingly per the family rule of 'yes.' This rule was in full force since he was borrowing the family car. Phil had a sport practice at Foster High School Saturday morning just about the same time Cathy was to be at Cady's parent's house to meet up with Dorothy. Cady's mom was enthusiastic when he asked if she could bring Cathy along with her to the ranch on Saturday. Dorothy loved the idea of having company and especially if it was Cathy. Dorothy knew Cady loved Cathy it was plain to see and they were so cute together. Dorothy also loved Cathy for her son, but there was a weak thread of jealousy that of the loss of her son's attention to this pretty girl. On the other hand, it would be nice to have a girl in the family, so she let this thought fill her heart. Cathy was glowing; she was going to not only see Cady again, but the ranch as well. She had been dreaming of this event since she had joyfully shown Cady all of her special places at the orchard. Cathy parted with Phil at the school without much conversation; he was not prone to use any extra words at least not with his sister. Cathy fairly skipped down the sidewalk along 144th to the Anderson household. Dorothy was on the front porch ready to go and smiled when she saw Cathy hurrying into the yard. "All ready to go?" Dorothy teased. "Yes, yes, yes!" Cathy responded lightheartedly. Dorothy with Cathy in the front seat with her pulled out of driveway and drove down the hill toward the I-405 freeway entrance. It was a cool and overcast day in western Washington very typical for late September in the 1970s. The trees were all full green, but giving serious thought to a color change in the next 30 days. Dorothy was a two handed driver who didn't have much trust in what other drivers would do. Because of this conversations came at best in short spurts. The changing scenery did most of the talking as they exited I-405 onto I-90 eastbound. The climb to Snoqualmie Pass was accomplished granting a restroom stopping point at the Pass itself. Cathy watched as they motored along, Lake Keechelus was shrunken in girth down to a small percent of what it was in early summer. Lake Keechelus supplied irrigation waters to the Kittitas Valley. More enduringly to the system that supplied the ranch via the Highline Canal partly diverting into Taneum Creek. Cathy thought about the water flowing from here to the ranch and felt akin to it. They passed Easton and Cle Elum just as Cathy and her family had done over the years except this time it was different; this time she was with a new family and only she and her betrothed knew the secret. Cathy liked Dorothy she was kind and sweet and she was Cady's mom. Dorothy exited the freeway at the Elk Heights exit just a few miles after the Indian John Hill rest stop. Cathy put this exit into her memory, it was a new one for her, but very important as this was the exit to the ranch. Dorothy drove assuredly down this country road; there were no houses or buildings here just old fences and wild grass. The country road brought them to distance ranch houses set far from the roadway. Cathy looked to Dorothy for an indication of distance to the ranch and got a smile in return. Suddenly Cathy spied a single very tall windswept pine tree along the road. She knew instinctively it was the tree, her Cady's tree, the one she had seen from the freeway as they had passed by traveling toward the orchard. Dorothy slowed down and pulled off the road stopping in front of a white fence near a small gate. A sign next to the gate proclaimed, "The Lawler's Live here," and there was Cady standing in the yard with the biggest smile she had ever seen him have. Dorothy said, "We're here!" Cady hugged both his mom and Cathy. Cady simply said to Cathy, "Hi Cathy I am so

194

glad you're here I thought maybe you got lost or something!" Just as Cathy had greeted him the second time at the orchard.

***

Cathy and Cady had only four hours together. Such a small amount of time to gather in the singular life experience that formed Cady and to impress that experience unto Cathy's eager heart that waited with open arms to receive all that was Cady. Cady led Cathy and Dorothy across the yard to the white plantation style ranch house. They climbed the half circle set of brick steps up to the front door that was framed on either side by six panes of textured yellow ochre colored glass. Cady loved the curved push-down handle-set on the front door and as a small child would stand on tippy-toe to pull down on the brass trigger to open it. Cady had never been so eager in his life to show all he loved to someone; he had always been a keeper of secrets, his own and his family's. Today with the giddiness of the expectation of both bringing Cathy into his inner sanctum and expressing his love for her by doing this act that he was sharply focused and blissfully overjoyed. Cady introduced Cathy to Grandpa Charley and Joyce. Grandpa's eyes twinkled as he welcomed Cathy. Cathy was wonderfully endearing to him in return. Cady asked Cathy if she would like to tour the ranch house and with bright blue eyes shining she nodded yes. Cady led her to each room save Grandpa Charley and Joyce's bedroom. The ranch house was split into two attached apartments on the main floor. To the left of the front door was a living room with fireplace. That fireplace was duplicated on the other side of the wall to serve another living room. That duplicate living room was attached to a separate kitchen space and bedroom. To the right of the front door was the main dining room with its own kitchen and master bedroom. There were only two bathrooms in the house these both on the main floor. Upstairs were four bedrooms arranged around the stairway. Cady told Cathy little personal stories about each room from his time of growing up here. He demonstrated the personality of doors that made strange noises as you closed them or floorboards that sang out as you stepped on them and of course, where in dark corners he was sure that ghosts must live. Cady took time to show Cathy his bedroom with the brick chimney right in the middle of the room. From here Cady made sure to let her hear the noises of the wind through the big pine tree and the song of I-90 traffic coming in through his windows. He showed her where he kept his letters from her in an old box that once held fireworks that Cady had shared with David one July 4th. Cathy opened the box to be greeted by the sight of her own letters to Cady each with its wax seal unbroken, Cady had carefully slit open the tops to so as to keep the seals intact.

"Oh, you have other letters in here too," Cathy exclaimed. "I see one from Michael."

Cady returned, "It's a new one he had just arrived at WSU. Go ahead and read it. In fact, there is one from his mother in there too! Go ahead and have fun reading while I pack some stuff!" Cady continued, "It was so cool, Mrs. Leona and daughter Beth after dropping Michael off at WSU stopped by here to visit with me on their way back home."

By the time Dorothy called upstairs that food was ready Cathy had read three from Grandma Ida Anderson, six from Dorothy Anderson, three from Leona (Michael's mom), three from Michael, two each from friends Lydia, Greg, and one from Cady's cousin Linda thanking him for fixing their television.

Dinnertime came, lunchtime to city folk, the family ate around the kitchen table country-style. Joyce served pot roast and a wilted green leaf salad Cathy had never tasted a wilted salad before. It was a simple dish, made of greens picked fresh from the garden with hot bacon grease poured over the top of it to soften the lettuce. Joyce always had fresh table pickles at dinner, they were made by slicing fresh cucumber, pouring vinegar and oil to cover, then let sit out overnight. Dinner was soon over and Dorothy suggested, "You kids go have fun exploring the ranch while I visited with Grandpa and Joyce." Cady was so thankful for his mom being here, she was going to run interference with his grandpa while Cady spirited Cathy away to introduce her to the ranch et al. Cady and Cathy walked hand in hand out the back door across the screen porch to the garden. Cady truly thought he was in heaven; Cathy listened intently to his words and seemed to relish his feelings of place. Cathy and Cady were nearly twins in that they shared so many common experiences of farm and ranch life. No experience here was foreign to Cathy, just as it wasn't to Cady at the orchard. Their souls seem to find a perfect match into each other as if one could complete the other's thoughts. They explored the shop seeing the workbench piled deep with work-worn tools of all sorts and then crossed the gravel drive to squeeze through the fence. After clearing the fence Cady helped Cathy cross the irrigation canal on a weatherworn wood plank they now were in the old orchard. Here were gnarled trees planted in the long ago time before Cady's grandparents' ownership, all lightly laden with wormy apples of ancient varieties. Cady showed Cathy how to open the metal water gate by spinning a wheel that lifted the gate up for irrigation water to flow into the orchard's ditches, but the water was so low now that only a trickle moved. They walked back to the gravel drive down to the barn where the horses were casually standing near the feed troughs. Cady opened the big barn door to show Cathy the inside of the structure. Cady scooped up some oats and soon Sandy and Red were munching away happily. Cathy watched as Cady deftly slipped ropes around the horses' necks, he formally introduced Cathy to Sandy and Red. Both horses accepted this new person into their world and soon Cady had them saddled and bridled. Cathy fell in step as naturally as if she had been around Red all of her life. She spoke to him while she stroked and scratched between his ears something he loved to have done. There wasn't any doubt within Cady's mind that Cathy wasn't capable to handle Red or Sandy and or for that matter there wasn't any doubt in Cathy's either. The moment Cathy was astride Red with feet planted properly in the stirrups and Cady was astride Sandy the couple became a single unit. Cathy was to Cady as Cady was to Cathy both linked together. They rode past the equipment shed where the silent baler sat dormant for the winter then toward the board gate leading down to the corral. Cady dismounted to open/close the gate carefully so that Rocky wouldn't follow them through it. They rode next to each other across the near dry irrigation canal to the somewhat sinister corral. These wood gates Cady opened while still on Sandy's back. Cathy felt Red's quirks in responding to neck reining in a slow and lazy matter and made adjustments to keep up with Sandy. Cady would stop from time to time to point out places where he would stand alone and sing out loud and places where he sat on the large smooth rocks along the creek to ponder whatever troubled him at the time. Cathy would mark each place mentally and match it to her own identical experience while at the orchard. Cady's mind was fixed exactly on the place he wanted to take Cathy to. Their destination lay across the big field north of the ranch house to the foothills that rise up from the old railroad bed. This place among all others called to him when his spirit needed lifting up from some dark mood spawned by an irreconcilable life. Up on the hills he had thought thoughts that called to God for help and he desperately needed Cathy to feel this place so she might understand it. There was no trouble with the horses the couple rode together as if they had been doing this all of their lives. Cathy felt this also, she was with her Cady she could not only keep up she belonged here. Cathy had confidence in her horsemanship in the same way Cady did she earned it by living it. Cathy's years of being around ponies at the orchard, hours of riding at Aqua Barn Ranch, and a backpack riding trip up at Goat Rocks Wilderness Area gave her a strong base to pull from. The two riders paused on the old railroad bed at the base of the hills. Cady rubbed Sandy's neck chasing away some of the mosquitoes as he told Cathy about the train almost a hundred years ago that came down the Taneum Canyon on this roadbed. Not much survived to show that the roadbed had once been here only a few telegraph poles and sleeper ties. The railway was dead now except in Cady's mind where he could still feel the life in it. Cady reined Sandy to climb a dirt road leading part way up to the top of the hill. As they climbed, the vampirish mosquitoes disappeared behind them preferring to stay near the damp ground of the field. Near the top where the road ended a lone apple tree gone wild clung to life in a little flat hollow. Cathy and Cady rode over to it Cady postulated that it might be the only thing left of some ancient Indian camp or maybe a homesteader. They followed cattle trails from here on up to the very top of the hill; here Cady reined Sandy to a stop so they might look out over the breadth of the ranch. The dry hill wasn't irrigated at all so it had become covered with clumps of low growing scrub sagebrush. The wind never completely stopped traveling across these arid hills and it was this that Cady wanted for Cathy to see and feel. He pointed to the green field below; Cathy reined Red to come close to Sandy so she could see what Cady was pointing at. Off in the distance she could see the back of the ranch house and the top of the tall pine but Cady gestured again with his arm. Cathy understood; it was the fields he was pointing at. As she focused her glaze outward the wind suddenly rose up and a strange scene unfolded across the field. The grass bent at the wind's insistence, but not in the same direction as the wind seemed to be blowing. Instead waves of tall grass seemed to dance in swirls and spirals forming complex patterns in a sea of undulation. Cathy watched with inspired amusement. Cady narrated, "There are a pair of eagles near here that dance together daily on the thermals formed from the flat fields meeting the hill. I feel small and God feels big to me here, I have died in this place and returned to the living as I rode back down. Isn't it amazing?" Cathy nodded and tilted her head slightly to the right as she looked at this beautiful person next to her astride a buckskin horse gazing out at the sky. Her thoughts dance back and forth, "Cady Anderson you are so different from anyone I have ever known and I think I feel just as you do." Cady reined Sandy to turn and head downhill. It's a tricky thing to ride a horse down a steep incline; you lean back in the saddle while pushing down on the stirrups toes pointed outward. There are times when the horse loses footing and slides. During such a time a rider's weight needs to pull into the hill not out away from it. It dawned on Cady as they started down just how hard this part of the ride might be for Cathy, he turned to warn her, but then marveled on how well she was doing. Cathy didn't falter she naturally balanced her body with the horse's direction of travel as Red lazily picked his way downhill. Back on the old roadbed they rode the length of the ranch chatting away in the joy of each other's company. The couple found that if you ride carefully enough you could hold hands... With the horses put away back at the barn Cady and Cathy with the childhood exuberance of two best friends explored the old International truck's cab, the clockworks of the baler, the greasy crawler tractor, and the rusty seed drill with its metal levers frozen in place. The afternoon wind made its daily appearance to alternately blow Cathy's brown hair from her eyes into Cady's eyes as they walked and laughed together falling deeper in love second by second. Dorothy had visited with her father and Joyce until she couldn't stand it any longer. The dichotomy of being in the ranch house that was full of reminders, on every wall, in every room of her deceased mother, while diligently laboring not to offend her new stepmother so that she wouldn't lose contact with her father, had Dorothy near her mental breaking point. To her great relief, Cady and Cathy burst through the door into the kitchen. Cady and Cathy were irrepressible in their joy for each other, it not only filled the room as they came in, but cleared the air of tenseness of Dorothy's dilemma. The two climbed the stairs to fetch Cady's things. It began to touch Cady that this was it, the summer adventure was over he was leaving the ranch; that odd sense touched him again. Cady looked around the room fixing the image in his memory while at the same time thinking he could be back soon. He had a fantasy that Cathy and he would live here forever, in love and joy. He would be Charley and Cathy would be Hazel, but there were difficulties that he just as soon not think about now. All of the personality of Cady was removed from the bedroom with the chimney in the center. It was drained of the youth that had sheltered here each night, the love that gave reason to ponder a future where there wasn't one, and of the hopeless tears shed by both mother and son. The material things of life were packed into boxes and carried downstairs to be put into the car's trunk. There were hugs; Cady was a hugger even with his reluctant grandpa. Cady judged the state people were in by a good hug, his grandmother had felt frail and hollow the last time he hugged her just before her death. Grandpa Charley felt less sturdy even a little vulnerable this time when Cady hugged him goodbye. Charley's voice or body language didn't show it, but Cady's hug was a foreboding feeling that spoke quietly to Cady. Cady drove with Cathy next to him and Dorothy in the back seat. In the rearview mirror as Cady started down the country road he watched Charley and Joyce turn and slowly walk back into the ranch house…

***

There was something solemn about that trip westward on I-90 but it was just a single discord in the music of going home sitting next to Cathy. On their schedule for all of next week was Bill Gothard's *Basic Youth Conflicts* seminar. Cady and Cathy both had purchased their seminar syllabus in anticipation of attending the week-long event held on the Seattle Center grounds at the Coliseum. It was the first step in their walk together as a Christian couple. During that seminar week Cady and Cathy as a couple would fellowship with their school-hood friends one last time, Michael, Janice, Beth, and new friend Cindy. They would sit in the upper rows of the Coliseum listening to Bill Gothard lay out his challenge to young people to understand that God is shaping their lives, his slogan button that everyone was wearing said, "Please be patient God isn't finished with me yet." It was the first time Cady had been to a Christian fellowship with any of his peers in his life. Yes, he had been to Sunday school off and on during his elementary school years and regular Sunday service with his mom and grandma Hazel, but not in a fellowship way with young people of his own age. Cathy had attended youth groups, but for Cady this was a new experience. Cady enjoyed the camaraderie of young believers, the message of each night's sermon, the chalk drawings that were created to illustrate the sermon, and especially being with Cathy. There was no closing night conversion event for Cady or Cathy they already shared a common love of Christ, neither could remember a time when they didn't. There were over the years, challenges to the understanding of their personal faiths. Cathy was driven back to church after a short absence of two years during the time of her move from one house to another. After a conversation with a friend Cathy felt a longing to find a church near her new home and did. Cady for the most part of his childhood didn't have a concept of a world outside of Christianity; it was everywhere you just didn't see it manifested, other than on Sunday. During each crisis Cady faced after the divorce of his parents, he prayed for intersession, healing, and forgiveness. Simply surviving through the event was always an acceptable answer from God. From the abandonment of to the reclamation by his dad, Cady began to push away from going to church with or without him. This angered Cady's dad and of course it hurt Cady, but such is nature of the time they were in. Cady during adolescence was a keeper of his own secrets and a reader of the Bible and had come across Old Testament verses in Deuteronomy 22:5, 23:1 seemly dooming him in mind and body. Biblically it was inescapable, Cady had this in his heart. It was a shock and a sickening blow to his spirituality, but not to the faith that Cady had relied on. God was always there when everyone else abandoned him. Prayers to God in Jesus' name were always heard. Cady's answer to this challenge was to leave the physical church his dad currently attended, but not leave God. Yet, there had to be an answer and there were Cathy's feelings to consider. Cathy and Cady as a couple began to look for a church in the area that they might become a part of and have trust in. Over the next two months they attended Sunday service in four churches they had searched out as possible places. None of these churches were welcoming in any way to this young couple, which seemed to match each other in action and thought. Cady had long feminine hair that clashed with his male beard. They prayed before each try but in the end were but ghosts in the sanctuary. So they kept to themselves holding their own Bible study and listening to Sunday sermons on the radio. Sometimes friends would join them in their little Sunday church in Cady's basement.

***

Cady and Cathy saw each other every day. Soon a routine came into being of visiting Grandma Ida Anderson every Saturday night for games. Most of the time Merrill came with them to make it a foursome. Grandma Ida loved to play Canasta they would gather in her little dining room and play until 11:00. Cathy loved chatting with Ida all about family history, they became closer with each visit. Dorothy was at the Riverton Heights Ice Creamery working away until closing around 1:00am on Saturdays. Saturday night as a game night would remain a custom for the next 47 years for Cady and Cathy as they moved through their lives, family members would come and go, but the custom remained. Cathy's senior year continued to trudge on without fanfare. The fanfare for her was time spent with Cady they would meet together at either house, hers or his, to play card games in the evenings. Looking at them you would guess they were already a married couple, they didn't seek out dark corners to kiss and squeeze tightly together, but instead were always hand in hand teasing each other.

October came and with it the realization of a weekend trip that had been long ago planned for Cady, Cathy, and Janice all to drive to Pullman to visit Michael at WSU. Cady drove while Cathy and Janice took turns reading the book *The Little Prince* by Antoine de Saint-Exupery aloud to pass the time. Cady thought this was the most pleasant trip he had ever taken. Cady also thought that Michael had planned all the details of their overnight accommodations, after all, he was doing Michael a big favor in bringing Janice along. Cady had never been to Pullman before, but had a secret weapon in Cathy who did all of their navigation; she was a wiz with a map. They found the dormitory Michael haunted, parked in what seemed to be a visitor spot, and tumbled out of the car. Janice was, as she put it, "Super excited" to see Michael; it had been six weeks since they had seen each other. She all but flew toward the main door of the building. The door was locked, but could be opened by a call box, Janice pushed the number for Michael's room, and the door buzzed open. A university dormitory was a very strange place; it smelled of the concrete that made up the floors, walls, and ceilings of the building. Everywhere was a chaotic flow of young coeds seemly unaware of anyone else around them; it had all the raw energy of a Saturday without anyone over twenty-two anywhere to be seen. The threesome found Michael sitting cross-legged on one of two single beds in his small room. Janice came running in and nailed Michael with a big hug that left him flat on his back. Michael was up in a flash and leading a tour of the building from top to bottom. Then as he and Janice poked at each other they left the dorm altogether and headed to a campus store that had a hidden staircase in one corner that led down to a small store within a store. Here in his true outrageous fashion Michael had found an adult only boutique of bongs and over the top comic books. Cady complimented him while at the same time backing everyone back upstairs as soon as possible. He realized this was Michael totally unchained; so this was only the opening salvo of the fireworks show he had planned. Michael led his group back to his dorm room where his roommate was gathering stuff together to be out for the night. The plan as put forth by Michael was another class-friend Paula from Foster had room for Janice and Cathy to sleep that night while Cady could stay with Michael in his room. Cathy wanted to check this out, so Michael led the way to the coed side of the building to find Paula and assure Cathy everything was okay. "Paula is out of town and no one told me about anyone staying here tonight," answered Paula's roommate as she closed the door on them. "Well that's strange," puzzled Michael. Cathy stared at Cady. The foursome returned to Michael's room where he and Janice camped out on his bed sitting side by side. It wasn't long before they hid under a blanket by pulling it up over their heads doing what physically estranged couples might be tempted to do when restrained by an audience, leaving Cathy and Cady to sit on the other bed and either stare at the giggling blanket or kiss like there was no tomorrow. It was too awkward and nowhere near their style of affection, so they grabbed their sleeping bags and retreated into the hallway shutting the door behind them. "Okay, we were taken advantage of. Where will we sleep any ideas?" Cathy asked. Cady thought about the car, but it would be cold tonight and once outside they couldn't get back in to use the bathrooms. "Let's walk around on this floor and see if we have any options," Cady offered. They did and found a little study carrel with a little two-person chair. Cathy could lay down on her side with her knees bent. Cady crawled under the chair and lay on the floor below her. At least it was heated space, but it was going to be a long night. Cady awoke first as the sunrise streaming across the Palouse hills filled the little carrel space with golden light. He wiggled out from under the chair and looked out the window giving thanks that the long night was over. As Cady turned to gaze at his love still asleep on the little makeshift chair-bed, he realized this was the first time they had slept together, well sort of. He smiled to himself as her eyelids twitched and opened revealing those beautiful blue eyes he loved so much. Cathy felt a warm glow seeing Cady standing there above her; it was an adventure and she was sharing it with her Cady. The challenge of the morning was no food service on Sundays and no local grocery stores were open. Cathy, Cady, and a very serene and somewhat sedate Janice all climbed into the car for the trip back home. Oh, and Michael had one more favor for Cady to do, he slipped a case of Coors beer out from under his bed to go into the car's trunk, a gift from Michael to his dad since Coors wasn't legal in Washington State. Cady wasn't happy he was under 21 and if stopped and his car searched (this kind of thing did happen close to WSU) he would have been it big trouble; in the end he did it anyway, who could say no to Michael. The trip back across the state on I-90 was much less enthusiastic and much more sleepy. Janice slept soundly the whole way and Cathy, even though she fought sleep, would nod off too.

***

Covid still demands barriers to be overcome as 2021 moves along forcing us to sit in our car waiting for the cellphone to ring. It does and we enter the outer lobby of La Belle Vie Cosmetic Surgery. Questions are asked and temperatures are taken, then the reward of the inner lobby is ours. Cathy and I are given Christi's attention as we stand near the reception desk. She asks us to wait a few minutes while the doctor catches up with her schedule. This is new for us this waiting in the inner lobby; we get to sit and watch the big aquarium's three fish swimming purposefully in circles while the office staff seemed to be doing the same. A pleasant medical assistant came and led us to a very familiar exam room. This time it is Cathy's turn to sit in the corner chair as the supporting wife while I take center stage on the exam chair. Cathy's turn was two months ago at center stage. The exam room is furnished with a simple straight-backed chair in the corner, a dental exam style chair centrally, a three by six foot mirror mounted long-ways on the wall beside the exam chair, and three square 24 inch paintings of bright white dogwood flowers that hang on a chocolate brown accent wall opposite the mirror wall. The medical assistant asks what we are here for and I reply a tummy tuck. We chat for a minute about her son, she hands me a paper gown telling me the open side goes to the front, strip to the waist, but leave your bra on, then she is off to go find Dr. Megan Dreveskracht who must be fulfilling someone else's body image dream at the moment. I do as asked and fidget moving around the room holding the gown closed with my tightly clenched hand. Cathy takes notion that the white flimsy plastic belt attached to the paper gown's waist should be tied; I differ and challenge her to try. If there was a hidden camera in the exam room they got lots of good comic material of two females trying to tie a belt with only one inch of overlap. I continue to hold my gown closed and soon Dr. Megan breezes in after a little knock at the door. She is so understated in demeanor; she's rail thin with short hair and about 5 foot 5 tall, "How's life going for you two? Did you have fun in the snow?" I answer, "Yes, we both thought we were younger and shoved like crazy to clear our driveway then discovered we weren't!" We both ask her about her little daughter. Dr. Megan asks us, "Would you like to see a picture?" Together we say, "Yes!" She zooms out and is back in far less than a minute. Her little girl is 14 months old and just had her picture taken for Valentines Day. She is so cute with curly golden hair and bright smile; she has her mother's eyes and ears. Dr. Megan aims us back to business with, "So you're after a tummy tuck?" "Yes," I try to sound unflappable. Dr. Megan asks to see my tummy and explains what she does, "Using your belly button as a middle point I remove a piece of skin around it in the shape of a rounded diamond, then pull the bottom and top together afterward. Any questions?" I ask, "What happens to the belly button?" Dr. Megan responds, "It is removed with the skin but we make you a new one." Cathy is using the opportunity to ask several she had left over from her consultation. Cathy asks, "Where is the scar located and do you need to do electrolysis in the bikini area." Dr. Megan answers by showing us a

206

little drawing she has. I stand up and ask, "Show Cathy where it will be on me." Dr. Megan points to an area about six inches down from my belly button. "As far as hair removal goes you don't have to, but if you would like to just stop it a week before surgery." Dr. Megan is chipper and eager to have more questions and we have more. I ask, "Could the surgery interfere with either GRS or BA (gender reassignment surgery or breast augmentation)?" She quickly responds with, "No it shouldn't." I ask about fat transfer, "Will I have any left to use in my face if needed?" She again quickly responds, "Yes we leave the fat on your backside so there should still be a good supply for simple transfer to the face." A thought forms in my mind and I take the opportunity to ask, "Can the fat you are removing be moved to my breast?" Dr. Megan carefully answers, "Yes we can do this, but it is with the understanding that as low as 70% of that fat may survive. You do recover quicker than with an implant even quicker than Cathy did her breast reduction. Also what is your expectation as to size? We deal in cup sizes here." I said, "I am a C cup now and would like to go to a D or in other words one-cup size up." Dr. Megan commented, "That should be doable we usually get around 1000 cc of fat, if transferred should give you at least one cup size increase. The trick is symmetry between the breasts, we inject fat into the breast not under your muscle, with an implant it is set, but with fat just don't know if one side or the other will hold onto the viable fat cells. Also with fat transfer I would do some taping to bring your breast together giving you some cleavage." I have another question, "Could you still get an implant later if the fat deserted me?" She quickly answered, "Yes." Dr. Megan poked her finger into my belly button to check if I had a hernia and no I didn't. Dr. Megan stated what I would need for surgery, "You need a letter from your doctor stating that you are fit for surgery, stop your estrogen two weeks before, and a negative Covid test result. No, having the vaccine didn't make any difference we still need the test as we don't know if the vaccine works." We asked her if she had the second shot. Dr. Megan answered, "Yes she did, my trick was to take the rescue packs of vitamins for a week, and no I didn't get sick, but what I hear from my patients it's running 50% of them having symptoms. I am having trouble getting the shot for my mother." Cathy commiserated with her she was having the same problem for her mother. (Side note Cathy managed to get an appointment for her mom for tomorrow at the Safeway up on top of the hill near her.) As our conversation flows over me my mood is getting better and better. It is almost too good to believe, as I am just as excited as Cathy has been to get this done. The relief is growing moment by moment this is the answer I have been missing I am tempted to stand up and hug Dr. Megan. This is a lifesaver and I try to share with both Cathy and Dr. Megan how this is making me feel. She was being summoned back to another exam room but was being slow in leaving us, as she does reluctantly leave she says, "I am so glad to see you today!" Cathy and I get ourselves together and start toward the exit only to be turned around by Christi, because she isn't ready with our quote yet so we return to the nice warm exam room. While we wait we can hear Dr. Megan in the next exam room giving a consult to another patient. Although it isn't polite we can't help hearing what is going on in the next room. A male voice is explaining about having to wait for retirement in order to get an Adam's apple reduction. Oh my, I think Dr. Megan has just gone from one transgender person right to another. We hear a few more snatches of conversation and I wonder just how many people are there just like me and will I see this person on the way out? It kind of makes me sad in a way, two things persist, I'm not so special after all and why did I wait so long? I also wonder what God has in mind giving me this experience? We drive away from the nondescript office building in Tukwila. Cathy is excited for me to get fat transfer into my breasts instead of the silicone implants, "It's your fat not some foreign object under your muscle just sounds better." Now with both of us doing a surgery we have to time the events so as one will be recovered enough to be the caregiver to the other.

***

Life moves through autumn and into the winter of 1973 Cady's dad has risen to the challenge of turning his youngest son David around in life to the extent he has returned to High School. It's a struggle for David; the responsibly of doing schoolwork that in many cases he can't compete against the tug of ample sources of ways to get high with friends. He does try; he faces his brother's shadow in school and ultimately succumbs to dropping out. Still the Anderson family holds on by the threads of the thin fabric it was made from. There are Friday night drive-in movies where Cady and Cathy join Merrill and David at the El Rancho drive-in and game nights at Grandma Ida's house. Cady struggles to find work in a very tight jobs market based on his high school electronic skills. Cathy and Cady continue to find contentment in each other's company day after day. Spring brings work for Cady at Redco controls a company making aftermarket electronic controls for the plywood manufacturing industry making $188.88 per week. It's Cady first experience of working in an enclosed factory as opposed to outdoor agricultural work. He is a final test assembler in a group that includes many women. At home David is arrested for breaking into a local store. He is released into his mom and dad's care. The cycle is up and down, good David bad David. David is 17 and has a group of less than desirable friends that hang out together. They forced open a back door to a grocery store and he got caught inside after the alarm sounded. Afterward a detective brought David home late that night and then had a talk with Mom and Dad, Cady wasn't included.

***

Cathy graduates in top ten from Foster High School in June 1974. She and Cady buy a used car together. David is at home asleep on the couch when Cathy and Cady drive up in their used ten-year-old Buick Special Station Wagon. Cady tries to wake him up, but he is on the down cycle from some drug. They can bring him to consciousness briefly, but can't hold him there; he just slips right back to a heavy narcotic sleep. Cady gives up and leaves him in peace to sleep whatever off. David drifts farther away from them each day and seems to be falling into a hopeless pit with no way to return. The tragic irony is David seems to be following a like addiction trail (drugs vs. alcohol) as his and Cady's mom had fallen prey to. For Cady it is another abandonment in life and another failure to find a way to help. Summer continues to be muggy from June into July, but goes without notice as Cady's world revolves around Cathy without any external notice of time and place. Cady's dad is seldom home until late at night and his mom reacts accordingly. Her work at Howard's Riverton Heights Ice Creamery does help to distract her. Cady and his dad were chatting with Howard the owner of the store one day when Howard made a statement to Merrill that both shocked and surprised Cady, he said, "I totally trust your oldest son with everything even handling money here in the store, but I don't trust your youngest son at all. He runs around with a bad crowd and we have to watch him every minute here in the store; he shoplifts." Cady's jaw dropped open, he was being complimented on one side, but damned on the other. What was going on with David? That store was a social hang out for the family, they had three pinball machines that Cady used to play while waiting for his mom to get off work. Cady also liked Howard and was impressed how he ran his business. Still Cady's heart ached for his brother. Cathy found work in a Daycare, she was drawn to the little kids and wondered if this was where her life might lead work-wise.

***

Cady needed something to do with Cathy tonight it was July 27th, 1974; he realized not only was it Saturday, but the Seattle Seafair Torch Light Parade was tonight. Cady picked Cathy up at her house, she mentioned that her parents were none too happy that they had purchased the station wagon together. Cady pointed out that Cathy was openly wearing the engagement ring he had bought for her so it is not like we are just friends. Cathy on her graduation night had slipped on the ring she and Cady had picked out to be her engagement ring. Cathy after her mom noticed the ring simply said, "It's a graduation gift from Cady." Cathy's mom persisted saying, "Does this mean you two are engaged!?" Cathy responded, "Yes mom it does," but quickly added, "We aren't planning on getting married for at least a year." This had mollified her worried mother and since then the subject was seldom mentioned again. It was late afternoon already as they drove

210

toward downtown Seattle. The parade route was all staked out through the center part of Seattle. Cady had a plan to head to the end of the route near the Seattle center in hopes of finding a place to view the parade that wasn't so crowded. They parked the car and found a high retaining wall to sit atop of. The plan worked, but by the time the parade had reached their spot near the end of the route both the participants were very tired and the floats showed signs of wear. Cady and Cathy walked through the Center grounds to reclaim their car and drive home. Cady dropped Cathy off at her house with a goodnight kiss and headed to his parents' house and to bed.

Cady pulled into the driveway after his date with Cathy to be met by his father standing at the bottom of the stairs nearest the driveway. His strained countenance sent alarm bells ringing. Cady had never seen his father cry and now through those tears he hears his father struggle to form strange terrible words, "David had been drowned." His dad was hysterically falling to pieces right before Cady's eyes. Cady is stunned then tells his father, "I'll be right back don't go anywhere." Cady quickly calls Cathy telling her he needs her and will be there to pick her up in ten minutes. He leaves to go get his wife to-be, and returns to his mother and father. This is too big for Cady to handle without help; he doesn't even try to plan on what to do until he has Cathy at his side. Cathy was at the front door and ready to go with him as he pulled into the driveway. Cady beckoned for her to get in and she did so without a moment of hesitation. Once out of the driveway Cady suddenly felt tears fill his eyes. With as much control as he could muster he told Cathy that David had drowned in the Green River not one mile from their house. Back at the Anderson household Cady and Cathy together face Merrill and Dorothy to try to comfort a loss that cannot be comforted. They hugged, all cried together, and Cathy became a pillar of a comforting daughter to Merrill and Dorothy, and wife to Cady. Cady had never experienced such complete brokenness of family and yet there was Cathy, just as broken as they were over a deceased brother and son, but she brought grace and God along with her tears. Without a word being said David was

Cathy's brother and Merrill and Dorothy her grieving parents. They cried from the bowels of their beings over the life that was torn from father, mother, brother, and sister leaving empty broken shells that a life had filled. It all settled down to a complete physical exhaustion for Merrill and Dorothy they moved into their bedroom to fall into bed in a spent stupor. Dorothy and Merrill were never so close in their whole married life to each other as they were on that awful night. Afterward, they would never again be a comfort to one another as husband and wife; their relationship was over. Cathy and Cady walked downstairs to Cady's bedroom. Cathy would not leave him, she called her parents to explain what had happened and that she would not be home tonight, to her surprise they agreed. She had seen Merrill and Dorothy fall to bits, but not Cady. Yes, there were his tears, but there was more to come in a different way. She didn't know how it might come, but she would be needed when this happened and she was all he had. For the second time in their relationship Cady and Cathy slept together in one room, Cady in his bed and Cathy in a sleeping bag on the floor next to his bed. All night long Cady's hand lay over the side of his bed, and it was held safe by a gentle loving hand near the floor. Cady's pillow was damp in the morning, his hand still hung down the side of the bed. Cady and Cathy talked together; better still Cathy let Cady talk it out. She knew Cady better than anyone now especially after this night, he would be okay as long as he talked, as long as he explained what he felt, as long as he was able to be observant of life around him. Cady was a complicated being made up of crisis, conflict, and love. In Cathy's heart she knew that's why she loved him.

The next morning the events around David's death began to come out. Earlier yesterday after Cathy and Cady had tried to wake him up David had indeed slept it off. He felt great and met up with a friend who he had camped with this last summer up at Lost Lake. It was hot so they headed down to the sand bar on the Green River to cool down. David didn't swim, but his friend David D did. The idea wasn't to swim, but to just splash around to cool down. David Anderson had spent his life playing in and out of Taneum Creek a shallow creek with a firm rocky bottom and he knew every rock. The Green River was nothing like this; David knew nothing of its undertows or mucky bed. They found an old glass Coke bottle and took turns tossing it out to be retrieved. David even saw his cousin Kevin for a short time while he was there and traded words in casual conversation before Kevin left. The exact details are lost, but it went something like this, David slipped out into a deep pocket of water and got trapped by an undercurrent against a submerged tree branch. In a panic his friend tried and tried to find him by diving deeper and deeper only to have David slipped away from him... His friend David D was heartbroken... People come to your house when someone dies, some are official, some are family, and some don't need to be there at all. To keep the ones who don't need to be there at all away and marshal support Merrill was telephoning family, friends, and a local newspaper. Dorothy was in the bedroom. From the official folks Cady and Cathy learned that sheriff drivers were looking for David's body and that there wasn't much hope of finding it. Cady and Cathy drove down to the Riverside Inn and parked in their parking lot near the trail to the sand bar. Cady had never been down to this river it wasn't his creek and right now it seemed an evil place. The couple walked the well-worn dirt trail to the water where divers in good spirits were dawning equipment to make the underwater search. Cady and Cathy found a spot out of the way on the bank to sit in the shade of the trees lining the river and wait on the cool earth. The day was sunny, the air still, the river silent as a snake that already had its prey. Cathy told Cady that she kept expecting David to come wandering down the trail wondering what was going on. They both laughed and wept bitterly. You could see where it happened, a sunken tree trunk stuck out a slim branch above the water at low tide; as the tide turned the whole structure disappeared below the water line. The couple watched as a husky framed diver floated on his back while he pulled on a mask. He was in no hurry, after all, no one expected to find anything or anyone. Cady revisited Cathy's hope that David would just wander along any minute now when suddenly a diver surfaced holding a pair of feet. Instantly Cady knew those feet and the jeans on the legs. He was up and pulling Cathy with him, Cady didn't want to see anymore it was enough to know that David would come home to be buried. As they walked away from the scene a newsman approached and Cady told him if he hurried he would see that they just found the body. The man broke into a run. Cady and Cathy drove home, the house was filling up with family and friends. Charley and Joyce were on their way from the ranch. All was bedlam and tears. The news had already reached the household that David's body had been found; this was greeted with joy and great sadness. Cathy was right about the delayed reaction of last night, the full weight of sorrow came to Cady right then when he didn't need to be the soul strength for his parents. They secreted themselves in Cady's bedroom and Cathy held on to Cady with all her strength while Cady came apart. Finding David's body brought the need for interment, a coffin, and a plot. Merrill and Dorothy simply didn't have enough money even adding what little Cady had to do all that was required. Margaret, Merrill's sister, and her husband Ole Hanson offered to sign over a cemetery plot at Washington Memorial to Merrill and Dorothy. Other family members helped with the coffin and liner. Merrill used up what little credit he had to get the headstone and funeral at Yarington's Funeral Home. The funeral was nice and a guitarist performed the song *If* by David Gates. David lay peacefully in an open coffin for viewing, his fingers interlaced gently together just as we had seen him do so often watching television. Cady and Cathy stood together loving David in their minds one last time then turned aside from their brother to take their places at the funeral service. At the graveside service Cady saw a somber faced Michael and Janice and other friends. Michael couldn't bring himself to speak to Cady. He didn't have to; Cady saw the expression on Michael's face speaking for him. David came to Cady in a waking dream that night. Cady in shock asked, "How could this be you're dead?" David told him, "I'm fine don't worry anymore." Then it was all over David would be forever 17 within a month of his 18th birthday. All that was left of the family he had been part of were just shattered pieces; there was nothing to hold onto. In Cady's vicarious never-ending search to help the people around him one profound problem remained. How to repair what had happened? Cady with Cathy's agreement decided to move their wedding up to October just three months after David's death; it was their thinking that the family needed a good thing to set things right after a tragedy and a wedding would be it.

***

Cady and Cathy took both sets of parents to the Royal Fork Buffet Restaurant for dinner. The party was to give Merrill and Dorothy Anderson, and Ainsley and Joyce Dixon a chance to get to know each other before the wedding. The big surprise was the announcement by Cady and Cathy that the wedding was no longer over a year away, but was moved up to October 5th. Cady had sincerely believed that everyone would be so very happy and pleased to look forward to a joyful event after the death. It didn't work this way at all... The happy announcement instead was met by the drama of Cathy's mom dropping her fork midway between mouth and plate. Then it went downhill from there.

The drama was centered between the notion of Cathy throwing her life away and the short planning time before the wedding. Both of these things had entered into Cady's mind also, but Cathy was resolute. Merrill and Dorothy were quick to volunteer what help they could to make things go smoothly, Ainsley philosophically continued on with his dinner. The battle was now the traditional one between daughter and mother. The reasoning for the advancement or delay of a wedding date stands on either good solid ground or bad shaky ground. You can get married too quickly and lose each other in the rush or you can wait too long causing a chain reaction of a grandparent never getting to see their first and only great-grandchild. (As a side note: Cathy would gently place her month old first-born son Casey into the arms of her grandfather Herman Tuttle. Herman despite his weakness from brain cancer beamed seeing his first great-grandchild. Cathy would treasure this moment in her heart. Casey would be the only great-grandchild Herman would see as eight months later he would be laid to eternal rest. Herman had been diagnosed with brain cancer after Cady and Cathy had wed.) After David's death waiting seem not to make any sense; the tragedy made clear the frailness of this mortal veil we call life and how easily it can be lost. There was no downside to moving the ceremony up, only gain. The wild card if there was one was Cady himself, Cady wanted in on the bridal experience. He was a virgin as Cathy was and he wanted to be married in white. They began to plan a very unusual wedding ceremony in that it allowed Cady to have as much of the bridal experience as possible. As a couple they picked Rev. Ruhlman a Baptist Minister near their home. Cathy went to high school with his daughter. The couple met with the Minister for a chat and to begin pre-marriage classes. He had told them over the telephone that there would be ten classes held over ten evenings and to expect to learn a lot about each other. Cathy and Cady met with Rev. Ruhlman; on what was to be the first night he chatted with the young couple and asked them to list life experiences they had in common stating, "That to become one in matrimony many differences would need to be overcome." Rev. Ruhlman used differences as teaching points to young couples. If the list was short, he asked about favorite color, music, and the like pointing out the need for a plan of understanding when their choices would be at odds. Rev. Ruhlman explained, "In Christian philosophy these are the challenges that must be faced and understood in their new relationship in order to continue to grow throughout life together."

The couple started their list:

1. They both loved the Lord and shared that love with each other.
2. They both spent every summer on farms and ranches near each other in Eastern Washington with their grandparents. Both grandfathers were born in the same area of the Kansas/Oklahoma border and found their way to Eastern Washington at very near the same time.
3. They both enjoyed riding horses and caring for them.
4. They enjoyed studying the Bible together.
5. They had confessed all personal secrets to each other.

6. They both started in the same school district as eighth graders
7. They had both been bullied in high school.
8. They both shared friends in common.
9. They both wrote letters to each other each day all summer long.
10. They enjoyed all the same music and had the same color choices.
11. They enjoyed playing the same games.
12. They both did darkroom photography.
13. Their paths seemed to cross back and forth all high school long.
14. They liked to bake the same things together.
15. If we could, we would spend all of our time together.
16. They are each other's best friends.
17. They are both virgins.
18. They split their life between city life and country life.
19. They both lived with maternal family who had mental health issues.
20. They both had been loners in life keeping their own company.

The good Reverend stopped them at 16 saying, "This is the thing with Christian couples! There is no need for any more classes for you two." He smiled broadly at them, "It will be a blessing to marry the two of you to each other." My only criticism is you don't have a home church. You need to find one, dear ones; you'd be a blessing to any church you choose. And with that Cathy and Cady were well on the road toward their shared wedding. The church Reverend Ruhlman pastored was a small one, too small to hold the big Anderson family so Cathy and Cady searched for a bigger church. They found a nice brick church to hold the ceremony in and Cathy got busy sewing on her dress. Cathy would have one Maid of Honor and Cady one Best Man, who to this day doesn't remember anything about the wedding.

In the hours before the event the bride and groom hung out together at the church painting clear-coat on each other's nails. After the church was full and seated the song *Follow Me* by John Denver began playing while a procession of the three sets of Grandparents, followed by two sets of Parents walked down the center isle to the front row pews and were seated. Next came the Maid of Honor escorted by the Best Man, they took positions on either side of the Minister at the altar. The guests didn't quite understand what was going on until the Wedding March started and everyone stood up and turned to see both Cady and Cathy walking together hand in hand to the altar where the Maid of Honor and Best Man were waiting for them. Two figures in white walked together down the aisle and left together at the end of the ceremony. It was a break with the old traditional way a church wedding was choreographed. Cady and Cathy were making the public statement acknowledging their grandparents and parents and most importantly that they would keep each other's company side by side forever. The wedding didn't center on the bride, but on both of them equally. Cathy told the wedding photographer that there were to be no pictures of her alone it is our shared wedding. Cathy's mom got so many complements on this unique take on a traditional wedding that she was all smiles. The only sad note was Cathy's Nanna live in Georgia and couldn't be there. After a weeklong honeymoon drive around Eastern Washington the couple took up temporary residence in the basement of Cady's parent's home. So closes the autumn of 1974 and part one of our book.

Part 2: The Time Between Being Joined Together and What Came After

Our wedding didn't repair anything Anderson family-wise with only one great exception, our longing for each other, and would lay the groundwork for Merrill to once again flee to freedom. He to his credit had served five years more than what was expected of him after the initial divorce. Cady at the time didn't see it this way, but came to this understanding many years later. The truth was there was nothing left to bind Merrill to Dorothy anymore except the loss of their son David and in that there was no solvency. Cady didn't understand as a male marrying Cathy that he was in essence stepping away from his birth family to join hers. The old saying of "A son is a son until he takes him a wife, a daughter is a daughter all of her life" holds true.

As life events are the interface of ocean to beach, they came falling upon Cady and Cathy in waves. Cathy lost her job at the daycare, Cady lost his job at Redco, beautiful baby Casey was born at 9-1/2 months after their vows, Merrill disappears altogether off to seek his own path, Dorothy begins work as a maid at a big motel, Cathy's grandfather Herman Tuttle passes away, Cathy's grandmother Freda's depression lifts for a time, Cady started work at Terra Technology, Cady's grandmother Ida Anderson passes away. The ranch is sold (1976) and an ugly ranch auction scratches across the face of the place that held Cady's childhood together, all the little bits he cherished, and all that was emotionally part of him. House-hold goods, tools, farm equipment, livestock, all listed on the sales brochure; not listed are little bits of Hazel, of David, of Dorothy, of Cady that are meaningless to strangers. It is an ugly rape of the emotional fabric that Cady clung to a hopeless tearing away of his spirit. Cady had one last chance to claim anything before the sale started as Grandpa has asked him to come and help at that Saturday auction. More than bittersweet but Cady promised to be there as not to be is unthinkable. He is defeated in this as early Saturday morning his mom who has been drinking all night can't be left alone; Cady is trapped while across the mountains bits of his past life are scattered to the winds. Grandpa Charley and Joyce move into Ellensburg, another beautiful baby Corin was born at 28-1/2 months after their vows, Dorothy moves out of the house that she had shared with Cady and Cathy and into her own little apartment along Highway 99, Dorothy after two years living alone loses her life in a drunken stupor. Grandpa Charley moves to New Mexico with his second wife Joyce and passes away there in 1981. After the death of Cathy's grandfather, the Orchard becomes a family run business and after a few years is sold off. With first the ranch and then the orchard gone there are no longer any physical ties to Eastern Washington for either Cady or Cathy but emotional ties remain.

***

There is no greater sorrow in any parent's life than to lose a child, I saw both my parents die inside that day. With all the hurt in my parent's lives this was the point of no return it was just a matter of time. I felt a strange feeling not so much remorse but relief; death was an end to David's suffering there seemed no other way. The people where I worked would even comment that I didn't seem as upset as I should have been in losing my only brother. I wondered about this, Christianity teaches that death is overcome through Christ thus giving us hope for eternal life. My life so far was filled with despair and constant suffering both internal and external to myself. Longing to be the opposite gender both inside and out and the hopeless states of my brother and mother all being ever present. So if life is short it is a good thing. Bad Cady I know, but this is how I felt at my brother's death, he is free now of all that held him down, free in a way that silently I longed for. I would feel this way again at my mom's death five years later. She, with almost three times the legal limit of alcohol (1979 limit of .1) in her blood stream, stepped into the path of a traveling car in an attempt to cross Highway 99 and died instantly. She called me earlier that evening to tell me she loved me and I told her I loved her too, this being completely unusual for her to do in her drunken state, usually we argued. She had gotten an apartment a year earlier leaving the house to us, each day it seemed I was up there because of her drinking. I was worn down to being numb. It was left to me to try to take care of Mom as Dad had just disappeared completely after Cathy and I had our first child. Now it is left for me to tell my grandpa Charley that his one and only child, his loving daughter Dorothy had just died. The ranch had been sold and Charley and Joyce were now living in a little house in Ellensburg; Grandpa would mostly just sit in a chair there. He would follow his daughter into death two years later. Cathy and I had wed a few months after David's death, it was my thinking that the whole family needed a life-affirming thing and our wedding would be it. It didn't go as planned. My dear sweet mother is buried at the head of her dear son David's grave; both are now at peace.

***

After the passing of my mom Cathy and I found we could steal away some late evening quiet time for just the two of us. I would crossdress and we would read books or play cards and enjoy each other's company. For a few precious hours I felt close to being a real person not a contradiction of my self-image, but it was just a band-aid; the real world was always just a few hours away. We borrowed the book *Conundrum* by Jan Morris; it came to our mailbox from the library wrapped clandestinely in plain brown paper. I read it first then Cathy had her turn. Cathy told me afterward if I wanted to change gender as Jan Morris had done she would understand and support our continued relationship. It was actually very settling to us both since our love was out in the open for both of us by way of our confessions to each other. "I love you as you are, in whatever form you are, it doesn't make a difference," Cathy assured me. Along came rearing our two beautiful children, my work career in electronics, many activities with Cathy's parents and her grandmother Freda. Our family world is built on being together; I swore never to do as my father had done. We had Saturday night games at our house, apple cider making in the fall at the orchard (before it was sold in the late 1980s), camping, car-trips across the country to see far flung relatives, school sports, extended family picnics, horseback riding, and museum trips. We took pains to show our kids the rural side of the mountains, the orchards and ranches that we both grew up with. Cathy and I took 9 year-old Casey and 7 year-old Corey to the livestock auction in Ellensburg that Grandpa Charley frequented for years. We sat in the very back of the arena and Cathy admonished the kids to sit on their hands lest we go home with a calf or horse. The kids got to hear the sounds and smell the scents of the place I knew as a child. Casey and Corey got to pick cherries in the orchard, as had all of the Dixon children. The two boys had a little fruit stand in our front yard and sold the cherries. And most importantly our family life was filled with humor and laughter as a bulkhead against heartbreak.

My greatest joy in life was to come home after work to Cathy, Casey, and Corey. No one would have really understood my affliction I thought, so as long as our kids and Cathy do well in life I don't mind diminishing, after all, I took a lot from my family when I was young, time to repay the debt. My gender conflict was even a factor in the naming of our kids. We wanted names that could follow them into either male or female roles if my experience fell upon them. Cathy's and my philosophy was to do everything possible to help our sons' education experiences, right down to cross-gender specific play experiences. We squeezed all we could from the public school system by participating every chance we were given as parents and then some. Cathy volunteered in the classrooms; this eventually led to an actual part-time position as a school employee working in the library and becoming an academic coach. Our house was full of textbooks that Cathy would find as she scoured school book-sales for educator sample sets of instruction books. We considered them a treasure, especially the teacher additions of math books. There was no roadmap for what we put together, it was all outlandishly outside-of-the-box of our time parenting. Casey and Corin responded in kind they seem to be up for all that was put before them, both are empathetic, loyal, and open-minded. They both did High School sports along with all the academics during the school year and summer also. Our sons and Cathy did do well; better than I could ever have hoped for. Sailing through school with the boys jumping grade levels until the three of them (mom and the two sons) graduated from Highline Community College (HCC) with a two-year degree (Associate of Arts with emphasis in Mathematics) all at the same time (Corin at age 16 graduating HCC one day before his high school graduation). That graduation night at HCC was a surreal affair with our local television news stations covering the unique angle of a mom and sons graduating together. The College was suddenly embracing them with open arms, when in fact, it had been an uphill battle for us to meet all the barriers the College put before us to allow Casey and Corin to attend there. Because of Cathy and my persistence Casey and Corin became some of the very first Running Start secondary school students to attend classes at Highline College at night while still enrolled in High School during the day. Then onto the University of Washington years: Cathy earns her BS with a minor in mathematics, Casey earns his BS/MS in computer engineering and Corin earns his BS/MS/PhD in computer science and engineering. They were all three bright engineering students and math wizards. There were no words to describe how proud I was of my little family. They were all I ever wanted to be and in that I am content or so I thought. My gender conflict never left me; in my loneliness I would sometimes crossdress in the evenings while the house was still and empty only to throw the clothes away promising myself never to do such a thing again. Why do I keep doing this when God has given me so much? Why would I ever do anything that had the potential to hurt my precious little family? They are not suffering as I had during my childhood and that should be enough for me. It must be enough for me. I have Cathy who loves me and I her, I will be a good husband for her, I will. I fold up my female persona and push her far back on a shelf to gather dust and soldier on. For years my gender conflict as a subject falls silent to myself and to Cathy.

223

Then it happens, Cathy begins a career at Microsoft, our sons leave home to pursue their own lives, my eighteen year career (one that I felt very fruitful in and that brought two patents from my little brain) in electronics as an engineering technician comes to a complete crashing end, then my father dies after I cared for him during his two months in hospice. The house I had helped design and build for Casey was completed, Cathy's father's health seriously falters, and I turn 50 years old. I am adrift and feelings that I have long been suppressed explode forcefully outward. Is it possible that the family obligations that I have set aside any gender congruence for, are no longer the impenetrable barrier they once were? I haven't crossdressed for many years making that sacrifice as payment for becoming a rock that our sons can always hold onto as they kick-off into adulthood; something I never had. Now though, the need to be myself on the outside is driving beyond any crossdressing Band-Aid I had held onto to from the past, leaving me with only the loud demand to have my body physically and properly changed. The conflict gets louder and louder way beyond anything I had experienced before and at age 51 (May/June 2005) I cry to Cathy for help, "What is happening to me?" I figured that since I had been playing the role of a man for this long I could just keep doing it until a merciful death found me, my sacrifice was just that a sacrifice in payment for the tremendous blessing of my family. All of a sudden I can't stand the thought of dying as a man, of staying something I am not any longer. Being transgender is something you hide, there is no general acceptance I've known this since my childhood. It was a hard lesson to learn then and I felt grateful this information was gained without violence toward me. What I am being driven to do now could bring disgrace and physical harm, yet I can't turn away from my conflict either. Cathy isn't happy and in tears tells me, "Nothing will ever be the same!" She shouts, "I couldn't even be with you!" I hadn't expected this response in any way, shape, or form, it was a lightning strike to me. My heart fell to my feet and the world closed in on me. We had our talk, our understanding, so long ago before getting married, about me, about this... I had always thought we were okay about this... I had always told myself Cathy's

224

got my back; it was how I had made it this far in life male-imaged. Now what? I am torn in half, can't go back, can't go forward, and can't even stay here and now. Perhaps I can hold on a little longer as I have always done. We claw a tattered normalcy out of a lightning strike and continue on.

Photo Interlude

Photos of the ranch, where Cady spent much of her childhood.

Orchard in Quincy, where Cathy spent much of her childhood. Cathy, Corin, and Casey as college graduates.

2005

Cady finds the very beginning threads of solace from the crisis of gender dysphoria by starting a personal journal in 2005. It becomes the deepest dive taken into understanding a lifetime of discord and a desperate attempt at surviving that life to its natural end.

So go ahead, read this part of my journal, it is the raw picture of a person who is transgender coming to terms late in life. It became my memory of daily events and most importantly it was my tool to share with my therapist to tell her my story in hopes of understanding it myself. It is a very intimate look at Cathy and Cady lifting the veil of privacy in some ways this is a risk but the benefit will be sharing that we stayed together; we found a loving way to be who we both truly are during and after transition. Read on curious reader read on...

August 2005. After all my phone calls to scary therapists there is no question that Sandy Fosshage is the right person for us; all that remains is to meet her in person. The day of my free first therapy visit with Sandy does come. Cathy will just sit in the van and work on her scrapbook of our recent trip to Victoria BC while I bare my soul to a stranger. I know that both Cathy and I have high hopes for this person, fingers crossed, and prayers to God. Just as I reach the old Craftsman style farmhouse that now serves as a little professional building standing stoically between a modern church and a new sleek apartment complex, the front door opens, and a short thin woman in her very early sixties says, "Hello" and asks if I am C----? My simple answer is, that I am. We shake hands; she leads me up a creaky dark stained wood stairway and into a converted office at the end of the dimly lit upstairs hall. The room still has a bedroom feel to it with two ancient double hung windows on the gable wall. I am aimed toward an antique high-armed couch directly across from a single high-armed chair. She takes her place in the chair notepad in hand. Sandy has steel blue eyes near the same shade of Cathy's eyes, short grey hair, a half smirk smile that you can only interpret as she is continually sharing a personal funny joke with herself, and is wearing a sweatshirt and jeans. She speaks better in person than on the phone and her casual caring demeanor quickly makes me feel comfortable in trusting her. I have brought along a write-up from my journal, which covers my childhood, a narrative that seems to have pointed me in the way of needing therapy. I wrote it with the hope of someone reading it someday and hopefully she will be the person. Her fee is $60 per session, which is a pleasant surprise as they can range up to $130 per 60-minute session (2005 prices). She asks about me in direct ways. Luckily, since I have done my write-up many of the facts are fresh in my mind. I do so need to talk to someone, until now I didn't know just how much. I react to each of her questions, instead of pondering them until the answer is no longer honest. "What brought you to me?" Sandy asked. I answered. The world conspired against me. It comes from series of events, because of a diet of soy protein forming into estrogen that began to affect my body, me turning 50, and family commitments waning, my female side has gotten very loud. I didn't present anything like female standing there in front of Sandy when we first met, wearing male clothes and raincoat. I still had part of my male beard around my mouth and my hair was short. I was truly desperate. I needed her to believe me, even though I didn't see why she would at that moment based on what I looked like. I so needed help to find a way through the crisis that was exploding within myself. I made a foolish statement; I want you to help cure me of this driving feeling I have to be female. Years later, I would understand its foolishness. Sandy in her wisdom and looking somewhat dubiously at me said quietly, "Okay, let's just see what comes as we go along." Sandy does know many other folks traveling along this line and asks the pertinent question, "If you didn't have any strings attached and everything was going to turn out fine in the end, who would be standing here in front of me right now?" Without thinking and to my own surprise I said, a middle-aged woman. Did I really say that!? Oh my, I am messed up. What brought me to reason that I was transsexual? I told Sandy my story of discovery when I was 9 years old leading me to understand that I was a girl inside. She asked in an even tone, "Did you crossdress?" Yes, but that was some time ago. Things are just spilling out of me at this point. She wanted to know if I had ever used a feminine name and I said for a short time I was Sheila, but only for a short time. I told her I like the 'she' part in that name. Sandy thought that was neat. I also told her that I folded Sheila up and put her away on a shelf to rear our sons. Sandy asks, "How did Sheila feel about that, not that you were two different persons." I told Sandy, yes I am only one person but existentially I thought Sheila understood the sacrifice in return for how well our sons and Cathy were doing in life and in a way I got to mother all three of them for a while.

In my mind, I can't believe what I am saying! My self-promise was to be totally honest, not hold back, and to just say whatever came to mind at that moment. I am doing just that. We talk about gender and how it is not always what is displayed on the outside. She tells me that she herself is a lesbian. Oh my. Sandy asks about Cathy and me. I tell her that I was honest with Cathy, telling her about me before we married. But, I don't think either of us fully understood the immensity of what I was saying. Cathy and I were such soul mates nothing else seemed to matter. We had so many things in common, one being the Eastern Washington farm towns of Thorp and Quincy; upon hearing this Sandy told me she was reared in Yakima. We swap stories about having to be careful in very conservative farming towns to keep bad things from happening to you. I ask about couples' therapy and we talk on how that might be accomplished. In the end, my free 30 minute talk ran to 45 minutes, and would have run longer if Sandy didn't have an appointment right after me. Sandy tells me again about her fee and gives me the number to open the front door lock for next time. I make an appointment for two weeks from now on November 5th, really too far in the future for me but Sandy will be out of town until then. She tells me she would like to help me on my journey for as far as we both will go and that she likes to play the devil's advocate but not too hard.

I leave my write-up with her to read. Okay, I am suddenly both tired and relieved at the same time. The next hard part will be downloading to Cathy in the appropriate manner.

We talk on the way home, Cathy is curious, somewhat suspicious, and concerned. Actually, just as I would have been if I were in her place. We will intensely discuss all about the whole problem again. Cathy doesn't see any support for her in this, and she is so very correct. She has fear that a therapist will somehow blame her for not letting me overcome this problem sooner. This is unfounded, since I was the one to wait until now. Anyway, this last part is just her hurting internally and I want so much to take that pain away. I have a deep abiding faith in Cathy and still haven't given up on the conversations we had together before marriage or after reading the book *Conundrum* by Jan Morris in 1976. Cathy is still that understanding and accepting woman inside; she is frightened, but the love of my life won't leave me, I know she won't…

***

Saturday December 10, 2005, and morning is suddenly here. We sleep in until 9:00; I turn and toss before getting up. We have to leave just after 10:00 to be at Sandy's office in plenty of time to pray before Cathy goes in. I finally bring up the subject of what Cathy might want to ask Sandy. Cathy has already thought about what she wants from the meeting. I add to her list that she can ask about the seriousness of the condition for both parties. It is time to leave, as we drive along I tell Cathy that I take old highway 99 to avoid the First Avenue Bridge, which just might be open and cause us to be late. We pass the Museum of Flight sporting two sleek fighter jets out front. I view these weapons as something hurtful that reminds us of what we shouldn't be in life, but are forced to all too often. So sad. Near Green Lake Cathy tries to help me navigate, but I tell her I have found a route that I can remember even if it is somewhat backtracking. Because of the divided roadway I drive past my turn off to a traffic light where I can make a U-turn. I find a park on a side street in front of the church next door to Sandy's office building. Cathy and I pray and we walk together toward

231

the old house that four therapists share as office space. I tease Cathy that now she is going to see a therapist, how yuppie! We climb the front stairs and I start to push the lock numbers when Sandy appears and opens the door. I'm a bit startled (I was hoping that we would sit in the waiting area for a few minutes) and make a quick introduction of Cathy to Sandy. They both send me packing and I walk back to the van all by myself. I pray, fret, and look at a Sunset magazine (an article about shopping in Ballard). My thoughts fly back and forth. I think of how I came to be in this spot of my life, and then try to visualize the most important woman in my life sitting on Sandy's couch in that little upstairs room. Will Sandy be kind to Cathy? Will Cathy accept Sandy? What will happen and how will it change everything or nothing at all? As the time passes, I think what if Cathy suddenly walks around the corner before the hour is up, leaving in a huff because of something Sandy said? I worry as each minute passes. I read in the Sunset magazine about trendy shops coming to fishy Ballard. It is only one hour, I think to myself, what could happen at a dollar a minute? Then all of a sudden a wispy silver-gray adorned smiling woman is walking toward me. It is like two minutes until 12:00. Cathy opens her door and looks at me, and tells me that we should go shopping. Okay, for what? For you, Sandy says that I need to take you shopping. I ask Cathy to tell me all about her session, "I like Sandy, she seems like a nice and knowledgeable person and she said I should take you shopping." I giggle and we drive toward home. Cathy tells me that Sandy suggested we shop for clothes for me that tend toward the androgynous side of things, which will let me express femininity while still maintaining some part of a male appearance. To give me some idea of just how her talk went with Sandy, Cathy now knows that there is a clerk at Nordstrom's that fits men for lingerie. Too much for me right now, I think. Right now as we drive I do feel so much better, Cathy and I are back together again. I am no longer doing something without it including her; my promise of this to myself is again kept. Seeing Sandy while greatly helpful to me was a separating action from Cathy for both of us. Cathy is on a little high right now having survived the Sandy trial. I know the feeling. This is Cathy's only solo meeting with Sandy. Sandy told us she would only do one. I am her client but we are always welcome to come as a couple.

Cadance & Catherine Anderson

2006

Saturday January 7, 2006. Cathy and I park right outside of the old converted farm house and chat for the few minutes before our appointment, just general stuff. We go inside so Cathy can use the restroom then sit in the waiting room. The magazines here today talk about 'Out and About Travel'. I never in my wildest dreams would have thought I would be sitting in the waiting room of a therapy practice filled with Gay Life and Travel magazines! A young noisy couple (man and woman) comes into the waiting room. I have often wondered what would happen if this occurred. Do you ask what they are in for? Sure… I do strike up some conversation about the old house just to diminish the tension of both of us being in the same room. We talk briefly, they are young and kind of at each other in a confrontational way most of the time. With great relief Sandy appears to spring us. We climb the stairs and find our places on her couch. After the greetings and little holiday stories it is down to business. I didn't know just what I needed to say before I got here this time, but stuff was spilling out, just not as coherent as I would have liked. Sandy asked the question of where we are right now in the gender issue and we generally explained the holidays sort of put it away for a time. I can't just put it away, but am happy to at least give others a break. I tried to tell Sandy that I had thought a lot about being transgender and had decided that indeed it was real. I really am this way, especially since I keep finding people on the forums that sound uncomfortably close to me. Sandy asked if this gives me some comfort to know that there are others? I say yes, to a great extent it does, but I also feel like I lose my personal identity from being grouped. She then asks if I do anything for just myself. An odd question; I am stumped because I

234

don't view anything I do as just for myself. Even as I write this, it is with the idea that it will be of value for some of the family sometime in the future. I am at a loss; Cathy pops up with my journal and that is close enough for me. It is really strange to be the center of what is being talked about, as both Sandy and Cathy seem to aim at me. It is like Cathy is outside of us I mean as a couple, just unnerving. It is also like being a kid again in the school office at a parent teacher meeting. Cathy and I do talk on the way back home. The whole thing has been pent up for three weeks and that it turns out was not a good thing.

***

Thursday September 7, 2006. Women seem to have a fascination with their men. He is like a painting that she has gazed at off and on all of her life until she knows most every detail and has stored them in her mind perfectly. She knows what to expect, but is still put out with some adverse reaction on his part even though she fully expected it. I think a woman yearns for an unexpected caring act from her man, something that opens a new facet unseen and enthralling. After thinking about this, I have this fascination with Cathy. Not very husband-like I know, but there it is. I know that a yes or no answer from her has to be interpreted correctly; case being, a 'no' that is slow to come or is drawn out actually means yes. Cathy lets experiences pass through her, then they are gone, and she is reset for the next one. Don't expect her to bask in any past experience they are gone in light of those coming tomorrow. I get put out at her reactions to emotional times for me even though I know this is what to expect. I will not be caressed or fondled physically in passing (sigh) and I do know this but I still miss it. Cathy will mentally caress me during the day by thinking of me and phoning to share something. Yet, I yearn for that unexpected intimate caring act and try to provide them for her. She fascinates me still. I touch her and I watch her trying to memorize the whole that makes up Cathy Dixon Anderson. Cathy is my painting that I gaze at, and in fascination I study day in and day out.

***

235

Friday September 8, 2006. I had my consultation at Caddell's Laser and Electrolysis clinic. The place is in a business building in Bellevue. Not a very welcoming warm fuzzy place at present. Marsha Morgan who is one of the operators is in her mid to late fifties and nice enough. She explained how the hair is killed by the laser (heat travels down the shaft and destroys the cells at the base) and didn't ask me why I wanted permanent hair removal on my face. I told Marsha that I wished I was younger and had more pigment since the laser doesn't work on white or grey hairs, she said she wished the same thing for herself. They use the GentleLase Plus machine by Candela with the cooling spray. The cost from Caddell's is $300 for the first three sessions then $200 for the next two and $100 thereafter. I asked Marsha if she could do a test shot so I could feel just how much it hurt. Sure, in fact she did three after she took my picture. There is the slight smell of burnt hair and a sting like a ring of needles suddenly poked into your face. The common word picture is a rubber band snapping against your face. Your eyes are covered, so you can't see and I find myself tensing as I guessed what was coming. It does hurt and having my entire face done will be an experience to say the least. Marsha just started up and if I had asked her to would have done my entire face right then and there.

***

Monday September 19, 2006. I got myself over to my first laser appointment for removing my beard. Cathy called me to wish me luck. I had decided that Marsha Morgan the nice late 50 to early 60's year old lady at Caddell's Laser & Electrolysis would be who I trusted to help me. Marsha has been doing electrolysis for folks for the last 20 plus years and two years ago got her Laser training. Caddell's has a GentleLase Plus machine and having done research, it is the one that seems to be the correct pick for my Fitzpatrick skin type of 2 to 3. The GentleLase Plus by Candela is an Alexandrite laser lasing at 755 nm and precedes each laser shot by spraying a cryo-liquid onto the skin milliseconds before the laser shoots. The liquid instantly cools/freezes the skin and the laser instantly heats to, well, very hot; in theory

236

between the two extremes the pain should be tolerable. So now my head is just spinning with excitement and fear. I have an appointment with my therapist Sandy Fosshage tomorrow and this could be really something to talk about! I had put together a plan; I have a tube of aloe along with several cold packs in our thermo picnic bag so if I need cold I'll have it. This makes me feel a little calmer but not all that much. I have felt so blue and depressed that I thought if I made myself do something extreme like this it would shake me a bit. It isn't that I want to die but I just can't see how I can keep living sort of thing.

On the way, I had said a little prayer as to the pain involved and about doing this at all. I have gone over this in my mind many times. The extreme is there is no way I could ever go back to being the C---- of the last 32 years. The truth is, it is scary to close the door on anything, even if it is something that bothers you. It shakes your anchor of self-image a bit.

The central reception area of the office building Caddell's has space in has a black leather couch and a large work area behind their reception desk; big enough for several people to be filing, appointment making, or just recepting. All this space is empty and quiet except for one lone lady with a headset on. I tell her my name and she puts in a call to Marsha, then has me sign in on a bleak looking clipboard. Before I really finish my name on the official clipboard and have time to jump fully into the anxiety of the moment, Marsha appears and calls out my name. She is standing at the mouth of a long hallway leading toward a little room full of humming laser equipment. I follow her at a trot; Marsha is one fast walking person! Trying to catch up to my lab coated laser operator, I haven't had time to fall back into fear. But this respite is about to come to an end. Fear and excitement swirls around in the damp basin of my current depression distracting it somewhat into abating for the moment. The dark pressure lessens and while I don't feel better, neither do I feel as bad. Marsha directs me to lie on the white terrycloth-spread treatment table. We chat briefly about our grandchildren and then she hands me a tiny set of dark glasses with a rubbery band to go around my head. The glasses are the type used on tanning beds, these let no light through at all. They have a black band across the nosepiece with white rubber top and bottom to seal against your skin. I shut my eyes tightly, just to be on the safe side. I remind Marsha that I want my entire beard gone, even the sideburns. I also ask about the meaning of numbers she was repeating to herself as she poked at the machine's control display. She replies that 18 is the spot size in millimeters for the laser shot (near a quarter in diameter, this I know is adjustable to 12, 15, 18mm from the web) and 14 is the number of joules per shot (adjustable from 10 to 50 joules inversely proportional to spot size). I have some idea of what to expect from the three test shots of a week ago and from reading about people's experiences on a forum about laser hair removal, but really don't know for sure given the much greater number of shots over the larger area to be treated. I lay blinded and listen intensely. The machine has a handpiece that includes a waveguide and coolant line. Marsha, who is shielded by protective glasses that excludes the laser wavelength, holds the handpiece in one hand and a ¾ inch vacuum hose to remove the burnt hair smell into a smoke evacuator in her other hand. The thing sounds very pneumatic something like the dentist office does when you are having a tooth drilled and they are sucking away the cooling water. Marsha pushes the business end of the handpiece against my sideburn pulls a trigger and snap! A flash of bright light burst into my eyes from behind my eyelids. Very unnerving! The laser is stimulating my optic nerve through my skin and muscles of my face! Just a millisecond ahead of the snap I felt a cold sensation on the skin under the hand piece. This would be the cryo-spray. After the flash comes the pain. I had thought it would be like a ring of needles stabbing my skin, but the classic rubber band snap against the face is closer. This rubber band is stretched far from your face as it can get and really hits with a snapping burn. I have learned from physical therapy that if I can keep from tensing during the pain infliction I am better off. But it is all that I can do to keep from flinching after each shot or anticipating the next as I felt the pressure of the thing against my face. The vacuum sound is continuous, I am glad of this since it does help with the smell and I do catch the smell of burning hair from time to time (more than yuk). I remember that smell from branding cattle during my youth (something I would like to forget actually). Marsha works in a flowing matter from down the side of the face toward the jaw. She holds her finger against each spot right after the laser shot then sometimes zaps the area again. By the time she gets to my jaw on one side I have made up my mind not to do this again, and maybe even stop right now! A rhythm forms there is the constant sound of the vacuum, then pressure on the skin, an annunciator beep, a pneumatic sound, cold, zap and burning heat. The beep must signal that the machine has a full charge and can be triggered again. This is evil because the sensory chain of pressure, sound, and feeling lets me anticipate what is going to happen next. Marsha finishes the less painful places on my face leaving the worst places to go. She checks in with me to see if I want to continue and I do; it both surprises me and strengthens me. These are the areas around my mouth, under my chin, lower neck, and under the jaw from ear to ear. Hurt, hurt, and extra hurt! I have to fight not to moan or jerk, I lose out when she does under my chin. I felt like I was being burnt and poked at the same time. Marsha was soothing to me saying, "I know how bad these areas hurt, you're doing great!" I tried to remain relaxed all that I can, but this is the hardest hurt I have ever felt that I willingly had done to myself. Zap and the bright light would now flood my eyes despite the metal shields of the goggles, another in the same place, and I would wilt inside. I try negotiating with myself, pretty soon it will be over and you will never have to do it again, and it is such a big thing to tell Sandy about in our next session! Zap! Now she is doing the mouth area aaaarrrrggghhh! The vacuum is turned off so she can move the hand piece carefully across my upper lip. I have to stop breathing to keep the smell away. Marsha tells me to hold my breath until after the zap then breath out through your nose. A little feminine voice drifts into my mind, it's one that I had not heard before she began to speak to me. 'Just think how nice it will be not to have that hair anymore; so very long ago you hated it, and tried to pull each one out as they appeared each morning, only to give up because of the pain. Now this pain is going to be better, because you're going to succeed; you can stand it, we can stand it.' Beep zap; beep zap, then silence as Marsha looks over her work. One more zap right on the chin and it is over. Soothing cold as Marsha rubs cold aloe on my face then removes my eye protection. What relief to be done! "There you go my dear!" Marsha tells me with a big smile. I sit up; my face is warm but not red hot. Marsha tells me that in about a week the hair should start to fall out of my face and in 4 to 6 weeks I'll need another treatment. I pay with a credit card and make another appointment 6 weeks from now. I tell her by then maybe I'll forget the pain. "It is just like childbirth, you wouldn't have another baby if you didn't forget the pain of the first!" She tells me with a laugh. I leave feeling sore and lightheaded from the laser and the fact that I really did this!!! Out in the car I open up my ice bag, get the cold aloe, and smear it on my face, it feels so good! The aloe seems to melt into my skin and in about ten minutes I am really for more. I start the car and turn the cooler on aimed right at my face; this really helps! I get goosebumps as the memory of the pain comes to the surface of my thoughts. I drive the back way through Bellevue to Microsoft campus to pick Cathy up at building 31. Most of the time Cathy will carpool with our son Casey who works in a different group at Microsoft. I call ahead and only have to wait a short time until she shows. As I wait I use more of the nice cold aloe cream. Cathy is excited that I did the laser treatment! Of all things! She tells me that she is proud of me! The pain was almost worth hearing this alone! We have a dance class tonight and I think I can go. My face is warm to the touch but the aloe is great in reducing the heat. Cathy is bubbly; I have finally done something instead of just mope in depression! I am afraid that the depression of the last few weeks hasn't let go all that much because of this, but it is so good to have her proud of me. We have our dance class, just one other couple and us, so we have lots of attention! Cathy is careful of my face and the secret we both share of why.

***

Friday November 3, 2006. Funny thing about what happens when your cat hides your office keys, you end up giving therapy in a van. Sandy couldn't find her office keys so I said, let's just sit in my van and talk. I have never had a bad session with her, but some are more or less just a rehash. This was a rehash as I keep wondering what the long hair and laser appointments are leading me to. Sandy suggested the Emerald City Transgender Social Club might be worth a visit. I looked them up and I don't think so… There is a lot of sorting out to do and I just don't see it in the future, but I really do have to find some sort of balance to have a future at all. And I don't see myself as a CD (crossdresser) person living by costume for a short time, then returning to the male world.

2007

Thursday August 30, 2007. I have not found any transsexual person (MtF) whose life hasn't lost all the safety of family, marriage, and love that they had before they took the action to remove the GID (gender identity disorder) pressure. I haven't found any person of strong Christian faith or wives that still love their transgender husbands after he takes actions to become more like her. It is true I only know of the people on Susan's place forum and the fact that they post for the world to see makes them much different from me, but they are all I have. I feel so alone and slipping toward a dark hole toward losing everything.

***

Tuesday September 4, 2007. I saw Dr. Marsden today; the office was quiet and peaceful so I decided to tell her all about me keeping it condensed as much as possible, a sort of Reader's Digest version. Dr. Marsden is not at all up on transgender people, as she has none as patients in her practice to treat so it is up to me to lay the groundwork. It is funny, as I was waiting I heard her refer another lady to a specialist saying that was outside her practice and if she knew all about the problem then she would be the specialist! Dr. Marsden came into room one, closed the door, sat down on her little wheeled stool, and listened while I admitted to having GID; I then had to explain what GID was! This is not unheard of; many other folks have to work with their physician to learn together. Once she understood and I had noticed she hadn't pushed her stool any further away from me and in fact wheeled a little closer, I told my story taking care to get clear my mother and father's place in it. Adding that I found a therapist I could trust and have been trying to do little things to bring the feminine parts into my life mainstream. I have removed (still have much to go) my male beard, worked on my voice, and let my hair grow out softly. This has helped along with Effexor but not enough. I have come to the painful realization that I must face the hormone question. (This is the great divider currently, the door leading to truth of facing just who you really are. People in care many times are put on HRT right away using it as a weeding out step; if you like what is going on with body changes, it is pretty positive indicator of being transgender, if you panic at the changes you can stop and have some assurance at where you stand gender wise.) I answered the few questions Dr. Marsden had about my story and she then said, "Where does that leave us? What is it that we need to do today?" I told her I think HRT is needed, as does my therapist, it will answer the question of how far I need to go to find some peace so that my life can continue. I then stood up to leave and Dr. Marsden came over and gave me a hug!

***

Tuesday October 23, 2007. Saw Marsha Moyer Morgan at her electrolysis clinic in Redmond to do my face. Thermo or flash electrolysis is less painful than the blend. Marsha also uses Teflon coated probes that you purchase ($25) from her and bring with you each time. The Teflon coating helps the thin needle probe to slip down the hair follicle with minimum pain. Marsha zaps the follicle in three places, at the bulb's bottom's blood supply, the nerve just above, and near another blood supply above the nerve. You can feel the heat/pain each time she does a hair. Marsha does work smoother and faster than Barbara Neumayer (consulted her a week ago) and I didn't notice Marsha removing the hair each time where with Barbara I could feel a painful pull. Thermo will leave you with scabs; I had a little trickle of dried blood on my chin when I check in the mirror in the van, and the blend doesn't do this, it gives you raised welts. Barbara charges $60 per hour and Marsha charges $59 per hour, seems like this business is pretty competitive after all. Marsha told me that if I came each week for an hour I should see a dramatic change in three months (12 treatment hours). The downside to Marsha is distance/traffic, so I can't get numb by Dr. Ken effectively and she only takes checks or cash. Barbara does take every credit card made, is close so Dr. Ken could effectively numb me for her. I think Marsha is definitely faster but I don't know if thermo is as effective as the blend so everything is a toss-up. I have come to trust Marsha from our laser treatments together. She is sincerely competent, honest, and caring. I think I will start with Marsha for electrolysis this next week and see how it goes for several appointments.

***

Thursday November 1, 2007. Well, am much better now that I have had a good solid 30-minute session of electrolysis under my belt. The burning wasn't unbearable and if Marsha had the time I would have done another 30 minutes! The area she did is so nice and clear, I can't put into words the relief this brings. I want more much more! I have dreamed about being clean-faced since the curse started around age 13. Funny how doing something affirming like this turns around my mood so dramatically and not doing the right thing drags me down even faster. With the sharp pain of each needle poke followed by the quick wave of intense heat I rejoiced that a hair was gone forever. Electrolysis is something that works on all the hairs whether dark or light and I have someone to fix my face permanently! The downside is length of time to do it and the cost. For now, I will simply be happy starting electrolysis.

***

Friday November 2, 2007. I really am looking forward to my next electrolysis session on this Tuesday. Cathy had a very nice facial with Mary at Caddell's last night and she also got to meet Marsha!

***

Friday November 30, 2007. I have officially started HRT (Hormone Replacement Therapy) I use one .1mg estradiol patch twice a week. This year has been so tough on both Cathy and me. Mix in all the work pressures she is going thought at MS along with all the changes I am physically going through. Adding to this turmoil, we haven't taken the time to really talk about what we are both going through. Got to do better...

2008

Monday February 11, 2008. My last shaving day was Saturday and it is no fun to go without shaving until after my Tuesday electrolysis visit with Marsha. It takes so long to remove the little mean hairs and so much money. At the moment I have right around $900 in electrolysis and at least twice that in laser cost. Man, I wonder if I am worth such a price. My breasts hurt all the time, all around the nipple area; my male parts are very quiet and have shrunk to half their size of a year ago. I still rattle around in this box of thoughts as to stopping HRT and knowing full well that I can't. It is one of those can't go forward or retreat. Can't give to Cathy what I used to and can't fathom gender anymore. I watch women in their roles and men in theirs only to feel as much or more removed than before. This has gone beyond feeling female inside to being overwhelmed by gender itself. I thought that if I started talking to a therapist about my past and this odd feeling of being wrong, I would get better, the dysphoria would disappear; it didn't seem to work all that well. I mean, there was great relief in voicing all this stuff with someone who knows what is going on, but it wasn't enough. Then I thought voice lessons and beard (I don't like this word, I prefer hair) removal would help and they did but still things are not right. I started on anti-depressant meds and couldn't stand each one offered until out of desperation, I forced myself to stay on Effexor only to lose how my thoughts used to be formed. I played my big card in hopes that magic would occur and started on medium dose HRT with Avodart as a suppresser. After three months I do feel different, but I don't really see any light at the end of the tunnel from here. There is pain, pain in HRT, pain in laser, pain in electrolysis, pain in addiction to Effexor and sadness in life. This is really awful of

245

me to be in this hole of my own making, but it is so hard to climb out. The more I try the more I realize I have been in this hole most of my life, to the extent that I don't know or can't fathom anything different. This can only lead to me never being any different than I have ever been. I think the answer at this point, other than taking my own life, is to give all this stuff time to work. In other words, just hang in for another year and see what becomes of me. I am God's child just as we all are and my path is set by Him; I do pray that He will give me strength to go where He leads. I love our sons so much, and what hurts me are the problems Casey and Mindy have in life, or how the world will be for Colby and B----, or any difficulties Corey and Melinda face together. This looks like meddling in their lives from the outside and I know this, but I just want so desperately to help sometimes. Yes, I know it isn't my place… I guess my color vision is fading, I am seeing the world only in dull shades of gray, mean, hard, and dying. Again, this comes back to holding myself together until I see what God may do with me, for in the end pleasing God in some way is all I can really ask for or want in life.

***

Tuesday February 19, 2008. Going along with the need to do what I am doing… I just can't image undoing anything that I have done so far but the size of what has happened shakes me sometimes. I continue to ponder the place women have in the world walking beside their men, mothering children, and just being so vulnerable the whole time. I ask myself is this me? Is this what I am? It is so hard to see myself living here, a lot like being a misshaped puzzle piece looking at a very square or round hole. I wonder how other women do it and realize that they simply have never done otherwise, like asking a man who is blind from birth what it's like not to see. I ponder men's place in the world, leading their women along as the woman guides from a half step behind him, and know that that is not my place either.

***

Tuesday March 18, 2008. Two more hours of electrolysis down; I am now at twenty-nine- and one-half hours total. I have been on HRT for close to four months now (I started one .1 patch twice a week on November 30th 2007). I haven't checked my blood levels for four months so it might be time again. Things I have noticed are nipple soreness (like a bruise would be), very little activity from my penis, softer skin, slower beard growth, and less body smell. I started electrolysis on November 9th 2007 and Marsha is now working around my mouth and chin area. I have upped my estrogen dose to one .1 patch and one .05 patch at one time twice weekly. I did this because the soreness in my breasts was fading away and somewhere deep down inside me I panicked thinking this was a sign that estrogen had done all that this was going to do. I had three .05 patches left so I added them to my .1 dose. The soreness returned in two days and along with this a swirl of thoughts about this whole thing. I seem to think on a high level and act on a much lower primal level. I argue with myself trying to find reason, cause, and effect while, in the end, acting purely on some basic primal need. What I mean to say is while I am waffling back and forth something deep inside me is sure of what is needed. I still am in a conversation with myself over just what I am going to do with this HRT treatment while right now I grant I do need to be on it. There is no addition, just a hope, as I go along that things will become clear up high in my mind. I spoke to Sandy about increasing the dose and got the turn-the-table-around answer of how I felt about it and at the same time a small note of encouragement to do so. Transgender folks talk about the family and friends they have lost addressing GID but what is not talked about is the life you lose to it. All of my life I have been haunted by it and as I reflect back, the startling thing I see is what of me I have lost. I see as the mist begins to thin on the picture of my life, all the fear that directed each movement of each day I made. I was afraid of so many things that life was a kind of a nightmare to get through each day. This was so wrong, so sad, and I am in no way over this, although I can start to see what was happening then. I was leading a life ruled by fear of life; I feared travel, work, child rearing, car breakdowns, being left helpless, or forced to do something, in short, I feared almost everything. I now wonder if GID was at the root of this along with the few childhood difficulties I had. I have never really actuated in life nor have I ever been comfortable that I could have in anyway. Could GID have done this over time and how in the world could it ever be undone? How would I even know if it had? At the moment, what I look forward to is just marking out time before I die. I wonder where all this is leading me?

***

Friday April 25, 2008. It is very hard to explain the sense of doing something wonderful for yourself that I have right now. It is a mix of finally removing a lifelong irritation and finding a treasure underneath. Today the burnt smell is gone and the skin is not as stubbly, but it will still take several days for the dead hairs to fall away. I look forward to it and it feels so good to know under my shirt I am as I should be… Makes me feel good about the path I am taking.

***

Thursday July 31, 2008. As a pre-teen I read the Bible and in Deuteronomy 22:5 my heart broke. I was drawn to these things and here in plain words I was an abomination to God, no way around it… As years went by, I was drawn further into the fantasy and dress of being a girl, reaching for this forbidden fruit, and this verse would haunt me more and more. I dreamed about not having testicles through some accident and came across Deuteronomy 23:1 and added the two verses together and felt terrible about myself. The Bible is the word of God both old and new; you can't dismiss one or the other is what I was always told and believed. I was trapped, no matter what I did, I always had a longing to be physically female and biblically doing something in your heart is the same as doing it physically. I watched as Christ brought Cathy's life and my life together, answering our needs, giving us wonderful children, and good health; all the while I had this blackness in me. I came to the thought that as long as I didn't do anything beyond some small amount (I gave into) I was at least trying to be as God would have me be. I would not be a stumbling block to my family. I thought God made me this way so I would grow stronger, and in doing so, help someone else in some time to come, so holding it at bay was okay. Now I have done much more and the ghost

248

words of long ago twist me in unceasing torment. I have chemically damaged my healthy testicles and wear ladies' jeans every day. More and more I hear about the wrongness of this on Christian/Catholic radio and my old fears are multiplied hundredfold. Am I damned or not? The idea of having the temptation placed before me of choosing one or the other is frightening to say the least. I need to face this whole question and understand if it is a trial God has put before me. A trial of life or death of my soul or is it something else... I spoke about this with Sandy in a tentative way. In a way I felt childish that I hadn't worked it out for myself, but I needed to voice the fears I had to someone before I could think them through. And I feel small speaking to Sandy sometimes; she has so much wisdom from her experience with so many people that it overwhelms me. She is so good that most of the time I feel I am offering her something new; silly me I wasn't. After I was able to get out the root of my fears, then she rattled off all I was thinking; "You fear being used by the evil one, going against God, etc." I didn't tell her another thing that I really needed to hear was that she was a Christian; somewhere deep inside of me I truly needed a kindred spirit. The weight that was lifted off me was huge and before the end of our talk I felt so much better! I can now start to face this roadblock to my faith. So what is my faith???

I believe that Jesus Christ was the true Son of God born to the Virgin Mary.

Jesus was God walking among us.

Jesus was the expected one of the Jews as called for by prophecy, but the Jews rejected Him as such leaving Him free to offer Himself to the entire world.

In suffering and death, Jesus free of sin, covered all of our sin debt so that we might dwell with God.

I believe that we are able to pray to God directly in Christ's name.

My faith is I believe in Jesus Christ, there is no way for me a sinner, to come to God except through the Christ.

I believe the Bible to be the words of God given to his creation.

I believe that the Holy Ghost enters your life after acceptance of Christ to guide you and teach you.

I also believe that Jesus Christ in His perfection fulfilled all the requirement of biblical law so that we who have faith in Him are free of that law, whose total fulfillment is required all during our earthy life for our souls to ascend to heaven. We are not free of the spirit of those laws, which Jesus summarizes the total to be in Matthew 22:37-40 as *" 'Love the Lord your God with all your heart and with all your soul and with all your mind.' This is the first and greatest commandment. And the second is like it: 'Love your neighbor as yourself.' All the law and the prophets hang on these two commandments."* In essence, this is what I have held onto to void Deuteronomy's hold over me if it is right to put it this way. And yet I have slipped, because of Christians of authority preaching the reverse on this subject. Am I free from the Old Testament laws after all? I am only free of them through my belief in Christ's purpose fulfilled and my resulting faith of relationship with Christ. This is what it comes down to. Everyone has a personal relationship with Jesus Christ each totally individual from everyone else (after all, God knows the very number of hairs on our heads). That relationship is guided by the Holy Ghost as promised in the book of John. So it is not legalism that guides us in our relationship but love of Christ. The Holy Ghost guides us in that love to follow the teaching of Christ in our own personal way by not looking at our own faults, but keeping our eyes on God's perfection. Still, even with all these words it is hard, because others will tell you they are right and you are broken... I will have to think about this much more before I am through.

***

Tuesday November 18, 2008. Another hour appointment with Marsha today. While she worked on my face, she told me, "I used to do transsexuals years ago when I was just getting started. I did a very sweet guy who was lots of fun as he changed from male to female her name was Marsha Botzer. She went on to be the head of an important organization and would screen clients to send to me. I didn't know just how much she was protecting me until I started getting transsexual clients from other places; some were very strange.

Marsha had me turn my head to the left. She continued, "Have you ever heard of her? Her hair cleared pretty quickly from treatment to treatment and she would say it was my expert work, but I think it was the hormones."

My heart skipped a beat. I know this name! Sandy works with but doesn't work for the Ingersoll Gender Center, which is the pioneering organization that was founded by Marsha Botzer in 1977. It is a broad group, which welcomes all forms of gender expression. They have support groups that Sandy has suggested to me but I'm not sure at this point.

Wow, I thought and began to twist inside, one half of me shouting for me to tell Marsha about being transgender, while the other half saying to just wait and find out more. So, what did you think of those folks generally? Marsha replied good-naturedly, "Well you do what you have to do in life. I don't have any trouble with people or make any judgments. As my appointment books filled up over the years, it was just simpler to limit my work to female clients only."

So, what I had cooked up in my mind was: I was being told by Marsha that she limited her client base to females and if a man wandered in she would only do his face. Suddenly I didn't want to be viewed as a man and I certainly didn't want any limitation on the area of my body being cleared of hair. I like Marsha in a friendly way and was also becoming more uncomfortable in this whole conversation being a male. Still, it is such a gamble to tell someone you are dependent on and consider a friend, even with positive feedback. I steady myself then fess up to Marsha, telling her I'm one of those people on hormones and added that she had probably already guess this.

Marsha was somewhat taken aback. "No, I hadn't. You mean you're on hormones?" Now the cats out of the bag and it is all play it by ear. Yes, I said quietly and I hope this doesn't lower your opinion of me. Of course, Marsha said no but there was tension for a few minutes after that, which I didn't know how to break. Marsha broke it with a question. "I have always been curious, it seems like as soon as a husband starts to transition, the wife packs up the kids and leaves." Poke, burn, pull, poke, burn, pull, she works away. Of all things to be curious about I think to myself. I told her that Cathy and I have been married for 34 years and I told Cathy before we married about this strange feeling I always had. We made it this far and I hope to continue for many years more. We went on to talk about how well-suited Cathy and I are together but the whole thing really tired me. We chatted about how an electrologist's office would make a great sitcom and Marsha did tell me if I ever meet Marsha Botzer to say hello for her but she would remember her by Marsha Moyer, her name then.

2009

Tuesday April 28, 2009. Cathy and I got to play grandparents this last Sunday. We picked up Colby and B---- in the morning and drove to Seahurst Park in Burien to visit the beach. It was a nice low tide (our luck!) and we all had rubber boots. I got to be a Boppa showing both Colby and B---- the magic of standing in a little creek in waterproof boots. I showed them the little places I had found special all of my life, where water flows under a bridge or a driftwood log, the dance of the water as it jumps over submerged rocks and the special sound it makes. I had B---- stand right at the saltwater's edge so the ocean could say 'hello' by lapping the toes of her boots. She pointed at each new thing and asked, "This?" I answered, revisiting a world I had almost forgotten. Cathy got to be a Nanna as she explains little crabs and kelp to Colby. He would repeat her words reverently. B----, at not quite 2, was wearing the little green sweater that Cathy had crocheted for our sons when they were the same the age B---- is now. The sweater fit little B---- perfectly and she loved the cat face on the back! So nice to pick up a little child and carry him or her as we walked the beach. Later, we all stopped at McDonalds for lunch. This is the first time it was just us and the grandkids.

***

Wednesday May 6, 2009. I had electrolysis with Marsha yesterday. My total hours are now at one hundred-seventeen and one-half hours. So let's figure out just how many pokes Marsha has done on me so far. If Marsha pokes and pulls one hair per minute and my total minute count is 7,050 (hours times minutes) then she has poked me 7,050 times. Marsha can easily do two or three times this rate so 14,100 to 21,150 pokes is closer to my real total!!! Each and every one of these pokes hurt, some so intense tears routinely ran down my face. I couldn't have possibly gone through this could I? Me, silly old me, no way, and yet I did... I question over and over in my mind as to whether or not this is just a phase that I am going through, while poking myself with 'I couldn't really be transgender.' Just as these questions travel through my mind over and over, something inside me (let's use she) marches right along unfazed past my defined safe areas, heading toward the unsafe ones (where conclusions lead to awakening facts). The first safe area she pushed me to was just learning gender terms (okay, kind of unsettling), then came therapy with Sandy (what could happen and I need someone to talk to), followed by herbs (not real meds, right), voice training (I just need to know if I could), hair (I've longed for it but dared not), laser (a little just to see what it's like), electrolysis (got to do it), HRT light (just to see for a week or two), and then HRT full (it's not really working or is it?). Looking

254

back, I don't think any of these areas were as safe as I thought at the time... I wish I were one of those really brave MtF folks I read about on the Susan's Place forums; the ones not looking side to side in a dither but with tunnel vision seeing straight forward. I am not one by nature of being me... Now, I must learn the language of dreams to understand just what God (perhaps a guardian angel) through my nocturnal meditative mind is trying to tell me.

In my dreams: I feel that the ranch house is no longer a safe place and belongs to other people whom I have no control over or standing with. My darkest fear is being abandoned alone and unable to care for myself. As I type this, my spirit is shaking at the realization of the naming of this fear. I have never been complete; something always was missing, a dichotomy of my soul if you will. Because of this I have always been separate from my fellow humans, hurt and alone. I guess we all are in some way. I thought I was a child of nature when my human family failed me. In seeking this, I walked in the hills and fields feeling that the very earth I walk on or sat on held me as its accepted kin. In turn, I listened to the breath of the world and the music therein. I ran my figures over old dry fence posts, touched rusty barbed wire and felt the vibrations the wind gave it. I lay on the damp grassy banks and watched the liquid world of the creek or ditch flow eternally by. Once, I lay on my back on a wooden plank bridge staring into the sky trying to be part of all there was around me, sort of thinning myself out into the air. I would sing to the creek and trees around me, but they didn't listen, they were eternal and I was just passing by; a thing unlike other things in the dusk of the day. Poor little thing, it thinks it can be part of us when it can't be part of the race of man. Still out of pity we will give it our care, our being, to remember, and to pine for... That is me I guess, lost between worlds between male and female between earth and mankind. I am tired, time is passing, I am changing, and there is that unknown. Can I exist without any part of me? I mean, am I becoming me or am I breaking into pieces? Is this what the dreams mean? I have only the smallest of clues at best. Boundaries are being set up inside me, but they haven't gotten around to telling me or I haven't accepted them yet. This is like revisiting the fearful time of an early teenager, to be hopeless, and alone. I don't know if I care to know what these dreams are telling me...

2010

Tuesday January 26, 2010. I babysat two days ago and got to experience so many little wonders from the little wonders. B---- came upstairs to find Boppa and Colby after her late morning rising only to have Colby hear his sister coming and go and hide from her. She looked at me with a questioning expression and said, "Dolby?" I told her to go and find him. She walked slowly around the room saying, "Dolby, Dolby Scott, Dolby Scott," in this little gentle voice so as if to lure him out of hiding. Colby popped up from his hiding place and B---- tackled him. So cute so wonderful to remember... Colby got to play Yahtzee with the big people at Grandma and Grandpa Dixon's house this last Saturday. He sat by me and I gave him a score sheet and told him to put his name on the name line. He took the pencil and with the most care and concentration printed his name!!! Those crooked beautiful letters, what a sight to see so proud a little boy (he is like three years and 9 months). What blessings grandchildren are to grandparents, it is a different experience than being a parent both are unique and rich.

***

Wednesday February 17, 2010. I babysat this last Monday Colby and B---- are so precious and I am learning so much from them. Colby loves playing the Wii with me (or anyone else) and I find myself in team play responding to him not as a three-year-old but as seven- or eight-year-old. Less as a pre-school child more as an understanding school kid. B---- teaches me to listen closely and be more discerning. She has reasons for her actions and in return I hope she is learning I too have reasons for my actions when I say "No" one minute, or "B---- stop." We played in the backyard for most of the day; it seems that this week's favorite thing to do is dig in the dirt! B---- loves this; she and the soil currently have a very close relationship, one that she has to be fully immersed in to fully enjoy. Colby and B---- both have scaled down shovels to dig with and soon they were bringing up earthworms to be fascinated with. B---- collected a worm family, mommy worm, daddy worm, and baby worm. I told Colby that birds sometimes hunt and eat worms so as soon as that was heard, the worm family had to go back underground! The kids dug a worm house and planted the family safe and sound! B---- is taking up her identity she asked if she was a girl? I said, "Yes and Colby is a boy." B---- tentatively accepted the girl for her but her Colby wasn't a boy he was her Colby!

***

Thursday August 19, 2010. August is the time of spiders their dusty webs are everywhere in a desperate bid for starving flying things. Sandy has been in my thoughts today… I can be very busy mowing lawns (all three today) but still the blackness creeps into my head. I don't know what to do about it; my tools to cope from Sandy's tool chest of advice help but don't put the fire out. I have got to get busy to push this away… Rest well and heal well from your surgery Sandy.

***

Monday September 13, 2010. I have been thinking of many justifications I have used to make it to this point in existence. I have been condensing and then stripping away layers to find the kernel of each. The excuses and distractions I have used are fading away crumbing as time eats them to dust. The ranch so important as a symbol of something real and lasting has been given another deathblow. We drove by it on our trip home from Eastern Washington. I stopped suddenly, just as our vehicle neared the creek that flowed through the ranch land. The dam was gone! The concrete irrigation dam put in place over a hundred years ago was completely removed… I felt so violated, so adrift, so powerless as I stood on the creek bank. Had I owned the ranch I could have never kept it whole I thought and it could never have kept me whole either. The water still flows in the ancient creek bed but never again will it flow gently through the irrigation ditches onto the grass fields bringing life.

2011

Thursday July 14, 2011. Had a very nice meeting with Sandy and got some good insights. Sandy also felt the personal discord in a couple's world that I have been struggling with. Day after day everywhere I look, it's a couple's world. Man and woman together moving as one unit through life, it is the one great rule that is so hard to accommodate. I love Cathy; I always have and always will. I am part of her and she me. I miss her while she is away at work and look forward to each evening together. The problem is the constant gender struggle cycling through my mind, it keeps me feeling out of place in this world. I believe Cathy and I were brought together by God I really do. That then leaves me with this struggle. If God gave me Cathy, and I believe it is so, then God gave me this gender struggle also... Package deal. So in my world it is all about an answer to the gender struggle, its validity, its purity, its charity, and its guiltlessness.

***

I have also been thinking what I think about. That is, how I focus in on the man and woman world. What's more, I focus in on the difficultly and pain in people I meet. I am always looking for clues on my state of being in the people I come across. Why do I have to look around externally and not into myself internally? I had a sudden thought: it is the reality of the world as it is that I can't mesh with! I'm at conflict with reality itself!!! Sure right... No, really! All of my life I have either directly been told or shown by observation what my correct place in life is. God, gender, and life. My literal knowledge of self as related to self and as self-related to others was constantly challenged. Moreover, my perception of God as loving and full of beauty was and is challenged externally, as I see all earthly creatures seemingly at war with each other resulting in a life of sorrow and pain. My self-knowledge is of a loving, unchanging God and is strongly rooted. My self-knowledge of gender is female, albeit battered through the years. I have learned to behave as someone else to match world reality, but I died a little each minute of each day from this external/internal discord, all the while not knowing the nature of the conflict within me. I will never mesh with reality; I can only get close on my learned/observational terms and then it will always be just out of reach. This is how reality is and it shouldn't change, as it is proper for the world to be as it is. Those of us out of mesh with this reality have the curse/gift of seeing reality as something that is external to our own. We then need to find some way to come along the side of external reality and make it a place for our true internal self-reality. A conflict with reality, sure sounds crazy, but on the other hand, this is just what is and is happening within my sad little brain.

***

Friday August 19, 2011. I feel much better but my brain is sore and the slightest conflict with anyone around me sets my stomach to hurting. I need to come up with a rigor of tapering off of this stuff. What was the reason for getting off of this again? Oh I remember; I had a suspicion it was having an effect on my sinus that I couldn't tolerate. Well, I might have to aim lower than just stopping Effexor altogether perhaps. A much lower dose is best to aim for… Hey, I just found a forum on the net about getting off of Effexor and its generic Venlafaxine! Not so encouraging for success. But at least what I am feeling, even the description of electric shock explosions by other people trying to beat it lets me know I am not alone… Today I am so grateful not to be so completely in pain while flooded by thoughts of dark mean death and hopeless life. It's hard to even describe being in such a pit yesterday both physically and mentally and having an uneasy relief today. Negative side: I am afraid of this medication just as I would be of the torture of both my mind and body. I am afraid of this medication because I am under its control. I am afraid of this medication because it shakes my mental foundations. Now on the positive side, it did help me when I desperately needed something… I think I have grown since then, thank you Sandy. So I will pursue the stopping of the war Effexor is waging on my brain and body. God help me.

***

Sunday October 23, 2011. Condensing the Effexor withdraw:

- April 2007 started Effexor (depression battle), one 37.5mg capsule per day.
- End of June 2007 doubled dose to two capsules (a normal dose per day)
- July 20, 2011 Four years later quit cold turkey lasted only 3½ days.
- July 24th Returned to only one 37.5mg capsule per day (half of normal dose).
- Sept 18th 57 days has now passed. Reduce to half of half or 18.75mg.
- Oct 7th 19 days on 18.75mg and will now go to 10mg (around).
- Oct 14th 7 days at 10mg, starting Effexor dose zero…

Looking back at my journal, I am surprised to see I had sinus reactions from the very start; they were subtle and ever increasing. I should have seen the handwriting on the wall… Right now, I have been at dose zero for nine days, withdrawal pains have been constant, but I have noticed in the last two days a change in emotions. I laugh out loud again, sometimes I can hold it in other times I can't. I also tear at sweet stuff or kindness. I guess the flatness of antidepressant high/low control is leaving me to feel in more of a full swing. My inner voice and outer voice match once again. I can now run music mentally and at the same time think more clearly.

***

Thursday October 27, 2011. I feel a little better with each passing day. My sinus is moist and the pressure/pain therein is all but gone!

My emotions are within check highs and lows, laughing or crying all expectable. It has now been 13 days at Effexor dose zero! The withdrawal pains are all but gone thank God! I am very nearly clean of this stuff and will never go back!

***

Thursday November 10, 2011. I had trouble praying last night; it was as if God wasn't accepting my prayers. My tears flowed at the rejection, the closed channel, the loss. Who was I to dress-down God even in hurt and anger? No one, that is who. Out of my pain and misery I shouted to God to hurt but that wasn't me. That wasn't C----. All my life I have tried to be a friend to God (how silly and little childlike). God was all I had; it wasn't in me to turn on God even in my deepest despair, even when my world was breaking into pieces. Who was I yesterday? What was I and why was my mind so muddled? I thought I was still me, but on the other hand I thought that part of me had died (of all things). This morning I awoke to brain zaps, the withdrawal pains that boom inside my head in groups of three, then pause and begin again. I also had throbbing pressure right between my eyes. Both of these had been the hallmark of Effexor withdrawal. I feel more myself this morning so was Effexor still having an effect on me even after 27 days? I think so and I worry how long these flash backs (if you allow the phase) will continue. Yesterday was not only troublesome but also terrifying in that I couldn't dismiss what was happening! I have asked God to forgive me but forgiving myself will take much more time. God forgives in a moment but I have failed myself in my own esteem, my own trust of me. I shook the only branch of my tree of life that I had carefully and lovingly protected so as to always have it to anchor to. It will be a long time before I am right in my own mind with God again… I am only just at the point of letting God forgive me and my prayers are only provisionally allowed to drift to God. I expect the provision is by me not God. When I allow that I was not in my right mind by the force of the Effexor flash back and accept God's forgiveness my prayers will again flow easily upward. Well C---- is back and (never really left I guess) my inner voice is bruised but unmuted. Effexor is mean, ugly stuff; it is humbling to understand its hold on your mind but trust in God who is bigger than all.

2012

Wednesday February 8, 2012. We are back from our little vacation to Canon Beach. We left flowers in the little cove (marked no beach access) below the Cape Disappointment Lighthouse, which sits high up on a cliff above. The tide seemed to flow out and wait for Cathy and me to creep to the water's edge and toss in our memorial flowers. They floated in the still of the moment then a wave suddenly took the little carnations to itself with a roar. A little up the trail I prayed aloud for us expressing our love, sadness, and hope for reunion one day. Lots of memories of Cathy's dad seem strong to us at that place, his resting place so to speak. Five months ago, the entire Dixon family together scattered Cathy's dad's ashes from a boat at N 46° 16.432, W 124° 03.389, which is just offshore of the base of the Cape Disappoint Lighthouse. He had died suddenly from a congenital heart issue on February 3, 2011.

The weekend weather was wonderful for February and Cathy had her wish to be away for her birthday, in some ways neither of us really wanted to go back home. A deep hurt from being beat up by the world...

I think I have looked too deeply at myself. Yes, I understand my lack of singularity more, but this price is handling that knowledge. What I mean is my hold on some base concepts like male, female, love, existence, and faith to name a few is in turmoil. They are up for questioning, for trying to understand, to tolerate, or accept. I am confused and tired of the search for peace in these things. I put all of such life questions into a dark corner of my brain as too hard to think about. Now all of this stuff is floating to the surface with no hope of being beaten down again. I really don't know what I am, isn't this odd?

I know I am unconformable, frightened, and lost. I am still having the withdraw effects from Effexor even after so many days, I guess you could figure mathematically from the half-life decay how long it will remain in my brain tissue, but this is beyond me at the moment. Sandy, I'm sorry this is just a stream of junk today; I will try harder tomorrow.

***

Monday July 23, 2012. Yesterday Julius Pierpont Patches (Chris Wedes) passed away. If you lived in the Seattle area and were born after the 1950 to the mid-1970s and watched TV, you were influenced by his children's show. He taught us what was funny; he shaped our sense of humor, and melted into our sense of local culture. His passing is our culture melting away, our time coming slowly to a close... God rest Chris Wedes, many eyes are close to tears today because of what you meant to so many kids that are now aging adults. Thank you for being a noble clown, funny and loved; you were steady and never tainted as we grew up watching you in your magic shack by the city dump. Sigh...

***

Thursday September 6, 2012. It has been five days since the tenderness has returned to both of my breasts. Changing your body chemistry is hard and uncomfortable at best and yet I am continuing to do it. Would I stop? It doesn't seem likely. I can't even see myself doing this. How strange this all is especially stepping back and looking at it. You would think you could just reason this stuff all away, just walk away from it; but somehow deep inside there is more to your soul, to your being that leads its own path.

2013

Wednesday January 2, 2013. Life is all about distracting yourself from mortality until you succumb to it. This dawned on me this morning as I was trying to help myself from a deep pit of depression. Cathy is back at work and the holiday is over; so with this lost distraction increasing the rate of my depression, I thought I would try talking to myself out loud as I do when I visit Sandy. I discovered that the running internal commentary within my brain goes quiet as I speak out loud. This is just what happens during my visits with Sandy. I am, in effect, someone else for that hour, a person without a running internal commentary. So I verbalized while I drove the car to the gas station, not letting my internal commentary be part of the moment. I was, as a way of description, totally in the moment; my mind didn't wander to the food of depression and feast upon it. I started talking to myself about being distracted and what that truly is. I postulated that distraction is how we survive being alive; it is the tool we all use to keep the face of mortality from coming into view. Everything we do is a distraction from mortality, whether it is work, play, pain, plans for the future, chemicals, religion, good behavior, and bad behavior. Just to name a few.

2014

Wednesday January 8, 2014. Had my appointments with both Sandy (evening) and Marsha (mid-day). My next two-hour Marsha appointment is March 11th. My talk with Sandy yielded the benefits of me taking the time to see and experience the good (fun, joyful) specks dotting each day among the unfortunate dark background I see so well. This is a skill I must develop no matter what the distraction is.

***

Monday January 13, 2014. Cathy and I (I go in with her for support memory-wise) had her Dr. Jarvela (Natural Med Doctor) appointment in Portland three days ago. This doctor has helped Cathy immensely with all her issues: thyroid, gluten intolerance, hormone, and MTHFR (Methylenetetrahydrofolate reductase) mutation. This mutation and allergies that we both have ensures we will have to be gluten-free for the rest of our lives.

The doctor was going over her blood test results and how to exactly treat Cathy's problems with her thyroid and hormones. I found myself so envious, I wanted someone to help me too. Dr. Marsden prescribes for me but it is left to me to do the research of how much and when. This is how the world works for transgender care. I wanted to get better and to have my hormone and sinus aliments understood. My headache was just swimming that day so in sudden desperation I asked if she was taking new patients. Her quick answer, "No, only special cases such as family members and I only see women 18 to 65 years old but my partner (a male natural doc) is great with men's health." I declined saying that wouldn't really help me… She dug in her heels and continued to point out how great her partner doctor was until I offered up an explanation involving me being transgender MtF needing help with a female hormone system and that didn't go over very smoothly. It didn't help either; she wouldn't even consider taking me on as a patient but was happy to continue treating Cathy. I am still getting over it. Stupid gender…

***

Tuesday April 15, 2014. Dr. Scopes graduated from the National College of Naturopathic Medicine in Portland and her practice is in Portland. She has been there since 1986 and volunteers at Outside clinic, which offers low-cost transgender health services to homeless and limited income clients. I had done my research and she looked very promising on paper.

We got through my Dr. Scopes appointment okay, but no great insight on my hormone regiment and it proved traumatic to Cathy afterward. Dr. Scopes seemed taken back when I told her I was transgender and not just another male seeking a new doctor. This both surprised me and rang alert bells in my mind; after all, on paper she was supposed to be all trans-friendly. She became all business like from this point on and forbade Cathy to say anything. I became very nervous there was no empathy here, but she made her examination and that was that. So ends my second attempt to find a naturopath doctor and in both events I felt rejected. We decided Dr. Scopes wasn't a good match for us.

2015

Friday January 9, 2015. Gender is beginning to trouble me again, not that it ever really goes away. It rises and falls depending on what is swirling around me at the moment. Family turmoil does an almost complete job of pushing it down. I try to listen to what 'she' wants, is it just attention or mourning the passage of time? You have to be so careful looking inward at yourself.

***

Wednesday January 21, 2015. Sandy asked me to think about how I could answer she-within-me's rising gender murmurings. (I'll split myself into two pieces for journaling's sake.) I find it so much easier to think of things I can't do because of physical limitations, voice, appearance, and fear. Fear particularly paralyzes me by making me see that it is safe where I am at currently, while pointing out going anywhere forward or backward could be disastrous. Still, I wasn't always paralyzed like this; so many years ago we would sometimes spend late evenings with me dressed as female and happily play cards together. There was always a feeling of daring and fulfillment in doing this but at the end of the evening a letdown also. So let's look at this in light of right now.

***

Thursday February 26, 2015. I dressed in a nice feminine top for my appointment with Sandy last Tuesday. There was more: I had on support garments to give me some definition; I matched my socks to go with my top and left my hair down. I would have done my eyes if I had the means. All this occurred to me to do forty-five minutes before I was to leave for my appointment with her... The look seemed to fall into place as I found articles of clothing here and there. As I dressed, I wondered if I was crossing some line toward trouble (risk taking) but that thought didn't seem to slow me down much. It has been a long time since I have dressed at all. I didn't seem to rely on it so much as I changed my body through electrolysis, laser, and hormones. It felt like the absolute right thing to have done as I drove all the way to Sandy's office. I still wonder just what has been driving this restlessness in me? It has me looking at an Orchiectomy, trachea shave, and clothes. Why the sudden burst in the dam? Sandy told me I should have a conversation with the her-in-myself and see just what she wants…

***

Wednesday March 4, 2015. So here I am after a week of thinking and listening to myself. Early in this past week I was overcome with the need to find information on bilateral orchiectomy surgeries. Who did them in the area and what you had to have to qualify for one. I also was driven to find out about trachea shaves. I searched for accounts of people who had gone through the process. One of their reasons for the surgery that impressed me, was to 'lock in' the feminine changes that cross gender hormones had brought to their bodies and I was all for that. I found Dr. Marci Bowers had moved to San Mateo and almost called to inquire as to the cost… In short, I realized just what 'she' was doing and it was nothing short of a jailbreak. And she had me more than half convinced, way more…

***

Sunday March 8, 2015. 'She' told me exactly what she wants and why we need it. All my life I have never had a concept of future, it was just a place I could not bear to go. I got to the point in childhood where I could not tell what having fun was. This is all old hat, but I now understand more. It's about a barrier to the future, something you have to overcome before you can exist there. If you don't overcome this barrier, the future coming toward you is simply an end; it's death. The future comes, no matter what, so you sit right at the barrier waiting out life to end in death. So what is this barrier to your future that keeps

271

you from existing there, from living each tomorrow without despair? It's the brain/body gender pressure to correct the gender mismatch of body and mind; sometimes it's loud sometimes only a whisper but never silent. You have to correct it, but it seems you can't really, so in a sort of cycle of despair you wait at this ephemeral wall, doing the only thing you can do you and that is to wait out life ending in death.

***

Tuesday March 17, 2015. Sandy gave me a newspaper article to read from 'The New York City Times Sunday Addition' dated March 8th. The title was *'Better Late Than Never'*. Sandy asked me to read it and tell her what I thought about it. The story was about transgender people transitioning late in life and I am grateful she gave it to me to read. For the most part, it was sad tales of lives spent trying to wait out the pressure of gender dysphoria. The main reason for waiting that was given was it simply wasn't possible, given the times we grew through. They also listed waiting for parents to pass so as not to hurt them, marriage, and then children came along, etc... And yes, I thought the pressure would drift away as time took bits of my life away, but just as one of the people voiced around age 50, it just gets stronger... Yes, I so identify with their plight and it is comforting in an odd way to know what it feels like for others. I am not alone in this age group.

***

Tuesday March 31, 2015. We have an appointment with Dr. Thomas Lamperti for this Friday at 11:15. The office lady asked, "How did you hear about Dr. Lamperti?" I told her from the web, and I was told because of this there was no charge for the consult on a trachea shave. Cathy seems fine with it and will come along with me. I wonder if a corner has been turned for us. I kind of feel like I am being swept along but that is okay really; it is just a consult appointment.

***

Thursday April 2, 2015. I just had a thought; a good share of the pressure I feel comes from the fear of not being able to escape/avoid becoming myself. I have always been able to avoid this, but now it seems inevitable. My favorite middle-school English teacher, Kate Ostrom, commented several years ago to me about aging, saying, "The older we get, the more like ourselves we become." I would add. Until finally we become who we really are.

***

Monday April 6, 2015. Okay me. Apparently I have an appointment for a feminizing trachea shave on May 8th with Dr. Thomas Lamperti at the Seattle Surgery Center! I seemed to have agreed to it after telling the doctor all about myself with Cathy sitting across from me. Cathy was listening in agreement as I told my tale. He is a nice man, giving us (both Cathy and me) almost an hour of his time. He asked the right questions and I was amazed I had the right answers. How long on HRT and what doctor was administrating it? Seven years and by our family doctor, Dr. Judith Marsden. Did I have a therapist? I gave Sandy's name and he recognized it. Dr. Lamperti was very excited with the idea of doing this for me and he has a passion to help transgender people.

This is a day later; I have my pre-op appointment on May 4th at 11:40 at Canyon Park in his Eastside office and my post-op on May 15th at Seattle. Oh my…

***

Friday April 10, 2015. My appointment with Sandy was kind of amazing really. I told her about my surgery date and she surprised me by being enthusiastic for me. She agreed probably no one would really notice looking at me, but I would know and that knowledge would change me. She told me she was happy for both Cathy and me! Cathy will be getting much more of the true C---- than she has now, less internally conflicted and less hidden. Sandy told me all the right things last Tuesday; I know this because as each day has passed this week, her words have come to my mind over and over. Each time brings a little more understanding and a little more peace with the whole issue.

***

Wednesday April 15, 2015. So I spoke with Sandy last night. I told her that the whole idea of having my Adam's apple flattened has drifted into the world of a done deal, a completely needed action, and the fear of having it done seems to have become minimal. I see myself past the surgery and having my scar faded away to almost not being noticeable. I also told her that arriving at this state had made my gender pressure very quiet; so much so that I can't recall the last time it was this quiet. Sandy rightly personified my gender pressure into that young woman within me. "Yes a young woman," she told me. Sandy continued, "She is trusting you. That is why she is quiet; you are doing something she needs."

As strange as this sounds from Sandy, it is dead on. Somewhere inside of me, I have always felt divided somehow. But right now I feel like one person undivided. This is all so very odd; I haven't felt anything like this completeness before in my life. Could this whole gender conflict thing be really true, I mean really true for me?! I have marched through laser, electrolysis, hormones, voice lessons, and hours of talk therapy all the while thinking that there is no real relief for this for me (couldn't even conceive of any in a tangible way), but still I was desperate to try... Looking back, I see that I had achieved a thin shadow of what I feel right now, but still that was a great reduction of the overall pressure, but no quietness. This feeling I now have is likened to someone who could never walk. Sure you keep doing the physical therapy, all the while knowing there is little or no chance of really feeling your legs move naturally like other people. Then one day, you feel a little shadow of response in one foot. You wake up after a restless night of the most vivid dreams containing the oddest images of physical movement and swing your legs over onto the floor, and stand up not even thinking about what had just happened. You just feel complete; there is no uneven drag from the waist down. You are yourself; it is the most inexperienced feeling you have ever had. I feel slammed by this, it is unreal to me and yet, it is so very real this togetherness feeling. Is this all because I accepted and acted upon the fact I needed to flatten my Adam's apple while not knowing the mental hurdle I was clearing? I wish I could truly understand what happened, it just seems like a miracle from God that has touched me. Yes it is that big to me. So here is my bunch of words to try to share the mental weight of where I am at right now. Please don't let this feeling fade away... You know this may be a coming challenge...

I revisit the thoughts of a few years ago about when Cathy told me, "I feel like I am losing you." My first response to this is: I am still the same person I always was. Thinking about it and giving in to what Cathy was trying to tell me using underlying symbols, I wonder if after all the talk of duality Cathy is telling me she is losing me to another woman who will come between us. The whole thought of that other woman emerging from me isn't a stretch I guess; except there is no duality in the end. The answer to this whole mess is the feeling of oneness I now seem to be experiencing for the first time in my life. I feel more like myself, not like becoming someone else. I so very much love Cathy and can't imagine life without her, and so very much want to continue completely with her. I now know I will be able to be an even better spouse after all this is done, I wish there were words...

***

April 23, 2015. I had a Sandy appointment this last Tuesday. For the last three weeks, I have been seeing her each Tuesday instead of every other. She asked me about how I felt about my upcoming trachea shave. Was I nervous? Just how did I feel about it? I told her it was really odd. I view myself past the surgery instead of it coming toward me in a few weeks. My feeling is of having it done and being relieved and free from discomfort. I seem to be putting it in the same category as a dentist appointment, something routine, even though it isn't and then viewing it as a done deal. My Adam's Apple doesn't cease to bother me daily, it aches just as an infected cyst needing to be removed, and this gives rise to looking forward to it being gone. This is also how I explain the whole affair to family and in truth; this is also a dimension to how I feel about it. It is a male marker to be removed for sure, but also a physical/mental pain I hope to be free of. Sandy wanted to know how Cathy was feeling about this change. I told her pretty much as I am in that it is needed and I will be better off after it is over. In a quiet and subtle way, she acknowledges it in the same fashion as HRT, etc.

I addressed the question that had been poking me. I asked Sandy about a person being gay then putting it aside to return to a straight relationship. What kind of hold does being gay have on you? Sandy asked me, "Does this have to do with you or Cathy?" No, it is a general question outside of us. I was curious if you could make the discovery, take action, and then walk back from it. Sandy told me, "It is not something you can walk forward into and then step back from. This is a time where being gay is trendy, especially on college campuses, so people experiment with it. Being gay churns away at you from the beginning of life and doesn't let go of you, ever. As an experiment someone can try it and go 'well that was interesting'. You then take a look at it and it looks back at you as two ships passing each other, then you move on and it fades away."

Then after hearing Sandy talking strongly about what it takes to be gay or what hold on you being gay has, I put forth a question in a small voice to her. Since an experimenter can back away from this, I wonder a little about me? "No!" She said sternly, "C----, you are what you are."

From when I first told Sandy about me to now suddenly finding myself with an appointment for an Adam's Apple reduction and then searching for a place to get an orchiectomy, I have had the impression Sandy has been expecting all of this to happen. I focused in this last meeting on her body language to this end.

"C----," Sandy said to me, "I have been treating transgender folks for over 25 years; there is a pattern. When you first came to me you told me you felt this way and could I help you not feel this way. You didn't want hormones; then after a while you were on them. We talked over the time you told me you would never alter your body ever, and now look. I have never had to lead you along because I have seen this so many times. People who are transgender don't back away because they can't; it will not let them alone. The brave ones find relief by actualizing into it, meeting its needs, and becoming themselves. This is different for each person but in every case, the need makes itself known. I refer to it as 'she or he' making herself or himself heard. When this need is met, the conflict quiets. You become a single person and life is bearable, even joyful. I have seen it over and over for this population that you are a part of. You are brave C----." Sandy then told me, "The transgender folks that aren't so brave self-medicate with alcohol or drugs to escape their condition; they don't do well, many die. I had seen many of these people also and I mourn their passing."

***

Thursday April 30, 2015. This is the next to the last day for Cathy at Microsoft (MS). She made a gluten-free, dairy-free, and egg-free apple cake (her signature goodie) to share with her group. We had to run around to find organic apples and finally did at Whole foods in Redmond near Asiana Bistro. Couldn't get near the Bellevue Whole Foods because of the traffic into Chick-fil-A! She was in such a dither about trying to remember everything for today. She has composed her so-long email including two poems, one a takeoff on *The Walrus and the Carpenter* and the other from *Both Sides Now* by Joni Mitchell. Today I will make cookies for her to take on her last day. This is such a special sweet/sad time, a once in a lifetime experience really. I find myself just as nervous by reflecting back on my last day at work experience of this rare day, so lots of prayers for Cathy today.

***

Friday May 1, 2015. Today is the day, Cathy's last day, and to send her off in style we used purple hair chalk to color her hair. In true fashion MS folks haven't said anything so I told Cathy to give them a window or permission to say something about it! All of our lives together, Cathy and I have worn similar clothes subject to our work conditions. Our retirement promise to each other was to always wear matching tie-dye t-shirts every day. Added bonus: this shielded me many times, changing the paradigm from people centering in on my vague gender presentation to seeing Cathy and me as a cute older couple. A side note: I have a picture from the late 1960s of my grandma Hazel and grandpa Charley wearing matching shirts. Grandma had made a top for herself and a western shirt for grandpa

277

out of the same fabric. A one-time deal as I only saw them wear it once.

***

Saturday June 20, 2015. I have had my surgery to remove a male marker and to relieve a physical pain occurring all along my trachea. My original surgical date was to be in May, but I had a minor break in my elbow (trying to ride a grandkid's scooter) so we moved the date into June. Cathy and I have had to weather the added pressure from the narrative of Caitlyn Jenner having this same surgery during this time. Suddenly, transitioning is all over the news outlets making Cathy grumpy and me distraught, until it came to a head yesterday. We talked and talked and agreed that I am not Caitlyn Jenner; she in her world is far removed from the two of us in our world. Her world is celebrity, headshots, and glitz; our world is real and bonded with our love for each other.

***

Saturday October 3, 2015. We are visiting at Corey and Melinda's house and I find I can no longer put off coming out to him. Much has happened to bring this about. Two months ago, Cathy and I got the courage to attend the Gender Odyssey conference held in Seattle. We both attended workshops together and separately. It was this huge window to the population we both belong to. There were kids to adults all with stories to tell of their struggles to be themselves. In the trans-elder workshop, I listened to life stories of people my own age and came to tears because these were my stories and struggles too. This experience and the removal of my male marker have changed everything. I have accepted who I am, no more beating around the gender bush. But part of this also caused the unsettling feeling of C----- dying. Sandy explained it as Cadance coming fully to the front of my identity. Sandy also explained it quite common to mourn the passing of this part of self. Understand it as being part of transition. So I invited Corey to sit with me in his backyard because I have something to share with him.

Corey I want to share with you a personal secret, I'm a werewolf and you are next in line. He laughs and grins at me.

I don't know how much you know about the conference Mom and I were at two months ago, I know you saw a picture I shared on Facebook and I allow location sharing... Your turn!

Corey replied with, "I did put two and two together."

I'm transgender Corey. I have always been but haven't acted upon it. I have lots to share, much of which has just come to fruition because of this conference and the surgery I have had.

Corey leaned closer to me and said, "Please do share I would love to hear it."

I walked back through my life from single digit age of discovery, hiding, hurting, falling in love, distraction, crisis, therapy, finishing a slow understanding on my part. All this as I did with his mother-to-be before I asked her to marry me. In both cases I received understanding and love in return.

Corey surprised me with, *"I know of other people at work going through the same thing, in fact someone in the group I manage just transitioned. We are careful to use the right pronouns. I can only imagine how hard it was for you to go through this for all these years, I'm proud of you!"*

2016

Friday July 15, 2016. We have had our annual Taneum Creek Cabin sleepover with the grandkids with lots of fun building dams on the creek and playing in the water behind them. The cabin was just as we left it last year and this year with no ban on campfires the kids got to cook over an open fire.

***

Wednesday August 31, 2016. Sandy had suggested Cathy and I get away from the constant mental storm I have been having about gender hormone mechanics; who to turn to, what steps to take, is there still time etc. This, along with the stormy times all around us, had been hurting me more then I realized. An emotional event brought this all to light; before kid sitting I got into the car to go somewhere and had a crushing wave-like of gloom/hopelessness simply twist my brain. It felt like someone I had loved and had loved me forever had just died and now all was over. This came along with a crushing pressure headache that has lasted and lasted. I have no idea what a breakdown would feel like so I can only expect this wasn't one, but it brought into focus the intense turmoil I really need a break from. And a break was to be had; we took B---- on a horseback ride adventure up at Crystal Mountain Ski Resort. It was the first B---- was ever on a horse by herself she did great and pumped the guide for how much does it cost to buy a horse and what does it eat if she got one! It was fun to ride again and, to top it off, the guide was born in Ellensburg as I was, so we had a nice ride.

***

Saturday November 26, 2016. Corey, Melinda, and little Quince all successfully stayed with us for four days! Quince was a free-range baby in our house so someone had to be with him every waking minute. He had a great time and we did too. All our work in preparing the house was well spent except for the fact that Cathy and I were both a bit worn out.

2017

Monday May 15, 2017. We rushed around today getting nothing done and pretending we have unlimited time. Right now, at 9:00pm, I am having a panic attack (I don't think I have ever had a real panic attack before) about going to the *Esprit Gala* tomorrow. Serves me right, after telling our learned therapist Sandy last Tuesday just how relaxed I was about going to this thing. I just don't feel prepared, also I feel like there is increasing hesitation from Cathy. I guess from me too. I have increasing fear that I am going to mess this whole thing up, that I will be tongue-tied with Dr. Marci Bowers, that the place will be full of beautiful women with perfect smiles, and in the end I will just look foolish... Perhaps this is what a panic attack is like, feeling completely unable to think, talk, or act, and full of desperation with no place to turn to for help that can't possibly ever come.

The other day, Cathy said I should remember that if I had been born a girl we wouldn't have ever been together. Without hesitation I replied the inverse. If I wasn't born transgender, we wouldn't have ever come together. My mind worked on this while I slept that night and I awoke to the realization that this was true. She and I fit together because we both are who we are, I would not be 'the me' that I am now if I was without the transgender part. Cathy wouldn't be who she is without the space she holds for someone like me to fill. It has taken an ocean of tears and a mountain of understanding to come to this point and we still haven't fully cleared the self-imposed barriers yet.

Tomorrow is so close and panic-buying clothes that just aren't right doesn't help to calm me at all. God be with Cathy and me, or I should say Cat and Cady.

***

Forever and Two Days More

Wednesday May 17, 2017. Yesterday the 16th went all wrong! I am convinced that everyone will be dressed to the nines and I will be completely out of place. I took a shower that seemed to take too long. Somewhere in my mind, I made a mental note that if we got out by noon, everything would be fine. Cathy packed very quickly and it looked like we would make it out much sooner. I insisted on taking too many clothes basically to still my fears that we wouldn't be attired properly. This led to a too heavy suitcase, which, in turn, led to a very sharp heartbreaking stabbing pain in my lower back and to an emergency chiropractic visit. Dr. Yael said my back was in crisis and pushed and pushed and twisted until I could stand erect again. Oh, and at the moment I hurt my back, I completely lost it. In my mind, the whole trip was off, lots of tears. Cathy did get me to the chiropractic doctor, we were on the road by 1:30, and arrived at the hotel by 5:00. The downside was that *Esprit* registration was closed for the day and wouldn't be open until 9:00 tomorrow morning. First impression at checking in at the lobby for our hotel room was positive. We were greeted as two ladies and were assured we would have a great time because of the location of our room was right in the heart of all the activities. Heading to our room, we began to run into many other attendees with perfectly coiffed hair and dressed in skirts or dresses. Oh, dear… My fears were all confirmed! We walked the hall and found a door opened to the free clothing exchange room. Three beautifully made up ladies inside looked us up and down, said a quiet 'hello' to us and told us to come on in. They didn't seem very warm, but here we are so in we go. After this, we retreated to our room where I tried to find some combination of dress that might work for this place. I own three tie-dye dresses and three tie-dye knot-shirt tops. Nothing to match the long-practiced crossdressers all around us, I quickly come to understand what I had read about *Esprit* is true. *Esprit* was formed like twenty-seven years ago to give crossdressers and drag folk a safe place to live 24 hours a day for a week as their presented gender. Only one blue dress came close, when to use it? In the end, we wore what we always wear with the exception of my hair is down. We eat dinner at the Kokopelli Grill (Southwest food for the Northwest mood) nearby to the hotel, the food was okay, but my stomach was a little unhappy that night. In fact, I wake up and have to get up every hour from midnight on suffering with foot cramps, all related to my hurt back. Even with the pressure of standing, my feet still wouldn't uncramp. I drink four bottles of water during this period.

Wednesday the 17th morning. Everything is so haphazardly organized here. At 9:00, the little registration desk opens up and is women-ed by an unenthusiastic Kaci. Part of our information was correct in their computers but parts were missing – Cathy's part. It was slow and arduous and unorganized. I really think this Gala is primarily set up for returning people, not new ones like us. We now have our badges and head to a Koffee Klatch, which was for newbies. We arrived a little late because of registration, and quietly came in and sat down. We were asked to each introduce ourselves and speak to whatever topic they were talking about. The long and short of it, Cathy (Cat) didn't feel particularly welcome there and I (Cady) was cut off in the middle of speaking. The result was, we really felt like turning around and going home but we held on.

When the Koffee Klatch was over, we looked at the schedule. Cathy decided to go to the SO session, this one being for 'Significant Others' only (couples session came later after lunch). She told me later about the session. Only two other people were there besides the facilitator. Cat asked about how many SOs were at the conference and Dotti (the facilitator) said about 1/3 of the attendees were SOs, but were probably off doing other things. Some were helping one couple get ready to renew their vows tomorrow (28 years) and would probably be there on Friday. Cat and the other two SOs introduced themselves and talked about their spouses: how long they had been together, did they have any kids, when did they first find out, etc. Turns out Cat and Roxy both knew before they got married and Linda knew 3 years into her marriage. Both Roxy and Linda's spouses have "come-out" full time and their families are nearly all supportive. Linda has two friends coming to stay with her (she's in a wheelchair and on oxygen) for a week while her spouse travels to Bangkok for gender surgery. Unfortunately, the friends are less than supportive and

284

Linda's anxieties are on high alert. Dotti helped to calm her and did some role-playing with her to help her come up with ways to minimize her discomfort. The hour long SO meeting has broken up and Cat is still in talking to Roxy and would be for 30 minutes more (Roxy gave Cat a friendship card).

Debbie Caddell is here doing electrolysis for those who would like to try it, so I visit with her while Cat naps in our room. Debbie does 15 minutes on my arms. I told her I wanted bragging rights to having had electro done by Debbie Caddell herself. We chatted (I put a plug in for Marsha) and I began to feel better about being here. So, between Dotti and Debbie, Cat and Cady began to heal somewhat. We have our lunch at H2O eating their Maguro Tuna poke rice bowl, so far so good.

1:30 comes and we go to the couples SO (significant other) program titled *Guilt, Shame, and how it affects your family*; it's all about transphobia from both sides. Eek! Cat really likes Dotti so we are off. Each couple is asked to introduce themselves individually. Things like how long married, when did you know you were transgender/or spouse was, who/children have you told etc. At my turn I ramble something switching from 3rd person to 1st person and call being transgender 'it' as how I distracted myself from it or how we distract ourselves from it. Dotti called me on this big time saying, "See just how powerful it was when she switched from 3rd person to 1st person! What, or more importantly, who are you distracting yourself from?" Cady that is who. Later I commented I sometimes feared Cady not being strong enough to survive on her own. There was discussion around not losing parts of yourself but adding to the whole. Cat was up to bat; she began to describe how she felt about Cady coming-out more publicly and big deep things about transition. Cat was silent for long periods waiting for words to come to her; this happened to me when I had just started therapy with Sandy. Words failed me as I was called to look at concepts that lay hidden about myself. It is a hard place and I wanted to hold Cat close at that minute. Dotti is nearly on par with Sandy, asking tough questions then backfilling around your answers. I sure missed talking to Sandy at this moment. A good therapist is just like a good personal trainer. A trainer works the long

285

forgotten distressed muscles of your body, bringing them to life again, but leaving you with sore muscles in places you never knew you had. The therapist works parts of your long suppressed psyche, bringing concepts to life again, but leaving you mentally sore in parts of your mind you never knew you had. Both are charged with bringing healing, freedom, and a regained future. In our room (162) before bed I try on the blue dress again and tell Cat that I would like to wear it out and about tomorrow and would she help me decide when. Cady was peeking out and Cat was mentally battling in silence on many fronts. We both were being faced with who we really are.

***

Thursday May 18, 2017. Today was the worst day of my life and the best day, in that order. I slept much better than the night before and got myself out of bed at 7:15 to shower. Cat continued to sleep while I showered. After I was done and she was up, she became agitated and restless. The SO program was a saving grace yesterday (Cat enjoyed meeting the other SOs) and last night her plan was for her to go the morning session (SOs only) while I went to a hormone talk (Dr. Sara K Becker). I asked what was up and it came down to she didn't want to go anymore. Oh…

"They are all about transitioning and I like us as we are, I'll go with you to the hormone talk," she told me after a little prying. I knew right away it was my announcing that I wanted to wear the blue dress and be like all the folks around us that caused this push back…

'Wearing the dress' had become this line-in-the-sand thing to her. I hadn't completely understood this, especially with everyone else here being in dresses, so I quickly capitulated saying that was fine I wouldn't wear it. She cheered up and offered to braid my damp ponytail but something inside me suddenly broke into little sharp pieces. I walked out onto our little deck and faced the ocean feeling that something of my being had been taken from me again and again. Cathy told me, "Your braid looks cute," and I suddenly pulled it out and said. Take it I don't wear my hair like this. This was the start of the worst part. Cathy burst into tears and I followed. I couldn't handle the dysphoria any more by giving parts of myself away to provide comfort to others. I wanted out of life; to walk into the nearby ocean and be done with it, but I couldn't because of all the human barriers, the kids, the grandkids, on and on all the resulting hurt I would push on them. What do you do when there is no escape? You spin around and around faster and faster until reason flies from you leaving you empty to thoughtlessly walk into one wall after another muttering. It was the strangest feeling I have ever had I felt so tired, empty, and broken. Is this what a break down feels like, staring straight ahead while reason pours out of you? Cathy sprang into action saying she was wrong, this is her problem; she needs to completely come to terms with me being transgender. Her words didn't seem to matter I was falling into a pit. I have never cried so hard, so uncontrollably for so long. I babbled through my tears. I can't escape because of the kids or you, everyone gets hurt I can't do it, and I can't stay, I am so tired just so tired… Then she started to talk to Cadance by name and slowly I regained some composure, it was in spurts with sudden sobs pushing out between. I had never been laid out so completely bare to anyone ever, completely vulnerable and I never want that feeling again. I think it comes down to 60 years of suppresses dysphoria finally bursting out. I was so exposed to all of these beautiful transwomen at one time that I was overwhelmed… With Cat's help I chose to return to the land of the living, and so started the best day of my life. With Cat's blessing I spent the day in a nice blue dress wearing nylons and a matching multi-colored fiber optic glass bead necklace. I was no one special, just a lady among other like-minded ladies. I cannot fully describe what it is like to be who you are, to have hope that this feeling will be yours day in and day out. Suddenly, I was one complete person and my mind seemed to clear. There was no sexual pleasure in being dressed at all, just this amazing completeness, and relief. Cat and Cady had just fought an epic storm and, amazingly, had overcome it! Cat and Cady attend a hormone talk done by Dr. Sara Becker 'retired,' where Cat is eager to learn. After this, Cat and I attended SO couples' group and shared with the other couples, learning, and slowly accepting each other just as we were. Later in the evening, we attend a wedding/vow renewal, two wives pledging love to each other in front of a group of carefully and beautifully dressed women, just amazing... I belong to this group, I do... On the way back to our room, I stop and make an appointment to have my eye makeup done tomorrow.

***

Friday May 19, 2017. Cat is pulling back some from SO stuff and the fear of Cady transitioning pops up again. This evens out with Cady again getting to wear a dress. A talk on *Christianity and the Transgender* done by Dr. Jennifer Burnett gave us lots of ways to defend ourselves as Christians who are transgender. She transitioned in the late 90s and is the dearest person. Cat and I would stop by her room and chat until 11:30pm after the days' events ended. Her story was she was the very perfect model of a male family practice doctor complete with her own family. She transitioned, losing employment, wife, and kids. She regained her kids and employment then married again to have a mom for her kids, only to again lose everything in a messy divorce. But in the end, she gained an understanding of God that is amazing. She explained, "I finally came to an understand that I had been coming to God in prayer and worship mimicking a male. Males have their relationship with God and females have their relationship, there is a difference. It wasn't until I accepted standing before God as a female, a daughter of God, and fully accepted that I had a female spirit that I truly came closer to God. All the time I mimicked a male spirit, there was a barrier between us."

This was enlightening to me! When Cat and I were first married we visited lots of churches and each gave me a cold feeling. It wasn't the churches; it was me bringing a false male mimic into the house of God. I am a daughter of God, part of the bride to Christ. Anyway, it was so encouraging to hear her speech of how God took her through one storm after another. She is a Bible scholar and defender of transgender's place in Christianity.

A luncheon and fashion show to experience next. You wouldn't know most of these women were anything but cis women. I have missed this world and have regrets, but they are tempered with the love I have for Cat. Cat and Cady have collected many friend cards and given out the same number. Several couples live near us in Western Washington.

Cat and Cady actually walk around town as themselves (Cady in a dress). Cady confuses a clerk at a store we had visited. It is so freeing to experience being dressed as me. We found a post office and I send my finished typed journal to Sandy. We did a Pokémon walk along the beautiful waterfront. Two dogs play a big role here: Piper a Border-Aussie owned by Suzanne and Bailey Joy, a Red Standard Poodle owned by Dotti and Robyanne. The dogs just spread love around.

Early evening, we have dinner and the talent show at the Elks Lodge (gluten-free is just barely adequate at all meals). We sit with Debbie, Renée, Katherine, Patrice, etc. Renée and Debbie are just enamored with all the transgender and crossdressers here they love this world. Renée is also so excited about meeting Dr. Bowers tomorrow. The talent show is a lot of fun and since Cady is dressed the ladies' bathroom is to be used but the line is just too long. Back at the hotel we spent the rest of the evening with Dr. Burnett. We listen to her stories and she listens to ours.

***

Saturday May 20, 2017. The big day where everything comes down to Dr. Bowers' talk on gender affirming surgeries. The fearful Cat is returning again; we go up and down about transition, as to how much. I am so nervous and jumpy that I can hardly contain my emotions. For breakfast, we have bread and bananas. Cat is all about packing to get on the road and this drives me to the edge of breaking down again. To me, this is a sign of putting this whole experience behind us as if it was just something to get through. Cat wants to go for a walk before the talk and I am nervous about not being there before the talk starts (I want to be there at least 15 minutes early). At this point, I even talk about leaving before the talk and going home. We fight again and make up again.

The time comes; I am wearing a knot shirt top, silver cross necklace, and black leggings. Renée is planning to be there but Debbie (who is so excited for Renée) at the last minute has been drafted to give a talk on hair removal, so she will come in halfway through. Cat and Cady meet Patrice just outside of the Olympic meeting room. Renée joins us and we all go inside to find an empty room. So we sit and wait. During our wait we are asked several times if any of us are Dr. Bowers, no not us. Then she walks in and I realize that Dr. Marci Bowers is indeed real! She is poised and pleasant and I am instantly in awe of her. I had no idea she would exceed what I have been told about her, it was an amazing moment for me. Our group is five people and I am thinking this simply can't be, it is just too perfect. Yes, the group will grow to twenty but most will just listen to her talk then leave. This gives those of us who are anxious plenty of time for questions with the doctor following her talk. She gave her PowerPoint talk adding in more information than the slides contained. All I can say is, she is the most gentle and passionate person one could ever hope for in a surgeon; I'm sold. Her talk is great; it mixes in history and a full explanation of all facets of the surgeries. I think Cat is very impressed. I have full confidence in her at this point. She offers a full GRS package for 30k hospital included but there is a 3year waiting list. My heart sinks. Dr. Bowers opens the floor for questions.

I get to ask all my questions:

Do you do the orchiectomy surgery? "Yes."

Does the three-year list pertain to orchiectomy also? "No, the list on day surgeries is something like a year."

Is a letter required? "Yes, just one and can be done by any therapist."

The formal talk ends and Dr. Bowers will continue to talk one-on-one with each of us to answer any questions we might have. A line forms but I am very near the front. I let Patrice go ahead of me just so I can try to remember what else I needed to ask. Renée is waiting and Cat is ready with her cellphone camera. My turn, I ask if she remembers Sandy Fosshage. Wow she sure does! I give her my introduction letter and tell her that I had an appointment with her on the 30th but now I think I will just consider this it. Dr. Bowers advices me to call her office and get a surgery date set. Right now I am just flying so high, this is such a big win, praise God!

Renée's turn (she was an OB/GYN patient of Dr. Bowers years ago before Dr. Bowers transitioned) and it is old home week, the two of them are so excited to see each other! Dr. Bowers has to leave and we head to our luncheon. Half way through it, Dr. Bowers quietly comes in to the back where we are sitting to give Renée a hug before she heads out. Cat and I leave the luncheon to finish our *Esprit* adventure by attending Sandy Hirsch's talk on voice. I ask if she remembers me and after reminding her about our adventure together, where she dismissed me from voice training on account of my physical problem, she is excited to hear all about what happened. So ends our *Esprit* adventure; it is back to C---- and Cathy both accepting that it is our transition now. Yes ours, the storm we came through brought to the surface that we both, in being so matched with each other, reflect deep aspects of each other. Transition isn't a single action of one of us, but as we two are one before God transition is mutual.

***

Thursday May 25, 2017. Blue Monday with its pullback from returning to the real word was manageable. I met with Sandy two days ago fully dressed as female in a little black dress and introduced myself as Cady (Cadance). Sandy just beamed and gave me several 'Wows;' it was so cool! She asked me what name I wanted her to refer to me as and either Cady or Cadance was just great. In our talk together, she wanted to hear all about our adventure and was especially concerned with how Cathy was doing. I told her about the couples' sessions we had attended separately and together. Cathy found some support in her first group but felt somewhat isolated as the others all were so far down the transition road with everyone being out, old news, done deal, etc. Sandy said, "I have a woman friend who is a therapist, is straight, happily married, and completely non-judgmental. If Cathy would like to have a place to share her feelings I would be happy to give her a call." I'll relay this to Cathy. Sandy gave me one especially good piece of advice, and that was to make time away from talking about transgender issues, "Give yourselves as a couple nights without mentioning it at all." Very good advice! As a side note, many times I hear the same advice from Sandy and Cathy independently; makes me wonder if they are in cahoots, a like-minds sort of thing.

One more visit back to Tuesday morning before I continue to Wednesday: *Esprit* had taught me that I really had no clothes past the real daily lifestyle I share with Cathy. I now really wanted to dress for my Sandy appointments in a more classic way. So, there are no coincidences, just aren't, because we had to visit Costco and right there in that big warehouse was the skirt I needed. In fact, a little black dress in my size was on the rack and I found the hardest part footwear in that place! Lastly, I have become convinced it is time to tell Casey. Cathy and Corey both agree too.

Wednesday morning, I make my plan. I know Casey is working at home this day so I call him and ask if he takes a break around noon. He tells me he could if I needed him to, no problem. Great! Mom and I would like to stop by and talk about summer stuff, etc. Now I panic some about what to say to our son in just four hours. Well, there was still time and Cathy had a Doctor Marsden appointment at 9:30, so I could think while in the waiting room. I didn't; I visited with Patty the office manager. I heard about her trip to Cabo and her unpleasant experience with the TSA. For some unknown reason, sixty-year-old Patty got tagged for a full body search. I said I'm not going to fly anymore! Can you imagine what would happen to me? She responded, "I sure understand and for good reason you being transgender." And in the oddest way I was just affirmed by her. And on the morning before me telling Casey! There are no coincidences I am being lead along. I remember just a few years ago coming-out to Dr. Marsden. It was a rocky time for both of us, but in the end she gave me a hug, and agreed to start me on HRT based on a letter from Sandy. After Dr. Marsden gives me back Cathy, we drive to Seahurst Park beach to check for any new Pokémon (a video game we play) that might be lurking there. Oh no, just one hour before we leave and panic about how to frame my talk. I call Corey and get him at work; again, there are no coincidences as this is near impossible to do normally. Not only do I get him on the first ring but he also has an hour free to talk.

Me: Hi Corey I am going to tell Casey about me at noon. Do you have some time to talk? I'm having trouble forming my approach.

Corey: "Great it's the thing to do! I do have time right now as I just got out of a meeting. Are you still holding onto your plan of asking him if he would keep it a personal secret?"

Me: Yes, well, that is one of the barriers I am facing, how to do it?

Corey: Do it just like this, "Casey I have something very personal to tell you, something very important to me, and I am not ready to share it any further yet."

Me: Wow that is perfect!!!

Corey: "You're not asking Casey to agree to anything you are simply telling him at this time you're sharing with him. Casey will accept this; he is grown up, he is reasonable, I know you know this. Don't worry this is the right thing to do for all of us."

Me: Thank you Corey I am so proud of you. You see so much so clearly. I have vague fears I think from being within my own secret for so long. One fear is because of all the hurt Casey has been through that he might not be as understanding but even this so unlikely, it isn't Casey like.

Corey: "Thanks! I think everything will turn out fine. I'll say a prayer for you and Casey. I am booked with two back-to-back meetings while you will be with Casey. But if things don't go as you hope them to, call me I will make time to take the call. Remember I will take the call don't hesitate."

Me: Thank you Corey, love you…

Corey: "Love you, you are doing the right thing!"

Wow! I have my frame for the conversation and at my back is our son Corey. Cathy and I discuss his advice on our drive to Casey and Mindy's house and call it good. I don't think the drive to their house in Auburn ever passed so quickly for me. I expect it was because of all the thoughts in my mind going back and forth about all the years of living with this issue coming to this day. I wonder if words will come to me when I need them and what it will feel like after I use all my words on Casey. Cathy and I talk tactics; she will head into the house if Mindy is there and I will see if Casey will walk with me. In their driveway, we pause before getting out to say a little payer that God will bring direction to us and will be glorified by all that is now to be.

Casey is right at the front door to meet us, Cathy heads in to visit with Mindy and I begin.

Casey: "What's up?"
Me: Will you go outside for a walk with me? I have something to tell you.
Casey: "Sure what's up?"

We go outside and walk over to their garden. A calm settles over me. There are no back and forth fearful thoughts now, just a gentle determined flow of speech. It is just like having the most pleasant father/son stroll and chat I haven't had for so long with Casey. He is easy and interested.

Me: How's your garden?
Casey: "I am having trouble with my tomatoes. They look better today but there is this browning on some of the leaves."
Me: Too much water or too little water so hard to know.
Casey: "Yup."

We turn to walk up Casey's driveway to the little private road servicing the ten or so homes in their neighborhood. As we walk I begin my speech.

Me: I have something very personal to tell you, something very important to me. I'm transgender a transsexual really. Do you know the term?
Casey: "Not really, I mean I know of it globally."

294

Me: Oh, I would have thought being at MS you come across folks and things in the news. I've seen you 'liked' same sex marriage on Facebook…

Casey: "Gays, sure I mean anyway."

So, at this point I stumble a bit because it looks like it is going to be me just talking at him. I was hoping with the world of late it would be more on his radar.

Me: I have a discord with my mind and body on gender. I'm male bodied but something in my brain is female, putting me in a conflict of identity gender-wise. It is something I had all my life.

As we walk down the road an odd thing happens, Oreo-baby, one of their tuxedo cats begins to meow and starts following us.

Casey: "Okay."

Me: The dysphoria traveled along through life with me and only seems to grow as I aged, just drowning happiness, and hope more and more. Don't misunderstand me; my life has had many happy times, but none that would distract from the dysphoria for long. You and your brother were great distractions.

Casey: "Thank you."

The cat seems determined to follow us no matter how long we walk and if we pause he lays down to listen.

Me: Does your cat often follow after you when you walk down the road?

Casey: "No never; this is something totally new."

Me: Must want to listen to our conversation pretty badly. I continue, I have always figured on just getting through life, never living it, and actually hoping it would be a short life. About ten years ago the discord became so unbearable I sought help. It was this or leave life altogether and that was not possible. I found a very good therapist and asked if she would take me on and perhaps give me the tools to end the discord. I have learned much, come to completely trust her, and follow her advice. Tuesdays are my therapy night and have been since around 2005.

Casey: "Okay."

He is listening to everything I say attentively without a grimace. Oreo-baby continues to follow and listen to us. I have the full attention of two beings.

Me: The discord is treated by accepting it as part of me, it being that I am female in identity, and allowing my body to follow my mind. I have been on hormones for something like ten years now, have had electrolysis, laser, surgery to reduce my Adam's apple, relocate an ear lobe, and been to two gender conferences."

Casey: "What about the voice training, was that part of it too and not something else?"

Me: Yes and no, as with my trachea shave there were other problems these solved. I was having trouble with my trachea physically catching on something from between it and my spine. The surgery fixed that and my voice did sound wrong after my sinus surgery. But yes, I also wanted both because they feminized me.

Casey: "How does Mom feel about all this?"

Me: We have decided to stay together through the fall. (I was joking, Casey looked shocked.) I told her about it before we married and she decided to stay with me albeit we didn't know the full effect this would have on me. We just came back from a conference/Gala that had couples therapy and we have both grown from this. Your brother knows about me already, because of the conference Gender Odyssey. I shared an anonymous selfie picture and he saw via tracking that we were at the downtown convention center. The only thing playing there was GO. He asked and I told him.

Casey: "I never keep track of where you are; it is your own business!"

Me: I just look at it as family being interested in each other, Casey.

We have walked the length of the private road and the cat is still with us.

Casey: "So what does this mean? How does this affect me?"

Me: I am still your dad if that is what you mean. Casey, to show you just how strong this discord was all of my life, when you and your brother were born, I gave you names that could be easily used by either gender if you had this happen to you.

Casey: "So that's why..."

Me: I am a little surprised you didn't notice me becoming so androgynous. Any questions?

Casey is still seemingly to be doing fine.

Me: Well, I'll play role reversal. "What do I call you now?" Dad will work, as I am your father. He laughs.

Casey: "How about where do you see yourself in five years?"

Me: I see myself higher up in the organization, as I have passion for this company and its products...

Casey: Laughs!

Casey: "I don't see that this affects me any."

Me: I'm not ready to share this openly yet. People tell me that once you tell a secret you lose control of it very quickly.

Casey: "I don't see that as a problem, especially if the person you tell it to keeps it." He gives me a hug.

Me: We were also curious about taking Colby and B---- to Victoria for a trip this summer...

Mindy has come out front and we both walk back to their house. Unfortunately the kids' passports have expired. Ah well...

On the drive back, I tell Cathy all about my talk with Casey. It didn't go as I expected. I have a sort of empty feeling. Casey was mostly concerned with how any of this affected him. No affirmation or acknowledgement of a difficult journey I have traveled. I call Corey to tell him about my and Casey's talk as he asked me too. I also ask him about his brother's reaction and Corey tells me look at it this way, "Knowing Casey, you can take it as a reaction of support. If it doesn't affect him, he is perfectly fine with it. Go for it Dad, is what he is saying." I think he is right...

It dawns on me that I am suddenly free to pierce my ears! Our children didn't disown us. Corey would call me the next day to discuss pronoun use; he will try to use the proper pronouns, it is just the right thing to do.

***

Thursday June 1, 2017. Sandy congratulated me on telling Casey as soon as I entered her office. We talked about what my next steps would be and she encouraged me to make an action plan. How in the world did I ever arrive to where I am right now? I have had surgeries and expect more, hormones, hair removal, and all the pitfalls along the way. We have told our sons. Cathy and I are still together and Jesus Christ is still our Lord. I feel a curtain being drawn closed between myself and the male population. When we come upon a group of guys, they don't interact with me, instead they talk toward Cathy in our conversation. How did I ever travel this far toward this sort of transition without fully realizing this? It is mind numbing, and as one weight is lifted another comes down heavily. I understand some as to why Sandy was keen on moving me along; the place I am at right now is a dangerous one to linger in. I can feel it, the isolation of being in between the past and the future, him and her, ending up as nothing in the end. It's a place where you can easily find yourself paralyzed to move at all. I think Sandy is right, so I have begun to collect information on things that were always out of reach to me like breast enhancement ($6 to 9K).

I have studied each person I met at *Esprit*, looking for me in them and I found little parts of me here and there. I never thought I looked at all presentably female until a very beautiful young wispy lady told me "You look so sage-like in your rose glasses, so wise, and pretty."

Other me stuff: I had a blood draw at Dr. Marsden's. So, in a few days I will know if reducing my Avodart dose to three per week has had any effect on my T levels. If not, then I would be able to further reduce the dose to twice a week.

Ever since I had my talk with Casey my mind has been much more clear in thought and memory! So perhaps it was stress hurting my memory. I also started vitamin B12 again so perhaps the combination of reducing stress and the B12…

Cathy bought a new cell phone for me! She loves new stuff and this one is very cool, works well, and looks nice. We were looking forward to driving to Idaho to see a friend of mine from working days. Dennis was a wonderful friend to work with. He came and sought me out in retirement to do little projects for his new employer. I was so grateful to be valued again for strobe light design. Anyway, he is now fully retired having had a stroke and a heart attack six months ago. I had built a table lamp out of one of the strobe lights he used to sell and had hoped to give it to him for his coming birthday. I had made so many proto-type units for him during our time together that I thought one final one would be so cool to do for him. At the last minute before we headed out I called to be sure of the timing for our visit. And was told by Dennis that his wife had a heart attack ten days ago and could he have a raincheck on our visit? Of course, but we were disappointed... The last raincheck was because of his health problems six months ago. I guess our disappointment was from us looking forward to visiting a dear friend and the fear of not seeing him again.

***

Thursday June 15, 2017. Things are not well. The specter of Corey and family moving is very much alive and they may not even be in this area when my surgery date with Dr. Bowers comes. On the other hand, we have had a nice visit with Quince (he is growing so fast) at his daycare center. Cathy has made dinner two times for them, the five of us visited the San Mateo County fair (a very windy Sunday and great petting zoo), and we have done lots of Pokémon playing.

Me stuff: On the drive through Oregon, I was addressed as female several times. This kind of shocked me; it happened at a gas station where I had taken off my glasses and my hair was pulled back in a ponytail before stopping. I thought I was very much in guy mode; it was my intention not to be anything else, so when he said, "Thank you, ma'am" I was more than a little taken back. This continues down here in San Mateo as Cathy and I are referred to as ladies many times. This is all new to me, it wasn't this way last time we were here. Cathy and I have struggled some as the realization of visiting Dr. Bowers

299

office is now at hand. She has fears that I will become absorbed in myself like Caitlyn Jenner (Cathy just finished her book), making myself the center of the universe leaving no room for us or for her. It is a rocky time; we are both nervous and shaken in our reality. We have no answer to any of this at the moment. I decide that the best thing to do is to get this visit over as soon as possible. Thinking that perhaps we both will feel better. To this end on Monday June 12th we fill out the forms asking questions like legal name, female name, how long on HRT, and when real-life trial started to name a few. This is both disturbing and calming at the same time, the fact I can answer them brings home a reality to both of us for better or worse. The hardest one for Cathy is 'female name;' I go with Cady short for Cadance, I realize that my letter spells it Cadence but that shouldn't be a problem, I hope.

We drive to Burlingame (15-minute trip), and have trouble finding Dr. Bowers office. After several around the block loops we finally find the place and then parked nearby. I don't feel very presentable; then I sigh and pop out of the car. We walk toward the office building at 345 Lorton Ave. The outer glass door wasn't scary; it opened passably unto the building's lobby. We walked inside and are now facing a sign stating, 'Bay Area Reproductive Health Care,' very nondescript and understated. There were several young teenagers sitting in the waiting room glued to their cellphones. I march over to the reception desk and tell the young lady that I am here to drop off forms and make my deposit. Her name was Erica and she was very nice to us. I had rehearsed my little talk over and over in my head on the drive here and so far, it was working fine. I could see Dr. Bowers talking to someone in the inner offices behind the reception desk. She was within hearing range, but I chose not to call out to her to say 'hello' as she was plainly very busy. I heard something about a phone consultation waiting on hold for her. I also silently thanked God for the fact that I was able to see and talk with her during *Esprit*. And yes Sandy, just as you said it was a much more comfortable and relaxed setting, here in her offices she was totally in doctor mode. Erica asked what procedure I was after I told her an orchiectomy and she said perfect and switched to referring to me as Cady Anderson. She listened with interest to our story about seeing Dr. Bowers at *Esprit*. We made my deposit of $1000 with a credit card and I asked if my letter made it here to their offices. She checked her computer and told me, yes, they have a letter from Sandra L. Fosshage M.A. LMHC, and she told me that Robin (Dr. Bowers surgery scheduler) would give me a call as to my surgery date. Erica also gives me Robin's phone number. Cathy surprised me by referring to me as 'she' to Erica in questions. All during the time of being here in this place, I have this surreal experience of my condition (if you will) being so normal; so matter of fact, just something you have to take care of and then move on. This waiting room is like any other waiting room. We left and I told Cathy, don't think that I didn't catch that you referred to me as she! We laughed a little. I try calling Robin several hours later only to get her voice mail.

***

Tuesday June 17, 2017. I try calling twice today and get Robin on the second time. She is pleasant and chatty, much different from the time I called her many months ago, having dropped off my forms and making a deposit makes a big difference it gives you credibility. The good news, she tells me, is that I am ahead of the game by leaving my forms in the right office to start, and I am after an orchiectomy with the shorter wait list. The harder news is they are booking appointments right now for October 11, 2018! Wow! I ask about my letter from Sandra Fosshage and yes, she has it. I correct her mispronunciation of Sandy's last name, telling her it means falling water in a Scandinavian dialect. Robin tells me she will definitely remember to get Sandy's name right in the future. So, my date is October 11th but Robin tells me there are always cancelations, and I am on a list now to that end. Robin also asked how long on HRT and about living as female; they would like a letter from my therapist listing the start date of HRT and viability of living as female. In turn, they can supply any needed documents for supporting a name change and gender marker change. Oh my…

***

Thursday June 22, 2017. So, my blood tests were not done right again. Patty says doctor didn't get enough blood so I will see her on this coming Wednesday to draw more; just as Sandy says, move forward no big deal. This is an ongoing problem; I need to be better informed of how much blood, and which vials are needed for my tests. My plan to remedy this is for a trip to local blood lab and ask them. This is also a good place to remind myself just how far Dr. Marsden has stretched herself in being my HRT administrator back in 2007. She brought both of our sons into the world, and has treated all of our medicinal needs, very family country doctor like. When I came-out to her she was stunned, she had never had any experience with anyone in the transgender world (it simply wasn't in any training for a country doc). It was a learning experience for both of us and she took on the challenge but still it remained an ongoing learning experience.

***

Friday June 23, 2017. We arrived home last night after a very long drive. I am all done in and experiencing motion sickness; an odd feeling of still being in motion all the time. We keep saying that the long drive needs to be broken with an overnight somewhere along the way. On returning home last night Cathy and I shared the same dour feeling of 'not really wanting to here anymore;' she was moved to tears. Some of this stems from the heartbreak we feel from leaving little Q or in turn leaving Colby and B----. And there is the fact of everyone going on with their lives, and in doing so, moving away from us emotionally and physically. This brings me into a continuous reflection of my being transgender may be driving this isolation of us with them.

After talking with Sandy on the phone last Tuesday I have been doing a lot of thinking. She always has this effect on me, but this time even more so. I'm tired and my mind has been running on and on about gender stuff. Cadance is faced with so much to overcome (couple-problems and life-problems) and has so little to look forward to really. That is the crux of the matter, life just gets harder from here on in, the progress Catherine and Cadance made at *Esprit* is somewhat lost in the reality of the labors of tomorrow. Perhaps I am just at a down swing right now. Cathy has talked about us going on a short trip with me more as Cadance (Cady); seems like a good idea…

***

Saturday July 1, 2017: Caddell's receptionist Hope and her spouse Tina had just returned from Tina's MtF surgery with Dr. Bowers, and several Caddell's folks who knew my need for experiences of other couples told me I should chat with Hope. Well, it didn't work at that time, but all of a sudden this day would bring a chance to talk with Hope! Cathy had a laser appointment so during her appointment in a treatment room I was beginning my memorable chat in the waiting area with Hope. We chatted about how they are still using a paper schedule book even though they have a new computer system, about how cool the new color purple is in the reception area, and was she looking forward to any adventures this summer?

"No, we have already had our adventure back in April." Hope responded.

Oh, of course that's right Tina's surgery! I returned smiling. I got to meet Dr. Bowers at *Esprit* and later traveled down to her offices to get a surgery date. I told my little story then felt brave enough in conversation to ask Hope if life was better now?

"Yes for Tina; for me there have been some hard bumps." She returned.

I tell her, oh I'm sorry for that. I mean I see Cathy's part, and yes she is right in saying that support for the cis spouse at best is thin. Hope smiles, she is such a sweet lovely person. I would love to make her feel better and I would feel better in the process of doing this; but right now, it's hurtful.

Hope confides to me, "For her (meaning Tina) now is the greatest time ever and she has blinders on to all else. The bumps come from our sons and to me especially on Mother's Day."

I tell her hoping to bring comfort to her, I read that after surgery the transitioning person almost goes through a second adolescence. That clumsy tunnel vision time we experienced as teenagers.

303

"That is exactly right!" Hope quips, "She hasn't come back to reality yet."

We continue on back and forth. I tell her a shorten story of my journey including that I told Cathy about me before we were married with the idea I didn't want to have any secrets from her. I really don't have a very interesting story compared to most, so I am amazed with each account I hear from transgender people. I take note that there are two other persons in the waiting room, a man with his son over in the corner, but the conversation we are having is too important to me to stymie it on their account.

"You are very thoughtful of other people; not everyone is." Hope smiles again and continues, "I found out several years into our marriage about Tina. I felt hurt and angry that she was keeping secrets from me. But in the end, 27 years of marriage and two sons is not something you just throw away without thought."

I'm so sorry that is so tough to go through, I reply compassionately. In my mind, I feel waves of hurt for Cathy, and I give thanks to God that I did tell her so many years ago.

Cathy comes out and conversation swings around to more normal pleasant things. I mention to Hope that she and Cathy could have quite the conversation if they wanted to. The wife of the man comes out of one of the treatment rooms and they make a quick exit. The quiet time of no phone ringing at Hope's desk is suddenly over. She gets busy and Cathy and I leave.

So, what just happened to me? I came face to face with many of my worst fears through someone else...

On another note, making a list for Sandy to use has led me to read my past journals from 2005 and up. It is sobering to see my words describe my experience and how painful each little baby step was for me. How gentle or tough Sandy was at the right times, how profound her advice, and how we waded through some very thorny stuff. Then I look at myself right now and still see the same intense battle/fear going on despite all this time. And without fully intending it I have transitioned. I kept trying to keep it down to just a little bit but it happened anyway. Now can I stand it?

***

Monday July 10, 2017. We had our weekend trip to Sisters, Oregon, for their annual Outdoor Quilt Show. Colorful and well-crafted quilts are hung up everywhere indoors and out. All were lots of fun to see and I was just one of the many ladies wandering the streets of Sisters. Many new things, Cathy and I were asked if we wanted separate checks at restaurants and being called sweetie to name two. Cathy has told me that we will just see where this road takes us together and she told me, "I love you, Cady."

***

Friday July 14, 2017. I feel odd or I should say uneasy or perhaps a little frightened. And what has brought on this feeling but being clocked as 'Cady' of all things, when it is C---- standing there, in other words being identified as female by random people and not the male C----. I thought I was presenting as C---- but it was Cady who was really there in person. It happens when I least expect it. This particular occurrence happened at a Starbucks we visit all the time, albeit with a new barista addressing Cathy and me with, "What can I get started for you ladies?" She never wavered on my gender all through the transaction. I was not at all especially female looking that day, standing there with my hair pulled into a tight ponytail, wearing blue jeans, and this seems to be happening daily in one way or the other. The outcome from this should be, "Right on, you go girl!"

Instead, I feel a little like I have lost myself altogether. I am experiencing my inner self differently. Hearing a different internal voice, wondering just how did this happen all of a sudden, and who am I now? Sandy has told me when she looks at me, she sees a middle-aged woman. I don't see 'her' in the broken mirror in our bathroom, but somehow I do feel this change inside. It just mashes the dysphoria to pieces, but also comes with the feelings as I typed in my first line. I didn't even understand the extent or the depth of this feeling beginning to come over me a few days ago, but must have had a clue when I typed the last line of the journal I sent to Sandy last visit with, 'now can I stand it?'

Sandy was already ahead of what was happening to me and even told me of her experiences with gentle people traveling this road and finding themselves also being frightened. I would like for our chat together this time to explore what is happening to me right now. I find myself unsteady or maybe ill-equipped as a better word in just daily interactions with people; anyways something in this vein.

***

Thursday July 20, 2017. Today we have B---- with us we picked her up after Colby's baseball game last evening. Colby played second base, right field, walked, and stole bases. Playing has helped him gain some control over his emotional breakdowns; tears and anguish still come with disappointment, but he is making gains. B---- slept all night, super good! She is lounging under our dining room table right now being lazy. We will pick up Colby tomorrow after our lunch with our electrologist Marsha over in Redmond. Colby told Nanna that he would be happy to go to lunch with us if it meant being pick up sooner. It is so nice to have him eager to visit with us.

Me stuff: Sandy told me I should find ways to be gentle with the time I am going through. To me, it is almost like getting used to being someone else; not completely someone else, but an internal shift from one place to another. From C---- up front to Cadance now being up front. The other side of this is a whole new set of vulnerabilities to cower before. Thinking about it, most of these vulnerabilities are not new and my way of dealing with them was never purely C---- (male), because I was always made up of Cadance being in the shadows so she has at least a seed to start with. There will be things to learn, unlearn, and things I find myself seemingly to already know. I have sent my question off to a trans support website about the hormone patch problem I have between Mylan vs. Sandoz and yes, other folks have had trouble with the Mylan patches also, so I am not alone in this. Sandy's experience with so many transgender people over the years is just a priceless resource and I benefit from it each time I visit with her. I mustn't get lost in other experiences either as I am prone to do; this is my own unique experience.

Forever and Two Days More

***

Sunday July 30, 2017. I didn't see Sandy last Tuesday as planned; there was a mix up. I did get to talk to her on the phone for a few minutes to wish her good sailing to Alaska! My next appointment with her is August 15th (the day before Jack-the-cat's birthday).

I had vivid dreams this morning, all about things coming to an end in life. I was in a big house, like the upstairs of the ranch house in a strange way. The feelings were all about loss and mourning the passing of life identities. I guess it was trans in some way, as I feel myself slipping away from myself. So many things are doing just that all around me.

Today is a get-ready day for the Taneum Creek Cabin trip; so much to do and in my mind lurks the thought, is this the last time? Colby and B---- are growing so fast. Corey and family will be here this Friday for the Tuttle family picnic just as we return from the Cabin. In one fell swoop all summer activities are done. I sure don't like August... Cathy and I are both feeling sad in this way. In my depression I am losing comfort in places, ones that I used to hold so dear. Anyway, to be honest in a journal is always a risk, this all sounds so dour when the fact is Cathy and I are still functional and still pushing forward albeit against great pressure. Talking to Sandy again will help.

***

Monday August 7, 2017. Our great family event has passed now. Cathy and I spent a good deal of money, worry, and physical work to get ready for it and now it is over. All the experiences, for all the people I hoped and prayed for, came to pass. Casey got to play with and enjoy little Quince, Casey and Mindy as a couple also got to play with and enjoy little Quince, Colby and B---- got to play with their little cousin, and Linda and Cathy's mom got to experience little Quince. Cathy and I got to give the Taneum Creek Cabin experience to Colby and B----, albeit not quite what we hoped for it to be. The Tuttle family picnic gave Corey and Melinda a chance to visit and show off little Quince to Cathy's side of the family. The order of events were Taneum Creek Cabin with Colby and B----, we return to our house in time for Corey and family to arrive, the Tuttle family picnic on Saturday, Casey hosts a smaller gathering on Sunday at his house, and finally Corey, Melinda, and Quince fly out Monday morning.

Taneum Creek Cabin. The world changed; for twenty years Thousand Trails Corp (TT) has contracted with the Nation Forest Service to manage its campgrounds (including the Cabin) and this year they chose not to. This left the NFS scrambling to find folks on their own. We had no clue as to the change except there was a note on the NFS website that the propane stove was broken at the cabin. How odd, the place was always so perfect we thought. We scrambled to find a butane burner to bring with us. There has been a lot of life pressures on Cathy and me and to this end we fail here and there; this time Cathy forgot to pack several things one of which was our state Discover Pass. To fix this we thought to stop at the ranger station at Snoqualmie Pass and just buy another one, but found the place closed, and being painted over. So no problem, there is another one in Cle Elum. Here we were asked if we had the code to get the key out of the key box. What? Don't we just get the key from the host couple as always? No, things are different this year... It sure was a good thing we happened to stop at the ranger station, but we still didn't understand just how different things would be... Colby and B---- are older now, they are just toying with pre-teen life. Some changes are Colby can eat like there is no tomorrow and B---- is more articulate both in speech and writing. Some things are still the same B---- is a huge hand-full and Colby still will break into tears as if the world has completely broken into dust... A nice surprise is the road to the cabin has been repaired so no potholes to fall into. The cabin is still intact and there is a host trailer nearby as before but here things have changed. The host is a young under thirty-year-old woman named Rose with 5 little kids and one more on the way this November. Her unemployed husband gives me a very hard stare. This is so different from the retired folks TT hires who are happy to spend summer after summer camping and seem to take such pride of ownership of the grounds and cabin. Ownership such as each year

308

adding paintings and little things like lawn chairs down by the creek would welcome you to the cabin. So different, now things are broken in the cabin and there are little dusty kids under foot. They did have the next day off and left to go somewhere, so we did have a nice day all to ourselves on the creek. The next day was too hot and smoke coming down from a forest fire somewhere drove us to leave early on Wednesday. On the upside, the four of us did get to do Pokémon hunting all around Ellensburg.

***

Thursday August 9, 2017. Tomorrow would have been my mother's 93rd birthday; then comes my brother David's birthday and my dad's. When my mom mindlessly stepped in front of a speeding car, the thought that came to me was she is free from the hellish trap that was her life. I thought this too after David passed, and even for my father. Today is bad for me. I feel trapped and hopelessly resigned to remaining trapped. I am tired also. Cadance was alive but lately she feels like a completely dried out potted plant with no expectation of being watered. All of the family experiences and connections between Casey and Corey's family have been successful now, so I don't have to worry so much anymore but I am so tired. If I am true to my promise and send this journal to Sandy, I had better explore what is happening to me.

Well, let's look at my experiences and feelings resulting from them. At the family picnic everyone (those that came) seemed to be broken in some way physically (backs, knees, eyes, hearts, etc.). Our family dentist seems to have lost interest in helping us dental-wise, our family doctor probably will not be in practice much longer, and Cathy's naturopath is becoming increasingly difficult to keep appointments with; all this leaving us high and dry. Sometimes I don't feel like my hormones are working right anymore. Even if you try not to listen to news it still leaks out all around telegraphing gloom and doom. I miss Cadance; I felt different as her but lately I feel all clunky and male. I am not sure just what is going on…

***

Thursday August 24, 2017. We changed our plans on the eclipse (that being just Cathy and me driving to a friend's house in Oregon) when Casey said we could take Colby and B---- with us as long as we had them back by Monday night. Casey told me that he wasn't going to do anything but work that day at home. Long and short of it is we had a car accident (no one was hurt but our hood wouldn't close completely). We traded seeing totality down in Oregon for sharing a view of the partial eclipse in Kennewick (this was as far from home as we could go and still be safe in returning Monday night) with the grandkids and I thought that was fine, but in the end I began to feel bad about Cathy and me missing seeing the total eclipse. Seeing the total eclipse was a very big deal to me and I let my need for fulfilling someone else's experience kill it. I'll never know if the experience we gave to Colby and B---- will make any difference in their future lives really, maybe it will. I am not selfish I don't think; I do so love Colby and B----. But never before has doing something for others so I could feel better through them hurt me so much or has it caused me so much internal conflict later. Originally our plan was for Cadance to make this trip with Cathy... Wow, I didn't realize until right this very minute that Cadance was such an important factor in this... I mean the experience of Cathy and me seeing our second and last total eclipse together in this area was to have Cadance sharing it too... This fact is very sobering in its own way.

***

Wednesday September 20, 2017. We are back home again from our trip to visit Corey and family and my letter from Sandy has been mailed to Dr. Bowers. This trip was cut short due to illness befalling both Cathy and me. We hurried home because we wanted the follow-up from Urgent Care in San Mateo to be with our family doctor.

Other stuff: Quince is so cute and this time in his little life is so precious! Corey took us along with Quince on all sorts of outings; Melinda stayed behind for one reason or another. She did come over to Kalmia (the little bungalow home Corey owns and allows us to stay in during visits) to see us one time and we enjoyed it. Just like his brother, Corey is the main caregiver for their child. This is not in any way a comparison of Melinda to Mindy but just a point in common of our sons' behavior. Corey and Melinda have been looking for age appropriate children books dealing with transgender and in their search found *The Red Crayon* by Michael Hall but thought it wasn't right for Q's age. Wow! I thought to myself, they are doing this because of me! It also brings me mixed feelings in some way. I caused a variation, a bump in the family road that they are busy working to incorporate into Quince's life. Also, somewhere in the back of my mind the tool I have used for all of my life to deny myself being transgender gets an electric poke when validation by family around me points it out and moves on past the issue. Just amazing.

***

Friday September 29, 2017. I had my last antibiotic pill on Wednesday night and the stuff is now out of my system. Some of my cough has returned but overall, I have much relief in my sinus and lungs. I have taken anti-yeast pills and will do one more either tonight or tomorrow night to stop the yeast bloom that happens when all the bacteria get knocked down (on probiotics now). We have done Pokémon raids (we love the Pokémon group we run around with especially Kevin and Sheryl) in Renton, attempted to get our internet upgraded (old story our landline wires outside are too noisy so waiting for more work to be done on our street), and have gotten help for our backs over at the Burien Wellness Center.

Me stuff: I had a deep tissue massage with Natalie for my very stiff and painful back. She is both a skilled and loving single mom in her fifties with a 4 year old and a ten year old. I like to hear people's stories of their lives, it helps distract from the painful manipulation of my joints and shoulders. The long and short of this is I told her about me being transgender. It came about as she was telling me at fifty she was thinking of dating again, but finding herself wondering if other women would be better company than men. It is customary to be naked under the sheet for this massage and my patches attracted attention so I just fessed-up (it just happened on the spur of the

311

moment and I had the feeling Natalie was trustworthy from her life story) asking her to not say anything to Cathy's mom who is also her client. I guess I could have made up some story, but I was just tired of denying things to myself or anyone else. So, Natalie and I talked about gender and about relationships while she stretched my very sore tendons. I talked about how I have been an observer of male and female all of my life, and then moved on to things I thought about both. At some point, she had a little gasp and said, "You would be perfect! I need the company of a trans-woman! You have the most unique perspective, I need to find someone like you!" Anyway, she told Cathy, who had her massage right after me, that she was enamored with me. All this was fun but it tires me to talk about me in this way.

Sandy asked me (she of course planted this seed that would pop up later) if I felt vulnerable moving from a privilege level to a minority level. Such a thought had never occurred to me before, the dysphoria hides so much until you start to treat it, and then the tug-of-war rises up. So yes, I feel that vulnerability and it is the same vulnerability I have pointed out to myself all of my life as a means of mentally slapping myself for the thought of pining to be female bodied. It is hard to recover from a lifetime of mental slaps to a state of 'it will be okay now.' My problem (if you would call it that) is space. I have known, but been dysphoric in, male space and the associated privileges there just fed my dysphoria. In this space, to survive I parroted the tools including privilege I had observed there. I kind of locked myself in there for a sad and hopefully short lifetime. I guess what I am trying to convey is I never internally actuated the associated privileges of that male space; there was always the negative feedback from gender dysphoria standing in the way. Turning all this onto its head continues to be a bumpy road. Lately, I find myself interested in breast forms or breast enhancers. I mean what I really want in the end is for my breasts to be real. So, I guess this is just some path my mind has set upon to move myself down the gender road. I'll talk more to Sandy about it this Tuesday…

***

Friday October 6, 2017. Cathy and Cady spent our 43 anniversary in Victoria BC. Weather, food, carriage ride, Laurel Point Hotel (they provided a memory foam mattress topper for us), BC Museum, reflexology, and shopping were all very pleasant. Folks in Victoria were just tolerant of us in our tie-dye but that was all. Even so we kept our chins up, thinking what all this really amounts to is a learning experience in being outside of the norm. We were referred to as ladies one time and I did thank the woman for it. I learned that you engage people one on one and they will either relax with you as you are or not. You can't really move them one way or the other. Somehow, we stuck out in a sea of people who were themselves trying very hard to stick out. The piercing place we learned about last year was no longer around but we did look for it anyway. All in all, we walked 22 miles in our three-day stay and have happy but tired feet to show for it. Cadance (Cady as Cathy calls me) poked her head in many clothing stores but didn't find anything appealing. Cady longs to fit into life among the women we pass as we walk; she always has done this, but quietly without any expectation of actual movement. The realization is never before has she been so close to doing just this. More and more this seems possible, but in the form of a barely discernible steady continual movement coming towards her. I'll chat with Sandy on Monday…

***

Thursday November 9, 2017. Me stuff: I got up this last Monday (11/6/17) morning and told Cathy I wanted to get my ears pierced that day and she told me that was fine because she wanted to get her ears pierced that day too. We had two names given to us by Debbie Caddell who is knowledgeable in that world; she gained her place in that world from the business of laser removal of unwanted tattoos. The two picks are Skin and Soul Tattoo and Pierced Hearts Tattoo. Skin and Soul Tattoo was in downtown Bellevue while Pierced Hearts Tattoo was north of Sandy's office and toward the UW, both places opened at 11:00am. To pick which one we nervously searched for reviews on the Internet. We tentatively chose Pierced Hearts but reserved final choice

313

after phoning the place to see if they were friendly and they were. We made an appointment for 12:30 and raced there in our car. We found Pierced Hearts in a somewhat scary neighborhood near a food bank and sad empty buildings. We had to circle the block twice to find a park. We walked in the wrong direction and in doing so passed a line at the food bank where one of the people took offence to me for some reason and threw a ball at my back. It fell short and we just kept walking. Things got much better when we walked into the Tattoo shop. The counter lady was bright and cheerful despite having to use a knee-scooter for a hurt ankle. She helped us pick out earrings and do paper work. Cathy and I picked the same style (barbell type) but with different color opal stones. We met Joey a very gentle, assuring and multi-pierced husky fellow who would do our piercings. He led us to the back of their office past busy tattooing stations and explained every step that he would do in piercing our ears. I was to be first per Cathy so I got to sit in the treatment chair. First, Joey marked a dot and asked me to verify that it was the right place. I told him I had my left ear lobe moved to be more symmetrical so he remarked the dots to balance that. He told me he was just going to feel the placement of the piercing, then I was to take a deep breath and as I let it out through my mouth he would pierce my ear. He said take the breath and I felt a poke a little greater than electrolysis gave and breathed out and it was done. The other one was just the same. Yes, some pain but nothing great and I kept reminding myself how much Cadance wanted this. Joey put my earrings in and I got to see in the mirror. It was so cool!!! I was so happy! It was Cathy's turn now, during this time we all got to talking about gemstone jewelry. Joey was very interested in the subject especially about what we knew about BC Jade. We were pierced and felt like we made a new friend. A funny thing during our time here, one or the other of the tattoo artist would suddenly let out a piercing scream every now and then. Joey laughed and told us it was just part of working here. He walked us back to the front and told us what to do to care for our earrings and piercings. Spray saline solution on the them twice a day and dab them dry, no need to twist them just leave them alone, other than that treat them as if they were already healed up. It will take 4 to 5 months for healing to be complete but if we find we really didn't like our earrings and wanted to changed them out just come back in and it is possible to do before this time. On the way back to the car I thought to myself, when I finally do something I always wonder why I didn't do it sooner. After this adventure we had a time of both being down/sad. I did post on Facebook about the earrings no great shakes, a lunch with Dr. Ken was canceled, so to break the sad time we went to the movie *Thor: Ragnarok*.

***

Thursday November 16, 2017. I used progesterone cream last night hoping I would wake up to a clearer head both in breathing and thinking. Instead, I woke up this morning to a bad dream; one full of me being out of control saying and doing angry things, and Cathy parting from me to go to some event on her own. It was an awful mean dream and I woke up with all kinds of anxieties that persisted most of today. All I can figure was the progesterone cream and my reduction of Avodart/Dutasteride (T blockers) had something to do with it. T blockers prevent/block certain receptors in your brain from acting on receipt of testosterone metabolites, these receptors affect a lot of brain functions including mood (blocked receptors can cause depression, etc.). Progesterone also stimulates these same receptors (it is nicknamed the female feel-good hormone) elevating mood and opposing metabolites of estrogen (these gum up other brain function). Anyway my receptors were totally opened up since I reduced my T-blockers and like a dummy, I reasoned backward (yes I am dyslexic) and used too much progesterone at a wrong time with so many receptors fully open. What a wave of emotional turmoil! Fortunately adding a blocker pill and just waiting the day out returns me to a more balanced state. So, to try to pull out something positive from this, I got to look at all my anxieties and fears amplified many times. You see and feel every little hidden facet so very strongly. Just a bad day overall I hope tomorrow will be closer to normal for me.

I also took an anti-yeast pill before bed, as my sinus is not happy either.

***

Thursday November 30, 2017. Cathy and I had dinner at Bai Tong with our high school friend Barb two days ago on Tuesday. I dressed in the same way as I do for my sessions with Sandy. We stayed until they insisted we leave and then Barbara invited us for tea at the house where she is currently staying. She said, "I want to continue talking about this." The 'this' was me offering to swap stories, mine being that I was TS, and hers about her transgender son. The dinner started off with all kinds of small talk mostly between Cathy and Barb but after we finished eating I put out my offer. I came-out to her about being transgender and I supposed because of her son she had guessed about me being transgender some time ago. No, no she hadn't and she was taken back about me but came back with, "It all makes sense." It was amazing really, I just trusted that Barb would take it the right way and she did. The grounds I had for that reasoning were that we had learned about her son being trans from a comment of hers on Facebook. But I am hypervigilant about being transgender and forget other people aren't. We had to leave the restaurant as they needed the table, but Barb really wanted to keep talking so we ended up at her late parents' house here in Tukwila. It was a nice long evening full of drama on both sides. Barb told about her experience with her daughter being a lesbian on the way out to college, to return home a transgender son. Lots more heartache ensued but not from transitioning, from other issues he had. More drama, Barb and her husband are taking a time out so she is staying here in Tukwila in her late parents' empty home. Barb understands trans stuff from her son's experience so we had a really good talk. It was a three-way talk Cathy included. We parted just before being all talked out. I felt as if some huge weight had been lifted from me but really didn't fully understand what it was. In fact, I slept so deeply and serenely that night it was just amazing, it was something I haven't done in many years. Below is the message thread that I sent to Barb. I started to understand just what had happened and why a weight was at least temporarily lifted from me, and perhaps why a new weight has taken its place...

316

Me: Hi Barb; the enormity of our talk has come to me today. You are the first person, outside of the circle of professional healthcare people and very select family, that I have outed myself to or should I say admitted to being TS too. Stuff like this never dawns on me until a day or two passes after the fact. I always tell my therapist that she plants seeds during our sessions that will flower in my mind sometime later in the week. Anyway, it turns out that you being outside of this protective shell is indeed very special to me. You knew me ages ago as just another guy in school so admitting this to you is like opening a door I kept shut years ago... I slept so completely serene last night just as if a weight had been lifted from me. Thank you again dear friend.

Barb: I'm so glad to hear all of this my dear girl. I was thinking a lot about it too and I felt and feel incredibly honored that you told me and I hoped our rambling talk helped. Yes, let's do keep talking and hopefully get together again before Christmas.

***

Friday December 15, 2017. Cathy and I are cleaning our house like crazy to make room for Corey and family. We have purchased ten plastic bins to fill up with all the loose stuff piled in the corners of each room. The next step is to find places out of sight to stack the bins then comes cleaning, and finally the Christmas tree.

I am still worried about this coming gathering at Christmas, but on the other hand what happens certainly will not be what I dream up out of fear. I am tired, which means depression is up; one of the clues to this is things we used to find comfort in doing or a respite from the gloom of the political world, are not working. Going to Starbucks, playing the Pokémon game with other folks, eating out, everyone is too busy to be caught up in the gloom I guess. I could sure use a positive note or two right about now. It is a hard time, a time that magnifies all your emotional stresses. My time with Sandy this Tuesday is something I will look forward to but the next one in two weeks will have lots of things to talk out and that one I will really appreciate.

***

Thursday December 28, 2017. Christmas 2017 has been the most memorable Christmas in recent memory. All of Cathy's siblings were together for Christmas Day Linda, Mark, and Phil. We had a truly white Christmas so little Quince could not only experience his first snow but his first Christmas snow! Corey, Melinda, and little Q were wonderful houseguests in our little place, filling our home with Quince joy, laughter, and a few diapers (well worth all the work prior to tidy up and Quince-proofing our house). All the work Casey put into getting his house repaired and serviceable for hosting Christmas Day came to fruition and all his guests raved about the Christmas feast he prepared. He did it all, every dish, and all were just great. We really did have a wonderful Christmas, one that will be very hard, if not impossible, to even come close to matching in the years to come. And this makes it bitter-sweet to think of it as the last big Anderson/Dixon Family Christmas...

The highlights were:

Having fun (yes Sandy I said fun, it's easy to see Q having fun and so did I too) playing with Quince and looking at things through his eyes. When put to bed he talks to himself going over the day, I listened outside his door and heard 'Nanna, Boppa, Colby, B----, Casey' all named and 'uh-oh' a few times, his toys and books were mentioned. I realized he was putting the day to rest and I wondered if I did that, too, at night just before I sleep.

Having my plans for Casey to babysit Quince one day while Corey, Melinda, Cathy, and I had lunch with Uncle Ray and Pat worked out. I could see that Casey longed to be with Quince and be a caregiver again of a little one and this gave that to him.

Seeing Christmas morning with Casey's and us and have it flow to afternoon with everyone else arriving despite the snow and then more Christmas gift opening followed by visiting and dinner.

The lowlights were:

The snow trapped us at our house Christmas morning so Casey had to come get us in his big four-wheel drive vehicle. The result was we forgot some key gifts (a battery ride-on excavator that really digs, a Harry Potter clue game) in rush to get back to his house and they had to wait until the next day. I was very sad as a special gift for Quince that I had worked so hard to get was forgotten and this colored most of my Christmas morning experience.

Being on all the time and constantly performing for everyone was just so draining for me. I needed to make people happy and moving along in a funny way every minute; this would just fatigue me mentally.

Okay Sandy, me stuff: One morning before Corey's arrived I was getting dressed in our bedroom and couldn't find a top to wear. I was poking around a pile of clothes with only a pair of tights on and nothing on top. I was bare on top and suddenly realized I felt no discomfort in being this way. How crazy is this I thought. I do have my two little breasts, just a little too big for a guy my size to have and yet I felt perfectly balanced with nothing on; in fact it was no big deal at all. I never felt this way when I had a hairy guy chest, I would have been grabbing for anything to cover my top. Just what has happened to me to go from complete hiding/shame to being more than fine with modest exposure of my chest???

Health: I have had a terrible time with my hands, so very dry and painful. The pointing/index finger on my right hand burns and is so stiff I can't make a fist or open a bottle without great pain; it's the same on the left hand but not as bad. My skin cracks and bleeds at bend points on both pointers. They wake me up at night, itching like crazy. I scratch and get some relief but it doesn't last at all. If I put them under burning hot water until I can't stand it, the pain reduces some but again this doesn't last. I have tried several creams, salt water, anti-yeast, and antibiotics; nothing helps. Yesterday it started to improve, hopes it continues. I wonder if the low T has anything to do with it?

I got my missing labs redone this is the lowest my T has ever been! Realigning my hormone system is the biggest and most hurtful medical challenge I have ever faced. Yes, my skin is suffering because of this. There aren't any doctors within my reach who have skill in transgender medicine, as it is a closeted small population. Even so, since 2005, so much has changed for the better…

2018

Monday January 8, 2018. As of the first, I have reduced my dutasteride to twice a week. I have read that progesterone will counter the hair loss I am having so I will give that another try, especially since I can get it over the counter as a cream. Last time my one attempt to balance these two meds brought on an emotional wave of anxiety and sadness. There is some kind of bounce from the extremely low T I now have plus almost no Avodart/dutasteride when adding progesterone… We are just leaving to drive down to see Corey in San Mateo.

***

Thursday January 11, 2018. Today is a beautiful January day here, cool but not cold and sunshine. Cathy and I spent the day walking through Central Park here in San Mateo playing our Pokémon Go game and sitting enjoying life happing around us. The past few days were a different story. We left home on the 8th and arrived at Kalmia on Tuesday the 9th at 7:30pm. Walking through the house revealed that yes other folks had stayed here. Things were mostly okay but not as we left them. Cathy threw herself like a whirlwind into unpacking and wouldn't stop until every last thing was out the car, the bed remade, bathroom arranged, and kitchen restored. She didn't slow down until bedtime. Corey came over to welcome us back, show us his new car, and to take us to the store so we could get supplies.

We slept fitfully and awoke to Quince's 2nd birthday day. We spent the day getting ready for our little party with Quince in the evening after Corey, Melinda, and little Q get home. We shopped for a card and any little gift for him that took our fancy. We still aren't comfortable re-establishing ourselves at Kalmia yet, some things are changed such as the neighbor (Scotty) across the street has moved

321

away and the big tree in the front yard has been removed. Thankfully other familiar attributes are very much the same. Kalmia was a smart looking two-bedroom rental home Corey owned about a quarter mile from their house. When the last renter moved away before Quince was born, Corey left Kalmia empty for us to stay in and whoever else might come to visit them. In many ways Kalmia had become our second home, we assembled all the IKEA furniture that filled each room and welcomed little Q there each time he visited Nanna and Boppa. Cathy and I made gluten-free spice cake cupcakes and a fruit cocktail molded Jell-O treat for Quince's Birthday Cake. We drove over to Corey's place just as he and Quince were getting out of the car. Quince was overjoyed to see us and it was great fun to pick him up and carry him around while cars were unpacked. Melinda arrived a few minutes later in her little car. So Quince had his birthday dinner, cake, and presents, all enjoyed to the highest levels. He was measured against the bedroom wall and is growing up right along. He uses much longer sentences and is just great fun to play with.

***

Thursday January 25, 2018. We are home again in Tukwila. We celebrate Linda and Cathy's birthday in a week from this Saturday. Quince is adapting to his right arm being in a cast, he's back to running, smiling, and teasing. This is a great blessing! Quince doesn't seem to be in any great discomfort and has mastered sleeping on a bed made up of the crib mattress and body pillows directly on the floor in his room. He is free to get up during the night and does, but so far stays in his room and returns to his little bed after his walk around. The reason for being on the floor is all about his cast not getting damaged.

Switching grandchildren: We went to Colby's school's Science Night tonight to see his poster on Grace Hopper, a pioneer in early computing and creator of the computer language Basic. He is in full pre-adolescence and feeling the first effects of T that his body is starting to produce in larger quantities. That little loving boy with the gentle spirit, who hugged us whenever we came to visit, has been replaced by someone much more firm and aggressive. His sister's aggression has mediated somewhat and she has become more of a hug bug. B---- will be staying with us this Sunday trading off to Colby on Monday (he has a day off from school). Watching your grandchildren grow up isn't as much fun as you might think as it happens so quickly...

Me stuff: I am glum, depressed, and tired. My mind seems to bring up more hurtful memories to reinforce this state each day. I don't feel right not male nor female. I know that is a vague statement but it is as close as I have to explain where I am at this minute. Cadance is hardy with me at all; this is a loss, this hurts, and adds to being glum. So, let's try to figure what might be driving this mean cycle. There are lots of negative world events around me and negative personal events also. On top of these, I am at the lowest level of Testosterone (free, total, and bioavailable) I have ever experienced. So, after mind numbingly wading through miles of dreary text on the net, bringing no good answers, but some explanations, I think I understand a little of what is going on. And that is the very low T level is known to bring depression as a side effect and so is the T blocker Avodart/dutasteride. The answer seems to be in adding progesterone in place of the blockers but you shouldn't do this until E (estradiol) is high enough (whatever that level is) and the blockers are out of your body for some time (however long that is). Adding progesterone with T blockers in your body just messes everything up mood wise. So next month I will further reduce blockers to just one pill every week and after a month I will stop completely then add progesterone and perhaps pregnenolone also. Why does this have to be so hard? Everything was so much simpler just a few years ago! Medical resources for treating transgender hormone replacement therapy (HRT) are still hard to come by, leaving the research up to the patient. That's just the depression talking again… So, all this typing is just me thinking out-loud in trying to overcome what is happening to me. Oh yes I forgot I am still ill; the center of my forehead is full of constant pressure/pain; this must be added to the effects of low T and mood. There is hope: I'll be off the amoxicillin, which is helping, in four more days then I'll take a pink anti-yeast pill and with this I have high expectations of great relief. You know what I think? I think I will make an appointment for some electrolysis this next week that is a good thing to wake up Cadance…

***

Thursday February 8, 2018. First, my struggle getting off of dutasteride, my last pill was on January 24th. Upside, depression is much less, I can recall music and images, and thinking is much clearer. Downside, hair is thinning, and a less feminine feeling over all. Someone suggested something brilliant on the HRT forum about patches! Instead of simply removing all of your patches every three days and putting on new ones, leave one from the last three days on for three more days in addition to the three new ones. They are good for longer just not at the same strength. It works! I feel much better as my E numbers were low (200ish and I needed more in the 300 area) for some reason and this didn't require more money or a new script. I will try cycling in progesterone soon (when I feel well again) and see how I feel.

While depression from the dutasteride is less, it is still a problem and will remain so in the state I am in. The answer is to find a way out of this state and see what happens. By the way, I have no regrets from starting HRT despite the years of painful trial and error looking for a balance point; this is all balanced out by the relief it brings to me gender wise. I did have an electrolysis appointment with Marsha and it proved therapeutic for both of us. Catherine and Cadance both have deep tissue massages from Natalie (she is fast becoming our friend). She is also eager to learn about my journey and I find it affirming and therapeutic to talk to her. It turns out she has had schooling and is just short of her MS as a therapist. Her life story is quite amazing; falling, battling back, falling again, finding Christ, and rebuilding her life with her two sons to take care of. Oh, and very learned in physical therapeutic massage, she has been a godsend to my back.

Unfortunate stuff: Cathy and I have both been ill, me more so this last week. Colby and B---- came down with whatever is going around (and it is not nice at all) so they passed it on to us and to Casey. Our car's transmission died we will have to use a rental for our planned to drive down for Corey's birthday.

Cathy's birthday was nice; we ate at Capitol Cider, a completely gluten-free restaurant downtown and a very rainbow friendly place. The French fries were very good as were the burgers and French onion soup. I gave Cathy the birthday present of a facial appointment with Mary at Caddell's and she used it on Friday the 9th. Casey catered a party at Grandma Dixon's house for two birthdays (Cathy's and Linda's); his food was great. We played Saturday night games with everyone and it went tolerably well with the exception of Colby trying to control his emotions and Linda and Grandma not really understanding this. But in the end even Cathy's brother Mark had a good time. There was talk about doing this kind of thing on a cruise; we'll see. Also, this was the seventh anniversary of Cathy's dad Ainsley's passing and his absence was keenly felt, especially by Cathy. A cruise was instigated by Mark and his wife last October and flowered into a Dixon family cruise through the Panama Canal this April. All the Dixon brothers and sisters plus spouses along with mother Joyce. Cathy and I will cruise back alone as everyone else is flying home. Cathy and Cady have special plans for this return trip…

***

Friday February 23, 2018. We are here in San Mateo getting ready to leave for home. The rental SUV has been okay but it will sure be nice to have our old car back. (Note added on 12/31/18: The four-wheel drive was a godsend as we came back into a blinding snowstorm just south of Olympia.) The guess when the car would be fixed was today, but it was finished two days ago! I got Quince to say, "Happy Birthday Baba" on a little video and Corey loved it. Melinda is in Alabama interviewing and will be back late tonight so we will not see her before we leave. Corey has an offsite next week and was teasing Melinda she will have to do Quince duty… Cathy and I visited Quince's daycare to have fun with all the little toddlers and to see what illness we might catch this trip. The weather here has been sunny and chilly for the area.

Me stuff: I can't deny being transgender no matter how closely I look back through my life for signs of something else to explain things. I have put myself in an uncomfortable place seeking relief from being TS and I have put Cathy in discomfort too. I need to get my blood numbers to see if E only will work for me; I feel like I have lost some breast volume from this also. All this is just venting, not a lot of good stuff lately. On the other hand, I have been sir'd so much that I've gotten to telling myself it doesn't matter anymore so I keep my hair back and wear nothing to give a female clue. I tell myself it's okay; everyone is comfortable with me, then out of nowhere on the drive here I get called ma'am, honey, and sweetie in a gas station, and again at a store. And it is so relieving to me…

***

Thursday March 1, 2018. This last appointment Sandy asked me what was the biggest thing bothering me right at that moment, then added, "Don't think just tell me." This gray haired-pixie (a mental giant in a small package) in her seventh decade sat directly across from me, legs crossed loosely at the knee, and was looking right through me into the very heart of the pain (that I didn't know was so strong) that I was having. And I answered, the passing of time. I am up against it: our family doctor is talking about retiring in just over a year from now,

I have a surgery date with Dr. Bowers coming in October, and the very office Sandy and I are sitting in will be gone sometime after April. This last is the hardest since it brings an end to my time with her; that precious gift I value so. I have been so slow moving toward a resting place gender-wise, but in my own defense, and looking back to affirm this, I think I really have traveled as fast as was possible for me.

Let's look at each part of the time issue:

Dr. Marsden retiring. She has been our family doctor for the last forty-three years but directly to the point, she is the support of my HRT meds and blood tests. There is no joy in looking for a new doctor at all and this weighs on both Cathy and me.

My surgery date with Dr. Bowers. Upcoming blood tests will help me to set aside doubts about the value of surgery to me hormone wise.

Sandy retiring. I have only 4 or 5 more possible face-to-face appointments left with her. What an amazing resource she is and what a blessing she has been to me! She has opened my eyes to a whole world I didn't know at all and to a person within me I needed to come to know. In a true sense she saved my life. Imagine her at the wheel of a BMW racing down the autobahn in Germany twenty years after the end of World War II! She did this in the 1960s. She had gathered herself up and traveled alone to Germany to find herself, just amazing. I find great joy in her life story. Cady is going to make the most use possible of these last face-to-face appointments to refresh memories of things Sandy has shared that may have faded from our memory.

Me stuff: We have Colby this Sunday and B---- this Monday. During their spring break (April 9 to April 13) Casey, Mindy, Colby, and B---- will all drive down to San Mateo and stay the week at Kalmia. The kids are so looking forward to playing with Quince and so is Casey. They will do the tourist thing in SF also. Cathy and I will stay at Corey and Melinda's house during this same time. Quince has spring break during this week so he will be home with a babysitter and Corey has said that he will take a few days off to have fun with everyone. I am hoping this will be the best visit yet for everyone!

***

Thursday March 9, 2018. Cadance stuff: Cady feels much better today; I am more myself with the reservation of a dull headache from pollens. So wonderful to be able to think again and enjoying the relief that decreased sinus pressure/pain gives. I have an appointment with Dr. Marsden for a blood draw for hormone levels on Monday; this should answer several questions, and put my mind more at ease. What I want to see in the results is a reduced free T level and an E level above 250. I am optimistic that the pregnenolone I have started will improve my mental health given some time. This is a pressing time for me though, mainly because so much has been thrown at me in the way of forcing issues at an accelerated timetable. I just got a perfectly timed call from Robin, the scheduler at Dr. Bowers office, asking if I would like to fill a cancellation they suddenly had for my surgery. Perfect in a bad way of course, as it feeds the-everything-coming-at-once and too quickly pressure we have. Frankly the call was a bit of a jolt; October being a good way out gave me so much more time to prepare. I work with C---- little by little as he recedes so we can be whole. We are together in our fears of making a misstep. The call was for Cady and I told Robin that I couldn't take the appointment since we are out of town until June first. She responded that was fine and I was still at the head of the list for cancellations. Oh my. I had a nice visit/appointment with Marsha Morgan my electrologist and laser friend. We chatted longer than the time spent in electrolysis. It is such an amazing thing to have fallen into company with Marsha and Sandy, and to have them both have Marsha Botzer's transition in common. While at Caddell's, Debbie asked if she would see us at *Esprit* in May. No, unfortunately we will be down south. Debbie has become a good friend to Cathy and Cady; her story is a remarkable one also.

I am husband to Cathy and she is wife to me, we are just an interesting couple in both a standard way and non-standard way. I would like to chat more about this with Sandy on this Tuesday.

***

Thursday March 15, 2018. My last appointment with Sandy included Cathy and was very helpful for the both of us. Cathy got to voice things that were under the surface such as our identity as a couple. We all left together from Sandy's shared office going down the creaky stairs and out to the street. Outside on the sideway Cathy walked next to Sandy the two of them chatting and I followed appreciating the moment.

***

Yesterday we drove to Decent Exposure in Lake City to see about some custom leggings for Cathy. Their manufacturing shop is on the second floor with a door at street level leading to a flight of stairs. You buzz the intercom to get someone to come let you in. There were only two ladies at the place, one busy on a power sewing machine, and the other in charge of taking orders and fittings. Cathy tried on several types of leggings and chose L with the modification of waist increased and length adjusted. I worked up the courage to ask to try on some leggings also, no problem. This was good because the enormity of what I had just done was having its way with me. I was nervous to the point of being clumsy in trying things on. The L was close but I ended up with M with the modification of adding two inches on the length and at the waist. We both chose several colors and finally, in what was a watershed moment for Cadance, I asked about a bra for me. It didn't bother the lady at all; she got right down to business, measured my band size and set about pointing out several to try on.

She pointed out, "You need at least two inches added to the shoulder strap length, around 39 inches in the band and a C cup. Here try the racer back with front closure made with organic cotton and a little Lycra. How does that feel?"

It felt amazingly right! No rib or back pain that I normally get from the off-the-shelf almost-fitting-but-not bras I own. Those garments were all about tolerating the discomfort. These fitted bras have the promise of an appropriate place on my body and with comfort... We ordered two one in black with a racer back and one in beige in a standard back at $44 each. Our custom clothing bill was over $400 on seven pairs of leggings and two bras. Yes, it was an expense but we expect the garments to last a long time and the experience for me was very valuable. I was flying high after we returned to the car; it was a big thing I had just overcome and Cathy was beaming with pride for us both.

Cathy and I had dental appointments and I ended up telling Jennifer (Dr. Ken's dental Jill-of-all-trades/office manager) I was transgender. It was the oddest thing, she had finished polishing my teeth and I was looking in the mirror. I exclaimed my eyebrows were full of little white hairs that I need to remove; this led on to a discussion about hair and eyebrows. Right in the middle of this girl-to-girl talk, something screamed inside me to tell her and before I could catch myself, I did. It wasn't a mistake but I was queasy to my stomach that I would do such a thing... After I told her I felt like apologizing but Jennifer said, "Don't, it is a beautiful thing!"

Cathy found a cute green t-shirt (medium) to give to Sandy; it had the outline of a cat filled with white shamrocks. She loved it and told us that she would wear it during her daily workouts.

A note: a typical Sandy outfit is a polo shirt and jeans, matching colored socks, many with cats on them. Sandy is 4'11 and thin she wears a boy's sized skiing coat (shoes too) and used to lug a backpack around everywhere (not anymore). Her backpacks generally have a Disney theme and sometimes the addition of a big sticker bearing Keep Abortion Safe and Legal on them. Over the time I have known her, her right arm has recovered enough from the stroke to slowly begin to gesture in a natural way while speaking. She can't really use it to move or lift much, writing is all left handed as well as steering her little red car. She is so amazing, so sharp (her sky blue eyes can look right inside you), and so wise with experience of all the years (30 some) at the Crisis Clinic and in private counseling for transgender. She spent her youth in Yakima; she has two sisters and her father was in real estate. She came-out as gay late in high school but never acted upon it. After graduation and with some college, she spent several years in Germany. She marched in the first Gay Pride Parade in Seattle and counseled some of the first MtF persons (38 years ago) here. What is amazing is that Marsha Morgan (then Marsha Moyer) my electrologist did that MtF's hair removal. In Sandy's private practice

330

over the years, she has seen both MtF and FtM in pretty much equal numbers. She told me flatly that no one in her practice has ever regretted or not been relieved by moving toward the gender that they felt was true to them. Many had checked back in with her over the years after transitioning, but with other life issues external to the steps addressing GID.

Sandy has warned me many times that I can't go back gender-wise to where I was before after experiencing the steps I have taken. Once you know the truth it changes you.

Journal stuff: Caddell's Laser and Electrolysis Clinic had a flood from a broken pipe, again shutting them down for a few days just when I need to get private parts' hair removal done for surgery. This was the second time such a thing happened to Debbie. Luckily none of her machines were damaged just wet carpet everywhere. The first time this happened, she needed to repaint in places. We went to B----'s culture fair at Lake View Elementary. I called to see if cousin Carol was acting on the Anderson picnic. Cathy and I both have had back spasms and have had a painful Dr. Yale appointment. Tomorrow we will have massages with Natalie.

***

Thursday March 22, 2018. Sandy gave me two names that I might use as a counseling resource. Rachel, her practice is full but she could recommend folks to me and Calvin, he is young but up to date with all the current stuff.

We talked about my experience at Descent Exposure, which comes down to most people really don't care anymore male or female, and about my vivid dream, a very productive appointment with her. I also got to show her my good blood numbers from successfully getting off dutasteride and how positive pregnenolone seems to be for me. The trouble is dutasteride is a 5-alpha-reductase inhibitor; its action depletes allopregnanolone, and many other neurosteroids in your brain. This causes memory trouble as well as depression, etc. Pregnenolone metabolically becomes allopregnanolone and begins to resupply shortages; so I have read. I can feel my body trying to come to terms of estradiol blocking testosterone without dutasteride. Little erections disturb my sleep once again. I will just have to wait and see how it all turns out...

I have been to Caddell's and found out from Marsha that she doesn't do genital hair removal but Debbie has taken training in it. So, I caught Debbie after my Marsha appointment and she told me exactly what I needed and where. She would need 15 minutes of laser time and any white hairs would have to be removed with electrolysis, which she no longer does, but she does refer to someone who does... I have an appointment with Debbie for laser on April 4th at 6:30. As with other stuff' there is no question I will feel better after getting this done as hair removal can be applied to either bottom surgery. I still don't completely understand what drives me or has driven me to do the few things I have done gender-wise. Half of me is quite surprised at the moment of an action, and the other half is quite confident and calm at that very moment (like making the appointment with Debbie), so off I go... This last time at Caddell's, there was an MtF waiting in the lobby. She was dressed in a brave outfit of a skirt, nylons, top with a sweater, and a pink scarf covering lack of hair. I told Cathy I thought she was pretty brave and what did Cathy think about her? Cathy told me she liked how I wore my femininity better... I would have liked to ask Sandy a question or two at that moment.

**

Thursday March 29, 2018. Well, I have two appointments left with Sandy April 3rd and the 17th. We will be in San Mateo with our two son's families the week of the 7th until the 14th and then get aboard ship with the Dixons on the 19th and be back home again on May 27th.

I wear a bra that is fitted just for me most of the time now, in fact, it feels strange not to have it on during the day. I also have three pairs of tights sized for me that I don't look good in at all because of my fat roll. It's going to take more work to put together clothes for the return part of our trip and it is feeling like a very time consuming task. I have an appointment with Debbie Caddell this coming Wednesday to have my personal parts lasered. Just a note about private-area laser hair removal. Wow! It burns with the most exquisite pain I have had from any other area. I can hardly hold still for it and consider myself pretty tough in standing laser pain. Electrolysis in this area is just as bad.

Sandy I use my journal to record and straighten my thoughts the ones that need to come to the surface and I promised to share these with you. I think it is the right thing to do even if this includes you in them...

The seriousness of the fact that my time with Sandy Fosshage is coming to an end is upon me. The mental weight of this is bearing down on me more and more as it gets closer and closer. There is so much more I should have done, while I was under her wing, and I knew she had my back. Just like she had the backs of so many transgender folks over the years. I expect each of them felt very fortunate for her support then and when it was time to move on went through what I am going through now. What a singular honor I have had and what an amazing experience has been mine to be guided by Sandy at this time in her practice... I am a huge fan of Sandra L. Fosshage!!!

Now I need to move this back to me because this is what Sandy will do when I see her in a few days.

So how is this bearing down on me, what parts, and what did I feel I didn't do?

I would have liked to have been able to show Sandy the finished product from our time together, me at a gender resting place. I would have liked to have met Marsha Botzer (she established the Ingersoll Gender Center Sandy has known her for years), made appointments to explore different surgeries (tummy, breast, face, waist, etc.), walked through Southcenter in appropriate dress, get my ears pierced (oh, I already did this), see what a wig could do, and stuff like this. I just would have like for her to have known Cady better.

I don't want to lose Sandy, this historical link to the LGBT world that I have each time I had an appointment with her. A lot of the time I don't even feel that I am part of this world but with her it is at least

333

possible. And the movement of time always drags on me and this is a strong expression of that movement.

Now an odd thing to report: In a very strange way, the fact that our normal appointments are coming to an end seems to give me a sense of accomplishment. Right there in amongst the fear and sadness, lies the feeling of something of great importance that I seemed to have done, to have completed. I look forward to talking with Sandy about all of this come Tuesday.

***

Friday April 13, 2018. I type this from Kalmia. Casey and family just left to drive home and we will leave very early tomorrow morning also. The sad news is Melinda is expecting an offer from a University in San Diego to start there this coming October. They will be selling both homes here and be relocated well before she starts in SD. So, this chapter in the Cathy and C---- story is coming to a complete end. So many things are coming to an end, really. Of course, why couldn't we just continue to drive down to SD and visit Corey's family there? Yes, we could, but there is a note of separation in Corey's attitude toward us now that wasn't there before. Cathy and I feel like we are begrudgingly tolerated company as opposed to welcome visitors. This is also how we feel visiting at Casey's house, especially after Casey and Mindy got back together. I am glum. Cathy and I both feel abandoned and in a true sense don't care about much anymore. It was more than convenient that Dr. Bowers was near Kalmia for my surgery. I felt that we benefited along with Corey's family by being here during this time and now we're just strangers in a strange place; the whole thing just seems empty. Cathy surprised me by telling me she wasn't going to let me give up on Cady. Anyway, I am tired and it is affecting my emotions. We have been short on sleep this whole last week. It is odd; at times I don't even know who I am other than being different from who I was. There is the good news that Casey and family all got to have the experiences I so hoped they would have with Corey's family. Lots of game nights with Uncle Corey plus Casey got to share with his brother some of his accomplishments that he is proud of. We had my early birthday together since my birthday will come while Cathy and I are away on a cruise with the Dixon family.

It was both a good and hard visit. Using the tools Sandy has given me over our time together, I tried to look at all the interaction of our sons from all angles, knowing all they are going through with holding their families together. All this to understand the movement of their lives and ours.

Thank you, Sandy, for all you have given me in our time together. You have introduced me to myself. She thanks you with all of her heart and promises not to despair in silence but to stubbornly guide her life forward.

***

Wednesday April 18, 2018. Yesterday was my final session with Sandra L. Fosshage in her office that she shares with her business partner Patricia M. Kalafus. Pat owns the old farmhouse turned office building and is retiring also. At least, she will return their shared office for rent or at the most, sell the building out right. I had baked Sandy gluten-free chocolate chip cookies and included the recipe so she could make them herself. Each Christmas, I have given her a tin of my cookies and in return she praises them. I know she enjoys them greatly (it is not in her nature to give false praise for anything). We talked about all I had written in my journal about the San Mateo trip, even the part about me not caring about anything anymore. I had planned to just chat with her about light stuff, this being the end of our time together, but this was not to be. It was instead a very productive typical session hitting directly on each spot I was hurting from.

I told Sandy that all my current stress revolved around my deep desire to give her something to thank her for all the time she has spent guiding, teaching, and supporting me for over ten years. And this amazing lady said, "Why?" To me then went on to say, "I should thank you!"

This floored me and stopped me cold. What? I stumbled back.

She said in a matter-of-fact tone, "I mean you allowed me to go on this journey of yours with you and I am grateful."

She explained, "This is why I do what I do; it fulfills me, it is an honor you have done to allow me to come along. I remember the person who first stood in front of me all those years ago, strong enough to seek help, but unsure what to do from there. You have come a long way and I got to travel along side of you, thank you!"

I was so close to tears and so thankful...

We continued our talk by me asking how she was doing and Sandy said it had been a long hard day at the Crisis Clinic where she has been the coordinator of the volunteers for over thirty years. With a sigh she explained, "We were short staffed and some new people who hadn't read the instructions kept raising their hands for me to come help with each call. I kept telling them to, 'Keep listening and I will be there soon.'" I in return said. A t-shirt with that phrase on it would be just the thing for you to wear to work! She laughed and laughed.

Sandy had told me stories about herself as our years had gone by and today was no different. I have felt privileged to be her last client and that she would share with me. Sandy told me she was a World War II buff and that was why, just out of school, she decided to travel to Germany to see what she had been reading about. She reminisced, "It was just twenty or so years after the war then, and I just up and went all by myself and was glad I did; what an experience!" She also shared some life advice, "You should not only view things coming to an end but what is to come next, the experience to come is the thing."

***

Thursday May 31, 2018. Sandy and her business partner Pat have cleared out their shared office of many years last weekend. Had I not gone on this trip, I could have had three maybe four more sessions with Sandy there...

On the other hand, I would not have had the most remarkable experience of being Cady (Cadance) 24 hours a day for 18 days on our return home cruise. And I was Cady, my ship's card was in her name, every receipt came out printed Ms. Cady on it, everyone at our dining room table was introduced to Cady and Cate as a female couple and they accepted us just as that. We both dressed the same as always with matching tie-dye tops. No one bothered to care otherwise. I didn't really believe I passed but figured people didn't care as long as it didn't directly involve them... But on shore tours, much to my surprise, local people constantly address me as female even though I wasn't trying very hard with my hair pulled back, etc. It was, "Señora come buy this" at each shore excursion we took. What we did to lay the groundwork for this to happen was to change our names at the front desk when we got on board. It was surprisingly easy. Cathy always wanted to be a 'Cate' so we both went incognito and everyone was quite cool with it. I never used a male restroom or changing room, always opting to return to our cabin for this. I was offered female changing room keys by staff upon entering the thermal suite but never used them (I did once but only to store our bags). We visited the thermal suite daily; it offered six heated ceramic lounges to relax on. We would both lounge for at least an hour or more, each of us in our two-piece female swimsuits. I was always taken for female here even though the place was open to men also. It was funny how folks on the ship seem to adopt us as that odd female couple always in matching tie-dye clothes. They would stop us to tell us how cute we were and make us feel special. One lady stopped Cate to tell her that her hair was such an inspiration, "It gives me courage to let my hair go its natural color!" I lost my male identity with the two men (who were on opposite sides of the political spectrum from each other) at our dining room table as they would talk together leaving me to chat with the other gals. I listened to them take turns in conversation as men do while I tried to get used to group speak with the women. Cate and Peggy passionately chatted together about beadwork. Peggy was never without a beading project at her side and as we strolled all over the ship we would invariably come across them, he with a book and she beading away. In fact, once we returned home Cathy took up beading again. It is odd to lose your sense of self, I didn't feel like C---- and in that empty place was a gal named Cady. She had no life tales to share, which didn't matter, as Peggy and Dan (two of our table-mates) had so many life adventures from being missionaries for over 30 years. No one could even come close to competing with such life experiences, so I didn't have to try, just sit quietly and listen. A rough question did arise as Peggy asked us how we gained our children, adopt? "No," Cate answered sternly that they were ours, which lead to the unasked question of which one of us or both gave birth… Again, having never passed before in any way, this sure pointed that I was at this moment. There were other adventures both positive and negative, but suddenly Cady was resolute and simply couldn't wait to have all sorts of surgeries to have a standing as female among other females. There were no doubts in her pretty little head, no reason not to, only full steam ahead; I am and shall continue to be Cady. I wore shape-wear, a bra, and matching tops along with Cate and my hair was never pulled back always down around my shoulders. On formal nights lipstick, black slacks with shimmery electric blue over the shoulder drapes or other matching tops we found on the trip. On shore, leggings and tops, but sometimes I would ponytail my hair back, and even with this I would still be addressed as female by local people. The only time I gave up on being Cady was going through customs to show my passport at the end of the cruise. Now it's over and I am totally drained emotionally. Crashing back down into the world of C---- without being him as much as I was before the trip. Cathy is all excited to travel as Cady and Cate again, but right now I don't feel like myself anymore. So odd to be who I was and return to who I am not so much anymore. So much to think about, God brought us together with a Baptist missionary couple Peggy and Dan (early 70s just celebrating their 50th anniversary) retired from 30 years of living his calling in Tanzania, full of the most amazing experiences, and more than willing to share them with us. There was a very tense few minutes when we first sat down with them at our dining room table and they perceived us to be a female couple with children. I saw a conflict flash within Dan's face and as it rose I wondered if he was going to bolt from the table! Then suddenly he came to some terms with it deciding to put up with us. I am glad he did; they had much to tell us over our time together and I think we really didn't do much for them except be an attentive audience of their stories. Diane (60s), another of our tablemates, was traveling by herself; she had some mild form of

Tourette's Syndrome compelling her to talk about some random little fact about the ship over and over repeating it day after day. Jim a very liberal man (80s) was the other man at our table. He was traveling by himself for the first time since his wife had passed away recently. He would sit quietly staring and respond to questions with just a few words (Dan, a very conservative man, would try to connect with him but with no great success). Either God brought them to us or us to them; I have no idea but I learned from each person. Two tables from our table, a young woman with red hair, part of a family group, would repeatedly glance at me during dinner. She seemed excited to see me. I got so I would wave hello to her, it turned out she was just a few cabins down from our cabin. We would see her and her family when they were out on their veranda and we on ours. She seemed excited to see us whenever our paths crossed and I let that excitement be a positive thing. Verandas were very important on this trip as it passes through the Panama Canal. We would engage with people on either side of us, sharing the wonder of passing through the canal. Another person, seemly very interested in us was a ship's shop lady Ronel. Her home was in South Africa; she was in her fifties, and was suddenly free of children (they are now adults) and husband (now divorced). She did the midlife crisis thing, which turned into joining as crew on this cruise ship for a 180-day contract and in doing so got to see the world. She was fascinated with me; my name, my height, and long hair, but never to the point of being derogatory. I never let our short conversations rise to that level; instead, I was simply who I claim to be: Cady Anderson. I never let the idea that I didn't pass as female with someone I came in contact with break the spirit of me being female. You can view it in terms of an actor who never broke character; except I wasn't acting, I was being my true self. I held it as me giving people we met an experience for them to take away, hopefully for the better. I figure Cate and I did stick out but to each other we didn't. We are just as we always are at home. It was on the last day of our cruise that I began to appreciate how our presence on the ship had affected other people. The red haired lady came up to us and told us how much she and her family enjoyed seeing us each day and how brave I was. As we waited to disembark another young woman with her little boy cornered us to tell us how proud she was of us and how seeing us added to their experience in a positive way. We chatted until our time to disembark came. There were several encounters with crew where I was addressed as sir-ma'am but many others with both crew and passengers who never gave thought to me as anything other than an older woman. One thing more about the cruise: we had bad luck playing Pokémon Go because the local cell service was so slow we couldn't connect to the game. On the other hand, we discovered there is a Pokémon gym on either end of the Panama Canal locks. After, the cruise was only a memory and we were home again. Cathy and I stopped in a rest area during a drive and as I was waiting outside of the restroom for Cathy I heard someone calling for Cady and Cate. It turned out it was the red haired lady; they live here in Western Washington!

***

Friday June 15, 2018. These last two weeks have been hard for me. I had my last official contact with Sandy on June 1st via a phone session. She was in awe in my recounting of our cruise as Cate and Cady. "Blown away," she would say and "So happy for me." It was exciting for me also to tell her all I/we had accomplished. I felt as if I was showing my mentor that all of her work spent on me over these years (13 years) was worth the effort. I had worth, I was real, it wasn't just some broken thought coming from my broken mind, this gender thing… Then the reality curtain opened. Sandy asked me if I had contacted any of the therapists she had given me. No, I hadn't. I asked if the office was still around at all? "No, someone else is renting now." I wondered aloud if we could even see each other face to face again sometime? I had some pictures I would like to share. Maybe some Saturday in late June in a coffee shop or such… Bye Sandy, thanks for all you have done for me… I guess I had hoped for something else, a few phone sessions I guess. I felt like I had earned them, but the reality is my time with Sandy is over. Things just started sliding downward from that moment as more support people will drift away.

Over at Caddell's, Debbie will do laser on my personal area but not electro nor will Marsha and the names they gave me of other electrolysis providers only led to dry phone calls ending in long list of 'what I am' and 'why would I want this done' or 'why wouldn't my current operator do it'… I am left feeling lost, alone, and unworthy in a world of 'we do lots of transgender people, how do you rate'… So, what I am left with is a world of strangers to contact for the most touchy and hurtful area for hair removal. I have to prove myself worthy and safe to them, not the other way around, as they have no connection with my lost support network. Debbie who or Marsha who or Sandy who?

We have planned a trip to take Colby and B---- on the train to see Quince for four days. Cathy is a go-girl and needs this trip. I feel it may be our last chance to get the cousins together like this. It is playing out as the last trip we will travel to see Q and family again before they all move to a new place and totally new lives. We left from Seattle Union Station on the Coast Starlighter heading south to San Jose. It was an overnight trip and the grandkids had a great time. Yes, there were bumps in our trip but overall, a wonderful journey and visit with Q and family, a very grandparent time to remember. I had planned this trip carefully so we will return in time for our Saturday June 30th appointments at Caddell's. I wanted to chat with the receptionist about Cady and Cate's cruise. I count her as another support person in a causal way as her mate was in the same place as I am and I crave to know her story as a wife of an MtF to be able to learn from it. But there was a train tunnel collapse and the train trip was delayed enough so as to miss our Caddell's appointment (this was last chance this summer to chat with her). I count this as another loss of support and increase of isolation for me. Anyway, this is a steady loss of support people in our lives. So, I am becoming more and more on edge, with a reverse pushback dysphoria roaring away to put Cady away completely. But now, who am I with her gone? I go to sleep each night pondering what a wretched thing I am. Does all I have done to quiet the dysphoria and its constant mental storm come from good or evil? After sleep comes awaking to the same problem playing over and over, but to no acceptable end. C---- died along the way, it felt like that anyway. I actually mourned him to tears and all. Sounds crazy and it is impossible to express it in any way to make anyone outside the transgender world understand what it is like to have yourself die like that. I didn't cease to be, but I wasn't C---- anymore nor was I completely Cady. It was like standing on the far side of a bridge you have just crossed that has suddenly and sharply collapsed behind you. You look back and see your homeland and mourn the fact that it is gone from you. You can't really know that you belong to this side, so you just stand there quaking. A dangerous thing quaking; it leaves you frozen in place in fear without the emotional resource to move forward. Assurance is part and parcel of the currency you pay for self-acceptance... Support people helped me cross that bridge slowly when others just ran across it, their arms open in an embrace. But I now stand alone and tired, so very tired and I am old. The great temptation is for Cady to curl up and go away (though she couldn't). There is no great joy in accepting you're transgender, just a nagging isolation. I guess I'm just at a low point with all that has happened support wise, facing surgery, mourning, and my age. Being trans for me is being sort of gay in that I yearn to be physically female but truly love Cathy. I don't even fit into what being trans is today. It has turned into some of the most varied and continually evolving things. All this is just a stream of thought.

Back to what is going on right now.

I don't feel I have a place in the female world as I am. The orchiectomy surgery was to fix that, something I could point to in my mind to say to myself, see I belong. Sandy helped me understand three things some time ago: first, I was transgender, no question about it; second, I can't go back to being the way I was before I started down this path; and third, she has never had anyone in her practice regret transitioning, not one... She didn't say just how hard it was to proceed from one side to the other for everyone. One great blessing in this entire storm is Cathy. She has lovingly walked beside C---- for all of our years together and has just as lovingly switched to walking beside

342

Cady. There isn't any doubt in my mind that it was God who paired us together.

***

Monday August 13, 2018. Well, I have come back to this journal after two months of silence. It has been Cathy urging me to start again. My reason for silence, without Sandy who would I write it for? I haven't contacted the two names Sandy had given me. I just couldn't see how either could take up where Sandy left off. Marsha had a therapist retire on her and just continued on without one, so I thought I could too. What has happened instead of me being self-reliant is I find myself seeking advice from other people that God had brought into our lives. One such is Natalie, our massage therapist. Both Cathy and I connected with her and I found Natalie to be a good sounding board.

So, let's get up to date: I have a new orchiectomy surgery date of September 14th (a month from tomorrow), my pre-surgery checkup with Dr. Marsden is on August 22nd. I need to call Patty this week and check about getting an EKG. I have become more resolute in having this operation. For the past two months, I have gone back and forth, day after day, over and over, on whether or not to have it. Finally, about three weeks ago I started to have some pain in my groin area and erections returning at night, both very disturbing to me. It was as if I was de-transitioning, returning back toward the male I was and it shocked me. I would awake from vivid dreams of male function thinking that I couldn't stand it, I wouldn't stand it, and I wasn't going back! The result was I sort of made peace with the idea of losing this part of my body, it was not only right but needed to be done. I equate the whole experience as those of someone needing a limb amputated and the surgeon leaving it attached until the pain was so great that, in the patient's mind, it would be a greater relief to have the limb removed than to still be with it. So that milestone was passed and I didn't fully understand this until Robin from Dr. Bowers office called to ask if I would like an earlier date (than Oct) and without a second's pause I said, yes! This works to both Cathy and my advantage in that

Kalmia will still be available. Corey will be back from a trip sometime on the 14th and the surgery center is just two blocks from Kalmia so Cathy will not have trouble driving me back.

I have orthodontics Invisalign tray number one in my mouth busily straightening my teeth and will go to tray two out of thirty-seven this Wednesday. The clear plastic top and bottom trays have little pockets, which the attachments that are attached to several teeth push into. The thing gives me a low-grade headache since I grind on it day and night. Natalie did give me a TMJ (Temporomandibular Joint) massage of all the facial muscles and I have never until this blessed day known such relief from my grinding problem. This gives me hope to continue my orthodontic treatment of the next 18 months ahead of me. After all the failed attempts to find someone to do electrolysis on my personal, area Marsha very generously agreed to do it for me. During a normal appointment she asked me how the search was coming and I told her it was all a bust and I was at a total loss to find someone. I had consults with several providers, none of which had experience doing that area, but were happy to learn as we went along. Marsha told me, "That is terrible, I'll do it for you!" This is such a relief to me as I will not only be ready for my orchiectomy, but in theory, I would be in good shape for SRS (Sex Reassignment Surgery). But one thing at a time. I seem to have to be either planning some gender body changing event or actually doing one. Either way, I need to be always making progress toward a final goal in this battle with time and dysphoria. It is a battle; I keep waiting for Cadance to step out from me and vanquish this life-long malady and she keeps waiting for the path to do so. Go figure. Some months ago, I told Jennifer over at Dr. Ken's about me for some reason, just all of sudden when we were alone in the office after a cleaning. She was very supportive but I am not sure why I did it back then, just needed to at that moment. Suddenly during that short time, I was someone else and that was Cady talking. I am toying with telling Dr. Ken at lunch this Wednesday.

Corey and family will own a house in San Diego this Wednesday. Corey offered to keep Kalmia just for me to have a place to recover from my upcoming surgery, bless his heart.

***

Tuesday August 14, 2018. I chat with Natalie as she works on my tight muscles. I voice that I have been falling back to questioning my place with God. Natalie told me I should just sit down and have a face-to-face talk with Jesus. The very next thing I know Jesus arranged to have me happen to find some journal pages I wrote ten years ago (July 16-17, 2008) on this very question. I marvel how I have come back from answering this question ten years ago to forgetting and having to rediscover my answer…

***

Thursday July 17, 2008 (ten years ago). A thought that came to me in the shower (of all places) was everyone has their own relationship with Jesus Christ each individually unique from all others, but with all holding the central truths of Christ's divinity and His sacrificial death, giving forgiveness for our sins, allowing us to come before our almighty God. This is what is troubling me; I am looking at others who are voicing their relationships as to who is a Christian and who is not, then measuring myself thusly. I have always believed that the Holy Ghost guides our growth in Christ so we know personally what is right and what is wrong for ourselves. This doesn't mean that I am free from the Bible. It only means that the Bible is the source of truths, but the Holy Ghost is the source of understanding these truths. Somewhere inside me I know that when I pray God hears me, and when I am doing something wrong, I feel it. I know of no other way to explain it. So, with this gender resolve I don't feel I am going against God's will for me. I pray that I always follow his will, but with so much external talk by professed Godly men and women against such things, I end up questioning that which God had given me. This is, as I sit calmly, why any evilness of gender change flows away from me; I am again listening to the spirit dwelling inside me, and not the world outside of me.

345

I haven't laughed in so long, I don't even remember the last time. I don't mean a little giggle but a real deep laugh that is almost uncontrollable and hard to stop. I have lost my anchor in being and knowing myself just like before starting elementary school so many years ago. Back then I hounded my mom constantly as I had learned she was the source of all the answers. I would lean with my bottom against the warm clothes dryer in the kitchen holding a cup of milk asking about what she was doing and why. I didn't know me, why was I, what was I, and who was God? I had bottomless questions, everything bothered me, and she was my place for answers. In the back of my little mind, there was something wrong; I was adrift trying to catch ahold of something to stop the rocking of being. The more I asked the less rocking and blackness. I have come back to this point in life again just like that little child. Everything is up for grabs, leaving me so empty and confused, because just like then at the end of the all the questions, which is how I as a little child felt. I can't fathom ever again shaving my face, having erections, giving the male sex act or having thick chest hair. My electric razor hurts my skin and is now so foreign to me. It is as if I were a child again grasping for an anchor trying to be right with God, understand me, and life around me somehow. I just came to a shaky truce then and let the years go by into adulthood. It worked for so long; now the terms are broken on my part and I lay in bed thinking that I am but a bunch of chemistry and atoms. Is that me, male because of one chemical and female because of another? I had no idea how great this turmoil had become in my mind or how much energy my mind was using to solve it each night, until it began to wake me as it did tonight. I need a rock to hold onto so I know I am more than biochemistry. I need to know God is on my side. I came to this as a child and need it now more than ever. God was always there for me no matter how odd my parents were acting or how alone I was. Time to go back to bed…

***

Wednesday August 29, 2018. Sandy has been in my thoughts for the last five days in the form of needing to talk to her. There is this nagging feeling of discord and I need to know she is okay. I tried the other day, only to reach her voicemail and even though I left a message, the thought still persisted that she might not be there to hear it... This morning, all I wanted to do was to get back home again (from Cathy's Marsha appointment) and call Sandy's number; the feeling had become very strong and urgent. It was important for me to tell her about my upcoming surgery. To let her know that she did so well with me, and to know she was still doing as always in her world. So, I tried again and again finally got her voicemail. I told it I just wanted to check in, to touch base, and that my surgery date was coming very soon. I hung up in low hopes of hearing from her at all. Twenty minutes later she called me. What a relief, but big things had happened to her! Sandy told me she had just retired completely from the Crisis Line and was lying low trying to pull herself together. She told me there were so many new policies and procedures and she could learned them but didn't want to do it any more, her brain was closed to learning, "I can do it, but I don't want to anymore." This was very big stuff for her, she had tried two times this last year to step back from her work coordinating the volunteers and making the-buck-stops-here decision of sending police services. Each time she would step right back into the game after a short time of regret. Now something physical must have pushed her beyond return and my heart felt her pain. Her voice was the same one that guided me through all of my wounds back towards life, but now there was a little tremble in it. She hadn't been answering her phone instead letting everything go to voicemail. She told me that there have been lunches and dinners for her retirement and now she just needed to be away by herself, to ruminate about what life was going to be like. She told me she wasn't planning anything at all, "That's unlike me; I'll see how long that lasts, for now I just go check on my laundry." She asked me all about my fast-upcoming surgery and we talked and I thanked her again; this time she told me you're welcome. If I had not caught her today, I would have missed her as she leaves tomorrow for Birch Bay for two weeks with her family. She got a vet-tech to stay with her cats Jack (19) and Chloe (16) for two weeks. This just shows you how big this step is in her life, for her to leave the cats at all. This is a very quaking time for Sandy to completely be stripped of her way of life, even if it is her decision to do so. She made me promise to call her after my surgery; I hope and pray for us both to find a new way in life.

***

Monday September 10, 2018. Here I am at Kalmia waiting for Thursday morning with Dr. Bowers and Friday morning at the surgery center. I just have had a long phone conversation with Casey and he asked good questions to which I had fair answers. Such questions as, "Will you just have to turn around and now take testosterone to replace what you just had removed and what does this buy you in the form of reducing meds?" These questions and a few more have played out in my mind over and over. I have pat answers to share, but one fact that I can't describe clear enough is the fear of reverting to being male. This is so strong and continually compelling and so very hard to verbalize to myself or anyone else. Plus, there is this feeling of mourning the death of being C----. With each day that I move closer to surgery a little more of C---- dies a real death. So, who is it that I am to replace him, who is Cadance (Cady) Alane Anderson? I am so spent, so drained that I am having trouble keeping myself together. Simple thoughts escape me, my voice is flat and low pitched; I reach for words and come back empty and am left in a panic of a standing stupor. Panic is the true word; it is being backed into a corner and totally unable to make my mind work. Very frightening. My memory is just plain broken. I got a call from the surgery center (Kenya was her name there) to ask about meds (we had already sent that stuff to Dr. B to share) and everything she told me was gone within minutes of handing up…

What is wrong with my brain and will it just get worse after surgery? The surgery is a big deal for me; it defines me as female in my mind and I am hoping for two things from it: first, the continual discord feeling of body and mind gender will fall into a quiet sync; second, my health will not suffer. I'll add one more, that I can reduce patches to two and not need to add DHEA or straight testosterone for the rest of my life. I worry about Cathy and meeting her needs each day and how the world will see us. Truth is, I don't think it will be any different than how folks have seen us for the last ten years. I won't look any different than I do now, but I wonder if I will project myself differently. In fact, I know I will, but how much and in what way is a mystery to be seen. The little surgery center is very close to us here and doesn't look very impressive from the outside; I guess we'll see in two days at 7am. I got a call yesterday from the center asking for my health information apparently my paper work, which was mailed to Robin, has yet to find its way to Kenya at the San Mateo Surgery Center. Also no one has shared with me if I have to stop my HRT or not. I have stopped the supplements (fish oil, flaxseed oil and my multi-vitamin containing E oil) that thin blood; I hope that is enough. I guess my plan is to remove my patches on Thursday and start with new ones on Saturday if I don't hear otherwise. Oh, and Cathy and I have been at each other over all sort of little stuff only to make up and start at each other again… There is so much stress coming at us not only from the surgery, but that this is the last time to stay at Kalmia house (we have to start packing our stuff up), or visit little Q at Quince house, and our future relationship with our family.

***

Wednesday September 12, 2018. Cathy and I are going to wear our purple tie-dye tomorrow morning. We tried on all the tie-dyed tops we brought with us; I feel the most presentable and the most comfortable in the purple tights and a tie-dye shirt. I have showered, picked out clothes, bought tasty gluten-free treats at the Ferry Building (a guy there asked to take our picture to share with a friend), posted in a vague way about surgery on Facebook, so all that is left is the final unstoppable slide to my pre-op appointment with Dr. Bowers tomorrow morning at 9am. So many things can go wrong; I haven't stopped my patches (never heard to do so from Robin), some funny supplement I am taking might jinxed it, or Dr. Bowers might look at me and decide I am not sincere (kind of like Linus' Pumpkin Patch). Corey was very nice to call me today to check up on how I am doing, as we probably won't see them before Monday evening (they have a moving party on Sunday and a birthday on Saturday). We were asked to pick up little Q at the Wetlands (daycare) yesterday. Quince's daycare isn't the same as when we first came to know it. The kids sure have grown along with Q. Quince has been in three daycare classes there, Morning Dove as an infant (8 months), Snowy Plover as toddler (20 months), and lastly Tiger Beetle (near 30 months). The Tiger Beetle class is sort of a running *Lord of the Flies* group. When we picked up Q, he had to use the bathroom before leaving, so I helped. The place had a very public restroom feel to it of need-to-clean the sink, etc.

So how do I feel right now? I feel ready to have my appointment in the morning, kind of looking forward to it and at the same time worried about what will come of it. I guess I feel like I can't stay where I am right now and yearn to have them out and done with. Still there is something so weighty about doing this; but so many do, and I am so tired of my internal pressure to act, just need to get through it. Hopefully after tomorrow the on-edge that both Cathy and I feel with each other and all that is going on extraneous to us, such as Corey moving his family just after their vacation in New Zealand (Oct 13th) to San Diego will calm down. Right now, we both feel lonely, drifting away from our sons, Cathy's mom and Linda, or should I say they are drifting away from us. It is a very pressure-filled time of life we are traveling through… I am so tired and it's only 9pm; need to sleep.

***

Thursday September 13, 2018. Wow Dr. Bowers is the coolest person!!! She totally blew both Cathy and me away, we chatted together for over 45 minutes! Here is the how our morning went:

I sleep soundly here so 6:30 comes suddenly to me. Cathy is up out of bed at 6:50 and I convince her to come back for ten minutes after all my appointment is at 9am. At 7:00 Cathy is up again and poking me to get going and if I don't she has very cold hands (just a warning). I am glad Cathy was as insistent because after breakfast and Invisalign stuff, it is 8:20 and time to go! Burlingame is a 12 minutes' drive and then we need to find parking. There we find street parking, insert 10 quarters into the meter for two and a half hours of parking, it is 8:45. Cathy is still nervous about time and the appointment, I am feeling resigned and kind of looking forward to it. We walk the short distance to 345 Lorton Ave and inside we find the door marked Dr. Marci Bowers suite 101; it is 8:55 and the door is locked. Panic sets in; is this the right place? I call their phone number and the message tells me it is. I need to go to the bathroom and there is nothing for it because the building restrooms are combination locked. All we can do is wait; a fellow rushes in past us and keys the combination to the restroom. My plan now is to wait until he comes out and either get the combination or grab the door. It's 9:03 now and the fellow has been in the bathroom for eight minutes. I am near the door and when he comes out, I go in, yay! I have become bathroom phobic I am uncomfortable in the men's room and won't go into the gal's, leaves me with hoping for single bathrooms. To my great relief, the men's room is totally empty because of the time of day. Out into the lobby again, it's 9:07 so we sit and wait; then a lady hurries to the office door, unlocks it, and closes it behind her quickly. We decide to wait a few minutes more, then at 9:10 we open the door and walk in. Erica, a tall thin lady with short dark hair and a very business-like demeanor, greets us. She asked for my last name, photo ID, and insurance card. I asked why the insurance card and she tells me meds will probably be covered. She gives me a clipboard of stuff to sign and when this is done and my cards returned she 'Sirs' me. Fine, I let that roll off my back. Karen arrives, steps behind the desk, and the two of them start talking about getting sick on a flight back from Hawaii. I pop up with we simply don't fly anymore because of this happening to us; this breaks the ice. Cathy tells Karen about having tooth problems from our last flights and all about our family cruise. Karen has never been on a cruise before, but her mom has always wanted to take Karen's kids on a Disney cruise, in fact, Karen has worked for the Disney Company and thought they were a very fine bunch. Karen is the office manager here and is gentle and calming. She is a good pairing against Erica the physician assistant's business-like demeanor. There are incoming phone calls, most Karen handles with gentle assuring words like, "Yes we are excited for you too, fill out a surgical application and you will need a thousand-dollar deposit to get your date." There is a steady stream of same response that will occur all morning long. We chat about Butchart Gardens; Karen would like to visit there she has a horticultural degree and since it is one of our favorite haunts we tell her all the great insider things to see. Another phone call handled in the same gentle matter. I asked her what the waiting time for SRS and she told me 3 to 4 years. I instantly began regretting just having an orchiectomy, so long to wait… Erica called my name (Cady) and I asked her if Cathy could come also and she said sure, it's your consultation. We were led into a standard exam room decked out with art on the walls and a framed mirror hanging right next to the door. One piece of art titled 'pussy in blue' reminded me of 'Natasha' of Rocky and Bullwinkle fame with a small blue cat. There were two ceramic masks on the right-hand wall (as you come in) in blues and oranges very much like some you pick up in Mexico. On the wall directly across from the door hangs a Southwest sort of painting in varying reds, yellows, and oranges. Erica tells me to sit on the exam table and takes my BP and told us about prescriptions waiting for us at Walgreens. She gave me a drape then told me to undress waist down, sit on the table and Dr. Bowers would be in soon. Cathy and I chat and wait, I listen to any sounds coming from the other side of the door like a chart being read. While waiting I have Cathy straighten the small mirror hanging on the wall next to the door and notice the odd way the linoleum is curved up from the floor all around the room especial on the bottom of the sink/drawer unit, here they did a ruff curve to meet the floor with the unit. I note the assorted containers on the counter by the sink and swing my legs some.

Dr. Bowers does come in and says, "Hello," to us and sits down with her laptop. But her Surface Pro connection malfunctions, so she excuses herself and leaves. We wait, speaking to each other in whispers for some reason. She does return, telling us that Microsoft isn't one of her favorite companies anymore. It seems like they are profiting from the pains of others, we join in saying that it just isn't the same from when Cathy was first working there. We have a nice conversation in this direction, Dr. Bowers telling of some of her experiences and Cathy of hers working there. In fact, Dr. Bowers told us she has sold most of her stock although the street seems to love it and I guess we have been too. Dr. Bowers started asking health questions about meds and past surgeries, luckily Cathy had my list all printed up, so we referred to it for dates. Also Dr. Bowers didn't seem to care if I had my patches on during surgery.

I told Dr. Bowers 'Hi' from Renée and told her about my experience at *Esprit* with Debbie Caddell and Renée. And I told her 'Hi' from Sandy Fosshage.

Hearing Sandy's name got a big reaction from Dr. Bowers!

"Is she still around?" she exclaimed.

I told her she was, and she had just retired from the Crisis Line a few weeks ago. I came to know her in 2005 right after she was recovering from a stroke. She was just getting her practice back up and running then. I ask what Sandy was like when Dr. Bowers met her.

"She was a firecracker!" Dr. Bowers returned smiling, "She was old when I knew her and that was back in the nineties! She was a real force to be reckoned with."

I told Dr. Bowers about my connection between Sandy my therapist and Marsha Morgan my electrologist. Both had tries to Marsha Botzer.

"Marsha Botzer," Dr. Bowers exclaimed! "I haven't seen her for quite a while do you know how she is doing? I think the world of her and what history there is with both Marsha Botzer and Sandy Fosshage!"

I returned, "I haven't met Marsha Botzer, but it is on my bucket list to do. I think since I was so close to the end of Sandy's taking on clients that I got to hear just the smallest amount of history of it all. I know it is personal stuff, but there is such history in all of this. Also, from what I understand, Sandy was a bit toned down from her stoke during my time with her."

I mention how I value her doing what she does.

Dr. Bowers tells me, "Back around 2003, Dr. Stanley Biber, who was like 80 at the time, was looking for someone to take over his SRS practice. He chose me, saying that I had the hands, the heart, and the courage the to do it. It was one of the nicest things I have had said to me."

Dr. gets her laptop all adjusted on a little metal exam tray table.

"So, Cady," she asks me, "How long have you been full time as female?"

I surprised myself by my quick reply, I made it through life until the year 2000 and I couldn't go any further without doing something, by 2005 I was in therapy with Sandy and wearing female clothing.

Dr. Bowers then asked me, "So tell me your story, when did you first come to know you're not the right gender?" She is typing all this into to her laptop as she asks me.

This took me back a little, I figured she heard so many experiences over the years that my little experience wouldn't be worth hearing. Even so I regroup and was happy to share.

I gave her my short story, I was nine-ish staying at my grandparents' ranch, it was a big old house, historic really, and in exploring I came across my grandmother's closet under the stairs. I remember the hinges made the shape of HL and my grandmother's name was Hazel Lawler, anyway suddenly I was moved to try on one of her dresses. In the hall, next to the closet, hung a full-length mirror; I stared in that mirror at my image thinking this is so good so right and I had a unique sense of completeness. I even tried on my grandfather's cowboy boots and hat but got no sense of that completeness."

Dr. Bowers then asked me, "Facebook has like a hundred and some different ways to identify your gender, what way do you identify?"

I told her, I'm old, I just see myself as female.

Dr. Bowers returned, "Right answer!"

Dr. Bowers asked, "How do you list your sexually?"

I stumble at this point, Well I have been with Cathy for 44 years.

Dr. Bowers returned, "So, you're a Lesbian?"

I stumble again, I know that this is Cathy's super-hot spot; I have to be very careful.

I answered, for 44 years, I don't know, I guess I am then or now.

Dr. Bowers said, "44 years wow that is something!"

I put in; I shared my internal feeling about being female with Cathy before we were got married. We just didn't know then where they would finally lead us.

Now was the time to talk about the surgery.

Dr. Bowers begins by explaining, "What you are having done is a Bilateral Orchiectomy. I do the work of two surgeons in this procedure. I do more than just remove the testicles; I remove the cording and then do the work of a hernia surgeon by closing the natural openings on either side. So, you don't ever have to worry about getting a hernia! A few years ago, Victor T. Cheney author of the book *Castration-The Advantages and Disadvantages* sent me a signed copy. He lays out all the heath advantages even includes Biblical references to benefits. It is all there; in fact, the statistics show that this extends lifespan some 13 years! So, this procedure is not a life taking one it actually is a life giving one!"

I relate, I actually found that book years ago at Powell's in Portland Oregon in the little area they had for transgender books. I looked through it and at the same time kept looking around to make sure no one was watching, I was sure temped to buy it but not brave enough at the time

"Okay sweetie," Dr. Bowers tells me, "Lay back and put your heels up on the edge of the table and let's take a look."

"Well you don't have the longest candle on the cake, but there is enough tissue to form a good amount of depth, not great but good enough, if you want the full procedure," She continued, "What we do is split the scrotum tissue top to bottom right along the fusion point to form your labia majora just as the Good Lord intended for you."

She asked me what my plans were, "Why aren't you doing the full procedure now? You understand what you are having done is the most painful part of the full procedure."

I told her, it seems that I have to do things little at a time.

"Well," she returned, "What you are having done is a big part of the full procedure, so you will be ahead of the game!" She is a bright, reassuring, and upbeat person and I am now a great fan!

I sit back up again and Dr. Bower's listens to my heart and lungs. I'm glad I have a bra on under my top; it's saying, 'see this is who I am.' We chat again for a few minutes and she's on to her next patient (an FtM who will also be a patient tomorrow at the surgery center).

***

Saturday September 15, 2018. Yesterday's surgery story: Cathy sets our alarm for 5am to allow for the 7am appointment, but I had been awake off and on since we went to bed at 11:00. At 4:00 I lay staring at the ceiling waiting for the alarm to sound, wondering if I should just get up at that moment and head for the shower. I decided that two hours were enough since all I had to do is shower. The alarm did sound and up we got to the morning darkness. I didn't wash my hair but did shower paying careful attention to the area to be worked on. The anesthesiologist (Dr. Jeff Shapiro) had called yesterday, we talked about my Invisalign braces, he decided for me to leave them in during surgery because the little attachments could be broken off when he inserts the breathing tube down my throat. As soon as I ended that call a panic attack hit me; suddenly the fact of surgery coming in just 12 hours totally overwhelmed me. I physically shook all over and tears flowed freely. This morning was all about doing, going through the motions, and trying not to think. Cathy and I pick at each other out of nervousness, in the end we leave early at 6:15 with the idea we will do some Pokémon spinning at a spin point near the center. We had checked out where the parking lot was located for the little surgery center (which was all of a 5-minute drive from Kalmia House) the day before and parked at 6:45, 15 minutes before my 7:00am appointment. The door to the building was locked, but a gal who worked there (turned out to be my recovery room nurse Laura) was on her way in and opened it for us. The place was compact, the waiting room had six chairs and a one-person reception desk. One other person was already occupying a chair. As we entered the busy receptionist looked up from her screen long enough to invite us to sit and wait. Soon it was Cady's turn at the reception desk, more papers to sign, it was good thing I had been practicing my Cady Anderson signature; I needed it for all of the paperwork. We waited again until my name (Cady) was called and into the surgical end of the center I went leaving Cathy outside in the little waiting room. She would get to come see me after I was prepped. I was taken into a changing/locker room, told to change into a gown and put all my stuff into a plastic bag. The bag was to go into a locker and I was to take the key. I could easily enough undress but tying the gown behind me wasn't going well at all! Finally, I hit upon tying the ties first then putting the gown on over my head. I put all my stuff in the bag and the bag into locker #12 and took the key. I wandered out the door gown on properly but hair net out of place; the nurse was quick to fix it for me. The prep area had two hospital beds one was already in use and the other was to be mine. Kenya was my prep nurse she covered me with a warm blanket, inserted an IV port into the back of my right hand (this hurts all the while it is in there), slipped cuffs on each of my legs, and hooked up monitors for heart, etc. I asked if Cathy could come see me and that sent Kenya off to fetch her. Cathy sat with me and we listened to the gal on the other side of the curtain talk about being a bush pilot in Alaska, and a teacher there. She left Alaska several years ago and still misses it; her son is still there and he didn't want her to leave. I think Alaska never really let's go of you, once you have been there long enough for that sense of innocent freedom Alaska is famous for takes hold of you. Once it has, and you leave the state, that sense of innocence is lost along with the freedom it empowers and you are left with a continuous mournful loss. Our friend Michael mourns it longingly and lovingly, as do several other of our friends. Anyway, her story is a good distraction for us since Dr. Bowers is running over 30 minutes late. Warm air blowing into my heated blanket is nice, but I am beginning to get a little too warm. My hand aches from the needle sticking in it and when the attached tube is moved at all I get a sharp stick. All around us, the little place is kind of out of whack, Kenya knocks the hand sanitizer unit off the wall trying to use it and chases it around the floor. The anesthesiologist (Dr. Jeff Shapiro) came by to verify stuff and was impressed by my drug list so much so to give us a lecture on the evil of supplements. We dutifully listen, and he does have several points, thankfully when he starts to talk about how bad statin drugs are, Cathy pops up in agreement. She gives her personal story of her trouble with them, so we can all agree in this area. We hear a now familiar feminine voice and Dr. Bowers plunges through the curtain, which has been closed with a clip so that the gal next to us can rest with privacy. Dr. Bowers tells us, "Hello," and Cathy mentions she found a copy of *Castration-The Advantages and Disadvantages* by Victor T. Cheney and Dr. Bowers says, "Wow great find!" She turns to me with, "Are you ready for this?" And then is off pushing through the curtains to be greeted by the nurses as she heads someplace to get ready. Within a very few minutes, Cathy is dismissed, and I am in tow by Kenya who is handling my IV bag for me. I like the idea of the IV; I have been so parched these last few days leaving me dehydrated even though I have been pushing water into me. Kenya opens the door to the chilly OR and that same cross-shaped table I had seen on my last OR visit is just in front of me. Kenya is gone leaving me for the OR nurse who directs me onto the table. She tells me, "Scoot down honey," until I am in just the right spot. I am female here to everyone; it's just routine as they see lots of Dr. Bowers' patients. I remember getting positioned on the table and resting each arm on the side tables then looking at the ceiling lights, but after that everything is blank, just like a switch has been thrown off. I awake; to me it is like a switch has been thrown to the ON position again. I returned to the land of the living and to my recovery nurse Laura putting an apple juice box straw in my mouth. I am totally confused and ask her what her name is twice before getting it straight. Here I am, suddenly back in the bed I started with just like I never left here. Thankfully, someone had gone to get Cathy because I was still not with the concept of being awake. Laura was relieved to see Cathy so she could explain homecare to someone able to understand what she was saying. Cathy was dispatched to get our car, while Laura was pushing on my shoes, unhooking monitors, and

358

getting me onto a wheelchair. I remember the wheelchair itself, but not being in it nor do I remember going to the car or getting in the passenger side. Continuing, I don't remember the drive home except there was a bump that hurt to go over. Cathy tells me she got me out of the car and held on to me until we got to the front door; there, she had me hold on to the door frame until she got it unlocked. From there, she got me into bed and propped up. I am now much more awake and aware of what is going on but don't remember getting here. There is pain on my right side of my groin up a bit I get relief by applying pressure to both sides. Instructions were that I drink lots of clear liquids; this would lead me to have to use the bathroom, which means a look at the area of concern. It turns out I am wearing a sanitary pad and fishnet true-waist panty, there is blood on a gauze pad on the sanitary pad toward the lower part of the scrotum. Any pulling on my cowering little penis or pressure in the area brings sharp pain. I relieve my bladder of lots and lots of fluid; what went in is now coming out. Going from a sitting position to standing brings pain (level 6.5 out of 10) so I learn to slowly straighten up just like dealing with a leg cramp. I expect what is left of the spermatic cords is cramping up in the now closed inguinal canals. Cathy has me ice every twenty minutes and the cold does help deaden the pain, which comes on that right side and from the center if I twist too quickly or spread my legs. She is in total charge of me, my meds (Cephalexin 500mg three times daily for seven days, Hydrocodone/Acetaminophen5-300 TB 4 to 6 hours), and needs. The pain meds worked well, I could find a position in bed sitting up where I didn't hurt so much. I would use only three of the Hydrocodone pills (last one late Friday night) because the ice packs worked well to reduce swelling and pain and a familiar pain formed right at the top of my head that I knew was caused from the Hydrocodone itself. I had noticed after a surgery several years ago that I quickly became addicted to this stuff, so this particular top-of-the-head pain would come and only go away with each Hydrocodone pill; in short, this stuff is just magic for the first 12 hours for me but after that I have to get off of it. Still, I very much appreciated it during those 12 hours. Our day is made up with me in bed distracting myself with an iPad or phone and contemplating what I just had done to myself. Cathy administered bone broth and toast; she metered out my pills and saw to all my needs including my bathroom trips. Bathroom trips were tricky; I needed to stand to urinate because I couldn't stand any pressure on the surgery area by sitting. So, each time I was reminded by a bloody gauze pad that yes, I was still bleeding and hurting. I needed help to get all my dressing on and off each time too. I dreaded the coming time when I would have to move my bowels. So, the day passed with little out-of-bed walks to the bathroom and back. The pain was manageable and the socks they gave me to wear were soft with good treads (I still don't know how Laura got my shoes on over them). Lying flat to sleep for the night was tolerable too and I fell asleep very quickly. I had to get up one time to use the bathroom, but other than that I did slept very soundly scoring a 93% on my sleep monitor, this was unheard of for me!

Waking Saturday morning was the most emotional moving experience I have ever had! I opened my eyes to the most amazing feeling of release, my jaw was resting limp and my facial muscles didn't ache. I hadn't ground my teeth at all during the night! At that precious moment, that beautiful wonderful precious moment, I felt the greatest weight lifted off from my soul after 64 years of it pushing down. I didn't want this feeling to ever leave me! I just wanted to lie there forever, letting it flow over me pushing out all darkness from the hidden scars formed from a lifetime of this conflict. After 64 years, I am finally me! This sort of thing only happens once in a lifetime, a hidden blessing God has just given me. I started regretting a little by only doing the orchiectomy but for this moment, all was grand! Saturday would find me mostly in bed icing while Cathy beaded either in the dining room or at a TV tray near me in our bedroom. Cathy had returned to beading with a passion after meeting Peggy, a beading enthusiast, on our last cruise. The weather was blue sky and my only job was to slowly travel through the pain (7 out of 10), which now was controlled by two ibuprofen and ice. Each time I had to stand up very carefully and slowly to stretch myself straight up through the cramp like pain this brought. Bleeding was slowing and to our great luck we

360

had 10 3x4 inch gauze non-stick pads on hand here, I was wearing a sanitary pad and on top of that a gauze pad both held to my scrotum by my panties and the fishnet panty. We would change out the gauze as it soaked through. Eating, drinking water, resting, and going to the bathroom filled all of Saturday. Oh, if I used incense, I could catch a few Pokémon during the day too.

Sunday morning, my sleep score was 90% again, which was very high for me. In the last few months, I would be lucky to get 87% (according to my Samsung Gear Fit tracker). The temperatures here have been cooling at night; enough so, to have to use the furnace each morning for a short time; this is perfect sleeping and waking weather. Today I took a shower being careful of the surgery area; my goal is to shampoo my dirty hair more than scrub my body. The shower was clumsy for me, but I felt much better afterward. We also changed my patches (just three new ones with no fourth hold over). More and more it dawns on me just what I have done; my job now is to process just what this is coming to mean to me. Cathy, too, is processing her side of what has just come to pass. She surprises me with she is okay if I want to put down another deposit for more surgery… So much to think about, to experience, to understand, and now the need to walk some despite a little higher level of pain (8 out of 10). We go for a walk down Kalmia Street to the Pokémon spin point nearest us called Seventeen Stones sculpture. The day is fair, I start with good intentions; slowly walking along the sidewalk is both painful and a relief all at once. We make our goal. I foolishly decide to try for a full around-the-block walk, find part way along that my pain level is increasing more and more. The pain is from the sides of my personals and toward the bottom of them (8.5 out of 10 now) my right foot is starting to point out away from straight more and more. This is from my back being stressed by all the sitting in bed. By the time we make it back home I am totally spent. Cathy gets me into bed and all I want to do is lay flat; soon I am in a heavy dosing sleep that I will awake from in almost two hours. Our Sunday walking adventure is over for today. Being stuck inside is no fun so we try a little drive to do some Pokémon spinning for gifts to give and the chance to hatch some eggs by distance. We find that if we drive very slowly and move our phones rhythmically it tricks the game to registering us as walking! Since it is Sunday, business parking lots near us are empty so we use these to our advantage by driving below 10 miles per hour, waving our cellphones back and forth. I hatch a Farfetch'd, not so good, but the trick did work. I used B----'s account and got her a Kangaskhan, lucky girl. Cathy didn't have any luck at all. We drove to Central Park and Cathy got out to walk through the park to spin and hatch while I waited in the car. We returned home with me spent again. Corey did come over after their moving-away party (which we couldn't go to because of my condition) after 9:00pm with some bottled water we needed. He stayed for over an hour to talk with me about my quandary on who to tell about my surgery and what I have come to realize about myself. I clumsily try to form good concept questions of what is going on in my mind, how I feel disingenuous toward myself by hiding what surgery I have just had. I also at the same time am still trying to get my mind around the fact I have had parts of my body removed because of this mind/body conflict. It's so apparent that Corey has a very keen sense of problem solving and I suddenly wondered when did he develop this? When did he became this amazing man that he is?! He suggested I make a list putting family and friends' names above and below a line denoting who to talk directly with and who to just let the information come to. Of both groups, individually consider how I would feel if I lost their acquaintance letting this give weight to me making direct contact at some point. In the converse, noting in both groups those who are most likely not to care and would remain in contact with Cathy and me. This was all sensible stuff, I just wish I had more time with him; in just a few days, they would be gone… I had in my mind felt like Cathy and I would travel and stay at Kalmia for the next ten years, watching Quince grow, and having Colby and B---- come stay with us here, and now it is to be all over. So very hard on top of becoming someone else and knowing how hard it must be for Corey, too.

***

On to Monday the 17th. I again slept very deeply; we were up by 9:00am. My pain on either side is less (6 out of 10). Breakfast for me has been one egg over easy with two slices of Canyon Bakehouse raisin bread to make a sandwich; Cathy has been having goat yoghurt. We are slowly running low on our supply of gluten-free treats from Mariposa Bakery. I call Casey; he has been keeping us at arm's length with no calls or just short conversations when he does call, and I wonder just what is going on. Is it me/us? When I asked Corey for his opinion about this, he said he doubted that I was the issue, and that the drama in Casey life from family or his job hunt is probably more likely. I call Casey and ask what he thinks about me telling people about my gender surgery: the quandary of who and what the outcome might be, and my fears of losing acquaintances with family and friends. I figure this is a good springboard to get a wedge into what might be going on with him. Anyway, Casey was quite cut and dry about telling folks, "If they won't accept you as you are, then they aren't really healthy to have as family or friends." He told me that he lost one of his very best friends when she just up and walked away from him because she couldn't accept his stand on family issues. We talk all around my issues (including what to tell the kids) and part on good terms. I still don't know the exact root cause of his hurting but am satisfied it is not me at the moment. He would later text me a nice note telling me 'He just wants me to be happy;' and that is exactly what I want for him. This morning belongs to Cathy. We go for a short walk to spin a Pokémon Go Pokestop, then return to our home away from home. I shower again, this time to clean my body for my appointment with Dr. Bowers. Cathy chooses red tie-dye for us to wear with black leggings for her and black flowy lounge pants for me. We eat our mid-day meal, I fuss about wearing lipstick and then it is time to go to our post-op appointment.

The drive to Burlingame is uneventful and we find parking in the lot near 345 Lorton Ave suite 101. It is blue sky with a little breeze; this place is so nice in the fall. Cathy and I do stand out in our loud red and purple spiral shirts, but no one seems to care enough to notice. In the lobby of 345 right in front of the door to suite 101, stands an 18-

year-old thin frail girl dressed in white thigh stockings and matching dress looking confused and bewildered. I ask if the door is locked and she says very quietly that she can hear voices inside. I try the door handle and it opens right up to the little waiting area of seven chairs. One has been claimed by a purse belonging to a lady near my age wearing a light burnt orange dress. She is currently standing at the desk talking to Erica. Cathy and I sit down and the girl in white comes into the room and stands looking dazed and confused. Karen gently asks her if she can help her; this starts a line of disjoint conversation that wouldn't be cleared up until her mother comes in from finding a parking spot. Rona, the owner of the burnt orange dress, sits down next to me and introduces herself to me. I reply with I'm Cady. Rona asks if I am there for a consultation and I tell her no, I'm post-op; she congratulates me. What a cool thing I realized just happened: I am a post-op MtF! Rona is a talker, which isn't bad at the moment, she tells me she is here to consult with Dr. Bowers about a poor job of GRS/SRS done by another surgeon on her. I reply that I hear Dr. Bowers is very good and Rona tells me she is the leading expert on female multination repair. I hear about Rona's many neck injuries from being in the Navy, that she is from Olympia, originally from San Jose, and when asked if we drove here she tells me that is the lowest carbon impact way to travel. (A note here about what I would discover later about Rona, she is a Rabbi and has a website.) Kara the girl in white is sitting next to Rona now and since there are no empty chairs near us, Kara's mom is on the floor near her daughter. Christian (FtM) and his dad come in and sit in the two seats on the right side of the door, there is only one empty seat left. Christian has had some form of bottom surgery at the same place I did and is in a lot of pain from it. During my surgery, Cathy sat in the waiting room and listened to his dad talk to another guy about flying all sorts of aircraft. Rona leans over to tell Kara's mother how nice it was that she was supporting her daughter. Rona went on to tell her she worked with teenagers that don't get support. To this, Kara's mother told Rona that they just wanted to get this done and the name change over and behind them. Like all the moms I would see here today, she was juggling taking care of her daughter while doing the needed paperwork with Karen. Kara would drone on in a perfect quiet little girl voice about some video game she plays much too much; she passes perfectly as the young lady she is. Rona tells me, a little too loudly, she had a 2:00 appointment here and was still waiting, she sighs and says it better than no appointment. When Karen asks if anyone would like some water Rona chimes in, "Isn't it the cocktail hour?" A dad and his daughter who is quite lovely and you wouldn't think anything other than female (assume when I say daughter or son it's MtF and FtM) come in and find no place to sit so they decide to sit outside in the lobby. Another perfectly passing young woman comes in looks around and leaves a cellphone number with Karen so she can wait in outside her car. It is well past my appointment time by 45 minutes and we come to find out that Dr. Bowers isn't in the building yet and more and more folks keep coming in. What has happened is Dr. Bowers suddenly had to travel to New York for a week and this has totally broken her schedule to pieces. How I found this out is I volunteer to come back tomorrow and find that isn't an option. Christian and I have some priority since we both are here for our post-op checkups. The most gorgeous young thin thing comes in wearing jeans and a great top, Rona compliments her on her bold eye shadow. She tells Rona in a very passable voice that it took her like two hours to find the perfect match. Rona is the type that says things I would be afraid to. Rona is also jolted each time by the slamming sound the waiting room door makes because the return spring is far too tight. The young thing who just came in looks around, makes a comment about no place to sit, and finds a clear spot on the floor. There are eight in the waiting room and near the same number in the lobby. A family comes in mom, dad, son-in-law, and daughter with a stroller; in that stroller is a month-old baby. They check in and leave their cell number and go somewhere else to wait. Dr. Bowers comes hurrying in, saying I'm sorry everyone and heads to the back. It is almost six o'clock. I reflect, I was so worried about how I would look, that I wouldn't pass, and I would offend all the beautiful people here. Yes, there have been many perfectly (the young ones are amazing, nailing fashion in a way to make a personal statement but still blending right in) passing MtFs in and out of this little office in the last hour and some odd minutes, and none has given me notice except that I am one of this group and we are all here for the same reason. We are here because of Dr. Bowers, each of us equally. Okay, folks are beginning to go into the two exams rooms. Rona makes a comment as to which is the world-famous exam room where Jazz Jennings saw Dr. Bowers. Jazz Jennings has a popular YouTube and television show. They brought in a video crew when she had her appointment with Dr. Bowers. Karen told Rona loud enough for everyone in the waiting room to hear that we were more important than Jazz because we are the ones who make up the real population and it is a privilege to be helping us! Wow, Karen is a dear person she has expressed concern several times about the pain Christian is in (thankfully he goes in before me). She also asks about me and I tell her I am doing fine as long as Christian goes in first. I have been putting off going to the bathroom for as long as I can. This is a problem for me; the men's or ladies' room each has two stalls. I figure I can't use the ladies', there are so many perfectly passing and cis folks around and I don't want to use the men's room what if someone from the office sees me or if one of the FtMs are in there. I can't wait, I will just hold my head up and use the men's room no matter what happens. I head out to the lobby over to the restrooms, which are out of line sight from the lobby. I try the code to open the men's room door and it doesn't work, darn my poor memory the number is just gone; no time left I head to the ladies' room door, of course that code is still in my head, thankfully the light turns green and the place is empty. Once in a stall with the door closed and locked, I feel a little better but not much. Going to the bathroom is tricky for me; I have a sanitary pad to deal with and a gauze pad that sits on top of it. There are two panties that hold all of it together and I am in fear someone will come in at any time. Had I been smart I would have had Cathy run interference for me, but I had planned to be in the men's room feeling guilty. It turns out where I'm at is better equipped for what I have to do. I do my business and get myself back together and no one comes in... Safe back in my seat in the waiting room once more. I watch the family with the stroller now in the back behind the reception desk. Apparently their time with Dr. Bowers has been successful, everyone is cooing over the little newborn. I wonder what is their story, the guy pushing the stroller looks a little FtM like and the mom walking with him is very cis and the proud older grandparents well, are proud... My name is called. Cathy and I are led into one of the exam rooms. Erica held a drape and asked how I am. I tell her and we chat for a minute or two; she doesn't seem rushed in spite of the big backlog behind me. She tells me, "You know the drill get undress and cover yourself with the drape and doctor will be in very soon." Cathy and I wait and chat away the time. She takes a picture of an interesting art print in the room. We have come a long way. Cathy is now a champion of me having full GRS/SRS surgery and has told me I could put a deposit down for it. Dr. Marci Bowers breezes in followed by a thin young lady named Casey who is shadowing her. I don't think to ask what this is all about but do ask her name. First, I show Dr. Bowers Sandy's picture I have on my phone.

"Wow she looks just as she did when I knew her!" Dr. Bowers exclaimed.

Dr. Bowers tells me, "Let's see how we did."

I lay back with my heels hooked on the corner of the exam table legs spread out. I thought to myself, you sure lose your modesty fast in this new world.

"Wow!" Dr. Bowers exclaims, "You wouldn't even know you had a surgery by looking! Great job taking care of it! Wash the area normally, but don't scrub and just pat dry. Don't lift heavy stuff for at least ten days. Tell us about right any spreading redness away and continue using Polysporin as you have been doing."

Dr. Bowers tells Casey, "Cady had a bilateral orchiectomy, she already looks feminine." I break in with I don't think I do, and Dr. Bowers tells me, "That's because you always see yourself! In fact, you're glowing, orchiectomies have this magic to them!"

I tell Dr. Bowers that we have decided to have complete GRS/SRS.

She exclaims, "Well I will be here, I'm not going anywhere any time soon; there doesn't seem to be anyone here to replace me at the moment! You can have the surgery anytime really and you have already had the most painful part done! You should get your deposit down soon to get a date. I am getting a bigger backlog every day. Hair removal is nice but not necessary we do that during the procedure. I'll look forward to seeing you again, do you guys always match?"

Yes we do, I quipped.

The waiting room is so packed now and Rona is wearing sunglasses and kind of slumped down in her chair, poor thing. We leave light-hearted; my 4:45 appointment turned out to a 6:10 one and no playing with Quince tonight it is 6:35 and he will be heading to bath-time soon.

***

Tuesday September 19, 2018. We awoke to our nest cameras reporting a car prowler. The camera showed a guy walking to our old truck, trying the door and then leave, very unnerving. We walked over to the surgery center to drop off the survey and say 'thank you' for the care. On the way back we spoke to our next-door neighbor and I told her I had had surgery and walking seem to be a good idea. She asked what surgery and I told her gender surgery, she was taken back and after moment or two said, "I still love you anyway." Next, we drove to Dr. Bowers' office to place our deposit and say thanks. I really needed to use the restroom and Cathy was determine I should use the ladies' room I resisted but relented because I really needed to go, and Cathy went with me. We did a really good walk through the park afterward. I felt really pretty good, only a very low discomfort level, so a good walk seemed like the thing to do. Home again and it suddenly hit me that I needed a nap very badly; my body seemed to have hit a wall after the walk. Cathy made a very nice lunch with leftover chicken patties and fries. Spent the rest of the afternoon waiting for Corey and Quince to come over for a play date. They showed up at 4:45 and we played until 6:00. Melinda was too busy to

368

come over. I started typing in my journal after Jeopardy and Wheel of Fortune…

***

Friday September 21, 2018. Okay three days have now passed without my journaling. I will go back and forth to cover Tuesday, Wednesday, Thursday, and Friday so hang on and try to follow my randomness.

Tuesday, I feel better and cut back on ibuprofen some. I called Corey on his way from work and asked if he and Q could come to Kalmia instead us going to Quince house and he said an energetic, "Yes!" I got busy putting together the hot wheels track set and the track for the little battery powered truck (like Stompers). I would have to be very careful not to lift Quince up or let him bounce into my lap. The two of them arrived and Quince came running up to the door and into playland. He squealed with delight and stomped/ran all over the place. This night, the big winners for toys were the battery trucks and their colorful track. The backyard was popular for Cathy then Corey helicoptering Quince round and round with Q squealing again! I used a pillow when I needed to get down on the floor with Q and it all worked out grand. Yes, I was sore afterwards but intact.

Wednesday, our routine is to get to bed around midnight and wake up after 8am heading toward 9am. I get up and shower being very gentle with my surgery area. We change my patches still using three per time with one holdover. This morning's pain level at the surgery sight was up some and a little more swelling due to no pain reliever. We got dressed in matching blue leggings and blue spiral tie-dye shirts. Our plan was to drive to Dr. Bowers' office to pick up my Surgical Declaration letters (2 copies). We drive the 15-minute route (2.7 miles) all on El Camino to Burlingame. There we park in a lot very near the office building where suite 101 lives. Cathy and I do get noticed as we walk along, but not to any reaction. I open the office door to an empty and very quiet waiting room. It was unlocked so we sit down and wait. Soon Karen comes in the door and the door slams shut behind her on its too tight spring. She is so pleased to see us, and

I thank her several times for the care she has given us, I also tell her what it is like for me to finally be me. We chat, and she gets my letter and I remark how amazing they are signed by Dr. Marci Bowes and notarized by Karen. We get hugs from her and are on our way out to our car when I thought to check the spelling of Cadance. Oh no! It was spelled Cadence. So back we go with me thinking that it was probably my fault. I told her there was a spelling problem. Didn't faze Karen or Erica at all; in fact, Erica thought the 'dance' part of Cadance was pretty cool. They would just redo it and we could pick it up Thursday. I complimented Karen on interesting necklace she was wearing. She told us she got it in a little town to the south called Ben Lomond. She told us about how artsy it was and told us we should visit it sometime. That put a seed in our heads to do a test drive. On the way out of their office, Cathy headed to the women's restroom and said I should come to. I told her I was comfortable at the moment and would wait for her in the lobby. We go back and forth; she makes the argument that we can go directly to the park without stopping at home, until with all the talk I began to really have to go to the bathroom. So, we both share the ladies' room; it is empty and convenient.

We drive over to Central Park, the top of my head hurts to the touch and the pain travels deeper into my skull. We go home to make pizza for our dinner and after that I again need a nap. Before I nap I realize that the headache I am having is being caused by estrogen dominance. I pulled off the carry-over patch so now I only have three on. With so little T in my body E is having its full way with me. I even flushed at my appointment with Dr. Bowers and now I understand why. Normally, I would take Diim (diindolymethane) to counter the E metabolites floating around in my bloodstream or a little progesterone. But now it is going to be just a juggling game for a while. I will have my blood tested on the 12th and go from there. Now I really need that nap. Corey and Quince come over again to play and Melinda shows up too. The big toy this time is the hot wheels set, he loves to send them down the loopy loop and then go running after them across the wood floor. Corey and Melinda chat with each other about all their move stuff coming up. Quince is really coming along with potty training almost to the point he could use the bathroom by himself. On Tuesday, Wednesday, and Thursday nights, Corey comes back to chat with us after Quince is in bed. In all our conversation we come to understand he is moving all of the Kalmia stuff down to Carnegie house, so it will be equipped for us to come stay as we did at Kalmia. Takes a lot of pressure from us having to come back with a minivan to get stuff. Also, we decide to do a driving trip from home to Kalmia to Carnegie house like the first weekend in November; we can pick up anything that got left behind if needed.

Thursday, I feel better headache-wise, so we will do our two-hour test drive to Ben Lomond. Karen calls us early in the morning to tell us the letter isn't ready yet because Dr. Bowers got in too late last night. It will be ready on Friday from 9am to 1pm. Ben Lomond is very small; the high points are the Mountain Feed and Farm Supply store with its old city bus permanently parked on the back of a garden nursery that houses a veterinarian for folks hard up for money. There is an art store full of local pottery and an old church founded in 1890 that is now a doctor's office. We beat the traffic home in plenty of time for another nap. We don't see Quince tonight because they had dinner with friends, but Corey does come over for the last time to visit with us. I am filled with all that had happened to me but sharing this just doesn't work smoothly because of its contents running roughshod through our father-son relation; still Corey is exceptional in trying.

***

Friday September 22, 2018. My pain level is way down to a minor level unless I do something to aggravate it, such as get up too quickly from sitting and torquing my body. I learn this pretty quickly and am careful, after all there are internal structures stitched up inside me. Be that as it may, I am confident that come this Tuesday morning I will be able to drive all the way home. It is too bad we couldn't be home for Pokémon Go community day tomorrow, but it is well worth getting to see Quince on Monday night before their big vacation trip to New Zealand. I shower again, and we drive to Dr. Bowers' office for my letter. We thank both Erica and Karen then share the picture of Ben Lomond with Karen.

Erica is busy on a cellphone telling someone, "And we are excited for you, just get the application in along with your deposit."

I told Karen, I just want to thank you again, I feel complete after 64 years so amazing to finally be me just like starting a new life! And the experience on Monday, with the waiting room so full, was such a wonder for me to have had. Funny as it sounds from your point of view, but I wouldn't have missed it for the world. You were so good to hunker down yet show how much you cared for each person coming in, especially Christian and Kara, just thank you for what you do!

Karen returns, "You two bring such a positive energy in here. Thank you for that! And for the added contact these two days. I think the older people coming through here have a brighter outlook before and especially afterward. That is how I learned about Ben Lomond from an older gal who had surgery here and was so happy that she lived so close to us. The younger ones seem to have to process it differently, more internally, they pull into themselves."

I add to her comment; for me it is this great relief, a weight lifted off, I do think it is all about the many years in conflict before resolution. I did see Kara just pull into herself and the other girls being very quiet.

We turn to head to the door saying. Thanks again and see you in two years!

Cathy checks the letter for spelling and we head out to the car. There I actually take time to read the letter carefully it's very sobering.

Cadance Anderson aka C---- Anderson
To Whom it May Concern:
This letter is to certify that the above named individual underwent irreversible and permanent Genital Surgery performed by myself, Dr. Marci L. Bowers, MD, in San Mateo, California. The surgery constitutes appropriate clinic treatment for gender transition to female. The surgery was completed in accordance with the standards

established by the World Professional Association for Transgender Health. Accordingly, all documentation should reflect this individual's current and final gender status as female.

Wow! This gives me a sudden pause to reflect and take a very deep breath.

***

Monday September 24, 2018. This is our last day for a normal visit here, one that involves Quince house and family. We will be back for a two-night stay in the first part of November as a stopover point for our drive to San Diego Carnegie house. This visit will be for three nights just to see the place and if there was something missed in the move we could bring it down then.

So, I am very thankful that I got to have my surgery at this time and place. Just in time as it were, while Corey and family are still here. I do wish I hadn't been so frightened of the outcome and been brave enough to do the full procedure of gender reconstruction. Seeing especially that Cathy is now my biggest supporter of my surgery and has no trouble with me doing the next step. I had come to know the Dr. Bowers I know now, giving me total trust in her; it is enough that I now have a surgery date with her in three years Oct 2021. There won't be this little house to recover in or Corey nearby to visit with but there will be someplace for sure and it's three years into the future. So now it is packing stuff up day. Cathy and I did a handful of last minute jobs, wash the car, the needed yard work of pruning the dead wood out of the olive trees in the back yard (they look so much better), the wisteria, a mean thorny rose, and bug infested bush. We repaired a corner cabinet door in the kitchen, replaced the burned out special bulb in the floor lamp in the dining room, transferred the stand mixer to Q house, and changed the furnace filter. We both have our minds set on getting going tomorrow early, they aren't set on what we will find for us at home just the trip back. There are going to be a lot of things for my mind to settle down on post-surgery wise, but that is safety into the future at the moment. As far as I feel physically, everything seems to be just fine, things are all functional in the bathroom, soreness level continues to drop, and I feel comfortable walking and driving. The reality is I am not healed yet and still will have to be careful moving and lifting for a month or more; but my brain does seem to be clearing more and more as the days pass. My short-term memory is slowly improving and spelling is slowly coming back, fingers crossed.

***

Wednesday September 26, 2018. We are home, we pulled into our driveway all bug covered at 9:00pm after sixteen hours of travel time. I wore jeans with my hair pulled back; it didn't feel so good to be a guy again even if it was convenient for travel. We are both spent after a drive of this length and feeling sick from the constant motion. It is a good thing on our upcoming drive to San Diego in November that we will have the use of Kalmia house as a waypoint and stay two nights then drive onto San Diego. I have almost no pain from the surgery anymore, just some internal soreness. Cathy has become very learned on the steps to change names. I still need a nap and crash in the early afternoon. I don't know if this will continue or not. The sleep from this nap is an odd mix of a deep doze without achieving true sleep. It is very hard to wake up from but doesn't seem to interfere with my nighttime sleep.

***

September 26, 2018. Both Cathy and I had massages with Natalie at 8:30 and 9:30. She was all excited to hear about our trip and my surgery. My face muscles were on fire as Natalie put pressure on each point to release their spasms. I told her of our adventure and left her with some of my journal pages for her to read, if she would be interested and return them afterward. Natalie wanted to know why I wasn't Cady there at the clinic and I told her C---- is my legal name and it is health stuff but there again we do pay cash... After we were finished, Natalie had to French braid Cathy's and my hair, we had fun. Natalie told us she sank a nineteen-foot putt! Wow! Golf is a passion of Natalie's that she picked up when she was married to a well-to-do man. They were country club people, she had all that money could buy, the whole nine yards, and then she walked away from that affluent world to be her true self. Now it is a treat to play golf, which only happens if she can find the time and money from the physical work of being an independent contract massage therapist. She is amazing, a single mom with two sons totally dependent only on her. Thanks for being our friend, Natalie!

I am pretty much without pain but have noticed what seems to be a mass in my empty scrotum. I use salt spray to clean the area daily then apply Polysporin and massage the incision up and down. This seems to bring relief to the soreness and the mass sort of flattens out… I still use 3 x 4 gauze pads to keep the surgery sight separate from my underwear.

***

September 27th. Stopped at Caddell's to visit with Renée for a minute or two. I had been feeling the need to do this and it was a good thing as Renée just gave notice. Her last day at Caddell's is to be November 15th. We had the nicest visit, the phone was pretty quiet, and she showed us pictures of the neighborhood they would be living in Bend Oregon, all like a little Hobbit village.

***

September 29th. Spent the day with Colby; had the best time especially at Saturday Night Games with Grandma Dixon, we play Mexican Train and all used funny names. I was 'dear' Cathy was 'honey', Colby was 'the kid', Linda was 'sweetie' and Grandma 'Mommy Bear'. Everyone had the best time especially Colby. We tried to do all Colby's favorite things, Minecraft, Pokémon Go raiding, cribbage, Saturday night games, had pizza and even a little walk to please Nanna.

***

September 30th: This was B----'s day with us so we went shopping, did a Pokémon Go raid, ate pizza, and did a puzzle. The puzzle was a big winner it is still waiting on our tabletop for her to return and finish it.

***

Wednesday October 10, 2018. My journaling is sure piecemeal now. Not having Sandy to read it before each appointment is sure telling. In fact, it is hard to come up with a reason to continue with the exception of a store for my failing memory. To this extent, it is useful but still a little sad. Let's go with the last contact I had with Sandy. I had sent to her a twenty-seven-page portion of my journal for the time of my surgery along with a letter stating 'that it meant a lot to me for someone else (meaning her) to know what my experience had been.' I also enclosed sixty dollars cash 'because her time is valuable now that she is retired! Well, it worked, I got a cell phone call from her while we were on a walk up in Victoria BC. The connection was noisy and I was standing on a sidewalk on a busy street (Pandora Ave). Still, I could understand her and she me. She was very excited with all that had happened to me and congratulated me for how far I had come. Her exact words were, "You've come a long way, baby!" She also asked me to confirm that I had more surgery coming up, yes I did.

"I remember the day you first came into my office, you had what was left of a beard and told me you wanted to be free of the condition that had bothered you for most of your life." She continued, "You weren't going to do any hormones or dressing just wanted help to be free of it. And the money you sent to me, I can't accept."

I thanked her again for all she had done for me and told her I meant the money for her and she could do anything she wanted with it, she returned she would donate it to an animal shelter. I expect it was her way of telling me she was completely retired, no going back in any way for anyone, therapy wise. Sandy does not dither, what is done is done. She did ask for me to keep in touch with her as time goes on… Oh, and confirmed that Dr. Bowers had never been in her office, what she is remembering is the time they all met together at the Ingersoll Center. So bitter sweet, I have done all that I hoped would meet with her approval and that would give her a sense of personal accomplishment at the end of her amazing career in helping so many people. That is what I do, it is not the only reason for my surgery(s) but I need to admit it is one. I did this for myself, so I could continue in life; it is just this simple. I feel the loss of Sandy keenly; there is an emptiness that I can't envision ever being filled. This leaves me adrift in somewhat troubled waters and I find myself casting around blindly for replacement. Natalie, in some ways has become a stepping-stone I seem to be using as I stumble around. So odd, as God brings people into your life for His purposes, is it for you or them? This is also a new and difficult time in Cathy and my life, frightening in some ways…

What I wanted to journal tonight was about my surgery as an update. I am now at a place where I feel almost back to normal. No pain to speak of except on the right side of my groin, and that occurs only if I stretch my legs out from each other in either direction or if I lift something heavy. I have been using a Scar Away pad on my incision and it has begun to itch, I'm thinking it's a sign of healing. I got a B12 shot from Dr. Ayla Hopkins today.

***

Friday October 26, 2018. Patty confided to us that Dr. Marsden will be closing her practice this coming June. Patty told us it was because of her decision to retire, not Dr. Marsden's, and since Dr. Marsden said she would not train anyone else, the practice would close. Patty told us she just had had enough dealing with insurance problems and all the buyouts of hospitals has become too much of a headache… So, we have lost our doctor and soon our dentist, we fear. All of our life support structures are disappearing from around us; our little house is becoming just an island with empty space all around it. In a real way, there is less and less to hold us here, but also nowhere to go either… I feel like I am losing myself, my identity of self.

2019

Thursday January 31, 2019. So many experiences to have had and watched go by. But no driving force to type since October 2018… So, I'll just try to get into the groove again by touching on high spots, sore spots, and spots that take the life out of you.

Early November 2018. I was seven weeks into my recovery when I noticed a sore spot right in the middle of the incision on my empty scrotum. The area seemed to pull inward making a plus shape and was very sore to the touch. This happened at the very time Erica called from Dr. Bowers' office to check on me. I told her everything was great except for this one sore spot. She suggested I text Dr. Bowers, which I did, she requested a picture of the area. Dr. Bowers thought it looked like a cyst or trapped hair then told me to make an appointment and she would fix it in her office. I got the very next appointment available on December 5th 2018, six weeks from the texts back and forth. As I waited, the area became more inflamed. I tried warm compresses, Scar Away silicone dressings, and just plan direct pressure; nothing seemed to diminish the pain for any length of time. I would turn over in bed at night and that motion would pull on the area and awaken me from sleep.

Here we are in December 2018 making our way to stay at the Holiday Inn at the Airport in Burlingame, California for my appointment on the 5th. Kalmia house was now empty of furniture and no longer ours to stay in. I had my appointment in a perfect storm of a Jet-laggy doctor who was just in from Australia. She was very much under the weather with a cold and her office staff following suit. She looked at my sore spot and exclaimed, "Where is the drainage and redness?" Well things spiraled downward from there. I was having pain but she didn't want to open the site… So, I was to wait another six weeks and hope for the best while applying warm compresses.

**

We returned on the 22nd of January 2019 for my next try with Dr. Bowers in Burlingame. I had expectations of her opening my incision since I had followed all of her instructions and still had pain. My appointment time came to be, Karen the receptionist wasn't there anymore and Dr. Bowers who was being shadowed by Dr. Parikh was running over an hour late. Erica, Dr. Bowers MA suggested we go out and have coffee or walk around in the sunshine and we did just that. My appointment was for 12:45 and I got to see the doctor at 2:05. She chatted with Dr. Parikh (Plastic Surgery) about my problem and both were puzzled as to what to do. She tells me, "You won the battle but lost the war." I was getting pretty sore from all the examining and I feel that I am irritating Doctor Bowers by being there with this small (to her) problem. Dr. Bowers said to me, "I expect you want me to open that site up," but she clearly didn't want to. She even suggested that Dr. Parikh could do it since his practice was in Seattle. In the end, I was to give it two more months and we left for home right after that.

I am trying laser with Debbie Caddell in that area to see if this will bring some relief. Cathy and I are increasingly more isolated; Doctor Marsden will be retired this summer sometime and Doctor Ken's practice just seems to be not as welcoming anymore. Cathy and I did attend the makeup workshop event that Debbie organized at Caddell's. She got two makeup artists from Nordstrom's to come in and give lessons to her transgender MtF clients. It was great fun. But the place was full of twenty-something T gals; kids to us. We did enjoy talking to Shawn and Amani; they are mother and daughter who act as receptionists at Caddell's, but we were still the odd old folks out. Debbie works very hard to be an ally to the transgender folk who come seeking services at Caddell's. The place seems almost like a second home to us each time we come in the door and it should after all the transitioning time I/we have spent here. I remember the first time I fearfully came in with my head down. It seemed so sterile and forbidding; now it is a joy to be here in this affirming place. I have watched the place grow over the years of my transition. We have become friendly with Debbie and I am always interested in people's life stories.

***

Monday January 28, 2019. The outing problem: Cathy and I both have Facebook pages for Cate and Cady that we created to share with the very few folks who know us in this way from a cruise we were on last May. That cruise was a milestone in me accepting who I am as Cady. Cathy's brother Mark's wife received a friend suggestion on Facebook for Cady along with a profile picture of the two of us. This piqued her attention and she texted us with, "I just received this shall I accept it?" This message led me to taking down the pages quickly and to Mark's wife poking around trying to find them again. So, this coupled with Mark's sudden and odd behavior of taking my picture several times at a recent birthday event has me feeling vulnerable. I don't want to be forced to come-out by Mark's wife poking at me. I want it on our terms; I would like people to be respectful. I'm not just this odd person on display for their amusement. There is more to this process (accepting, coming-out, transitioning) than just making sort of a declarative statement and things are all better. It has to do with me accepting it and with that comes acknowledging all the fears formed from 60 years of a split life being put to rest. To top this off my short-term memory is failing more and more each day. There is only empty space in places in my mind that once held words, ideas, pictures, and concepts. I mumble when I talk and miss turns as I drive because my mind wanders. My emotions scream in agony that I waited until my mind and body function are at an end to address my GID problem. I am very tired. Cathy and I have to make a movement in our lives someway, somewhere, and somehow. So, there you have what is going on. Only in short listings, each should be described more fully but I find it like going back and visiting hurts over and over. Growing old is no fun, perhaps it is just that we haven't found the joy in it yet…

***

Wednesday May 29, 2019. May 1st, we were in Victoria BC at the time when my retina detached in my right eye. The process started on April 12th but didn't immediately point to a retinal detachment, just a vitreous humor detachment. I had twice the normal floaters and a few flashes of light in the vision field of my right eye. It was scary, but was explained to me as something that comes with age and should settle down given a little time. We had a trip planned to Victoria BC as my birthday outing. I was given the go ahead to travel by Dr. Bucher with the warning about returning if other symptoms occurred. We were off to one of our favorite place to travel to. We booked first class tickets on the new Victoria clipper, and such was a new experience for us, a very comfortable ship. We cleared customs and walked to our hotel; this will be home for us for the next four days. Cathy and Cady wandered the shops and unique eateries in the area. The weather was beautiful and two days and two nights passed without sadness. Then we were walking along and I took note of the people we passed with white canes announcing their vision impairment. We passed three people walking with spouses helping them to avoid obstacles. A dark curtain suddenly drifted across the vision field of my right eye, I stopped dead in my tracks. I have only one good eye and right then something had happened to it. The symbolism of all those white cane folks hit me; what an awful coincidence! I told Cathy what was happening and she called our eye specialist who confirmed my now detaching retina. When told we were so far from home, he said it wasn't a problem as long as he gets to it within the next few days. Cathy took my hand and we became just another white cane couple except I didn't have a white cane. We arranged to leave on the next clipper that day for home.

May 2nd was Thursday and I saw Dr. Griggs. He had me booked for surgery on Monday the 6th. The surgery had to be done in a hospital by our trusted Dr. Griggs and was successful, leaving a bubble to hold the repair to my tear in place. The bubble disappeared on Thursday the 23rd bringing back my eyesight in that eye (albeit my glasses don't work right but an older 2017 set seem pretty good). So, praise God for restoring my eyesight!!! I was unable to get enough sight from my left eye to drive, read, use a computer, or just see clearly because of the central vision problem it has. Quite the experience to go through, losing then regaining your vision; the day I did I read a book and just looked around everywhere… On the weekend of my birthday, Corey and family were here. Corey volunteered to stay to help us through the eye surgery. Melinda returned home and little Q stayed. Casey and family (minus Mindy since she was ill) took care of little Q while Corey took care of us. All in all, it was the most amazing birthday I have ever had, our sons and their families were with us and they rose to my needs; so cool!

***

Tomorrow May 30th and I have an appointment with Dr. Elizabeth Eaman. I am so nervous and sad at the same time. All my adult life it has been Dr. Marsden that I have turned to, even to the point of her confiding in me at times, and now that is all over… Symbolic of this time in life of saying goodbye to things held as everyday anchors in our lives: people, places, and things. Add the turmoil of gender transition's death-of-my-male-persona. Now we face crossing over to some unknown, unsure, and perhaps untrustable doctor. Life itself seems almost impossible to handle must less the eventual coming end of it. At sixty-five, I feel time running away from me, the cup draining so low now. I really needed to get my revision surgery done on my orchi. Now due to the eye trouble, my date has moved off until August 9th almost at the end of the summer of 2019. So much of the time draining away, I am so tired…

***

Wednesday July 31, 2019. Trying to end the downward spiral by returning to journaling again. So, my appointment with Dr. E was just okay, she almost always has a med student in her office, and this one was very curious about me being transgender. I felt like I was on trial trying to justify myself as I answered her questions; it drove my BP up, and I couldn't get it down... I have ordered Novartis Estradiol patches from a Canadian pharmacy for $595 for a 90 supply. We had to create a checking account just for this purpose, as they don't do credit cards. By using an isolated account with a limited balance, we hope to limit any loss from misuse. This price, as high as it sounds, is better than anywhere else, and insurance doesn't cover this med for me. I prefer patches to gels, injectables, and pills (orally dissolved). All can deliver the level of estradiol my body requires but each has its downside. Gels containing estradiol are messy in the amount needed for me. Injectable (well it's a shot) estradiol produces a depot of estradiol in your body that leaches out in a decaying fashion over time. It is prone to unpredictable worldwide shortages (most folks as a buffer against shortages keep a years' supply on hand all the time); other than this, it is less expensive than patches. Pills require that you take them several times a day. You don't simply swallow them as your stomach/liver changes estradiol to estrone; the trick is to dissolve them in your mouth without swallowing. There are three forms of human estrogens: estrone (E1), estradiol (E2), and estriol (E3). Patches work for me; they produce a steady intake of estradiol over their life of three days (less of the ups and downs you experience with a shot), have been in steady supply, and are convenient to use. All are important because this is something I will be on for the rest of my life…

My body's muscles have been wasting and my weight is down to 162 and dropping. My mind has been very foggy; common words aren't there when I need them in conversations, and my short-term memory is all but gone. Good news is my E is sure high, bad news I all but have no T (less than .3). The very low T number is well below female normal and I have a feeling my brain function and muscle wasting is the result. Well Dr. E will get to give me some advice on this; good advice I hope. My detached retina is currently stable and I am off the prescription eye-drops completely. My new normal is dry-eye over the counter products. I must remember to ask for a blood test for Sjögren's syndrome from Dr. E; there is a suspicion that because of the new hormone cycle I have that it may be a partial cause for the dryness in my eyes. The Anderson picnic was a success, but only eight of the first cousins came and we really missed cousin Orlyn and his family.

***

Thursday August 1, 2019. Yesterday, I took a DHEA capsule seeing that my T level was so low. Mind fog has been so thick; I did feel better after taking a DHEA capsule along with a Fluconazole, and Diim two weeks ago. The risk is hair loss at the crown of my head so I have to be very careful in dosing. I wonder if a little T gel might be better in raising my T level to female normal. Pregnenolone is my attempt to compensate for low T but Pregnenolone can metabolize to either T or E. Since my E level is higher now, it looks like it metabolized to E. With the electrolysis today on my private place with Marsha (Moyer) Morgan, I now have done everything possible outside of surgery to address the sore spot that has developed on my scrotum. Today she hit some very sore places right near the bunched scar area from me orchi last September. This for some reason dulls the overall soreness for a while but the soreness does return. So, I am resigned to going through with surgery in seven days with Dr. Parikh. He seems enthusiastic and caring; I feel better about it now that he stated he had spoken with Dr. Bowers and will not remove the remaining scrotum tissue. On my last visit with Dr. P before my detached retina problem, he was all about removing all tissue saying it was not needed for GRS/SRS. This was opposite of what Dr. Bowers had told me, so I was on edge… Speaking of Marsha, she was in a lot of pain when I saw her today for both laser and electrolysis. It was her right shoulder aching in a way to frighten her with the idea of needing surgery and a long recovery. I promised to get her a copy of the book on shoulder health that Natalie had me get for myself. Also, I promised to scan some photos of her granddaughter swimming with the sharks for her.

Now me: My back is full of spasms, my right foot has a very sharp heel pain (enough so I can't walk on it without a support), my bottom gets sore whenever I sit on any surface in just a short time, my hips ache after driving short distances, I have no energy, and I tend list to

384

the right as I walk (almost dizzy at times). I feel like I really need the middle of my back adjusted; there is a hot spot of pain right in the middle and I hope this helps all of the other problems. We see Natalie tomorrow, fingers crossed, for pain reduction…

Our 45th anniversary is coming at us and we still don't know how to celebrate it. An idea I had was to see if Casey would fly his family down for the weekend at Corey's. We all could do something together there; but this sure puts a burden on him. It's a long way for only two days. Something that should be a happy time is just becoming a bump to get over. I wonder if things will become clearer once this surgery is over; fingers crossed.

***

Friday August 2, 2019. I have one week left until revision surgery on my scrotum. The antibiotic Dr. Parihk prescribed wasn't paid for my by insurance. No explanation just not covered, it's the world we live in today, and appears this will be the new normal of fighting over everything with them. Too hard, just pay the $25 for something that was covered a few months ago. I am hurting from the center of my back down my right leg into my foot. Natalie did a very intense massage on me and found many places that were very sore. She had me roll my back on a foam roller that left bruise marks but did give me some relief. She also told me my problem was I had no fat left to protect my muscles and bones, which were now all aching, "You are starving your muscles and they in turn are wasting and hurting." I am right around 162 pounds and have no appetite, but when I lay on my back I have a flat tummy! Something I have dreamed about all of my life. That flat tummy disappears when I stand up again, that fat is permanent… Anyway, I desperately need to have my back adjusted, hopefully Monday will bring help. I don't know just what to do about my weight. I don't want to hurt and this keeps me from driving long distances. It is mean to regain weight; when I do it goes right to my tummy area before all else…

***

385

Monday August 12, 2019. Happy Birthday Mom! You would have been 95 years old this year. Well, I had my surgery two days ago (Friday 9th) in Dr. Parihk's surgery center attached to his office in Bellevue. Sam was my surgical nurse; this is her first job after completing her training. She chatted with me in the center while we waited for Dr. Parihk to join us. We talked about video games and the 'divide by zero' joke Siri will tell if asked. I was placed on the edge of a reclining exam table with each of my legs resting on a step stool on either side to take the place of standard stirrups. I am Cady here nothing special. I had changed into a gown leaving my clothes with Cathy. We were together as Dr. Parihk marked my skin with a pen and he got to see that the area did in fact weep; a very good thing as he could see there was something going on. In the OR the worse part was injecting the anesthetic; after that, I would busy myself counting beeps and blood pressure cuff inflation cycles. He told me as he worked that at first he didn't see any trapped hairs then later told me he cut out two of them. My appointment was for 12:30 and we left their office at 2:30 with the surgery taking a little over one hour. I could drive home (making Cathy very happy) and walk without discomfort. The low level pain didn't start until near 8:00 and one pain pill (Perocet) let me sleep on my back lying still all night long (95% sleep level). Yesterday we entertained Colby and B---- while Casey and Mindy saw a play downtown. We made it through including games at Great-Grandma Dixon's; it was just the four of us and B---- even played Yahtzee with us. The two kids will have that memory for a long time I hope. I used another Perocet before bed, which was a mistake; it did let me sleep undisturbed but I woke up in the morning dizzy and my head ached. This has happen before. Perocet works great for a day and maybe two, but after that it is the source of pain not whatever I was taking it for. Right now, at 8:30pm I am finally getting over the effects of the pill I took twenty hours ago…

So how am I feeling about the surgery? I am uncomfortable but not in dire pain. It is dawning on me that I just had the same surgery again that I had all almost one year ago. I have to repeat the same healing cycle. This time without the gain of anything gender wise…

On the other hand, I have suffered for almost a year with a constant sore area and my prayer is this surgery will, once and for all, cure this and we can move on…

We are switching to Dr. Grace (mid twenty-something) for chiropractic care. She is maybe too gentle, but we will give her a try. I outed myself to her to explain my drug list and got no reaction one way or the other. My insurance name is C---- so I am C---- to her. So, the only places I am truly Cady or Cadance is Caddell's, Natalie's, and Dr. Parihk, these places are paid with cash or card. I am stuck between genders, totally on the outside looking in, and the world is moving away from me, from us. And then I wonder if, without realizing it, I have transitioned and no one cares.

When I see Dr. Eaman I need to remember two things: Dr. William Powers' trick of going on a month of oral E at 2mg to spur breast growth, and the test for Sjögren's. Dr. Powers is located in Michigan and has focused his practice on transgender care; he is fast becoming the go-to doctor for this specialty.

***

Monday August 19, 2019. This week is so important to us and it will be a relief when it is over with (although maybe not). Cathy has a first appointment with Dr. Crider (general doctor with gynecology) who if everything works out, will be her new primary care physician. A lot rides on this appointment; Cathy is deeply worried (and that means I am also) about her protruding stomach being a sign of tumors in her uterus. She has had a fibroid tumor in the past that shrank on its own, but this time even with strict dieting Cathy has not been able to reduce her stomach bulge. Natalie had the same bulge happening to her and she is now scheduled for surgery. Dr. Crider is in Tacoma so it will be quite a trip just to get to her office but she is covered by Cathy's insurance. Cathy has the female super power of ignoring whatever scary physical that faces her. This time though for only one day. I also saw the unprotected break-down of pure fear and hopelessness in her face that the fear of cancer can bring. The next day she was better. I asked her what has changed and she told me that she slept on it and now can go on. I have been sick to my inner core at all that might happen to her and us. All in all, I am worried for Cathy; she is my all and what happens to her happens to me. Praying each day for God to give Cathy a good doctor she can trust and feel confident in. The loss of doctor Marsden is felt so very acutely for us both right now. I am to have my first real appointment with Dr. Eaman on the 22nd and she has not responded to my emails I have sent containing labs and a link to Dr. Powers' video. Dr. Powers had some important comments on Estrone levels that I thought would pertain to my transition. In my own way, I am facing the same loss of someone to medically care for my problem as Cathy has.

So, what are we hoping for from this week?

First, a physical exam leading to imaging done on Cathy's uterus by an understanding doctor and if there is a problem that it doesn't involve cancer or any hospital use. This would be a blessing.

Second, Natalie's surgery will go well and she will recover quickly, even if she refuses pain meds she will only have a short time of discomfort.

Third, Dr. Eaman will put me at ease, agree to look up Dr. Powers' stuff, and apply it to me.

Fourth, Dr. Parihk will remove my sutures on the 23rd, be kind to us by answering our question, and most importantly, the returning pain I am having in the same spot as before will fade away very soon.

Fifth, our time with Colby tomorrow and Wednesday will be a lasting memory for him and us.

Sixth, the isolation coming from the loss of family structure we both are feeling will be relieved.

***

August 22, 2019. I have my appointment with Dr. Eaman one day before my appointment with Dr. Parihk for my suture removal. I did have a conversation with Dr. Eaman about Dr. Powers' video and yes she had given it a once over. After I pointed out the areas I was interested in (oral E for a month and adding P) she promised to view the video from start to end. She told me we could get together right after Cathy and I return from our anniversary trip to Corey's family's house and at that time do blood testing (including Sjögren's) and other physical exams. So, it was a positive appointment. Cathy had asked me not to go with her for her new Doctor (Dr. Crider) appointment later today. Okay I guess, but I had gotten used to being her extra memory and kind of felt left out. Cathy told me on my appointment with Dr. Eaman she would just stay in the little waiting room during any exam I might have to have. This felt odd to me; she had been with me during exams at Dr. Parihk's office and Dr. Bowers, why now? Cathy hasn't warmed up to Dr. Eaman and is leery of Dr. Crider seeing us together. We both have to come to trust again.

***

Sunday September 8, 2019. I am 30 days past my revision surgery with Dr. Parihk. I am still applying Vaseline each day and using a gauze pad between my underwear and me. The pain level has returned to what it was just before surgery so I have neither gained nor lost ground... On my last post-op appointment (15 days ago) where my sutures were removed (didn't hurt but he did leave several in), Dr. Parihk had at that time great expectations of all of the pain being gone. I didn't want to disappoint him, so I only reported a little soreness adding that it was getting much better, it looks better anyway... In my view there is still something wrong but I have now tried all that I can think of to address it. Dr. Parihk was very careful to address me as Cadance, and his office staff was equally as careful. He also let me know he was more than willing to work with me on any other surgeries I might feel I need in the future (face and body feminization).

I got depressed after my Dr. Parihk visit and went over and over in my mind asking myself if I had tried everything or blaming myself for not going back to Dr. Bowers for my revision. I still have the problem with the only path to address it being GRS/SRS, this being a several years wait and then no guarantee really. So, I read, thought and wondered if I could have possibly picked up some form of strep from my original surgery way back a year ago, I mean surgeons offer surgeons' fixes so perhaps a general doctor might have a different view. I would try one last avenue of treatment and if that didn't produce anything, I would just be stuck... I called Dr. Eaman and asked to get in to see her in the next few days and here we are today. Anyway Dr. Eaman did view all the cocky Dr. Powers' (as she calls him) video and understands his findings. In fact, she is from the same area (Michigan) and may even know people in the med-school he went to. She did an exam and found some sutures still in place and asked me why? I didn't know but I would ask on my next visit to him. She suggests that I try applying testosterone cream directly to my scrotum, "The pain came with time as your testosterone levels dropped so adding some back may help with healing and revitalization of the tissue." I was all for this; I had read that mind fog is reduced by adding some T back into your system and her idea sounded good. Dr. Eaman also prescribed Progesterone (200mg) as a suppository to help with my breast development. She also took Dr. Parihk's cards so I felt I had done my duty.

***

Sunday September 15, 2019. I am now taking Progesterone (Micronized 200mg) via rectum before bed each night. I started 9/9/19, Cathy also measured me 37 inch ban by 39 inch bust. The side effect of Progesterone is I sleep very soundly (89 to 92% each night at a $1.50 per pill); my dreams are muted as well as my memory. We have made the acquaintance of Key Compounding Pharmacy (I am Cady there). I now get Testosterone cream 20.25mg/0.1ml to apply to my scrotum nightly to hopefully help healing and memory. I started this on 9/11/19 and don't know if it is helping yet as I am still sore; (my last appointment is tomorrow with Dr. Parikh. He will not be happy to hear that I am still sore but he did all I asked him to do. I have given his cards to Dr. Eaman, did a nice review on Real Self, and will give him Caddell's cards.

***

Tuesday September 17, 2019. I had my checkup with Dr. Parihk. I didn't tell him that the soreness was persisting and instead told him I was steadily getting better. There was no need to do otherwise; as I said before, he did all he could do... I loaded my big cannon in a final attempt for healing and fired. This was to take a course of Cephalexin (500mg 3times daily) one that I had been saving from Dr. Marsden. The first pill was at bedtime last night, so I should know pretty soon if this will help. On the positive side, it has helped the right-between-the-eyes pain I have developed in the last few weeks. Fingers crossed, I don't expect I will ever have this prescribed for me again...

***

Saturday September 21, 2019. My GID dysphoria is just shouting at me today; so very loud, so mean, so irritated, and I am deeply hurting from this. I was even moved to call Sandy; all I needed to know was that she was okay. One Eyed Jack cat passed away just a few days ago on the 15th. We talked for twenty minutes about her and she continually called me C----; it didn't matter, it was Sandy and she was hurting too. She told me she has lots of support. Folks bring food and comfort, but what she really needs is to be alone for a while to internalize her loss; tomorrow she will turn off her phone... Sandy is volunteering at an animal shelter and doing things with her younger sister (Sandy is the oldest of three sisters) like some traveling. She was sitting in her place wondering what it was going to be like without Jack, without any cats for the first time in decades, when she heard a meow outside. It kept going on, but she didn't see any cats around and soon it stopped. She even had a big yellow cat come up to her the other day, and she told herself thank you Jack for the comfort. She wanted to hear about me. I told her my adventure and in return she told me it was not my problem but Dr. Bowers'. Sandy gave me the name 'Rachel' and phone number to call for possible help in finding a trans friendly Urologist.

I don't know why I am hurting so much. Was it the book I just read? The book was *Love Lives Here* by Amanda Jette Knox. I haven't had so big a flare, so extreme feelings in years...

I am almost through my course of Cephalexin; it did help with sinus pain, but didn't reduce the soreness of my personal area. I had Debbie shoot a laser near the site around the shaft. Not directly at the scar tissue but this didn't help either. So, two more things tried to no avail. I think this issue is driving this almost overwhelming transgender dysphoria feeling I am having. I have to work very hard not to do anything rash like coming-out to anyone without first thinking very hard…

Another note; I am cutting back the T cream to like once a week, it just drives uncomfortable night erections and I just don't need this. My eye has been inflamed several times forcing me to use the prescription eye drops for a short time.

***

Friday November 1, 2019. My chest is 37 x 39.5 from 53 days on 200mg Progesterone per day. I weigh 160 pounds or so with my clothes on. So there…

It has been 40 days since I last typed in my journal. All of October has passed and much has happened! I find myself fatigued from the flow of events; so instead of recording the experiences, I have been living them one by one… I was mindful enough to take the time, while Cathy is packing our bags for our trip to LA, to record our adventure of our 45th anniversary party last month at Corey's home:

Our 45th anniversary is this year and much of our family is going to be out of town. In fact, Grandma Dixon and Linda are both going to be visiting San Diego as they have a timeshare condo near Corey. They were pushing for us to come down and spend our anniversary with them, but it just seemed so much like an also ran event to us, not the important benchmark it is to us. Cathy was sad, she wanted (me too) for this year's anniversary to be a special one. It has deep meaning for us; we are still together and after 45 years of a transgender sword of Damocles dangling over our union. 50 years is the big one, but there is much in this resting place of 45 years… We poked at each other from June through August until I could finally see a solution. Let's throw ourselves a party down at Corey's house! There was no reason that Casey couldn't fly his family down to San Diego for one weekend, other than the price of the tickets, and we would pay for them. After all, it is our party, so to speak. We would have both our sons and their families along with Grandma Dixon, Linda, and, because Cathy's brother Phil lived nearby, he and his wife could come also. Cathy has a second cousin Joan living in Vallejo who was happy to come if she could bunk in with Grandma Dixon and Linda at their timeshare condo. Unfortunately, Mark and his wife couldn't make the sudden trip but still it seemed pretty special with most of our family to be with us... Still, what more could we do???

We wanted to make our 45th anniversary on October 5th really special so I suggested coming-out to Joyce (Cathy's mom), Phil (Cathy's brother), Tamara (Phil's wife), Linda (Cathy's sister), and Joan (Cathy's second cousin Joan just because she happened to come). Standing on Corey's grand staircase we will make a grand announcement to the gathering there that we are Cady and Cathy and after 45 years we are coming-out as transgender! What could be more dramatic or memorable than that? Cathy was at first very trepidatious, but as she thought about it she resolved that it needed to be done. It was getting harder and harder to lead a double hidden life as a couple. Cathy was all in!

Trouble was already in place, starting from our arrival four days before the party at Carnegie house in San Diego. The new beautiful backyard was in dismal shape with the ground covered in crunchy dry leaves. Corey was deathly ill and wasn't getting any better. He was worse than we had ever seen before. (The last time he was this bad, he had Mono back in grad school.) He was pretty much bedridden all the time with a mean cough, so we took over Quince care and party prep. We couldn't keep from being parents to our sick son and ended up on eggshells all the time. Corey had no energy and looked spent; finally, he made the decision to see another doctor. Previously he had been to urgent care five days ago, but they had just passed it off as a sinus thing and patted him on the head. It sure looked like pneumonia to me and I did have firsthand experience from my several bouts with pneumonia to pull from. What is so disheartening is how broken healthcare is now even for someone who has all the resources to afford it. This time by the grace of God Corey got to see a doctor who had 30 years plus experience. He looked Corey directly in his eyes and asked all the right questions, an x-ray confirmed pneumonia and a Z-Pak was prescribed. Yay! With Corey still in bed but getting the right meds Cathy and I started much needed party prep work. It's touchy going as Corey pushes back about us doing stuff but still it needs to be done. We drove all over finding stores to source food for the party and equipment for cleaning up their newly installed backyard. This beautiful new backyard was marred by a thick layer of dried leaves from a centerpiece tree that wasn't deciduous, but was in transplant shock causing the leaf drop, and the result was simply a mess. We needed tools to remove this debris from the new artificial lawn and freshly created granite dust paths without damage. We sought out a hardware store; I had figured a leaf blower would do it and I had an idea to add some outdoor lighting for a party mood.

Pacific Beach Ace Hardware was a narrow, deep, two-story place full of stuff. We asked about leaf blower and were escorted to 'The Yard', which had outdoor garden tools and lumber. We found a light duty electric leaf blower for $40, done deal. On the way back to the front I spied a poly-scoop shovel that would be great for leaf scooping (they had exactly one in stock at any one time). At the cash register I asked about strings of white lights (after all San Diego is all about living outside and you see these lights everywhere) but they were in transition to holiday lighting at the moment. I had it in my brain that Costco carried these things, so we will check for them there. I wasn't worried about spending money on this party as it was for Cathy and me as a love gift to each other (if Corey could have done the whole thing he would have but bedridden is bedridden). The airplane tickets for Casey family to get here was all part of experience for us. We decided to have Casey cook us a prime rib roast, so it was on our list to find a meat market and we found Siesel's Meats not too far from the hardware store. They did have Choice Rib Roast, but we are headed to Costco (Casey told us Costco had the best cuts of meats around) and will check for a roast there along with the lights.

Hurray! Costco has the same LED strings of outdoor lights but much longer and for less money, we pick-up two 48-foot strings. At the meat counter they have a 5-pound prime rib roast, but we hesitate.

Would it be big enough? We dither and finally ask one of the counter fellas if they had a bigger one. Yes almost seven pounds! Close enough! Pricey but hey, once every 45years right! As side note, we also will have a small ham because Melinda and Colby don't like roast. But guess what? No one sells a ham around here! We settle for several ham steaks, which Casey can work his magic on…

Back to home base and to start the labor of de-leafing the backyard. I announce to Corey that we have two 'new backyard' gifts for him (it has been ten days since the completion of the backyard and most of that time Corey has been sick): the outdoor lights and a leaf blower. I ask if he would like to give it a try? He does but soon he is headed back upstairs to lay down… Corey was happy about the lights and the leaf blower and did give me the blessing to install the lights and de-leaf the yard. Cathy did ground support with me on a ladder attaching the string bulb by bulb with tie-wraps to their new pergola. By using tie-wraps it would be easy to remove the string if Corey took a notion too. I am poor at figuring out how/where to string the lights so I must physically lay the string on the ground below the overhang of the pergola and then lift and attach it foot by foot. Part way through, I have to start over; in theory, math and measurement would solve the problem, but my mind is so slow anymore… We have to stop just before completing the job to go and pick up Quince at the daycare. He is put to work holding Boppa's ladder as safety-kid and tie-wrap picker upper. Corey's Pergola is strong enough for me to stand on this is very handy in finishing the job. Now the leave problem; the dry leaves have worked themselves into the artificial lawn, and the only way to remove them is with teamwork. Cathy and I take turns raking while the other uses the blower aimed at the area being raked. Slowly foot-by-foot the artificial grass is cleared. Of course, Quince thinks this is all for his amusement, which I guess is partly true. By carefully applying the blower, little by little the leaves are herded into a pile leaving behind the granite dust and little rocks. The poly-scoop shovel works like the perfect dustpan and after a hard day's work we are treated to a beautifully clean backyard aglow at dusk. I know Melinda didn't really care what it was going to look like for party time versus how it does look now that we have cleared and lighted the place, but I think Corey was deeply grateful for our help. We have been here three days at his point, have gotten much done and Corey is improved enough to go shopping with us this Friday afternoon at Costco, Ralph's, and Whole Foods (after we pick up Q at his daycare). Cathy even worked in baking two loaves of banana bread and a happy anniversary spice cake during this day (Casey will decorate the cake when he is here tomorrow).

Cathy and I stay up late waiting for Casey and family to arrive to drop off Colby who is going to stay with us here at Corey's. Honestly there is a lot of stress in this house, at least for us. Corey is not his normal congenial self at all and, to get along with Melinda, we must walk on eggshells at times. It is understandable them being this way made so much greater because of Corey being so far under the weather. Corey really is the linchpin of his family and right now it's a bit wobbly without him. There is the specter of us coming-out at the close of the party in our minds also. Quince does demand our time; giving into his demand returns much joy, it is fun to pick him up at daycare each afternoon and see him come running over to us all excited. Each morning right at 6:30, Quince comes running into our room before we get up to spend time in bed with us for 20 minutes of videos (mostly Paw Patrol). He squirms continually and delights in each twenty-minute episode until his Baba comes in to take him down to breakfast. Truth is by us being here, we change their tightly held normal routine. We feel this intrusion all the more but there is such joy from Quince…

Cathy and I make sure Colby's bed is ready for him when he arrives to get right into as it will be well past his bedtime. We put some of Quince's stuffies on the pillow as a welcome from Little Q to his cousin Colby. The house is very quiet; everyone is asleep except for us right now. Normal bedtime for Q is 8:00 and 9:30 for Corey and Melinda (and us too).

Casey shows up in the driveway at 10:30pm and drops off a sleepy Colby. They pull out right away to head to where they are staying tonight to get B---- to bed. No sooner did Colby's head hit the pillow and he moved my hand to rub his back he was asleep. The next morning (October 5th our anniversary) Q was in our room, right on time at 6:30 wanting Paw Patrol videos. We watch several to give Colby some extra sleep time then suggest to Quince that cousin Colby needs to wake up in the other bedroom. Q is off in a flash and we can hear giggles as Q is up on the bed with Colby. Casey and family will be here any time this morning to shower (wherever they are staying has a pretty sad shower) and everyone else sometime after 10:30am for the party. Corey is a little better this morning and we tackle moving tables from the garage into the big dining room. Melinda did a run to find Sudafed for Corey and I asked her to look for a Happy Anniversary sign while at the Pharmacy. She misunderstood and got me a really nice card to give to Cathy! Cathy's mom, sister Linda, and cousin Joan Barker showed up and the home tours began. Lauren Grace, the lady giving the painting class that Corey has arranged for, comes to the front door pulling a little wagon behind her filled with easels and paints. She sets the dining tables up for the class as Phil and Tamara show up. Everyone is here and more home tours go by, then it is class time. Casey is the only one not painting and is doing the camera thing. I become frustrated as the lesson goes along because of my eyesight; I had forgotten to use eye drops last night and my eyes are becoming sore and dry. I convince Casey to take over for me and he turns my mess into a nice painting. Yay! Painting is over and Corey had a bunch of pictures printed for us to pass around as did Phil; so, we all visited while Casey and Mindy prepared our dinner. Mindy asked Corey if she could take his kitchen home with her. Quince-care, at this point, is mostly handled by Colby and B---- hanging out with him, as cousins are apt to do. Another joyous thing to remember.

As soon as dinner was in the oven Casey and Colby made the rounds to get drink orders for a Starbucks run (nine drinks in all $40 total and Casey put $80 on Colby's Starbucks card to pay for it and he got to keep the change)! A wonderful dinner came from the hands of Chef Casey and Sous Chef Mindy. The roast was perfect and the gravy was the best I have ever tasted! Everything was the best it could have been during that dinner, it just was!

Dusk had fallen, the lights outside did justice to the new backyard and Q was heading to bed. Before everyone began to gather their stuff up to leave, Cathy and I walked upstairs and each changed into black and white dresses to introduce Cady as Cathy's spouse. There was hesitancy on Cathy part and some on mine also. This was throwing all our cards down on the table, ones we have held so close for so long. We walked downstairs and stopped on the last step then Cathy told everyone this was Cady her spouse. There was a moment of confusion before I told my little audience that I was transgender. I offered that I have been transgender all my life, and that Cathy and I discussed this before we were married, then asked if anyone had questions. Everyone seemed okay except Cathy's sister Linda; she just stood staring with her mouth open, and Cathy's cousin Joan went silent. Questions were "What do we call you?" (This came from a smiling Grandma Dixon.) My name is Cadance and Cady for short. "What do the grandkids call you?" Cathy answered, "They call her Boppa." "Are you planning for surgeries?" (This came from Mindy) and I told her gently that is one question you really shouldn't ask transgender folks. Linda seemed to be mumbling something to herself I took note to talk to her by herself later. Tamara chatted with me about her perception of me and added some hidden things about herself. I asked Cathy later if she had talked to Linda at all and she told me yes she had. Cathy asked if she was okay and Linda said, "Yes," but kept mumbling, "How did he know for sure" over and over. It wouldn't be until two days later that we would find out just how negative Linda's view on me was...

***

Sunday October 6th brings Legoland with Corey, Quince, Casey, Mindy, Colby, B----, Boppa, and Nanna. After two hours, we all have lunch together and Boppa, Nanna, Corey, and little Q all go home leaving Casey's family more time to enjoy the park. We all meet up back at Corey's place around 3:00 for more visiting and then it was off to the airport for Casey's family.

***

Monday October 7th and we haven't heard from Linda and Grandma Dixon they all were doing stuff with Phil and Tamara and Joan...

***

Tuesday October 8th today we meet up with Linda and Grandma Dixon to visit the Birch Aquarium and Museum (Quince is in daycare). We drive our car and they drive their rental to La Jolla and have a nice time visiting every corner of the place. I take lots of pictures of the three ladies having fun. We leave the two of them to have lunch at the aquarium and we head out to pick up Quince. The plan is to have dinner at Corey's place (he is ordering in). We all are together except for Melinda who is working a little late, but did show up toward the end of our meal. This is the start of Linda poking at me. During dinner she sirs me, I pass her a plate and she sirs me again this time with a big grin... Why is she doing this? I make it a point to make sure to talk to her alone before they leave tonight (this is their last night here).

So the evening comes; Quince is headed up to get ready for bed, Linda and Grandma Dixon are getting ready leave. I turn on the outdoor lights and ask Linda if I could chat with her outside before they leave. She says okay and heads toward the backyard door with Grandma Dixon following right behind. I guess I am talking with two people... Cathy is up with Quince so it is just the three of us. I tell them that they really didn't get much of a chance to ask questions the other night and I was sure they had some (especially after 'sir'ing me, something Linda never normally does). Linda says she doesn't know what to ask and then asks me belligerently; what should she ask? So, I offer a little more about me. I tell them I think that Cathy and I are not doing anything Biblically wrong; we were married before God and still are. Then she leveled into me with "Why now, why did you wait so long?" "What about your grandchildren, do you realize what you are going to do to them?" "What about the radical transgender agenda?" "What about the bathrooms?" "Are you gay?" "You don't look female, I will never see you as female!" "I can't ever use your

399

name!" "Don't expect me to use your name or pronouns!" Cathy's mom chimed in with "I was very much hurt that you didn't tell me sooner."

I got all hot and flustered; I was being attacked with a collected group of standard bashing questions that now I am sure was the result of either conversations between Phil, Joan, Linda, possibly Cathy's mom, and Tamara or a web search by only Linda into the world of trans-bashers. What is worse, this is the very thing I have been so fearful of happening to me, to us. I have read about this over and over; it has kept me closeted in both fear and self-loathing. Cathy came to my defense as I found myself trying to justify me against each question/accusation. Cathy's mom poked at how Cathy was going to deal about not having sex in the normal way anymore. Cathy told them that I was the same person she fell in love with 45 years ago, the very same person.

Still trying to justify myself, I pointed out that at 65 years old I had only a small handful of years left in my life. Shouldn't I be allowed to be happy?' Linda blared, "When were you not happy!" I returned, most of my life this kept me from being happy. I tried to tell Linda that she most likely had already shared a restroom with a transgender person at some point in her life and never knew it. I got louder and Linda pointed this out by shouting, "Stop being angry." I was flustered and felt battered. Now I grabbed at calming down. No, I am not gay. Cathy and I have been careful to be gender neutral with all three grandkids, the use of Boppa instead of Grandpa for one of the ways. I have given myself to Casey and Corey as Father well into their forties. I have seen most of my birth family pass away. Just how long do I have to wait? I turned to Mom Dixon and said, so many game nights I have sat across from you wanting to tell you but it was never the right time and our sons were the first to know as is right. Back to Linda, I have had surgeries to help my face and neck look more feminine, spent many hours in hair removal and on hormones. She returns, "I'll still not get pronouns right." To this I respond, I can't make you use them or my name but neither can I tell you it won't hurt me when you don't. My feeling is Linda is looking for permission to be exempted and I am tempted, it would be so easy to say I didn't care at all if she still just referred to me as C----. No big deal, doesn't bother me, but truth is something in me is changing even as we talk... Sex, the radical transgender agenda, and the bathroom are left unresolved; they're just bashing points. Linda tells me, "Perhaps I'll just call you C." In the end, I think the cruelty of her words began to make Linda feel dirty; they weren't going to gain her anything, but once the seed is planted who knows what will grow from it.

That is how it is left and in the end I do give hugs to Linda and Mom Dixon as they leave. Linda and Cathy's mom left the San Diego area on Thursday October 10th. We all have much to think about and I have faith things will calm down.

Cathy and I have decided to leave Corey's Friday morning but Corey asks us to stay until Saturday morning the 13th. Corey wanted us to stay until then because Melinda wasn't feeling well and it gave us a chance to pick up Quince at the daycare while all three of us could match tie-dye shirts. It's time for us to leave even though we had planned to stay another week. Corey will be gone to San Francisco just after we leave and while, on the face of it, we would be there to help it just doesn't feel comfortable this time. Also, by leaving early we can visit Universal Studios Park and attend the Open Salt Collectors Meeting in Costa Mesa! Most of the members are ten to twenty years older than we are and several have passed away recently. Still, it is fun to have a lunch meeting with them.

Linda's words bothered me and coming-out took a lot from me, more than I realized. I couldn't eat, the thought of food seemed to turn my stomach, and the only stuff I could stomach was a soft fried egg and potatoes. So, we search for little organic eateries along our drive home all the while my stomach flipped flopped. We arrived home early in the evening on October 17th to rain and chill. It was quite a once in a lifetime adventure, life changing as such adventures should be. I lost something of myself in this one, in fact I think I have lost who I was, or had been trying to be, or resolved to be, and haven't fully understood who I am to be yet...

***

Thursday November 7, 2019. Filling in from arriving home on 10/17. We skipped game night with Grandma Dixon and Linda (10/19). I just couldn't bring myself to face any sort of confrontation or trust myself not to cave into giving my life away. Nothing has changed... We played Saturday night games until 7:00pm at Casey's house (Machi Koro) with Casey, Colby, and B----. We had arrived at their house at 2:00 with the big bag of Lego stuff from Legoland Casey had purchased for his family and some to give out to others. It was so fun to watch Colby and B---- give Lego kits to CJ and Caleb, they were so gentle with the two neighbor boys, heartwarming. Cathy gave Casey's neighbor Jen the dog tags she had decorated for sale in a holiday craft bazaar for her Bags of Hope charity. Sunday's weather is very nice for this time of year and we walk along the river and in the afternoon video visited with Quince. I play with the car set after he and Nanna both build it and he laughs away. Corey shows us his decorations for Halloween that he and Q have put up in their house.

On 10/21 we visit Deb Montgomery at her little apartment. We had told her all about me on 9/24 and she was very nice about it. On that visit we learned about her daughter-in-law being transgender, that she had once known another MtF years ago, and some other of Deb's life adventures. On this visit I told her about the reaction someone had with my news. I was searching for advice about how to proceed with that person in the coming days ahead. The three of us chatted together for like three hours (Deb is so unique and her life is so amazing). She asked me many question including, "Which do I prefer, trans woman or woman?" I struggled having 'trans' as a tag; it cuts at the self-identity that I am trying to come to address. The whole point is I am female... When I got home I had this amazing message in instant massager:

"Cady I really enjoyed our visit today. How brave you were to open up to so many. That person you spoke about will take a bit of time to reframe her reality, you don't own that. From what little I have

been told about her she seems fairly self-absorbed in many ways. Often our social identities, or the groups to which we belong, help us to define our personal identities. To the extent that the boundaries around the groups that are important to our identities become blurred, we may experience a distinctiveness threat. In short, the uniqueness of who we are as an individual comes under threat when the boundaries around group definitions that we use to define ourselves shift or become malleable. Does that make sense? Her PERCEPTION of your malleable gender has shifted her perception of who she is and that makes her uncomfortable. Something that she has looked at as an essential, immutable, human trait: gender and, by extension, the connection between sex and gender. Has now been changed and she doesn't know what to do with it. Give her time. It took you a great many years to embrace your own truth enough to embrace yourself. She might need a month or two. Be the beautiful gracious woman you know you are and everything will settle. Let your children stand behind you. Let your family be your strength, it is their turn. You were theirs for a very long time give them that honour. They earned it my friend."

What a marvelously focused thought for me to ponder! It really helped me understand where Linda might be coming from. This didn't instantly fix the situation for me, but I did feel a bit of the weight come off of my being. It is interesting; the two people I felt in the back of my mind who would cause me the most worry were Mindy and Linda. I worried that Mindy would adopt some form of gender fluid thing or ownership of such by association with my state; this did happen. First thing she did after I came-out in a limited way (I asked the people I told that night not to out me to anyone as I wasn't completely out yet) was to call her cousin who is openly gay with the news that she now shared in his world by her association to me. His reaction (and bless his heart because of this) was to tell her, "Don't out-her; we shouldn't even be having this phone conversation unless she told you that it was okay." Mindy would tell Cathy about her 'slip up' the next day, but do the same thing several days later with Sherry her family friend. Mindy

403

told me she did have my back. I know it is very hard for her to keep something like this quiet so the beat goes on.

With Linda I hadn't foreseen just how negative her reaction would be or how much it would affect me so deeply.

Opening up or coming-out on our anniversary changed things, changed me, and changed us. More of myself became Cady and Cathy became not only Cady's spouse but her advocate as well. Where Boppa would remain for our grandchildren, we now routinely use Cady between the two of us in conversation. Cathy was in full support of changing my name sooner rather than later. We even kicked around changing the name with changing the gender marker just to speed up the process. I now experienced a twinge each time Cathy needed to use 'C----' as my name in public and Cathy told me she did also. "I don't think of you as C---- anymore," she told me. Pronouns also gave us discomfort, it was Cathy's challenge to always use proper female pronouns for me whenever talking to her mother or Linda. She didn't want to get caught by either of them while on the other hand with other people it was still he and C----. Each gender name event would spur my internal conversation about who I was to be. Slowly little by little the back and forth conversation became less and Cady not only became more comfortable as my name but required. For the last fourteen years I have read about and studied many MtF transitioning accounts, each full of rejection, pain, loss of spouse, family, personal safety, and security. These filled me with fear and an internal conversation that kept me from seeing myself in any of these painful experiences. Sandy would point out the flipside of these experiences, joy, freedom, relief, and self-love in place of self-hate. I would surprise myself with each little step I would take placing me further into sharing these experiences but with the disclaimer of not going much further mostly because of fear, so I hung onto the ever diminishing male C----. I ponytailed my hair and was constantly reminded by the continuing pain from my surgery site to stand still as far as physical change goes. C---- was safe but now I can't be him anymore… So, the negative attack by Linda, so fully in tune with the many transitioning experiences I have read about, brings me face to

404

face with my deepest fears while at the same time in an odd way validating my transitioning position. In an ironic way Linda unintentionally did me a great favor as being a sort of devil's advocate. Simply put, I am a transitioning MtF person; their journey is now my journey. In fact, I am very close to having transitioned! Cathy and I have both come very close to fully transitioning together. She tells me she only sees Cady now, her spouse, and she sees herself as a transgender spouse. Still even at this point there is so much more to reconcile for me...

Casey both surprised and endeared me with the forceful proclamation that next time, Cathy and I were to play games at Grandma Dixon's house with Linda there, he and his family were going to be there too. He told me, "I want my kids to see that I don't stand for bad behavior and mis-gendering you is bad behavior." Wow! In none of the experiences I had studied had anyone done this for their parent. This was so touching I felt so loved and relieved. So, Saturday night (10/26) came and Casey was there along with Mindy, Colby, and B----. I was Boppa Cady she/her all evening, Linda avoided using my name but did use proper pronouns. We played Mexican Train with lots of laughing all around. Grandma Dixon did call Cathy to see if she and Cady could come up to fix the telephone earlier in the week. I tried but failed because after three hours I realized it was the phone company's box failing not the old brittle house wires; this would need them to fix their problem. On the other hand, Casey and Colby working as a team did fix Grandma Dixon's computer so she could print a picture she really wanted to print! I thanked Casey and Mindy for their support. Casey in turn told me he would be back for games next time too. What I came to understand through Casey's comment was the problem with Linda wasn't going to fixed quickly; it would take more time and so the next time would be on 11/9/19.

***

Monday November 11, 2019. Another Saturday night games at Grandma Dixon's have passed. Casey was true to his word; he, with his whole family, was in attendance right at 6:30 pm to support me.

Cathy and I arrived first and Casey's came next. I noticed that Grandma Dixon seemed lost having us in her house without Linda being there also. How odd to be a familiar stranger in her house. Not unlike my experience of the summer of 1973 which would be my last summer at the ranch. The relationship now between Grandma Dixon and Linda is one as a couple. I had déjà vu at that moment from my time taking care of my dad during his hospice. I was there but he was always longing for Butch (Wayne) to show up to take care of him. My dad loved Butch in a way I can't yet understand but I can appreciate, as it was clearly evident. All in all, I was a poor substitute for Butch. Grandma Dixon only fully relaxed when Linda showed up.

We played Mexican Train (except for B----) and despite my name being used around the table Linda found ways to avoid using 'Cady'. She would use 'Boppa' instead. After half of the evening had gone by I resigned myself to the loss of a relationship with her. I thought to myself, what value is there in this kind of rejection of a relationship? Linda was pitiful to look at that night. She had been to her dermatologist and he had found and frozen dozens of suspicious bumps on her arms and nose. So, I was all resigned to letting go of any chance for a relationship with Linda and was thinking how wise Casey had been. When out of the blue she used 'Cady' two times. Surprised me in fact! But it is still way too early for any solid hope to hang onto… Thinking about it now Deb's familiar stranger description was maybe as much as can expect…

Saturday during the day we did Christmas Craft Fairs with Casey and family. B---- spent all of her grade money ($45) she earned from us on Christmas presents for teachers, family, and stuff for herself. Colby, who has lost his electronics until he clears two Ds from missing assignments, earned less ($40); he did have more As than B----. Colby was really hurting from no electronics but it gives him incentive to due diligence on his schoolwork.

B---- did one more Craft Show shopping with us then on to our house to help Nanna with Christmas craft planning she was doing. Later after games, we would trade for Colby, as B---- doesn't like to sleep over at our place. Colby is now 5'9" tall and has grown two inches in four months. Sunday morning Nanna made pumpkin pancakes for breakfast and then we played Ticket To Ride and Sail board game for four hours. After a short walk that I needed because of stiffness, we play Clue for almost an hour. Nanna and Colby played two games of cribbage while Boppa made dinner of camp food. Wow! A whole visit with Boppa and Nanna without any electronic games! Instead of meeting in a video world, we chatted in the real world. I asked Colby if his parents had talked to him about my transition and he said 'no'. So, I asked if he was at all curious about what was happening with me and again he said 'no'. Pronoun use during our chatting was 'she/her' in relation to me; he didn't have any problem with that at all. But again, not even a little bit curious? So, I didn't force the issue and considered myself lucky. We do a video Hangout with Quince to virtually babysit while Corey made dinner for them. Colby and Quince played together on toys we had at our house and Nanna read a Paw Patrol story. We ended our time together with a camp food dinner; Colby and B---- both sure can put away food...

***

Round up time with my stuff:

Dr. Eaman gave me a script (9/10/19) for Testosterone cream and I have been using it at a half dose level for little over a month, emptying one syringe of 1ml dose of cream, on my scrotum. I had hope that this might help the persistence soreness there but that didn't come to be. Instead, I got night-erections and my penis gained in diameter and length. I did have more energy but didn't notice much relief from the persistent brain fog as I had hoped for and more derogatory unwanted black hair growth in places I didn't want. I even had a small ejaculation one night of clear fluid from my now sore prostate. I had my appointment with Dr. E and she took blood and we chatted about what test to run, total T and fractionated E for two of them.

I got my blood numbers back a few days later:
Estradiol 281 pg/ml and Testosterone 618.5 ng/dl!!!

I panicked, I haven't had Testosterone levels this high since 2007 and then it was in the mid 500's and at that time my Estradiol level was 130!!! My 6/6/19 T blood level was less than 3 ng/dl; what an increase! There are studies done that claim having high Testosterone levels while also having high Estradiol levels greatly increases prostate cancer risk. The two don't normally occur together. So here I am hating myself for letting this happen to me but thankfully I had not used any T cream since the day before my test. Still the erections continued for ten days and dropped off three nights ago. I have been so tired during this time and my mind and memory are very foggy. I calmed down; this is the world I live in now and these are the necessary trial and errors I have to go through. This is the world of 'Informed Consent' medical treatment; basically, it is left up to me to do the research and then partner with a doctor for HRT treatment meds. When I started HRT it wasn't at a doctor's direction, it was me stating that I was starting HRT at a particular level, it was my choice and I accepted and understood the risk in doing so. Transgender medicine at best was on the very fringe of modern care not so long ago; trial and error was not something defining standard doctor care but a patient could consent to it. The bulk of the problem is because transitioning gender is on the fringe, there is very little interest in doing research on treatment meds, etc. Dr. Eaman is very brave in focusing her family practice on LGBTQ+ needs. We are both learning together…

I will get my blood test tomorrow for total T as well as progesterone and Sjögren's Syndrome. I am hoping for a T level well below double digits. So best case, I will now have a T level under 40 ng/dl and dropping and understand just how powerful this new tool is for me to use sparingly; also, I will have two more test results to add to my collection.

More me stuff:
We have 19 trick-or-treaters this night, many are little ones with parents just at the bottom step and yes I have bought too much candy.

I have read about the love of Halloween that so many transgender folks have, the adventures that come from the freedom to dress up as your true-self one night a year… In a way my father had such a story one Halloween in his youth, I have always wondered about this…

***

Tuesday November 12, 2019. I called Uncle Ray to check in on him and Pat. Pat answered my call with she is okay and would give me over to Ray for him to tell me about what is going on. Uncle Ray told me he is still here but hasn't improved since finally getting over the flu in July. He no longer drives and can't walk very far so they don't go out. He told me he is so weak in his legs, balance, and just has no energy. He is focused on the fact that he needs to start physical rehab but there is a difference in opinion between he and Pat as to his doctor ordering it. His mind has become fogged, he reaches for words that don't come and it frustrates him. He shares with me his ailments and my heart sinks little by little; he is still there, this amazing man just as Ainsley was amazing, but now he falters. I ask about church and he and Pat did get to one service but he couldn't stand all the way through one hymn and couldn't rise at all for another. The pastor announced from the pulpit that it was good to see Ray and Pat there that day. Ray told me he would have liked to stay after service for the fellowship time but was just too weak too. Jeanette comes each weekend to visit her father (bless her heart). I learned of the news of his children and their children. We talked about it being his and Jean's anniversary 11/11/55 and that Costco had changed the way you pay for your membership. Our conversation became a reminiscence of precious times that had passed. I thought to question myself, should Cathy and I go visit Ray and Pat? Yes we should. Should I tell them about me being transgender? Not so clear on that one, and yet how can I not. On the other hand, to whose benefit would it be? The world is becoming lonely, there isn't going to be anymore lunches with Uncle Ray and Pat for us and Corey to enjoy…

I had my Dr. E appointment this morning to get a blood draw to test for total testosterone, progesterone and antinuclear antibodies

409

(Sjögren's). We arrived just as she drove up so we all walked together to her office. She was in a good mood and gave us all a spirit lift. I am calmed down from my high T level shock and feel confident it will continue to go down again. Cathy has an appointment with Marsha at Caddell's for electro (electrolysis) after my doctor appointment. I watch Debbie scurry between clients as they come and go. I think how I used to belong here right in this rhythm, sort of growing up here over the last twelve years trans-wise. I feel like an outsider and have lost my place in line, as a newly transitioning MtF seeking the forbidden services at Caddell's to feminize my body.

***

Monday November 18, 2019. The excitement of this weekend's visit with Corey and Quince is still with us. It was a wonderful experience full of family time at our house where the house was full to bursting with the joy of a three-year-old. We didn't expect to see Mindy and B---- because they had been ill for the three days prior to our weekend, but to our great pleasure all four of the Casey Andersons came for a visit! Cathy's and my hearts were full of family support and love this last weekend. Mornings starting with little Quince hopping into our bed at 6:30 with us for videos (Paw Patrol, Theodore Tug Boat) for thirty minutes before we all would get up. Days would end with bubble baths, storybooks, and prayers. Cathy made the whole family (all eight of us) a pumpkin pancake lunch in our little house and we would snack on her pumpkin bread all weekend. All I heard all weekend long was her/she pronouns. It was an odd experience to be addressed this way, almost surreal, almost disquieting in some deep way, as if you suddenly received a life-long sought after treasure, one you had made up your mind would never be yours.

As I followed Quince into the bathroom to get his hands washed, he began to chant, "He she he she."

He was reacting to the change in pronoun use in referring to me by family.

He asked me something like, "Are you a 'he' or a 'she'?"

I answered simply; I'm a 'she' inside and out. I have looked like a 'he' on the outside but knew I was a 'she' on the inside. So I have become what I am inside.

He thought about this and said in a very precise and definite tone, "I'm a 'he' on the outside and a 'he' on the inside."

I returned. What a wonderful way to be!!!

We both left the bathroom secure in our gender identities!

***

Tuesday November 19, 2019. I had an appointment with Debbie Caddell for laser in my personal area; with the sudden recent increase in my T level many dark hairs began growing there. I just don't need this; it is just like walking backwards. Debbie called me into the treatment room and asked me if I still loved her. Apparently several of the new clients have come in asking for anybody except her! Yes, Debbie I still love you! We decided to laser my whole scrotum.

Michael's mom is in a new care facility after her fall in the old one. Michael doesn't expect her to be around much longer as a result of her fall so he has been visiting her every day. Cathy and I will go see Leona this Thursday.

My massage with Natalie gave me great relief! I told Natalie (who was in her normal great spirits) that Cathy's mom knows all about me and if I came up in conversation to feel free to use the proper pronouns. Also, Cathy's mom offered a suggestion for my middle name of Alane. I feel so safe in talking to Natalie (who is just a little shy of her masters in mental health therapy) that I find myself opening up to any current challenges Cathy and my transition have brought us. This time I said something about losing my sense of self from C---- to Cady, almost like the death of part of me. Cathy hears all the conversation that goes on and I hear all of hers with Natalie. So, I realized we would both need to talk about this on the way home to clarify what my fuzzy comment was really about. I would come to understand just what was going on later. It would dawn on me that transition is a process, which is moving day by day. And that it involved not only me but also Cathy's transitioning.

***

Saturday November 23, 2019. We did visit with Leona. Michael was waiting for us in the parking lot of Hallmark Manor right at 10:00am when we arrived. The place is full of broken older people and those who take care of them. Leona is in a two-bed room and she was sitting up on a chair when we came in. Michael had brought his guitar and played for us all; his first piece was *Reverie* the one he wrote just for his mom; he also played another he wrote *Bear the Weight* and finished with *Classical Gas.* She was alert and sure enjoyed it! She really enjoyed us being there too. Cathy was the lady with the long beautiful hair and I was the man with the long beautiful hair. No, I didn't correct her or come out to her, although I did think about it very carefully. I have been her 'other son' so she says for many years, a funny foil to and with Michael. To what end, I thought hers or mine, and who will benefit? It is a tricky thing this; it just seems giving comfort is the key with someone so short on life's time. I wish we knew if coming-out would make a difference or just a hurt... Cathy and I prayed with her, as I held her now seemingly small hand; we asked God for his comfort for this little family. She loves her son Michael so much and he her, her joy is Michael playing music and his losing weight. With the grace of God all of Michael's family with have Thanksgiving Dinner there at the Manor in one of the family dining rooms. The prosecutors who Beth works with paid for a complete dinner to be delivered to her home. Just shows how much she is appreciated and valued at her work.

Me stuff: Cathy had an appointment yesterday at Caddell's Laser and Electrolysis Clinic for laser. While she was in one of the treatment rooms the receptionist and I chatted in the waiting room. She had brought me back the book *Love Lives Here* by Amanda Jette Knox that I had loaned her unread. I was intensely curious if there was a single event between her and her spouse that brought about the decision for them to separate. I asked if I could ask a personal question she said, "Yes."

I explained why I was curious, I worry about Cathy in our transition and it would really help me by knowing your experience.

To our great benefit the waiting room remained empty giving us privacy and time to talk.

She turned to me with a girlfriend-to-girlfriend expression telling me, "It really wasn't a single verbal fight or someone else; it was more intimate."

I felt honored that she would share with me like this, but at the same time I felt innocently embarrassed to having this talk; I felt like I was prying.

There is a base directness women have with each other in confiding intimate problems. If you have shared with someone then in return they share with you tit for tat, we are all women here.

I expressed, I hurt for you two and understand how this all came about. I wish the cis-side of the transitioning couple's story, the struggle that is there and the need for their own transition tools, would be honored. I worry about the pain I cause and want to be better for Cathy…

She told me, "You don't know just how awesome you are."

***

Sunday November 24, 2019. We had such a nice game night with Cathy's mom last evening. It was just her, Cathy, and Cady all playing Yahtzee. Cathy's mom was the big winner in five out of six games. We also discussed food plans for this coming Thanksgiving (there will be twelve of us if everyone comes) and all moaned about how expensive medical services have become. The experience is much different than other nights with more people at the table; much more relaxed and less restrictive. My status as Cady is being normalized with Cathy's mom now, and there was even a little conversation about Dr. Marsden being my hormone doctor. I signed my Yahtzee score sheet as 'Cady' and I would sit and look at the name there on the sheet on and off all evening long; thinking that it is truly becoming me. My signature is balanced with the 'C' making a gentle loop followed by an old classic 'a' then 'd' and looped 'y'. Somehow it looks pleasant and personal to me, not so much forced anymore. How can this be I wonder; when did a switch get flipped from C---- to Cady? Whatever that switch is, I think it is traveling bit by bit from one position to the other without my notice until the time is right for me to notice. Cadance Alane Anderson is still a work in progress, but Cady has ready moved over. I noticed this the other day when I needed to write 'C----' and I had to pause to think how to do it. In other words, 'Cady' is now the default.

Cathy has been baking this week to do three pies, and I need to plan cookie baking for Marsha, Debbie C (for 12/12), Natalie, and Sandy (if I can arrange visiting her somewhere). I love sending cookies in a tin to each of them.

Me stuff: I have had a continuing storm in my brain with thoughts going round and round smashing into each all this weekend. My talk with our friend at the Caddell's reception desk truly bothered me with its issue of physical intimacy. This central issue has been on my mind for a very long time, that being how I am taking something away from Cathy. In my mind, I tried to look at both sides of our friend and her spouse's challenge. She put it that her spouse had worked to craft her body to match her soul; a body capable of providing all the dimensions of joy a woman can experience in all the places possible. And this is true; working genitalia, how could you not use them to give yourself and your partner pleasure and in doing so, acknowledging your true female self? Then there is the cost of your cis-partners' identity before you transitioned, that relationship being lost. So, with our friend's spouse now completely transitioned and she remaining unchanged creates an impossible impasse despite the love between the two of them. In this rests my greatest fear for Cathy and me, and why seeing it playing out with this couple bothers me deeply to distraction. On top of this is the realization of GRS/SRS leaving me with a lifetime of dilating a portion of my body to keep it open for use, then never using it. What is the point of this? On the other hand, it is an icon of being female. So, the long and short of this is finding an acceptable path through this minefield. Here is the rub: my mind's numbingly constant and completely fatiguing search over and over for that one path without success. Success is the right combination of the sub paths of compromise and sacrifice to follow to that so important single path of

414

harmony for the two of us. Unnoticed to me, something has been happening in the background of this constant battle within me, something flowering from a conversation we had so very long ago. Cathy has been transitioning also. Little by little almost without notice by herself or me, she has been transitioning to what we call a trans spouse, the other half of my transitioning self. I had finally prayed to God that His will be done with my transition, not asking for it to be taken away from me or me taken away from it anymore. I think this is when Cathy's journey started to be defined within her. We began to mesh together again even though the gender storms continued to push at me. Now the two of us began to push back together looking for resolve and wholeness.

***

Wednesday November 27, 2019. Leona, Michael's mom, seems to be holding her own. After Michael's gig at the extended care facility where she is now at; he texted me that his mom told him she was very proud of him. What a wonderful memory this will be for Michael from his mom to hold on to in the weeks to come.

Greg came by three nights ago and visited with us. He is slowly coming to terms with his daughter being out on her own and so very far away from him. He tears up as he read us her last text to him. Greg kept making the point of how he had been so unbending and judgmental years ago. He told us, "I was just an awful person then, now I'm trying to be less judgmental."

I fought the temptation, as he sat across our living room from us, to tell him about me being transgender. I could never explain it to him really and I am unsure why he was sharing what he was sharing. Telling people I am female then having to justify myself in every way to them is so very draining. It sucks the life out of you. I realize now, that over the years I have internally gone over this justification cycle over and over again with myself; to do it with someone externally just shakes up old sores and tears at scars. Then there is the chance of rejection and disdain after all you do and say. I hope I will be stronger after I complete my name change…

This week has been out of balance for me. I keep thinking it is the weekend all week. Cathy has been drawn and out of sorts, emotionally strained, and short tempered. Her naturopath doctor in Portland has been very slow in communicating with her. It is like pulling teeth to get information on blood tests to be done this week. Cathy's new GP doctor is still an unknown, so between the two doctors, Cathy feels powerless and abandoned. She did see her new doctor and the doctor did tell Cathy she would take over prescribing NP Throid for Cathy. This was a very good thing since the Portland doctor's one service is prescribing this stuff. Cathy does love the Portland doctor but it has become clear she doesn't love us. Despite the need being removed we are still going to Portland to see this doctor one more time. I'm not sure it is a good idea, because it just seems like it is not going to end well. On the other hand, Cathy almost seems a little frightened by her new doctor. Don't know could be just the storm our little world is going through.

Cathy also has found and joined a Facebook support group for Trans Spouse Support. They are the spouses of transitioning MtFs and FtMs. Most of which are aiming to find a way to continue to stay together as couples. We hope this will be good support for her as she transitions along with me. So, it is good, this has led to more comfortable conversations between us about this world, but Cathy is still stressed oddly tight and anxious in a new way. We have had many little arguments and I don't know how to help her. Even though this Facebook group was specific to spouses, it was made up of mostly young people leaving Cathy as a small mature minority. Cathy had many years of life experience in our relationship and because of this her need of support was far different than someone under 35ish. After a very few years of being partners, the majority of these young spouses had been broadsided by the sudden announcement that their partner was transitioning right now! As a result, there was much self-centered concern in the minds of these young spouses. A natural stance since they had little long-term relationship experience to draw on. Cathy came to our transitioning armed with many years in our relationship and prior knowledge of me. She could see past some issues that they couldn't. So common ground was thin.

I wondered also if this could be the effect of her own transition at work? It would make sense but it is awful if this is it. Transition is not to be wished upon another; case in point, continuously for these last twenty years the thread that has run in my brain is that there is a good chance I will not survive this transition, and that might not be so bad. I think this comes from years upon years of mental torment someone at my age experiences before acquiescing to transition. Transition is the answer, but sometimes it's so dark that you can't see the light at the end. So after all this rambling, what is left is Cathy and I are feeling isolated, especially after Cathy's recent Facebook experience with the spouse support group. Although no one was derogatory of Cathy's posts or her comments on other posts, she only rarely felt support flowing her way. Cathy decided to completely leave the group after its focus suddenly changed even further away from Cathy and my situation. We appear unique and therefore isolated. I need to love Cathy more deeply to give her whatever she needs to be calm and feel valued…

Other stuff: Cathy is really bothered when she has to use my old male name; she tells me it just doesn't feel right any more. I have been complaining about a storm blowing away in my mind; I took a DHEA capsule (10mg) and the next day no more storm. The effect DHEA (Dehydroepiandrosterone) has is different than Testosterone cream, more toward the clearing the brain fog in a very short time, and then producing night erections. T brings on erections then seems to spread to the rest of the body before slowly clearing some of the brain fog. DHEA is quick to cause hair to fall out also… I will use T again but it will be a long time before I use DHEA!

***

Saturday December 7, 2019. I have been experimenting with four new patches at a time and the result has been very encouraging. I have been on progesterone (200mg) for 90 days now; my chest was 37 x 39.5 at 53 days, and today I measure near 40.25 inches. My breasts

417

have been tender especially around the nipple, but that feeling slowly died down until three weeks ago when I switched to four patches. So much changed at that point. My breasts are very tender and that feeling spreads from the nipple outward radially and deeply. They feel as if they were rounding out as opposed to growing out. The other odd new thing is I blush/flush very easily at the pressure of Cathy touching them. It also happens if I am the subject of conversation. This hasn't happen since my orchi over a year ago in Dr. Bowers' office. I have read from other folks on the HRT page that a sudden change in estradiol intake can spur development. I was going to try a short course of oral E from Dr. Eaman for this effect but two applications of four fresh patches seem to have done the trick big time. The experiment was four patches twice a week and then back to three fresh patches with one holdover twice a week routine. Other things I have noticed are my skin seems softer, my hair is less oily, the pain in my scrotum seems to be lessening (not leaving) as time passes. There has been a spot of discharge from my prostrate every morning, emotions tend to cycle up and down more and my short-term memory is increasingly failing. My memory problem is very disturbing. I panic when words don't come when I need them to in face-to-face conversations. All I have is an empty place in my brain and I find myself completely dumbfounded; names, dates, and descriptive words all completely gone. Sometimes a word will surface well after I needed it but more often than not they don't. Is this caused by the stress of becoming Cady or a punishment for letting Cady happen at all? I can't help myself in thinking it's the latter. Truth is, there are enormous amounts of stress in disassembling C---- and uncovering Cadance for the weak and fearful thing I am. So, this might be the undoing of my frail memory system...

My/our idea of giving Grandma Dixon $85 for her 85th birthday has been accepted by all of the family. My journal is drifting so back to now. Colby will stay with us tonight and he is so looking forward to it! We are too and I hope games will happen with Grandma Dixon for Colby's sake. I had a very bad day of depression, which hit me two days ago, very deep hopeless depression that left me limp. I just knew something was coming and it was going to be just awful. I had been worried about Natalie for some unknown reason before Thanksgiving but she and her family were fine. I had an appointment with her two days ago with me still in the depth of depression. She explained all the really awful things that had happen to her since our last time together. My depression lifted; here is what I was dreading and that dread had been growing since our last visit. So, the event was real after all, and with that knowledge I had something to pray for.

***

Wednesday December 11, 2019. I wrote fifteen days ago that it would be a long time before I took DHEA again; so, with that in mind I took it again this evening. It was a five-milligram dose, which was half of what I had before. Why I did this goes like this. To be honest, I have been battling a really mean bout of depression these last few weeks. Some of the deepest I have ever had. Add to this the fragileness of my short-term memory and the return of sharp pain to the middle of my scrotum. The scrotum pain was the clincher! It now hurt continuously without any pressure. Before, it was only sore to the touch. Up to that point I had decided to cancel my appointment with the UW urologist. Reasoning that the pain was seemingly going away by itself, but that suddenly changed… So, I tried a small bit of T cream last night and woke up to a much-reduced level of pain, none without pressure and some with touch. My depression was less, memory seemed to be better, and my brain-fog less. I have read of other post-op MtF folks having depression as their T levels dropped to near zero and feeling better by adding T. Just a note: all during transition I have had to do extensive research on all aspects of the medical treatment needed. Everything from scholarly research papers to medical textbooks; there was no other way. This evening my depression drifted down upon me once again and I decided to give DHEA a try again but at a reduced dose. This just drips of irony. I remove male parts in an effort to feel whole and instead, I gain a painful reminder; win the battle but lose the war. Two surgeries to no avail and a constant psychic battle over further transition rages on. I feel the need to continue to make progress in transition especially as each day I am that much older. While at the same time I feel struck in place by the battle of the painful area. This is also such an oppressive time in our country, I see it each day in people I met, and this just adds to my burdens as I hurt for them. I find myself so fatigued each night that staying up past 11:00 is near impossible. I crave sleep so much especially to be next to Cathy in bed; it really is the best part of the day for me.

We will see Sandy Fosshage on the twenty-first to have coffee and chat. What I really want is to give her the traditional box of my cookies.

2020

Friday January 10, 2020. Thirty days since I journaled. I have been sort of paralyzed from this for many reasons, none of which are really beneficial. Cathy and I did have coffee with Sandy Fosshage at a Starbucks in Ballard on 12/21. She was sitting by herself sipping on a mocha waiting for us. She stood up as we came in and was all smiles. There stood the same old Sandy in spirit but with shorter hair and thinner frame. She wanted to know all about what had been happening with me/us and I wanted to know all that has been happening with her. She had left the Crisis Line on her own terms, but it was clear she couldn't continue with the new format and new management structure now in place. The new structure was going statewide bringing along with it so many changes and losing so much... With both of her cats gone now, Sandy is recovering by volunteering at a cat shelter showing love to strays. She connected with her sisters and a niece watches out for her. Sandy takes great solace in the fact that Rachel LordKenaga agreed to see me when I would need help. Sandy lit up when I gave her my gift of cookies and said, "I should hold on to these for Christmas (2019) at my sister's place but I'll probability eat them all myself before that!" Sandy is still driving herself but avoids any distance driving. We chatted for over an hour before saying our goodbyes. After seeing Sandy, we drove to the Market (Pike Place) and met up with Shane who minds a sales booth for Marcus, our favorite tie-dye artist. We had two custom tie-dye shirts waiting there for us to pick up.

Christmas (2019) was nice; we had it at Casey's and the seven days Corey, little Q, and Melinda stayed with us was all fun. We still have a rough daughter-in-law relationship with both Mindy and

Melinda. Mindy pretty much has outed me to all of her family in Wisconsin (yes I know it was too good for her to keep to herself, I understand this). We enjoy her going with Casey and being a companion to him now; it's good for him. Melinda is always distant and detached, sitting and looking at screens or reading a book while someone else plays/attends to Q. This is just Melinda being Melinda, still she is so much better at being an active companion to Corey. I just wish she liked us; yes, I know I try too hard to entertain, looking for love, and always end up irritating her. I look back on the relationship Cathy's dad had with his daughters-in-law; they completely adored the time spent with him, so I figured that at least liking me was achievable… The world has changed… On the other hand, both seem to accept me as 'she' without any problem, but at the same or slightly reduced status level as before. The coolest thing to reach our ears each morning right at 6:30 was the sound of little running feet coming into our bedroom to see videos with me. And the most convenient thing was all the food that Casey provided us to feed our household that Christmas week.

Me stuff: I quit journaling last year well before Christmas. I just didn't have it in me to do; a lot had happened, family was being restructured, and Cathy and I were in an acknowledged joint transition. Acknowledged only by us intuitively. I did have a very accepting/affirming experience Christmas day while at Casey and Mindy's house for family gift opening. We were waiting for Grandma Dixon and Linda to arrive to start our gift opening. I was sitting in corner of the living room on a little bench next to the fireplace while Cathy was off in the kitchen with Casey. The room had been arranged in circular fashion but, at the moment, I was the only one hanging out there on the little bench. I still had my coat on since Casey's house is cold in the winter, they are used to it I am not. I see Linda's car pull up outside and I suggest Colby go out to help with bringing stuff in. Grandma comes in, looks at me and gives me a big smile! She makes a beeline to where I am sitting and sits herself down right next to me! Wow! What was that all about? She told me sweetly she was just glad to see me. I would find out what was going on during gift opening when I opened Grandma's gift to me. It was a book that I had placed on my Christmas list. The book was *It Never Goes Away* by Dr. Anne L. Koch that deals with gender transition at a mature age. I wanted to read it and thought that since I had come out in October to family, it was perfectly legit to be on my list. As I open the now unwrapped box Grandma announced that she hoped that I didn't mind getting a used book as she had taken the opportunity to read it! She was all smiles! I entered her name in my 'ally list' I keep mentally; it's so very nice to have an ally, especially a mother-in-law! After all the unwrapping was over I talked to her and she told me that the book answered many questions about transitioning for her, the need for it and the process for people in their senior years. Wow! After I read the book I came to understand that this was a very good book for her to have read. To honor my supporting mother-in-law, I took 'Alane' as my new middle name, after her middle name of 'Elaine'.

I have been on four patches now for 33 days. There is soreness right around my nipples, I have had many intense headaches, depression, and my bust remains about the same. The four-patch dose is so easy since I have a big supply of Mylan patches that I had quit using, and this is a nice way to dispose of them one at a time. Cathy tells me my face has changed quite a bit this last month also. I have had spells of blushing when Cathy pokes at me in fun but this has faded in the last two weeks and scrotum pain has increased. I am going to take a DHEA pill and a little T cream tonight to see the effect it might have. Speaking of scrotum pain, Cathy and I saw Dr. Walsh yesterday at the University of Washington Medicine Center and the experience hurt me mentally. Dr. Eaman recommended I see him saying he is the best urologist in the state (head of the Urology department at the UW) and if an answer to my scrotum pain is to be found, he would find it. We made an appointment and found out he practices out of the men's clinic. I was the odd person out at the men's clinic; the reception person skipped a beat when he asked me if I use 'them,' 'they,' or 'he' and I answered 'she.' Even though my medical records were faxed in from Dr. Eaman, we had to manually enter my drug list with the Physician Assistant. She was polite enough, but distant, until she asked me what I was here for and I told her about my problem. She faltered at me going through the operation twice and still hurting. I had to comfort her and in the end she loved my new name and was so glad we had come to see Dr. Walsh. That was the last of the good stuff... I had to see a gate-keeping resident doctor before Dr. Walsh (it is a teaching hospital). He came in, joked about Cathy and my clothes, finding it hilarious that we matched. Then after a good laugh on his part, not ours, asked me about my problem and examined me. I told him about the constant pain in the center of my scrotum. He asked who the doctor was who did my orchiectomy and I answered Dr. Marci Bowers. He boasted that he had never heard of her, then demanded what qualifications did this doctor have? I told him obstetrician/gynecologist/gynecologic surgeon. He openly mocked the idea that this Dr. Bowers had any of these qualifications. What! I was shocked at his ignorance and his condescending behavior. He didn't know who Dr. Bowers is? How could he not know of her?! She is a legend as a long time surgeon in the transgender world. On the other hand, he was fully showing his tunnel vision and lack of patient respect to us. He continued to scoff at the very idea that Dr. Bowers might have had any skill as a surgeon. He went on to tell me of all the hours of training he had with Dr. Dugi (a male doctor) who is the only one he would ever recommend for bottom surgery. He told me loftily that my problem had to be something nerve related. If I was going to have full bottom surgery, I should just wait it out and why couldn't I do that? This has boiled down to verbal combat with me in a corner trying to defend my identity. I told him surgery was a long way off since booking times are years in advance, the pain is here and now. It is in total opposition to me presenting as my female self. His retort was asking me how much did that mean to me? The conversation just went downhill from there. I felt disdain from him. In the end, he reluctantly deemed me worthy to see Dr. Walsh. After he left, depression just dropped right on top of me; somewhere after seeing the PA I had began to hope again and now it was just slammed in my face by a cocky young Indian doctor who thought Dr. Bowers was some amateur-come-lately. And without reason, my confidence in her was shaken. I was suddenly all alone; without Sandy, Dr. Bowers, Dr. Marsden, and Dr. Ken. None of them were germane anymore; the world was done with me... Still, we waited for Dr. Walsh some twenty minutes. Cathy and I talked about just leaving before he showed up; after all, it was clear they couldn't do anything. And it was clear that I was just comedy relief for the staff in this department... Dr. Walsh did come in, spoke softly, and examined me carefully. He told me he was trying to put himself in my place, to feel what I was feeling. This was so different from the other doctor; I also tried very hard to work with him during the exam pointing out the area of pain. I asked him if he had any experience with any other patient having persistent pain after an orchi and no he didn't even after doing over a hundred of them. He told me he couldn't find any mass to remove and gave me two choices that he could do. I could try low dose Citalopram Hydrobromide 10mg tablet and/or direct injection into the scrotum of an anesthetic (it would hurt but be over quickly). We left without any path to follow; I was deeply hurt mentally from being treated so disrespectfully and demeaningly. This mental sting persists and lingers as each day goes by.

***

Monday January 13, 2020. Cathy and I have been reading several different transgender journey books. Each story chronicles an individual transition's peaks and valleys, mostly valleys. They are all different; Dr. Anne Koch vs. Jennifer Boylan vs. Amanda Knox's family, but one common thread runs through all of them. A continuing movement, a progression, always some sort of progress along a transition timeline. Without fail, transition is a momentum of movement forward and not a dead standing in place. Standing in place seems to be a deadly thing, a hopeless thing, and spirit quicksand. Whereas movement forward brings life, God, and salvation. I have been standing in place, using pain as an excuse for inaction. The result is my spirit decaying, my life dimming, (hurting Cathy in this way) and God is further away. My mind treads in quicksand denying my inner identity over and over again. There is also chronicling of how the wife of an MtF feels; that being she had no control or say as her transitioning spouse just continually rolls along unstoppable. So, stuck in a quicksand of my own making, feeling that life would be better to be over with, and how in turn that would hurt Cathy. I had a thought, a simple clear thought, one whose time has surely come and perhaps one that I should have had sooner. Cathy can be in charge of doing stuff like my name change; in fact, I need her to be. I get lost and am lost right now. My transition may have started off as my transition but it has become our transition, we both have changed or are being changed by the love we communally share as one in spirit before God. My slow transition was paced by God to match Cathy's transition so that we might fall into step with each other at some critical point. Cathy my love, would you take charge of this part of our transition? Cady is lost, she needs to be whole, her name and identity made legally whole, would you take on our burden to gain us both life? Cathy was in full agreement and we went to bed.

Cathy told me this morning before we got up, "We are going over to the King County District Court in Burien to get your name changed this morning." I started to waffle in the quicksand but remembered that this was her say in the matter; so even though it was lightly snowing outside, off to the courts we went. On the way we prayed (we do each morning in the car) and afterward I wondered if I would start to feel a coming regret or panic at the whole deal I had made with Cathy last night; after all, this is putting 'C----' away not to be he again... As I drove, I waited for the sick feeling to come to be followed by a sudden abort off in another direction from the road to Burien. This didn't happen; no sick feeling or fear of what legally changing names really means, and no sudden turning away at the last minute from the parking lot at the court. I was surprised, we parked in the almost empty lot and I said another little prayer asking that God's name be glorified in our errand. We wondered if the court building was even open, a light snow was covering nothing really but even so traffic was so light everywhere it was eerie. The place was open; we opened the door and walked into the security search station, emptied our pockets, handed over our purses and walked through the metal detector. The whole lobby was empty. We walked up to a teller window and a nice lady helped us. The form Cathy downloaded wasn't the right one but that didn't slow Cathy down at all. No pressure, Cathy made out the right form and we paid our fee, then chatted with the lady for a few minutes. She told us that normally the place would be full of people and noisy kids but today is a nice surprise. Our court date was today at 1:15pm so we had two hours to go home and wait. Even on the way home no negative feelings, no dread, just a sudden expectation that I was so close to changing my name and what a positive thing this was going to be for both of us. At home, I sat feeling how slow time was going by then realized that this was Monday and we could go visit Jennifer over at Dr. Ken's. So, we headed off to see her with the idea we could visit for thirty minutes then leave to drive to the court. Both Jennifer and Dr. Ken were at the office so we got to talk to them both; this was great, as we really needed to share our exciting news! We chatted and I watched the clock and got nervous at 12:40 so we left. At the court, the parking lot had a dozen cars just barely making a small dent in the empty lot. We now know how to get through the security search station and find a place to sit and wait. I sent messages to Casey and Corey and start to feel more and more nervous; not about the name change itself but about standing up before the judge in explanation for the action. We had listed 'gender change' as reason but we didn't know if this was too much information and if that information would be shared before the folks in the courtroom… I felt cold and began to shake. The other people waiting in the lobby for the most part were non-English speakers, and the remaining few just folks. We had a court date in courtroom three and the clock was moving so slowly… The court opened at 1:17 and we all filed into the room. We sat four rows back on the aisle side. Name changes were first up and I so hoped that someone else would be first. God was good to us, one other lady whose demeanor was sullen was called first. She was asked to come forward. I watched her leave her seat and walk quietly down the aisle toward the front of the courtroom coming to rest at the tables used by opposing counsel. All eyes in the courtroom followed her journey and now focused on her figure from the back. The female judge said, "You seek this because of a divorce, sorry about your divorce, and you want to remove the hyphenation?" The sullen lady simply said, "Yes." The judge then asks her to come closer and view the change paper that the clerk was now holding and check that it was just as she wanted it to be. The lady was then instructed to wait out in the lobby for her processed order. Then she called 'Candace' and I stood and corrected with Cadance, the judge looked at the paper before and agreed that it said Cadance. I had looked around the room before I was called to see who all was going to get to share my 'gender changing' news and now I steeled myself for the judge's coming questions. I stood as tall as possible despite being nervous and walked the same path to the proper spot as the sad lady before me. I was ready for the judge's questions; all that came was, "You spell it C-a-d-a-n-c-e?" I said, yes and was sent on my way to pick up my papers without any more questions! We left the courtroom and a seed of jubilance began to sprout inside of me. Again in the lobby, we sat on a hard bench near the teller windows of the office workers to wait. A middle-aged lady and her daughter were at the teller window of the nice lady who had help us earlier. She was filing some sort of damage suit against a building owner. The sullen lady sat quietly dejected at the far end of the bench we were on. I was slowly and steadily feeling more and more jubilant inside, the feeling was electric, and spilling out onto Cathy. After maybe fifteen minutes, one of the other teller window ladies came out from behind the teller barrier and walked over to the name-changing sullen lady (she was all by herself and this made me glad I had Cathy with me). We had noticed this office lady when we first came in, she was at the window to our left as we filled out paperwork, she had chalk rust red colored hair, a long sweater, and leggings. I now noticed what seemed to be a faint shadow of a much-thinned beard and a telltale low toned voice. We listen carefully as she answered the few questions from the other name changer. Yes, the order is good forever, for SS they will just look at it then give it back as will WDL. Our turn, she came over to us and instantly she and I were Trans-sisters! Cathy asked great questions about gender markers on birth certificates, SS, WDL, and Passports. She answered Cathy and me with things that she had happen to her personally, such as, "I couldn't get my birth certificate changed because I'm from North Carolina, no hope there. I did get my SS name change; be sure to get there 30 minutes before they open. The WDL wasn't a problem; I should get my passport but I have been lazy." That feeling of jubilation that was growing within me was now close to giddiness as she looked directly at me smiled and said, "Sure feels good don't it!" I answered, after sixty-five years it sure does!!! I asked her if I could give her a hug and she said, "Yes!" This just fed my giddiness to the max!

Walking out of the court building I couldn't contain this joyous, giddy, wonderful feeling inside of me. It was the best I have ever felt in so very long. Tears came at the very same time as giggles did; I had to hold my hand over my mouth to hold myself together; it was so very lovely. In the car the feeling washed over me again and again, I couldn't drive yet because I couldn't contain the joyous waves spilling out all over. At the crest of one of those wonderful waves, I realized that I would never again question whether I was truly transgender or not. It was so affirming, freeing, and releasing all at the same time. Just amazing, blessedly amazing! I was given a wonderful gift from God today; in fact, God had lowered all barriers that had stood in our way, and I will never be the same as I was before; I will forever be me.

Cathy, sharing in the euphoria that was quickly filling our car, now wanted to know where we were going to go eat to celebrate! Bai Tong sounds good! Cathy added, "But first let's stop at PCC market for a rest stop." I started the car; it seemed to purr in the most pleasing way. The world passing by as we drove the short distance to a market was so bright just like I had never seen it before. The feeling was infectious between us as we walked into the market. Produce is right at the entrance and time seemed a great luxury to be savored even here among the green leafy veggies. Cathy came upon something she hadn't see before baby turnips; she squealed with delight! Well, we will always have the joy of discovering baby turnips to remember this day with...

***

Thursday January 16, 2020. Cathy started my name change on Monday the 13th with the court order, Tuesday 14th would be for my gender marker change with Social Security keeping my same number, Wednesday 15th was electrolysis with Marsha at Caddell's to spread joy, finally Thursday was Dept of Licensing, First Tech banking accounts, and Costco.

***

Tuesday the 14th. Cathy got us up early so as to be to the Social Security Building in Burien before it opened at 9:00 so we might have the same experience as we did at the King County Court Building. That experience was that few people braved the cold and snowy roads at that hour, leaving a light client count and happy clerks. This time, we arrived at 8:35 expecting a twenty-five minute wait in our warm car. A lady holding a big cup of salt came over to us to tell us they were opening an hour late at 10:00 because of the frozen weather. The idea of this weather delay flies in the face of the light dusting of snow, very little ice, and mostly dry streets in our local area. What has happened is from Seattle south there has been a ribbon of no snow with most of the snow to the west and north, leaving our little area as sort of a no snow oasis. Normally, the ocean beaches are free of snow and this is where we will go to get out of the snow, but not this time… Anyway, there are only three cars in the parking lot (so our strategy would have worked great); we left to warm up at a Starbucks. We came back at 9:10 to find eight cars in the lot. From our warm car we watched as guys in trucks started to further fill the lot. I voiced that maybe we should abort; of course Cathy's spirit fell at this utterance and it was the wrong thing to do. The right thing, was to wait it out and see just when someone drifted out of their car to stand in line at the door. Lining up at the door was problematic because of the wind chill making it more than uncomfortable. A young black woman pulled in to the lot at 9:40 and immediately got out and lined up at the door. This started the flood of everyone in the parking lot to leave the warmth of their vehicles to go stand in the cold for twenty minutes.

Cathy bolted, giving us a place sixth in line at the door. I came along shortly but couldn't stand the cold (part of this is my nervousness chilling down my whole body) so I returned to our car for a raincoat to protect me from the wind. It worked somewhat and we casually chatted with the lady next to us in line. She had just this one day to fix a problem with some kind of documentation of a family member or would have to wait until the weather was completely better. At the courthouse, you have to go through security to get in and it is the same at SS, but the difference is no metal detector. When they opened, a large uniformed guy came outside to officiate our going through one by one in a controlled manner. They searched our purses, then one by one we got to go inside the warm building either to sit down or stand. The lady who was apparently in charge was very good at handling us as a crowd. We were herded into the building, little by little, to be seated in many rows of chairs in the center of an open lobby. When all the rows were full folks then stood in another line near the wall. We were lucky, we got to sit and wait to be called to one of ten clerk security windows lining one wall of the lobby. I was called to a window (Cathy remained seated) and asked what I needed to have done. The lady doing the asking was the one handling the flow of the crowd. She had all the earmarks of authority; my guess is she was the one in charge of the place. I gathered up my nervous self and using the pass-through hole, answered the boss lady saying that I was here for a name change and gender marker change. She raised her eyebrows a little and hurriedly wrote something down on a notepad avoiding eye contact with me. I then was asked to return to my seat. I was a little worried because of the note she wrote. If I had any bravado at all, it was of the completely false type. Glancing around me yielded a growing sea of disgruntled older folks, totally filling the waiting room. We were still sitting next to the lady we came in with and continued to chat. In our conversation with her we were vague about why we were there. Looking back, I should have told her directly; it was nothing I should have hidden and I regret not doing so. The time was 10:17am when we (Cathy came with me, she was in charge of all the paper work) were called to another window protected with thick desk to ceiling high Plexiglas that allowed two pass-through holes. According to his nametag, the young man at the terminal there was Jeff. He was casually dressed in a camouflage baseball hat and jacket (like hunters wear). His bravado was fully intact; he told us in a low serious tone he was going to process my request. Cathy and I sat nervously together on the black chairs on the petitioner side of the Plexiglas with our fingers crossed; Jeff on his side kept a straight professional face while his fingers danced across the keyboard. We had prayed before each place that God would grant that the people would be kind to us, helpful to us, enjoy us during our time together, and above all His name would be glorified. We passed our precious and hard fought for documents through the lower pass-through hole to Jeff and waited for questions to be asked. But first came the stern warning that any attempt to defraud Social Security by giving untrue information was a crime and I had to understand this and swear to it. I solemnly did so. He cracked a little smile as I answered his questions about my requested changes, in ten minutes he pushed back from his computer to go get printouts, then returns and hands us a receipt for my letter that stated:

'This letter is to certify that the above named individual underwent irreversible and permanent Genital Surgery performed by myself, Dr. Marci L. Bowers, MD, in San Mateo, California. The surgery constitutes appropriate clinic treatment for gender transition to female. The surgery was completed in accordance with the standards established by the World Professional Association for Transgender Health. Accordingly, all documentation should reflect this individual's current and final gender status as female.'

The receipt bore my new name Cadance Alane Anderson. Jeff stated in a flat controlled tone that the new card would be in the mail within two weeks; Cathy and I both felt a huge burden melt away, and at the fifteen minute mark the computer screen seemed to satisfy him and with a bigger smile Jeff handed my original papers back to me along with congratulations! As we started to leave the office, the lady who was handling the crowd waved to us, as did other folks who worked there. What a surprise! I guess my request got around the office quietly, so cool! What a blessing to have had such support in this process so far! We had started out our errand at 8:15 and were at 10:35... I was shaking both with cold and that same giddy jubilant feeling that would return over and over in the next few days. We drove over to PCC market for Cathy to use the rest room and me to stay in the car motor running to try to warm up. I was riding this wonderful emotional roller coaster up and down flying so high with each breathtaking turn. Since this is also Cathy's transition experience, she sailed along too. She came back from PCC Market with a purchase that had suddenly become the most incredible wonderful bunch of baby turnips ever. She was so excited when she showed me her treasure, yes we will always remember these two days by the Court, the Social Security office, and these beautiful baby turnips...

***

Wednesday the 15th. Cathy has electrolysis with Marsha Morgan at Caddell's. I am looking forward to chatting with Shawn (who happens to be Marsha's daughter) about the wedding of her daughter while Cathy is in with Marsha. Our appointment time was at 1:30 and since the weather was cold outside and spitting snow, I wondered if Marsha had had any cancelations that I might take advantage of since we were there. Yes, there was one when I called before we left; her 4:30 had canceled. Shawn asked if I wanted it and I said yes! Where Tukwila didn't have much snow at all, Bellevue had a bit more and since we would be there from 1:30 to 5:00 we hoped that no new snow would be coming our way. Cathy and I arrive at Caddell's at 1:10 to find Shawn is out to lunch and the office is pretty empty. Marsha comes out to get Cathy and I sit down to wait. Darn, no one to talk to, all I can do is listen to the message machine answer incoming calls. The speaker is on and I hear some lady calling in to cancel her appointment with Marsha at 2:45, apparently Whidbey Island is getting hit hard with snowfall to the point that schools are closed and roads are impassable. Wow! On the other hand, it has started to snow here but I wouldn't mind taking that 2:45 cancelation with Marsha... Another lady comes into the lobby/waiting room. She is here to get a product she ordered and is waiting for Shawn but no one is around except me. We chat and she tells me Woodinville north of Bellevue has 10 inches and she would really like to pay for her pickup and get on the road. After twenty minutes, we decided that she would leave a check and I would point it out to Shawn along with an explanation when she comes back. It all works out, Shawn finally returns just before 2:00, and we chat about her daughter's wedding and my name change. Shawn is so excited by my name change and wants to know every detail. She is so sweet, and listens on pins and needles. That giddy jubilant feeling rains down upon me once again as I recount all that has come this week to Cathy and me. Cathy's time is over with Marsha and another young lady is here for her forty-five minutes, then it is my turn. Outside, the snow is increasing moment by moment even though the weather report says it will stop precisely at 4:00. My turn comes and Marsha gives me her full attention; we talk of the wedding, my name change, and my idea to get in contact with Marsha Botzer. She tells me to be sure to mention her old name Marsha Moyer in my email to Marsha Botzer. The snow outside is worrying Marsha and she decides to cancel the rest of her appointments for the day and head home. Caddell's was so empty when I went into Marsha's room and now I come out to a full waiting room. Debbie is here now and greets me warmly, adding that she is enjoying the book I gave her. Shawn gives Cathy and me a big hug goodbye. That affirming joyful feeling is just staying with me all the way home…

***

Thursday the 16th. We arrived at the Renton DOL just before it opened and go to the end of a twelve-person line forming outside the front door. It was cold and I was cold, but we didn't have to wait any more than fifteen minutes to get into the warm building. While we waited in line, a man in jeans and winter coat walked the length of the line asking us what we were here for? I ponied up about the name change wondering if he worked there or not. It turned out he ran the office! He told us to get a number as we came in and tell the desk person what we were here for. We did and their computers went down

434

as he assigned us a number (112). The system came back up as soon as we were seated. Oddly enough, there was a line at the door before opening but no one else came after the doors were open. Everyone was so nice and seemed to be so happy for me. A few minutes later we were told that we didn't have to wait just go get into line at the exam desks. Cathy stood by me all the time holding her envelope full of ID papers. When it was our time, Cathy walked up to an exam desk with me and the next thing I knew was I was Cadance Anderson with an 'F' on my temporary license. The clerk congratulated me and also updated my voter registration! That same giddy feeling of warm happiness flooded my body again. I wondered if it would just whither out, but no, there it was again, the joyful feeling of completeness and good cheer. Can you imagine after decades of hiding because of the fear of condemnation suddenly to be joyfully supported? The feeling is just indescribable. I didn't drive well, so scatter brained, more so than I have ever been before. It was not that I was going to have an accident or anything; it was I had to keep making myself focus on what I was doing. I wonder if people taking recreational drugs or alcohol have this kind of high feeling? I mean, if this was what being high felt like, I understand why they would continue to use and use… I awoke this morning feeling differently; my mind has for the longest time upon awakening focused on all the trouble in life, all the hopelessness. And this normally forces me out of bed just to stop the cycle from building. But these last few morning things have been different. My mind drifts to what the day will bring and how wonderful it is to wake up next to Cathy each morning. For that matter, I look forward each night to going to bed with her and being next to her all night long; so blissful and so blessed.

We continue our drive to get more changes done today, this time Costco. Cathy figures the best place to start is membership services so we gather ourselves up and head over there. At the desk, they needed to see the court order, the old driver's license, and the temp driver's license. All done, got to get a new picture and I have a new membership card. The new credit card will come in two weeks. Cool! Okay, lets now try First Tech. We drive back to Bellevue to First Tech.

This will be the hardest experience we have so far. They want the court order, a new SS card, and a new Drivers' license. Since we don't have all the stuff we are tasked to send copies when they arrive in the mail to them via email... This time we are tired but still feeling up. Big day change wise... We call Citibank and they confirmed that the change Costco put it is already active, we did the right thing then!

Other transition stuff: I believe that something fundamentally changed in my mind over these last few day... For one, suddenly I can spell words! This alone is something amazingly different from where I was mentally. And two, I can type like crazy! I haven't been able to do anything like this for as long as I can remember.

And there is the poem I wrote *Transition* that came to me all at once yesterday. I love this, my heart is in this, and it came totally out of the blue. Mind you, this rises up to the way I suddenly feel and contained in that remarkable spirit is the confidence that I can achieve things, is simply a miracle so truly a miracle! It is like waking up one morning to find to your amazement, that you have become someone else. You feel with her fingers, see with her eyes, and think with her brain, it is no less than that to me. Can't begin to explain it but maybe I already have... Will it last, oh please let it last...

Transition
By Cadance Alane Anderson

I shall dream a dream
No matter what reality seems
And in myself I shall abide
And no longer will I hide
I shall dream a dream

I shall dream a whole dream
No matter what reality seems
And in completeness will abide
And with no need to ever hide

Forever and Two Days More

I shall dream a whole dream

I shall dream a true dream
No matter what reality seems
And in myself truthfully abide
And acceptance no longer hide
I shall dream a true dream

I shall dream a loving dream
No matter what reality seems
And within myself love abides
And forgiveness no longer hides
I shall dream a loving dream

I shall dream a peaceful dream
No matter what reality seems
And in myself hope abides
And joy no longer hides
I shall dream a peaceful dream

I shall dream a prophetic dream
No matter what reality seems
And outside ourselves we will abide
And outside ourselves no longer hide
I shall dream a prophetic dream.

***

On Sunday January 19, 2020. I came out on Facebook. I changed my profile gender and name to Cady. I posted pictures of Cathy and me at the Court, Social Security, DOL, and one of me jumping for joy. I posted that it has been quite a week---new name, new me, fun! It took the longest time for me to push the button but with Cathy reminding me of who I am now, I did do it. Everyone was so nice and every comment affirming. I got 57 comments and 37 likes and I was in Heaven. I answered every comment with 'thank you' and a little explanation of some part of my journey. We had fifteen family members react to my post, all in a positive way, and ten no-shows. I was elated but worried. I know Janet and Karen both who were no-shows and did regularly see stuff on Facebook; others may or may not have seen it at all. So, I have read of many coming-out strategies; in the end the advice comes down to. There is no right way to do it. In my mind, I thought of the times Orlyn had poked at me as well as Tony in what I thought was a good-natured way, but Orlyn did refuse to come to the Reunion last summer (yes, I know I'm hypervigilant but that comes with the territory). What really was in my mind was the old Anderson family feud splitting the family along the lines of Hanson and Smith and I didn't want anything like that to happen again. Of course, this was me being paranoid, things are different now, and the way I was treated during my name change is sure telling of this. Also, there are the senior family to think about Uncle Ray, Aunt Luella, Cousin Audrey, and Uncle Fred, none of these see Facebook and my FB post really didn't explain what was going on with me. I dreamed about this and I fretted during the day about how to come-out to these family members; I mean over the phone, drive to meet with each one, and on and on, until Cathy and I decided I would start with Audrey. She is hard, she is a long drive to see in person and even if we did, dropping a bomb in person didn't work so well with Linda and Cathy's mom, so maybe some other way. I thought of sending an email to her and set down to type one. I started typing and this is what suddenly appeared on my screen, a story of my journey in short form:

Hi Audrey,

I don't know if my Facebook news has gotten to you so I would like to explain as if it hadn't.

I'm transgender, wow that was easy, but falls short of the explaining part...

As long as I can remember I have had a disconnect between what I saw in the mirror each day with the reflection of myself mentally, gender wise. It was a painful, grating, mean trick played on me over and over without end. What I saw wasn't me just the opposite; on the other hand, what I saw in the mirror matched the boys I saw around

438

me. Being very young, the best defense was denial, so I went blank in my mind as to my gender identity and played as if I wasn't anything. This is isolating, not belonging to either group male or female but as I was numb then, a kid is a kid nothing more. Somewhere near eight years old, it dawned on me that I was to be a girl when I grew up. It would just happen naturally and everything was going to be okay. I prayed little prayers to God about it, who I knew was listening to me. Time moved forward, the grinding discord just got worse and now I had shame to add to my daily life. There were family upsets, divorce, and loss of our home. I was a mismatched male in Eastern Washington, there was no hope otherwise, so I learn to copy the other boys around me and figured life would be short. I felt no joy just daily dread, Dad was gone, Mom struggled, and one day I crossed dressed and I was gone too, all of us broken.

God never left me; He brought us back to the west side of the mountains, there would be the loss of David but the true gift of love in Cathy Dixon. With David gone, my mother and father were broken apart forever. I wanted to be with Cathy forever to love and be loved, but the gender discord was a secret I was not going to hide from her, it wasn't fair, it wasn't right, so I told her everything before we were married. It never dawned on me that she might just turn and walk away, I had prayed to God for her understanding and I still have it to this day... I kept dragging along through the years, holding the never-ending mental storm of discord at bay by the distractions of family. They needed a husband and father and I needed them. Everything came crashing down after my dad passed away and the kids left home. I couldn't hold my false shape anymore and live... God came along in 2005 and brought me to a therapist and she helped me become whole; this would take 15 years... So, I never was a guy but I played one in 65 years of life...

Last week Cathy and I went to the county court to get a name change order from 'C---- A--- Anderson' to 'Cadance Alane Anderson'. God placed me in the hands of a clerk there, who happened to also be transgender and had gone through the same change process. She looked at me and said, "Feels good don't it." It was the most amazing

439

feeling of completeness I have ever felt; at that very minute a weight was lifted off my shoulders, I could actually feel it lifting! Cathy and I giggled, cried, and giggled again! Social Security was next and the folks there smiled and waved to us as we left with my marker changed from an M to an F. The drivers' license changed was just as smooth and jubilant for me... I feel so blessed.

If you have any questions or want to chat with us, don't hesitate to call.

I attached the images from my Facebook post and a copy of my poem 'My Transition' and emailed it to her.

I got this reply: *Love runs deeply. There are no choices in life that you could possibly make, that I would love you any less. I hope your life is always successful and happy. Love Audrey.*

So, with this reply in hand, I thought about what Cathy's mom had poked at us about dropping bombs (I thought I had honored her with my information in person). Okay, there might be something to that. I was dreading calling all the senior folks with my news as well as the no-shows, so a letter would let them ponder my information on their own terms. So, we added to the to line:

Hi Family,

And

Love,

Cadance and Cathy

After we checked with Casey and Corey to see if this was worded well and even if this was a good idea, we printed our ten copies on white paper. Cathy hand addressed ten business envelopes to Fred Tuttle, Ray Bothel, Janet Reynolds, Orlyn Hanson, Karen McClintock, Kevin Smith, Luella Pratt, Jim Sura, Tami Smith, and Gail Boisseau. I looked at the white envelopes with the white business letter stock and shuddered; it was so sterile, then I thought this is happy news, I am happy they should be happy. What to do? I packed up Cathy and we drove to Bartell Drug Store to get stickers. They had their Valentines stuff out so I thought there has to be all sort of happy things to put in our envelopes as a sort of happy bribe. Fun! They don't sell kids Valentines things anymore; the kind you would buy for your child to take to school and hand out; so sad, but we did find stickers and Paw Patrol tattoos! And some of the stickers had butterflies! At first, Cathy wasn't on board with the idea but I wanted her to have fun and sure enough as she sorted the stickers as to which to use to decorate the letter and which to use as a bribe, she got into the swing of the thing. I hope people will remember the stuff falling out of our letter as they opened it as a happy surprise, and remember Cathy and me as loving family members who wanted to honor them with our joy. I am currently on pins and needles with the idea some of our letters will be to their destinations tomorrow. The ones to the Hanson folks may have been there today! Then the trick is for me not to call before giving people a chance to think about our news. This will be a hard time for the next few days. I can watch for hits on my Facebook post to see if anyone new has reacted but I guess that's all for now.

Note added February 20th. We also sent the letter in email to Audrey Gregg, Jeanette Bothel, and Linda Ramuta (paper copy). After thirty days, only one person replied back to us from the paper letters: Mary Ann, she was supportive. I guess the stickers didn't work…

***

Thursday January 23, 2020. Important hormone stuff: I began a four patch per dose 47 days ago and I have been on progesterone (200mg) for 114 days. My chest measures 37inch band and 40inch bust. Three weeks ago the breast tenderness I was experiencing pretty much faded. I went from feeling anything brushing against them to only if I pinched the nipples. I felt again as if I had stalled out. I had reset development by using four patches plus progesterone and it was very heartening to be developing again after what amounts to years of very little increase breast-wise. Over my HRT history I have increased Estradiol levels to keep feminizing but this stalled until Doctor Eaman added progesterone 114 days ago. This drove breast tenderness and new development until I stalled again thirty days ago. I reminded myself of Dr. Powers' idea of increasing Estrone levels as a tool to restart development. His theory was estrone is depleted over time and the only way to rebuild it is with estradiol taken by mouth. He found in his patients by just adding a 2mg pill swallowed whole had very noticeable effects. The trick is when you swallow an estradiol pill it is processed first-pass through the liver and changed to mostly estrone. If you just keep it in your mouth until it is dissolved, without going down your throat, it bypasses this first pass, and remains intact estradiol entering your bloodstream through mouth tissues. So, I asked Dr. E for the med and she had it in stock, which was perfect. She also told me to reduce my patch number by one while I use it. I didn't after reviewing Dr. Powers' plan; he said to add it to the ongoing estradiol dose. His thought is, lowering your estradiol dose that is first pass liver exempt (in my case by taking away one patch) and then adding an estradiol tablet, which is subject to the first pass through the liver just nulls out the estrone creation, so I am continuing my E at my current intake and adding oral E on top of it. If anything bad happens, I was following Dr. Powers plan not Dr. E's advice, but I am adding a baby aspirin each day in case of blood clotting issues. This is my third day on this routine and my breasts are very tender even more than when I started four patches plus progesterone! I feel like my breasts are filling across as opposed to out. The downside is the Reynaud's syndrome symptom of turning some of my fingers white from lack of blood flow is back, but this experiment is limited to only nineteen days so keeping fingers crossed (some of them are white and hurt now). After this, we will ascertain any gain vs. risk. Some folks go on oral for a week, then off for month; it is all new to everyone, and yes it is experimenting. I have notice that pain in my scrotum is dropping with this new HRT; so odd. I have also notice that pain there would drop somewhat when I added T cream. Somehow the area is reacting to hormone levels in some strange way. I don't think doctors would believe me if I told them; after all, no one studies transgender medicine per se being a small marginalized population. I also told Dr. Eaman face to face about my negative experience with Dr. K (Dr. Walsh's resident at the UW) and she thought he was too big for his britches, as he didn't know the premier gender reassignment doctor!!! She urged me to do the survey they will send…

***

Saturday January 25, 2020. Word is Greg has decided to step away from our friendship. Michael shared this from a conversation the two of them had the other day. Greg wanted to talk about me but Michael didn't so he kept changing the subject. Also, in that conversation Greg said that he had deep concerns on how my news would influence Cathy and my grandchildren. I sent a book describing Biblical references affirming my faith as a Christian, who happens to be transgender, with Michael to share with Greg if possible and he wasn't interested in seeing it. All this I guess was to come but it still bothers me deeply. Greg has a very close walk with God and I admire this greatly.

Again, there is no one scheme on 'coming-out' that provides a predictable mechanic where emotions are concerned. In short, no matter how hard you try to set the stage or judge the time and place correctly, it all comes down to a sudden emotional reaction to you sharing your true self with another person. In a soul-baring face-to-face setting, at least both parties have the luxury of body language. Of course, this is not the case in phone conversations, for better or worse, mostly for worse. This is how I came-out to my friend Greg; I didn't plan it this way, it just happened. Greg has visited us at our house on and off since his divorce from his wife ten years ago. The divorce was a very messy one, and particularly hard on Greg. He wanted no part of it, he felt that it was affront to God, but he himself had no earthly choice in the matter and it was tearing him up inside. Nothing in his Seminary training accepted this. One night, deeply depressed and full of despair with no place to go he came to our house. He was seeking help, looking to be with supportive friends and had nowhere to go; God lead him to us and he spent the night in our spare bedroom. The next day he turned a corner of sorts and left us to go back to his work. From this time forward Greg has visited us and turned to me/us for life advice. Over the years, Greg has grown as we all have; he also poked at me wondering what the heck I was doing wearing an ankle bracelet, etc. We continued to have had lots of phone conversations about God, life, and the world around us. Caitlyn Jenner came out in 2015 bringing with her the world of transgender people to the masses. And so, it happened one night after a windstorm had made its mean way through our area. I got a cell phone call that evening from Greg as he was driving home from work to his house on the Olympic Peninsula. Greg was in a good mood he hadn't been back to his house for a while choosing instead to stay closer to work until the weekend came; he had an arrangement to be able to do this. Greg loves to call me and address me in a low heavy tone as, "Mister Anderson." Done in the fashion from the *Matrix* movie. It's his little joke and I give it to him, but mentally I wince each time, especially this time because, well, I am very close to coming-out myself. We talk about the windstorm of a few days ago and then turned to world events. Greg laments transgender people, he doesn't understand them, the kids or the adults, and wishes someone would explain the whole concept to him. This hits a nerve in me; after all, who better could he turn to, to explain it, than someone who is transgender? Something in my mind screams, "Tell him! You'd be doing him a great service and it would be helping him just as you have done many times before." I resisted for a moment not really thinking clearly, and as I stumble the window God had opened in our conversation quickly closes, as Greg moves on to something else. At this point in this narrative, I should have moved on also and left the idea alone, but I didn't; instead I tried to bring the conversation back to the transgender topic. This was a mistake on my part; Greg was just about at his house and the natural ending of our conversation. Hindsight is 20/20. I should have wished him a 'good night' and laid the seed of let's-talk-about-transgender-stuff' I will have good information for you next time. Unfortunately, part of me was desperate to come-out to Greg given the right time as I had already come out to Michael. Anyway, I persisted in the conversation telling Greg, "I am transgender. I can explain things to you." Greg was shocked into dead silence; I had unleashed the unthinkable torment of hearing a friend confess to falling away from God. This had to have been the concept he had in his mind at that moment. He had reached his driveway and had to come to a dead stop because he could go no further mentally or physically. The windstorm that brought with it no good, had taken particular pleasure in blocking his driveway with several downed trees. I tried to get Greg to return to our conversation, but all he was going to say was how he had to get a chainsaw to unblock his driveway. He continued to tell me that he had one in his shed. There was nothing for it now; all I could do was to say goodbye to a friend, one who had been our best man at our wedding. I'm so sorry Greg... As before, there is no right way to come-out, but the longer you wait in life the less time there is for lost friends to possibility reconcile...

I had previously done better with Michael. Cathy and I had invited him to our house for a chat. I was dressed as I normally am, that is in women's jeans and matching tie-dye shirt with Cathy. I had the benefit of face-to-face body language and the advantage that Michael prides himself on being unshockable in any social instant. I told Michael straight out using succinct direct words. He responded with, "Bet you thought I might be adverse, well I'm not." No Michael, I expected you to be you, my friend.

No fallout from the letters yet; I did call Jeanette to ask how her dad was doing health-wise. Since he has had my letter for a while I was worried about his reaction to it, in short, I wanted to know if I was welcome to call him once again. We had a wonderful conversation; she had watched the television series *Transparent* and was so happy for Cathy and me. We talked for almost an hour; she would let me know when was a good time and day to call her dad and for Cathy and me to come visit her!

***

Monday February 3, 2020. We sent in the application for new passports for both Cathy and Cadance. This means we don't have passports as we had to send them in along with the paperwork, fingers crossed...

***

445

Tuesday February 4, 2020. Bits and pieces: We only have had one response to the ten letters sent; Mary Ann, Uncle Fred's wife, emailed a supportive response. Gail did post a generally inclusive piece on Facebook. I called Linda Ramuta because I had sent a letter to her sister Tami, not her and suddenly thought that could be interpreted as a slight and I didn't want to start a family feud. We talked together; she wasn't slighted at all and I was relieved to hear this.

Linda quietly told me, "My sister Tami and I had talked together about you. We agreed I should tell you something that our mother (Alma/Sally) told me about your father. Your father (Merrill) had confided to my mother that he had always felt that there was a woman inside of him trying to get out. He was troubled by this constant feeling and didn't know what to do. My poor mom told me she had no idea how to help him and felt so bad. This is verbatim what my mom told me and I hope it helps you."

Linda also told me that she has a granddaughter that is gender fluid and she tries to be very careful to use the pronouns they/them, "I get what is going on with you."

I was dumbfounded by Linda's news. This very important piece of the 'Merrill Anderson puzzle' she gave me just rocks my world all around! So many unanswered questions for so long and suddenly a key puzzle piece comes at the most important time for me, or maybe the perfect time for me, to understand it. This was more than just a key puzzle piece; it was an enormous leap in understanding, akin to the level of the Rosetta Stone in pointing out what was unfathomable as far as my father's life behavior had been. Thank you Cousin Linda, thank you many times over!!!

Then I pondered the remarkable way this message had remained intact, from the past to the present, and had made its way from Merrill confiding in his sister Sally, to be kept by her daughters after her death, to be given to me at just the right time. It was an obscure and troubling confession he had made, one that could have easily been lost to the passage of time. But it wasn't; simply because of the very loving relationship between Aunt Sally and her brother Merrill. Sally gave it to her daughters to keep and they did because of their love for both their mother and Uncle Merrill. This is the path God laid for me to have this intimate piece of my father's struggle just as I struggled too. Praise God in every way, heart-to-heart when hand-to-hand doesn't reach.

I am finally on the road to understanding all that my dad was and why he lived the way he lived. Dad was either gay or transgender. On reflection, I think he was a closeted transgender MtF; it just all fits together from all of his actions over the years combined with what I know now. So, this forces me now to visit long put away memories about our fractured time as a family, many of which are just plain painful to the point of being emotionally scarring. I have a lot of thinking to do...

Our Journeys (a tribute of understanding)
By Cadance Alane Anderson

My father wasn't able
Her time didn't come
Our world wasn't ready
Acceptance not begun

My father wasn't living
She knew no simple hope
We share a common labor
In spirit we were broke

My father ever searching
Her rest never to fulfill
We in other lives abide
Their fountains ours to fill

My father's journey ended
Her gentle eyes I closed
I journey on past her now
On the path neither chose.

Cadance & Catherine Anderson

I will complete this journey
My mind and body whole
I am a woman born of conflict
Reaching oneness in my soul.

***

Monday March 2, 2020. I wish I had kept this journal up. I miss keeping my memories here to rediscover. I miss having a place to empty my emotions. I miss having an ear to think out loud too.

Apart from Mary Ann's supportive response in email to my letter, we only got dead silence... I decided I had better start calling people...

Cousin Audrey was my first call. I had emailed my letter to her first along with some images and a poem I had written. She was all about poems and such so I had high hopes. Also, I had what seemed to be a very supportive email from her; so a voice-to-voice encounter shouldn't be a problem, or so I thought. The call didn't go smoothly; I suddenly found myself in a defensive conversation ending with, "as long as your happy." This shook me up I wasn't very good about defending myself, words didn't come when I needed them most...

Cousin Linda Ramuta was second. Now Linda had posted a 'like' to my Facebook post, which came before the letter (letter was a try because few Anderson family reacted to my initial post) so the call was as described in the journal 2/4/20. Linda, who wasn't on FB much, is now following me closely.

Aunt Luella was third. Luella is the last surviving member of the original Anderson family of twelve brothers and sisters. When she answered I didn't use any name hoping my voice was enough to identify me. It was, and as it turned out, she hadn't received my letter yet very strange. We never talked about my coming-out at all; instead, she went on and on about her new guy friend. It was so sweet about how she asked the children of this widowed man if it was okay to see their father. They knew each other from church over many years. So since she had not seen my letter, I let it go even to this day...

Cousin Janet was fourth. I thought I had a way in with the information about Luella as a starter. Again, it didn't go very smoothly; as would happen over and over, people would talk about themselves to avoid the issue. Janet came close to tears over the loss of her cousin C---- and I could only listen helplessly with no means to comfort her. It was like attending your own funeral in a way, I will never be the same but I do understand. After this call, I admit to self-loathing for hurting a dear loved cousin since it was in a way Cady's fault.

Cousin Karen was fifth. Again, she talked on and on about her health to avoid the subject, but she was kind and asked for my forgiveness if she used the wrong name from time to time. "It's hard because this goes against what we are taught."

Uncle Ray was last. Last because I found I couldn't do anymore. I had planned Kevin and maybe Orlyn but no, I just didn't have the words or the strength to. It was never my plan to hurt those who I loved and I can't stand doing this.

Anyway back to Uncle Ray. We spoke and in the end, he told me the letter was the proper way to bring this to his attention. He didn't see as this change made any difference, why should it? A surprise came in the form of Jeanette she was very supportive and helped me to pick a time to call Uncle after a family funeral. She also affirmed what Uncle Ray had told me that the change didn't make difference to him. Jeanette also was the best informed about the transgender experience of all of the family and quickly became an ally to Cathy and me. Thanks for the love cousin!

***

Friday March 13, 2020. The virus brings Bedlam. Panic in the year 2020. Our governor doesn't care for our President, so instead of squashing the wildly untrue rumor that the entire state of Washington was going to be quarantined by the President, he used the time in presser to insult and left it hanging. The result was a panic run on Costco to buy food and all the toilet paper they had... All day, as we did everyday stops, there was a panic feeling in each local store we entered. I woke up thinking of all the damage done to all of the businesses from the over reaction of the west coast states; so very troubling and depressing. All the schools and the churches closed up tight; so sad.

More bad news. My passport gender marker request was denied; we were told by the clerk at the courthouse to use form DS 83 and now the Fed told us no, use DS 11. Can't fix it until Monday, so it will just sit and irritate us all weekend. We will have to use our last certified copy of my surgery letter and maybe even have to get Dr. Eaman to write one too.

I still hurt at the one place on my scrotum, it seems to come and go with hormone changes. Speaking of hormones, I can't find the right combination of progesterone/estradiol/DHEA/testosterone. This has been an ongoing battle since I started HRT back in 2007. I find some relief in knowing it is a common battle transgender MtF folks share. We are always adjusting doses based on perceived development or lack thereof. In addition, there are all the physical discomforts that female hormone use causes (I do make adjustments based on how much I hurt e.g., Estrogen headache, hot flashes, or flat muscle cramps). I use progesterone in a suppository nightly and as a cream I rub onto my breasts. I am using patches, pills, and cream and no one adjustment seems to be the sweet spot. The sweet spot being breast soreness, low skin dryness, hair growth, and high mental/memory function. Whenever I question my place as transgender, I review just what I put up with to get to where I am now and that puts the question to rest...

Cathy's brother Phil did come and help Grandma Dixon clear out her garage; it was good for the four Dixon kids (especially the brothers) and Grandma Dixon. Phil has clicked me right into the sister-in-law box. There was plenty of stuff to discard after everyone got what they wanted to keep out of the garage. As Phil put it, "It was a trip down memory lane." Grandma Dixon's emotions ranged from relief through distress and at times numbness. Cathy and I loved seeing her father's drivers' license number scratched on each screwdriver grip...

I keep going over and over about GRS surgery; this is good really as I need to be very sure. I also now have even more information about

450

the world of young Merrill Anderson. Dad's father Amer (who passed away in 1946 when Merrill was 16) attacked his young son Merrill with a knife; I am here so the attack didn't work. I was told by Aunt Sally and Aunt Leatha the same story that the fight ended when his mother, Ida Anderson, walked in on it and fainted dead away falling to the floor. The story was Merrill was somewhat effeminate and would rather do what was viewed as women's work in the household than outside doing what was viewed as men's work on the family farm. Amer perceived this and struck out at him in disgust or perhaps in fear; either way, he wanted no part of his son. The same story is well known with other Anderson first cousins, so it must have some truth in it. What is new now is that Amer had a beautiful singing voice, and loved to go to church and use it; this was told to me by Aunt Luella. In fact, he liked to hear pre-adolescent Merrill sing in church. Cousin Linda told me that Amer had this strange divide in his personally; like two opposite sides, continually fighting each other. Here was this beautiful voiced man, who regularly beat up his wife and children, to the point that none of them had missed him much after his death. Linda also told me that her mom, Sally/Alma, always said, "Merrill was the spitting image of Amer right down to his beautiful singing voice." Based now on more than just a guess, Merrill was transgender in much the same way as I am, but didn't have the concept or the words we now use to voice it. So many little pieces have come to the surface pointing to this other than being gay. This leaves me with trying to both separate and own a trans-thread, running from Father to Son (ironically perhaps trans mother to trans daughter) that binds me to him/her. I am not my father, but we both share this and now Amer, I wonder… Did Amer react out of fear against Merrill or out of anger? Two very different reactions and each shows us something completely different about Amer himself. If it was anger that drove Amer to try to mortally harm his son, then a moral high ground was driving him to remove useless beings, especially one that was an affront to God. But he didn't try to remove Orval; a sickly son. If it was fear then, Merrill represented something Amer feared about himself; Merrill was somehow a mirror reflecting something Amer couldn't tolerate to exist. This is as far as I can take this pattern of him. Amer is completely hidden from me. I only have vague memories from older family members and they are of someone, well, is best left out of memory. So, I have to accept the thread I am most sure of, that being the one Merrill has with C----. And now it is left up to Cady to complete wherever this thread leads and to find its end. Who knows how many generations that thread has run through. Hopefully to the benefit of Casey and Corin, for all three of us, to learn what God has set out for us to learn.

***

Wednesday March 25, 2020. This is the last time we have heard Rush Limbaugh's live voice over the radio. Lately his show has been anchored by a continuous list of guest hosts. Rush is sure missed in this time of trouble. You would think that I couldn't stand Rush's view of transgender people and you would be right, but I value both sides of issues. Looking back on the last few days...

***

Monday March 16th. We try our local elections office and yes it is locked down. We find that the city office in Port Townsend that did passports was still open until 5:00 so we jump in our car and race over. There I, in person, with my right hand up, swore before the city clerk that the information on the passport application was true so now it is up to that office to mail out my properly completed name/gender form. This office would be closed due to the State ordered lockdown the very next day.

***

Tuesday March 17th. Our home-base Starbucks run brings news that this is their last day. There is great sadness in this for us; many of the baristas here have become friends over the years. To top this off; this was the first public place that I came-out to that used my new name and gender marker; I love them for this. Everyone is moving to the classic Starbucks across from Azteca but it is not the same...

***

Thursday March 19th. Another drink run: this time to the classic Starbucks near Target. This time we see old Dave, a long time hangout customer at our now closed home-base Starbucks, sitting with his drink in the open trunk of his car looking very forlorn. We find out that tomorrow this store will be closed too. Now due to the lockdown only Starbucks with drive-thru attached to them with remain open with no lobby hours.

***

Friday March 20th. My growing fear that my passport papers were now sitting in the Port Townsend office doing nothing was relieved by an email acceptance of receipt of them arriving back east. Now, I just have to wait some more but I'm good at waiting…

***

Wednesday March 25th. Cathy and I took the chance to get a massage with Natalie today. She is only doing two per day. We were all so starved for conversation that we talked and talked. Natalie had binge watched all of *I am Jazz* and was very supportive of me now.

***

Wednesday April 1, 2020. My dysphoria/discord is so loud now; this feeling of mind-body irritation just grows daily. I don't feel right and I won't ever feel together. I have thoughts of death, regret, and hopelessness all this despite of the things I have done, which now suddenly seem so little. I have always lived with thoughts of death and internally cried each time at how wrong this is. Life was very rich with love, family, and more love. Even so, I realized that I started to sign off of life little by little, year by year. What had always held me together were Cathy, Casey, and Corin. But bit-by-bit I was slipping away until 2005 came and Cadance began to live little by little. I like to think that Cadance chose life. She slowly emerged from the rubble of a collapsing construct that no longer could hold itself together. I dragged my feet even in surgery in 2018, opting for a lesser procedure; it was all about fear and hopelessness.

I have typed that I was on the fence about GRS until all surgeries stopped dead and there was no options anymore for the foreseeable future. And suddenly, I came to understand just how much I really needed GRS and other feminizing surgeries. No, I am not at a resting point; I am Cadance and to survive as her I have to physically be whole; this gives me both resolve and depression. Things are all shut down and I grow older each day. Will the world return with any hope for an old woman who happens to be transgender? This is what drives my discord right now and my regret at time passing. I know what I type is very hard, but right now in this place and time this is how I feel. I don't feel as though I would act on advancing death, it just isn't me. It isn't right, but dark thoughts do come and do hurt as they have always done. I just know this time 'why' and must allow resolve to lead me even if the path is hard to walk...

Some other things running in my mind: My father left me for a second time in my early twenties and passed away when I was in my early mid-forties. Casey and Corin in their forties lost C---- their dad. I wonder how I compare or even if it is possible to compare experiences. Both Cathy and I feel as if our sons are sending very strong signals that we need to keep away from their households (and not just because of Covid-19). Our daughters-in-law would not be dismayed if we dropped completely out of their worlds, only to surface very rarely for a short time, say every five years or so. And perhaps this is a good thing, they do have their lives to live, but this is a very hard thing for us. I have always lived vicariously, it was all I could do, it was the only path I had. From this Cathy and I poured all that we were and all that we had lovely into our kids. Then came grandkids, could we short them of this? After all, we were still in the same place in our living of life (the same life philosophy, this is love). No, we were bound to the same behavior out of our sons' need for our help and the love for our grandkids they asked for both. So now we are thrown completely out of work as grandparents and this gives us great sadness, loss of purpose, and direction in life...

***

Wednesday April 15, 2020. So how do I explain the isolation, loneness, hopelessness, grief, and a continuous sense of mourning that each day brings with it for us? A malaise has settled in on us; we don't even attempt projects as we first did with our newfound alone time. We have no place to drive to escape this cycle. And even if we did, there are barriers, like restrooms are mostly closed for one. Gas is cheap, the car has new tires, but travel over two hours is just too hard to accomplish. All the gender-affirming things: Caddell's, consultations on plastic surgery, and the thought of my four-year away appointment of GRS getting closer; all these things I did to keep my dysphoria down are now out of reach. The greatest loss is personal contact, especially hugs, game night at Casey's or Grandma Dixon's home, and trips to San Diego. There is no one to call for a conversation, because there is nothing to talk about. The mainstream news media constantly rains fear and doom down upon us (things will never be the same as they were before, etc.) until we just don't listen to them anymore. Thank God for Rush Limbaugh as a counter view, but he is gone from most live broadcasts and still there is no light at the end of this everlasting dark tunnel, 'always Spring and never Easter'. Easter has passed as if it never was; no Casey roasted ham or egg hunt or grandkids' hug. Just being alone, the two of us watching a video of Colby and B----'s treasure hunting last Easter...

So I fess up, I have always had thoughts of taking my own life for as long as I can remember, all interwoven with my gender discord. Thoughts not actions, well, none that would have really worked anyway, I always thought everyone else had these same thoughts as a normal life experience. These times we are living in with hopelessness being the only emotional currency accumulated, bringing wave after wave of thoughts of self-harm. With each wave, a feeling of sadness washes over me and cold tears fill my eyes. You see, I feel that the thought of self-harm is as real as the act of doing it physically (the Bible tells us that even though a man does something physically or just thinks it, both are equal). I feel like a little part of my soul dies with each event, even though my body has not been damaged. So to avoid this, I try to find anything affirming like posting in Facebook, getting identity documents notarized despite all the closures, or buying female pronoun buttons, and posting color palettes of our tie-dye shirts each day.

Politics fill our times in a very grim way; I will put it this way, "I will never vote for another Democrat again in my lifetime." We have watched one no-holds-barred attempt after another to get President Trump out of office. It's not that we have a high opinion about him personally, but with each failed attempt we see a very dark, dishonest, and soul-selling Democratic Party that we want no part of anymore. Odd, me being trans and all, but the reality is how can you trust the untrustworthy to protect your safety and at the price of every other issue for everyone else? We are now members of the Independent Disillusioned Party; our current membership is two, but we are growing.

So other experiences to note: Cathy has muscled through the malaise and found a way to make masks to match our tie-dye shirts. This was no small task as she cried with each misstep she made and each experiment that didn't turn out right. She couldn't find a successful pattern to use or materials to purchase (out of stock or store closed everywhere). We have loved each other more than before and at the same time have verbally battled more often too. Schools are all closed for the year, but at home learning is to start next week. Cathy and Cady are trying to find an existence outside of our sons' families and Cathy's mom and sister's lives. We are losing the battle of being self-contained; my glasses broke and no place to go get them fixed. I had a deep tooth ache, and our teeth need cleaning but no dentist is open, my bank card quite working, forcing us into our bank that didn't want us there. Anyone we meet on a walk avoids the ground we step on out of fear. We did get the card fixed and by taking parts from my spare glasses I made one workable pair for now anyway. We get a little human contact by shopping at PCC market once a week and at our only drive-thru Starbucks (Chris is an old timer we know at the Interurban Starbucks) pretty much daily. At PCC, we feel a thrill if the stuff we need is on the shelves, many things are gone, eggs are in stock but not the choice we like, flour is gone (but gluten-free was the last to disappear), no clue on its return.

We have used up all my gender surgery letters and I'm low on court order letters. The courts are all closed but I did order two more surgery letters from a non-friendly office person at Dr. Bowers' office. This rattles me. Has her office become a non-caring faceless business? Has she???

Things have to return to the normal rhythm of the time before C-19. There really is no other way; we cannot survive in this artificial world of isolation controlled by local despots.

***

Saturday May 23, 2020. We are about to leave to drive to Quincy for our seasonal Memorial Day day-trip to leave flowers on graves. Just a drive but I'm nervous about leaving home…

***

Friday June 5, 2020. I should be journaling daily about this very sad time in our and our nation's lives, but the weight on my soul is just too much to allow this. All I can do is make a few notes.

We did drive over to Quincy and Ellensburg to leave flowers (we had to use little African Violets in place of the mums because it was all we could find). The social conditions were much freer over there few if any masked faces with sad eyes. We have been under curfew for five days after organized breaking and looting in Tukwila. Cathy and I have listened to gunfire, police sirens, fire sirens, explosions, and seen broken glass everywhere all week.

***

Tuesday June 30, 2020. Even in this time of times my journey still demands movement. There is even a little hope for the future in this…

I have my quotes from Dr. Rikesh Parikh:

- Forehead Reduction set back with hairline lowering: $1500 + $5750=$7250!!!
- Facelift with neck lift, Fat transfer to full face: $9700+$2500+$4750(discount$1250) =$15700
- Lip lift, Upper Eyelid Lift: $3100+$2500(discount$550)=$6450

***

Saturday July 4, 2020. Check-in time: Transition in the time of Covid 19:

The imprisonment of this time hangs over our lives and touches every second of everyday. It has brought life to a halt and holds it in place including transition. I have at times blamed myself for the whole mess, after all, things started to fall apart after I came out… God does give hope to keep Cathy and me stable. We were blessed in two important things in the last week. I received my Passport in my new legal name and with gender as female!!! I had no idea just how important this was for my mental health, I cried. I have a surgery date of July 9th for two facial feminization procedures with Dr. Rikesh Parikh!!! Dr. Parikh reopened my orchi wound a year ago and I know he does a great suture line but he has such an ego, I thought I wouldn't go back to him. I got quotes from Dr. Lamperti (who did my trachea shave) on a complete facelift, lip-lift, eyelids, brow-lift and nose. I had a great experience with Dr. Lamperti and he is such a nice guy. For a second set of quotes, I tracked down Dr. Parikh. He is very competent and very busy doing surgeries. Dr. Parikh is very interested in doing brow-lift and forehead contouring for trans women. He has taken a course from the Facial Team group in Marbella, Spain (they are world renowned in this new procedure). He told me if I would trust him with my face, he would do the procedure for a very low price just to have someone to be his first patient. The two quotes were very close to each other but Dr. Parikh has two dedicated OR units for just his practice where I would have to go through a separate hospital for Dr. Lamperti. Dr. Parikh is closer and I don't have to walk through a medical building to get to his OR. I called his nurse Stacy after getting the quote just to ask how soon I could get the two local anesthetic procedures (lips and lids) and got a call back of July 9th! To my surprise, my whole being leapt for joy and I thought, what the heck is going on with me. Then I thought, oh no I have only six days before we go with Colby and B---- to Thorp on the 15th. So, I told Stacy that I couldn't take the date and felt sick at the pit of my stomach. After the call I began to fret and Cathy told me the State could be shut down again because of Covid and maybe I should reconsider. It took me just a minute and I was back on the phone to Stacy who told me my stitches would be out before the 15th. I need this so badly I'll take the date!!! I should have been frighten at the thought of the procedures, dragging my feet, and dreading the risk I was taking... There was none of this in me, only joy at the idea of this affirming surgery.

I have running doubts from a lifetime of coping with GID but I shouldn't; I am what I am. I need to do what I must do and with each step a little more of the weight is lifted off me.

***

Wednesday July 8, 2020: So, tomorrow Cathy and I will spend $6450 on me... And at the risk of interfering with our Colby and B---- trip... I don't want to put it off, but have no assurance of the shape I will be in for our trip. At this very moment tomorrow is still my surgery date. I had a thought about transitioning, it really is a battle fought on two fronts: the first front is social acceptance and the second is personal dysphoria/body discord. In our little world socially, I'm being accepted as female, my ID is all female. This is slowly sinking into my personal reality; the battle here has strong measurable progress via external feedback. I have no idea of the larger world outside of our city and state. On the personal front of dysphoria/discord, the life-long battle continues, even with the progress so far. This battle/war is the hardest to reconcile, to show progress in, or to come to a place of final rest from. I don't think it will ever actually be completely over, but instead comes to a place of manageable victory. Why do I need these procedures at all? I have to move forward, to see a change in the broken mirror that is affirming and real, not an aging androgynous male anymore. This is all so disjoint, but there is something deep inside of my being that is undeniable, a feeling that I will not doubt anymore. It shakes me when it takes charge and I wonder, where did that come from? A feeling that is right and sure. I am a daughter in the Kingdom of God no matter how odd that seems to me.

This binary that was so impossible for me to reach sixty years ago is now mercifully within reach, while at the same time that binary has also been cleaved into so many unimaginable pieces, that I ponder if there is room for me at the end of my battle anymore...

***

Friday July 10, 2020: Money spent and in return I have received an upper eyelid Blepharoplasty and an upper lip-lift from Dr. Rikesh Parikh. I feel like I climbed a mountain and stood on it's top!

Here is the experience beginning yesterday morning: Cathy and I didn't get to bed until midnight, dragging our feet to this day. We wake up on the day of surgery at 8:00 am; I open my eyes, stare at the ceiling fan going round, and think that this is the day, my day. Each morning, since we made the appointment for my surgery, I have reminded myself of the mathematical position of that day to The Day. This gave me relief that there was still time between here and there. This morning no time remained anymore, it was time for the planning we had done to come to life; Thursday July 9th was here at last. There is calmness in having a planned path of actions to follow from showering (I used antibiotic soap on my face per my own idea and let the hot water stream over my face since I didn't know the next time I would be able to do this), dressing in matching clothes and masks, and having breakfast. We went for our walk, returned home to read our iPads and wait for Casey. Casey was taking the day off to be our hero, our rock; he was to come between 1:00 and 1:30 to make our 2:00 appointment with destiny... A little back-story, one reason we picked Dr. P is because he was in a private office in Bellevue, not one small office in a big hospital complex. This way we don't have to wade through a crowd of patients all trying to be six feet apart. I put the garbage out to be ready for tomorrow and was trying to think of anything else that I needed to do especially since it was near 11:00 and I still had some time. My phone rang and it was Stacy at Dr. Parikh office asking if I could come in earlier at 1:30, oh my, I think so. I had a panic attack screaming to get out and called Casey to ask if he could come earlier. His reply was, "I will get going right now." Okay. Suddenly everything became very serious, no more relaxed attitude. Cathy sprang into action gathering up stuff into a bag that she may need during her waiting room time. My nerves are jumping left and right, but at my core some part of me is so very excited to get going. Casey arrives at 12:30 and is more or less ready to go except he sees two now high-strung females about to pop. He tells us, "Okay it's time to do a deep breathing exercise to get rid of some of this stress." He won't let us get into his car until Cathy and I both take a deep breath, hold it, and then push it out twice. That turned out to be kind of hard for me, darn panic stress stuff! Okay then, all breathed out I open the door and wait until everyone passes outside, then close the door and stay inside the house. We all have a good laugh when they come back to get me! Inside Casey's SUV, he starts to talk about when he had surgery on his leg and suddenly I let out a scream. Cathy calmly tells Casey that I have been doing that all morning... Casey wants to make sure we have all our stuff and reminds his mom that it is not a camp out only a few hour appointment. Casey zips around a backroad way via Grady Way to get onto I-405; he prides himself on his knowledge of such stuff. Casey's audio system started playing *Sweet Home Alabama* and Cathy commented she really likes this song. Cathy navigates us off I-405 at the carpool exit for Bellevue then across the overpass to Whole Foods. We turn left and then straight until we turn right at the Bel-Red center. Casey tells us he thinks this is the same building where Mindy had an appointment for a consultation with a plastic surgeon 13 months ago. Cathy tells Casey that Grandma Dixon thought she might like her eyes done after I told her about my upcoming surgery. The time is 1:05 as we park. I am content to sit and wait until 1:30, but Casey reminds us that there is always some sort of paperwork to fill out so might as well go inside and get it done. Cathy and I walk into the joint corridor linking Dr. Parikh's office and the office of Dr. Zemplenyi (Dr. Z). The shared operation rooms are located here. We can't remember which office to go into so we go left to Dr. Parikh's office waiting room and find that we are the only people in the empty waiting room. Stacy was behind the reception desk, on top of which is a display of implantable breast forms of various sizes and shapes. These just scream to be touched, I always keep in mind just how many people have done just this; so it's hands off for me. Dr. Parikh was just behind Stacy in an open office lounging in a chair. It was all so casual and undirected; Dr. Parikh greeted us with, "Hello Cadance!" He was in light blue scrubs with a mask. He loves to call me by my formal name. Stacy was in dark navy scrubs, no mask, and did have another form for us (Cathy) to fill out. Dr. Parikh told me that he had something to tell me about the lip lift. He wanted to make sure I understood that only the center part of my upper lip would be lifted up and out. The sides remain where they are; if I wanted to do the sides it would be another fee and a small scar on either side. Dr. Parikh makes a point then revisits it multiple times. I assure him I understand and I do, I have researched all about the procedure. He has a release form for me to sign so he can take photos and use them as he sees fit. I am fine with this especially if they help some other person to understand his work. Dr. P has me come with him leaving Cathy with Stacy (Casey in his truck). We walk down a hall to what he calls the photo room. He measures me and revisits the lip lift point again in depth to make sure I fully understand and we chat about it. We return to Stacy and Cathy in the waiting room and I surrender for safe keeping my purse, phone, mask, and glasses. I would realize later giving up the phone was a mistake… Cathy pays the bill of $6,450 dollars with our Costco card and in just a few minutes gets a notification on her phone of the transaction. We all walk into the connecting corridor over to the other office. Here is a bigger waiting room and a reception desk with two oblivious office ladies working away. The two ladies remain consistently oblivious to Cathy during the time she is waiting here. Cathy, overhearing them laboring over sending a document through their interweb, thought seriously about asking if they needed some help. But remained mute reminding herself how oblivious they were to her.

Dr. Parikh has me follow him around the reception desk to where the OR door stood open. He tells the oblivious ladies at the reception desk that he is going to use the OR for a local procedure and they continue to remain oblivious. He leads me to what he calls the picture room different from the photo room. One wall is painted photo-blue and has footprints on the floor to mark where to stand. There are two photo strobes mounted on the walls opposite, pointing to this photo-blue wall, a desk with rolling chair is pushed up against the wall to the right and two chairs stand near the door. There is a Canon SLR on the desk and Dr. P gets busy taking direct on, 45 degree, and profile, pictures of my face while I sit on a chair because I am so tall. He continues a constant banter about the lip lift problem, marks a centerline with a ballpoint pen down from my nose to the pigment line of my upper lip. Dr. P loves to use the phrase 'you know what I mean' sometimes changing it to 'you know what I'm saying' as a check to make sure you understand his point. He leaves me for a few minutes and returns with a gown and a set of footy socks. He tells me I can leave my leggings on but doesn't want to get blood on my custom tie-dye shirt (I'm in full agreement on this) and turns to leaves while I change. I remove my shirt, shoes, and socks leaving my bra and leggings on. I remember to tie the gown before I pull it on over my head. Dr. P comes back and begins to mark my upper lip and upper eyelids up with a purple skin pen. He has a running stream of consciousness about how he is going to accomplish the surgery. The conversation centers around being aggressive or conservative on the size of the skin wedge to be removed from the top of my upper lip just under my nose. He goes on about how the ideal female length for this distance from the nose to lip pigment line is 1.2 cm and marks a line on my lip for this length then marks out lines at 1.4 for a more conservative length. My current length before surgery was like 1.9 to 2.0. Dr. P tells me that he has lately seen some overly aggressive lip lifts that leave the lip unnaturally curled up too high and it is very hard to undo or add the lost length back again. Funny this, Cathy told me this morning that I should be conservative in how much to remove, so I am very careful in considering our conversation on this point. And at the same time, I pretty much agree to whatever Dr. P has to say; after all, he has all the experience, I have none. He marks and marks using this space of my face as his art canvas; it really is an experience to be going through, to be part of this his artwork as he plans each incision individually. He finishes and has me stand in front of a full-length mirror while he explains each purple line.

Dr. Parikh explains, "Instead of a smooth cut line, I'm going to try cutting out connected radial segments all across under the nose with the idea like the spokes of a wheel; each segment will pull up more of the lip overall. I've marked out 1.2 and 1.4 centimeters I think it is best to go with the 1.4 and be conservative, so hard to add length back in. You know what I'm saying Cadance?"

I assure him I do, he is full of energy and I am full of compliance. We both are on a shared mission to reach a common goal. He tells me that Cathy may be waiting out in the car as he leaves me to check on the OR. I sit in the chair by the desk thinking that giving up my phone was a mistake. I should have kept it to take some pictures of my face all marked up before being cut up. I could have texted Cathy to check on her and she on me; just darn… I get a crafty dark thought; there is a phone there on the desk I wonder if I could get away with just calling her. She could even bring my phone to me. I don't want to get caught on the phone by Dr. P, but I try using it anyway. I run into trouble right away I don't have my glasses anymore and then I remember I don't remember Cathy phone number either; darn again. I am still alone so I summon up courage and take a stab at remembering her number, 57 something 4*** it's the third number, maybe 575 4***. I add the 2*6 and feel the keypad to identify 2*6 575 4***, busy signal darn. I hang up just before Dr. P comes in, that was close! The telephone adventure did distract me while he was gone, but the truth is, I had no trepidations within me about this surgery itself. I am looking forward to it with only one exception and that is the local anesthetic; this remains a bump I have to get over. It's odd not to worry, but I do have the experience with Dr. P doing surgery on me to take from and this is a big plus. Add to this that just after our calming circle breathing (think *Hocus Pocus* video) that Casey directed us to do before we left home, I held his and Cathy's hand in prayer for God's blessing for us. I prayed most of the drive here and felt very calm afterward; a sense of doing something right at the right time. Dr. P takes my shirt and shoes and leads me into the hallway, he puts my stuff into a locker just outside the OR door.

I walk into the OR with Dr. P. I am in a gown, have my hair in a ponytail down my back, no cap, but I figure they know what they are doing; it's all just so casual. The inside of the spacious OR is very bright from outside light streaming in through opaque window coverings. At the center of the room surrounded by machines with lots of switches and lights is the table/bed that is to be my home for the next 90 minutes. A nurse (Lisa, she has blond hair) is puttering around and Stacey pops in and out, masks aren't on them yet and elevator music is playing in the background. I am directed to lay on the narrow bed, which does have armrest on either side and cover myself with a light spread. Dr. P fastens a big black belt over my legs, he then asks me to scoot up on the bed, the belt makes this a trick, but I manage to wiggle into the place they want me to be in. I stare at the white ceiling, a central LED OR adjustable light fixture is above me; to one side of this is a red fire alarm thingy. Other than this, the ceiling is uninteresting; so no distraction there for me to find. Nurse Lisa helps Dr. P into a surgical gown that covers his scrubs, he is masked up and ready to go. The nurse assisting Dr. P raises up the light spread covering me to put a cold sticky square on my side for some reason, she seems surprise that I still have my leggings on. The background music suddenly stops playing and no one takes notice, something about not knowing how it works. Dr. P drapes my head until only my face is showing, my arms are under the light spread and I think to myself this OR isn't cold like the others I have been in. I take comfort in the big belt across my legs as something I could push against if I ready needed to... Dr. Parikh tells me he is going to do a video now and will be doing some talking.

Dr. P begins his narration, "This is Dr. Parikh and today we are doing a Blepharoplasty and an upper lip lift on this patient. It will bring her eyebrows up and give her eyelids more depth. The lip lift will bring her upper lip up and out, revealing a fuller set of lips." The video is stopped. I look up at Dr. Parikh now standing near the left side of my head and a serene surrender comes into my trepidatious brain. My inner voice spoke, Dr. P has dark eyes and calls me Cadance, I'll be okay. He tells me, "It's time to administer the anesthetic Cadance, a poke at the side of the eye Cadance." Okay, I have read that this is the worst part of the surgery. I'll be okay; I have gotten through dental pokes, electrolysis pokes, and a breathtaking anesthetic poke in my scrotum that I will long remember. That last poke, I figure would be the true benchmark for such things to be measured against as to severity until now... One thing I'll say about Dr. P is he never let a bloody object cross my field of view, nor did he allow any long needled mean looking syringe to appear anywhere I could see it, and in any event I could always count on the big black belt holding me safely down to be my friend in fear. I now have a benchmark that far surpasses the scrotum poke. I had started to count out the time tones that were occurring around the OR to see if they repeated. It is a good trick for distraction; it worked for me when Dr. P did my scrotum. The poke came on my right eye at the outside corner of my upper lid, time stood still while all my muscles sharply contracted. Both eyelids snapped shut in a panic reaction and the most pain I have ever felt flooded in through that mean needle as it slowly moved along. It was everything I could do to remain on that table; I grabbed the armrest with my fingernails and dug in. My brain was fighting to have my body remain still for the sake of the needle traveling within my eyelid across its width. The needle broke the skin surface and sprayed my face twice before diving back down into my eyelid. Even as this trauma developed, for some reason my brain continued counting audible beeps; poor brain, I think it was cowering in some deep place in my skull. After several days had seemingly passed by, I made it through the first eyelid; then the poke came into the other side. A thought floated into my pain busy brain; it was that I really loved Cathy so very much. I loved our life together, waking up to her every day; just wow... I also knew at that moment that I couldn't stand to have him do my lip. I was going to tell him to forget that part just as soon as the now spraying needle crawled out of my eyelid. Dr. P told me he was done with the eyelids and said, "You did very well through a difficult part Cadance." My inner voice returned, Cadance, that's my name, he just used it, so nice to hear, and he has dark eyes. The pain had stopped, I remembered to open my hands again and undig my fingernails from the armrest. This memory to move my hands, although abstract at the time, came from the depth of a pit coming back

466

to life again. Dr. P said something vaguely sounding like, "Now to do the lip." My inner voice pleaded, this is supposed to be the time to tell him to abort the lip, this is the time, open your mouth, and say the word 'stop,' come on do it! Then the brain that had stopped counting and lovemaking had another thought. Could I ever bring myself to do this again at another time knowing what I now know? Well could I? No, better not wait, now is still the time, the right time; darn smart reasoning brain… Drapes were moved over my eyes, I became aware that tears had freely run down both sides of my face forming two salty streambeds that had run dry. Gently Dr. P murmured, "A poke Cadance." My inner voice swooned, He said Cadance again. I had in my brain at that very moment the experience of just how much an electrolysis probe hurts when poked into the spot just inside of my nose. There is the pain of the invasive poking that travels deeply into the sinus, looking for the little branch of the trigeminal nerve and then the pain of burning from the heat of the probe that further infuriates said nerve. Some call the trigeminal the suicide nerve. I'm ready I thought, no I wasn't my brain returned. Everything came as it did with my eyelids plus a few degrees more. The nurse commented about how much it hurts to pop a pimple under your nose and I managed to say try electrolysis… I was disappointed in myself for not holding still, but once the needle had traveled through the length of the area under my nose, it became a thing of the past, an ugly mean memory in contrast to hearing the name Cadance. I was also so thankful it was over, such a relief! The drape is moved from my eyes to my nose and mouth. Dr. P asked, "How are doing Cadance?" My inner voice purred, Cadance again, I'm okay. His eyes are dark and they are looking right into mine, as this is their focus now. Dr. P tests to see if there are any spots not numb, ouch oh no! I thought that mean needle wasn't over as if in some horror movie replay, it came back; even briefly for one last bite.

Dr. P then moved onto the surgery part of my Blepharoplasty. He commanded, "Open your eyes Cadance." I obey the dark eyes as they stare into my eyes. His next commanded, "Close eyes." Now is the time of surrender, resolve, and release. I surrender to who I truly am and to the hands now cutting my skin, I resolve to this surgery and the hands reshaping my face, and I release my spirit to become me fully and the hands to do their talented work in attaining this. Now the reality of those actions: I hold my eyes closed with no thought to open them unless directed to. I feel Dr. P take a firm hold of my top right orbit near the bridge of my nose; he is squeezing it very tightly and orders the nurse to hold it in this matter. She takes over the pressure and I silently think of Cathy again. I feel a sharp stick and winch slightly. "You feel pain Cadance?" And I return just a little, he responds, "It should only happen in the corners." I'm okay with this; I just compare it to the needle poke and opt for the lesser of momentary pain. I feel my eyelid being pulled out and the numb sensation of a scalpel cutting across the eyelid. Cathy floats all across my thoughts as I try not to guess what the strange pressures I am feeling are in reality, cutting and snipping. Dr. P has the nurse modify her position and pressure on my orbit, he then asks for dabbing squares. A new noise in the OR, a deep beep; it happens at the same time I feel an electric shock on the eyelid. The smell of cauterized blood floats up. The nurse points out another bleeding area and the deep beep announces the shocking, smoking, cauterizing, probe at work; just like the little Dutch boy's finger stopping the flow against the great pressure. The cutting seems to be done but cauterizing has taken its place. I think, if he gets my eyelids done, I'll tell him I can't do the lip, it will be too much for me so only the eyelids; I must remember to tell him this after the eyelids are done. Dr. P's voice, "How are doing Cadance?" My murmur, Oh Cadance again, I'm okay. The cauterizing is making me ill to my stomach; I have become so hot under the light spread and a plastic sheet that has now been added on top of it that I am sweating profusely. I thought what would happen if I had to vomit? I then thought I've got to calm down… Dr. P moves on to suturing my eyelids back on. He asks me to open my eyes and I try to but it doesn't work quite right; then I am to close them again. The nurse marvels at Dr. P's developing suture line, telling him it's such delicate work, she hasn't seen an eyelid lift in person before. Dr. P leans out putting pressure onto me as he stretches to suture across the length of my eyelid. My obit and the skin above my right eyebrow has been stretched tight and it isn't numb like the eyelid itself; it is a discomfort but not painful. As Dr. P continues suturing, my nausea forces me to move my arms out unto the armrest to find a cool place. It works for a while then turns around to me being chilled like I am going to pass out. The game for me is find some place between these two extremes until this is all over. The suturing is done but Dr. P has more cauterizing to do and the nurse finds even more places for it. My right eye is done I am asked to open my eyes and close them. My right eye does work but no longer closes all the way down. My one eye is done now to begin the other one. Some lady comes into the OR and nurse Lisa asks what happened to the music? The lady responds (sounds like a female voice) telling her she is already connected to some four-digit number so all you have to do is swipe, the music restarts. My left eye is a repeat of my right but with less skin to be removed. As Dr. P moves through each step, I make out what song is being played during each step. I remember *Piano Man* and *Hey Jude* then some that were unrecognizable because my attention was somewhere else. I remember listing to the nurse quietly mouthing the words to *Piano Man* as it was played in the background. It was comforting to me, making it seem like the things happening all around me were just common everyday occurrences. I could have been in a store or elevator somewhere, not having my eyelids shortened and reattached. Dr. P ordered me to open my eyes and when I did I noticed the air of the OR was full of blue grey smoke from all the cauterizing. He then told me to close and now both of my eyelids only close 75% leaving a crescent of light at the bottom. My eyes are done I open them again as requested and stare directly into the dark eyes of Dr. P searching for any pieces of skin out of place before he moves on to my lip.

The drape is moved from my mouth to my eyes in preparation for my upper lip lift. In my brain, a memory is stirred up to consciousness level. It told me to say something about not doing my lip when this moment came; it seems like a very old memory from a really different time and didn't seem appropriate anymore. I looked at the memory in light of all I had gone through today, all the reasoning I had looked at, all of the Cadances I had heard, all of the mountains I had dragged myself over. I told myself, I'll do the lip, but thanks for being there for me and I wished me well. Dr. P moves to begin on my lip and as the scalpel is poked into my skin I feel a sharp stabbing pain, Dr. P says, "It's the corners again. Cadance, I would give you more anesthetic but it distorts the shape of the skin, can you tolerate the pain? It will just be in the corners." My inner voice, Cadance again, yes of course. The pokes are sharp and stabbing but short of much of the pain for me this past day. Dr. P has to really lean down on me to get at my lower face because of the width of the bed/table. It doesn't bother me any except I have to concentrate on not wincing so as not to move at the wrong moment. The lip is a very different experience from the eyelids. The upper lip skin is much thicker where the eyelid is the thinnest and most delicate of all our skin. Both Dr. P and the nurse are quiet as he moves along. There is more cauterizing than with the eyelids (I guess because of the thickness) and the whole area is under tension after the suturing is done. I hear Dr. P ask for several sizes of sutures where I didn't remember him asking for different kinds on my eyelids. He tells me, "I am using lots of suture types here. This is a good thing and will give a good result, but when it comes time for us to remove them; it will take quite some time to do. You know what I am saying Cadance." I do Dr. P. There is a noticeable change from both Dr. P and the nurse and I realize they are wrapping everything up; I'm done! Dr. P tells me he is going to video again and ask if this is okay and I say sure. The nurse holds a phone up to do the video. Dr. P begins his narration, "This is Dr. Parikh again and we have just finished Blepharoplasty and a lip lift on this patient. You can see how beautifully it has turned out! Her lips are now fuller (he points to my lips) and her eyebrows are raised to reveal brighter eyes (he gestures around my eyes)!" The nurse stops the video.

Dr. P asks if I would like to see my face and I say yes! He brings over a mirror and gives it to me. I look at the person in mirror and squeal with delight, amazement, and joy. All of the pain is instantly forgotten. The nurse tells Dr. P, "We stopped the video too soon!!! What a great reaction!!!" I was truly speechless at the me I saw in mirror! The me whose reflection was so someone else. What I saw in that reflection was the shadow of the true me and it was so moving I couldn't stop looking at it! The nurse was so tickled and happy for me and so was Dr. Parikh. I sat while the nurse got my shirt and shoes. She pulled off my hospital socks and saw my painted toes. "Wow so many colors!" I explained I have a granddaughter and she loved this. She put my shoes on my feet for me and helped me with my shirt. So, there I sat with my gown off to reveal me in my bra just like any other woman. We got my shirt on and I floated off the table. I got hugs from the nurse, Stacey, and Dr. Parikh as we walked to meet up with Cathy in the waiting room. I opened the door and said joyfully. I'm done get a picture!!! Cathy is sitting in a chair with chairs on either side sporting do not sit here signs. She gets up and comes over to us. Dr. P. says that everything went well and says that Cadance can shower on Saturday. He goes on to say that she got an antibiotic shot in her rear, and that she should start taking the prescription starting in the evening. Dr. P. says he will send more instructions and we are free to go. Cathy goes over to the chair and collects all her stuff. As we leave the room, Cathy suddenly says, "Cady, where's your mask?" She is in a dither as we look all over the room but don't find the mask. Stacy helps look by taking us back to Dr. P's office and looking there. No mask. Then we check the restroom – Stacy says she has never been in this restroom before. Still no mask, but we go ahead and leave. Ah, well. Cathy plans on making more masks anyway.

Casey is waiting for us and we climb into his vehicle. Just as we get ready to leave, Cathy starts laughing. She went to take off her mask and put it in her pouch, only to discover that my mask was already in there just grinning at her!

***

Saturday July 18, 2020. Nine days since I have journaled! Let's start with a day by day from my weak memory:

July 9th. Casey takes us to Starbucks and I get to show off my surgical battle scars to Thomas and Bryan. They were duly impressed. Casey dropped us at home; he is on his way to Bartell's to pick up my meds and anything else he thinks we might need. Cathy has directed me to our couch and gave me one Tylenol to start my pain reduce/control routine. I am numb, can't close my eyes fully, and moving my mouth brings soreness. Pain level right at this point is five out of ten. Casey returns with gauze squares, Polysporin ointment, a bag of Seattle Chocolates, and Doxycycline (100 mg capsules one twice daily). He has nursed his household enough to know just what to get. Casey has more advice for taking care of me to give, then he leaves with our promise we would keep him posted. Cathy makes me mashed potatoes and an egg to eat. I take my first Doxycycline dose with this food. As the anesthetic wears off my pain level as an overall ache rises to level seven. Cathy procures ice packs to apply to my eyes and forehead, not my lips per doctor's instructions. Speaking of this, no one at the doctor's office offers us any written instructions for my care. He later sends a short list via text on my phone. I have to sleep on my back and figure it would be a good thing to patch both eyes to keep the overhead fan in our bedroom from drying them out and to keep me from touching the area by accident. This is especially important because they don't completely close anymore.

July 10th. I slept poorly and woke up tired but grateful that one night has passed. I had taken both Oxycodone and Tylenol before bed only to wake up with a dull deep headache. So no more of that; in fact, I didn't notice any pain reduction from Oxycodone at all over just Tylenol. Soft food is the order of the day. Ice packs are the best relief ever in this, my current world. Another dose of Doxycycline with breakfast and that deep dull headache is becoming more annoying as the day drags along. Cathy and I decide to walk our loop to see if being out and about clears my headache and helps healing in general. I know it was good to walk but I need ice when we get home. I do more ice; there is a deep ache on the top of head down to the sides and forehead. This pain is separate from the local pain of my eye sockets and upper lip. I take my evening Doxycycline dose with food and notice that I am developing a bad taste in my mouth. I guess all the good bacteria are being killed off as well as the bad bacteria by the Doxycycline. I sleep poorly on my back with my eyes taped over to keep them safe.

July 11th. After a restless night, I awake to increasing brain pain and pressure in my sinus; I take a yellow pill and ibuprofen in hopes it will help. I also have a sort of dizziness developing whenever I turn sharply. It's back to only soft food again; Cathy and I walk our loop, this time it is harder to balance properly. As we walk on 46th Ave approaching the corner of 144th, our neighbor John is in his fenced yard with a new puppy and waves us over to him. We say hello to his new puppy Keko and chat with him. John tells us Keko loves their bedroom and hangs out in the closet there. He tells us that his two sons have both come out of the closet as gay and now he has a new dog coming out of that same closet! I ask him about his sons and he has no problem with them being gay; in fact, as he comes from Fiji he has never understood why there is such a fuss about it here. I tell him cool, well I feel comfortable telling you I'm transgender. I'm female and my new legal name is Cadance. We chat; he is delighted and tells me I should Google 'acquiring a daughter and Fiji or fa'afine'. He tells us he will always say hi to us as C&C each time we pass. Back home I shower carefully to keep my face dry and still clean my hair. Ice packs to my eye and forehead bring relief and I can even nap with them in place. We do Saturday night games with Grandma Dixon and Linda; both are in moods from forced retirement for Linda and giving up driving for Joyce... I take my nighttime Doxycycline dose with food and tape up my eyes for bed.

July 12th. Another hard night of not sleeping and hoping for the morning to come. I want to rub my eyes so much! The ointment I use to keep them moist gets into my eyes and down my lip. I clean the sutures with vinegar/water and apply the ointment several times a day. After waking this morning, I pull off my eye patches and hold my forehead with my hands. The deep painful ache is much worse. I turn my head to the left side of the bed and suddenly the whole room begins to move, just like being on a ship in a storm! I know it can't be moving, but it feels like motion via my eyes and deep in my head. I pull my head back to straight up and the motions stops. I am on my back looking up at the ceiling again. I try to turn on my right side and this brings violent motion and headache. Cathy helps me get out of bed and things settle down again… I feel like I am moving through Jell-O as I walk, so odd. The day is a repeat of meds and soft food.

The dizziness is increasing and yellow pills don't help nor did a Fluconazole pill, it just keeps me awake. I took my Doxycycline dose at breakfast and as the day slowly moves along the dizziness becomes alarming. Cathy has me call Dr. Parikh's office and Stacey answers. I tell her about the dizziness and ask if it could be the Doxycycline and could I switch to another antibiotic. She Googles the drug and found that indeed dizziness is an unwanted side effect and told me she would check with Dr. Parikh. I get a call back to just stop the med altogether, thank goodness. I would continue to spend all day in fits of dizziness…

July 13th. I don't think I'll ever get a goodnight's sleep again. The days bring more of the same regular chores of ice packs, cleaning, reapplying ointment, and eating more protein. The dizziness is slowly decreasing, but at times I have to hold onto something to keep me from falling onto the floor. We walk late in the afternoon holding hands mostly to keep me upright. We have to plan what to pack for our trip with Colby and B---- on July 15th. That means getting all the things together we need to pack tomorrow.

July 14th. Again broken sleep, this time I didn't patch my eyes. Before getting up I test to see if the dizziness is still with me by turning over onto my right side. Still a little but much better; you wonder how an antibiotic would cause such a side effect? We have breakfast and get ready for our 10:00 appointment with our chiropractor, Dr. Grace. She is very impressed with my surgery and we ask her about her wedding plans. It looks like it will be a Thanksgiving wedding this fall for them. Cathy has found an Airbnb just outside of Thorp for us in lieu of the little cabin on Taneum Creek that we normally use. Unfortunately, the little cabin along with many of the camp grounds are closed this sad year. Anyway, we now need to go to the bank for cash and shopping for stuff we will need for our upcoming trip to the Airbnb. A problem has arisen; we had planned on Casey driving Colby and B---- over to Thorp to drop them off with us there and return to take them home later. This would give Casey and Mindy a nice drive

474

and they could see the Airbnb for themselves. The upside is this would give much more room in our car for supplies of food etc. Casey had to cancel because of work so Cathy and I formed a plan to take just the very basics and buy food in Ellensburg when we get there. Cathy checked out Super 1 Foods website for our gluten-free needs and yes, the website had what we needed so we felt confident in just bringing money. There would be ample room in our car for the grandkids and our other non-food stuff.

July 15th. We pack our car carefully leaving the backseat empty for the kids, score! We leave our little house stopping at Starbucks for drinks for everyone and arrive at Casey's near 1:00. B---- is outside waiting for us holding her stuffies and backpack. Casey's work did get canceled at the last minute, but he was feeling under the weather so it was still a go in our car only. Colby organized getting stuff into our car and we said our goodbyes and were on the road by 1:30. We stopped at Snoqualmie Pass for restrooms, the single use toilet's door was broken and wouldn't lock so I had to be very resourceful and fast. We arrived at the Airbnb at 3:30. We met up with Dan Leavitt the manager of this Airbnb, and he walked us all around the property while lecturing to us on the attributes of the nearby Yakima River and the little village of Thorp. I was quiet, I felt vulnerable with my eyes all sutured up and he just didn't give a break in his narration big enough to start a conversation. But before he left us to our vacation, I told him I was from Thorp and I went to school here for several years. It turned out he had too. He graduated from the High School in 1977 and knew Mr. Dudley Tailor, my sixth grader teacher. Dan's wife also went to school here and her brother Kevin Chandler was a friend of my brother David. She remembered David was blonde and even knew he had drowned... Small world. Left to ourselves we move into the guesthouse and the kids were given their choice of rooms. B---- picked the upstairs loft and Colby the downstairs bedroom while we would use the master bedroom. Now to get everyone back into the car to head to Ellensburg for promised supplies. Quick story is we shopped Super 1 Foods and found none of what we needed; the website was wrong, we tried Fred Meyer and had to make do with fries instead of hash

475

browns and poor gluten-free Franz bread. So, in retrospect bring your own food from home even if you don't have room in your car... The afternoon wind is blowing strongly and the sun is burning down on us as we pull into the parking place back at the house. Food this night was Cathy's homemade mac and cheese and I cooked eggs for Colby and myself. Afterward we play games; Tenzie for all of us (B---- won) and three-hand cribbage for Cathy, Cady, and Colby (Cathy won). It was a treat to hear prayers for B---- and to sing goodnight songs for Colby to sleep too. I don't know if this will be the last time for songs so I will cherish this moment with my grandson as if it were... The master bedroom is nice and spotless, but the bed has two worn indents on either side of the bed so even with our foam mattress topper, it was a back killer for me.

July 16th. The night is accomplished with broken sleep for me, seven hours for B----, more for Cathy and Colby. This is the big breakfast day; we found a simple gluten-free pancake mix that looked like it might work. I cooked bacon and sausage while Cathy cooked many pancakes. We brought maple syrup from home. After breakfast, our plan was to head to Taneum Creek to find a place to play and see the sad empty cabin. We stopped on the road climbing up Taneum Canyon to listen to the water racing down the hill in the old concrete flue. This is the source of water to irrigate the upper Kittitas Valley and then, with Colby as lookout for holes in the now unpaved road we headed up Taneum Creek. The road was full of tire damaging holes so Cathy and Colby had to be my extra eyes. As we approached the first stop, I could see a trailer camping there so I drove past to the next. This one I crossed off because of the dead animal Cathy and I had come upon two weeks ago, but maybe if I walked further in there might be a place for us. I did and yes there was a perfect place to wade and rock look. We played for over an hour until the wind and sun tired us out. We return to the house and the kids announce that they are extremely hungry! We had bought a pound of sausage and one of ground lamb in town. I had used a quarter of the sausage for breakfast so now I cooked all of this meat together. We found some spices in the cupboard to add to the meat mixture. I set this aside and took a

476

thawed 16 oz package of French fries and cut them into little cubes. I fried up these cubes along with a package of root vegetables and then added the meat mixture and heated it through. It worked!!! Colby and B---- devoured the stuff!!! So cool! All you have to do to get them to eat is starve them beforehand! The Thorp Fruit Stand was our last attraction of the day; here are treats and shopping for stuff like old Nancy Drew books. More game playing time on the Airbnb's screen porch. Actually, the best game time we have ever had with Colby and B---- together. I will remember this experience for as long as my memory will allow me to. We played Uncle Fred's version of gin rummy and the kids loved it; there up in Heaven Fred Booth must have been grinning down at us. I loved this so much, Cathy laughed so hard and beautifully, I was so happy for us all… Bedtime prayer-time song singing-time… And to think Cathy and I were almost ready to head home this evening, thank you God for this blessing of staying here for tonight!

July 17th. Yes more broken sleep but this is the last of it. We have breakfast of left over pancakes, ham sandwiches, and anything else left over. We pack up, load the car, and head to Ellensburg for Starbucks for us and gasoline for our car. On the way toward home, Cathy texts with Sheryl Leavitt and she shares even more memories of her Thorp school years with us. B---- tells us all about this story she is putting together; it an epic full of conflicts in a universe that would rival Star Wars. She explains each character, their powers, and lineage in a complicated family tree structure. Wow! We drive until they are delivered home again and we find ourselves at our home too. Cathy and I laid on our couch together and napped for hours…

***

Monday July 20, 2020. We have a 7:00am appointment at Dr. Parikh's office to remove my sutures. So here is back-story: I was to have my sutures removed two days ago on the morning of Saturday 18th. Dr. P attempted to first remove them from my left eyelid and found that half of the eyelid itself had not fused together; he stopped at that point telling me to wait until Monday to give it more time. I was at nine days past my surgery at that point. I guess I was a slow healer, so we waited until today. Just a note, removing sutures hurts just shy of the pain level of getting a shot in your eyelid. This time I was prepared though, I had taken two ibuprofen pills and a yellow pill one-hour before. It was uncomfortable but not as bad as two days ago; Dr. P removed all the sutures from my left eyelid (except one small area) and my upper lip, but had the same non-fusing problem on half of my right eye. We will try again this Thursday the 23rd at 7am. We chatted with Dr. P (who now refers to me as his special patient) and Cathy asked if he did breast reduction; yes he does. My upper lip looks great and I am using Scar-away strips to reduce scarring. Most of my right eyelid is free of suture and all of my left. I am so looking forward to healing all the way so I can wash my face again without fear…

***

Friday July 24, 2020. Cathy and I had our appointment with Dr. Parikh yesterday at 7:00am. The office was quiet but Stacey told us the day before it was full of building problems. She explained, "They are doing construction on the upper floors of the building and accidently cut a water pipe that flooded our blood lab and knocked down some of the overhead lights." Stacey takes us back to room five and Dr. Parikh comes in. He goes right to cutting out the remaining sutures out of both eyelids. He tells me, "All done, you healed well and I think this is the best eyelid lift I have done!" We chat about the facelift work he has quoted me, he tells me I can have anything I want done; it is a blanket price. He starts going over my face telling me how he will make an incision below my chin and I might want to have my chin shaved down. Suddenly panic is right at the edge of my thoughts. Dr. P explains, "Put a deposit on a surgery date, we are booking in October and you can move it around if need be." Cathy and I look at each other, who should get the next date: her or me? As Dr. Parikh turns to leave us to go give a consult in the next exam room, he tells us, "I need so see you back in three weeks for pictures." Cathy and I walk to check with Stacey about an appointment in three weeks and book another surgery date. We chat with Stacey as several patients come into the waiting room. Cathy asks about what she needs to get ready for her surgery and what I might need for my next surgery. Stacey's causal tales of all these procedures gives us confidence that she and Dr. P do these things routinely. We book the date for my follow up (August 13th) and (Oct 22nd) with a $500 deposit, we don't commit to who will use it, but it sure looks like it might be me... I suddenly wonder just what have I done? It felt so right back in the exam room and right up to the minute Stacey took our deposit, but now I wonder about me again. There is a new trepidation moving around in my mind as I drive us home. Something is changing the 'me' that is 'me'; I'm trying to understand what this shifting foundational feeling within my psyche is doing to who I am to become...

A whole new veil has been lifted from my consciousness. The surgery was a 'transition victory,' a validation action really, but even more than this a no-turning-back milestone, because now there truly is a future. In this last handful of days, my body has become truly home to Cadance Alane. Before this surgery, all I could see in the mirror was an immutable shell that was forever male. A shell Cadance didn't own because she just couldn't; the conflict was too great, the discord too painful. No way out in life, but somewhere in this last handful of days a crack formed in that shell and it was changed. IT WAS CHANGED! Cadance could own this shell; she could flow into each crafted recognizably female portion and be one mind and body. This was subtly taking place day by day and that foundation being built was now very real; I am becoming her and she me.

***

Tuesday July 28, 2020. Too hot! We didn't sleep at all well last night. I clipped out a knot poking out from my lip on the left side. The stitch was white and when I clipped out the knotted end the rest slid down inside. I also clipped off another loose end near the knot. I had checked with doctor first and sent him a picture; he said it was okay to do. He also told me earlier that any blue sutures I could just pull out.

I want to remember that I felt odd at my last orthodontic appointment on July 22nd. On this appointment, I was told I didn't have to use elastics anymore; my new aligners don't even have hooks for them. Tina popped off the buttons so no more little rubber bands in my mouth... I feel so mixed about it. I was so used to playing with them and making them squeak that I miss them. Also, it was so amazing to be able to put my lower jaw out beyond my front teeth. I worry that without the rubber bands my jaw will move back... On the bright side, I can now speak much clearer.

This last Thursday I got out the last of my sutures, it took two weeks for me to finally heal enough to allow it. The surgeries on my face are healing but I still have some black and blue under my eyes. My upper lip is also turning down again, it is so sad to see the fullness of my lip slid away. I still have a little more lip fullness than I did but this loss is still disappointing. Doctor recommended being conservative and I agreed (he made a point about having seen some bad lip lifts lately). At the same time in the OR, he told me if I wasn't satisfied he would do the whole thing over for free; I hope he remembers because I think I'm going to need it...

***

Monday August 10, 2020. Healing stuff: It has been five weeks this Thursday, on which I happen to have an appointment with Dr. P for pictures. I don't know how good I'll look. I still have a red scar line under my nose with bumps on either side. The bumps are the ends of buried sutures on either side of my scar. On my right the bump was full of pus and on my left I keep clipping off white suture as my body pushes it out little by little as the swelling goes down. As that swelling goes down, my lip reveal grows less... My eyelid scars are fading nicely, but little raised bumps come and go on the scar on the right eyelid. I push them down and that seems to take care of it for a while. The one big problem is the eyebrow on my right side has drooped down and needs to go higher to maintain symmetry; otherwise one eye looks hooded. Hopefully Dr. P will be able to fix this in October as he does my facelifts. I have become very cognizant of the width of the bridge of my nose and may have to have it done along with everything else. As far as pain goes, only my lip is sore. I have tried scar gel, silicon scar strips, and Vaseline to lessen the scar color and soreness. The silicon scar gel by Aroamas seems my best hope at soothing the scar. My three times daily routine is to clean my face including the under nose scar with a Stridex pad and dry with gauze then repeat. My face has been so dry and flaky since the surgery that I have to scrub off the dead skin and use face cream. I then apply scar gel to both eyelids and my under nose scar each time. I shower normally including scrubbing my face with a light sisal scrub pad; this seems fine. During these last weeks I have taken one Fluconazole pill because of the pressure pain between my eyes across the bridge of my nose; this is something I normally do whenever I have to take antibiotics. And it worked; in the morning the pressure was gone.

Car stuff: We had the oil changed in our car at the dealership. It was an affirming outing when our service advisor (Cage), who clocked me as a woman talked down to me. He explained that we needed a valve adjustment. Looking right at me he used the simplest words to describe what valves were and why cars needed them. As he was talking down to me I realized that I was having an amazing female affirming experience. I didn't push back just thanked him and said we didn't have time today to do it. Cathy laughed after we walked to the waiting area, "There you go, girly!"

Trip to visit Quince stuff: We miss Quince so much! This awful Covid disaster of the last six months is so carefully manipulated and full of fear that we need to somehow break out to see him. So many plans: Corey offered to fly up here and stay five days with us. Cathy and I were even thinking about breaking our rule on flying. Why didn't we just drive? Bathrooms in so many of the places that we would stop at were closed to the public. I didn't feel passable to use the women's restrooms along the Interstate and didn't feel safe in the men's restrooms. The long and short of it is we didn't feel that we could ask Corey to take the chance of flying with Q... Cathy and I will just have to suck it up and drive...

Transition stuff: Cathy has wanted to have her breasts reduced in size for twenty years; a running joke with us is she would gladly trade with me. It is just another way we were matched together. In my many searches for gender affirming plastic surgery for myself, I had come across La Belle Vie cosmetic surgery center right here in Tukwila. This is the longtime home of Dr. Tony Mangubat and Dr. Megan Dreveskracht (she is a recent addition in last four years). Dr. Megan was new and Cathy called and got an appointment with her for today. We waited in our car in their parking lot for an hour past our appointment time of 2:30 before Doreen (she does scheduling and manages the office) lead us to an exam room. A tolerable lady named Grace took Cathy's information down. She was mildly pleasant and listened to Cathy's explanations of what she would like to have done. Cathy was given an open-in-the-front gown to change into, then she seated herself in the center-stage exam chair and we waited for Dr. Megan. Dr. Megan entered the room and introduced herself and asked what brought Cathy to see her. Cathy explained that she was tired of back, shoulder, and neck pain from her heavy breasts. Dr. Megan said okay and had Cathy stand up to do some measurements. She measured from the notch at the bottom of the neck to each nipple and then from each nipple to the base of the fold under each breast. Dr. Megan is direct and self-assured. She explains what the surgery would involve, how long it would take (2 to 3 hours), what the anesthesia would be, and what the recovery would be like (four weeks of no lifting, sleeping at 45 degree level). She talked about possible complications, she doesn't use drains, what the incisions would look like, she has never had to do a free nipple graft, and would keep in mind to go as small a cup size as possible (C cup). It will be four to six weeks before the swelling goes down enough to start to see what the resulting cup size will be and a year before finally settling down to a stable cup size. Cathy would need to wear a surgical bra but could take small breaks. Cathy was told she would need a mammogram and doctor clearance. With all the serious stuff out of the way, we settled down to chat with Dr. Megan. It was pleasant and she learned about us and we about her. She had a baby seven and a half months ago and her family hasn't been able to see it yet. Cathy commiserated, adding about us not being able to see little Quince. Time to go, we are pointed to Doreen who keeps the schedule and orders Dr. Megan around the office with a management flair. Doreen has the price list quote ready ($8865) and told us September has several open dates, a $1000 deposit is needed and payment is to be made at the pre-surgery appointment. Cathy is certainly impressed by Dr. Megan. The only failing is they don't seem to be interested in us as people. We look unique and have a good story, but there is no touchy-feely here. This time that we are in could be to blame and most certainly is. A toxic time driving everyone to be self-contained and self-centered. I did long for someone here to care…

***

Tuesday August 11, 2020. Happy Birthday in heaven Mom… She would be 96 years old here on earth. It has been 41 years since she passed. Hazel, David, Dorothy, and finally Charley. I had never thought about it before, he was the last surviving member of his little family. Memories are all mixed with images of today and so many images of yesteryears.

Cathy is settled in on having breast reduction surgery in just a few weeks, just like I was about my eyes. I don't know if it will astonish her as mine did me. We have much to juggle with the idea to drive down to San Diego. There is something new to consider; Corey's sitter may have had contact with someone who has Covid. I want to remember the experience of Cathy's consultation something very important will come from this…

***

Thursday August 13, 2020. Cathy has a date for her surgery and we will be back by Labor Day to meet it. She has to have a mammogram and a release from her GP. I got her to act on scheduling one and today she called to get her doctor to write a release. There was a panic when the doctor's office told Cathy, "You will have to come in and see the doctor in person." Cathy responded, "We are to leave for San Diego in just a few days. How soon can she see me?" The short answer was, "3:30 today." So, we race down to Tacoma all the while Cathy is fretting about gate-keeping. I was thinking just how important this surgery is to her as mine was to me. Good news! Cathy got her letter at that appointment and is all ready to go; her body problem will be completely addressed in just a few weeks. There will be pain, but also healing and in the end done is done giving relief. Me, on the other hand is an open question to when my body problem will ever be given relief... I rejoice for her but mourn my situation.

***

Saturday August 15, 2020. We had a pool party at Casey's for his belated birthday. Linda finally got to go into the pool... Yesterday, we had Colby all day long so very cool! The first thing he wanted to do here was play cards. We played all day long, gin, Careers, and Can't Stop. He and I even played Paddle Battle. The most fun in so long. We did Starbucks and I made camp food; Colby watches me cook, telling me he just can't make it like I do... We just had the best time since May.

***

Tuesday September 1, 2020. In the time since I last journaled we have driven to Corey's and returned safely. We left home on August 21st and slept in our own bed on August 31st. On to our trip and visit with Corey and family:

The big barrier for me in driving to San Diego is finding bathrooms along our route. Other barriers are finding gluten-free food, avoiding protests, and staying in motels. For memories sake, I'll review the conditions making these barriers almost a showstopper to us even attempting to travel this familiar route to Grandson Quince's home. Covid has done much to closet us in our house; it has closed bathroom facilities, restaurants, restricted motels, and limited store hours. The main problem is the single-use bathrooms we normally use as we travel are all closed to us. Starbucks has long been our trusted rest stop as most have single-use restrooms and are open very late hours. So here is the deal; I have avoided my fear of using public facilities matching the letter 'F' on my driver's license by using non-gender specific single-use facilities. My fear comes in the form of violence against my person from some burly husband. Cathy even has a map on her phone pointing to the location of each Starbucks or single-use place all along I-5. I don't feel that I pass enough to be confident in the women's restroom and do pass enough to be totally uncomfortable in the men's restroom. In fact, it really bothers me to go into the men's room now, to the point that it triggers my dysphoria in the same panicky way that kept me out of the boy's locker-room years ago. I just don't belong there and couldn't go in. At the same time, my fear of being violently outed or just shocking little girls with their moms nearby is huge. Most rest stops along the freeway are multi-stall and, although Starbucks are open, their restrooms are not. Corey wanting us to come visit; he felt Quince would just love us being there but he understood that we couldn't fly. Each time Cathy has flown, she has had tooth trouble to the point of losing a tooth completely. I had fear of TSA scanners marking me for close inspection. Cathy has breast reduction surgery on September 17th with a pre-op appointment on the 8th. The only two weeks we could make the drive and visit was August 21 to September 4th. We just have to find a way somehow. The motels we normally stay in are open, but with no gluten-free food available and the gluten-free restaurants we counted on have been driven out of business. Our answer to this is to pack three days of sandwiches along with snack stuff. The restroom problem lingers; Cathy tries to call Starbucks to enquire with very little luck. Several are closed altogether, and what is left close early now anyway. I actually ponder the idea of getting adult diapers; this just shows how big the issue is I am facing. There doesn't seem to be an answer other than just using the ladies' room and I am so torn about this.

Friday we get up just after 7:00am and get busy. I pack the trunk, check the oil, and Cathy packs the rest of the car. Cathy waits in the car while I bar the front door and leave by the basement door to join her, it is 10:30am. No, I didn't get diapers so I have forced the issue; at least I have tried to force it. Traffic is unnaturally light because of Covid, and my mind is still dwelling on my problem. Jansen Beach, Oregon, is three hours from home; I don't drink anything with the idea of making it to the Starbucks there, which we knew was open. We stop at the Toutle River rest stop for Cathy; the place was very busy and when I see men, women, and kids all over the place, I just can't get the courage to leave the car. I need to go to the bathroom, but feel I can make it to Jansen Beach. We use the restroom there and buy drinks for the road. I have used the ladies' room a couple of times near home, but only when Cathy checked to see if they were empty. Leaving Jansen Beach, we motor all the way down to Albany where we try another Starbucks to find its lobby closed tight. A Fred Meyer was nearby and we both really had to go to the bathroom so we stopped and I thought this is it, I am doomed. What we found was a single use all gender restroom and then we added Fred Meyer to our list of places to make rest stops. This was our rigor now and it worked. The rest stop in Canyonville had a single used bathroom and we just needed to make it to our motel in Medford. So, this worked all the way down to Lathrop, California. We left Lathrop at 9am and stopped at Buttonwillow at noon. Here I was forced to use the ladies' room, it was a dash in to an empty restroom, use the handicap stall, and get out. No problem, other than a lot of anxiety and we were greeted as 'Hi ladies as we came in. So yes, I did use several ladies' rooms but they were always empty and I figure as long as I could just get into a stall I was okay. Still upon leaving my fear would always be to hear 'it's a man call the police.' Cathy did show me the trick of using the ladies' restroom side closest to the where the big semi-trucks were parked at public rest areas; they were usually empty because most truckers are guys. Other women in the restroom have never challenged me while I was in a stall or waiting to use a stall. I would become undone on our trip back home from this fear and dysphoria it triggers. It would happen at a Chevron station just off the freeway. We have discovered that many Chevron stations had outside facilities that worked pretty well. I pulled around the side of the station only to find they were the four-stall type of rest rooms. I needed to go and from our car I watched three young dark-haired ladies enter right when Cathy entered the restroom. I couldn't just go in with all those women inside waiting to get to a stall and I desperately did not want to use the men's side. I

486

surrendered; pulled my hair into a tight ponytail, put on dark sunglasses, and a hat, so I would look masculine. I headed toward the guy's door all the while my mind was rebelling at the action I was about to take. The door from the ladies' room opened and the three young women came out and lingered near the men's room in the shade of a tree there. Next a thin androgynous young woman with a short hair-cut literally marched out of the ladies' room turned and marched right into the guys' room while the other three women looked on. This all occurred as I had begun to walk from our car to the restrooms. At this point, I should have just turned into the ladies' room that was where I belonged, but I didn't and I greatly regret it. I marched into the guy's room to find both stalls occupied. The young androgynous woman had finished in a stall, exited, and hurried out past me, I took their stall. I sit always now and while I was there I heard congratulatory shouts from the young women outside for their friend's brave act. It dawned on me he was an FtM and had just got up the courage to use the right restroom for his true gender. My heart sank and my world collapsed; I was the failure here. I didn't have the courage to be who and what I am, it would have been so cool if only I had just done as he had done with the help of his friends. I returned to our car heartsick; this is all so real even as I deny it out of weakness, day by day. More and more, it is not other people who out me, it is I myself doing it. I worry about my voice sounding masculine and just mumble to cover it; I seek body modifications to give me confidence to be in the world I already belong to. This is a hard path to travel but I must travel it. I belong to the female world; there is no question or middle ground here. I can't hold onto an untrue bridge to being male. How odd that I tried to do just little bits over time to feminize, resulting in me not entering female spaces while my mind screamed at me for being in male spaces. After we left that Chevron station I suddenly and convulsively screamed, the irony of what had happen brought overwhelming mental pain, in other words it triggered me beyond tolerance. In Medford's Fred Meyer, my cashier lady was a pretty trans woman taller than I am; she desperately wanted to sign me up for a Fred Meyer reward card, just another reminder.

Our stay in San Diego began with backing into the garage to unload with Quince dancing around giggling with delight. It is hot in the eighties with humidity in the eighties. Corey and Quince both are so very welcoming to us; Melinda is somewhere in the house doing something else. Corey has reset the middle bedroom back into being our bedroom and with an air conditioner/dehumidifier, which is happily and loudly cooling our room. We unpack and play with little Q. Our days start at seven with Quince knocking on our door to come in and snuggle in our bed with us. He and I watch three episodes of *Paw Patrol* until Corey comes to take Quince downstairs to his caregiver Heather. We get along okay with Heather; she isn't interested very much outside of making sure Quince is in the bathroom hourly. Both Cathy and I work at being friendly but it becomes clear she is here for Quince and nothing else. It's okay really; she is quick to let us totally entertain him while she looks at her phone and keeps track of bathroom breaks. She also takes care of feeding little Q. So we get up, shower, and dress, without hurrying each morning. We seldom see Melinda at all; she has an office in the empty bedroom and seldom leaves it. Corey has done the same as Casey in keeping their wives in isolation while the guys run all the risky errands and do the cooking. Corey, too, spends most of his time in his office doing meetings so it was Nanna, Boppa, and Heather playing with Quince all week. We had big guns with us: a glow in the dark car/track set, the Donald Duck comic books we had saved from when Corey was a kid to read to Q, along with Disney Lego mini-figures to go along with the comics, Lego kits to build, including one Technic kit and ingredients for making banana bread. We played and played; I got down on the floor only to get back up again over and over, we also climbed the stairs over and over. I folded myself into Quince's downstairs closet hideout to build a glow in the dark car track that was very cool. It was sure stuffy in that closet but Quince loved the cars in the dark. Corey would cook us one big breakfast of pancakes with his own banana compote. He would play cribbage with his mom and all of us would play Go Fish sans Melinda. There were multiple Starbucks runs, several store runs, and one Costco run. One day Corey's car was detailed by a nice young lady named Ashley who was from Bremerton, Washington; she turned us on to tight yoga pants with pockets and just assumed I was female. I don't know if people are just being polite to me or if I pass better than I give myself credit for.

So, our stay was only seven days instead of the ten we originally planned. The truth is, Melinda is only tolerant of us for about that long and she perked right up when I said we had to leave early. I did have a little tiff with my daughter-in-law as she poked at me for Quince being so fond of playing with me. She admonished Q for leaving her side as I came downstairs so I just said okay then, and went right back upstairs again... I have two daughters-in-law neither of whom are very excited about me before or after transition. I had seen how Cathy's dad was so loved by both of his daughters-in-law Dale, Marks first wife, and Tamera, Phil's wife; they treasured him. Since I study how the men around me act, and were received, I tried to mimic Cathy's dad's decorum expecting like results from my daughters-in-law, but wow it was just the opposite... Our new benchmark is to stay no longer than one full week. This amount of time seems to be within Melinda's tolerance. As our car was packed Corey and little Q hung out together outside with us, Q even made a place in our back seat to ride in case we said he could come with us! Love you Q!!!

Our trip home would, as I said, bring my undoing at a gas station. We stayed in Lathrop and from there drove the rest of the way home in one stretch. Both of us slept so wonderfully in our own beds that night... This is the third day since returning and Cathy's rash, which we attributed to the heat and humidity of California is steadily fading. With luck, it will not be an issue for her appointment on this coming Tuesday. Cathy's breast reduction surgery is no small thing coming in just two weeks we both will be praying.

***

Tuesday September 8, 2020. Cathy's rash wasn't an issue; the pre-op appointment was with a MA named Jasmine filling us both in on all that will happen next week on surgery day. She is also asking her own set of questions of Cathy. Cathy is very prepared; she has a copy of the mammogram finding and the clearance from her Primary Care Doctor for surgery, just in case they didn't happen to get to their office by mail. Yes, they both were needed; for some reason the two reports didn't get delivered to their office. Score Cathy! I offer my name and Cathy offers my relation to her as 'wife' to Jasmine for her to record in Cathy's chart. It is dawning on Cathy that this is really going to happen, and now the excitement is beginning to build up. I know this feeling well now, having a problem for like always, then suddenly, there is this physical correction available and it's going to happen right now! Cathy stops at the reception desk to pay for the surgery in full before we leave. Cathy is on cloud nine, but we will be back tomorrow for my consult with Dr. Megan. I had this idea that it would be good to have Dr. Megan on my list of surgeons also. I would have all of Cathy's experience with her to give me confidence and Cathy would get one more chance to chat with Dr. Megan Dreveskracht in person before surgery day since she would be at my side tomorrow.

***

Wednesday September 9th: 2:00. My plan was to explore lots of FFS (Facial Feminization Surgery) questions and then maybe BA (Breast Augmentation or enhancement) information. If Cathy needed to ask a question or two about her upcoming surgery, she could do this also. My plan began to fail with simply filling out the paperwork while we waited out in the building's common lobby. The lady seemed to be confused as to what form I was to fill out. She came out three times to add to my paper pile or delete from it. Finally, we were taken back to an exam room (the one Cathy had been in the day before) and a nice medical assistant named Grace help us to straighten out the paperwork. She asked about face or breast being a priority and then said she would bring in the sizing stuff either way. Cathy is sitting in the corner chair and I take my turn in the center-stage exam-chair waiting for Dr. Megan. She pops in suddenly with, "Good to see you and how are you two doing?" There is a pile of breast forms in a plastic crate sitting on the counter. A pile of them! Cathy had already poked at one of them just before doctor came in; hard to resist not to. I tell

Dr. Megan I am interested in FFS stuff and breast enhancement. She quietly confides she doesn't do face stuff; that is left to her partner Dr. Mangubat (the scary older doctor) so I can come see him on another day. I tell her cool, I am so into getting information on breast implants with you! At this point, something in my brain sort of stutters to a stop, leaving me on autopilot. Clouds decent on my ability to think let alone speak clearly. Dr. M tells me to stand and slip off my shirt, so she can measure me. I comply then ask my bra also? Yes, that too. I am standing bare-chested with a female doctor judging my insignificant little breasts; for as tall as I am I feel very small. I always keep my chest hidden even from me. It is traumatic; I haven't had to face anyone bare-chested for many years. Never has my whole transitioning identity, as female, been stripped naked to be judged. She tells me I already have quite a good amount of breast tissue, more than she is used to seeing. I focus on the comment it gives me an anchor to hold onto as she makes her measurement from each nipple to the crease below my neck. She helps me into a tight bra she uses to size different breast forms and has me slip my t-shirt back on. She chats idly with us for a few minutes and I am pretty sure it is to let me calm down. Breast form sizing is kind of like what the eye doctor does as she asks which lens is clearer 1 or 2, A or B. Dr. Megan hands me a breast form to slip into the bra and quickly learns that I am not very good at centering the sticky forms on my nibble. To my relief, she steps up to center them herself; I am tall and she is beautifully short so I bend my knees. She starts with smaller forms asking me what I thought of each from looking in the mirror. I am lost really with the realization of this huge step I find myself taking. The only person to have ever seen me with breast curves has been Cathy. Thankfully, both Dr. M and Cathy offer to help me. Cathy doesn't think the first forms at 375cc fill out my chest width and Dr. M agrees. She tells me to get the width I need, we should use a medium profile form and since I am so tall I could easily carry 475 to 500cc under the muscle. She works those two forms between my breast tissue and the bra, the forms stick to my skin so it is a chore to center each of them. My left breast is smaller than my right and using a 500cc on it and a 475cc in the other evens them out. As Dr. Megan says, they are sisters but not twins. I have been looking in the mirror without my glasses and ask Cathy for them. This does no good, as they just steam up as soon as I put them on from me being so nervous. When I do look at my reflection in the mirror, I see someone else looking back and I really like what she looks like. Cathy approves; also this lightens my heart as we both move forward step by step. This is a milestone in my transition, one that I never thought I would reach. The whole time, in these last fifteen years with my therapist Sandy, I have always approached the idea of transition in tiny steps. In my mind I held onto the concept that I could hop back any number of those steps at any time and stand still. My world was full of examples of reasons to do just this; someone's failure in their transition could be found if I looked long enough on the web. What I wouldn't fully face, as I moved along, was even though I held on to that concept of reversal, I didn't actually possess the option to use it. That concept is still with me, as broken as it is, as I find surprise in a mirror that my continuing transition is marching along leaving the male world well behind me. The idea of having permanent breast curves, which pretty much completely locks me out of men's spaces, doesn't hold as much fear as that reversal concept demands. On the contrary, those curves complete Cadance; they open a world up to her. The only problem is recognizing the extent of needing such things. I have my face to do now also my bust, and even lower. All that I ask of myself is to finish it within the coming year and not be afraid anymore... Cathy has even pointed out with faces being masked perhaps I should move breast enhancement higher up in priority it would give a better clue as to my gender.

***

Tuesday September 15, 2020. My upper lip has refused to heal on either side. The left side has abscessed several times and I have had to lance it and then painfully squeeze the pus out per Dr P's texted instructions. These two spots are the knotted ends of a buried absorbable suture brand-named Vicryl. Vicryl is a braided material as opposed to a monofilament material. Natalie called my attention, three

492

days ago to the fact that I had a constant soreness from being stitched up from my orchi. Now, I have sore spots from stitches on my lip. She had seen on the television show *Botched* that this sort of thing had happened to another plastic surgery patient. Even after the stitch had dissolved, the soreness remained and was only cured by removing the tissue that had come in contact with the Vicryl product. I don't know for sure that the white braided stitch that my body has steadily pushed out little by little is this Vicryl stuff and I need to find out. A call in to Dr. P and yes it is Vicryl. Good to know for future surgery, but now what?

This whole issue had been weighing on me along with the issue of breast implants in general. Two very important problems: If I can't tolerate stitches then no more surgeries and I openly wonder if Casey and/or Corey will be able to tolerate me having a bust. Does it become a question of trading off transition for family relations and can I tolerate that? Having a bust really does cross a line in transiting; it is hard for people to ignore this visual key of gender identity and additionally it is also very affirming for me.

I am in such trouble future surgery wise... My very tired brain needs a nap, as does Cathy's. After our nap, the full force of what just happened triggers me into a sudden mean depression pit. I voiced the doom of my situation and it shakes out in the meanest way. One that pokes at Cathy having something I now physically can't. So, I can't have plastic surgery because I don't heal, I can't transition so what is the point, it is all over for me.

Cathy broke down with tears in her eyes saying, "I will not have surgery either! Every time you look at me you will be reminded of what you couldn't have." The emotional dam had burst. I realized the meanness of my words and fought them back saying, I was wrong, it was hurt talking, you have to have your surgery simply because if you don't, every time I look at you or you look at me I'll be reminded of the happiness I denied you. There has to be some way for me, for now it is your turn to shine. Right now I am just a little lost.

***

Wednesday September 16, 2020. In the morning we are up early for appointments with our friend Natalie for 90 minutes massages. My mood is even darker now and I resolve to not let it spoil our time with our friend if I can help it. It is such fun to chat with her as she unwinds our knots, both physical and mental. Natalie was one the first outsiders I came out to four years ago. She is highly skilled in physical therapy and near a master's degree in counseling therapy of the mental kind. Her mother is on hospice and Natalie has life issues that need to be worked through with her mother before time runs out. Today she has reached a truth in this journey with her mom and wants to share. "I've come to understand my mother is an apple tree that I am continually trying to get pineapples from." She tells us. "She isn't capable of giving me what I am in need of." Natalie explains by going on, "I have to face this and understand I have developed a new extended family to make up for what the two of us can't do for each other. This is the source from which to fulfill the void I have." Natalie, Cathy, and Cady spent over three hours doing girl talk, laughing, and trying to solve each other's problems. I hope Cathy and I are part of her new extended family, one that brings her comfort, as she sure brings us comfort both physically and mentally… I have come to understand that God passes on wisdom continually to me in every life lesson I am party to. This includes our time with Natalie; her revelation about finding support from a new extended family isn't lost on me. I wonder why has God given this to me at this time? After our time with Natalie, we shop for more supplies to last us and comfort us through Cathy's surgery. Tomorrow will start early; Cathy is to be at the surgical entrance at 8:15.

***

Thursday September 17, 2020. Cathy's surgery day: We are up by 6:00 to follow a plan Cathy has all laid out for the morning. She hasn't eaten or drunk anything since ten o'clock last night and neither have I. We will continue this fast until she is home again this afternoon. Cathy has to shower with special cleaning supplies then dry her top with a special disposable medicated towel. All this week, I have met each day by acknowledging that 'today was not that day.' This morning to my fatally nervous mind I had to acknowledge that 'today is that day.' I am nervous, fearful, lonely, and a little jealous all rolled into one. On the balance, Cathy is more excited than fearful. With my help her shower is completed and she is squeaky clean and dressed in the new extra loose PJs that she bought for the occasion. They button up in the front and should be easy to get into and out of. Cathy wants me to have something to eat, but that is not in my plan nor is coming back to wait in our house during her surgery. I'll wait as close to her as possible, one nice thing is, even with Covid, because this OR is in-house Cathy can have one person with her right up to surgery. This is such a blessing! I can help remember Cathy aftercare instructions given at this time and add any forgotten questions she wanted to ask. La Belle Vie cosmetic surgery is just ten minutes from our home so we leave home at 8:00 and arrive ten minutes later. I park at the side door as instructed, we say a little prayer, and put on our tie-dye masks. Cathy grabs the tote bag she has packed and as we approach the door it opens. Colleen one of the nurses, is waiting for us with Covid questions and to take our temperatures; we both pass. Colleen is somewhere in her late forties and will be Cathy's intake nurse. Just as we enter the building, a man who is to our right at a workstation looks at me and says, "Didn't I just see you in here the other day?" I didn't remember seeing him, but Cathy and I were here at the front office several times in the last month; so yes, that was me! We are walked into an exam room and Cathy gets the center-stage chair; I am just happy to there in the corner as support. Colleen works away at all the medical questions that are-needed-to-be asked before surgery like 'what are you here for'. When she gets to the ones about drinking or vaping Cathy answers no and I add we are kind of boring people. She laughs and adds that is how she replies to that question too! We commiserate about the social aspect of being boring; it was good for an icebreaker between her and us. Cathy and I as a couple work hard at trying to draw people we meet closer to us relationship wise; in other words be friendly toward them. Colleen hands Cathy a paper gown asking her to undress from the neck down she can keep her PJ pants on. Colleen tells me to put her clothes and shoes on the counter. I make sure about the shoes going on the counter part, since in my mind floor dirty counter clean, but yes put them on the counter. Cathy also has compression stockings to put on, her regular socks will go back over them, she will walk sock footed into the attached surgical suite (OR). The compression stockings will stay on for the next four days until Cathy has her post-op appointment on Monday. Colleen leaves us with instructions that only Cathy's clothes remain here in the exam room, no cell phones, etc. Cathy had a little box of gluten-free crackers with us because, many times before, she was offered a cracker in recovery but couldn't eat it since it was full of gluten. No personal items, only clothes; I guess I will keep the cell phone and crackers in the bag with me... Dr. Megan Dreveskracht comes in as Colleen leaves us. She is perky, full of energy, and chats with us asking Cathy, "How are you doing? All rearing to go?" Cathy replies with a laugh that Cady is more nervous than she is. Dr. M has a camera with her and takes four before-pictures right in a row then begins to mark the roadmap lines needed for guiding the surgery. Dr. M makes measurement after measurement in a rapid-fire matter until she is finally satisfied. Dr. Megan leaves, telling Cathy, "See you in the OR." The man we saw at the door when we first came in to the building pops in. He introduces himself as Zack and is a nurse anesthesiologist for Cathy's surgery, he needs a little information and would love to answer any questions. We both fall in love with Zack; he is very friendly, pleasant, and calming. He draws us in just as we like to draw other people in to us. We share little everyday things about vitamin B12, and it was a good move to get a shot of it before surgery, and about the MTHF (methylenetrahydrofolate reductase) stuff, it is because of this genetic mutation we both have to be gluten-free. The most important part was that Cathy really liked him and came to trust him. Cathy doesn't remember much about her surgery except the care that Zack offered her stuck in her memory. Zack leaves us to ourselves there in the exam room to look at the framed pictures of poppies on the walls; one was yellow, and the other orange. Soon nurse Grace comes in to explain that the surgery is scheduled to be completed by

11:30; she will call me 30 minutes before the surgery is completed so I can get back here in time to pick Cathy up. We make sure both our cell phone numbers are listed on the call sheet. Grace tells us, "You go that way toward the front exit and Cathy goes this way toward the OR." Cathy tells her she needs to use the restroom first, so I wait with Grace until Cathy comes back. Grace tells me, "Go ahead give her hug," and I do one last hug... I turn toward the exit sign and then look back to see the door closing on Cathy... It is hard to explain the bond of completeness I have with Cathy. When we are physically separated, I intensely feel the emptiness of the place, which I feel God has made in me for her. My spirit cries for that space to be filled and nothing else fits except Cathy. It is not a dependency; it is a completeness I find with her with me. She is not a possession; it is I who has given her me, in the most loving way. So, I stay in the car and watch the world move ever so slowly around me. People come and go, a disheveled homeless guy wanders aimlessly through the parking lot and turns to stare directly at me; I look away and he wanders on. The radio is just noise. I pray off and on, over and over, until 10:45 comes and I have to break my promise to myself of staying in the parking lot. I drive the ten-minute trip home to use the bathroom as quickly as possible. I lock our front door on the way out only to return as a thought crosses my mind. The antiseptic towel Cathy used also helped the sore on my lip, I return to save the towel for later use. I am back in the parking lot to wait some more. Grace does call me at 11:30 to tell me, "This is your 30-minute warning call." She also tells me to call when I get back to the parking lot and she will let me know if it is time. Well, I am in the parking lot now but wait 15 minutes before calling to tell her that I have arrived. I call and get the front office and they tell me Cathy is still in surgery and I will get a call when she is awake. I began a new wait for a call to come. One hour later at 12:45, I can't wait anymore, no call has come and dread is settling in to a displacing reality. I leave the car carrying the bag with all of Cathy's personal stuff in it. The things she holds as part of her, those things that you very rarely see her without, part of which is her purse and cell phone. I have stuff that Cathy will need and I am going to see what

497

has happened. I enter the front office and ask what has happened? I see Colleen in the background glancing at me then ducking out. I am told that Grace will call me very soon so I march out to sit at the front door. It is getting hot outside, I sit with my entrusted bag and I wait. I begin to think about my official position as spouse/wife to Cathy. Does this title mean as much to the people in that office or have the same weight as title of husband does? In other words, if I were still Cathy's husband would I get better answers from these people? Did I give up a measure of official access to Cathy by my transition? If so I need to understand this and find ways around the loss. Suddenly my phone rings, and it is Grace telling me she will meet me at the front door. The mixed feeling of relief and dread washes over me. I am up in a second at the door just as Grace comes to it. She takes me to the little recovery room where Cathy sits in an almost comatose state. Everyone is gone except Grace and she has been trying to wake Cathy up for the last hour. I talk to Cathy, telling her I am here and she half opens her eye and mumbles in a strange low tone voice. It's a little scary this is the voice I heard from her on the times she would pass out… Grace and I work at bringing Cathy back to the awake world. Dr. Megan comes in to tell me everything went fine and Cathy would soon be awake and leaves. This happened to me at the end of my orchi surgery, the thing ran late because my doctor was late, and I was slow to wake up, so they wanted me out of recovery even before I was ready because other surgeries were right behind me. Grace would like to be done, so we get Cathy fully into the wheelchair, and head out to the parking lot. This was not the original plan, I was to move the car to a special spot but now the idea is to get Cathy home. I am thoroughly on board with this when suddenly I remember I didn't have Cathy's tote bag, the one she entrusted me with. All of her most important stuff gone and me with someone who can't stand up to explain it to! I run ahead of Grace and find the bag where I, in my excitement left it in full view outside on the bench. Thank you God! I move the car so we can sort of roll Cathy out of the wheelchair and into the car. Grace is gone in the wink of an eye and I am left with the car running in the middle of the parking lot. I close Cathy's door and run to the drivers' side and get in. I turn to put Cathy's seatbelt on but she is flat on her back! She must have come to in time to pull the seat back lever. I run to her door and pull the lever and lift her back up. I run to the drivers' side and get in, fasten my seatbelt and then do hers. I remember to put a pillow under the belt to cushion her breasts. Cathy comes in and out of consciousness. I try to encourage her to wake up by talking to her and asking questions. It kind of works, but each time I have to turn the car I also have to hold onto Cathy's shoulder as she will just plop over to whatever side we turn to. It is the strangest drive home, Cathy asking for water and me trying to hold her up. I pull into the driveway and stop at the point where it is the straightest, flattest path to our front steps. I lift Cathy's legs one at time to get them out of the car and onto the ground. She does lift herself up to standing but can't keep from swaying enough to cause her to fall down. I steady her and we walk one step at a time toward the front steps. All this time, I am thinking if she falls I can't begin to catch her in any way that would keep us both from go down; it's a very scary time. Cathy does slowly make each step then into the house and onto a waiting rolly-chair, there she shouts, "I'm home!" I get her safely into the recliner chair and breathe a big sigh of relief. Cathy is pretty much awake now, but will drift off for a few minutes from time to time. I had her take a Tylenol at 1:34 and Zofran at 2:20 per Grace's instructions.

***

Monday September 21, 2020. I found a little bell to give to Cathy to use if she needs something from me. We decided on strict bell etiquette, no over-ringing, under-ringing, and no false alarms. The doctor had told us it is more than okay to take walks. We find that going up to nearby Foster High School and back is all that Cathy can tolerate. The surprising aspect as Cathy's recovery moves slowly along is we both are dead tired and nap on and off all day long. I have been sleeping in the living room on our broken down couch right across from Cathy's recliner. Even though we nap a lot we still sleep through the night. Cathy has to sleep on her back and the recliner is just the thing, but still it is hard for her. We both yearn for our bedroom

499

and our comfortable bed. Cathy has had no bleeding from her stitches or any nausea. This is a great blessing!

Today the 21ˢᵗ was her post-op checkup so we were up for the 9:30 appointment. We are taken to an exam room by medical assist Grace, she chats with us while making notes of Cathy's experiences. Grace leaves as doctor comes in. Dr. Megan Dreveskracht is very pleased with how everything is healing. She removes one layer of tape from all the suture lines then tells us the remaining layer of tape is steri-strips and will come off by themselves. Cathy's nipples look like they have been through a lot there is tape all around the diameter of each of them. Cathy tells me she still has feeling in her nipples, a very good thing.

[I'm going to interject my reactions at this point: I sat in the support chair in the corner watching and listening to Dr. Megan and Cathy's conversation as Dr. Megan removed the tape on Cathy's much reduced breasts. I am holding the blood stained surgical bra in my lap that the doctor had just helped Cathy to take off. Right now, in this moment, I am in a very intimate female space and I don't feel worthy of being in this space. Cathy is a complete natural female having her natural breast reduced by a woman doctor who can relate completely woman to woman with her. What kind of unnatural construct am I in this space, thinking to have my small breast artificially increased in the future by this same doctor? Will she relate to me in the same way or even more pointedly can she? I am only female here because of their consent that I am, as my body doesn't reveal my mind. In a flash, I realize this is what being triggered is like. I am female in a female space, but I also have to grow into that space in steps. The same steps each developing human takes into their gender space. I calm down; I do have a natural place here albeit one that requires faith and strength to grow into... The only unnatural construct was the one I formed of me as a male.]

Dr. M takes after pictures and answers Cathy's questions (Cathy has a list she made). Here are the answers; you can shower now no restrictions, I removed 300 grams on the left and 625 grams on the right for a total of 2 pounds, and yes, I do tummy tucks, but let's get you through this first, the bra size is 38, no pressure on the breast, half side sleep only, nothing went to pathology the tissue looked fine. Dr. M had instructions; you will be swollen for up to two months so use ice and meds, the swelling is mostly on the top of the breast, it really has nowhere else to go, wear the bra 24 hours a day. Dr. M had a warning, "Cathy, everything is going great with your recovery, couldn't be better, the big trouble with this is it will give you a false sense of security and you will overdo, don't overdo! You have lots of sutures deep in your breasts; don't do anything to strain them. If you do, you will come back to a very angry Dr. Megan!" We leave in good spirits and stop at the front desk to make Cathy's next appointment (Oct 8th); the ladies there are super friendly and complement us on our matching tie-dye. What a difference being on the other side of self-paid surgery, when we started they were so cold to us…

So, I realized two big things. Two years ago, I had bottom surgery and now Cathy has had top surgery; kind of unique for a couple in the transgender-world. I had been fitted for breast implants; the total of my implants are in the 900cc range; this is near the same amount Cathy just had removed from her breasts. So, I could have the exact amount added to my breast as Cathy had removed from hers, fulfilling her longstanding offer to do just this. This would be the ultimate intimate physical sharing between the two of us (well okay we do share many other things too, like one of our little fingers are both hooked).

When we return home Cathy has me take after pictures with her phone so she can share them with her support group. It's a Facebook support group for those seeking to have their breasts reduced. Cathy even has several surgery sisters who all had surgery on the same day!

***

Tuesday September 22, 2020. This is Cathy's 5th day of post-op recovery. The swelling looks to be going down. We have iced three to four times a day for 15 minutes each. Cathy controls her pain with ibuprofen four doses of two pills daily. Today, I've noticed her energy level is much higher as well as her spirits; we did outings to Costco, Starbucks, and walked farther doing our short block route. Cathy can also ride comfortably in our car for short trips. We will drive a little farther and see how she does tomorrow; also, tomorrow we will get her a vitamin B shot. Our sleeping arrangement with me on the couch and her in the recliner is tolerable as we are within touching distance. We played *Wizards Unite*, (we so miss our Pogo friends but they have moved on without us) watched *Escape to the Country* on channel 11.4 with Cathy sitting by me on the couch. The new black medical bra is doing its job and Cathy says she is less tight today.

***

Friday September 25, 2020: Cathy's 8th day of recovery. Cathy is comfortable sleeping in the recliner and hesitant to return to our bed. She is a side sleeper and sleeping on her side puts pressure on the sutured breasts especially her right breast; it is the one that had twice as much tissue removed. I have become comfortable sleeping on the couch; I can open my eyes anytime and see how Cathy is doing. I also side sleep and I find that the pressure the couch back cushion gives against my body brings the feeling that Cathy's next to me. The downside of this sleeping arrangement is both of us do not move much during the night and in the morning we both have congested lungs to clear. The upside of sitting up is gravity aids in reducing the swelling. It has cooled down to the mid-fifties at night. We sleep with the windows closed but we each have a fan pointed at us on the low setting. Cathy no longer rests during the day with her feet elevated, she has found that she sleeps better during the night if she doesn't. She does elevate her feet to sleep at night. Cathy has reported sharp shooting pains she calls zingers every now and then during the day. It is almost like a rubber band snapped against her breasts. The pain from these zingers last anywhere from less than a minute to a max of five minutes; it is also notable that they don't wake her up from sleep. The occurrence has been the same over the last few days. We find time to walk each day, at least up to and around the nearby public pool. Cathy enjoys the walk but is ready to rest when we get home. As far as pain medications use Cathy takes four 200mg ibuprofen tablets and a yellow pill right before going to bed. She uses no other meds during the day. She still ices daily but it has become only once a day at this point.

Today was rainy and windy. The gift of rain that so joyously clears out the smoke has switched to an irritant keeping us housebound for another reason. It's a gift to awake each morning to an empty calendar other than reading a book. Cathy has been reading books by Lynette Eason and Lyn Cote. I have read two transgender memoirs *Farm Boy/City Girl* by John (Gene) Dawson and *Trans-formations from Field Boots to Sensible Heels* by Erika Shepard. Their stories were disturbing for me to read, things hit too deeply at home.

Cathy also busies herself by reading her Facebook groups and posts regularly on the 'breast reduction group'. My 'FFS surgery support groups' go on and on but don't give me much relief. Speaking of this, the combination of the two books I have read and the dead end I have hit on surgery options have made me miserable. My scar under my nose is a little better but the raised bump on my left side is hard and painful. I have had confirmation about the suture material Vicryl being the cause of the trouble. Cathy's successful surgery is wonderful, but I am left without a path for mine. I do have a path for breast implants with Dr. Megan, who told me she could do them without using Vicryl. If I do this, it shuts down any path for face work for at least six months and vice versa. It really is a bad place to be in for me and I have to face it every minute of every day. I think I have to get a consult with Dr. Tony Mangubat for his take on FFS.

***

Saturday September 26, 2020. Colby visited us today and we had a lovely time playing cards and enjoying each other. Each day, Cathy is feeling more and more back to her old self. The swelling goes down little by little, her weight hangs around 174 pounds. We took Colby home at 5:00 after feeding him camp food and two dipping eggs with cinnamon toast. We saw the new retaining wall at Casey's, looks good. Casey's household is getting ready for the arrival of their new puppy next week. Never have I before felt the togetherness of his household with each other. It was like walking into a complete family unit where

Cathy and I were just foreign visitors. Colby and B---- were doing tasks assigned by their parents, aimed at the common goal of getting the house ready for the puppy, just amazing. Cathy and I drove home in time for Saturday night games at Grandma Dixon's. Joyce, Linda, Cathy, and Cady all play Yahtzee. Cathy would like to talk about her surgery and how she is progressing with healing, but no opening is made for this. Both Cathy and I know that this evening probably would spin around Linda and Joyce's adventures not ours. Natalie, was right you couldn't get pineapples from apple trees...

***

Sunday September 27, 2020. Today was a beautiful blue skyed early fall day. Cathy and I did our color palette post on Facebook. We feature our color picks in tie-dyed shirts to match our current mood; this time Cathy was wearing a large, tie-dyed t-shirt instead of extra-large, she was so proud and it look very good on her. Cathy's recovery news is a new soreness/tightness on her right side under her arm; she feels a pull when she moves her arm while walking even in a normal walking movement. We are trying ice on the area to see if this helps. We will continue to sleep in the living room to see if this helps.

I truly don't know what to do about surgeries. This troubles my mind day in and day out. I am locked into a desperate search to come to some kind of resolution on this question. The question just keeps getting broader and broader to include the very nature of my transition. Just what do I need to do to be complete? Are the troubles I am having from the surgeries a sign to stop everything and stay as I am? Should I just do nothing and go back to waiting for life to come to an end? I am getting more than just tired from these unanswerable questions; I am sliding down into a pit of hopeless oblivion where I was climbing up toward life not so long ago. It would be so easy to just check out in both mind and body. I see how unified Casey's family has become, and Corey's also. I'm a diminishing presence from them both day by day. I can only speed up this diminishment by further transition actions especially surgery. What price happiness for Cadance, to lose everything now as opposed to losing it in the near future anyway? I want life with Cathy each day and to see myself in the broken mirror knowing I have done all I could to be myself. I want my dysphoria to stop before I lose everything in the battle to stop it. Okay I have vented my soul. Yes, I am in a storm and yes, Cathy is right by my side. I realized I had not come before God using my female name in prayer. I was always 'I' or 'me'; I had subconsciously avoided it, this realization made me sad. It wasn't right, God knows who I am and has put me in this time and place. So now I pray for guidance for Cady and Cathy's transition each night and feel a burden lifted from me. Perhaps tomorrow will bring relief by a consultation by Dr. Tony Mangubat…

***

Monday September 28, 2020. Cathy's right breast just under her arm drained during the night through the bra and onto her pajama top. Extracellular fluid, not bloody or infected, and she has no temperature. There was also a little drainage from her left nipple scar. Cathy says this area is less sore than yesterday, I think we might have pulled it yesterday during pictures. We will do a sponge bath this evening. Cathy emailed a picture to Dr. Megan along with a question this morning, we will see how long it takes to get a response. This is my laser day with Debbie Caddell and I have a consultation with Dr. Tony Mangubat this Wednesday at 4:00. My memory short term and otherwise is getting worse and playing the never-ending game of trying to find the right hormone balance adds to this turmoil. I reach for a word as I speak, it is not there when I need it, and other words I'm certain I know I can't find a way to voice them. I can't spell very common words even if they are just a handful of letters. Normally, I keep mental pictures of the correctly spelled word to pull from, now no picture is available, and I'm stymied. I will say an incorrect word knowing that it isn't the right word and have trouble correcting myself. I will even say the wrong word again just as if I am stuck over and over. Words look foreign to me in reading as if I had never seen them before. So odd, to feel yourself slipping away, so helpless, and so guilty that I waited to transition until it was too late. Soon mentally I will just be an empty shell. I don't know how much time I have left or if the dysphoric stress that is currently draining me is speeding the process up. These last few journals sure have been depressing, we will continue praying for better…

What an afternoon does for a person! I had an appointment at Caddell's with Debbie to laser my scar. I was very worried about being lased with a CO2 fractional laser. Since Debbie directed I be numbed first, I was fearful that this would be the most painful laser procedure I had ever had. I have had many painful laser shots; for some I had our dentist numb me, and for others I used a numbing cream. But mostly I just toughed it out. I was worried that my sore scar would just become a very sore large bluster. I put together a laser kit to take with us of two ice packs, a towel, and aloe gel, then took two ibuprofen pills and one antihistamine pill. We arrived at 1:20 in time for Cathy and me to use the ladies' room. We popped out at the same time to wash our hands and headed to Caddell's door. Cathy was just going to say, "Hi" and then go back to our car, which I carefully parked in a shady spot for her comfort. Hope and Debbie were holding down the fort so to speak, Hope on the phones and Debbie doing everything else. Debbie has become the dearest friend to both Cathy and me ever since we all attended the week long *Esprit Gala* three years ago. Today is controlled chaos at Caddell's. Debbie is pointing Hope in a direction to do some task while at the same time, keeping to her own client schedule. She greets us and points me in the direction of the storeroom for before-pictures of my lip. She picks up her camera and positions me while Hope comes in to be pointed toward a new task. I de-mask because this show is center staged on my lip. After my lip is all documented image-wise, Debbie points me to treatment room #5 right next to the storeroom. This is the largest treatment room they have. Debbie and I chat about what I need done. I tell her my story along with showing pictures of the damage from the Vicryl. She has me lay down on the treatment table to put numbing cream on my lip. I also confide that I am nervous about the pain level. She buzzes out to get the laser and comes back wheeling in an Ellman Matrix LS-40 fractional CO2 freestanding laser unit. She parallel parks it next to the table I am lounging expectantly on, telling me to relax for 45 minutes and she will be back. She also tells me not to touch the cling wrap she has put over the numbing cream on my face. Just before she leaves she asks me if I need anything and yes my phone from my bag. I lay on the treatment table staring at the machine with its fix laser head on the end of a positional articulated arm. It is so different from the other lasers. They all have a flexible waveguide ending in a hand-piece that the operator moves as needed. Picture yourself shaving with an electric razor moving it all around your face (or leg), then picture that razor fixed to an arm that has to be moved each time the area is cleared. The room is steadily getting cooler and cooler. I realize I have my phone so I text Cathy to tell her what is going on at the moment (and to get hearts and happy faces). She commiserates with me about the wait and tells me I should take a nap. I close my eyes then another realization comes into my mind my phone has a camera. I take pictures of the laser machine staring at me, I take pictures of my cling wrapped upper lip, and I take pictures of the kitchen witch right above me hanging from the ceiling. Debbie likes to hang one of these in each treatment room and has done so for time out of mind. During my time at Caddell's (I started treatments in 2006), the treatment rooms have been referred to by color, number, and the name of operator who uses that room the most. So today I am in the purple Debbie five room. After my picture taking has become old hat, I have another realization. I can search the Internet, so of course, I search about the laser next to me. This turns out to be not such a good idea after all. Google tells me all about the laser drilling hundreds of little holes down through your epidermis into your dermis skin layer. You can expect blood to come to the surface and some oozing during healing… Oh okay… I decide I'm done searching, I'll just take what comes at this point. I begin to wonder if my lip is numb at all but completely resist touching to test it; after all, Debbie did ask me not too. I have been waiting almost 30 minute alone in anticipation of the treatment when a knock at the door brings Hope in to have me do the Covid paperwork we missed. She wanders out and closes the door. I have been listening to the sounds coming from the reception area where Hope is making and answering phone calls. I hear her answering questions I know the answers to and I hear information about prices I had no idea about. Half a leg treated by laser for hair removal cost $275 per treatment, after four treatments it drops down to $250 per treatment. I have spent a lot of money here being treated from head to toe, but now the max charge for any treatment for laser hair removal is far less for me. And when I started back in 2006, prices were only a little lower than they are now. I don't remember by how much, but I could look in my journal though. Hair removal is a very expensive cost for transgender women; you get all the dark hairs you can with a laser and then settle down for years to get the rest with electrolysis. Marsha charged me $60 an hour over my 1000 plus hour history of electrolysis with her. Sandy my therapist, charged me $60 an hour over my ten-year history with her. Both were bargains at the time as prices have more than doubled. If you figure I saw Sandy once a week normally for ten years that equates to over five hundred one hour appointments; I did the same with Marsha but with two-hour appointments. Wow!!! I am becoming anxious now; I want to get this over with. I have waited 50 minutes when a knock at the door brings Debbie in.

She looks coyly at me and says, "This will happen fast, you'll know the truth about the pain of CO_2 treatments, and it will set you free."

She blindfolds me after setting my glasses next to me on the treatment table. I feel the pressure from the metal ring at the end of the laser head on the base of my nose and my upper lip.

Debbie tells me, "I have to make a measurement then we'll get started. It will be over and you'll know the truth." Her measurement is to not overlap lasered areas. "Okay here we go…"

I feel dozens and dozens of stings; the pain level is much less than the hair removal lasers. The feeling is more sophisticated, not the blast of burning energy of a hair removing shot. After three matrix group shots; I have the neat pattern of perfect rows of ashen dots all across my lip under my nose. Debbie was right it wasn't a fearful experience, but an interesting one. The truth did set me free! Debbie had the machine set at 24 watts power and 35% density, units that I don't

508

understand right now; perhaps I'll research this. I expect the power is directly related to the laser output and the density the number of dots per unit area. Debbie told me the dots are actually triangularly shaped not round. Debbie cleaned the area and then put an oil of some kind on it to soothe the skin. She asked if she could use the images of my treatment area I said, of course!

Debbie told me, "Come back in three months for a check to see if we need to do it again; also, just stop by any time so I can see it healing."

Bottom line time: My scar feels so much better even after the numbing cream had completely lost its effect. I am sore across my lip as I was after my surgery, but the point soreness in either corner is gone! Pondering time: each time Debbie did laser hair reduction on my scrotum, the one continually sore spot would go away for a few days to a week. Unfortunately, the soreness would come back with time. It is safe to equate the cause of both the soreness on my lip and the soreness on my scrotum to a sensitivity to a particular type of suture. If this is true, whatever cures one should cure the other. So, we will say a prayer that this laser treatment, from a different type of laser, will be extreme enough to solve the contamination problem from the Vicryl type of suture. Additionally, that cure could be extended to the problem on my scrotum.

I would have loved to have been an author. I would have written the life stories of the people I have met and would have enjoyed every second of doing so. It is true that I have lived much of my life vicariously because my dysphoria filters all my emotions to a dull grey. So, to experience uplifting emotions like joy, I have to see it in or help it develop in another person, and let myself be part of their experience. I have no trouble experiencing depressed emotions on my own. Think of it in this way, there is a duality at work in me. I know I am female, but male bodied, and to survive I have to mimic the male behavior from the examples I am given. I am an actor who continuously studies their real-world part being played; this is paramount to me in this role that I cannot escape. At my core, I am undeniably female; one whose life experience is stifled to only that of

509

the artificial male role I am playing. At the close of every curtain, the actress is left empty; nature abhors a vacuum so the rise of being vicarious takes place when no other way is possible. This instills a great interest in me about the life stories primarily but not limited to, women. It also has given me a deep appreciation of those life stories and the great value each life has had. As I transition, I have had the honor of people who had an important part in it share their stories with me. Debbie is such a person.

If someone writes a book about Debbie Caddell, the title should be *The Woman Who Loved Lasers*. She is so in love with them that her business has eight different machines. Debbie, with a gleam in her eyes, once told me, "Life is so good right now. I have enough money from my business to buy any laser that impresses me!"

So, thinking about Debbie Caddell as *The Woman who loved Lasers* here is her story in her own words responding to my curious questions about it.

My questions to my friend Debbie:

o   *What brought you on this path of Electrolysis as a career?*

    o   *What moved you away from your degree in textiles?*

o   *When did Caddell's form as a business?*

    o   *Where were your business's first few locations?*

    o   *Was it Caddell's Electrolysis at the start?*

    o   *How many employees did you start with?*

    o   *Love to know the story about you and Karen?*

o   *When and how did you get hooked on using a laser for hair removal?*

    o   *The Alex was your first laser machine, what year did you get it?*

    o   *How big of a gamble was it investing in the machine?*

    o   *Was the Alex trouble free the first year?*

o   *Do you remember your first exposure to people who are transgender?*

> o   *When did you start going to events as a vendor like Esprit?*

Debbie responded: Here are my answers to your questions:

I was hairy and getting electrolysis at 19 years of age. I asked lots of questions. My electrologist (Karen Pecota) wanted to have kids and needed someone to work for her. She asked and I said no. I had just finished my degree in Textiles & Clothing. Six months later, I decided to supplement my income. I could do electrolysis part time and fabric design part time. Long story short... My electrolysis job grew and grew.

I worked for Karen for three yrs. I was born an owner, so I branched out on my own in 1986. I was in Federal Way for three years, then started one day a week in Bellevue, at my Dermatologists office. My original name was Caddell's Electrolysis Clinic. I became incorporated when I added laser and changed my business name to Caddell's Laser & Electrolysis Clinic, inc. in 2000.

I started with just one employee. Three years later, I added another. I was working full time and decided to have kids. I trained six ladies and hired four. I then worked two days a week. All of my employees have always worked two to three days per week.

25 years later, I spotted Karen's name in the AEA (American Electrology Association) roster. I searched for her on Facebook, thinking I could use another employee. She and her husband were missionaries in Germany for 25 yrs. She had just opened her business and needed to supplement while growing. She started two days a week, then several years later dropped to one day a week.

I was always interested in laser; the technology and potential fascinated me. I read any articles I could find. Most talked negatively about lasers downplaying them, because they were written by electrologists trying to keep lasers out of the business. I watched and watched. Then I heard Judy Adams speak at an electrology conference. She was the president of SCME (Society of Clinical and Medical Electrolysis). She told us laser is here to stay and it works! I emailed her with a litany of questions for six months, then decided to go get trained. At the time, there were only two competitors in the area. Both went out of business shortly thereafter.

I started with the Candela GentleLase Plus Alexandrite laser in 2000. Two years later the Yag came on the market. I bought a Cutera Nd:Yag for use on darker skin.

I am a risk taker. My first laser was on a five-year lease. I paid $1.00 at the end of the lease and it was mine. Another electrologist in Seattle went out of business three months after I got my first laser. She contacted me and asked if I wanted her clients? Another place went out of business in Bellevue a couple months later. They also asked if I wanted their clients. The trick was that I had to do them for free, because these clients had purchased packages. My hope was that they would continue laser after the package was over. Some did, but many didn't. But it got me started and on my way. I have never sold packages because of that experience.

I can't remember if the Alex laser was trouble free at the start. I had a service contract and so it was always repaired for free. I'm sure it broke down a few times.

My first exposure to Transgender clients was as an electrologist. I didn't have many in the 1980s.

Over the years, more and more have come in.

I went to an electrology conference in 2016. The gal was speaking about doing electrolysis on transgender clients. She said it takes 30-50 hours to clear the face one time.

I was so upset! Why would you put someone through that much pain and charge them that much money when you can do laser in 20 minutes at a fraction of the cost?

So I came home and wrote a page for my website. I decided to market to the transgender community. My receptionist Renée, heard about Esprit gala. I had a laser colleague who attended and she invited me. I fell in love with the ladies there. I speak there about the differences between laser and electrolysis.

We have continued to grow the transgender part of my business.

Me here: I wanted to know a little more, so I asked Debbie right after my laser session about dates and transgender experiences. She got right back to me in email.

I became an electrologist in June 1982. I became a Licensed Master Esthetician in June 2007. (We called it Medical Esthetician back then).

In the beginning, my transgender clients were few and far between. I always liked them. They seemed to be a little distant. The world was against them. Maybe they were worried I would be as well. But, knowing my personality, we always bonded. There were a few, and there are a few at this time, who were odd. We did not bond, but I still did my job.

I have one client I would like to share a story about. She was so much fun to work on! We bonded. However, she was homeless and living out of her car. I was training a gal at the time and this client came in often as a test model to get a free treatment. It was Christmas and she was staying at the state park in Federal Way. She would use showers there or at the local pool. My husband and our two boys and I took her Christmas cookies. We drove to the state park and drove around until we found her car. It was a moving experience for my family that we will never forget...

Debbie Caddell.

Debbie has a big heart...

I feel like Caddell's has kind of become a second home for me, in a real way I transitioned here over the last fifteen years. The place was clinically bleak to me when I first shyly got the courage to sneak in for a consult with Marsha Moyer-Morgan for laser hair reduction in treatment room #5. That day along with the day I met Sandy L. Fosshage changed the angle of my life's arc forever. Caddell's was five treatment rooms connected by a central hub room. You as a client used a remote waiting room that was shared by several other businesses. In 2016 Debbie transformed the hub room into her dedicated waiting room with Renée as receptionist. The feeling became more informal and homey; there was talk with other clients as we gathered in the purple waiting room. Debbie loves purple, so it was natural to extend the color into her new waiting room. As more transgender clients used Debbie's services she in turn started to arrange events for them, such as a make-up demonstrations and lessons. Her transgender client base was still a small part of her business, but she spread the love around! There have been tragedies for the business such as two building floods that shut down her business for a few days. And for Debbie herself when her house caught fire and she lost her dogs. I mourned for her loss during the fire and felt for her during the floods. As I said in my journal, I came out here and was more than welcomed. It has since become an even more welcoming place for the transgender community. I can think of no better place than Caddell's.

***

Tuesday September 29, 2020. Today, Cathy was feeling much better, so we tackled our normal long block walk. She felt pretty good afterward but a bit fatigued. We did a Pokémon Go raid with Kevin at the bottom of our hill in the afternoon. Kevin was starved for human-to-human conversation; in every raid he has been doing lately he was the only one to physically show up, everyone else were virtual. When I came out as female to the group of Pokémon Go trainers we raid, hunt, and even picnic with, it was met with mixed reactions. We had a dozen or more in our normal group, all of which were friends on our Pokémon Go Tukwila Facebook page. Over half of the group distanced themselves from Cathy and me without comment forming what amounts to separate group, the other few were indifferent about it. Kevin and Sheryl remain friendly to us and we picked up Tim a trans supportive gay friend. With this, our Pokémon Go playing days are over, but the memory lingers.

I am so thankful that Cathy has gotten the surgery that she so longed for. I thought I could separate out her surgery achievement from my surgery failure and sort of wall them off from each other. Turns out to be very hard to do. So, I'm in a cycle of who-even-needs-surgery, to the deep end of I-look-ugly-without it. The area under my nose that was treated with the CO_2 laser was all angry red this morning when I awoke. I dabbed hydrogen peroxide on the area and then washed it off with salt water. That did the trick! The redness lightened up to a passable pink. My lip is sore if I curl it; otherwise, there is no pain but lots of little scabs. The soreness at the trouble spot is gone and it has flatted quite a bit. So far, this has been a win as far as relief goes.

***

Thursday October 1, 2020. I had a consultation for FFS with Dr. Tony Mangubat yesterday at 4:00 pm. Jasmine came to the door, greeted us, took our temperatures, and had us sign the Covid papers. The office staff is much more cordial with us now; they complimented us on our matching tie-dye as we passed by following Jasmine. Jasmine leads us to an exam room we haven't been in yet. I get the center-stage chair and Cathy the corner chair. Today for some reason, I feel trepidatious and would have preferred the corner chair. Cathy and I settle ourselves down to wait. I explore the room with my eyes moving place to place as opposed to my body moving. The exam rooms all have a large wall mounted mirror running parallel to one side of the exam chair. The wall opposite has all the medical trappings of a sink and cabinets. Our wait is not long at all; in walk a grey headed Dr. Tony Mangubat followed by a young man. Dr. Mangubat tells me, "Good to see you again. This is our new young doctor Dr. Bawlatly, the old young doctor you probably knew is gone." I have been puzzled about this; the folks here act like they know me or someone who looks like me. I say hello to them both. Dr. Bawlatly is wearing scrubs; he stays at the doorway and leans on the doorjamb. Dr. Bawlatly has my file and is making notes. Dr. T has all the mannerisms of an older experienced self-assured controlling plastic surgeon. He is blunt and completely intolerant of any conversation outside of the one he has set forth. Dr. T sat down on some sort of stool and takes off his glasses. They are the kind held together by a magnet at the nose bridge and break in two to dangle on a strap down his front on either side of his neck. Dr. Mangubat goes on to say, "The landmarks of masculinity on your face are: the brow bone; these can be reduced but we would have to have a CT scan to see how thick the bone is. If it is too thin we still have things we can do. Your hairline; this can be made more rounded I wouldn't lower the central part that looks good. You have nice cheekbones and they are your best feature. The fat under your eyes has to come out and the skin there is sagging." He has me look straight ahead without blinking while he pulls some of the skin below my eye down then releases it. He continues, "See here how long it takes to return? A portion of this skin should be removed and the remaining tightened up. You're lucky your jaw isn't very wide so you wouldn't need to narrow it with surgery. Your chin needs to come out further; a chin implant would accomplish this. Ideally breaking the jawbone to move it out would do it too. Age is very masculinizing to the face and a mark of age in your face is the skin becoming loose forming deep wrinkles. A facelift reverses this and is the one most important thing you can do to feminize your face. The skin on your neck can be tightened also, but this will cause your Adam apple to be noticeable." I try to explain that I have had a trach shave already with Dr. Lamperti, but he bats this away saying, "We would address this when the procedure is being done. Your nose needs to be reduced and the bump removed on the bridge; you don't have much tip support, hopefully the previous surgeon left some cartilage. I would encourage you to find images of faces that you really like and we can try to incorporate the look into your new face." This is all good information for me even at the cost of not being heard. I have long suspected a full facelift would be the one best procedure I could have done and if I coupled it with lower eye Blepharoplasty that would do the trick. This would be the easiest to recover from also. The idea of having my brow bone made flat is very enticing, but I have read that the recovery from this is lengthy and painful. The meeting is over, we all walk out to the reception desk. The system didn't do well; I guess Dr. Bawlatly didn't take exact notes, because the price quotes are not done and there is confusion on what was to be done... Cathy and I check out the fish tank while Dr. T dictates to Doreen the office manager who is now busy working on the quotes. We say our good-byes to Dr. T and he tells me, "You have started quite a journey, one that will go on and on. I guess we all have." We walk out to our car feeling drained. At home we look at the quotes, there are two of them. First, Facelift (standard) $9800, Chin implant $3118.50, Lower lid laser $ 750 total of $13,668.50. Second, Browlift $5755.50, Rhinoplasty & Septoplasty revision $9,295 total $15,050.50. Looks like these two are separated from each other as surgeries. Dr. T also wants me to get a letter from a mental health or PCP professional indicating my competence in pursuing feminization. I guess the fact that I have had irreversible gender surgery and my name change isn't enough for him. He would have known this if he had looked at my file! He didn't. The whole problem is his arrogance really, which comes from being an accomplished surgeon, but one with an awful bedside matter. I have a Facebook friend, Jery, who is also looking at getting work done with him. It is nice to have someone to commiserate with.

***

Saturday October 3, 2020. Cathy has busied herself with reading *Dead Heat* by Susan Sleeman, she started it yesterday. Cathy has focused on her reading during most of our days; I have tried to write both in our book and in my journal. Our plan for our anniversary this Monday is to go for a drive to 5 B's Bakery for treats and return to GhostFish Brewery for take-out to eat at home in the evening. Quince is reading number 14 in the Cam Jamsen series of chapter books. School seems to be working out for little Quince.

***

Sunday October 4, 2020. Tomorrow is our 46th anniversary. Today was a get the house ready for winter day. Me stuff: I have had two plastic surgeries that left me in pain at a suture point. Is this going to happen over and over? My scrotum soreness is still with me after two years and now the same sort of pain is at the base of my nose at the knot site of a suture...

***

Monday October 5, 2020. Happy 46th Anniversary to us! Or as Mindy puts it, "To two of the most important women in our lives." I don't know how I feel about this sentiment… A few days ago, it didn't look like we would be doing much of anything for our anniversary, but a plan came together and worked. Cathy and I left to go on a drive to the 5 B's Bakery in Concrete as soon as we were up this morning. The round trip drive is just over four hours including shopping at the bakery. I was so tired from sleeping this morning. It was a good thing we had a *Nero Wolfe* mystery to listen to as I drove; it kept me awake. When we returned home, Cathy placed a takeout order at GhostFish for gluten-free fish and chips and pawns and chips. The place is about a fifteen-minute drive from our house. We spent the rest of the day feasting. Corey gave us $100 at GhostFish and Casey had a flower arrangement complete with purple balloons delivered to our house.

***

Tuesday October 6, 2020. We had a very good time yesterday. Cathy is becoming less afraid of me writing our book. I don't know if it will ever get done or if I will just give up. I have over 1300 pages of notes but have only 12 pages written toward the book. The trouble is it's so personal; I have to relive trying times and accept that other people might read about them.

***

Thursday October 8, 2020. Cathy just had her three-week post-op checkup with Dr. Megan Dreveskracht. Doctor was very pleased with Cathy's healing and Cathy is now pretty much off all restrictions. Yay!!! Dr. M told us that by four weeks she even lets her weight lifting patients go back to lifting. She told Cathy that arms over the head was okay but with incremental stretches to get the muscles used to this action again. Cathy can wear any bra that is comfortable for her and we can go back to sleeping in our bed. Our instructions are to keep the scars moist; she recommends scar sheets over ointments. You should use a good lotion on the flaky skin, which by the way is normal to have happen. Dr. M removed all the remaining tape and clipped the end of any sutures showing. She told us just trim off any suture that pops out. Cathy's next appointment is December 17th at 9:30am. Dr. Megan was very relaxed with us and didn't seem to be in a great hurry, so I got in several questions. I asked about how the experience of what Cathy had done compares to augmentation. She told us they were similar. Augmentation has fewer incisions to heal up but because the muscle is disturbed you get deep muscle pain liked to a strain. Most patients feel a great pressure pushing down on the chest. We all chatted some more and I told her about my experience consulting with Dr. T. I didn't feel heard; I had no doubt about his skill or experience, but I worried about care if I had some difficulty after surgery. In other words, his bedside manner left me feeling empty. She commiserated having been both on the patient side and doctor side about this. She told us, "It is hard; you have to look for both the skill set and what you need emotionally from your surgeon. You really need the whole package." I was grateful for her caring advice. We found out that Dr. M was doing top surgery over at St Anne's. She told us that she just started to do it, "Better to ask forgiveness than permission. Overall, the hospital seems pretty supportive so I guess it worked." Her baby is nine months old now and trying to balance standing up with sights on walking.

***

Tuesday October 13, 2020. I had electrolysis with Marsha today; for an hour she cleared my personal area and I got to talk with her about stuff. I now have a disc of the CT scan of my head and that data, per his request, was emailed to Dr. T. Dr. Eaman will draft a letter to send to Dr. T on my behalf. And I still don't know what to do about Dr. T, but I am checking off all the required boxes just in case. The scar under my nose hurts on either side and it has been fourteen weeks. The top sutures weren't a problem it was the buried Vicryl sutures that caused the pain and abscess. And it appears I am a slow healer. Does this mean I shouldn't do any more surgeries at all? I think I had better start praying for some guidance in this. If I do decide to have another surgery, what should I have: breast augmentation or Facelift including neck?

Writing a book about Cathy and me is draining emotionally; having to go back over so many years of hurt brings tears to both of us. An unintentional result surfaced; Cathy has a deep trauma from her first relationship with a boyfriend. I was relationship number two. She has never spoken much about that first relationship before, it was in the past and gone. But it wasn't completely gone; Cathy was hurt very deeply by him. Because of their age difference (she 15 and he 20) that relationship could have been considered statutory rape at the time. In any event, I fully agree that if she wants it left in the past that is where it is going to stay. He has no place in our story and Cathy tells me with relief in her voice that I am certainly not anything like he was.

***

Thursday October 15, 2020. Today is Cathy's appointment with Dr. Crider in Tacoma. She was all smiles coming out of the doctor's office, no pap smear, no breast exam, no problem with pulse on either side of her neck, she didn't have to have a BP med, and her NP thyroid med was renewed for the year. During her time at the doctor's office, I sat in the car and waited. My mind working away more or less in fits on the situation I was facing. A cloud was lifted; I called La Belle Vie to see how far out surgery for BA would be with Dr. Dreveskracht. You can have an appointment in five days, the procedure lasts an hour. This news gives me a sudden jolt of pure joy, which in itself shocks me. I am near giddy with the thought of having this. I had no idea my inner desire for this was so very great. I wonder if anyone truly knows themselves deeply. I had no clue it was so great, the feeling was akin to when I got my name changed legally. I go along in a constant state of denial of being female inside; it has been a lifelong survival habit. There is simply no question of who I am when the true extent of my true self is given a path to life. I wonder how could I ever explain this in words to anyone when I myself don't fully see it. All I can say is you have to feel it rise up from within to know it; there are no words to form a picture.

***

Wednesday October 28, 2020. Robin called! I am scheduled for October 5, 2021. This was the call I had been dreading, I guess the part I was dreading was I couldn't say no to it... Robin was cheery she could get me in sooner if I wanted to. She told me Medicare covered the hospital and the anesthesiologist leaving Dr. Bowers fee of $14000. I could get in first quarter of next year but I declined staying with my original date. This is a huge thing for me to figure out. Please Cadance think this through…

***

Friday November 13, 2020. No Thanksgiving at Casey's house.

***

Wednesday November 18, 2020. And just like that our family was broken asunder. Cathy and I are all that's left to each other. The threads we had held onto with both Corey and Casey have become just spider silk; still there, but in name only. Cathy and Cady are heartbroken and there is nothing we can do about it; just as sure as death will come to us, so too will our hearts forever ache.

***

Sunday November 22, 2020. Casey needs to be free of me; it will be better for him to be his own person. What kept Cathy and me seeking a close physical presence was our grandchildren. And the learned need to come to his assistance when there was a crisis. Although it worked, this was the hardest way to break up that I could have dreamed of. Because of his early death, I never experienced my grandfather Amer on my dad's side of the family. Had I seen the intense familial strain happening between my father and his father when coming to our home or vice versa; it might have made a lasting impression on me, but again I didn't have this experience. What I saw instead was my dad constantly taking care of his mother at her house and if she came to our home she was honored. In fact, my dad was the only male in his family to have shown me a physically caring relationship with his aged mother. He was forever over at her house mowing the lawn or playing games on weekends. Dad's brothers got away from her as soon as they could where Dad tarried. To me this is just more evidence that dad was transgender; 'she' was trying to be a good daughter to her mother. If you look at Cathy's brothers, they got away from their dad as soon as possible. The daughters flocked to be with him and, after his death, the daughters remained to care for their mother. Cathy didn't have the experience of a grandfather on her dad's side either; he had passed away just a year after her birth. So, she, just as me, didn't grok the grandfather stress against father experience. So, neither of us has a deep clue to this programming. In a way, this is just another thing to add to the list of things we have in common. All these typed words trying to make some sense of thoughtless reactions and all full of nothing...

***

Wednesday December 2, 2020. Days are running together, opening eyes each morning to empty days of lost hope. I had electrolysis with Marsha today, it was a 30 minute appointment. The area we did was around my mouth and two dark hairs on my arms. It was nice to have my upper and lower lip cleared. I had an hour appointment a week ago to do my personal area clearing. I will keep clearing this area just as if I will keep my appointment with Dr. Bowers in early October 2021. I baked cookies and packed them in holiday tins for Debbie Caddell and Marsha Morgan; everyone seemed happy with them. I am trying to get in contact with Sandy just to see how she is and if she would like cookies this year; all I can do is leave a voice message at her old business number. I had a very hard day two days ago. I am starving to do something positive for someone so I tried to repair two light fixtures Marsha brought me. One I put back together. The other one that I thought was successfully brought back from the grave, suddenly had the plastic pieces all shattered.

***

Thursday December 3, 2020. I called Sandy Fosshage's phone number yesterday and she called me back today! I did search the obituary notices first and kept my fingers crossed. She sounded good and wanted an update on me. I gave her one. Sandy now has two kittens one is Loki and the other Olaf. They have learned to flush her toilet among other mischief. I asked her if she would like some cookies and she was very enthusiastic so I will mail a care package to her very soon. Update: I baked two-dozen cookies; we bought a pair of golden cat socks, and a cat themed Christmas card. We boxed them all in a priority box and she had them the very next day! So nice that she loves my cookies; this makes me feel like I have done something nice for a great lady…

***

Friday December 4, 2020. I saw Natalie this morning for a 90 PT massage to get ready for an adjustment by Dr. Grace our chiropractor right afterward at 12:30. My back has been so stiff and sore centered at the lower back. From that area everything from my head and neck down to below my hips is restricted in movement. Natalie explained this was due to my core muscles being weak. It seems all the other muscles that I have been exercising are now compensating for the core, which I haven't paid much attention too. Also, my descending colon is sore from my waist on down for some reason. Cathy and I have been nit picking at each other all this week. Both of us are hurting, she with an itchy rash that doesn't seem to go away and me by stiff achy back.

***

Sunday December 6, 2020. We had B---- at our house today to play gin, Racko, and a little cribbage. Just like Colby, she is maturing into a teenager. She can be sweet at times, funny at times, and much less angry than in her pre-medication days. Parents think they grow fast, but grandparents know they grow fast. I lay in bed last night thinking about death just as I have for most of my life. In each hopeless state I was in from child to adult, it lurked as the only way out. There was always some other way in the morning after the long night had passed.

***

Friday December 11, 2020. I am at the place in our book where my cousin Tony was staying at our house. This was mid July 1973 according to letters to me at the ranch from my mom. I had been in Thorp all of June and was returning home for an eleven day stretch over the July 4th weekend. I don't have much memory of my brother that summer because I was gone. When I read my mom's letter to me

523

dated July 31, she said it was nice to have Tony staying for a while. I realized I had access to Tony and his memory of that time. So, I called Carol to get his phone number and called him. I don't know Tony very well really; mostly my memory of him was from that summer of 1973 when he was here. His mother Beverly had passed away in October 1972 and his father Paul was faced with caring for seven kids. The result was Paul sent his kids out to visit relatives for the summer. I called Tony to ask if I could borrow his memory of that time he was staying with us. I was nervous and tongue tied. Tony of all the Andersons comes the closes to having knowledge of my transgender experience, he is openly gay and has been for over 30 years. The trick about this is it has only been in the last two decades that there has been general acceptance of transgender people by the gay population. So, before that time there was no T in the LGB. He doesn't seem to care one way or the other; but this doesn't make any difference as long as we can talk as cousins with each other. I didn't ask him and he didn't tell. So his memory was a goldmine; Tony remembers his stay and time with my brother. He told me he had his first sunny-side up egg at our house. Tony slept in David's and my bedroom, he used David's bed while David slept in mine. He told me that he and David bonded together having both lost close people over the winter. David had lost Richard Mathisen a friend living next door to us and Tony of course, had lost his mother. Tony continued to tell me that David was just so cool and laid back; he didn't care what the Hell anyone thought about him. David was just turning 17 at the time of the visit and Tony was 13. Tony told me, "We would get up and have breakfast that your mom made, then leave for the day. David showed me a marijuana plant he had growing in the closet of the bedroom and one he had growing in the back yard. We would make the rounds of your neighborhood seeing his friends, David D and David P." That was about all he remembered but he was greatly impressed with David describing him as, "A real cool rebel who didn't care what the Hell anyone else thought!"

***

Friday December 18, 2020. It is all about my back. Today I had a massage with Natalie. These things hurt, she finds spots all over my body that, when pressure is applied to them, pain is reported. The good news is after 90 minutes of pain, I have at least a week of relief. Right now it is my lower back that is on fire, it limits how far I can walk to half the distance of our normal daily walks. We think we finally have an idea of what is going on. I am full time now wearing female clothes that Cathy and I match; our outfits are tie-dye tees and cotton leggings. Being the modest type, I have for the longest time worn a gaff. This amount to a woman's foundation garment that holds in the tummy and most importantly gives me a flat appearance between my legs; it hides my penis. I love it, I can wear natural-waist leggings without showing anything male hanging down. So here is the rub. The foundation garment holds my gut in by transferring pressure to my lower back. Over time, my abdominal muscles have become very weak. They don't do any work anymore, leaving my leg muscles to compensate for my overworked back muscles. I get leg cramps all the time and I have a continual lower back ache. Natalie poked around my navel and found all sorts of pain spots where the weak abs muscles didn't protect my intestines anymore. The answer is to strengthen my abs and stretch out my spasming back muscles. Quit wearing the gaff and start contracting my abs daily. Stretching out my back is another matter. I have to use a spiky roller placed on the floor. I lower myself down on the thing and roll it from the center of my back to the center of my bottom. As I do this, both my legs cramp and Cathy has to pull them straight out because my bottom is up on the roller and my back is flat on the floor. It is very painful, I also use an overhead bar to take some of the weight off my back during the stretch. I have to remember during the day to contract my abs off and on all day long.

***

Wednesday December 23, 2020. Cathy had her three-month post-op checkup today. Dr. Megan Dreveskracht was amazed on how well Cathy has healed. Cathy has a little dog-ear scar on either side, but Dr. M told us she would fix it for free anytime Cathy wanted. Dr.

Dreveskracht was genuinely happy for Cathy and was quick to respond to Cathy's request for a quote for a tummy tuck. Which includes muscle plication along with abdominoplasty. We didn't make an appointment yet; with all that is happening it is hard to pick a sure date.

***

Thursday December 24, 2020. Our last Christmas Eve as we have known them. Who knows what the world will be like in one year from now; but best guess being all that our family has known as a culture, over my lifetime, will be gone from sight and practice. This one remaining little puddle of Christmas practice we have tomorrow is but a dry simulation of what was.

2021

February 18, 2021. Rush Limbaugh whose talent as he said, "Was on loan from God," has personally brought it back to the Creator of all that is or ever will be. I have been so sad these last days; Rush was a very important counterweight to the balance between extremes, now he is gone and seemly devils dance. I try not to hate, but many live for it now, as a way of life, and wishing/following a man into the grave with only hate in your heart is not God's way.

***

Wednesday February 24, 2021. Okay, I still need to journal. Cathy and I both have had consults with Dr. Megan Dreveskracht for tummy tucks. I had my consult today while she had hers last December 23rd. The only difference between the two procedures is Cathy will have a muscle repair (plication) from giving birth and I'll have my fat transferred to my breast to add fullness. Cathy's will run in the $10k range and Cady's will be near $13k...

Cathy has been so happy after she scheduled her tummy tuck with Dr. M for April 6th that I started to consider my roll around my middle. I have had a spare tire around my middle for as long as I can remember. It never completely goes away no matter how much weight I lose; even when I was down to 147 pounds I still had a roll of flabby deflated skin hanging there. It has been an ugly physical reminder of my body conflict by destroying any attempt I will ever have at a feminine waist. I need to do something to actuate my transition along. I have been in a painful holding pattern of self-doubt and despair and as a result the darkness of depression follows me. I can be so much better for my family in these last years of my life; all I have to do is actuate, to move, as I am led into transition.

527

Covid still demands barriers to be overcome forcing us to sit in our car waiting for the cellphone to ring. It does and we enter the outer lobby of La Belle Vie. Questions are asked and temperatures are taken, then the reward of the inner lobby is ours. Cathy and I are given Christi's attention as we stand near the reception desk. She asks us to wait a few minutes while the doctor catches up with her schedule. This is new for us, we get to sit and watch their big aquarium's three fish swimming purposefully in circles while the office staff seemed to be doing the same. A medical assistant came and led us to a very familiar exam room. This time it is Cathy's turn to sit in the corner as the supporting wife while I take center stage on the exam chair. Cathy's turn was two months ago at center stage. The exam room is furnished with a simple straight-backed chair in the corner, a dental exam like chair centrally, a three by six foot mirror mounted long-ways on the wall beside the exam chair, and three square twenty-four inch paintings of bright white dogwood flowers that hang on a chocolate brown accent wall opposite the mirror wall. The medical assistant asks what we are here for and I reply a tummy tuck. We chat for a minute about her son, she hands me a paper gown telling me the open side goes to the front, strip to the waist, but leave your bra on then she is off to go find Dr. Megan. I do as asked and fidget moving around the room holding the gown closed with my hand. Cathy takes the notion that the white flimsy plastic belt attached to the paper gown's waist should be tied; I differ and challenge her to try. If there was a hidden camera in the room they got lots of good comic material of two females trying to tie a flimsy plastic belt with only one inch of overlap. I continue to hold my gown closed; soon there is a little knock at the door and Dr. Megan breezes in. She is so understated in demeanor, she's rail thin with short hair and about 5 feet 5 tall. "How's life going for you two?" Fine, the weather is better. "Did you have fun in the snow?" Yup, we both thought we were younger and shoved like crazy to clear our driveway then discovered we weren't! We both ask her about her little daughter. Dr. Megan asks us, "Would you like to see a picture?" Yes! She zooms out and is back in far less than a minute. Her little girl is 14 months old and just had her picture taken for

528

Valentines Day. She is so cute with golden hair and bright smile. "So you're after a tummy tuck?" Yes. Dr. Megan asks to see my tummy and explains what she does, "Using your belly button as a middle I remove a piece of skin around it in the shape of a rounded diamond, then pull the bottom and top together afterward. Any questions?" I ask what happens to the belly button? Dr. Megan responds, "It is removed with the skin but we make you a new one." Cathy is using the opportunity to ask several questions she had left over from her consult. Cathy asks about the position of the scar and do you need to do electrolysis in the bikini area. Dr. Megan answers by showing us a little drawing she has. I stand up and ask her to show Cathy where it will be on me. Dr. Megan points to an area about six inches down from my belly button. "As far as hair removal goes, you don't have to but if you would like to, just stop it a week before surgery." Dr. Megan is chipper and eager to have more questions and we have more. I ask if the surgery would interfere with either GRS or BA. She quickly responds with, "No it shouldn't." I ask about fat transfer, will I have any left to use in my face if needed?" She again quickly responds, "Yes we leave the fat on your back so there should still be a good supply for simple transfer to the face." A thought forms in my mind and I take the opportunity to ask, can the fat you are removing be moved to my breast? Dr. Megan carefully answers, "Yes, we can do this but it is with the understanding that as low as 70% fat may only survive. You do recover quicker than with an implant even quicker than Cathy did her reduction. Also what is your expectation as to size? We deal in cup sizes here." I said that I was a C cup now and would like to go to a D or in other words one-cup size up. Dr. Megan commented, "That should be doable we usually get around 1000cc of fat and that split between the two breasts should give you at least one cup size increase. The trick is symmetry between the breasts, we inject fat into the breast not under your muscle; with an implant it is set, but with fat we just don't know if one side or the other will hold onto the viable fat cells. Also with fat transfer, I would do some taping to bring your breast together giving you some cleavage." Could I still get an implant later if the fat deserted me? She quickly answered, "Yes." Dr.

Megan poked her finger into my belly button to check if I had a hernia and no I didn't. Dr. Megan stated what I would need for surgery, "You need a letter from your doctor stating that you are fit for surgery, stop your estrogen two weeks before, and a negative Covid test result. No, having the vaccine didn't make any difference we still need the test as we don't know if the vaccine works." As our conversation flows over me my mood is getting better and better. It is almost too good to believe, as I am just as excited as Cathy has been to get this done. The relief is growing moment by moment this is the answer I have been missing; I am so tempted to stand up and hug Dr. Megan. This is a lifesaver and I try to share with both Cathy and Dr. Megan how this is making me feel. She was being summoned back to another exam room but was being slow in leaving us, as she does reluctantly leave she says, "I am so glad to see you today!" Cathy and I get ourselves together and start toward the exit only to be turned around by Christi because she isn't ready with our quote yet so we return to the nice warm exam room. While we wait we can hear Dr. Megan in the next exam room giving a consult to another patient. Although it isn't polite we can't help hearing what is going on in the next room. A male voice is explaining about having to wait for retirement in order to get an Adam's apple reduction. Oh my, I think Dr. Megan has just gone from one transgender person right to another. We hear a few more snatches of conversation and I wonder just how many people are there just like me and will I see this person on the way out? It kind of makes me sad in a way, two things persist, I'm not so special after all and why did I wait so long. I also wonder what God has in mind giving me this experience? We drive away from the nondescript office building in Tukwila. Cathy is excited for me to get fat transferred into my breasts instead of the silicone implants. It's your fat not some foreign object under your muscle just sounds better. Now with both of us doing a surgery we have to time the events so as one will be recovered enough to be the caregiver to the other. We did a rest stop at home and then drove south down I-5 to Marlene's Market to get vitamin B shots in preparation for the demon second-shot next week. Our normal 15mg Zinc Citrate dose is now augmented with an additional 30 mg of Zinc

Picolinate. With the help of God these steps will ease the severity of the side effects for us.

***

Wednesday March 3, 2021. And the journal goes on. Today we got our second shot of the Pfizer stuff (our first was on February 8th). I had never been completely over the first injection really, low energy, achy muscles, poor digestion, intermitted chills, and a constant dull headache. Two days ago, I began to feel better say 80% and attributed this to adding 30 mg more zinc to our daily vitamins seven days ago. In addition, both of us got vitamin B12 injections from Dr. Ayla (Voda health) last Wednesday to be ready for today's Pfizer injection. Looking back preparing for the shot, I see that we were trying all kinds of schemes to ready ourselves for possibly being incapacitated after today's injection, including sort of saying goodbye to friends for the near-term time to come.

Back to getting the second shot: Our experience of getting the first shot had bumps in it when they couldn't find me in their system, I had to out myself as C---- then everything was good and the lady said they would merge the files together. I thought that was a good thing and maybe it would be okay to use this hospital in the future. Wrong! This time all the paperwork came under C---- and they couldn't understand who Cadance was. The folks were apologetic of course but they couldn't change anything. I was asked for my assigned gender at birth m/f all very nice, not! Moving to the shot station the nurse was dumbfounded into what to do, as C---- wasn't me. I tried to tell her I had no ID as C----; I could show her ID as Cadance so she just froze up. Finally, she gave me the shot to move me along knowing that anyone in the future checking to see if I had had the injection wouldn't be able to verify Cadance as getting it.

***

Monday March 15, 2021. I had my ortho appointment on the 10th and surprise! I have 20 more weeks of new aligners. The miserable part is I now have eight metal buttons, four to a side to hold two rubber bands. Each rubber band is stretched around four buttons to form a

531

sort of box. The idea is the rubber bands are going to pull up on four of my molars so that top and bottom will meet together as currently they do not meet at all. Also, those molars need to be squeezed together to give space someplace else in my mouth. In short, this is the most discomfort I have had so far. On the other hand, it is a fair price to pay for the smile I never had...

New subject: I currently have three surgery appointments booked: Dr. Dreveskracht, Dr. Parikh, and Dr. Bowers. We have put deposits down on all three of them and only one has a refund policy. Dr. Dreveskracht is first on May 5th, Dr. Parikh is on the May 25th, and Dr. Bowers is in October. I am so torn by all of this. I have to choose between Dr. Megan and Dr. Parikh; I can't do both. A Dr. Bowers' decision can be put off for a while. Dr. Megan forces me to stop hormones two weeks before surgery and I don't know if I can tolerate this; other than this she has my complete confidence. I have lost some confidence in Dr. Parikh and staff. What this all comes down to is what I need to do to fully address my GID. I have done much to cross the proverbial bridge in this aspect by way of actuating transition but there is still a final distance to complete. So far I have battled between what I am internally and what my image is externally, keeping back just enough so that a shadow of C---- is still present. Why? I don't want to completely take this façade, this shadow no matter how weak it is, from the grandkids or our sons. I have this unreasonable fear of losing my familial place with our sons. Yes, it is unreasonable but so is living your life as something you are not. So, I teeter just short of success for my self-image thinking death will be a relief because I can't stand to stay where I am. I am, in doing this, denying myself the tools to put to rest my disjoint self. Sandy pointed out that I am also denying our sons and grandchildren the true me... It's a gamble this late in life, but I have already rolled the dice and can just see the finish line. I think this is all about a particular fear that has held me in a place of misery. After all of this time, it is very hard to completely let go of it and I need to for all of us.

***

Thursday March 25, 2021. We did get our Internet back up on the 18th. Cathy had her pre-op yesterday, Colleen asked all the med questions and told us Cathy needed a negative Covid 19 test five days or less before the surgery. This is a bigger surgery than the breast reduction. Cathy will also have to wear a compression garment and a binder. Cathy is having her belly button removed completely; she is done with it and the problems it has caused her. We have made attempts to visit all the Starbucks where our friends have ended up at but other than to say hi most of the stores aren't welcoming. The two we will continue to visit are in Burien; they seem the most welcoming to us. Today as we left PCC market an older lady called out to us as we walked in the parking lot. She said, "Love that you match; are you mother and daughter?" She was being sweet. Cathy and I are trying to decide which of us was the mother and which was the daughter!

***

Tuesday March 30, 2021. We had our massage with Natalie this evening. Cathy had made a new backpack to replace the one stolen from her the last time we were together. Cathy also made a new nametag with a dragon on it to hang from it. The backpack had Natalie's business name and location on it. Natalie gave Cathy the biggest hug ever! Cathy had also made a mug with Natalie's name and business name on it also again a very big hug! My little part was two Ravi Zacharias books for her that we had talked about last time. I wasn't sure what to expect for this evening's appointment as at our last appointment the trauma of her car being broken into was awful. Cathy was first and we both let Natalie talk about all that had happened to her.

***

Monday April 5, 2021. Tomorrow is Cathy's 11:00 tummy tuck surgery with Dr. Megan Dreveskracht. Cathy is really looking forward to it with the exception of the recovery. She will have to wear a compression binder for one week and a body Faja for two weeks all the time. We haven't gotten too much family support, Casey hasn't volunteered or anything. I did ask a favor of him to bring us a refill of our water from Costco this week and he said he would. It's so odd to have no one really interested in us. I guess it is the new world we live in now, very self-facing. I on the other hand have scheduled this same surgery for four weeks after Cathy's. The difference is Cathy will discard all of her fat cells and I will have mine added to my breasts. So, at the moment I sit here with two surgeries for May, Dr. M and Dr. P. I can't do them both and wonder what to do about this? And with either, am I making a mistake in doing this? It is the same feelings that have plagued me for these last fifteen years since I acted upon my transition. It doesn't get better until you find some resting place where what you lost and what you have gained balance in some form. Until then, I'll just be continuously tired from the battle for life.

I have learned from Jonathan that his dad, Dr. Ken Nishimoto, who was our recently retired family dentist is in Overlake Hospital and has been there for two weeks in the ICU unit. He had two light strokes and heart issues. He will probably be there for another week at least then handed off to physical therapy before ending up in a convalescent home... He only made it one year into retirement so sad.

***

Wednesday April 7, 2021. Cathy's tummy tuck surgery was at 11:00. I was called to come get her at 2:30. I was left waiting until 4:00 and got to go see a very sleepy Cathy in recovery. Last time Cathy was very slow to wake up, this time she was a little better. Dr. Megan stopped in to tell me the surgery went off without any bumps in the road just as the previous one had. I had Cathy home at 4:45 settled in the recovery chair in our living room. I gave her Tyl-3 and a Zofran it was near 5:00. Cathy got some Jello I had made and napped on and off until bedtime at 9:40. At that time I gave her one syringe of Enoxaparin (Lovenox) 40 MG/.4 ML SYR and Keflex. We went to sleep me on the couch and Cathy in her chair. Our world is shattered after the short sleep as Cathy repeatedly blackouts after we try to get her up from the chair. I hold her for what seems hour until she perks up a little and we can get back in the chair and I check her BP the machine chews for the longest time then reports it to be 76/54, Oh no!

She stumbles in using words but otherwise is coming back. By 11:00 she is losing more words and goes silent then tells me to go to bed everything is okay. It is not! I call the emergency on call doctor. I get Dr. Mangubat and I describe what is happening and he tells me this is not normal in any way. I call 911, as I talk to the operator Cathy passes out sitting in the chair, her eyes roll up into her head and she slumps. I plead with the operator for help and they assure me the EMT will be there soon, although since Cathy is still breathing on her own she can't tell me when... Cathy now is staring straight ahead with unblinking and unseeing eyes. I call Casey to come help and Dr. Mangubat back just as Casey and the EMTs show up. Cathy is non responsive and our house is full of people all doing stuff, while I run around trying to help. Dr. Mangubat is still on the line so I give him to one of the EMT guys and tell the others we would like to go to Valley General. Dr. Mangubat pops up with Dr. Megan can go treat Cathy over at Highline now St Anne's so we switch. This was a very good choice; Dr. Megan will be a godsend for us there. I ride in the ambulance with Cathy and Casey follows behind us....

***

Thursday April 8, 2021. It is just after midnight when we arrive at the ER and Cathy and I are separated. I sit with Casey in the waiting area and we talk. Soon a nurse is out with us seeking information. I have information for him and he returns to the ER. This will happen two more times until the nurse asks me to come with him into the ER. For the next twenty hours ER room nine is our home. Casey spends the night in the waiting area; I have no way of contacting him because my cell is blocked here. What I can do is send text and if Cathy is moved outside the ER to get imaged my phone sends the pending lot and can receive any to me. Cathy is totally confused she is functioning on a very low level something less than say a two year old. She doesn't know where she is or where she lives. My great fear is a stroke, what will our life be like after this, will Cathy be a shell of herself? I pray over and over again while I try to keep Cathy from tearing off her wires and IV lines. She tears at them as well as her top, stretching it until you can hear ripping sounds. We are told that her sodium blood level is dangerously low; they use a unit of 1.0 (100 mEq/L). One nurse was excited because it wasn't a stroke he told me it doesn't look like it right now so chances are good she will recover. At the same time, I am told her sodium level is near fatal right now so they will be giving her an emergency bag of 3% Hypertonic Sodium Chloride. Cathy has begun to thrash around tearing at her cloths and wires. She is just completely confused and wants out of this place. Two nurses come in to try to establish a main line in her forearm. Cathy keeps pushing so I hold her and stroke her head speaking quietly to comfort her. They switch to the other arm it seems to take forever then success. Cathy is hooked up to the emergency sodium bag; it becomes clear despite my best efforts I can't keep her still so they tie her wrist to the bed and give her an injection to quiet her. She sleeps for an hour then awakes to find herself bound in bed and screams at me, "Please, please, please, Cady untie me!" Repeated over and over. This will continue for hours and I die a little bit each time. It wouldn't dawn on me until days later that Cathy didn't know what day it was or if she had children or where she was, but she always referred to me as Cady! She never skipped a beat I was completely Cady to her. Even as she asked me to untie her and I would respond that since I didn't tie the knot it wasn't proper for me to untie it. The 3% emergency sodium bag gave her back some words by raising her level to 1.1 (110) reasoning and memory were still nowhere to be found. She would tell me she wanted to get up and I would ask her why? "I have to go to the bathroom." I would respond we can't go outside of this room and there is a bedside toilet right there; "No I need to go to the bathroom out there." If she tried to walk more than a few steps she would simply collapse. Once the emergency 3% was inside Cathy they switched to .9% to slowly raise her level .1 per hour. There were many attempts to show the return of mental function that would allow her wrists to be untied, but she could never answer the simple questions they would ask her. I sang to her, touched her cheek, and stroked her hair all the while silently praying. She would fall asleep for a half hour so I would lay my head on her bed rail and nap. At 4:00 her level reached 1.9

(190) and she calmed down. She demanded in a firm tone, "Cady untie my wrist." This tone was new. She was still so I told her; here is the deal if you want this we have to practice. First what city do we live in she struggled and I said 'Tukwila' say it with me, she did. What are your sons' names? Again she struggled and then said, "Colby and Quince?" I said, close, those are our grandsons. Casey and Corey are our sons. Say it with me. She did carefully. My heart was bounding I wanted this to be real. The nurse came in and Cathy demanded for him to untie her wrists. He explained the reason for not doing this and I interceded telling him she is so much better. Then the questions came. What month is it? Cathy struggled Marr, Febb no its April. What year? 2020eeee it is 2021! I was ecstatic these were not our practice questions and she was doing it on her own! We got a lecture on how he had been fooled before and how important that the main line was and in the end he looked directly at me, "Are you going to be here all the time?" Yes I will, I have for the last twenty hours. He dogmatically said, "Don't even leave for a second without someone taking your place. I charge you to keep that main line intact." I hadn't left Cathy's side for over twenty hours; I have had no water or food in that time. I used the bathroom once when I came out of the ER to speak to Casey and Mindy. Now when Cathy did need to go to the bathroom we called for a nurse but I was the one to get her up. I would help her to stand and hold her like we did in dance class. We would turn in a clockwise circle to the freestanding toilet and she would sit down. After she was through I would help get up back to our dance class mode and again turn in a clockwise circle until she was pointed again to the bed. Cathy would only turn clockwise I couldn't get her to do the reverse. I was all set to be with Cathy for the next twenty hours when shift changed and was told Cathy's level was now at 1.2 (120) for sodium and they were going to move her upstairs to the 5th floor and I couldn't go along... All this time no one could figure out why Cathy's levels dropped so much and so fast. She was also anemic and had a big hematoma under her incision. Dr. Megan tried to dig it out there in the ER but it was too big so Cathy would have to have surgery on Friday to remove it. Dr. Megan visited Cathy many times during the course

of the malady. There were only two things different from the last surgery Cathy breezed right through. First was an injectable blood thinner Enoxaparin (Lovenox) 40 MG/.4 ML SYR. The second was the second vaccination of Covid vaccine. Dr. Megan after Friday's repair surgery there in the hospital told us as she opened up the skin Cathy's tissue seemed to ooze blood it was strange she had never seen this happen before usually you get one or two bleeders throwing a clot but this was odd. Here we have two surgeries to compare with drastically different outcomes. Cathy's problem attracted the curiosity of many high-ranking doctors at the hospital but that is not a good thing. It never is, it means you are on the outside of their understanding. Cathy condition was near fatal, there was a real chance she could have died and God gave her back to me. Praise God! What a wonderful blessing!!! This blessing puts all other conflicts into perspective for me. We are still left with not knowing what caused it but that knowledge may never come to us. I got two of the greatest life blessings an answer to prayer in Cathy coming home and the fact that Cathy thinks of me completely as Cady… Praise God in the Highest!!! That which was the most precious to me has been returned…

***

Saturday April 10, 2021. Cathy is up in room 518, the surgery to repair the bleeding and reset everything happened last night after 5:00 pm, two hours after it was scheduled to happen. Dr. Megan texted me after she finished. It all went well but she put in two drains just to be on the safe side. I am so broken hearted and so alone here at home. I continually give thanks to the Lord and in two more days I get to bring Cathy home again.

***

Sunday April 18, 2021. Our good family friend and dentist Ken Nishimoto passed away today while at Overlake Hospital ICU he had been there several weeks. He was a dear friend to me, we lunched together often and chatted about all the inventions he had dreamed up. None of his dream inventions was without merit. His favorite saying to me was, "Let's think outside the box on this one." He only made it into retirement a little over one year before a light stroke forced him into hospital and there when his heart rhythm became unstable he lost his chance of ever leaving the place. He died alone without any family near him, just as so many others have during this awful time of our lives. We will miss him for the rest of our lives especially each time we pass his little corner office space over in Burien. It has hit me especially hard because it is just another door slamming shut to a time of life that is forever gone to me, to us… Dr. Ken was loved, a great achievement in life, and each day he brought relief to so many people through his dental practice. As I was transitioning he would deaden my face for free so my electrolysis treatments wouldn't be so painful. He never asked why I was doing them just how could he help. Rest in heaven with your family there before you Dr. Ken, may all the joys of your earthly life be multiplied a thousand times and added to the final joy of being with your God.

***

Friday April 23, 2021. Drains removed at 1 pm two weeks from the reset surgery at the hospital. Cathy's sodium level is back up to 132, Ferritin 121, hemoglobin 9.0, hematocrit 28.4, prothrombin time 10.2, INR 1.0. Cathy is so relieved to have the drains out. I have hurt myself somehow at my sternum clavicle connection on my right side, had an X-ray which didn't show much but I am still hurting and can't move my right arm much…

***

Tuesday April 27, 2021. I have an overuse injury of my right clavicle, a perfect storm thing. A combination of supporting Cathy's dead weight, falling down the stairs, a deep tissue massage, and using loppers over my head to cut through a thick thorn bush. The pain at the start was just a slight point where my collarbone connects to my sternum. Two days later it's a painful swollen lump that sends me to Dr. Eaman, I am so glad I did. She knew right away what had happened. Cathy ordered a clavicle support harness (it is like a backpack without the pack part) and it does give some relief. Dr. Eaman commented on how pale Cathy looked and yes she is… Cathy and I are again sharing experiences. We both hurt and are wearing tight restrictive bands around our abdomen... I worry about Cathy other than just how pale she is and that she is easily tired out but she is much improved over a week ago. Still, I worry and Cathy's doctor (Dr. Crider) is missing in action so we have to find a replacement. I think Cathy will sign up with Dr. Eaman for now so she will at least have someone. It will cost us $75 a month but meets a pressing need. The first bill we got from the Hospital was almost $100,000 before insurance. So, it is near my 67th birthday and we are pretty low right now, both of us are laid up, hurting, and recovery will take lots of days. Cathy's mom will have surgery sometime in the next two week to fix a prolapse this will be done at St Anne's and will keep her overnight.

***

Thursday April 29, 2021. A random thought about myself created from my childhood understand of my mother's odd behavior that has led me to constantly compare my GID to her mental illnesses. I have had a constant fear that I was like my mom and the only way to protect my own family was to hide my uniqueness and behave in an opposite manner. I took a vow to never consume alcohol, smoke, use any recreational drug, and always be reliably steady. Even as my GID progressed as I aged, that vow kept me in fear that I was doomed to follow my mom's path if I slipped up in any way. I guess what I am trying to get to is I have always had this fear of a mental illness implanted in me from my mom's genes. I created defenses to protect my family and myself. On the other hand, during the time my father reclaimed us from the ranch I would look to him as a great resource of non-mental illness or just plain normalcy. I would look at my father's not drinking or not being a paranoid schizophrenic and silently thank God for my dad's normalcy. So, I had a lock on this, just follow my own set limits and I could give our sons a steady childhood. But as life has brought me more information about my father I find that he was the one I should have looked toward as a warning. So ironic, I worried about becoming my mother to the point of studying her behavior carefully and setting up vows to keep me from her path all to the exclusion of what was happening with my father. For the sake of normalcy, I disregarded Merrill's odd behaviors all except abandonment. I vowed never to do this to Cathy and our sons and to always be there for them. Here I sit in my sixth decade of life accepting myself as transgender with the gained knowledge that Merrill was well within the transgender umbrella if not just like me... The irony is I steeled myself from my mother's but not from my father's troubling times. It is a gift really, if I as a child had understood my father's uniqueness and acted to steel myself from ever becoming anything like him, it would truly been a hellish life for me... Thank God!

***

May 6, 2021. Cathy had a very disappointing phone call from Doreen at La Belle Vue. She was businesslike as to the point of her call, "Dr. Megan Dreveskracht is leaving the practice as of the 23rd of June." Cathy reacted with a loud, "What!" My pre-op appointment was to be the 24th. Doreen told us I could still have my surgery but with Dr. Mangubat instead. We were both shocked and deflated. To explain, after Cathy's return home from the ER I canceled my upcoming surgery date with Dr. Megan that was for a few weeks after Cathy's tummy tuck. We had planned for her normal recovery then she could in theory care for my recovery. Things were different now Cathy needed more time. I was going to give her all the time she needed, simply put she was my everything. Cathy did steadily recover and insisted we continue our transition with my surgery so we rescheduled another date a month after the original date. We had both come to understand many things because of Cathy's brush with death: life is best lived in the here and now. I even had the misguided thought that Dr. Megan might not too excited to have me as a patient after that awful time Cathy had in the ER.

***

Friday May 14, 2021. Dr. Eaman is now Cathy's doctor too. Cathy's blood numbers as far as Hemoglobin (12.4) and Hematocrit (38.5) are now in the normal range. Yay! They were both significantly low 9.0 and 28.4. This was two and a half weeks between the tests. So,

Cathy is normal in blood count back from being very low. Her sodium level has dropped from 132 on the first test down now to 125. A new problem is Phosphorus is now high out of range...

Me stuff: I called Dr. Megan's cellphone today and Dr. Megan is happy for me to come to her new office for surgery! In a very cordial voice she told me, "You should have called me right away! We can work you in and how is Cathy doing?" Without a missing a beat I signed up remembering to tell the office lady at Dr. Megan's new office that I had an original surgery date at Dr. Megan's old practice of July 9th. She found an opening on July 7th and put a hold on it for me. Dr. Megan was cordial with us and assured me we had nothing to do with her leaving La Belle Vie. We chatted and got to see pictures of Dr. Megan's very cute little 16-month-old girl. Dr. Megan even had an offer to partner at Dr. Phil Young's practice after she left Dr. Tony.

So yesterday my worry with Dr. M was resolved. This morning I awoke to the darkest depression I can remember, way darker than any time in the last several years. I couldn't overcome it; the mood was too mean. Was it because I have signed up with Dr. Megan again and have a date for surgery? Is it because I have been revisiting my journals from 2005, 2006, and 2007? I had forgotten the pain that was going on with me, and the separation from Cathy's sympathies for my condition. I just can't do food either. What the devil has caused this today? I have made it to 3:00pm by beating my head mentally against a wall. I hope this doesn't mean something horrible is going to happen within our family. Cathy's mom is due for surgery on the 18th or some irreversible side effect from my planned surgery leading to lifelong pain could happen. Will my collarbone joint just become another new life long ailment? One more thought, this weekend is the last time grandkids will be open to us and the last time they will have their own bedrooms and the last time they will be the only children of their house. The entire affair of Mindy's sister Lisa's coming to live with them and bringing her three kids and two big dogs along, just looks like a huge trap for Casey. Casey is not a big boy; he is a middle-aged man, in charge of his own family and future. He knows what is going on. My trouble is he reminds me of my dad Merrill adopting outsiders into our family, the result was we diminished, as they became his focus. He had a new son over me; he had new grandkids over Casey and Corey. If he had trouble with them it reflected back in the form of a strained relationship between he and me. David and I over the years had to compete for the attention of our dad with whatever kids had drifted into our family. The same thing is going to happen to B---- and Colby they will have to compete with Lisa's kids big time. And B---- and Colby will be at the big disadvantage of their past history of known behavior. There are so many things that are going to crash around me including me personally. Cathy and I are going to be alone and thought ill of. There is no hope otherwise really. I am very tired and have no gift to fix things. My only worth was to fix relationships with our sons and the opposite always resulted. I am in a bad place right now time for tears…

***

Sunday May 16, 2021. Took anti-yeast tonight because of sores inside my nose.

***

Monday May 17, 2021. We decided to drive up to Mountlake Terrace and deliver my forms to them. It will give us a chance to see where the place is and what it is like to drive there. Baxter Plastic Surgery is in the same office building as several services for the City of Mountlake Terrace. They are on the second floor suite 290. Sara and Kim run the office both seem to be nice enough. They loved our matching tie-dye stuff so there is hope that they will be nice to us when we need them to be.

Cathy's mom's surgery is tomorrow at 10:00; she will be in our prayers.

***

Saturday May 22, 2021. Cathy's mom had her surgery and her sodium levels puzzled her doctor until Cathy had a conversation with him. It was good that Cathy thought to talk to the doctor; he was forearmed with information about family low iron levels, sodium levels, and how to deal with them. They got her sodium level up but

543

the hematocrit keeps trending lower to hold right at 22%, at 21% you would normally give the patient whole blood. The doctor waited on release for the morning's reading, which was starting to climb once again. So, she was released and is recovering at home, she has big iron supplements to take three times a day. Today she sounds much more perky and the four of us will do games tonight.

Me stuff: Erica called me about SRS; I knew this was coming and now I have to face it. I was expecting to hear from Robin Dr. Bowers' long time surgical coordinator, but she might not be with Dr. Bowers' office anymore... Erica wants eligibility letters. I wonder about going somewhere else closer than Burlingame, California. Checking around it comes to two places one in Spokane and the other in Portland. I can't even get any date for a consultation with these two without first having like three eligibility letters in hand. Dr. Bowers will let me get by with just one if I pay for all phases of the surgery out of pocket and it comes from a PhD therapist. The problem is Sandy is retired and I haven't replaced her so I am without a therapist. I am so weirded out that no one is taking new therapy clients and the thought of starting anew seems to be an impossible mountain to climb. Add the pressure of my surgery of July 7 being far away up north of Seattle. Oh yes and there is also my collarbone that was injured and no one had a good plan to help me. So, Natalie pointed me to a PT (physical therapy) clinic run by Chris Lee. He was magic and pushed my bone back into joint and will start me on an exercise program to strengthen the muscles to hold the joint in place. I was so happy everyone in the place was affirming to me and I was going to be fixed! We saw Dr. Eaman a day later and she and Cathy got along great! Dr. Eaman was happy to send referrals for my PT. Super Great! I got home and looked at the referral and saw 'Gender: male (identifies as female).' Death and doom fell upon me... I have never been triggered before, I had no reason to be because I didn't feel authentic as female, there was no hope I was just nothing really. Now I had let myself feel as if I could be fixed, it was going to happen, surgeries were coming, but that all came crashing to the ground knowing that a male gender marker was making its way to my new PT place. I was just one of those broken guys who was

544

pretending. I had just gotten over to the other side as it were, knowing that it wasn't an identification it was real to me and always had been… So I crashed. What point is transition, of all the pain, expense, and loss; if the male 'M' marker just follows you around everywhere, followed by a brief explanation in brackets of mental confusion, wink, wink. If this is going to happen there is no point in continuing forward, in transition or in life itself. I told Cathy she would have to be understanding in the only choice left for me was ending my life. We both cried as a part of me died right then and there. I had chosen life almost twenty years ago when my crisis had come. I had waited keeping distracted until the crisis stopped me cold forcing a decision. Life would be hard but it gave hope of becoming whole if I did all that was required. Now with one little group of words all that work was worth nothing. So I broke down, I couldn't go to PT; I would just get better all by myself. I'm not going to have any more surgeries either, they will just make the hurt worse each time that 'M' gender marker comes around. I can't continue in life like this with a thin female façade as that 'M' gender marker comes around to strip it away. So this is what being triggered is like. I tried sleeping last night only to awaken to the sadness of the place I have found myself in. I couldn't shake the malady of hopelessness. In the morning I thought I had one chance and that was to call Dr. Eaman and explain how that 'M' needed to be an 'F' on that paper and nothing more. If she pushed back with an explanation of it being a proper marker even in the face of DOL, Birth certificate, and Passport, then I am doomed and have to look for a new doctor. I never asked her on her personal view if a trans woman was a woman to her. I expect she wouldn't be straightforward as it is now politically correct… Anyway, I called and got Terina the office manager and the one who made out the referral. I stumbled asking if doctor might call me sometime today. No, okay I'll tell you. I explained how the gender line hurt me and how it is kind of a slur to point out 'identified as.' She was heartbroken that this happened and I now had guilt in bringing it to her attention! That's okay I just need for it to be fixed and resent, I can't bring myself to go to the PT place knowing the gender was this way. She told me she would and that was that. It was the only fix I could find that gave me hope. Now it was left to me to find a path back to being Cadance once again.

***

Tuesday May 25, 2021. Yesterday I got a text from Dr. Eaman apologizing and saying they have gone through all the files and updated them to female. I looked in my email and sure enough a new fax had just been sent a few minutes ago. I opened the thing to find that male was still listed. I called Terina to tell her about it. No, she hadn't checked before sending and the darn system hadn't updated yet... So she sent it again and now it is fixed! The fact remains that the PT place now has at least three faxes, which must scream 'look at me!' I so dread going to PT tonight... Then something happened, my phone rang while Cathy was getting a Natalie massage. It was the PT place, I answered and found out that none of the faxes ever got to them! So, they didn't see any of the mean gender male ones at all!!! God saved me, so wonderful just as God is...

***

Saturday May 29, 2021. Cathy and I had our Memorial Day drive over to Thorp and Quincy yesterday to leave flowers on my grandparents Lawler and Cathy's grandparents Tuttle graves. Cathy also left flowers on her Aunt Gladys' Pearson grave. The drive was a much needed getaway, we really haven't gone anywhere for over a year. We got out of the house just after 9:00am meeting fairly light traffic clear over to the mountains. Our companion was an audio book of *Perry Mason's The Deadly Toy,* we hear half the story on the trip. Our rest stop was at Snoqualmie Pass's public restroom facility, this turned out to be quite the experience. I normally gravitate to single use bathrooms, I just don't want anyone to be upset, and it is sort of a crutch on my part chiefly from fear of an altercation. We found a park near the entrance doors even though the place was pretty busy. The single use bathroom was just before the women's and men's separate units. I tried the door on the single use bathroom and it was locked tight, I didn't want to knock or anything and told Cathy I would just wait until whoever was in there to be finished. Cathy took my arm and turned me into the women's side saying, "That stall is open use it." I did and I was frighten the whole time setting there with women on either side of me. A funny thing mixed with the fear was a strange sense of belonging there. I finished got myself together and walked out past two ladies chatting with each other to find Cathy waiting outside. She asked me how I was and then told me bluntly, "You are female Cadance; use the right facility." Cathy told me once she had had a dream one night where she and I went into the lady's room and after I had finished I walked past two women with my head held up high as they stared at me, Cathy told me she felt so proud of me during that moment. The desperate search for single use bathrooms stymied our travel plans and to be confident in using the multiple stall restrooms gives us so many more options in travel. I have used small female restrooms a good number of times but this was the first really big one. The experience brought on a further shift in my identity as being female even after all this time.

We did the local cemeteries around home today and ran into Aunt Luella, Denise, and her husband Ken as we made our way to Grandma Ida Anderson's grave. This year it was my idea to leave flowers on the Hanson's and Smith's graves as well as Orval's. Afterward we came home to ponder how different life is without family. I have asked Corey to come help us on my Tummy tuck/BA surgery of July 7th. He would be a backup to Casey in case Casey was too busy to help out...

I have my sources for letters of surgical recommendation for vaginoplasty. Rachel LordKenaga will be my therapist. I got her name after Sandy called me back from a voice mail I had left. It seems that Rachel is a very good friend of Sandy's and would be happy to help. An email to a group of psychiatrists was answered that they too would be happy to help me. Dr. Eaman I'm sure would be the source for my Hormone Provider letter. So here I sit with a handle on getting the three letters, something I thought impossible to do just a week ago... One set for Dr. Bowers and the other for a consult with Dr. Geoffrey Stiller who is still unknown to me.

***

Thursday June 3, 2021. I just heard from Patricia Fawver PhD, she would be happy to help me with a letter too. Just amazing one day there is no hope and I know only despair, then God just turns things around. Tomorrow I see Dr. Eaman; I want to get my blood tested for Ferritin levels and an overall blood panel done in preparation for July 7 as well as a release letter for surgery, and ask where do I go to get an EKG done.

The book I am writing is such a big project to do. I have the basic narrative down but integrating my journals pages into the body of the story is just immensely hard for me. It is this high mountain to climb full of twists, turns, and so very many pitfalls... I can't see the end at all... If you want to feel overwhelmed and hopeless, write a book...

***

Friday June 4, 2021. Cathy and I drive over to Dr. Eaman's office for my 2:00 appointment. I have four issues to address during this visit and have not written them down. The mental list is as follows: Do a blood draw to test for Ferritin, electrolytes, Hematocrit, sodium, chloride (CMP); letters of support for Dr. Bowers and Dr. Stiller; a letter of surgical clearance for Dr. Dreveskracht, a referral for an EKG. I told my tale of upcoming surgeries needing letters and Dr. Eaman told us no problem she knows Dr. Stiller's practice and knows exactly what to do and she can do an EKG in her office. She is almost too good to be true none of my problems causes any effort for her to fix, consider it done... Dr. E was very glad to see Cathy because she had gotten her sodium blood-level test back and it was back down at the 126 level; "Can you stop the Triamterene Hydrochlorothiazide for a week? I have been speaking with a Naturopath friend about your meds bringing the sodium level down and all we could figure was the Triamterene. We will retest after five days and perhaps have an answer." Dr. Eaman loves being a doctor, the whole solving a puzzle part of it, and she is pumped to be on the road to unraveling Cathy's mystery. For my part Dr. Eaman's expertise in trans medicine is both a blessing and a challenge. It is a blessing that she knows so much, but the challenge comes in my weakened communication skills. There was a time I knew so much more about hormone interaction from all the research I had read about than I do now. For the most part, it is all gone along with my short-term memory, I just can't bring anything up. I blame the memory lapses and the clouding of my ability to focus directly on the androgen blockers (5a-Reductase inhibitor) that were my rigor in HRT over the years. Avodart and Dutasteride combined with anti-depression medications took a great toll on my mental function.

***

Thursday June 10, 2021. PT is going well. Cathy had a massage appointment with Natalie at 3:00 and a very thought-provoking conversation came from chatting with Natalie. Natalie also works at the PT place and often we will get to say hello to her while I'm doing PT therapy.

So, while Cathy is on the table and Natalie is giving her all to chase away Cathy's aches and pains we all chat together. I will sit on the floor out of the way of the massage table but very much within the conversation circle. I had everyone laughing off and on along with serious conversation about our health concerns. The main topic was tummy tucks, Cathy's past one and my future one in July. It is girlfriend talk and I relate that I am nervous/fearful as my time gets closer and closer. The two of them soothe my fear but Natalie has some questions about the whole process. Cathy and I explain about liposuction and how the fat from my middle will be moved to my breasts. The debate about having a belly button or not comes up to everyone's delight. Natalie suddenly pops up, "Will you be big enough from the fat alone and doesn't the fat slowly disappears over a short time?" Well the doctor told me up to 70% stays. Natalie is dubious, "What will you do if more goes away? Why don't you just get implants, they look and feel great, believe me you are going to love your boobs and if they deflate because the fat dissolves you are going to feel bad like you wasted a surgery." I respond that I should recover faster with fat transfer but yea that could happen… Then Natalie said something that backed me into a corner, "When you got your orchi,

549

didn't you instantly regret doing only the orchi and not the full SRS?" I stumbled in answering her. Yes this is exactly what happen and then the next day we put down money for the full SRS surgery. But I had a reason! I could get the orchi done quickly and would have to wait for three years otherwise... I started thinking about the one MtF I came in contact with at GO. She constantly was tormenting herself about waiting so late in life to transition. Her repeated lament was, "I'll never forgive myself for waiting so long."

Natalie you're right and I'll have to think about this some more, I get to talk to Dr. Megan on Monday. Natalie, as if to gather in what just happened told us she didn't want to cause any trouble she just cares so much about us... I have Emma for PT today.

***

Thursday June 17, 2021. In this last week:

Friday, Cathy had an appointment with Dr. Eaman for a blood draw. Cathy showed Dr. Eaman and Terina a beaded ball she made using 5000 tiny glass beads. All hand stitched one by one using a Peyote stitch (a classic hand beading stitch). Suffice it to say, it wowed both of them. I talked to Terina about fat transfer to the breast since she used to work in a plastic surgery office and no she didn't have any positive or negative to share. I asked for everyone's opinions on bellybuttons, Terina was neutral and Dr. E was pro. We begin our house cleaning attack on our clutter corner stair cap.

Saturday, we have Colby with us from 9:30am to 9:00pm. We got him before ten because Casey was expecting a nurse to give Mindy her first feeding into her TPN port. We played train at Saturday night games at Grandma Dixon's.

Sunday, our cleaning attack was focused on the living room computer area. We had a ten-minute call with Quince.

Monday, Physical Therapy appointment with Kimmy; she has a different style of PT than Chris. Our Dr. Megan appointment was afterward at La Belle Vie. The office ladies were friendly to us but we felt like we were sneaking into this meeting. A new nurse showed us to exam room one and told Cathy to take all of her clothes off. Cathy left her bra and underwear on anyway. A tired Dr. Megan came in and greeted us, it seems she had another patient have a bleeding problem after the anti-coagulant was administered, so she was not free to leave on vacation tomorrow and have to miss at least one day of her vacation (her husband's 40th birthday). Cathy and I had come to the understanding with each other that half of this appointment was for answering my coming surgery questions. So, after pictures and while Cathy dresses it is my turn. Dr. Megan was thoughtful and careful to answer all my worries about fat transfer and told me to find pictures of how I want my breast to look like afterward. She looks at my belly again and told us she could come up with 1000cc of fat to use. This matches the amount Cathy had removed from her breasts. Dr. M also told me my recovery is much quicker with fat transfer than with an implant and no she doesn't think she will need drains but doesn't guarantee not too. She also told me I was going to need Enoxaparin... This scares me after Cathy's problem with it... We also show her the booklet from Dr. Baxter office and confirmed I needed an EKG. Also, I need a surgery clearance letter from my PCP. Fun... Well, I told her I do trust her and my worry is much reduced over fat transfer... Dr. Megan gives me her card and tells me not to look for advice on the net but to email her my questions instead. We part with hugs.

Tuesday, cleaning attack for me was focused on the downstairs bedrooms and for Cathy it was cleaning the kitchen. I had a massage with Natalie where we wade into our problems seeking answers from one another. I tell Natalie that I have made peace with having fat transfer instead of implants and she is curious about how came to this. I had found on FB a nice write-up of a T gal who had done exactly the procedure I was to have that is a tummy tuck and BA using her own fat. In addition, she had the abdominoplasty part of narrowing her waist to more of a female curve. Her before pictures look a lot like my breast with my little sad nipples and her after pictures looked very promising. Her write-up had lots of good research and information. I still would like more projection than she got and more of a teardrop shape. So, I am okay with fat transfer; in fact, I am resolute to get this over with and on with life. At home Cathy does pulled pork and house cleaning continues.

Wednesday, all day cleaning with a little grocery shopping at Marlene's, Costco, Bartell's, and PCC. We were the walking dead in cleaning but we got the whole house done! We bought a new air cleaner at Costco ($129) for Quince's room so now both downstairs bedrooms will each have its own air cleaner. I took a much-needed shower. I have a very touchy phone call with Corey; he called me early in the day, which was unusual, to ask a personal question, "What about Father's Day, do we get to say happy Father's Day?" We waded into am I a trans-woman or a woman, does Father's Day discredit this, are you offended etc. It was a triggering conversation for me, Cathy touched on how Mother's Day was for mothers which seemed to shut the door to that for me and Father's Day didn't belong to me anymore either. Mean problem. The call got interrupted and Corey had to go attend to a crying Quince. So, I retreated into myself with tears. I began to think about who is a mother and who is a father. To be a mother do you have to be female and if you are female are you still a mother without birthing children. If being a mother is nurturing a child i.e., mothering them, then I have been a mother just as much as anyone is who steps into that role when no mother is to be found. The same with being a father; I have been a father to our children as well despite being a female who is male bodied. I don't know what will come of this quandary this weekend, or how it will play out with Quince. Will it confuse him? As far as Casey is concerned I am one of his mothers, end of discussion. This hurts Cathy but works for Casey. My take with Cathy on this is no one is taking your position as Casey's mom but on occasion I have mothered him too just as you on occasion have pushed into the father role. It is an uneasy truce at best, but as our mothering time and fathering time is now past us, taking on our last roles of grandparents is what is important. And we are still transitioning as a couple; it is this transition that will be our last as two females with molded gender roles to suit each other in everlasting love.

We had a Dr. Eaman appointment it was just her alone in her office. She did an EKG for me and was fascinated by my chest anatomy being non symmetrical and long. Dr. Eaman would happily do a clearance letter for me to take to Dr. Megan and she did a good job of calming my fears of having to take anticoagulants for surgery. She did also validate my fear but guided me toward an understanding of why the med was worth the risk. Dr. Eaman shared with us that one of her eyes need a correction of -14! Cathy's correction is -5.

PT today was full of new exercises and I was so tired afterward but my body was in better shape for doing them. The PT room was very busy and a gal who came in just as I was finishing with heat on my shoulder asked us if we were sisters. She loved our matching shirts. I said we are sort of sister as we have been married for a long time. I didn't have my glasses on and my hair was pulled back in a ponytail and she still thought I was female! You never know when someone will come along and make your day!!!

***

Wednesday June 23, 2021. Last night everything fell apart for surgery for me. I had been churning about whether Dr. Megan was going to do all that I wanted done to my body. Yes fat transfer to my breast, and a tummy tuck but I wasn't sure if she understood I also wanted a feminine waist. I wanted curves. I found experiences of folks getting body sculpting and even reached out to Jery for advice on how to articulate this to my doctor. Jery almost a year ago had a mini tummy tuck and waist narrowing with Dr Mangubat. She reported frustration in getting her need across too. If you don't have the technical language it is a mountain to climb in communicating this. Yesterday Cathy had helped me find images of breasts that would be acceptable to show Dr. Megan; these were printed and added to the other paperwork such as an EKG, surgery release letter from Dr. Eaman, blood labs, and clotting time to take with us to my pre-op appointment. I was as ready as I could be, still nervous, but ready. Then it all fell apart, Cathy tried on a new pair of yoga pants, and they looked good on her with her new slimmer waist. I tried to get a flattering picture for her to see the difference when it all went south. It is true that Cathy, at this moment, still has more around her waist than it was her dream not to have. It comes from a combination of swelling and scar tissue forming. Somewhere in the mix Cathy began to tear up saying no one had even acknowledged her new shape. Her sister, mother, Casey, Corey, and Melinda all have said nothing about it. To top this all off, Cathy still feels pudgy compared to some other women on her support group after surgery. Truthfully I had begun to wonder about this and how my surgery might turn out to be less pleasing than expected but Cathy's tears shook me into the darker side of this whole thing. That part being that this was a mistake to do at all. Then Cathy expressed that she was hurt that I also hadn't been appreciative for things she was doing for me. Her tears of failure of the surgery to fix what was wrong about her body, and a direct blow to my self-worth by me hurting her emotionally, shattered my weak hold I had on my fears. Now in the darkest of moods I realized this surgery wasn't going to fix my body either. In the bathroom I pulled up my shirt and for the first time in a long time looked at my misshapen chest, the one my doctor told me was so asymmetrical and thin-walled. I was repulsed by what I saw in our broken mirror. I could see my chest ribs just under the skin, what breast tissue I have hung down deflated and mocking me. How in the world did I get the idea this could all be fixed!? Where did I get this false hope of being made a whole female? Why didn't anyone stop me and point out the ugly reality, that I could never be anything except the broken misshapen freak I was born to be… Every emotional prop I had slowly built up broke to pieces, this was all an impossible mistake I have made. Cathy saw the dark change in my countenance and began to make excuses for the hurt I had given her but it was too late. I was a bad narcissistic person there were no excuses for this; the surgery is a sham it can't fix me because I am unfixable. Tears came, my voice fell to a low hollow monotone and I just didn't care anymore. We went to bed with me hating my unfixable body. I slept a night of horrible waking dreams as I lay all alone by myself on my side of the bed. In the morning, I awoke to the same defeated and dispirited brain fog that plagued the night. Cathy had reconsidered her surgery outcome during the night and in the light of morning saw it in a very positive light. She was better than before and her weight was still dropping. She resolved to make sure I didn't get the idea she had any regrets in doing it with Dr. Megan. Cathy wanted me talking; she wanted me finding my way through my hopelessness back to her. Her persistence in the face of my defeat gave rise to a spark of hope again. Cathy told me, "This is the real you and you can be whole. I know it is true, you are Cady and have always been her." I didn't eat anything but did get dressed and as we drove toward Mountlake Terrace a return to the resolve to do what is needed in spite of yesterday filled the empty place within me. Cathy had pulled my shirt back tight and pointed out that I did have breasts and this surgery would only make them better looking.

Seven o'clock. Our alarm clock app demanded we awake and we acquiesced. My dour mood was still in the need of propping up, Cathy insisted on an early morning walk. The air that greeted us was cool and welcoming giving all the room that I might need to lift each trampled part of my psyche for propping up once again. We only had time to walk to the high school and back but it was enough for me to consider Cathy's advice and accept it. I centered in on making sure not to miss this opportunity to talk again with Dr. Megan about all I wanted done. We are to be at Dr. Baxter's office by 10:00, which means we need to leave home by 8:30. Cathy gathers all the important papers and I grab my iPad for the images it contains. Our car awakes from its slumber and we are off into early morning traffic. Rush hour traffic through downtown Seattle is slow but nothing like it was back in 2019. That near gridlock image persisted in my worried memory but that image was not today's reality; today it was a rolling mass right past the unused convention center. The area north of the University of Washington holds the construction of the light rail project along I-5 all the way up to and beyond the Mountlake Terrace exit 179. We parked outside a five story brick and dark glass business building just off the freeway in Mountlake Terrance. The building is multi-use and holds many City of Mountlake Terrance services as well as Baxter Plastic Surgery where Dr. Megan now practices. As is our custom we pray that God might guide us and his name might be glorified in what we are about to do. Cathy and I are dressed in our matching orange

555

and black tie-dye shirts with matching masks. I almost make it to the elevator before I realize I left my iPad in the car. With our bundle of the book Dr. Baxter's office sent to us to fill out, med lists, EKG, letters of clearance, and my iPad now safely in tow we enter the Lobby's lifting machine and choose floor two. The book of loosely bound pages of to-be-signed forms is problematic to us as it lists Dr. Baxter as the surgeon doing the surgery on me. We had shared this with Dr. Megan on the last visit we had with her in Tukwila. She told us not to sign it until she was present and could countersign it. The restrooms were just outside of their office door and since I really needed it I made a beeline to the woman's restroom. Cathy was right behind me and since the place was empty hung around and waited for me to finish. She told me she was greatly impressed that I showed no hesitation in coming in here. The door to Dr. Baxter's office is propped open and all the chairs in the empty reception area were wrapped with a piece of white ribbon complete with a bow on each chair making them unusable for sitting. Sara greeted us hesitantly. The office waiting room feels sort of empty of business and we feel more like intruders at the moment. Sara leaves the reception desk and pops out of the door to where we are standing and hands me a clipboard loaded with a short pile of to-be-signed pages then asks me to take a clean pen from the cup she is holding. She leads us to an exam room and tells us to complete the important paperwork and for me to sign it then ring the bell on the counter and someone will be with us shortly. Cathy and I set to work checking boxes and initialing one statement after another. We run afoul of the full signature required pages stating Dr. Baxter is doing the surgery and ring the bell as everything else is done. In comes Tabitha who is the director of nursing for the office. She is in blue scrubs complete with character adorned yellow cap. Her body language gives us the feeling that we will be tolerated but are intruders here. She is thin, athletic, and mousey in some ways, but in reality she is a controlled powerhouse. She is in charge of the orchestra and Cathy and I the clueless struggling rhythm section. She asks who is Cady and I return that I am and tell her this is Cathy. I explain I didn't sign the paper because it states that Dr. Baxter is doing the surgery. She apologizes and offers that everyone is excited here because of the change of being a single doctor office to now a two-doctor office, we have to get used to doing things a new way, "For as long as I have been with Dr. Baxter it has always just been him as the surgeon." It dawns on me that everything is suddenly up for grabs in their routine way of doing things and we are the first of Dr. Megan's patients to come along making waves. Tabitha is impressed with our med and health history list. All we can see of her is her eyes and hear her voice which reminds me of another of our friends, Debbie Caddell, who herself is also a controlled powerhouse. Our challenge is not to challenge Tabitha as she tells us what they will do to me and for me, but to find openings for our questions to be asked. Tabitha keeps getting my pronouns wrong. At this point Dr. Megan pops into the room explaining she is a fly on the wall for this pre-op meeting. She doesn't get to remain in this role long as contrary information pops up especially about drains. Tabitha goes down her list explaining each action that will happen on surgery day and what Cathy will be responsible to learn to do in after care for me. Tabitha mentions that I will be prescribed Lovenox injections starting the day after surgery so Cathy will get some training on how to give them to me. The idea of getting the same medication that almost took Cathy's life just freezes me to the bone. But it is a routine drug for surgery as explained to me by Dr. Eaman and Dr. Megan and I am neither Cathy nor my father Merrill who had trouble with another blood thinner. The choice is this if I want the surgery I have to take the drug… Strangely no one cares if I continue on my estradiol patches or progesterone pills. It wasn't too long ago that I would have had to stop them four weeks in advance. It was all about unwanted blood clots from estradiol but there are good studies now showing the risk is very low. Anyway, the idea of taking Lovenox is still scary to me. Tabitha continues with telling me about Alprazolam I get two of these pills one for the night before as a sleep aid and the other if in the morning anxiety gets the best of me. It is my choice as to whether to take them or not. Also, there is Zofran for anti-nausea sublingual every six hours as needed. Cathy and I had talked about how La Belle Vie used Emend as a nausea preventer and asked

Tabitha about using it for me. She asked if I had a history of nausea after anesthesia and no I didn't so much but vomiting is so traumatic for me that I would do anything to completely suppress it. Tabitha accepted this and ordered the drug for me. Cathy asked about antibiotics and no they don't use them after surgery without an infection. Another big difference from La Belle Vie! Tabitha moves on to me having drains and the training Cathy will need to care for this. Cathy looks to Dr. Megan about drains and she tells Tabitha that I did not need drains; Tabitha is a little startled but moves right along to another bullet point. Tabitha tells me that I will be getting a compression garment that acts as a binder and compression leggings all in one. It is a one-piece garment covering from the ankle to right under the breast with openings for going to the bathroom. Wow! This again is very different from La Belle Vie using the flat Velcro binder that was such a pain to keep in place. A side discussion occurs between Tabitha and Dr. Megan about the garment and during this Tabitha keeps throwing out male pronouns in referring to me. I speak up asking that my proper pronouns be used, there is a pause in the discussion, an adjustment is made mentally on Tabitha's part, and the discussion continues but I no longer hear anymore-male pronouns. Even after I mention this is Cathy and my 47th year together to which both of them seem impressed by. Tabitha tells me later that all she needs is the right partner for this to happen for her. Tabitha tells me on surgery morning to wear an open front blouse and slip-on shoes. She is very specific about the shoes; this is a hot spot for her because it is hard to get a hospital-socked foot in a laced shoe. We will get parking information on the day of surgery and Cathy is welcome to wait with me in the photo room until I am taken into surgery. I thank Tabitha for using my female pronouns and she tells me it is especially important to her also. Tabitha gets a cloth gown for me to change into and she and Dr. Megan both leave us for me to change. I take off my shirt and bra but leave my tights on. I had worked up the courage to ask Dr. Megan about my waist being made more feminine by tightening my muscles and perhaps my abdomen muscles were also stretched from my fatter days. This was as important to me as the fat transfer. Dr. Megan knocked at the door and entered to look at my belly. She checked again for a hernia at my belly button while I lay on my back with my legs raised holding them in that position. She told me my abs were fine and I wouldn't benefit from doing anything with them, but doing lipo on my sides and putting in stitches on either side would help to shape my waist. She told Tabitha who had returned to write plication to the side on the chart. This was perfect it was just what Jery had recommended I do! We are left alone to wait for Lori the patient care coordinator to take our credit card as payment. Tabitha pops back with my Covid test kit, it is a little plastic cup that I drool into on July 1st and then FedEx it to some test lab somewhere in Texas. Lori replaces her and hands us a copy of my prescriptions then takes our Costco card telling us that the bill is split in two: one is for anesthesia and the other for the surgeon. The bigger of the two charges will happen right away. Cathy looks at the prescription and yes there is a mistake on the Lovenox it reads to take it the morning before surgery and should say the day after surgery. Tabitha is called in to verify this, she pops in with her mask and no cap. Cathy doesn't recognize her; she is speaking in a lower tone and has dark shoulder length hair! I recognize her cap in her back pocket. We are free to leave; my surgery will be at 8:15 on the morning of Wednesday July 7th and I will return on Friday the 9th for a post-op check. So, the plan is all set, amazing just 24 hours ago I was ready to throw it and myself all away…

***

Thursday July 1, 2021. At some point a while ago I had resolved to stop journaling. I was writing a book and the journal wasn't needed anymore. It was kind of a relief but the book is not done yet just as my surgical transition is not done yet. So de facto my journal needs to go on to support me, and the natural end of the book.

I now have all the letters needed to meet the requirement for surgery with Dr. Bowers and to consult with Dr. Stiller. Dr. Eaman did my medical letter of surgical release and referral, Rachel LordKenaga supplied support as my Therapist with an MA, and

Marissa Ohlstrom wrote a nice support letter I needed from a PsyD. I met with these last two very nice and very professional ladies via Zoom meetings. Marissa was yesterday and Rachel several days ago. Marissa is a very kind and learned person; she typed the letter in real time as she asked the required questions about me. Cathy and I sat together in front of her laptop for the meeting, we discovered iPads didn't function because they didn't run the Zoom app very well. Cathy's machine came to our rescue! It was an upbeat meeting. Marissa was kind in letting me talk about myself even if it wasn't pertinent to the letter. She apologized for the insurance driven bureaucratic hoops I had to jump through considering my history. I told her it was a benefit because I got to meet her as a new friend! She finished the letter and sent me a draft to okay then made a little adjustment and I had my letter! She also told me if anything needed to be changed just let her know!

***

Friday July 2, 2021. I did two Covid tests, the first by drooling into a little container and dropping it off at a FedEx drop box. The second was at a free testing site at a nearby church parking lot, just in case FedEx ran late. These last two weeks have hung over me as each day I am getting closer and closer to my surgery day of July 7th. I had settled away from the worry of the surgery itself but held onto the fear of making a mistake by not communicating what I needed done. In other words, did I tell Dr. Megan in coherent precise words about such and such? Of course, there is the nagging fear that what I really needed was breast implants not just fat transfer. And another downside to the two Zoom meetings was I sat and looked at my face for two hours. I became very aware of how wrinkled and old it had become this was going to have to be fixed also. The mountain I must climb just seems higher and higher and I am getting older and older. Then the idea that fat transfer wasn't enough and I will have to have another surgery after this one brings on the wish that I had been more aggressive years ago… It is not the surgeries themselves but the time you have to wait between them, and then there is variable of the time spent in healing

560

that must be dealt with. God give me strength to endure this all to become what I must become to be whole. I just have to let this surgery do to me what it does, if it comes up short I just had to have another.

***

Tuesday July 6, 2021. I had my day-before-surgery-call from Jennifer the nurse who will do my anesthesia and who promised to take good care of me. In a blink of an eye my mood went from dread to elation! How odd is that? Dread has been my constant companion for weeks now but yesterday it became let's-get-this-over-with! I call the Smart Orthodontic Group and when I hear Gwen speaking know that I have a chance to get this fixed today. Gwen is the nicest lady and is always very friendly to Cathy and me; in fact, she sent a get-well card to Cathy after her awful experience in the ER. I explain my problem with its deadline of today and she offers me a 10:00 appointment that morning! Perfect, as Cathy has an 8:30am appointment with Dr. Kageyama about some skin moles that she wanted to take care of while I could still drive. The appointment was success with no skin cancer and the mean moles were removed to Cathy's relief. Although Cathy's upper lip and cheek look a little worse for wear. The orthodontist office is the next step in our to do list this last morning. Here it will take three appointments one with Tina, one with Ali, and one with Dr. Leigh to finally fix the problem. Tina glued the button back on again no problem, but the angle wasn't right and at home the rubber band just wouldn't stay in place. Ali next tries bending the perpendicular shaft, but again the band slipped off as soon as I returned home. The final time Ali confers with Dr. Leigh then removes the button completely and glues it back on again with a buildup on one side this worked perfectly. Dr. Leigh instructs me to only wear the rubber bands at night from here on in. Gwen, Ali, and Tina all love the idea of my surgery matching Cathy's but with the twist of BA and are eager to see the result when I am better. Fifteen minutes after my ortho appointment, we leave to pick up Corey at the airport and then it is just a waiting game until tomorrow… I am resigned to the surgery now and looking forward to being home again

561

after it is over. I must remember to remind Dr. Megan she is welcome to harvest fat from below my breasts as she suggested it was a very viable fat supply. We will be in God's care just as our prayers petition it to be. I dare not to even dream at this point as to how it will feel to have a waist and breasts... Corey's flight is set to land at 1:50 at the airport. We station ourselves at the exits from C and D gates and stand where we can clearly see all the human traffic streaming through the one-way exit gate duly guarding by a single security person. We stand at a corner pillar across from the exit, just as we have so many times awaiting Corey and family, this time it is only Corey here to help us through my adventure. It was very important to have Corey here to give support to Cathy if something happened to me as it did to Cathy. We share many things in life, hopefully a visit to the ER right after surgery will not be one of them. Again if it is, Corey will be right at hand as Casey was for me that awful night. Cathy and I are wearing our matching white, blue, and purple spiral t-shirts and are garnering lots of looks from bypassing folks. Cathy has an app on her phone that tracks the location of airplanes so we can see the plane Corey is on as it taxis toward one of the open gangways. Soon Corey comes through the gate all smiles. At home, Corey and Cathy establish a running cribbage game. Cathy is having a great time with him. The first things he wanted to know about tomorrow were the timeline and did I want cremation or burial if things went badly. He realized we had never spoken about this... We have a clumsy conversation leading to a non-determinant end but this is okay the future will hold for now. Corey and Cathy play cribbage as I prepare food for us. Corey and Cathy will have what we call a Cathy dinner plate of cold strips of steak, with raw veggies, Kalamata olives, and goat cheese. This was the food staple for Cathy after surgery to bring up her blood count and sodium level. I am having trouble with my appetite; food isn't something appealing to me. I have been working to gain a little weight to improve the fat harvest but I haven't gain much at all. My take on food is one egg and one slice of toast. I did rotate in some rice and chicken recently. After dinner, Casey and B---- stopped by to give me hugs for good luck; so nice! Casey assured me that everything would go fine and he would say a prayer for us. I also decided to post on FB about Corey being here to help us through the ordeal. Phil was first to like the post and wish me good luck. Tonight, we will sleep for the last time in our bed and Corey will sleep downstairs in his room. I shower before bed as per instructed with soap only, it will be a while before I can shower again. We are as set as we can be now. From here on in it is all mechanical: one action following another all laid out without thought.

***

Wednesday July 7, 2021. Today is the day of my life changing surgery. We are up by 6:00am, Cathy and I go for a mile walk while Corey is busy showering. The weather is cool at 58 degrees I am wearing a recovery top complete with special pockets for drains, if I need them, and a matching hoodie to the one Cathy is wearing. Since Cathy and I can't match today, Corey has stepped up to match his mom's tie-dye shirt to keep the spirit alive. We have to be on the road by 7:00 to make our 8:15 appointment time. Cathy has packed her take-a-long bag holding all the stuff she may need, along with some that are required to have (such as all my meds) and a Kindle for passing the time. While I'm in the OR, she and Corey will have several hours to while away. This is the great blessing of having Corey here during that time; he can be my stand-in to comfort his mom. Cathy sees that I take my pre-surgery meds before we leave the house: these are one Emend and two Tylenol 500mg tablets. I had the option of taking a Xanax (alprazolam) before bed last night but decided against it. I wasn't anxious about this surgery at all. I had seen the worst that could happen with Cathy's turn at it. Her experience had triggered long discussions within my mind, all of which had already been the running threads of years before now. Years of smoldering gender dysphoria tamped down to make it through to another day while knowing that with the passing of that day a little bit of me was dying away. The three of us load ourselves into our car with me behind the wheel. Me doing the driving is a normal thing and this morning I fully appreciate any normality provided to me. Cathy is right beside me in the front passenger seat just like she has been for the last 47 years. I always joked that I had no idea how to run that side of the car at all. Corey is in the backseat and reports on the disheveled condition the grandkids have left it in. As we drive, Corey graciously accepts my advice on how to drive the car through downtown Seattle. This is another blessing because it helps me feel as though I have done all I can this morning in preparations for both the surgery and the return home. We park in front of a brick business building that houses both city of Mountlake Terrace offices and a plastic surgery office. It is 7:55. I have done my morning prayer as I drove along and now another prayer before we enter the lobby of the building wearing our masks. Cathy and Corey proudly wear matching tie-dye t-shirts and me in a drab recovery top. One thing we did forget was slip-on shoes for me. Tabitha, the in-charge nurse, had made a point of telling me not to wear laced up shoes as it was hard to get them on after surgery; too late now. We ride the elevator up to the second floor and exit into a hallway. I have to go to the bathroom of course but we know it is right across from the office. I make a beeline for the women's multi-stall restroom while Cathy waits for me. Corey heads into the men's restroom and I note the symbolism of the moment. The restroom is empty, a great relief to me even though I know I am in the proper place and while I clear away my inners a thought occurs to me that this is the last time it will be comfortable to use bathroom for quite some time because of the surgery. The restroom is still empty as I exit the stall and wash my hands thinking score! I didn't bother anyone. The next thing I know the door opens and in breezes Dr. Dreveskracht! She sees me and cheerfully says, "Oh Hi! Are you excited for today?" I answered, yes I am! And I meant it, although I was taken back for the moment but proud to have recovered. What was the chance of running into your surgeon in the women's restroom before surgery? Especially for me while thinking I had pulled off a quick in-and-out without anyone noticing. I took it as an affirming sign from the prayer I had offered up. It is what these surgeries are all about for me, to bring my body into line with my mind, and to allow me to be a complete female being. This morning I was being led step by step along a path that was formed for me before I was born. Cathy and Corey were outside the restroom just standing there waiting for me to return. Cathy was wearing a little smirky smile and when I asked why 'no heads-up' about the Doctor coming in she said, "Why would I? You're female, after 47 years I'm sure of it, every piece of ID you have says your female it's past time for you to realize it." (Wow! I thought we had come a long way, you and I.) The three of us enter the waiting room and are greeted by Sara. Standing at the glass walled reception desk she on her side and us on ours we turn our attention to her. Sara gives us the low down on parking and the estimated length of my surgery, which is currently set to be over at 1:00-ish. Sara has an odd habit of looking away from me as she talks to me, especially when there is a pronoun being used. She will look to either Cathy or Corey whose pronouns are easy to align. Sara asks where Cathy and Corey will be waiting at and Cathy says there is a Starbuck nearby. At this point Dr. Megan opens a side door to the waiting room telling us it is a nice Starbuck too. She has just discovered it and there is a trick to parking she shares with Cathy. Corey makes sure his cell phone number is on the office's list along with Cathy's. It is time to cross the threshold from the waiting room to the inner exam rooms and, specifically, the photo room. Corey pops up with he was just going to wait in the newly reopened waiting room for Cathy's return. I take a last look at Corey who is also wearing one of my tie-dye hoodies he has borrowed and notice he had removed the pins I normally wear. I guess he didn't want to announce to the world his pronouns are She, Her, Hers, or that he hearts Cathy. Cathy and I follow Sara into the photo room where all the magic will start to happen. Sara hands me a comfy cloth hospital gown, a mask, hairnet, and nice teal colored gripper socks with the instructions to open the door after I am changed. She leaves us on our own to explore the photo room after Cathy helps me change. The photo room is a narrow room with the far wall painted photo-neutral blue-gray with a little half round six-inch high stage I will soon stand on labeled Photographic Measurement Station. The far side of the little room has an exam bench against the wall and on the last wall is some sort of fixed camera machine with a little desk attached to it. Lastly, just off center of the room is the standard exam chair. Tabitha shows up before we become antsy and sits at the little desk with a pile of papers to go through. I try to make conversation with her by asking about her 4th of July weekend and how it went but she waves it away with, "Let's focus on you right now." I am asked my name, who is my surgeon, and which procedures are happening to me today. I parrot my name, tummy tuck, fat transfer to my breasts, and waist narrowing all done by Dr. Megan. This meets with her approval. Then comes a long list of things that might go wrong ending with me signing at the bottom to verify my doom. Cathy needs to sign a few pages as caregiver. Dr. Megan comes in, confers with Tabitha for a moment, and then turns her attention in my direction. I am asked to take off my gown, which I hand to Cathy who has been seated in a chair opposite the photo-wall and step up onto the stage. I am so glad they let me keep my bikini panties on. I stand semi-naked and Dr. Megan asks if I have any questions before she starts marking me up. Yes I do, I just want to say that you are welcome to harvest fat from anywhere you can find, you mentioned below my breast as a good source of viable fat. Cathy wanted to know if implants might be needed down the road, could I still get them, and received a yes to this. Dr. Megan asked for a pen and began to mark guide points on my front. I am dead quiet and she is serious in her work. It is an odd experience to be a human canvas; you feel each pen stroke across your body delineating areas of reduction, augmentation, and gradation. I have ceased being me and now belong to Dr. Megan as a work in progress. Dr. Megan is done and Tabitha has taken all the notes down on my chart. While the two of them check the surgery notes I have Cathy take a picture so I can see the marks on my body. The image is just as I hoped it would be, I am relieved and assured. I put my gown back on and Dr. Megan asks if it was okay to use my images if they blurred my face. I said sure whatever they want to do was okay with me especially if it helps someone else. Tabitha asks about getting a release and I tell her sure. In a few minutes I am signing a whole bunch of uses for my image. I have no problem giving permission. Who would want my image for anything? Tabitha announces that the time has come for hugs for Cathy and me. Ours is a hug of expectation and love with formality of

566

reunion in a short time to celebrate a life achievement gained. Tabitha leads me out of the photo room in one direction while Cathy hurries away toward the waiting room in the other. We walk into an anteroom with storage closets on one side, an alcove on the opposite wall, and a large heavy door marked with No Admittance Surgical Area in bold dark lettering. Tabitha steers us into the alcove, which has lockers and a sink. She selects a locker to store my recovery clothes in for the joyful after surgery get-together with Cathy and Corey. My clothes are safely behind an oddly shaped locker door and the key is in Tabitha's scrub pocket. Tabitha is an all businessperson, we are here for one purpose and let's get to it. It is soothing in its nature of a set predicable routine leading to the get-together-happy-ending. Now is the time for the ominous door to be opened for me to enter the OR. Tabitha has given me the instruction to sit upright on the table so Jennifer, the anesthesia nurse, can attach data cables to my back. I am armed with this one goal as I step into the OR. It's cooler inside but I was also promised a blanket. It is also brighter inside and not so crowded with machines as I had imaged it would be. Sure enough, the picture Cathy and I found of the kind of breast shape I would like to have was posted on a board near the operating table to serve as a guide. I don't know who the lady was who had those perfect breasts, but I envied them to be my own. I have three nurses of varying titles coming at me from all directions. Things are happening all around and my only instruction of sitting upright is immediately negated, I need to lie on my back looking up at the light fixture manufactured by the Philips company mounted from the ceiling. Philips is a good company I should take heart from this. A difficulty with my person has arisen in conversation between the ladies; I am six feet tall, the table is too short for me. They scoot me up as far as they can and talk about needing to get an extension as my feet are just off the table. I apologize for my length and one of the nurses tells me don't apologize we all would love to have your beautiful long legs. Still, in my mind I note that this place sees mostly women and feel that old out-of-place feeling from my childhood once again. Jennifer compliments me on my nice veins as she establishes an IV line in my left arm. I look up at the Philips light fixture with its three arms loaded with sparkly light emitters thinking past this one thing nothing on the ceiling is worthy of my last few minutes of consciousness. Jennifer has put a breathing mask over my mouth and nose; the smell reminds me of the respirator I used one summer long ago while bailing hay. A soft rubber institutional smell that I ponder as Jennifer tells me she doesn't ask people to count backward anymore because you're out in less than sixty seconds...

I rejoin my other fellow beings in the state of consciousness we have come to know as ourselves, but at the moment mine is slow in regaining its focus of being. I'm in the recovery room and nurse Deena is attempting to wake me up or so they tell me. The first realization I have is recognizing Cathy followed by Corey coming into the room through a doorway, and then the post-surgery elation flows over me with its so-cool-to-be-done tingle; it is a joyful thing. Cathy gets right to work widening my tennis shoes out so Deena will have no problem getting my hospital socked foot into them. Cathy blames herself for forgetting the slip-on shoes, but it was for the better; those shoes were shot and dirty inside. Deena has lots of aftercare instructing to share with Cathy and Corey too; the one ominous paper instruction was how and where to inject my daily Lovenox shot. I was aware but still had no sense of pain yet. A wheelchair appeared and Corey vanished. I was loaded into it with Deena's help thinking the joyful thought that I was done and on my way home. The recovery top was baggie so I had no clue what I looked like underneath it, there was the tightness of a compression garment hindering my breathing somewhat and keeping me very stiff. Corey had reappeared he had moved our car in the under-building garage to be right next to the elevator so it was a short distance to get me to the car. Deena parked the wheelchair right next to the car door and I surprised myself that although I can't bend at the waist I was able to stand up on my own! Well almost, Corey and Deena did help aim my direction of travel. From a standing position I gently and in slow motion let myself down onto the front passenger seat with Cathy in the backseat guiding my descent. Cathy had a pillow ready to keep the seatbelt off my breasts; imagine I thought I have breasts under all the recovery stuff. Cathy also gave me two Tylenol 500mg pills for our drive home. My surgery had run long by two hours the result is it is 4:00pm and we will be facing rush hour traffic through downtown on the way home. I just watch outside the window and marvel at all we pass, it is a very heady feeling to have accomplished a life goal, especially one that you never really thought was within your reach. This afternoon it happened and I was so thankful for everything around me, and then ouch we roll over an expansion joint on I-5 and then another. This kind of breaks the mood but not the reality of the accomplishment; that joy will linger a long time. I feel compelled to give Corey directions as we drive along but of course he doesn't need them. He has his good and pacifying son hat on this day. We are pulling into our driveway and only the front steps stand in our way from journey complete. I surprise myself again in getting out of the car but fail in walking without Cathy and Corey on either side of me. My strong legs, as Nurse Deena called them, did get me up with Corey and Cathy's guidance and into the house then across the living room into our recovery recliner. Touch down! Here I will sleep as long as I have to. Cathy posts on Facebook that we are home and doing fine then makes dinner for us all; all I could stomach was a piece of toast. Corey makes a bed out of our couch right next to the recovery recliner. After dinner I discover that to use the toilet I have to stand, thank goodness at present my body is empty except for urine. There is no way for me to bend in a way to accommodate now swelling body parts in a sitting position on the toilet; yes to sitting in the recliner its seat is a bigger target. Corey calls his couch bed a taco bed since it is one sheet folded over and the blankets become toppings. One blanket is the sour cream and another guacamole. All very cute; on that note, it becomes very important to dial back the constant humor our house is noted for; because it hurts for me to laugh, giggle, or chortle. Corey's humor is very crafted and refined, he has great talent in this, enough that it is second nature in his conversations, and I love it. But something that is second nature does take work to dial back, thank you Corey for doing this. I sit upright in our recliner with my feet propped up on a footstool. Cathy and I decide to use one Tylenol 3 for pain control tonight. Sleeping is in spurts no longer than an hour followed by waking Corey up to help me get out of the recliner to shuffle to the bathroom. I hate to wake him and apologize but each time he responds with "That's what I'm here for!" Corey hands me off to Cathy at the bathroom. Back in the recliner, I sit and watch the clock move ever so slowly, I listen to the street noises, and follow headlight shadows across the room. Time moves so slow waiting for any sign of sleep to return. The longest I stayed awake between dozes is forty-five minutes. What keeps sleep away is all the little aches across my back from my sitting position. I can't lie down in any other position than I am in because of the smile shaped hip-to-hip incision across my middle. I watch the living room fill with the sunrise from the dark of twilight of the before time. Amazing, the gradient from dark to light and the sadness of lost sleep...

***

This would be a good time to take a break from my narrative of the events of July 6 to10 and allow Corey's voice to guide us...

Tuesday July 6, 2021. Corey here: Everyone in our house left around the same time Tuesday morning. Melinda loaded Quince into the Model X and drove to UCSD, while Yulin, Edwin, and I loaded into their rental car and I drove to San Diego airport (they needed to visit the rental agency, anyway, so the trip wasn't wasted for them, either). I got to the airport about 80 minutes before my flight, but as a solo passenger with no checked luggage this was 70 minutes earlier than I absolutely needed. I still enjoyed the lax time. It was a bit odd flying without Quince - as I walked around the airport I kept feeling that I needed to get back to something, thinking that Melinda and Quince were waiting for me somewhere. But, no - I was solo and I could go as quickly or as slowly as I wanted through the terminal.

I arrived in Seattle early afternoon Tuesday and Mom and Dad greeted me at their usual place (the security exit at Terminals C & D). We found the car and drove home. I had eaten on the plane so we didn't need to stop for Starbucks or anything (plus, I'd gotten a coffee in the San Diego airport). I brought my bags inside the house but I didn't have much to bring, considering it was just me. We visited at

570

home, but I seem to recall that there wasn't too much we had to get prepared for Tuesday itself. Dad made dinner (bacon and eggs, yum), which was lovely. In the evening I got an IM from Tessa, whom I hadn't spoken to since last May, so that was a welcome surprise. She was in Seattle for business so we had a phone call in the evening to catch up. I also spoke to Melinda and she said everything was fine at home. Great!

We all got to bed somewhat early (before 11pm) because we had an early start Wednesday. I slept in my old room and it was a lovely, restful sleep.

***

Wednesday July 7, 2021. Corey here: I woke, I think, around 4:30am for some reason then went back to sleep. I woke and stayed awake at 5:45am, and finally got out of bed around 6am. I showered and such upstairs and Mom and Dad were out for a walk (I think?). I had something small for breakfast (I think it was a NuGo bar) and we drove to the surgical center.

We were aiming to arrive at 8am but got there about 7:40am. Fortunately, the doors were already open so we went inside. The center is way up north - at least 45 minutes of driving in good conditions, and more than an hour in typical conditions. We were happy we weren't late.

We went up to the center and, awkwardly, Dad bumped into the doctor (Dr. Megan Dreveskracht) while visiting the restroom. Back in the center for the proper meeting, there were hellos and welcomes and Dr. Megan escorted Dad into the back, with Mom in tow. Soon Mom came back out, though, and she and I were in the waiting room. The receptionist told us that the completion time was estimated at 1pm so we could go out and check back at 12:30. Great! So that's what we did.

I drove the car to a CVS pharmacy not far from the clinic and filled a prescription for pain medication. We then drove to a Starbucks for my good-morning coffee and a drink for Mom. We thought we'd stay there for a while during the surgery but the Starbucks was rather full of patrons, the bathrooms were always busy and code-locked, and it just wasn't very comfortable. So we decamped, drove back to the CVS to collect the prescription and then returned to the clinic to wait.

The waiting room wasn't so bad. They had Wi-Fi, I brought my laptop and charger, and the chairs were padded. I managed to get a half-day of work in so I counted it as only a half-day of vacation. Mom read a book on her Kindle. We saw a handful of middle-aged women come through the lobby for consultations. I didn't see anyone else coming in for surgery.

Around 11am the receptionist (or someone?) told us that the surgery was going longer than expected (but, nothing's wrong!) and that it would be more like 2pm before they would be done. Mom and I used that as a chance to get lunch, by returning to the same Starbucks and getting food and drinks. Mom and Dad have developed several friends among the baristas they frequent and Dad confided to me to always ask a barista what is best in their store. Who else knows better? I asked the barista who was stocking the display case what her recommendations for what was tasty here. She pointed out her favorite was the Chicken Bacon sandwich so I had them heat it for me. We ate and drank there, then returned to the clinic around 12:45. We waited and waited but around 2:30 someone (Dr. Megan?) came out and gave us an update - all done! The surgery had gone well, and the delay had been because they had to use a 20cc syringe for the lipo work rather than a 60cc; also, some machine didn't work as expected and they had to figure that out. But, no complications in the surgery itself, which was great! Dad was in the recovery area and we could go back to see her.

During recovery near 3:00, Mom and I went to the recovery area and sat with Dad. Mom seemed concerned that something was wrong - she asked Dad "is something wrong?" or "are you okay?" a few times. Maybe because she thought Dad wasn't responding normally? Dad was still out of it on account of anesthetic. Nurse Deena explained the home care but I didn't worry about remembering the details - it was all written down. I excused myself when the person suggested taking a look at Dad's surgery dressing - only then did the person ask

572

me - "do you get lightheaded about these things?" I didn't say, but "yes" was what I was thinking. And I knew I had some of the tells - I was yawning a lot, which is an early sign that I should excuse myself. So I did, and I moved the car into the wheelchair accessible spot downstairs. I waited down there, messaged Casey, and within a few minutes Mom, Dad, and the nurse arrived with Dad in a wheelchair. Everyone helped Dad into the car and then we adjusted things with pillows, etc. Then, off to home!

Driving home was fine but traffic is terrible in Seattle, all the time. Also, every slight bump in the road was a bit of a pain for Dad, and King County doesn't seem to maintain I-5 very well. We drove directly home but got there around 5pm, I think. Dad was tired (more like fatigued) but alert in a drowsy sort of way. She had no trouble getting her body up the stairs but we helped steady her so she knew which way was up. Then, down into the chair. [Whew!]

Mom and I ate dinner (did Dad sleep through it? I'm not sure; she was pretty drowsy) and played cribbage to pass the time. Lots of time passed, and Dad did a little bit of getting up and shuffling around. It was challenging for her. She was still drowsy / fatigued but she was her usual self-underneath. Eventually it was bedtime and I made a bed on the couch, in what I called a taco: the shell was a sheet folded in half, in which I slept, and I had a few blankets on top. Not exactly a taco but still funny.

We woke a few times overnight: 2:30, 6:30, and 8:45. I helped walk Dad to the bathroom and Mom helped her in the bathroom. Then, all back to sleep after the middle-of-night calls. The sun rose before 6am but we slept despite the light. Not too bad.

***

Thursday July 8, 2021. Corey here: Thursday was much better. By Thursday Dad had a clear head but was still in pain on and off. She took pain medication of various sorts and it helped, but she also had a hematoma develop, which was especially painful.

Midday, I drove to Grandma Dixon's house to do laundry. We knew that Friday would be somewhat busy, because of the post-op appointment midday, so today seemed like a good one to catch up on laundry. I started a load mid-afternoon then left; when I came back to move it to the dryer I stayed for the cycle and visited with Grandma. We talked about her upcoming travel plans (she and Linda will visit San Diego in December), about her yard and garden (she's bought a bunch more plants to plant), and I asked her what part of Boeing Computer Services she worked in ("Spares" for the military division). It was nice to visit with Grandma!

Dad had me read a little from her book - it's good! I read perhaps ten pages (of the 330+ she's written!) and I wanted to read more. The writing is engaging and I wanted to know what happened to the characters (of course, I already know!).

We had lunch and dinner, which were tasty (thanks, Mom!) and I played more cribbage with Mom. I think I won a bunch of the hands this evening fun! We also played a little Josephine solitaire before bed.

***

Friday July 9, 2021. Corey here: Friday was the post-op appointment, at 11am. We couldn't dally in the morning so we woke, I showered, we had simple breakfast, and we drove to the surgery center. Seattle traffic is officially bad all day long. I was expecting a 30-60 minute appointment so I brought my backpack with laptop, charger, book, etc. I was just settling into doing work when Mom and Dad were already coming back out of the office! It couldn't have been 10 minutes. Apparently, everything was going well (or, at least, not concerning in any way) so we could head home. Another 50-minute drive and we were home after 2.5 hours for the 10-minute appointment (Heh).

On the way home we stopped at Bartell's to buy water and the cashier noticed that Mom and I were wearing matching shirts. She wanted to know if we made them (no, sorry, we didn't). I was itching to get out and do something more so I volunteered to drive to Costco, which I did while Mom stayed with Dad. Costco was pretty busy but I took my time and bought what Mom and Dad asked for. Shopping at Costco is more fun when you can buy more things -- Mom and Dad didn't need most of the things I saw (ground bison! snacks!). In the evening we played more cribbage (Mom won most of the games this evening!), finished the gin game (I had the high score! Dad won...), and played Josephine solitaire. I'm getting better but still not as fast as Mom. Something to work on.

Friday evening I also showed Mom and Dad that they could use InstaCart to order things from PCC Market. They didn't entirely need anything, but we found a few items we could buy and the order arrived about 90 minutes later. It wasn't perfect -- the tomatoes included a moldy one, but it showed that, if they really needed something, they could get it without making the drive if the drive would be too inconvenient. Great!

***

Saturday July 10, 2021. Corey here: I slept in until 7:30, for the third night in my taco bed, but got going about then because it's a travel day. I showered and ate a brief breakfast, then packed in about 5 minutes. I added a few books for Quince and an old laptop of mine from college to my luggage, because I had plenty of room. Dad's doing well but still stiff and sore to stand up and walk around the house. The road to recovery is still a long one.

Friday night I messaged Casey to ask if he could take me to the airport Saturday morning. He agreed, and he arrived around 9:30 Saturday morning. Colby, Casey, and Eli came in and Colby and Casey visited with Mom, Dad, and me for about 10 minutes. It was cordial but Casey seemed eager to not engage and to get on being elsewhere. I took the clue and started my good-byes with Mom and Dad about 15 minutes earlier than I needed to. We were soon out to Casey's car and on the road.

Casey dropped me at the airport without issue and there was no line at the Pre-Check clearance point. I walked around SeaTac for a bit and bought Seattle Chocolates for the people back in San Diego. The terminal was busy but I didn't mind walking around to pass the time (about 45 minutes). I hadn't had coffee since Thursday and I contemplated getting a treat, but the lines at all the Starbucks and *other coffee stands were too long. Plus, I kind of wanted to continue resetting my caffeine reaction levels; and, coffee goes right through me and I didn't want to need to use the toilet so often during the flight. So I just passed the time by walking around and wearing a mask.*

Eventually, they started loading the aircraft. I sat in first class and had a window seat this time, directly above the cargo-loading door. I watched several bags glide up the loading conveyor, and soon I watched as we pushed back from the gate. I was surprised to see 11 other planes ahead of us to take off, but that wasn't much time to wait. The airplane took off, headed high above Puget Sound, and south toward California.

After landing in San Diego I messaged Melinda that I had landed and she headed out from home to collect me. I soon saw a familiar Model X driving up to the arrivals section, and Quince and Melinda greeted me. I'm sure Quince was bigger than when I had seen him last. But he was happy to see me when I climbed into the car, and I was happy to see him, too.

***

Back to me again, love you Corey!

Thursday July 8, 2021. My status is I have a compression garment around my waist from under my breast down to bikini area. I had electrolysis to clear my bikini area before surgery knowing that area was going to be home to the tummy tuck incision scar. This smile shaped scar runs the full distance hip to hip just low enough to be hidden by bikini panties. This was a good choice as it is so much better not to have hair growing up through the scar. Anyway back to the garment: it has three five-inch wide heavy elastic bands with Velcro attachment at the ends. These bands overlap each other giving a width in the front of nine and a half inches. In the back the width of the garment covers 12 inches of my body top to bottom. Caromed, the company that made this garment has different sizes 9, 12, 15 inches; again, I have the 12 inch one. My natural waist is snatched tightly by one band, the area that once held my belly button by another band, and the ribcage above my natural waist the final band. I will wear this all the time unless told differently at my appointment tomorrow. I had expected to wake up from surgery in a faja compression garment and wondered where they would get one to fit me as my height is six feet. The faja compresses from the ankle to just under the breasts with an opening so that you can use the bathroom without taking it off. This garment is worn 24 by 7 for up to a month or more. I had resolved in my mind to have to bear this along with the other pains of recovery. These things were fully known to me, I had seen Cathy's pains and despite all of this, I simply could not 'not' have the surgery. After 50 years of 'not,' the concept of not having it was not acceptable anymore. I so needed to feel my body and myself together as one complete being… On arriving back at home, I have the binder only and no compression socks. A surprise since Cathy's surgical garb, after her surgery, was a simple ill-fitting binder (that was just a pain to keep straight) and compression socks. We had to promise not to disturb either for a week; here I am with just a binder, albeit a good one, to hold me together. I have a sneaky feeling that this is what happens when you enter a mostly female space and are too tall to fit. Also, it's my guess I am a rarity there being transgender to this practice. I have no complaint; I was treated wonderfully and heartfully recommend Phase Plastic Surgery and especially Dr. Megan Dreveskracht! I was her first surgery at her new practice and wanted to be the best patient for her. She was Cathy's surgeon at her previous practice. Cathy had an unexpected adverse reaction to a drug given her, one that landed her in the ER. For the whole time in the ER (20 hours) and the following three days in the hospital, Dr. Megan checked in on Cathy with frequent daily visits. I don't know exactly what I look like under my dressings but I can see a little cleavage so cool. I have Tylenol 3 and Hydromorphone for pain control if I need them. Yes, I do have increasing pain in several forms. The skin from my chest down to below my missing belly button is painfully tight. My surgery was a combination tummy-tuck and fat transfer to my breast along with having my waist snatched. Fat is removed mostly from my belly area and also some from just under my breast. That fat is treated in a way to separate the good from the bad and injected back into my breast to increase their size. To this end, Cathy and I supplied a picture at the request of Dr. Megan of how I wanted my breasts to look. It was an odd experience searching for images of bare breasts; it feels like doing something naughty. I had never done stuff like this before. There was no turn-on in it for me in any way, just the opposite; it was like rubbing salt in a psychic wound. Now as I was looking, it was very different experience. I felt as if I was looking at me, just as anyone seeing themselves after a shower does. The good along with the not so good, but all in all you see yourself and that is what I have missed for so very long. And we had been clinical as we narrowed down the search to transgender before and after photos. This gave a good chance of the result I might actually have a chance of achieving. Today a quick measurement around my bustline reads 43 inches that would be a gain of almost 3 inches if I can retain the fat...

Thursday morning. Cathy makes us a wonderful pancake breakfast, a victory celebration breakfast for getting through the surgery, and I was so looking forward to it. Along with gluten-free pancakes I had two eggs over easy; all of it tasted so good. The swelling around my groin is steadily and painfully growing making using the bathroom difficult. My morning meds will be an injection of the blood thinner Lovenox (Enoxaparin) given me by Cathy and the anti-nausea Zofran under my tongue. Cathy had taken my blood pressure before we ate and it stood at 120 over 75. After my injection I was doing okay, I was a little fearful because of the awful interaction of this drug for Cathy but just sitting in the recliner now things were fine. Cathy then gave me a Zofran pill to hold under my tongue. I was sitting there looking at the wall with all of Cathy's glass salt cellars in their display cases when suddenly the scene began to shake, it was my vision going strange. I didn't feel faint in the normal way I experience it; that is, darkness closing around from the sides, but instead I was losing clear vision and thought. Cathy quickly put the blood pressure cuff on me and yes my BP had dropped to 60 over 40 and my breathing was becoming short and shallow. I was still there but was having trouble functioning. I wonder if that was what it was like for Cathy? My BP slowly came back and since it happened after using Zofran I refuse to take it again. I was back and stable (BP 106 over 65) so we chalked it up to perhaps Zofran or perhaps a panic attack; whatever we continued on. Corey headed to Grandma Dixon's house to start a load of laundry and then returned back to our house.

Thursday PM. The swelling problem is getting worse very painful I now have a large hematoma in place of my genitals. I expect this is what a hernia is like. The position I have been given of sitting up seems to allow all the swelling to flow right down into this ever-increasing hematoma. It is a good thing I see Dr. Megan tomorrow but for now I need better pain management as I can hardly walk. At 3:30, I take a Tylenol 3 and a regular Tylenol 500mg. I have a very light dinner of soup and toast. Cathy hardly had any incision pain so this is what I was expecting, my reality is a pain level well up the scale in the 8 to 9 area. Corey is back from a second trip to Grandma Dixon's with our finished laundry. He had stayed there during the drying cycle to visit with his grandma. Cathy and Corey play cribbage and I act as an appreciative audience. I have come to dread bedtime with its sleeplessness and inescapable aches no matter what position I tried. At 10:30pm I take another Tylenol 3 and a regular Tylenol 500mg say my bedtime prayer and settle down with Corey next to me on the couch. Sleep was sporadic and wakefulness abundant this night. I am thankful Corey can sleep through much of my wakefulness. It is torture to get up and down over and over to use the bathroom then have to walk the house until the soreness lessens. Each time I have to wake Corey up, he is always quick to get up to help me; he is being a jewel about it.

***

Friday July 9, 2021. I need something to cancel the pain right now! It is 3am and the night has been full of anxieties and radiating pain. I wake up Corey to go get Cathy, for most of the night I have tried to come up with a plan to get control of the pain level so I could make it to my appointment in a few hours. There hasn't been any sleep so all I can do is take a hydromorphone pill now and switch to a Tylenol 3 at 10am just before we drive to Dr. Megan's office. Cathy desperately

579

needs eight continuous hours of sleep to function normally, but I need her now. She helps me in the bathroom and then gets me a hydromorphone pill. Such a little pill, you wonder if it will do anything at all. It did, it knocked me out for four hours. I awoke for breakfast at 9:00am. The downside is I feel awful the benefit of sleep is totally canceled by the groggy feeling afterward. My appointment is at 11:00 so we need to leave a little after 10:00. I don't see how I am going to make it from the car up to the office when we get there. Traffic is light today on I-5; Corey drives with confidence, and I surprise myself in being able to walk when needed. I even use the restroom at their office on my own although Cathy does come in with me just in case. We are greeted by Sara with praise that I can walk so well (if she only knew the cost in pain). Corey sets up his portable office in the waiting room and Dr. Megan leads Cathy and me down to an empty exam room. This room is new to her as well as us. The center of the place is the exam chair, an older mechanical one. I sit and Dr. Megan tries to figure out how to lay me back. Pop! Down it goes and ouch for me. I take off my recovery top and Dr. Megan undoes the gauze that is wrapped around my bustline to give a slight support to my plump little breasts. She tells me she doesn't want any pressure against them but they do need some support, so I should try a bralette or camisole with a built in shelf support. I ask how much she injected into them and she tells me 350cc each. She confides to us, "I pushed in as much as I could without it pushing back out." How much fat did you remove from my body? I have to ask and she answers, "The accumulator jar had over 1200cc in it when I last looked." Dr. Megan tells us that my incision looks great and is open to questions. Cathy and I relate all that has happened since yesterday and I focus on my grossly swollen scrotum. Her response is, "Yes, this does happen I saw it in med-school, the problem is gravity pulls the fluids down. All that they offered us to help was to put a towel below the scrotum to slow the swelling." We chat for a few minutes more leaving me with: I'm to keep up with the binder, sleep positions, and walking each day until my next appointment on July 30 at 11:30. Cathy also has a 12:00 appointment right after for consult on Blepharoplasty for her. We rejoin Corey in the waiting room; he is surprised to see us so soon. Traffic is tolerable on the drive home, all that is left of the day is dinner consisting of a Cathy dinner plate for her and Corey and soup for me. I have talked to Casey, he uses Naproxen for swelling and pain relief so I am going to try this tonight. For now, it is one game of cribbage after another between Cathy and Corey. Cathy loves this and Corey is being very gallant in playing. Some games it is all Corey and others Cathy comes back, no one gets skunked. Corey is too tall to stretch out completely on our couch so he sleeps curled up, so now his bed has switched from being a taco to an empanada, the bedding is not spread but crimped, and each blanket is an empanada filling. Funny Corey funny! I watch over Corey while he sleeps if he kicks off covers I turn on the window fan to cool the room and conversely if he huddles under the covers I turn off the window fan; I can do this using my cell phone. I take two Naproxen before bedtime in hopes this will not only let me sleep but reduce the painful swelling between my legs. This side effect has helped me make up my mind to be done with this thing down there. Right now, this is the most dysphoric I have ever been all because of this awful hematoma. Night is a repeat of sleepless cycles although each sleep cycle is almost one and a half hours long before I have to get up use the bathroom and then walk the house for ten minutes before going back to bed.

***

Saturday July 11, 2021. I hate nighttime; there is no real rest for me just staring at the clock or walking around the house. Casey will be here at 9:00 to give Corey a ride to the airport. I have been awake since before sunrise watching the clock. I wake Corey up at 7:30 in time for him to get a shower. Corey also wakes Cathy. Cathy has found two camisoles for me to wear; I wear them as a first layer to protect me from the binder. The camisoles have a slight push-up bra built into them; we have also replaced the gauze around my bustline so that it pulls gently on my breasts giving me a slight cleavage. These things seem to bother Corey so we rearrange my clothes to cover most of this up, seeing that Casey will be here soon also. After a very light breakfast for Corey of a protein bar we hear a knock at the front door. Casey is here with Eli and Colby. It is very nice to see Colby as he has gotten older he is busier and visits with us are farther apart. B---- is also with them but chose to stay in the car. There is light conversation, Casey is reserved, and a hug from Colby. In no time Corey is leaving with Casey and we are standing on the front porch waving goodbye to them...

The day passes into the dreaded night, Cathy will try sleeping in the recovery chair and I am going to try an experience of sleeping on my back flat on the couch with my legs up and over the arm of the couch. I figure gravity will be my friend this way and pull some of the swelling back toward my belly away from my poor private parts. Cathy and I both say our prayers and try for sleep. We find it, but after a few hours Cathy is fighting the chair with her restless legs giving her no peace, so I call off the experiment and we both switch back to me in the chair and Cathy on the couch. This gives Cathy much relief and I did notice a slight reduction in my swelling, enough to try it again during the day tomorrow.

***

Sunday July 12, 2021. So here is a wrap up after several days of trying in vain to fix things. I get no relief from meds until I do the opposite of suggestions calling for increasing the dose. I reduce down to a normal dose of one ibuprofen pill. I begin sleeping in the opposite position as directed by Dr. Megan of setting up with my feet propped up. I switch to lying on my back with my feet higher than my heart and wearing a support panty to squeeze the area of my groin tight as the binder does my belly. This brings great relief to the swelling of my genitals to the point they are recognizable again. A side note, the whole area of my scrotum is so stretched out that it hangs down more than it did before. I loathe this. Before this tragedy, it had been just a small version of what I had years ago, to my relief. Cathy and I both found a way to sleep in the living room together side by side. She modified a footstool to better support her legs when in the recliner and I configured pillows to let me sleep once again with a head at a slight elevation as per Dr. Megan direction, but much less than before. I also use a pillow against the opposite arm of the couch to keep me from slipping down to an uncomfortable angle. This works for several days. Also sometimes Cathy did have to retreat to our bedroom because the recliner was just too uncomfortable. When the recliner did work Cathy and I could hold hands for payers or to just touch one another during the night.

***

So right now, on Friday July 23, 2021, I cannot sleep in our bed but can find sleep on the couch but it is a night-by-night gamble. My scrotum is tolerable but when I get up from a sitting position I get a burning pain on my right side that forces me back down again. This pain can also come on the left side. Cathy and I have walked over twenty-five miles since my surgery, we walk our neighborhood two times each day. On a good day, we will get to talk to one or two of our neighbors, a not-so-good day, we are just strangers to people we pass; although, I try very hard to say good morning, or good evening to folks and to wave to passing cars. I feel like the swelling has gone down, which is good but just like Cathy I feel that I'm still left with fat under my belly skin. I also feel like my breasts are growing smaller. I have added progesterone back into my nightly meds with the hope that it will help keep the fat alive. With this I have begun to rub some progesterone cream on them also especially the areolas. Nerves trying to reconnect are giving me what Cathy calls zingers, a sudden pain that travels across my body similar to what a TENS machine does. I still have to walk the house after sitting for a while before I can stand straight. I do feel better with each passing day but recovery is so slow and it seems like returning to our bed is light-years away. My weight is around 160 lbs with clothes and I seem to only eat eggs, as my protein source nothing else seems tolerable. We have had several sad experiences as Cathy and Cady. Our eye doctor would not engage with us in our eye appointment, she was all business and seemed irritated with us. I wanted to compliment her on her new hair color and how she looked great but it landed on deaf ears. So very sad. On the other

583

hand, Tom, cousin Tony's main squeeze sent me a Facebook message with a link to Tommy Dorfman transition pointing out her transition is very much as Cathy and mine is unfolding out to be. He told us he was looking forward to pictures. I read the article and began to understand that we are right in the middle of a medical transition. It hadn't dawned on me that it really was happening. I will call Allie and add top BA to my consult in September. It wouldn't hurt to talk about implants and by then my breast will be settled into whatever size they will be. I survived all my Lovenox shots but the bruising is still slow to go away. Finally Cathy had to go back to our bedroom to sleep last night and it is really bothering me to sleep apart. I know Cathy is just two rooms away but her absence during the night brings a great sadness to my soul. I guess what is happening tonight is I don't feel as if the surgery has made any difference to me gender-wise. My waist isn't suddenly more feminine shaped. It is not that my breasts suddenly stand out they are just a little rounder and project a small amount more. Natalie was right I should have had implants done along with my tummy-tuck. This question of making a mistake is trying to settle within my brain, was I right or wrong? It does look like wrong is ahead this time.

***

Sunday July 25, 2021. Casey's birthday/pool party was very nice. It was a little like the Walton's household with the addition of three more kids, an adult, two more dogs for a total of 11 under Casey and Mindy's roof. Linda, Cathy's mom Joyce, and Mindy's aunt Roberta attended along with Felicia and her two kids who were there for only half the party. Mindy is down to 12 hours a day on intravenous feeding, an improvement from 24 hours a day. It was a good party, Casey seemed to appreciate all the gifts and the fact we signed his card love from your mothers. Casey calling me Mom rubs against Cathy but he is insistent that I am now one of his mothers and we are grandmothers to his children. Cathy and I have talked about this issue and we have finally settled ourselves to it as just one part of a new relationship that Casey has delineated our part in with he and his family.

***

Friday July 30, 2021. We had our appointments with Dr. Megan today. My appointment was my three-week check-up and Cathy's was a consult for eye blepharoplasty both upper and lower. Cathy asked Dr. Megan if she would be a good candidate and Dr. Megan told her she would be a great candidate! Lori will email Cathy a cost quote Monday. Cathy and I arrived at their offices 30 minutes early, my appointment was at 11:30 but traffic was very normal for this time of day without incident. I drove and did fine; the discomfort comes when I get out of the car and can't straighten up until we walk around for a while. The office of Phase Plastic Surgery is still very much in transition from a single surgeon practice to multiple surgeon practice.

So, the appointment goes like this: We are greeted in the waiting room by a rushed Sara, her gray shoulder length hair revealing the tizzy she is in at the moment. She pounces on us being early and we are by 20 minutes but the waiting room is empty and there are plenty of chairs to sit in. The office seems empty other than Sara and a man in a smart business suit. She is explaining forms she has used in the past that the new surgeons want to change. From his bearing with Sara, it is my guess he is Dr. Baxter the sole owner of the practice, which is now a shared practice. From the tone of his voice, he is trying to be soothing to Sara, she has been with him for many years. He affirms the changes in a very even matter, careful to be respectful of Sara's opinions in each case. Sara is zooming in and out from behind the reception desk to gather papers from all the extremities of the office complex. We are busy looking at our phones to pass the time and at this time the reception area is still empty. A door opens and a couple comes out from the exam rooms to stand at the desk window. Dr. Megan pops into the other side of the desk looking for Sara who is out paper gathering. She is a bit like a mother hen trying to keep her chicks in place. Dr. Megan takes on the task of making an appointment for her patient and looking for the paper handout on taking care of drains.

Sara pops in long enough to get the request of the handout for drain care, then tells the room as she zooms away the handout isn't in here. We have no clue what the lady who is now waiting with her husband had done, just that it is her post-op appointment and she now has drains to take care of. She moves very slowly and holds her middle all the time. I so understand this; it is just as I have been doing these last three weeks. She is told that the drains can't come out until the 24-hour total output is under the 25 ml mark. Been there and done that with Cathy so I understand the guy's grumblings about the amount. They leave and we wait just a few minutes more until Sara comes back. She takes us to an exam room, now equipped with a new electric positioning exam chair. Sara hands me a robe, instructs me to have the opening to the front, hands Cathy a form to fill out and scoots away. I get busy undressing from all my layers down to just panties. It takes a while; I need to remove my shoes and socks to get my tights off. We are still alone so I look around and try the scale in the corner; 163 lbs. I am center stage for the first half of our appointment but sitting in the exam chair hurts my middle so I am resigned to standing or pacing. A knock at the door, it is Dr. Megan breezing into the room. She is bright and looks sincerely happy to see us. Dr. Megan thought my incision looked great, I can sleep on my sides or back lying flat but not on my stomach. Most of my restrictions are lifted within reason. She would like me to continue to wear the compression garment for two months. I asked her if she does any face-lifts and she told me not now. She did offer to give me advice on any other surgeons I was considering going with. So cool! I remembered to share my tool of lying on my back with my feet above my heart to take care of the swelling of my personal area. Cathy's turn comes next so we switch; she now sits in the exam chair while Dr. Megan does her exam. Using a Q-tip, she explores the tissues around Cathy's eye sockets. Apparently Cathy has dense brow tissues. Dr. Megan tests tissues using gentle pressure while explaining what she will do in each area around Cathy's eyes. There is talk about a browlift and extending sutures beyond the eye crease to address Cathy's anatomy while she continues to explain each surgical technique she could use in each area. She will spend over a full hour

586

between Cathy and me answering questions and carefully explaining blepharoplasty to us both. Cathy and I fully appreciate this, along with all the little chitchat about family both hers and ours. We love seeing pictures of her toddler daughter and hearing about cute things she has done lately. I do so wish she could do my face but I understand her side of the coin. It is wonderful that she will share her knowledge of different surgeons with me. Dr. Megan wants pictures of my progress so I close up my robe and we walk down to the photo room so that the pictures are consistently in the same place. We say our goodbyes and head to the reception room to make an appointment for my three-month checkup, October 4th. Cathy and I walk around the parking garage before we leave so my middle will calm down from sitting so long then it is off to join southbound traffic on I-5.

***

Sunday August 1, 2021. August is one of my least favorite months of the year. It's full of the three birthdays of my family (father, mother, and brother) that live only in my ever-fading memory. Last night was the best I have slept in our bed since before surgery. If I had to only remain on my back all night I couldn't have done it but being able to go one side then the other all night allowed me a sleep score of 85%. I had to get up two times to use the bathroom and then walk off the soreness. I have sharp pains intermittently all over my stomach area. There is soreness below the tummy tuck scar and it helps to rub that area. I also have full feeling in this area, but above this is still numb to the touch. When I touch the above scar area, I get a pressure feeling that radiates out from the point of touch, a muted sensation of light ache. In a way, it is like the sensation of needing to have your back scratched. When one of the traveling zingers makes itself known, I can dismiss it by scratching or tapping my binder. I shared on Facebook about medically transitioning and received no negatives out of 39 reactions.

***

Sunday August 8, 2021. I am one day past my one-month mark from my surgery. It's all about the binder and reducing swelling.

587

Cathy has gotten a spare three-band binder and a two-band binder. Her thought was to try the two-band for herself. Along with these we now own several other compression garments seeing as the longer you wear them the more the swelling goes down, in theory anyway. I thought that since I am at the one month mark I would return to my shoulder exercises and do a simple leg lift just to help keep my ABS from atrophying. I have also continued to tighten my binder adjustment bands a little more each day thinking this also will encourage my middle to shrink into a more hourglass shape. Well, things began to go awry. I have been feeling better and moving more like before, I can get into and out of bed with much less discomfort and more grace. If we tuck our t-shirts in my waist and breasts come right out as female. As I feel better I have actually sat normally in chairs, especially as the call to get back to typing gets loud. Unfortunately, after sitting upright for several hours, my three-band binder starts to rub my scar pushing down on it. It gets sore but not enough to stop typing or playing a game. I got ready for bed several nights ago and noticed that the swelling was returning in and around my scrotum, yikes! The skin there is already stretched out and is now re-inflating and along with it my mons pubis is ballooning out again. What has happened is when I sit, I put a downward pressure past the area were my belly button had been, this pressure forces the extracellular fluids to drain down past the forming scar at my bikini line where there is no external pressure to hold the fluid in place. Sort of like squeezing a toothpaste tube in the center. When I am standing the bottom of the compression belt gives some backward pressure against this. My first thought was I have no compression in this area even with the compression panty since the panty goes on over the binder. So I changed to wearing my bikini panty and compression panty under my binder so that the binder itself squeezes them both into the scrotum area. This worked somewhat to reduce the swelling back down but had the difficulty of me having to undress to use the bathroom. Also, the problem of sitting upright still existed. I also still have to walk around after sitting to stretch out to be able to stand upright and to walk off the pain. I switched to a two-band binder while I am at the computer; it is shorter

588

so the force pushing down is now above my scar, not below. It is all a Band-Aid fix until another month goes by. A new problem has arisen; horizontal cramps across my abdomen below my bustline. When I have to bend over to sit on the toilet, a cramp forms right above my scar line, just like the muscle is folding over on itself. Also pushing down to pass a stool causes pain in the same area, no fun. In a big way, my whole belly area now feels like it has fallen in. Where it was all swollen out, I feel like pushing out with my muscles to get relief, very strange. I am proud of my natural waist and feel the need to keep the binder bands very tight across it, my fear is losing my curves if I don't. So bottom line, I don't know what to do to help healing along, aside from walking that is. Conversely I don't know what will hurt the healing process either. Oh, and my bust seems to want to spread out under my armpits as opposed to project outward. To this end we use gauze to wrap my breasts back into a shape that also allows a little cleavage along with projection. This is just another thing that is either bad or good, who knows. I slept the best as far as sleep-score goes last night with a score of 91%.

Cathy and I are lonely as so many are now. We had tea with Dr. Marsden but she didn't want to talk about herself, she was all about us. She kept us for three hours wanting to know all about our journey right up to now. The experience was not unlike what happened to me at the orthodontist office the first time after my surgery, they were reluctant for us to leave. It seemed in both cases like they wanted to escape what was happening all around us by experiencing our adventure. As a person who has spent her whole life living vicariously, it is unnerving to be the subject of this action by someone else. This is August the month of birthdays of past family, this and it has always been the month of ending for me, end of summer and the downward spiral toward winter. I wonder if as I look back in years to come things will change.

***

Monday August 9, 2021. I just saw Dr. Pat Benca our dentist. She told me to tell my orthodontist that it would be great to push my two

589

front teeth up 4mm! She made a note to talk to them. I will mention this Wednesday when I have an ortho appointment. I am wearing my two-band binder since I plan to type today, the three-band binder pinches just below my scar forcing swelling down into that area…

***

Friday September 3, 2021. Today, Corey called me at 6:29pm to tell me Quince had broken his arm, not the same arm from his two-year-old jump to the changing table from his crib but the other arm from a parkour style jump on a climbing gym. They were at the ER waiting for treatment.

Cathy's sister Linda had her hand surgery three days ago and spent the first night afterward at Cathy's mom's house.

This coming Tuesday will be two months of me being in my three-band compression binder. Dr. Megan told me two months would be a really good idea to do. My swelling has gone down leaving my snatch waist intact but the tissue around my scrotum is flabby and dark colored from my compressing panty. I have decided to quit the panty for now and continue the body binder for a while longer. If I go without the support the binder gives me, it feels like I have to hold my stomach in with my arms. It is all about core muscles also without the binder my breasts spread out to under my arms.

***

Thursday September 9, 2021. I now have standard braces on the upper arch of my mouth. Dr. Leigh, my orthodontist, told me she had spoken with my dentist. The only way to move my front teeth up the 4mm is to use standard braces; that is, a bracket on each tooth of the top arch and the wire between them. It was my choice; I could go another 36 weeks of Invisalign aligners and Dr. Benca could cap all my upper front teeth but the bottom teeth most likely would hit the backs of the upper teeth. Dr. Leigh said, "If we band your top arch, I can lift those front teeth up enough to clear the bottom one." I really didn't want to hear this as right now, for the first time in my life I have a smile. I guess I need to do what is best in the long run but still after almost four years… Anyway, now I have a metal smile for the next eight months…

We had a massage with our friend Natalie. I had texted Dr. Megan to ask if putting pressure on my breasts is still off limits, and yes it is. So it is a face up massage for me.

***

Sunday September 19, 2021. Lots to journal about, I just need to carve out space to do it; this day I will record some past days' events keep that promise.

Thursday the 9th: Cathy and I had an appointment with Dr. Eaman. Dr. Eaman is quite unique in that she is the first in her family to become a doctor, there is no trail of medicine following down a family tree but there is a trail of activism. Most of her family lean toward law and follow activism therein. Her activism follows two paths: her practice being Direct Primary Care and her focus on LGBT+ care. Dr. Eaman's philosophy gives a hug to hour-long appointments and shuns corporate medicine's ten-minute appointments. She likes me to come in on Thursdays because this is her medical student day. Since her practice is sort of centered on LGBT, this gives med-students exposure to the actual population in an office setting. Also, it is Cathy and my custom to always match tie-dye shirts; we had made a gift to Dr. Eaman of one of our collection of shirts so on her whim she can match us. She loves to prank her med students by doing just this. Cathy had made two unique 3D beaded icosahedron balls of 1900 glass beads each to give to Dr. Eaman and MA Terina as gifts. Cathy loves to make people happy and in return gets mounds of compliments. My gift was myself as transgender to the fourth-year med-student Nathan as he did my health appointment and took blood. In the end, both Cathy and I had a blood draw this day. My numbers were Estradiol 591.0 pg/ml, Estrone 341.9 pg/ml, Estrogens total 932.9, Progesterone 1.5 ng/mL, and Testosterone Total 8 ng/dl. Cathy's numbers were sodium 132, chloride 96, and Ferritin 76.5, all acceptable for her.

Friday the 10th: Michael texted me that Gary True Prentice, a classmate of ours from Foster HS, had passed away. Michael and Gary ran around together during their senior year and afterward. During senior year they both had classes at the Occupational Skills Center on the beach near Seahurst Park. These classes occurred during the last half of each school day; it was all about seamanship and marine biology, the perfect playground for extreme guy play. Gary had a fast car and good times were had by all. Gary had reconnected with Michael in a deeper way in these last few months as both of them were facing family mortality issues. Michael was shaken to the core at the news of Gary's passing because of this. Gary at best was an old school high school acquaintance to me. I was removed from the teenage party-driven male world, I could observe it but had no place in it. I have no stories of high-flying or high-speed antics to look back on as Michael does. Gary redirected his life and found Christ and was better for it, a great blessing and in death is once again with his wife in the presence of our Lord.

Saturday the 11th: Cathy and I do game night with her mom Joyce and sister Linda. Linda is in a cast from hand surgery and is mournful. Cathy guided everyone into playing Yahtzee this was a good move on her part as the game is less combative. Linda has finger pain and loss of sensation. We spoke briefly about our coming trip to Spokane, but not in much detail, as it didn't seem prudent in the face of Linda's recovery.

Sunday the 12th: I have been spending hours searching the web for information on Dr. Stiller. Reviews are hard to come by, as were people's actual experiences with vulvoplasty and FFS from him. I have been churning away about the whole issue of zero depth/minimal depth/vulvoplasty vs. full vaginoplasty. This is the main issue but there is a whole subset of questions I want to arm myself with about zero depth to ask Dr. Stiller when I see him.

First the main issue: There is heavy bias toward full depth vaginoplasty and against zero depth vulvoplasty. Dr. Bowers makes a strong case against it on her homepage. Dr. Z (Zhikhareva) is careful to explain the finality that this procedure brings. These things are not

592

lost on me as I ponder this decision for myself. In fact, as each day has gone by this week, the enormity of this one decision I am now facing has cast a new light on all the other transitional steps that I have taken over these last fifteen years. I justified each surgery in two ways. First, did I feel this surgery had the ability to reduce my dysphoria? And second, did the surgery itself limit me in any way from any future surgical/hormonal steps I might or might not need to take? As time passed I churned about every step I took, I always wanted the door left open to jump back. Even as each step was completed it was clear that going back was repugnant and progress was joyful, but still this mentality persisted in my decision-making. My last surgery of a tummy tuck, waist narrowing, and fat transfer to my breasts taught me a grave lesson about how long recovery can take and how painful it can be. This lesson has been duly added to my decision-making mentality making the action even weightier as to surgeries. Here is how I currently stand in my/our transition, I have completely bought into the transition from male to female; I no longer have any doubts or misgivings. This is who I am and this is who we are as a couple. With this in mind, I have come from a place of try-this-and-see-if-it-is-enough to now having surgical goals denoting completion of my/our transition. With all this being said here is my thinking as to the need for the current surgery. My penis, even as small as it, has become an obstacle of sorts. By its physical existence it has become a confidence barrier to me functioning both in female space and in daily life. I have a constant fear of not being legitimately female; this is both an internal conflict and an external fear of rejection. The external part rests with people's perceptions and their judgments made on those perceptions. I can certainly steel myself against this but I can't do this without completely addressing my internal mind/body conflict. As far as my conflict goes, I intrinsically know what is right to do gathered from my past experiences in feminizing, but my actions are tempered with the consequences of each past action. So here we have come back to the hard issue of vulvoplasty or vaginoplasty. It is one or the other, and as simple as this sounds, I have spent many hours trying to resolve and justify which to do.

My basic list of what I want from the outcome of either surgery is:

- I want my genitals to give the appearance of natural female genitals.
- I want to retain and repurpose as much tissue as possible from my current genitals. This is an issue with me; my body, even though not imaged right, is still my body and to bring it into alignment doesn't mean just cut and discard.
- I want function, to be able to urinate in a simple and hygienic manner.
- I want function, to have sensation from the appropriate external female structures, labia, and clitoris.

Given a skilled plastic surgeon, all this is accomplishable with either surgery.

Sigh, now I have to move onto the unique weaknesses and attributes of each surgery and the land of compromise.

The great attribute with full vaginoplasty is, well, a vagina albeit a neo-vagina. The construction of this female affirming structure uses the shaft of the penis via inversion. This is Dr. Bowers' technique; there are other techniques using other parts of the body each with its own attribute.

Vaginoplasty's gifts to the owner of such are the affirmation of being female and the ability to have penetrative sex. A lifelong dream for me, my heart ached from the discord of not being bodily female and all that came with it. Four years ago, after meeting Dr. Bowers, I would have, if it had been possible, signed up for a full vaginoplasty right there and then. The great weaknesses are a lifetime of dilation, douching, and a long painful recovery period in terms of a year or more. Even after recovery, many gals have to have revisions to correct poor healing or function. Yes some ladies just spring back from surgery, but I now know I am not one of the gifted in this.

The great attribute with vulvoplasty is in its reduced overall recovery time; you don't even spend one night in the hospital vs. up to a week or more with vaginoplasty. Because your surgeon doesn't enter the pelvic floor muscle or come near the rectum or prostrate, complications of this area are not likely. There is no dilation or douching and recovery is in terms of weeks in place of a year. Plain and simple, there are fewer traumas to your body. I would look correct for my gender, have clitoris sensation after a few months and much fewer health chores. The great weakness is there is no vagina, no ability to have penetrative sex in this way. No affirming knowledge that I could function in this very female way. No female talisman albeit a neo-vagina one.

Now comes the great debate, and at its end the great compromise. I hope what has been clear from these spattering of words I have written is the epic mental conversation I have been having with myself over this really big non-retractable step in transition. I have waded through so many experiences of painful extended recovery from vaginoplasty on the net not to respect this, and even in this painful state, the women labor on in a sort of triumph of achievement. It is a great burden that brings an amazing reward to these ladies in terms of relief from their discord. I think this is why Dr. Bowers is so passionate in her advice to get full vaginoplasty; she has been there and walked this path herself. So why would I not do this especially since I already have a fixed surgery date in three months with Dr. Bowers? Was this not my dream to have for so long? Good questions, which needed good answers or at least tolerable answers.

To be truthful with myself, I don't think I am up to the work that recovery demands from vaginoplasty. I have learned a lot from recovering from my tummy tuck and vaginoplasty recovery is much harder. Then there is the fact that my transition is not mine at all, it is our transition. It is easy for me to get distracted away from this fact by centering in on myself as I reach for words to explain actions. God matched Cathy and me so very closely. I do believe this. For every raised bump on her psyche a matching divot appears on mine, as we transition together we begin to fit each other just like two puzzle pieces. I am not tempting fate in pointing out what I actually see happening. Cathy and I both have a shared transition that is bringing us to a more comfortable place in our intimate relationship. Vulvoplasty fits this relationship and even though I do have a surgery date with Dr. Bowers for vaginoplasty I had already planned to change it to vulvoplasty. As Cathy says, "Vulvoplasty is not settling for second best."

***

Wednesday September 22, 2021. On Wednesday September 15th we left our house and began the drive across the state of Washington over to the city of Spokane. We had our normal good intentions of starting out early in the morning, followed by our normal dose of reality moving our out-of-the-door time to midday. It was me mostly, since I hadn't slept well the night before. I was slow to get up and get going. It had been a night of disturbing dreams, the kind that never let you lay still and my compression binder and I were at odds with each other for much of the night. All this was brought on by the simple fact that what I was about to do was huge. Two more surgeries and my medical transition would be complete. One would be on display daily and the other would be felt but unseen. I don't know which will come first. Some little time ago, I read that active transition moves right along faster than you realize and then all of a sudden you're done; you are no longer the star of the transition show anymore, you are just you. The moral of this story was pause, look, and appreciate for better or worse the experience you are currently having. Soon it will only be a memory and you will be the reality. This advice was specific to medical transition (I count this as any plastic surgery from head on down) in that after pain and healing is over, your body is different, perhaps your mind also for that matter. I have taken this advice to heart by pulling off my binder and standing naked in front of a mirror (albeit a broken one) tonight. Who was that person looking back at me? She sure looked more female than male. My body is hairless from face down, narrow curved waist, and perky diminutive breasts. It was amazing! I felt inside as I looked outside. The exception of course, was in my genital area, the penis, for a better way of putting it, looked out of place on this body. Cathy had just wandered by and made this point too. We have come such a long way since I started this journey; it was really good advice to pause, look, and appreciate the experience because there is no experience like it. No non-transgender person can fully understand this experience. Right now, I have unicorn status, but once this bit is removed the transitional experience will be a fading memory and life will continue on. I showered carefully keeping in mind that tomorrow a doctor would be judging my body as to its suitability for surgery. Cathy had gathered most of what we would take along with us on the trip. She has a system, which includes carefully crafted lists of things to pile up in the middle of our dining room. Those things move onto our bed where Cathy packs them into travel bags. The full travel bags and food cooler are then returned to the dining room pile as a staging area for hefting them out to the car. Once out there, I get to pack the trunk leaving the back seat for Cathy to pack. Both Cathy and I have to be gluten-free and since Covid we can't be sure of any place to eat that would be safe for us. So, we pack enough food for our three-day stay. Our other foible is we are old and have the gift of backaches, again mostly my problem. Because of this gift, we have a dedicated packed suitcase that holds a three-inch memory-foam mattress cover. I had been given a weight-lifting restriction because of my abdominoplasty that I think is over now; Cathy is of the mind that it isn't, so we compromise, kinda. We are packed and the car is full of its fuel and our backseat is full of our fuel for three days' time. I lock up the house, Cathy settles in on her side of the car, and I take my place on my side of our car. My side has the steering wheel but Cathy's side does the navigating for our trip. We drive on I-405 until we are able to turn east on I-90 toward Snoqualmie Pass. Traffic passes from moderate to light as we pass by Issaquah beginning the climb up into the Cascade Mountains toward Snoqualmie Pass. Cathy and I chat in place of listening to an audio book, this is my doing. I need to speak my thoughts about gender issues and sexuality. We seldom chat about sexuality per se; this topic through its dynamic nature continues to mold us as a couple. Cathy doesn't challenge the topic's power over us nor does she confront it even while its worldview is shaping our relationship. Cathy sees this as part of our transition and is content to let it do its thing. I, on the other hand, being a little closer to the full force of transitional movement, especially in seeing Dr. Stiller tomorrow, need reassurance. It is silly really and in a sense even derogatory. It is like taking the cake out of the oven halfway through the baking time, then cutting into it; all you are going to see in this physical dissection is goo. Half-cooked cake is just that, unfinished; the physical forces of heat and chemistry, not in themselves recognizable, are now interrupted. Best to return the cake to the oven and wait and see. An abstract way to picture the product of forming sexuality between two people, or should I say the revealing of an underlying sexuality… In short Cathy is content as the two of us bake together. So we chat up and down on whatever my brain brings to my mouth: transgender stuff and transitory things, such as the fall colors here and there among the foothills up to the mountain pass. It is good to be moving, we have been held captive in our little house for too long, and we both feel the relief of the road leading ever onward.

I am careful not to drink any water as we drive along. I know that Snoqualmie Pass is our next rest stop and I would like to skip it for the Starbucks in Ellensburg. Cathy is happy for us to stop at the pass. I find a nice park in front of the public restroom building and wait while Cathy goes inside. I watch people come and go, trying not to think about whether or not my bladder has anything in it. Cathy comes smiling back from the restroom to get in the car. As she opens the door I slide out. Puzzled, Cathy asks, "What are you doing?" I am undone I have been sabotaged by my own brain it has convinced my bladder that the next restroom is too far away. I have to go to the restroom. Cathy giggles. I head into the lobby and pause at the single use restroom to listen for a minute, someone is in there. I march into the lady's unit and find a stall at the very end. I'm not totally sure but once seated, yes I did have to go. The stall next to me has someone in it and I vow to myself to be quick and graceful. I still have on my three-band binder which is very noisy to remove; because of this I have placed it underneath all of my clothes so all I have to do is pull down my underwear. I do well! Even though it takes me a few minutes to get myself back together, I am finished before the other lady. While I was in the stall, it dawned on me the difference between the men's room and the ladies' room in social interaction. In the guys' space, it is not uncommon to urinate while standing next to each other. There is an unspoken common rigor of respect of space for this, but even so snatches of conversations do happen. Cathy's dad was always very chatty in this setting. I have had sixty plus years in this space and sort of expect this background noise; in an odd way, it is welcoming. Women are totally compartmentalized in their space. It is odd to urinate in this silence. Conversations do happen around the sink and in line waiting but it's a different format and is not welcoming to me yet. My thoughts are focused in this area because one of my medical transition goals would allow me to be more graceful in this space. Back in the car with Cathy, I feel freer to quench my thirst. We are on a mission to get to the motel in Spokane before evening and are eager for the sound of the road passing under our tires to signal our progress forward. We chat about family things, Casey's family and Corey's family, their kids and our kids. We speak of being lonely; it's the malady of the times we live in. I-90 east, the road we have both traveled so many times over so many years. We used to feel like we were coming home after we left Snoqualmie Pass behind us and were making for Ellensburg. Now that feeling is very faint to nonexistent. I now see Ellensburg not in the metaphor of nature and life but in the harshness of the relentless wind that tears at your body and stifles your heart. Cathy and I are curiosities here as we enter the college Starbucks. We match in our colorful clothes and receive warm smiles. This Starbucks has a Transgender flag displayed prominently in the window and a list of pronouns of the baristas posted near the register. For them, we are a welcome treat in human form. Cathy orders drinks while I use the restroom. I come back and find her chatting with a barista whose nameplate announced he had been brewing coffee for Starbucks for 19 years. He reminded us of our friend Thomas as the one steadfast barista at our favorite Starbucks for over 24 years. That Starbucks is closed forever like so many other Covid victims. Cathy has her turn in the restroom and I sit with our drinks. Other older folks come in and throw hard glances in my direction. I wish I could pass successfully; there are still many things about me that don't give the proper clue; perhaps someday they will. Cathy returns and we are on our way again. Oh by the way, if you are in Ellensburg and need a Starbucks be sure you go to the college one at 908 East 10th Ave, not the one right off the freeway on the east side of town. There is a world of difference between the two. We return to I-90 east and it will take us all the way to Spokane at the eastern border of our state. The travel distance from our house to the motel is 290 miles. Cathy and I keep each other company for most of the way, watching the country change in agricultural content as we drive along. We will stop in Ritzville at a Starbucks for more drinks and to use the bathroom. At this point, we are both talked-out so we begin an audio book, *Perry Mason in The Counterfeit Eye*. This book will last the trip all the way back home on Friday. Spokane appears unexpectedly as you approach it; the only clue that you are getting close is the sudden appearance of a few scattered Ponderosa Pine trees along the freeway. This announces the landscape change from desert scrub to Eastern Washington urban.

We find the Spokane downtown Holiday Inn Express quickly; it was even somewhat familiar, as we had stayed nearby to attend the wedding of Cathy's cousin's son in 2016. That motel was right across from Riverfront Park and this one only a short distance with a commanding view of the city. I park our car in a spot very near the lobby door; it's close enough so that there is no point in moving the car for unloading. I follow Cathy into the lobby. There are a few people about, giving the feeling of an active place but all of the empty chairs attest to something contrary. We all have our masks on as is required; ours are just more colorful than anyone else's at the moment. The reception desk has no line so Cathy walks right up at the clerk's beckoning. The clerk is a middle-aged lady and is friendly enough; she talks directly to Cathy as if I am not there even though I am standing beside Cathy. I don't mind or I guess it isn't new to me; even so, I try to enter the conversation they are having from time to time. It is almost like being a little child again standing next to my mom at some business desk, you're invisible unless you do something derogatory and I wasn't, so there. The closest I got to direct conversation with the clerk was an answer to my question about the place our car was parked in, yes that is fine... The clerk did tell Cathy that there would be a 'managers reception' tonight and hot dogs were to be catered by Oscar Mayer. I get the luggage trolley and we transfer our travel bags, lock the car, and trolley back inside heading to the elevator. Our room number is 227; it's on the second floor and the elevator has a personality all its own. It will get to the floor quickly but take the longest time to move the last inch to open the door. It does this with theatric moans, bangs, and creaks. The room is nice enough with two queen beds, I don't know if the lady at the desk thought we would use one or both. I unload the trolley and Cathy takes charge of populating our temporary home with all of our stuff. The trolley is much easier to move sans luggage, the elevator quirk is now a known foible to me, and the path to the lobby is still in my memory. I happily push the trolley out of the elevator, turn left toward the reception desk then stop dead for a moment. In the covered drive directly outside the lobby's sliding doors is the Oscar Mayer Wienermobile! I push the trolley closer since its home is in the space between the set of two sliding doors. I park the trolley and I beat it back up to the room to get Cathy. I want pictures of this! The symbolism of this coinciding with the reason for my appointment with Dr. Stiller is just too much. Cathy is quick to come with me when I tell her there is a surprise I what her to see outside of the lobby. So we trot ourselves back downstairs. As we get closer to the lobby doors, Cathy giggles. We walk out to the machine and ask the young lady if we can get a picture of ourselves with the Wienermobile. She says, "Sure, would you like me to take it for you?" Yes! Afterward she gives us each a wiener whistle! We both giggle at our private joke that no one else has a clue too. Here I am having traveled 290 miles and 67 years to lay the ground for removal of my male body part only to be met with this large slang childhood playground symbol of that part face to face. You can't make stuff like this up and have it sound true. We return to our room for dinner that Cathy is catering for us from our three-day supply. We have ham sandwiches and potato chips. Bedtime comes after we play our evening games on our iPads. It is good that we have our mattress pad with us. Our hotel bed has a worn out depression on either side making sleeping uncomfortable. It's like sleeping in a trough.

***

Thursday September 16th: Today is the day, but the appointment time isn't until 2:30pm. Yesterday before dinner, Cathy and I had driven to Dr. Stiller's office to be sure where it was and if parking was nearby, all this to lessen the panic of missing our appointment time. This morning we would breakfast down in the breakfast room, always a roll of the dice but with luck their fare of scrambled eggs and sausage will be okay for us to eat safely. We get our gear together and walk out into the parking lot, only to find that the Wienermobile is now parked near our car! This is kind of spooky; is there a message I should take from this? No matter, this day along with the all-important task of seeing Dr. Stiller face to face, we also need to drive around and see the area face to face. We may have to stay here for an extended time because of surgery, and need to answer the question; can we get by here? We find that there is a Costco with a gas station, good start; we fill our gas tank and shop inside to see what is available. The store is pretty much standard Costco fare but not as extensive as our home store. Next we visit a bakery/restaurant called Cole's; it is reported to be gluten-free. Everything was good, Cole's has great bakery treats for after we see Dr. Stiller, and we found a Natural Grocers market to supply our standard food needs. All thumbs up on if we have to stay for ten days. As we drive the area, we come across the Wienermobile several times in different locations; I am feeling a little stalked... We are back in the room by noon for a much need nap. Cathy has set an alarm for 1:30 and when it went off I was startled awake. Now the rush starts along with rising nerves. It takes a few minutes for me to select what shirts we will wear. They have to convey sincerity, femininity, and a joyful countenance. We make the choice together. I primp using the room's full-length mirror and, while doing so, repeat the questions I must ask Dr. Stiller to drive them deep into my memory. Cathy has a copy of my meds and surgeries list if they ask for it. We ride the elevator down with another guest; it is funny moment as we all sort of hold our breath for the elevator to finally drop the last inch and slowly open the door. Out in our car, we say a prayer for the success of our appointment with Dr. Stiller. It is not only Dr. Stiller himself we must trust, but his staff also. Will they be friendly or dismissive, respectful or uncaring? I know we will be judged as we judge them for these things. During initial consultations with plastic surgeons, we have been treated more as a number than as a person sincerely seeking services. Once we sign up with them, then the switch is flipped to being a valued client. We successfully drive the route we had driven yesterday. Their website talked about parking behind the building. We found the N lot on the street behind the building but it was posted reserved by permit only. We parked here but it didn't feel right and it left us with quite a walk to the front door. It is 2:15, going from the instructions on the website, we are to stay in our car and text that we are here, we will get a come in text when it is our turn. So I text and we wait until it becomes 2:30 and nothing happens. Cathy insists we go now I am stubborn but yield to her on this. We lock the car and start to walk downhill; the thought of it not being the right lot bothers me even as Cathy pushes us on, until I got stubborn and turned around and head back toward the car. There is still time, we haven't had any texts yet; I will move the car to street parking, but this means hurrying back up hill. We are both sweating and fearful. The car gets moved and the meter fed eight quarters, still no texts. Cathy double insists since it is 2:45, "Cady we have to go now!" Okay and I call the office while we walk toward the building doors, I do get a person and they acknowledge that no one on their end has been watching the texts, please come up right away! Cathy and I enter the first-floor lobby and scan the directory, Dr. Stiller is on the sixth floor. No problem, we call for the elevator it opens and we go in but there is no button for the sixth floor! We ride up to the fifth and pop out into a long hallway with a prize at its end, another elevator. This one does go up to the sixth floor and Dr. Stiller's office. We enter trepidatiously into a standard waiting room with a reception desk on our left. There are three ladies seated waiting their turn for whatever services this practice provides; the gal at the desk greets us and we play the name game. You are Candice? No I'm Cadance. Cool I'll fix the misspelling. Two more times of name guessing and I am Cadance to everyone. We are asked to wait; someone will come for us so we drift back from the desk into the waiting area. I am numbingly calm and Cathy is anticipatory. The waiting room has functional chairs nothing glitzy, and the walls have the bare minimum of pictures, overall, there is nothing pretentious about this practice. In addition, there are no notes of glamour either. A woman exits from the inner office door; she is transgender. How I know this is by the conversation she is having with the receptionist asking, "What the next step is?" The reply is clear enough, "We need to get your insurance to okay your vaginoplasty. This can take anywhere from four to eight weeks, then we can give you a surgery date."

She is at least half my age, about my height, and has a nice voice; I am sad about mine. Our turn, a smiling young woman pronounces my name correctly and we are lead through the inner office doorway, down a hall, and into an exam room. She told us we could sit wherever we were comfortable and Dr. Stiller would be with us in a few minutes. Cathy and I choose the bench along the interior wall facing the exterior windows. The exam room was done in light earth tones and the exterior windows with their louvered blinds open bathed the room in sunlight, a bright comfortable place to be. The only aesthetic here is a large acrylic painting done in the same earth tones depicting a seated nude female figure with her back to the viewer, that same painting hangs in the waiting room but done in rainbow colors. The center-stage exam chair rests between our bench and the windows, just waiting for a customer, it seemed to beckon to me, after all this is why we came here. I remain seated next to Cathy; this is our transition. An odd sign posted on the wall exclaims 'No smoking No vaping' it goes without saying, doesn't it? So far, so good; the people we have met are all good-natured, there is no way to know this except to be here. There is a virtual fence around the office to make personal contact possible only by permission. Dr. Stiller bursts into the room followed by a quiet young lady who is a certified Physician Assistant (PA-C).

She takes up her post in the corner bringing along with her the ubiquitous laptop to take notes on. These notes will translate into a quote to take home with us to ponder. Dr. Stiller is tall; square shouldered, has dark hair pulled back into a man-bun, and has a silver loop earring in each ear. He has a strong self-assured tenor voice and a friendly we-are-all-family-here demeanor. He comes over to us and we get an elbow-bump greeting and then asks us in a teasing voice, "Where is my shirt!" I return his quip with. We didn't know your size! Standard equipment in every plastic surgery exam room we have been in, during this journey, has been a round wheelie stool always close at hand for the doctor to perch on in a doctorally way. As Dr. Stiller takes his place on said stool, which brings him to our eyelevel, he asks in my general direction, "What's your story?" I give the briefest of pause before I start my narrative.

First an aside: I have no idea why I didn't think to have this ready in a practiced matter. It has been the first question asked of me in every consultation we have had. At first, I thought it was a form of gatekeeping, but I have come to understand that there is more to it than just this. Yes, the surgeon needs to make sure you fit the demographic as deemed by the faceless World Professional Association for Transgender Health (Wpath) for the surgeries you seek, but there is another facet the surgeon personally seeks also. If you have the trust of a transgender person, allowing them to share their story with you deepens that trust; just listen and do so without bias. It will delineate a remarkable lifelong struggle full of pitfalls and human suffering just to be who you naturally are. Dr. Stiller was asked how he got started in transgender care and he basically said that early in his career he attended to a bright cheerful female patient. She was pleasant to chat with but in checking her chart he was surprised to see she was transgender. He was curious and spent over an hour with her asking about her experience. It was a career-changing moment for him. He defined it by saying, "For someone to struggle that long and then become who they truly are, how could I not want to be part of that?" Surgeons crave to be the great healer of a life malady; it is meat to feed their ego and why not? Who wouldn't want to be the surgeon to

605

give sight to the blind, hearing to the deaf, or rest to the tormented? Gender dysphoria is a torment and can be all but cured by the hands of a plastic surgeon, yielding a great reward for both the patient and the surgeon.

I shared my story and our story; the words came to me, as I needed them tailored toward someone who understands Eastern Washington. Dr. Stiller is naturally engaging and we have a discourse that puts both Cathy and me at ease with him. When asked what he could do for me, my answer is I have two surgeries in my transition goal. One after the other, the order is based on which can come first: vulvoplasty and FFS. He smoothly tells me he can help with both. First let's do the exam, his PA hands me a gown to put on and the two of them leave the room. Cathy helps me to get undressed; I have to remove my binder along with all of my street clothes except for socks. The gown is cloth colored in crimson and grey, the colors of nearby WSU, a nice touch. I put it on with the opening to the front, and then sit down in the center-stage exam chair to wait. Soon a knock at the door and the two return. Dr. Stiller listens to my lungs and seems happy with what he hears and then asks me to remove my mask to exam my face. He asks me what I would like changed. My right eyebrow is lower than my left, I would like symmetry and for the brows to be lifted some. I have a lot of skin that hangs in wrinkles so a lower to mid face lift, and my nose done. Dr. Stiller tells me he would pull the brows up at the hairline, which would also lower it hiding the thinning areas I have on either side of center. He goes on saying, "As far as your brows go, not too high to avoid the Kenny Rogers' surprised look. If I am doing masculinization, I tighten the skin directly toward the back of the head. For FFS I bring it up toward the cheekbones giving a feminine look." He gives me a mirror and demonstrates by pulling on my loose skin and yes, that is what I want. I have fallen for this man as my surgeon and I have sudden trust in whatever he will do to me. I am enamored with him; he is saying all the right words just as if he already knows what I need. Sigh… Of course, he does know all the right words, as I am part of a population that he has chosen to focus his practice on. He moves on and asks, "What is it about your nose that you would like changed?" I have a hump on the bridge of my nose I would like reduced and my bridge narrowed in width. Dr. Stiller was in tune with this and suggested shorting the tip just a little bit also. Cool! On the other hand, he spoke about breaking my nose to reduce the hump. Oh. He would also do a facelift to remove the extra skin.

Now he asks me to stand to do the exam of my genital area, he probes and stretches my scrotum skin. He tells me he is looking for lumps and bumps. Dr. Stiller concludes and tells me I am in good shape for this surgery. He will also go in and clean out any cording that may have been left after my orchiectomy. Doctor Stiller tells me the benefits of vulvoplasty; it is done as an ambulatory surgery so you don't have to spend the night in the hospital. We send you home to rest. This is great news to me, staying the night in a hospital is the last thing I want to do. This is one of the reasons we decided on vulvoplasty over vaginoplasty; the latter has you several nights in the hospital... Doctor goes on to tell me that I don't need any more hair removal, I can stay on my HRT but will need to stop several of my supplements. Cathy asks about blood thinners and Dr. Stiller tells us he doesn't use them; instead he uses ibuprofen, it is all that is needed. I'm sold! He asks about what insurance we have and Cathy tells him Medicare and a supplement. He tells us no one covers FFS but Medicare might cover the hospital expense. He and his PA tell us it was nice meeting us and take their leave. I get dressed figuring we are to head out to the waiting room. Just as I am finished a knock at the door brings in Kelly; she is the surgical consultant for the FFS. She has a quote for my FFS with her. We sit together while she explains the quote. But first she told me I have a bad*ss name, it is so cool! I explain cadence is a rhythm and I felt like my rhythm was broken and if you change the 'e' to 'a' you get dance, kind of like the dance we do throughout our lives. My name, Cadance, reminds me to dance to the rhythm I have always had inside, not what was assigned to me at birth. She loved it! We return to the quote; it has three line-items face and neck lift, brow lift, and rhinoplasty. The total cost is spit into Surgery and Anesthesia. It is the price of a new car ($23,600) and they want fifty percent down to book a date... Kelly is fun to talk to and is quick to answer questions. There doesn't look like there are any surgery dates until after November, which is just as well as I have one more consultation for FFS in the first week of October. We part without signing anything and at the front desk are told that my quote for vulvoplasty will take four to eight weeks to complete while waiting on Medicare to okay it.

Yesterday on a forum I follow on Facebook about surgeries, a lady talked about being in Spokane for her surgery with Dr. Stiller. I commented on the post that I was here also to consult with him. This morning, she posted that her surgery was just canceled by the hospital. Deaconess Hospital had suddenly pulled all elective times for the foreseeable future because of Covid. Here the lady had traveled across country, paid for an Airbnb for sixteen days only to have it pulled away from her at the last moment. Bottom surgeries are done at the hospital while things like face work are done in Dr. Stiller's in-house surgical suite. Poor lady, such a terrible thing to have happen... The times we live in. Cathy and I return to the elevators leading down to the street in front of the medical building. Our car was patiently waiting for us. It is almost 5:30 when we park in the hotel parking lot. Wienermobile is parked nearby and along with it the symbolism it conveys in its own comic way. But I think my surgeries will happen now. Cathy caterers our dinner out of our supplies of ham sandwiches, potato chips, and gluten-free baked goodies from Cole's Gluten Free Bakery and Cafe. With our tummies full and minds fatigued, we decide to go for a walk down the hill from the motel and along W North River Dive until the light began to fade and we turned around. Tomorrow on our way back, we will do breakfast at Cole's, then turn south toward Moscow Idaho. Sleep comes pretty quickly despite how uncomfortable the bed is. Normally, we would sleep with a window cracked open but there is no opening window in this room; instead, a sliding glass door opening on to a very small balcony. This door must remain shut, not a rule but because of good sense, the air outside is full of tiny mosquito like flies that come right through the screen on the sliding door. Morning comes and we pack our stuff out to the car to get going. The Wienermobile is still asleep from its prowling of

Spokane the day before. An early morning motel guest is walking around it. I'm sure his take on it is vastly different from mine. Our time here has been an adventure, full of information and symbolism that will affect our near future selves. Now, though, it is time to go to Moscow to the shop of Arlene's Tie-Dye Everything business. She is our go-to artist for the kid sized tie-dye shirts we give to little Quince and his parents so they can match as a family. It will give us a different route home, now it's time to listen to our audio book and let our minds rest in the 1950s world of Perry Mason for the next five hours. Our last stop on the way home is the college Starbucks in Ellensburg. Cathy orders drinks and is first to use the restroom, I wait for our order. Cathy is out of the restroom and it's my turn. I return to the lobby and Cathy is over at the bar chatting a male barista up, I stand there smiling under my mask. I came over to her and she said goodbye to the barista, as we headed toward the door I say. You were flirting back there. Cathy blushed, "No I wasn't!" I teased back at her; it sure looked like flirting to me! We laugh together as our car was soon back on I-90 going west and home.

***

Sunday October 3, 2021. Our anniversary is coming very soon so yesterday we took a long test drive to see how we do on them. I still wear a compression binder and there is the bathroom issue. This time we drove to Cashmere home of the Aplets & Cotlets Candy factory, and two large antique malls (Apple Annie, and the Antique Mall at Cashmere). All have survived Covid intact except Liberty Orchards the family-owned company that manufactures Aplets & Cotlets, has been sold to an international conglomerate, KDV Group. We followed I-90 to Cle Elum and then took highway 970 to state route 97; this road crosses Blewett Pass. Just before 97 little orchards pop up along with fruit stands. We stopped at the first one we came to and I parked our car off the highway near some apple trees. As we got out a parked van began to leave to return to the highway. I was standing at our trunk and Cathy had just closed her door when the older lady in the van rolled down her window and said, "You match!" I turned my head toward her, she then asked in curious voice, "Are you two sisters?" I returned, well sort of. I was walking toward her van as it stood between us and the open-air fruit stand. She giggled a little and ventured, "Are you partners???" I realized she was convinced I was a woman. I didn't want to break the spell with the wrong answer so my reply was, yes we are and this is our forty-seventh year together. Cathy was standing taking this all in with a grin. The lady very impressed said, "Wow that is amazing!" And I added, we always match! The lady was beside herself hearing this she flustered, "You're kidding that is just too good!" We were walking past her van now, I answered back to her, not at all! She smiled and waved; it was really fun talking to her. We bought three different kinds of pears. I never think I pass at all especially if I have to use my voice, but it depends on the age of the person I have encountered. Older folks look at you and see who you are without quibbling about your physical form. Bless them! Oh, I seem to pass best if I am not worrying about; if I am nervous and self-conscious there is no hope for it…

***

Friday October 15, 2021. Funny thing about journaling for me; I've been putting it off despite life continuing. I put the very thing aside to work on our book, which currently is in itself all about my journaling! It has become apparent that I simply can't stop making daily entries without knowing when the book is done because it's dependent on my journal. Is this one of those catch-22 things? With what will the book end? A surgery perhaps, but which one? I have two that I am currently wrestling with, FFS and vulvoplasty. Will an end be born from their completion; like a Phoenix rising from the ashes? Kind of a cool idea really, Cathy and I arising from the ashes of transition to fly off together to spend the rest of our lives unencumbered by the shackles of cis gender. Did I just get sidetracked again? Yes I did. Well, best to get back to the chronicle of what my journal needs to record. There is a clue in the surgeries that is important but I need to get to something first.

Forever and Two Days More

Our anniversary! We have been married for forty-seven years today! It was a cool rainy day full of the news that most our potential celebratory places were either closed because it was a Tuesday or closed because of some virus going around. Cathy is a go-girl and we need to go be away from the four walls of our home on this day. We decide a Cathy-centric day of shopping at Shipwreck Beads (the Costco of bead shops) in Lacey would be our special venue. Cathy had also found a gluten-free bakery, Miss Moffet's Mystical Cupcakes near Shipwreck Beads; a double win! The day is shaping up from a broken ho hum anniversary to a totally acceptable one! Corey had called the day before to wish us an early happy anniversary and asked how we were going to celebrate it. I gave him our outline of bead store, bakery, and then dinner at Duke's Seafood near our home. He cheerfully told me to have a good time. The next morning he called me to tell me to ask about a gift at Miss Moffet's place and don't let Mom know so it would be a surprise! I promised I would work it for all it was worth. We drove in morning drizzle, listening to an audio book that we had started during our last long trip. We almost always have an audio book on pause waiting for the next long drive to come up. Traffic on I-5 through Tacoma was slow; it almost always is, even with the virus hanging around as a political hammer. Cathy is all set to visit Miss Moffet's first; I have no problem with that suggestion! Miss Moffet's Cupcakes turns out to be an award-winning bakery; they appeared on a Food Network show and won a cupcake challenge using gluten-free ingredients. Gluten-free wasn't a requirement at all, so they competed directly against wheat flour and won on taste and presentation! Very cool! We found the place in a little break away mall; I parked and we entered their storefront. It was just amazing all the varieties of cupcakes, doughnuts, cookies, and cakes. We walked up to the display cases all but giddy with what lay before us. The lady noticed we were wearing matching tie-dye and said she had something for us. I knew she did because Corey had told me, but apparently he had told them to look for the tie-dye matching couple. He gave us a hundred dollar gift certificate here; we were truly kids in a free candy store. It was so fun; all that restrained us was the idea we could come back over and over again! Our goodies today would be for when we get back home. Shipwreck Beads, which had moved and been restrained because of the virus still looked familiar inside. We walked and shopped every product aisle. Cathy had brought along some of her beadwork; a three-inch globe made up 7,600 little glass beads depicting a jungle scene to share with the crafty folks there. The cashier was agog at her handiwork! The morning was as pleasant as we hoped and more. Our return trip home was through less traffic and what was left of our audio book will have to wait for another long drive. We had a nice dinner at Duke's at Southcenter of a seafood salad for Cathy and a crab salad for me. We finished our anniversary day off at home by watching *Hotel Transylvania* in keeping with the October theme of Halloween.

***

Last Friday, October 8th; Colby came and stayed overnight with us, the next day we traded Colby for B---- in the afternoon. Our day and morning with Colby was such a treat! We did Colby care (he loves to have a foot massage and has since he was little), played old video games, played Nanna a card game of cribbage, we cooked together, I was on hand to give advice while he repaired his 3DS, we did our activity of silly selfies in matching tie-dye shirts outside in our front yard, and we took long walks through our neighborhood chatting with each other. Colby is just the most loving Grandson to us; I wish he remembered our time together while I cared for him and his sister during their single digit years but that's okay. Colby is kind and protective of us; we love him so much! It truly was a very nice visit and to wake up in the morning to him in our house was super special! We had the nicest time with B---- the next day. We all cleaned rocks (she had a pile she had collected) while binge-watching *My Little Pony*. B---- loves to share her stories with us; she describes all these characters she has created and their interactions in their world. They are all very involved; she has an amazing memory to use to keep her story lines straight and running strong. B---- is indefinable; she is 14 going on 24, tough as nails, strong willed, and easily hurt but never showing it. She suffers no fools gladly and sees through airs quickly. We drove down to Joann Fabrics & Crafts so she and Nanna could shop for beads to make a necklace from using some of the seashells that came along with her rocks. We walked our neighborhood together and chatted. Nanna had created a beautiful one and a half inch globe out of 1,900 tiny glass beads. All intricately strung together revealing millefiori flowers in the colors of the asexual community. B---- lays claim to this community, so to honor her claim we bought a small ACE flag at Pride fest last month to go along with Cathy's crafted globe. B---- would honor us by going to Saturday Night Games at Grandma Dixon's house. It was just the four of us and we played cards; this time it was Uncle Fred's gin rummy. She was tolerant of losing and supportive of Great Grandma Dixon winning. What was going on? B---- normally doesn't play; instead, she takes her phone into one of the back bedrooms to watch videos, but tonight she was interested in and present for the card game. It was a wonderful gift to Grandma Dixon; it had been several years since B---- played with us. Thank you B----. As I said B---- is indefinable and we wouldn't trade her for anyone else. Colby's and B----'s path through childhood was very rough one; especially B----'s. Colby has shut out memories of that time whereas B---- holds on to a few. Looking at B---- now in comparison with seven years ago and all I can say is we have been greatly blessed... The next day being Sunday we had a video visit with little Quince; this time it was building with LEGOs. He is so far away but it is a blessing to video visit with him each week.

***

The week of October 11th is getting ready for Cathy's pre-op appointment by gathering documents (EKG and letter of surgical release) from Dr. Eaman.

I had my three-month post-op with Dr. Megan. Dr. Megan now has her own MA Amanda to be her right hand. She hands me a gown to change into and leaves. I peal myself out of my binder and street clothes, then don the gown. The floor is stone tile and cold, even with socks on. I wander around the exam room, holding my gown closed.

The room is done in tan hues with one contrasting wall in a dark blue-violet mix; this wall is opposite of a tan wall with a tall wall mounted mirror in place, so that you can see yourself from the exam chair. A large watercolor of a lily pond hangs on the contrasting wall. This art along with a line drawing of female figure opposite bring the artist touch to the space. Dr. Megan with a little knock comes breezing in, she seems genuinely happy to see us, "Wow your scar looks great! You don't have to wear the binder anymore unless you want to and you can now lay on your tummy if needed." She asks what we are using on my scar and I answer scar sheets; it was just the answer she wanted to hear. Cathy told Dr. Megan and Amanda that tomorrow is our 47th anniversary and they both congratulated us. Cathy is looking forward to her surgery with Dr. Megan on November 4th and told her so. Cathy also mentions the fullness she wanted removed from below her bustline and Dr. Megan said she would take care of it. The conversation came back around to me with questions on how I was doing. I'm doing really well; I haven't measured my breasts cause I kinda don't want to know just how much has been lost but I am really good with what I have. I want you to know just what a life changing surgery this was for me; the quality of my life is so much better now, all in all a lifesaver! I wish I could express how much it means to me, thank you so very much! Dr. Megan wants her pictures to mark three-month progress in healing. As she and Cathy chat, I get dressed. I report on my consult with Dr. Stiller. I told her that Dr. Stiller did recognize her name from being associated with Dr. Mangubat.

We get hugs and give hugs.

***

Sunday October 17, 2021. It has been thirteen days since I was given the go-ahead to go without the binder. I didn't stop wearing it until this last Monday and that was only during the day. My experience at first was very uncomfortable; there was a sensation of swelling pushing out all across the area that my binder had been holding tightly in. I am still numb right above the bikini scar line; below the scar I can feel a touch, above this there is no feeling. In saying no feeling what I mean is, to pressure on the immediate area. Without my binder in place, the whole abdomen just generally aches with a dull pain and pressure. With my binder in place, I can hold my tummy concave with my muscles but without it I bulge out. So, I can only go an hour or two at the most, before returning to the binder. Each day, I try to get in a little more no binder time. I never sleep without it. In the last three days, I have done a total of eight hours and even gone on our walks without it. My rigor now is to use a support panty to give just a little pressure on my tummy during the day. If I have to do something physical, such as I had to mow the lawn the other day, I wrap myself tightly with the binder. I was so surprised that I could mow the whole lawn! It has been several years since I surrendered to having to pay to have it done. My body did as I asked it to, but in the end, I had cramps in my hands and legs from over use. I wore a mask, kept a slow and steady pace, and after it was done I was proud of how our yard looked. Cathy was in tears. I was taking a big chance in doing this and I had forgotten why I quit doing it. I dodged the bullet this time and in the end Cathy and I would do some more yard work over the weekend to get ready for winter; we both had some recovering to do afterwards. So for the foreseeable future, I will wear a support panty without a binder during the day and sleep in a three-belt binder at night. The three-belt binder does allow me to sleep in motel beds where it was almost impossible before; now I can tolerate two-night stays in a motel bed. I also do exercises each morning after waking up and removing my binder. The goal is to stretch my whole body and strengthen my core muscles. Leg lifts, shoulder work, and some light weight lifting, with lots of stretching. All before leaving our bedroom, if I do these I am able to hold my abdomen in for most of the day.

Okay finally back to the surgeries. The vulvoplasty is a non-issue; all that lays ahead for it is waiting for Medicare to say how much they will pay of the hospital portion and this is weeks away from happening. But the FFS can be scheduled right now! We can put down money right now to hold a date sometime this coming spring. There is no insurance it is all private payer. So, what is the problem with going ahead and doing it? Well, there is an issue, one that subconsciously has set me to dragging my feet and it is time to bring it to the surface. I'm not going to go to anyone else, Dr. Stiller fits the bill, but Dr. Bowers is why I can't pull the trigger. I had became enamored with the idea that Dr. Bowers would take good care of me, because I was someone worth taking care of to her. I knew this in my heart because we share a history in common through the relationship with Sandy, Renée, and Jude… This was a construct I put together in my mind at a stage so very early in my transition, akin to hero worship. Reality is I prayed for God to guide Cathy and me along this journey. We were guided to Dr. Stiller and are thankful for this.

***

Monday October 18, 2021. Today we had to be up by 8:00 because I had an appointment for a blood draw at 9:30. Cathy and I are not early risers anymore; we put off going to bed until 1:00 am. On the other end; we put off getting up as late as possible, sleep and the time around it is all we have to feel safe in… I had the nicest ten-minute conversation with the nurse drawing my blood; she had gotten my name right and I thanked her. She commented, "I bet you get called Candace a lot, they move the n around." I returned, yes that is exactly what happens; I think people look at the shape of the word and make a guess without looking at the letters. She laughed and got busy getting the stuff to draw blood. We talked about how our nails have become so brittle and what to take to make them stronger. She told me what she used and that she was taking prenatal vitamins, "I'm trying to get pregnant and anything that might help even a little, I'm up for!" I wish her luck as we parted company. It dawned on me at that moment that we were two women exchanging pleasantries on a dreary day. I rejoined Cathy in the waiting room and we walked to the car. At home, Cathy told me she was going to make breakfast and I should use the time to call Kelly at Dr. Stiller's office to book an FFS surgery date. I hesitated, Cathy asked, "Why not? I'm good with it, you will look beautiful go ahead. You know it is the right thing to do for both of us." I mumble, the money issue is still there. Cathy's reply, "Go look into the bathroom mirror, make peace with it, then come back out and call

616

Kelly." I did and called. I had to leave a message for her to call me back but that was enough movement in the right direction to break the ice dam on the subject for me. My voice message to her was a mumble of picking a date for surgery. Now all I have to do is wait for Kelly to call me. We have our breakfast of sliced fruit bowls, cupcakes from Miss Moffet's, I had an egg over easy and Cathy had a protein bar. Cathy is so very careful in cooking eggs, low heat and timed exactly, so as not to be runny, instead beautifully creamy. She learned the technique at her father's knee making Saturday morning breakfasts. Each egg she cooks has to be up to her dad's standard and all the memories she holds of him. We spend our day running errands, walking our neighborhood walks, and then our dinner. Cathy did a dry roast, learned at the knee of her mother. Dinner was past, it was 5:30, and I figured Kelly would at best call me tomorrow. That was okay; I was still a little reticent with myself. My phone sprang to life with the caller ID of Dr. Stiller's office. It was Kelly quite excited and asking forgiveness for calling so late. She told me she was just thinking of giving me a call as surgery dates were now posting out into January. I put her on speaker so Cathy could hear and share the conversation. I asked, what about March? "Girl, the whole month is open except for one date!" She answered as if this was the most fun she had had all day. Cathy and I pick March 10th with the idea that winter may have broken there in Spokane. Kelly is having such fun making this sale. She tells us, "This is why I love what I do, you are going to look great afterward and we are going to treat you like family!" I ask about weather problems. She tells me, "They are not unheard of and we just reschedule and move to a better weather day if we need to." I didn't realize the feeling of relief we were both going to have on booking a surgery date for me. Cathy seemed very pleased for us to be moving forward. Cathy handles giving Kelly our credit card number for the deposit. Cathy is excited; she has always been a go-girl moving forward, accomplishing and experiencing new things. This is our transition together; we both are becoming us even in this time of disenchanted discouragement. Cathy has her pre-op blepharoplasty appointment with Dr. Megan in two days; we will drive north to

Mountlake Terrace for this. We have done everything possible to have Cathy up and healthy; her sodium levels are into normal levels and blood ferritin is good. There were two possible troublemakers in that last event, the second dose of Covid vaccine and the blood thinner Lovenox. It is forbidden to even consider the Covid injection, but all the doctors involved that day in the ER with Cathy's care said it had to be considered a factor... So, we will not get the booster before her surgery, even though we qualify for it and no blood thinners will be used. Cathy's primary care doctor has given the okay for this surgery, her eye surgeon is on board with it, and Dr. Megan feels it is safe. The surgery is just for Cathy; she wants this and is excited to be getting it. I know the feeling well now. I will feel so relieved when it is over and Cathy is safely home in recovery and healing normally (if not super-fast).

***

Wednesday October 20, 2021. We have to be up by 7:00 tomorrow morning to get ready for Cathy's pre-op with Dr. Megan. No small thing, our normal wakeup time is well after 9:00. Even with the euphoric distraction of booking a date for my surgery, my depression level is very high right now. Transitioning in the time of Covid can be, well, as extreme as living through it. I am worried about Cathy's after surgery time, what will it challenge us with, and how will it change us? I hope it doesn't do any of these things, but Cathy and I are changing regardless of this. We aren't changing toward each other but the world is changing toward us. Not the world in general but our familial community world.

***

Thursday October 28, 2021. The rain has closed in on us holding us hostage in our home today. Yes we can go out anytime, but suppression sits on our shoulders holding us in. I have spent countless days going over each year of my journal, cleaning up vague words and thoughts, but being careful not to touch the spirit of what I had written in moments of depression, adulation, and realization. My journal holds me together, it stops a downhill slide commanding me to document before I hit bottom, and in doing so, gives me the chance to regroup and reverse… It is also my memory in the face of a diminishing ability to hold onto them. It can be strong when I am weak and can also accuse me of my mistakes. Sandy would greet me with, "How are you doing right now? Don't think just tell me." Catching me off guard mentally but this worked, as I would almost always have some thought crossing my psyche at her office door that would disappear as I sat down on her couch.

Thinking of Sandy:

When Sandy was in high school, she approached her pastor about becoming a youth pastor. Her pastor told her he didn't think that would be a good path for her in life. This was one of the bumps that sent her on a different arc while still leading her in the same overall direction. Embracing her sexually would come later, after an initial coming-out, and then traveling abroad to find herself. She came out as gay late in high school in Yakima. Imagine her at the wheel of a BMW racing down the autobahn in Germany some twenty-two years after the end of World War II! She did this in the mid to late 1960s; she gathered herself up and traveled alone to Germany to find herself and spent several years there. Being a WWII buff, she wanted to see the places she had been reading about. To support herself in Germany she gave dance lessons on a military base USO club. She marched in some of the first Gay Pride Parades in Seattle and counseled some of the first MtF clients (38 years ago). Sandy finally came out to her mom in her mid-30s. It took a while but her mom became very supportive. Sandy really didn't understand this until one day her mom called and asked why she see didn't see Sandy on TV protesting for Gay Rights at an event? Sandy explained she had been out front as an activist so many times and this time she had decided to step back from it. Her mother chided her because of this, saying, "This stuff is very important! You should be right out there in front!" Surprised her no end… Pat and Sandy had a little shared office on Lee Street on Capitol Hill back in the late 1960s where they could see clients. In 1969, she joined the staff of Seattle Counseling Services SCS; the place served mostly men and kids. Sandy as a woman was in the minority there. In perfect

Sandy fashion she decided to get more women involved and formed a Women's Night at the place. She became their first women coordinator. She was asked if she would help with transgender women clients and Sandy answered "Sure! What's a transgender woman?" There were only four therapists in the Seattle area working full time treating MtF. Sandy helped out part time, she had 10 clients a day. In the mid to late 1980's Sandy joined the Seattle 24-Hour Crisis Line and would be their volunteer coordinator until her retirement in 2018. These are the life and times of Sandra Lee Fosshage MA LMHC.

She shared herself with me; I think it was because I was her last client a singular honor that I cherish. I should keep her secrets although she never asked me too, but the time for that is draining away, age is taking it away and I see no harm but only good can come.

Okay this is a good warm-up for journaling, so let's do it! I have stopped wearing support panties during the day. I still sleep in the binder but will slowly over time reduce this also.

The hormone circus continues. My current hormone patch usage had been four fresh patches twice a week. I'm trying to reduce the number of patches (they are very expensive) by one. My cycle is now four patches twice a week, three of them new and one a holdover from last time. Also, I stopped taking a nightly oral dose of a 2mg estradiol tablet by swallowing it.

I became anxious and nervous on the second day of the three-day three-patch cycle. The feeling disappeared if I took a 2mg estradiol tablet by dissolving it in my mouth under my tongue, giving me a quick surge of estradiol.

I didn't get this anxious/nervous feeling on the four patches four day cycle. In addition to the feeling I was having, my hair was falling out. A return to four fresh patches all the time seems to stop both the feelings and the hair loss. I guess I'm a four-patch girl from here forward...

From reading my journals dated back to 2005, I see I have had lots of pain trying to find the right dose of hormones. Right now, at this four-patch dose I feel better than in years! I still get sinus pressure but it is much reduced by comparison. Dr. Eaman, for as progressive as she is, doesn't like high estrogen levels; this is older science that held high levels bring on blood clots and was kinda true, when we used equine sourced estrogen. I am unafraid of my current levels, which are based on current transgender research, but patches are expensive. This is a good place to explain to myself about the HRT quandary again. As I have said, this is the best I've felt on HRT, I am stable my hair remains on my head, my breasts feel as if they are growing, and I sleep well. But I still experience reduced memory, focus, and math skills. I have been so stable that I haven't taken a Diim (helps remove estradiol metabolites) for a long time. I have been hesitant even now to take one because it is such a balancing act. Once I do, hair loss can pop up and getting it stopped is painful, but on the plus side I'll regain my mental function. That is the quandary in a nutshell. Fun being an MtF...

Cathy has her surgery in seven days and Corey and Quince are here in twenty-four days. I'll be so relieved when Cathy's surgery is over and she is back home again and still herself. Lots of praying to do... Casey and Corey are now removed from us; Corey is good to call each day to touch bases. Casey we seldom hear from, but of the two Casey has the most on his plate at any time family wise. Cathy and I miss being included in their daily lives; our place now is as a remote relative separated by the barrier of distance. You don't consider a remote relative's daily life as they are just there abstractly. It is a proper place for us as grandparents, but still, I do yearn to know that we are thought about in a closer way. I called Casey to ask if I had trouble after Cathy's surgery, could I count on him coming to help if needed. Casey did tell me he would be available but didn't suggest any more than just that. Sigh. Again, it is our proper place with our sons and Cathy and I have each other in an us-against-the-world philosophy.

***

Monday November 1, 2021. I had never been spit at before nor has Cathy. This very thing happened to us two days ago at Bartell's parking lot. It was 2:30 and yes our rule was not to shop there after 2:00 but we hadn't had any trouble for quite a while now... I parked right in front of the store and as I shifted into park, a man stood up from behind the garbage can that stands near the entrance. It was the oddest place for him to be, down behind that garbage can. I know that homeless people go through it sometimes looking for whatever. Anyway, he looked directly at me and burst into a tirade, he cursed (we were still in the car so we didn't hear his words) then started spitting at us over and over. He moved away to our left by a car length and pulled down his zipper and started waving his penis in our direction. I started the car and told Cathy not to look in his direction. Even as I back the car up, he continued in his angry X-rated tirade toward us. It was as if by just being us, we set him off. Now sadly, I guess I can't say, that we have never been spat at... I drove home and didn't want to do our afternoon walk for fear of that person being so nearby. The walk we had that morning brought several guys out from behind bushes in yards of boarded up houses just as we passed, odd and sad times. Yesterday I started to reason that I would feel better if I told someone at Bartell's about the aggressive person keeping people out of their store so Cathy and I headed up to the place. It was very quiet and no sign of street people in the morning. I saw the manager, told him what had happened, and he apologized profusely. It made me feel heard and I needed this. I know that the police don't do anything about this stuff anymore, there isn't anything they can do but our lives still have to go on...

***

Wednesday November 3, 2021. Tomorrow is Cathy's surgery appointment. We will leave to drive to Mountlake Terrace by 10:00; with that goal in mind, our getting out of bedtime will be 8:00. Cathy has spoken to her anesthesia nurse making sure she understands about Cathy's low sodium condition. The nurse, Jen Tanguy, is a pleasant lady who did my anesthesia. After Cathy started to tell her story about having to go to the ER, Jen said, "You're the patient Chuck was telling me about!" Chuck did Cathy's anesthesia for her tummy tuck at La Belle Vie here in Tukwila; this is before Dr. Megan moved to Phase Plastic Surgery up north. Apparently anesthesia nurses have lunch together as a group, once in a while. The result of the phone conversation was Jen is fully armed with the special care that Cathy needs to have during this surgery tomorrow. We have spent the day running errands to get supplies (food, treats, and assorted recovery supplies). Cathy and I showered together, enjoying each other and being very careful to get every spot clean. Our breakfast this morning was apple crisp and an over easy egg, our dinner was ham and bagel for Cathy and ham and an over easy egg for me. It is now 10:30p, Cathy is reading a book sitting in the newly padded recovery chair and I am at my computer. It is a normal evening for us. What makes it abnormal is the worry I have for tomorrow's surgery. I nearly lost Cathy seven months ago after that tummy tuck but she recovered, praise God! We have taken every precaution, run blood tests, and gotten doctors' okay for this. It was a trauma that I thought I had put aside but I was wrong. This last week has found my mind loving Cathy moment by moment, noticing her touching me as we pass each other, waking up to her beside me, walking hand in hand each day, and just being together. I have noticed her holding me in a hug longer, kissing my lips more often, and calling me babe. It is not lost to me that she is nervous about surgery also, but she wants this for herself, just as I want it for myself. Words fail to describe, because you would have to be us to understand. So, we pray together and look beyond the surgery to the time Cathy is recovered and Corey and little Quince are here in our house visiting us for Thanksgiving and a little mini-Christmas the day afterwards. I love Cathy so much; we are becoming just us, falling in step with a shared transition. Each kiss I get from her is so memorable, so fully experienced by me in ways I have never known before transition, and her experience with me seems to be the same. We both have been freed from stereotypes we were trapped in. Now with that freedom we are both blossoming in our relationship to each other. Tomorrow if I need help Casey has said we can call on him. It is my plan too; if I do need help it would be getting Cathy from the car into the house. I will make that call based on how she is after the surgery. It will take us perhaps an hour to get home in traffic tomorrow, enough time for Casey to drive to our house from his… You know as I sit here typing, the realization is that this day has come very quickly. I guess you just can't dodge it as Uncle Fred Booth used to say…

***

Friday November 5, 2021. Yesterday Cathy had quad blepharoplasty and suction assisted lipectomy with Dr. Megan. The surgery was at Phase Plastic Surgery in their surgical suite. We arrived at 11:00 and Sara greeted us in a distracted so-you're-here sort of way. Sara has been with Dr. Baxter for many years and has decided to retire rather than continue on with the new practice. There is tension in the office and it shows in and around Sara. A new computer system is being installed replacing the paper system she is in charge of. This is a hard time we are living through of constantly being forced to do things, and being a short-timer does color your attitude. We were taken to an exam room at 11:30 by Amanda, Dr. Megan's PA. She then left us with instructions for Cathy to disrobe and don a gown. Dr. Megan pops in to do her markup of the places Cathy wanted liposuction done and for the eye area blepharoplasty; we chat together. Yes, there is the specter of the bump-in-the-road calamity of the tummy tuck but everyone is focused on doing everything to avoid this outcome. They are giving her fluids all during the surgery amounting to one liter in total. I am nervous and as such I did a bold thing for me to do, I asked if Dr. Megan was religious? She answered, "Not really, it has been years since I was in church." Well, I went on to tell her Cathy and I even as being transgender are. We are going to pray as we normally do, would you join us? Dr. Megan said, "I would be happy to!" We all formed a little circle and I asked for a blessing from God for Cathy during the surgery. Afterward Dr. Megan said, "I feel good about this, let's get going!" She left us and Nurse Lori came in to wrap up paper work and explain she would be doing Cathy's recovery afterward. Nurse Lori isn't too far from our age; she remembers the cartoon *The Jetsons* giving us a commonality. Cathy answered Lori's questions about her breakfast of pills this morning. At 12:22 I am dismissed and Lori takes Cathy into the surgical suite. I wait in the office waiting room, I settle down in a corner where I am out of direct line-of-sight of Sara. I view Facebook until there is nothing left that has a remote crumb of interest for me. I silently pray off and on as time passes. I play games of Thieves-Of-Egypt solitaire on my phone; it is a good match because it requires my slow and steady concentration and by the end of each game thirty minutes has passed. I also listen to the ebb and flow of this office, a steady flow of women come in and face Sara who I, as have said, is plowing through her work as if hiking through the Grand Canyon, looking only down at her feet. At 1:53 Sara announced to me that they are almost done! Then at 2:15 Amanda wanders into the office and tells me that no they just finished the eye part and now have to do the liposuction. An hour later I learn that Cathy is out of surgery and into recovery. I can hardly wait to see her, but I wait until 3:30 hoping that someone will come get me. Finally, I asked Sara about going back to see Cathy. Sara had been busy but did call the OR and told the other end of the line that she would send 'him' back. I roll my eyes… In recovery I find Nurse Lori attending to Cathy, who is pretty much fully awake and cognizant! This is so much different from her last surgery when she really didn't wake up until we had been home for hours. Lori explained that she was waiting until the entire IV bag was fully empty, to give Cathy the full benefit of the sodium solution. Nurse Lori went over all the care instructions with both Cathy and me. I helped to get Cathy dressed and put her shoes on her. We were back in matching tie-dye but no one noticed except she and me. Dr. Megan did come by to check on Cathy one more time. She told us everything went great the only challenge was the lipo; there is so much scar tissue in that area that it was tricky to move the probe around. She didn't want to use too much pressure and push on the wrong thing. At our car Lori told Cathy to use 'her strong legs to lift herself out of the wheelchair' at that moment a memory popped up into my brain. I realized she was the one in the recovery room with me after my surgery! We both got hugs from Nurse Lori and headed home. Cathy was fully alert and didn't complain of any pain, the trip right up to getting into the recovery chair in our house was a breeze compared to last time… I called Casey and told him the good news that I wouldn't need his help with Cathy. Today, Cathy has been steadily improving, eating well and we took two walks up to the pool and back. No pain to speak of, she took Gabapentin and Tylenol-3 for pain management but even at the end of a dose time she is still pain free, such a blessing! We have been icing her eyes three times a day with a specially made ice pack in the shape of a mask. Nurse Lori is adamant that frozen peas make the best ice packs and to only apply an ice pack around the eyes for five minutes at a time. We will ice one maybe two times tomorrow then that is it for the ice packs. Cathy's main complaint is that her eyes can get stuck closed from the sticky ooze from her incision line. There was some bleeding but that has pretty much stopped today. Tomorrow we will clean the eye a little more with warm water and Q-tips. Cathy also has an eye-drop containing Tobramycin and Dexamethasone that we use three times a day. I am anxious despite the fact Cathy is doing so well. I keep looking for any change in behavior or mental decline that might signal low sodium trouble. What I am seeing is a Cathy that is micro-managing me and at times distracted from the obvious. Is this normal? Is this because of what she has just gone through or from how life has changed for us both? I don't know because I'm not being normal either. Cathy wasn't back to her old self for several months after the ER trauma of the last surgery. At first, the little subtle behaviors and new demeanor shocked me into thinking the trauma had hurt her and the Cathy I knew was lost to me forever. I mean she was still with me, but unsure of her mental footing. A month passed then a second month; either Cathy was battling back or I was accommodating, perhaps both. Then one day it became clear to me Cathy was back to being herself! What I didn't realize was that same trauma had changed me also, so here I sit battling with it again because unlike Cathy I wasn't forced to terms with it. She battled back from it while I pushed it down deep inside. God is big, bigger than all things we know that can harm us. This next week will bring resolution to us both, why should it be any different than all the other battles we have been through...

***

Forever and Two Days More

Saturday November 6, 2021. I have had a sinking feeling that Cathy has changed mentally. Several things she had trouble with pointed to it today. We lost one of our matching facemasks, she had lapses while trying to order drinks at Starbucks, again while checking in at the blood lab. She maintained a continual running dialog of directing me how to do any simple task and was uncaring about serious situations. All these issues are not normal for Cathy. Cathy places great value on our matching tie-dye facemasks, when my surgery was over with Dr. P and she couldn't find my mask it was a disaster! Today when we realized we had somehow left Cathy's mask at Phase Plastic Surgery, she shrugged it off... At Starbucks today she couldn't get our drink orders straight and hovered right in the face of the barista to make sure she made it correctly. It was kind of embarrassing the way she crowed the lady when normally Cathy will give space and chat with them. At the blood lab Cathy couldn't figure out how to check in on her phone; this is so unlike Cathy, she is swift and sure at this place. With each little occurrence, my fear of losing her grew and grew and I became dour and short tempered. The trauma I pushed deep down came up and smacked me right in the face. I can't get over the near miss at the ER months ago and the weeks it took for Cathy to inch slowly along towards returning to being herself once again. And why not? It was a great trauma for her to go through, but God blessed us; Cathy has a strong personality where mine is not so much. Now after typing all of this and waiting for the other shoe to drop here at home I wondered why the mental change came without the blood pressure drop (she is maintaining 133/65) and the drunk-like passing out??? Cathy is taking Gabapentin a new drug that she hasn't had before. We looked it up and guess what! There under the list of side effects is a separate listing of 'amplifies rare conditions'. Gabapentin amplifies the effects of the rare condition of people who have trouble with sodium levels!!! A stern warning in bold type of '**Contact doctor if you notice a change in behavior or mental processes.**' Also '**Contact doctor if a rash occurs.**' Cathy has developed a red rash on her legs, trunk, and arms. I was in tears when I read this, I was so frightened about losing her mentally, this seemed to be starting, and here was this drug helping it along... But we know about it now and Cathy's next dose at bedtime will not be taken! Prayers tonight that tomorrow will bring hope. I do have a vulnerability, deep-seated fear of how a pill or drink can take people away from me...

***

Monday November 8, 2021. Cathy has not been herself and I have known this since I brought her home on Thursday. I saw Cathy slip away seven months ago after her tummy tuck surgery and I watched her come slowly back twenty hours afterward in the ER. What is so different this time is there was no crash to zero but in its place was a strange lessening of Cathy's personality. A blood test we had done on Saturday has come back confirming a sodium drop from low normal of 132 to an abnormal low of 125 mmol/L (chloride is 87 mmol/L). Last time the hospital wouldn't release her until she reached 125 and then they were hesitant. We took every step to keep this from happening including giving her one liter of normal saline fluid during the surgery. It happened anyway, but without the crash of last time. We have been pushing electrolytes hard for the last four days. During this time Cathy's blood pressure has been steadily climbing into the high 160's. Sodium level of 125 was as of Saturday; we have no idea what Cathy's level is today. It could be higher or lower; most likely, judging from her personality it is higher. I say this because of the changes I saw starting on Saturday and continuing to this day. A thing to note: Cathy has had almost no pain this sure wasn't my experience with this surgery. Looking back seven months ago in the ER Cathy didn't experience any pain even as Dr. Megan opened her suture. No sodium no pain? All of this is working itself out; Cathy has contacted Dr. Eaman and got a follow up appointment with her on the nineteenth. She also has a follow up with Dr. Megan this coming Thursday.

So, to center in on me for a moment: I had an awful feeling all of this time that I was losing Cathy. The feeling brought me full circle: tears, anger, and hopelessness. I felt that Cathy was becoming someone else; I could perceive how she acted emotionally and rationally in a modified matter. In some ways it was heartwarming and others disturbing. This Cathy was done with people who centered in on themselves, who didn't acknowledge us, and our needs, she was, "Let's move and leave them behind." She is so right but where did this come from? My heart ached with, oh she is gone, but she is still right in front of me beautiful long white hair and all. Then just as a lighting bolt illuminates the stormy sky making clear vision possible out of the darkness, it came to me. I know this scenario, I have lived it but from the other side. Early in my transition Cathy's words to me several times were, "I feel like I am losing you." When I spoke to my cousin Janet, she used, "I feel like I am losing my cousin C----." I thought in both times, I am right here don't you see me I am not gone! Cathy was seeing me act emotionally and rationally different just as if my personality had been altered. Had I not become someone else at that moment? Poor Cathy; her perception was true just as my perception of her at this moment is true. I had no idea just how much this hurts to be on this side; it feels like a death is taking place, someone you love more than life itself walked away from you never to return. You can reach out with all your strength for their personality and close your hand on nothing but empty air. The warmth of their body will never again come to you in times of chill; all that is left is a cruel empty space and nearby to that space, a vaguely familiar but unknown person stands yearning to be close to you. Cathy I am so sorry I did this to you and so blessed to have it happen to me. I can now share your pain and you mine…

***

Tuesday November 9, 2021. Casey just called me with the most amazing offer/request. "Would you like to have Colby and B---- for the entire weekend? I would drop the kids off at your place this Friday right after school and pick them up late Sunday." Wow! I told him. Sure, we can do that but you did mean only two kids right? I teased back at him. After all, there are four in your house. Casey surprised me with, "All the others will be gone." I asked where and he simply said, "Back to Wisconsin I told them they had to go." I was careful at this point not to express any opinion or rattle off questions. I'm sorry this had to be hard for you, I told him. He waved it off with "Not really" and told me, "This is what you do when someone tells you they don't respect you now or ever will." Again, no prying for details on my part if Casey wanted to share he would. I have no idea who slapped the hand that fed them or what brought this on. Casey is big hearted to spent money to equip his house to handle this wayward family, he became caregiver to the four teenaged kids in his and Mindy's house, so whatever happened had to slam the door shut on their stay...

***

Wednesday November 10, 2021. Nice clear day today. Mindy called my cell phone to thank Cathy and me for taking Colby and B---- for the weekend! We didn't pry about whatever was going on at their place but Mindy came right out with, "We are going to be much better off with only the four of us in the house." Mindy even said, "Love you," at the end of our conversation! Casey has carefully isolated Mindy, Colby, and B---- from whatever happens at their house this weekend.

***

Sunday November 28, 2021. Corey and Quince arrived on Saturday the 20th and we had a whirlwind of play for four days. Quince started each morning climbing into bed with Cathy and me to watch *Paw Patrol* or *Wild Kratts'* videos on my cellphone. We all played with Hot Wheels, LEGOs, and watched Christmas videos (right before bath-time). There were lots of toys we didn't get to but will still be here for the next visit. Nanna read Christmas books and did a Christmas present project with Quince for his Mama. Quince did a drawing using Infusible Ink pens and markers of the Milky Way, deeming it to be a Galaxy 5000 and Nanna heat-pressed it onto a t-shirt. Quince was very pleased with it. It was a real treat to have lots of Corey time all to ourselves! Thanksgiving was at Casey's and turned out wonderfully. There were twelve of us including Cathy's mom and sister Linda, Mindy's Aunt Berta; Melinda had joined us by then. The day after Thanksgiving, we had a mini-Christmas at our house since we will not get to see Corey here this year. Cathy and I

630

wanted to see Q open our gifts (it is half the fun) so gift giving was centered on Quince, the adults would do gifts with each other on Christmas day. It worked wonderfully (we even played the Minister's Cat game). Grandma Dixon and Linda will see Quince at his house this coming weekend so our little mini-Christmas was just us. We all (except Corey and family) will do Christmas together on the 25th. Corey's joke was since we worked in Christmas on Thanksgiving weekend we might as well squeeze in an Easter egg hunt and Fourth of July fireworks too!

Casey and Mindy's house was neat and tidy, such a change from when they had four more living there. Scarlette their dog was well behaved nothing like she was when there were two more uncontrollable dogs in the house along with her. This same thread continued to Colby and B---- both seemed to benefit from the exit of their cousins as well as getting their bedrooms back again.

***

Thursday December 2, 2021. I have had the hardest time returning to journaling since November 8th. There have been distractions with Corey and Quince staying with us Thanksgiving week but it was especially hard after they went home. Yes I did touch in to record some news but no heart to paper did flow. I would start my computer and it would sit idle, waiting for whatever was stopping me to resolve the block. What the block came down to was I both didn't want to/couldn't bring myself to/refused to put words to paper... I even used the excuse of too much had happened to ever catch up again with it. So, let's began with draining the top layer little by little.

Cathy's upper and lower blepharoplasty checkup with Dr. Megan was today. It has been four weeks and a good time for pictures and a check-in with Dr. M. Doctor Megan is the fourth generation of her family to become a medical doctor. Her great-great-grandfather started the father to son doctor thread and her grandfather's medical bag has been passed down and now rests with her. An amazing family! What more could you ask for in choosing a surgeon? Just to go over this one more time; Cathy has had a rough time in recovery. We took steps to be watchful of her blood sodium level after surgery, yes it did drop to 125 when measured two days after surgery. Cathy was dismayed even frightened by the result of the test. Before surgery she was at 132, a low normal. We had two possible causes last time: the blood thinner Lovenox and the Covid injection. This time, there was no blood thinner at all and the drop still occurred, so the finger points at the vaccine. But the vaccine cannot be questioned, it isn't allowed, which is a pity; we are forearmed with this information so we can be watchful with Cathy and any future surgery. Other folks with low sodium problems will have to discover it on their own... Another issue giving a rough time in recovery has been Cathy's eyelids, upper and lower, being highly inflamed and itchy. This turned out to be her sensitivity to Aquaphor and other thick ointments. Once the area became inflamed (especially at the corners) nothing seemed to help; we used Tobradex and Lotemax to no avail. Cathy was miserable, she couldn't show off her eyes because they looked so mean red and the pain from the itching was never ceasing. All we could do was to put nothing on the skin and wait. Through a coincidence, we ended up trying Amore Pacific's Moisture Bound Recovery Masque. It is a light crème and seemed to soothe Cathy's eyelids when nothing else did. I applied it twice a day: at bedtime and when we awoke each morning. The coincidence was in already having a little pile of samples of the stuff. How we came by them: Debbie Caddell several years ago had put together a make-up demo for her transgender clients, me being one of them. Debbie brought in two make-up vendors from Nordstrom's to do demonstrations; they of course, came with samples! I am so grateful we are pack rats and still had the samples, they turned out to be a Godsend! Cathy's eyes do look much better now and she has improved vision as a bonus!

Our little house is so quiet since Quince and family went back to San Diego. I told Corey this the other day and he shared that Quince, while at after-school care, told his teacher that he had been in Seattle. She asked him how he liked Seattle because she had family there too. Quince told her he liked Seattle better than San Diego. Why Quince?

Because it is where Boppa and Nanna live!!! This melts our hearts little Q.

I have put the book *Walking the Bridgeless Canyon (Repairing the breach between the Church and the LGBT community)* by Kathy Baldock on my Christmas List. Cathy and I watched several of her videos about 'unclobbering the tangled mess about Biblical translations' and really enjoyed them. She herself comes from an Evangelical Christian background and when she found herself going through a divorce that she didn't want, God put her on a path she never dreamed of taking.

Me stuff: I have made several attempts to do electronics building kits or trying to troubleshoot non-working circuits and have pretty much failed. My thinking is all muddled, focusing and concentrating is near impossible. My short-term memory is totally unreliable. The more I try, the more I panic at failing… I feel old and doddering both mentally and physically. Because of this, I also feel my place in the family is diminished. I have a continual headache centering between my eyes radiating back from that point up and over my cranium. Yesterday was a terrible day for me; I couldn't deal with the depression, all I could do was dwell in the dark. I now have two surgery dates with Dr. Stiller March 10, 2022, for FFS and August 16, 2022, for bottom surgery. The depression is so bad that this brings no light to me; in fact, I wonder if life would simply become more laborious by these surgeries… Is either a gain anymore in the face of what our daily lives have become? I can't think when I need to, this is the most troubling, and failing vision comes after this. Body pains aren't so bad; with daily stretching I can walk without pain, a wonderful gift! Cathy and I are moving closer together each day; our relationship had never been as close as we are right now as a couple. As the world moves away from us, we cling to each other tightly, comforting each other, and praying together. We are seen as two older ladies, sometime as sisters, other times as a gay couple, but always as a loving couple dedicated to God and each other. The part about God we leave to God to make use of.

The surgeries run around in my brain, it seems like a dream to be completely medically transitioned by my 69th birthday. Imagine not having dysphoria after a life of daily pokes and uncountable sighs of defeat. The price may be very high, though; it might bring never ending daily physical pain. Cathy and I have decided on zero depth vaginoplasty also known as vulvoplasty. This is a compromise between functionality and maintenance, no small thing this…

***

Sunday December 5, 2021. This is Christmas cookie time (gluten-free nut-free, dairy-free, chocolate chip) and I wanted to confirm if Sandy still was at her long time condo address. I called her cellphone and left a message at the beep yesterday and was surprised this morning with a call from her! Sandy was doing well and is still in her condo along with her two cats, just where she prefers to be. She wanted to know all the news with family and I was happy to trade for news about her family. The voice I chatted with was the same old Sandy, full of determination and pixie dust. I related the shock of having grandkids who are now teenagers and she about nieces and nephews who are in the same bracket. I began my therapy relationship with Sandy before our oldest grandchild was born and my last time with her as my therapist was after our youngest grandchild was two years old. Over our years together, she has been well versed by me about our grandchildren to the point of being sort of extended family. She has never met them in person, but knows them vicariously through me. She is a dear to want to know how they are doing and was duly impressed with how tall Colby has become. The eighty-one year young Sandy had her daily life to share with me. She has coffee with her business partner Pat a few times a week, she and Pat go way back it is wonderful that they maintain their friendship and in doing so comfort each other. Sandy's world is now all about her cats Loki and Olaf. They are eighteen months old now and are mirror images of each other physically and in temperament. She is their cat mom and her charges' antics fill each day for her. Six months ago, Sandy had a catio installed in one window of her condo so the cats could, if they have a mind to, wander outside. She told me she fully expected Loki to be the first to discover the catio and make it her go-to place each day. Loki, in her words, is constantly curious and ever exploring all over Sandy's place, Olaf not so much. So, it was a big surprise when Loki took aversion to the catio and avoids even going near the place. Loki will sit at a distance and stare at Olaf while he is lounging in the catio during the day. Sandy told me that her sister brought her pug-mix dog over to play with the cats one day; the dog had no experience with cats and the cats had no experience with dogs. The cats bowed to him; Sandy told me this was an invitation on their part to come play. Sandy concluded, "Well the dog didn't understand the cats and vice versa; even so, given time they might become playmates." Sandy went on to tell me that male cats tend to be left-pawed and female cats tend to be right-pawed. "I spend my time reading all about cat psychology and watch it unfold. I'm just full of odd bits of useless cat information." She told me jokingly. We chatted for a good amount of time and never end our conversations gracefully; I always want to continue even when it is time to move on. I told her to watch for a box of cookies to come her way and just as I did Sandy exclaimed, "Loki just walked into the catio!" Loki had done the totally unexpected, rocking her mom's world. It dawned on me that Sandy is practicing her trade, her life's work if you will. The work of psychology to care for the minds of others, except now that amazing mind of hers is focused on two cats. She arms herself by continually studying, ever growing in the most natural way to be of service to whomever she can. God bless you Sandy. I have been blessed by knowing you. Now it's time to bake cookies…

***

Monday December 13, 2021. Cathy's mom's house flooded last Wednesday; luckily, we were there at the time. An upstairs bathroom sink water supply hose blew out, flooding the bedroom below. It was a mess. Cathy and I called Casey for help and we all moved boxes out of harm's way. Casey got us started with ServPro right away.

***

I have lost the strength to journal, the drive to, or the importance of doing it anymore. It is all there now waiting to be put together, a story waiting to be told, but it hurts to go over it and I hurt just as everyone else is.

I need to write more in depth about my dad's life during my childhood and after mom's death. I understand so much more about him as I look back over his life from the place I am now at. Only one of the Anderson brothers held a steady life long relationship with a woman. Rollin was forever single never holding any relationship in his lifetime. Orval married for a brief time to a woman who had two sons. Merrill and Dorothy put together twenty years in two runs. Edward and Norma's long lasting forty plus relationship ended at the death of Ed.

2022

Sunday January 2, 2022. I haven't journaled for a long time, just couldn't bring myself to do it... I think I didn't want to remember the dour emotional colors that ran through all of December. There were good splashes here and there such as how warmly Sandy, Marsha, and Debbie received my cookies. Because Shawn works at Caddell's along with her mom Marsha, she knows I bring Christmas Cookies and will inevitably suggest to her mom to bring them along to Christmas dinner at her place. Well, this time I made two tins of cookies one big and one small. I told Marsha she had a choice to share either one of them, just the big one or just the small one or keep everything herself. She laughed out loud! After Christmas, she told me that she did share but kept some for herself and her grandson who loved them. I didn't ask which tin she kept... My plan was to give our friend Natalie cookies but we lost contact due to the snow and Covid. We have made the acquaintance of a young couple one of whom is transgender, he/they. On our daily walks we pass their house and sometimes will stop if we see someone outside to chat with. Cathy is friends with both of them on Facebook and a go-fund-me popped up to help pay for top surgery for our new friend. A few days later we saw their garage open so we popped in for a chat. He is going to have surgery with Dr. Mangubat! I chatted on and on; he was kind to listen to an old trans-elder who is so out of step with today's generation. Afterward I chastised myself. My world has passed away; it belongs to younger people now. I'll be better at keeping that in mind. Christmas was at Casey's; there were nine of us but it felt hollow because of the dour times. We all are drifting away from each other. Linda and Joyce, Cathy and Cady, Casey's family all of us are drifting away from each other. Casey has extended family to be close to, Linda and Grandma Dixon have trips to take, and we fall by the wayside... Again, the world belongs to new people and we are not new. We are aging while watching close acquaintances our age pass away. There is the transition we are going through further separating us from all we had once known.

***

Monday January 3, 2022. How do I start to journal again? Perhaps with just random unrelated bits and pieces. This last Christmas held hope, and then limped away in the face of the continued turmoil of social pressure bearing the weight of false truths. But this is everywhere and there is no escaping it, so lets focus on us... I have FFS in something like nine weeks, which sounds like a long time but it isn't. I view the window of canceling the surgery closing in like half that time. I don't fear the surgery itself but the recovery afterwards has me frightened. I am in my mind so very close to convincing myself to call it off but in reality remain diligent in doing everything required to be ready for it. Man, this is so hard to journal again. Every day, thoughts fill my mind about transitioning, gender, my relationship with Cathy, the past life experiences, of my dad, my mom, my brother, and those of family and friends who are still with us. All of these are well worth putting to paper to share with some ephemeral future reader who will be thirsty for this drama, but I tire easily from living this drama, from its thoughts and physical changes. Where there was once a catharsis in typing now becomes a mental burden. I worry what I will be after FFS and SRS/GRS. Will I be too much for our sons to accept? If I were in their place, could I embrace this stranger, this construct being, with only a very faint shadow remaining of the father I loved? And who would this being be to me? To turn it around again, what place do I hold with our sons after erasing all the male vestiges from my being? And yet I still seem to pursue doing just this. This is the heartbreak of being transgender and transitioning late in life. And I am in the very thick of it with this year 2022 holding both FFS and GRS... Truthfully, I don't know if I will survive this part of transition, I find myself suddenly screaming at the oddest of times. It just suddenly vomits out of my month loudly and leaves me shaken afterward. There is the same odd sense of mental relief as comes with actually throwing up and I have noticed that I get same odd precursor to the event. I feel an anxiety tension building up akin to what nausea brings but with no retching; in its place the overwhelming need to let out a frightened scream. I find if I fight to suppress it, it will simply lay there churning away until it bursts like a balloon later. Life pressure, I wonder if I am now broken too...

***

Sunday January 9, 2022. Quince's birthday month! I hope he likes the airplane clock with wings that tell time we made for him. Michael brought his mother by to visit with us this morning. They sat in his car and we visited via the windows. It was a really nice blue-sky day very rare this time of year. We thoroughly enjoyed our visit with the two of them. Leona at one point in our visit said to me, "My other son turns out to be a daughter!" Good enough acceptance for me, no need for lengthy conversations at this point in her life...

***

Monday January 10, 2022. I tagged Michael in a photo I posted on Facebook of his mom and him. Michael walked away from Facebook years ago when it didn't prove to be the tool he needed to market his music although, his profile page still remains and is followed by many of his friends and family. He doesn't have any interest in it at all but when I tag him in a picture I figure at least his friends know he is still alive. Michael had mentioned the other day to me that he just as soon have his account closed down. This current photo tag I did garnered the attention of lady up in Alaska whose husband had passed away after a long illness. She commented on the photo, "Hi Michael, looking good old friend. You outlived my husband, he passed away last March." I texted this to my fuzzy friend and he quietly asked if I could find a way to give her his cell phone number. I'll try. I replied to the comment telling her I had gone to high school with Michael and he isn't net friendly but he would like for you to have his cell number. It is not a good idea for me to post it here for

639

everyone to see so could I message you? She replied, "Sure thank you." So, I did just that. The lady thanked me again and said, "She and her husband go way back with Michael in Alaska and she would give him a call soon." Long story short, she called him today and they talked for over an hour. It was a Godsend for Michael; he was so in need of a connection to his past life in Alaska. It was a Godsend for the lady too; she got to touch those happy years again with someone who was there. Good deed done but, of course, Michael outed me again. Sigh. It wasn't enough that I might have been a female high school friend but Michael only knows to be outrageous but he assured me the lady was okay with my transition. Michael doesn't really get it but then why should he? He lives larger than life, he is his own twisting tornado wherever he goes and that has been the Michael I had come to know way back in middle school. Back then the tornado was just beginning to take hold and there was no going back to anything placid from there. Anyway, being casually outed by a friend does bother me; it seems to devalue me because my value as a human then rests on the opinion of a third party.

My FFS hangs over me like a dark cloud scratching at my depression to inflame it. I have fear that I will not heal well leaving me in pain that will continue for years. GRS/SRS is still too far away but if I get past FFS a new fear waits for me. So, don't do either right? I fear that with an even greater fear. I have come across an amazing author Kathy Baldock; her book is *Walking The Bridgeless Canyon*. She does a great job for LGB inclusion in the Church by researching the roots of the clobber passages. Her deep wade into the language of the Bible only just touches T issues though...

Debbie Caddell was so grateful for the book *God Doesn't Make Mistakes* by Laurie Suzanne Scott I gave her that she is going to loan to our mutual acquaintance Dr. Jen Burnett!

***

Tuesday January 11, 2022. I don't journal on and on about the plague. I guess I should, it is a world-changing event; the world we knew is being pushed away. There are no words for the sadness of this 'death of spirit' that is happening everywhere. This spirit had defined the simple day-to-day life we knew. There is nothing left untouched no ceremony, tradition, or social system left as it was. We are left with a post-apocalyptic frame but without any huge population loss. A totally bizarre condition, it is as if the people are still here but their spirit has been drained away. So dear reader there is my homage to plague as short as I can make it at the moment.

Cathy's mother no longer drives so it is left up to her daughters to get her to and from appointments and tasks. The flood from a broken water supply hose has all been cleaned up at her house. Servpro dried out the bathroom and downstairs bedroom completely without having to tear up floors or walls. A big win! We have to replace the supply lines to the sink in the upstairs bathroom and get some replacement ceiling tiles in the downstairs bedroom. Uncle Fred Tuttle sent a note to us thanking us for trying to arrange family contact.

My cousin Orlyn, who doesn't return my phone calls anymore, sent us a letter and in the envelope was an old letter he found from my Dad Merrill to Grandma Ida dated September 1955. On that date my mom and dad were living in Coulee Dam near the Grand Coulee Dam. The old torn yellowing envelope was addressed to Mrs. Ida Anderson RR#2 Goodhue, Minn. c/o Mr. August Meyer. With the return address of The Andersons 6-Central Dr. Coulee Dam, Wash. All in my dad's beautiful flowing script (I was so envious of his handwriting). He told me once that he worked and worked on his handwriting every single day until it looked as ornate as he could make it. Dad was very proud of his handwriting. I practiced but never achieved anything even close to his style.

The letter was written in pencil on a single sheet of lined printed-paper.

Below is the content, verbatim:

Sept 27 Coulee Dam, Wash. 1955
Dearest Mom and all,
So you sneaked out on us huh? Did you have a good trip back to Corals? Hope so. I called over to your place to find out when you were

going to leave and Orval told me all about the latest news. Orval must be feeling better now he sounded so good.

Dot told me to write to you and to let you know to be sure to tell us when you will be here. I hope this gets there in time.

Tell Coral and all Hello from us and when she gets caught up a little to write to us a line or two. Coral might get lonesome for the family out here but when she writes to us it makes us feel pretty good too.

We have some news to tell you when you get here.

The weather is a little cooler now and a little rain but we still have our sunshine.

Please, Don't forget to let us know.

All our love to the sweetest Mom.

Dorothy, Merrill, and C----.

Grandma Ida had left Burien to travel to Minnesota to visit her daughter Coral. Orval is my dad's brother. I wonder what the news was and why he wanted to make sure Ida stopped at their place on her way back. My brother David was born in August of 1956, so the news couldn't be that Dorothy was expecting, the dates were all wrong being eleven months apart. Perhaps my mom miscarried only to become pregnant two months later? The feeling of the special news points in this direction. With that in mind though my poor mom must have had a very hard time of it right at the time of this letter. On the other hand, maybe the news was Mom and Dad were going to move back over the mountain to be closer to Ida and family there. I know my dad loved his brothers and sisters, most of whom lived in Western Washington near their mother Ida. This is very likely and in that case Mom did become pregnant two months after this letter before they could move delaying their move back to Western Washington.

Orlyn did put a little note in the letter to the effect that he hoped this would bring a little joy into our lives and it did. I sent him a thank you card.

***

642

Forever and Two Days More

Sunday February 6, 2022. Cathy's birthday party was at our house; our local group all attended less Mark. Cathy spent hours decorating our gifts for her sister with wax seals and ribbons. Linda's birthday comes a week before Cathy's, so many times Cathy and Linda share a party. Most of the time Linda will take off on her birthday figuring she will return to share Cathy's day. We haven't seen Colby and B---- for over a month and sure enjoyed seeing them today. I spent hours decorating Cathy's gifts with wax seals and nesting gift boxes within gift boxes each carefully wrapped and sealed. We had take-out gluten-free fish-and-chips from GhostFish Brewery. It all went well but left us feeling hollow somehow.

I haven't been journaling properly it has been a month since my last time. I have been proofreading our book and am only on page 176. It goes so slow; the first part is done but there are over eight hundred pages (after a first pass) of free journals to organize and trim away at. I am almost at a loss for how to continue. I am also distracted; my surgery is five weeks away on March 10th. We have to book someplace to stay in Spokane for a ten-day space of time. At the end of that time Casey has volunteered to fly to Spokane to drive us back home in our car. I have been asked if I am excited for the surgery and my answer is kinda. What drags any excitement away is waking up seven hours later to face recovery. I sleep so nicely at night and breath so clearly right now; the idea of all of that coming to a end for months is hard to take. Still, I accept the need for the surgery and the gift that I have access to it. It will be hard on me and very hard on Cathy. She has to wait alone without knowing what is going on for the duration of the seven-hour surgery. Cathy also hasn't driven for a long time and isn't very comfortable taking over the wheel.

Grandma Dixon's house is all dried out and Cathy and I have replaced the water supply lines in the bathroom. Corey's gift of a decorated handrail leading down Grandma Dixon's front steps is moving forward.

Cathy and I had our six-month post op appointment with Dr. Megan and all is healing okay. Cathy has a sore keloid scar on her left breast that Dr. Megan offered to remove along with some more volume. This will be done with local anesthetic in a treatment room on April 11th at no charge, bless her heart! I got Dr. Megan's opinion about my face surgery and what to ask Dr. Stiller about (is he making an incision under my chin and to be conservative about my eyebrow height). I also asked if Dr. Megan could still treat me at St. Anne's if something went wrong after we returned home that required a visit to the ER and she told me she would. Very comforting! Tabitha was Dr. Megan's assistant at our appointment; she seemed much nicer to us this time and we chatted about relationships. I gave her a hug after hearing how happy she was with hers. We love hearing about how Dr. Megan's little girl is doing.

I have a CT scan that Dr. Mangubat had me get after my consult with him on face stuff so I thought I would send the images to Dr. Stiller. After all, I have them. I'll send the images via email to Kelly tonight and be done with it. Kelly is the scheduler for in-house cosmetic surgery and is so high energy happy about it. Alison is the scheduler for surgery done at the hospital and is so not Kelly-like. So, I am in Kelly's hands this time, next time in August it is Alison.

We had a Dr. Eaman appointment on February 1st to do a blood draw for Cathy to check on her sodium level (it was 135). For me I needed an EKG and medical clearance letter for my Dr. Stiller surgery. Dr. Eaman is very welcoming to us each time we come by but I'm always on edge. Dr. Eaman is very in-tune with the LGBT world and I am not so much, the result is me feeling like an impostor. I have had this explained to me giving it the name 'impostor syndrome'. I really don't need a syndrome at the moment but I guess if the shoe fits... Dr. Eaman had me undress and get into a robe then as I lay on the exam table she covered me with twelve electrodes all connected to a laptop. EKG all done all normal.

Casey doesn't call us much anymore and when he does, conversations are short and mostly vacuous. Colby and B---- have been strangers to our house for over a month so we feel detached from their family bubble. I asked Casey again if he was still up for driving us home on March 18th and he said he was. I feel a detachment from him it is almost like we are neighbors asking for a favor instead of family. Part of this is Colby and B---- growing up and away from us. This is to be expected I guess although Colby gave me the nicest hug last time I did see him. I miss Colby dearly and the whirlwind that is B----.

Corey called me and asked the name of my therapist; he had the Sandy part right but was fuzzy on her last name. I responded with 'Fosshage' and didn't grill him as to why. We talked again the next day and he told me what was going on. After I came out to Corey and we chatted a few times about my required treatment with a therapist, I gave him a verbal picture of my therapist. I told him not only of her qualifications but also of what made her who she is, that intangible part of a person. With Sandy, it was her work outside of her private therapist practice; there she coordinated volunteers at the Crisis Line in Seattle. She cared deeply about it and what it accomplished each night; all this defined her persona. Corey was impressed in a way that I had no indication of, he felt so strongly about the care I was getting and the work the Crisis Line was doing that he sent a check to them as part of his charitable giving each year. He never told me about it bless his heart. What happened to out his charitable giving, was someone at the Crisis Line got curious who this person was that was sending them a check for these last years. They called Corey and asked; so, as Corey put it, he 'fessed up' to donating to them because of his transitioning father and her caring therapist Sandy Fosshage. It was a wonderful thing our dear son did and I teared up when he told me. I thought a week afterward to call Sandy and tell her also; after all she has done for me. I hadn't chatted with Sandy for several months so when I heard her voice I was much relieved to hear how strong it was. Just like the past days of my time with her, I was so excited to share my joyful news. I left a message on her phone to have her call me as I had some nice news to share with her, something that might make her feel good. She called me the next morning exclaiming, "Your timing always seems to catch me out somewhere, even though I seldom leave my apartment nowadays." I told this dear lady my story about what Corey had done these last few years since my coming out to him. Corey had done this in her name, as he explained to folks he had gotten the call from. There was dead silence on end of the phone. I asked into the silence, Sandy are you alright??? Sandy, sounding almost breathless, told me, "I have never been so blown away in my life! Cady I can't describe what a wonderful feeling this brings. I'm just so blown away." We chatted for a long time about life in Eastern Washington around Yakima. About cold mornings causing smudge pots to burn in the orchards, their oily soot drifting into the houses covering everything. About other things she and I experienced in common just like we had at the end of so many of my appointments with her. "I'm so blown away," she would repeat. We ended our phone call as people do; I usually say love you to people I hold dear and Sandy would return with, "Take care." This time I said, take care and Sandy told me quietly, "Love you."

A few days later a thought entered into my mind about Corey's philosophy in giving a gift to someone. He likes his gift to really make a positive change in their lives. I wonder if that philosophy could be turned around and applied to the gift giver. Sandy's reaction was so succinctly beautiful change-wise, would this not be a joyful thing to him to know? So, I called him to report her reaction and my deep gratitude for it. I have never heard such joy in Corey's voice before. Corey's emotions are still waters but today the waters roared as waves against the shore in triumph.

My mind replays problems of life over and over again. I let this show of joy of two people, who have never met each other, fill my mind to smother the bad stuff for as long as I can hold it there...

***

Friday February 11, 2022. I got a jury duty summons today for March 8, 2022 it is for the King County Court. I can't do it since I have surgery in Spokane on March 10 and have to be there by the 8th. This leads me to begin my account of my journey into and through FFS (facial feminization surgery) with Dr. Geoffrey Stiller in Spokane. For the longest time I have put it out of my mind, after all, it was months away so why even think about it. Each day as I awoke I reminded myself not only was this not the day for surgery, but it was safely months away. Don't worry, I reminded myself, it is like forever away time-wise. Zen-like reassuring thoughts of how far away surgery was didn't stop me from reading peoples accounts of their experiences going through FFS on Facebook, RealSelf, and Reddit. Gentle people at the acme of change, of course, none came without complications. I would breathe through my nose with no obstruction; even while sleeping in any position that was comfortable, all the while thinking surgery might bring an end to this hard earned wonder. So here I am three weeks until surgery just three little weeks left. I shower twice a week, so just six showers to enjoy before bedlam comes to my world. Dr. Megan asked if I was excited; so, did Debbie Caddell, Marsha, and Shawn. Yes, I am excited and fearful all rolled together. I have no working expectation of Dr. Stiller other then he seems to be a very pleasant man doing what he has a passion to do. Debbie tells me she has heard only great things about his work from her other transgender clients. I worry about the seven hours Cathy will be alone waiting for me during the surgery. About the inevitable waking up to the long painful recovery afterwards. I haven't been healing well lately simple scratches seem to take months to heal completely. I wondered what has been happening with my body until on reflection it became apparent that I wasn't getting enough protein in my diet. Natalie gave me a clue as well as Dr. Eaman. Cathy worked it out that I only get ten to fifteen grams of protein per day and this has been my intake for a year or two. It is my fault especially after my tummy tuck I didn't want to eat properly I finally had a waist and couldn't stand the thought of getting fat again. So, my body began to waste away and Natalie reported this each time I had a massage. Okay it was a mistake; Cathy has now set our goal on taking in fifty grams daily for me. I actually have trouble eating the amount of food that is required for this; my stomach feels so stretched out. Such irony, all my life was a struggle to lose weight, year after year, and pound after pound. Now I need to gain a little to be able to have a healthy protein level for surgery. I have gone back and forth about how I feel about this surgery vs. the pain of recovery from it, a sort of benefit balance against the physical cost to my body. Right now, I am resigned to having it, to trusting Dr.

Stiller and his staff. Sometimes I mix up the two surgeries I have scheduled with him; this is the FFS and the other Vulvoplasty. I have to correct myself that this is not bottom surgery with its long list of compilations and long recovery time, in doing so, I feel better about FFS. It's a mental trick I am playing on my brain but turnabout is fair play. Debbie C had a face-lift five months ago and is still hurting around her ears from the incision tension, darn. Dr. Megan wants me to make sure Dr. Stiller makes an incision under my chin as part of the neck lift. My list of procedures for FFS is Face and Neck lift, Brow Lift, and Rhinoplasty. I had a CT scan of my nose and lower face several months ago; we printed several pictures of it and them to Kelly just in case Dr. Stiller would like to see them. Kelly reported back that they were not necessary but she would add them to my file.

I told Cathy tonight that what I would really like from this surgery is to be able to say, I wished I could have done it sooner. Three weeks and counting we have a video pre-opt video call on Monday. If Kelly is in on it I'll have to remind her that she offered to massage my feet in recovery after my surgery.

***

Tuesday February 22, 2022. Happy Birthday Corey! We had a wonderful President's Day weekend visit with Corey and Quince. I loved little Q running to us at the airport all smiles, picking him up and carrying him on my hip; what a blessing! Yes I know soon this will not be possible for me to do anymore but for today what a joy. They came at midday on Friday and left on Monday midday with Corey's birthday party on Sunday. I didn't obsess about playing with every toy we have for Quince but instead enjoyed a calming carefree time together. Letting it feel like we had all the time in the world to be together and play gently and lovingly. I don't know at this point when we will get to visit down in San Diego with them. The surgery/recovery is in charge of this not us. So, speaking of this, I at the moment am resigned to leaving our little home in two weeks to drive to Spokane to check in to an Airbnb house that is totally unknown to us. All that is left for me to do is find a picture of a nose

I would like to have for Dr. Stiller to use as a guide. A side note: Dr. Stiller's office has charged my insurance for an office visit and here I thought consults were free, it looks like it was $1000! Truthfully I don't know if I would have gone to him if I had known this (I can't find anything about a consult fee on his website nor did anyone mention it to me when we arrived). It looks as if insurance has paid all but $33 of it. As of this date, I have paid what I understand is the full amount for the surgery. Traditionally any consultation fee is told to you up front and deducted if you book a surgery; I guess he feels he is above the rest. Maybe he is, fingers crossed.

Yes, I have for the last several months, read every Facebook post in the surgery forums dealing with facial surgery recovery/complications. Very few report sailing through with just a few weeks of recovery and most talk about recovery taking months not weeks. So, this has been my turmoil these last two months weighing the benefits vs. the pain. I have cycled over and over about the question of why I am seeking this expensive surgery. GID is flat out mean; I want it to be over or at least at a resting point that I can live with. So, with this in mind I set transition goals: two surgeries to complete defining the end to our medical transition. We are in the care of Dr. Stiller for these. We pray that God has brought us to this doctor at this time. I say done with surgery but I accept from all I have read that some minor revisions are needed as you heal over the months. The broken bathroom mirror still holds me captive each time I look at it but it also shows me hope for the last years of our lives.

***

Sunday February 27, 2022. Twelve days until my surgery with Dr. Stiller. I have cut my patch dose down from four to three for these two weeks before surgery. The fish oils and flax oils have been stopped as of yesterday. Cathy is in charge of my pre-op care she tells me she will stop more of our supplements starting on Wednesday. So yes, we are in the home stretch to the surgery date of March tenth and at this point I am not so much excited for it to get here but resigned to it happening. I am nurturing the idea of the time to come after surgery where recovery is in full flower, defined as, the time on the other side of the hardest first seven days ending in dressing removal. We will have been through that intense week and are both safely home. I worry about Cathy during the surgery she will be alone for a long time as my surgery is scheduled for seven hours. Who will hold her hand or comfort her especially if something happens to me? Will Dr. Stiller's staff be respectful of her and be kind to her? This bothers me more with each passing day. Tonight, it is raining heavily, the sounds of cars whooshing in the wet stuff and the hammering of rain hitting our windows and porch covers roar right through our walls bringing the din inside. The lower patch dose seems to have triggered breast swelling, both breast are tight against my shelf bra today and are tender; I look at it as a good thing. The frustrating thing is there is no clear hormone regiment that you can count on to kick development forward at any point. It will happen with a sudden increase or decrease of E, changing methods of taking E such as switching from pills to injections, or combining E with progesterone in various strengths; all have an effect. And there are all the side effects such as hormone headaches, brain-fog, hot flashes, anxiety and depression. These all respond in a semi-predictable cycle with each mix of hormone intake. Oh, to have the natural hormonal feedback system of a cis-female...

There is an all-inclusive depressing mire all around us tonight as the cold rain falls outside. The war that portends death to any hope of ever returning to the world before the plague does much to generate this. I feel like I don't dare mention my upcoming surgery on Facebook or to other family. Their emotional string is just drawn so tight leaving no room for empathy and in the place empathy had occupied only apathy now lives.

B---- now has braces, as she was getting her initial brackets installed I was having what they called the finishing wire clicked onto my brackets. I go back to the ortho office on Tuesday to replace a bracket that came off. The end date for my ortho is sometime before the start of next year; I will have been in ortho for four years. Casey is planning for an Anderson family picnic on July 23rd of this summer. Extended family I have called are so ready for a picnic but are frighten too. I have the notion that with the completion of these two surgeries by Dr. Stiller our book will draw to an end. The book needs editing and most importantly needs Cathy's content, her thoughts and feelings.

***

Tuesday March 1, 2022. Nine days until surgery. I found a nice before and after picture of a nose done by Dr. Tommy Liu that I can share as a map for Dr. Stiller. Finding that Dr. Liu is now here in Seattle made me feel sad as perhaps I am again going to the wrong doctor. Dr. Liu never came up in any searching I had done on FFS so I expect he is fairly new in the area. It's a gut punch as he is in Seattle so we would have no travel to speak of and I could recover at home; darn… On the other hand, as Cathy pointed out God brought us Dr. Stiller. I am more accepting and excited as the time draws closer and closer to us leaving on the eighth. I find myself napping several times a day now. I think it is the stress of the coming surgery added to the stress we all have from the plague-war. Cathy and I are feeling even more isolated as the little circle of people we interact with grows smaller.

Other news: Four brackets popped off my teeth after Dr. Leigh put the finishing wire onto my brackets along with a power chain. The finishing wire is the last step to the close of my treatment. Sigh, after reattaching my brackets she switched me back to the old wire until my April twelfth appointment.

***

Wednesday March 2, 2022. One shower left (isn't it odd what I use to count time passing) at home before we leave for surgery. FFS (Facial Feminization Surgery) is a very big deal! It is one of the three signature surgeries in transitioning. This is a mountaintop reached in becoming you and from that plateau you can see your true reflection in the mirror of life, that wonderfully unbroken completely whole mirror of perfect reflection. The other two are breast enhancement and bottom surgery (although no one sees bottom surgery's outcome). The intensity and extent of each of these life-giving procedures are the direct throttle to gender dysphoria control. Here you have these three surgical levers to balance against each other to smother the dysphoria inferno whose fuel is your life's blood. Intensity and extent are the key but only known by the combination of the three levers together. Meaning only after touching all three levers can you know what is needed for the final outcome. Case in point, I was determined not to do surgery after my egg cracked (a euphemism for accepting being T) but accepted doing HRT. Time passed in therapy and it became evident I was not one of the few who could transition thereby successfully controlling dysphoria with HRT alone. I lightly pushed one of the surgical levers; it worked! I was a baby trans (again another euphemism) starting on my journey. More therapy leading to discovery and another lever is pushed, this time with a little more pressure than the other. A whole new world opens for me; I am who I have always been inside and out. A light is turned on where there was only darkness this is the only explanation I give and make no apology. Along with newfound harmony there is difficulty in this world for the people around me. I feel the offense I am to them and in turn it shakes my foundation as to who I am. In these times of masks faces are minimized but this time will not last forever. Gazing in the mirror I see the value of the last surgical lever of FFS most importantly for myself and then other people. FFS is an intensely powerful tool; it is your face, it deals with the window you use to display who you are to the world and all nuances of mood it communicates. No small matter in pushing this lever, but then, it is still the combination of the three surgical levers of transition and their final interplay. In using this last lever some adjustment of the intensity and extent of the other already used levers may have to be made. With all this aside, FFS is the most intense and at seven hours plus the longest transition surgery I have had yet. I will face a long recovery but I am resolved to complete it, this doesn't mean that I'm not nervous nor does it mean I am not excited.

***

Forever and Two Days More

Thursday March 3, 2022. Thursday I can't believe it's Thursday. Friday is just in a few hours. Friday holds a massage with Natalie; I'll bake cookies for her birthday on Monday and give them to her tomorrow. Friday is also Marsha's birthday, we sent her a card and I will give her a call too. Every woman we tell about my upcoming surgery is so excited for me, I should be excited too but part of me feels like I am being slowly dragged toward next week. I should 'let go and let God'. There are too many variables too many facets to this adventure my mind is weary with worry and foreboding. Add to this the feeling that I can't share with anyone who is not overburden themselves. In the end there is God and I have never felt like God has left me even as I hurt and was lost as where to turn for help. Cathy found a really helpful book for partners (spouses) of transitioning people. It really hit a homerun for her, as there is so little by way of support for wives of MtF. The book is *Reaching for Hope* by Suzanne DeWitt Hall. She wrote a companion book *Transfigured: A 40-day journey through scripture for gender-queer and transgender people.* It is a forty-day devotional offering scripture in many different translations of the Bible. I am really enjoying the points they make starting at 'God made them male and female.' The point is the language is specifically 'and' not 'or'. People who are transgender are real, I am real.

***

Friday March 4, 2022. It is 11:30 at night and I realize that a corner has been turned in my brain. I am excited to get going even becoming eager to leave home. There is family drama at Cathy's mom's house that Cathy needs to be away from. I think we are going into a time where being transgender is going to be accepted but silently loathed, as any forced mandate would be. I guess as Cathy puts it, medical transition is needed to be safe in the world of being silently loathed. Still, it is mainly for me but she is a stakeholder and does have a point. Somewhere in my mind until the vestiges of my male parts are gone I will always feel vulnerable to ridicule and violence by someone taking issue of my place in female spaces. There is also the heartache we have

653

over agreeing with some Republican views but knowing there is no place for us with them because of who we are. The flipside is disagreeing with almost all the Democrat views leaving us with no place with them either. We listen to Republican chatter and nod our heads at certain points until they unload with eager delight on anyone and anything transgender, while mentally slapping each other on the back while doing it. We listen to Democrats' awful-speak about Republicans and loathe that the Democrats are using transgender people as a club to gain advantage over their opponents. All the while we know we will be thrown under the bus at any time because we simply can't trust the Democrats on any issue. Given the choice we would vote Republican for the good of the country but at our expense and what a price to pay for this. Still, you can't force people into acceptance you can only hope change one mind at a time but this only works if the message rises above the rhetoric...

***

Monday March 7, 2022: It is 9:00 in the evening, just three days before my surgery and I can't think of a soul I could call for comfort. Cathy has a pile of stuff we need to take with us; it is sitting on the dining room floor waiting for tomorrow morning. Gas is at $4.20 a gallon at Costco and there is a line to get it. So here I am at a life-changing moment, while all around me a way of life is seemly falling apart. My fear is I am not doing enough to my face, isn't that funny. I am not having a brow shave or fat transfer or what all else is possible. It just seems like I fall short in picking surgeons and follow that up by falling short in communicating what I need done. Heck, finding a picture of a nose shape just seems overwhelming to me. This is classic journaling, me just typing all the random stuff that comes to me at the moment, any one thing being nothing but trivial, but put together and it creates a black hole sucking the life out of both Cathy and me. Cathy did have a nice experience at the blood lab. A lady at the front desk called Cathy 'her tie-dye lady' then asked how Cathy's mom was doing and following it up by asking about her wife'. She asked, "She is the tall one with long dark hair right?" Cathy answered, "That's right! She is going to have surgery in Spokane this week." The lady went on with, "I have watched her change little by little over time as she has come in with you. Lately, I can really see the changes happening and was so excited for her." Cathy got to tell her all about us, how she knew about me before we got married and how it took until now for me to transition. As Cathy passed by the front desk on her way out she told the lady, "See you in April when I bring in my mom!" The lady cheerfully said, "See you then, I'm looking forward to it!" Cathy was in a very good mood when she got to the car... You don't know who takes interest in our journey for the better or worse. God brings us to them and them to us when we both feel the need...

***

Tuesday March 8, 2022. Our drive over to Spokane was mile upon mile across state on I-90. We had left at the hour of ten in the morning thinking that traffic will have started to lighten up as the rush hour wanes. All of the pile of stuff that had been lying in wait on our dining room floor was carefully tucked into our car leaving room for one extra passenger on the return trip home. That trip was so abstract in concept at this moment in time that all I could hold onto was the distant faintly glowing ember of release that it symbolized. Right now is right now, the car is eating up each mile by mile and we are both engrossed in listing to a Perry Mason mystery. All the trepidations about surgery are put on hold; the mystery is the thing along with the familiar roadway we are traveling on. The trip will take around six hours, not long enough to complete our audio book but long enough to thoroughly wet our appetite for Perry's dramatic courtroom performance revealing who the murderer really was. Covid has settled enough for Starbucks to allow us to be mask-less in their stores. If by chance I am called upon to explain our trip as a surgery one, I work in the idea that with the masks coming off I had to get my face done... Our first restroom break was at the Starbucks in Ellensburg, where they boldly display a transgender flag in the window. The baristas are all full of energy and chat with Cathy and me. The next stop will be the Ritzville Starbucks on the part of I-90 that is unfamiliar to us. The turnoff at George, Washington, which leads to Quincy, ends our lifetime love affair with I-90. Now I-90 turns into a different less familiar venue but still the journey calls us forward. Perry Mason provides the cloak and dagger to our now developing life journey and in the distance Dr. Stiller provides hope and change. The Starbucks at Ritzville, around one hour from Spokane is our final restroom break. This Starbucks has dual-stall restrooms. I always cross my fingers that both stalls are empty as we enter, today both are. I have developed a resolve to use the proper restroom and the further my medical transition proceeds the greater this resolve grows. An hour more on I-90 east and Spokane suddenly appears as the jack pines make themselves noticeable along what had been desert farmland. Cathy's directions bring us to our Airbnb in a quiet residential neighborhood. We have arrived at our surgical wait-station, our home away from home in a strange land of extremes. Spokane is full of natural food stores and joy of joys a gluten-free bakery and café while still home to a very conservative farming population. It is a mix that Cathy and I find a home in. This Airbnb has a very special attribute in the way of a very comfortable recliner couch; no other place we have seen can boast this very handy attribute for recovery from surgery. We unpack and make camp; even though no bed is just right for us here, the couch is perfect for sleeping. We go out to eat an early dinner at Cole's Gluten-Free Bakery and Café, Cathy has fish-and-chips and I have pancakes. It is very important that I ingest as much protein as possible to aid healing so I add an egg to my meal. Cathy had me taking Bromelain (2000 mg per day) along with Arnica Montana both suggested by Dr. Stiller to aid in healing. We pick out some take out treats from the bakery and return to our wait-station. Before leaving home Cathy had loaded my files on her laptop machine to journal on and so I began. Below are my thoughts:

So here is the thing, I am ripping out my learned identity leaving a scary emptiness in its place. I need to rant to someone about this but there is no one I can rant to. Cathy is full to overflowing with the angst I shed already and is dealing with her own, which centered on having to drive me back from surgery. Then having to deal with the recovery care I will need. She too has no one to rant to, no one willing to listen. It is a sickness we all have from the continued forced world change that touches every one of us 24 hours a day. We both have this sickness just as everyone else does. There is no place to hide and no unaffected human to turn to. Instead, we are called (or I should say I am called) to be that nonexistent human in return for the continued feeling that acquaintances still will come to our aid in time of our crisis.

Things I worry about with the surgery: Will my center part hairline be pulled lower along with the sides? How can this be done and still keep the forehead smooth? Pills to take. The shape of my nose. I have looked and looked for a perfect shape and only have two pictures that kinda show what I am looking for. I must remember to tell them to be gentle with my neck and collarbone. I wish they were shaving down my forehead to remove the male brow but I don't think they are.

Back to my identity: It is dawning on me that I have transitioned with this surgery in this place. More people I meet are viewing me as female and the two of us together are being referred to as sisters as opposed as a couple let alone a married one. An 'I did it, now what' moment. What indeed, who is Cady and what is Cady? How do I know how to be her? I seem to be gaining tools to talk with women but fail with men using the guy-to-guy tools I used to rely on as C----. Do I have any worth being female? Do I have anything to give wisdom-wise as female? It is all pushing down on me from every direction. Cathy feels this anxiety from me and it steadily feeds her anxieties from the loss of me being a stable predictable partner. The surgery takes me from being her driver; the recovery takes me away from her Go-Girl enabling partner. Converting me to a stay-at-home drag. We both need a steadily flowing source of accolades and comfort at this time of our lives. Ah there is the return to the start of this rant. Since everyone is burdened beyond capacity to care for someone else empathy is almost unknown. I have got to be stronger, although I am affected I need to recognized it and push past that thorn in the side. I need to reclaim supporting Cathy as C---- had done but now as Cady my true self. Cathy will give me space to do this as long as I make

657

progress, fair enough… It's bedtime we pick out a bed to try and had a long night of broken sleep.

***

Wednesday March 9, 2022. Morning finally comes with the realization that we can't sleep in this bed again. Cathy has claimed the kitchen as her workspace. We have protein drinks she has invented, I have two eggs with toast, and Cathy has two protein bars. The goal is to consume at least 50 grams of protein each day. Spokane is trying to turn the switch from winter to spring and today winter wins. Today is a shopping day for supplies for the coming week and to scope out where the stores are all located. We are back before noon.

We are going to have a 2:00 drop-in appointment with Kelly at Dr. Stiller's office. The idea was to get answers to the pile of questions that had been building up in our minds since yesterday. Like, what were all the steps we need to take to be ready for surgery tomorrow morning? Kelly was enthusiastic at the idea of a meeting when I emailed her earlier. The closer we got on the drive over to Dr. Stiller's place the more I could hardly contain my excitement! I don't think I have ever been so little kid excited about anything in my life compared to what I am right now! I couldn't keep still there was such an uplifting energy surging in my brain really indescribable. Perhaps like the feeling Christmas morning would give so many Christmases ago. The central thought in my mind that I was really going to have my face, this ultimate totem of self-identity, taken care of was epically incredible. Kelly was like hummingbird-excited to see us giving Cathy and me strong generous hugs. I didn't get many of the questions on my mental list answered but Cathy did get her medication question answered. I hope to have one last chance tomorrow before I am prepped but that might not even happen. Kelly thought my surgery would be about three hours and done around 11:30. Wow! I remember Dr. Stiller telling me differently, more like 3:30! Makes me wonder if I am going to get all the procedures done that he quoted me on, such is the dark curtain of worry and the waning of faith… So along with the excitement come trepidation and maybe even a hopeless disappointment. Kelly is a beautiful youthful thin blonde full of energy wearing a gold letter 'K' necklace; she refers to us as ladies who bring beauty into their office with our tie-dye clothes. I asked what was the best way for Cathy to keep tabs on the progress of the surgery and her answer was to text the main number with, "This is Cathy how is Cady's surgery going?" Someone will return the text.

It is cold here 25 degrees this morning up to 34 by mid-day. Cathy will have to drive us both back from Dr. Stiller's OR (operating room/surgical suite) after my surgery, as I will be in no condition to drive. Today is Cathy's day to practice the drive from Dr. Stiller's office to the Airbnb. Cathy doesn't drive or I should say she only drives if really forced to and tomorrow she will be forced to. Anyway, she does fine today and we check off the need to practice box. Also, we scope out where Cathy will wait during the surgery. Back to our Airbnb wait-station all safe and sound.

The house is quiet no airplane or freeway noise to speak of. I have made a decision to share my surgery with family and friends on our main Facebook page and in addition to this I will share on a private FFS support Facebook page. We had come out publicly on Facebook to family and friends two years ago. Considering March is transgender visibility time we decided to lift the veil of me medically transitioning and what exactly I am having done right now. Cathy was courageous in agreeing to this as it does lay open our private lives. I was making it clear that it is our transition not just mine…

***

Thursday March 10, 2022. Good morning! It is six o'clock, dark, and cold outside. Whatever I wear will not keep me warm but then again all I have to do is get into the Stiller OR. This morning is all laid out each task simply leads to the next no thinking needed and this is fine with me. I am wearing loose clothes that are good to get into and out of but not to keep the cold away. All I have inside of me is plain Tylenol so I am still the driver this morning. Before we leave our wait-station I recite my morning prayer in the car while it warms up; my prayer is modified this morning because of the coming surgery touching what both of us will soon go through. Spokane is quiet this time of the morning we pass an old sign stating 'Crescent Machine Shop Welding Restaurant Parts & Service' it hits my funny bone as a machine shop with a restaurant in it. Cathy and I drive the narrow pothole filled back alley to the rear entrance of the medical building where Stiller Aesthetics has its offices. People all bundled up against the cold of the morning are making their way from the parking lot toward the sliding door of the rear entrance. I park our car by backing in so it will be easy for Cathy to drive straight out when needed. One more prayer and it is time to get out into the cold Spokane morning air. We are a few minutes early Kelly had made it very clear that we were to be there at seven o'clock sharp! The sliding door opens and we walk past the closed door of their onsite OR itself then on down the hall to the reception office. The door here is locked but it is our time to be here so we feel empowered in knocking and waving through the glass window. Someone hears us and opens the door telling us to check in at the kiosk. Okay, we fumble with finding ID cards for the demeaning machine to scan, nothing like having a task to distract you... After feeding the machine information the lady behind the desk tells us someone will be out to get you. We wait fifteen minutes and yes we are gathered up by Kelly and led to the exam room we had been in before. She is so excited by the idea of me having this surgery and that even now we still match our tie-dye coats. Kelly explains why so much of the stuff in the exam room is wrapped up with handy wrap that doesn't need to be. "It's a joke we are pulling on Dr. Stiller! Just go with it. He pulled one on us so it is payback in this little way." They had even handy wrapped his chair! It was fun to be in on the joke! Kelly asked what kind of music I liked and we said seventies stuff but currently I do like Pink. She asked Alexa to play 'Pink' radio. I felt special and kinda with it at that moment. Kelly asked me if they could use any of my images and then told me I didn't have to they understood that transgender people guard their privacy. I told Kelly that they were welcome to use any of my images as they liked especially if it helped someone else. It was very hard to find images when I was searching for them to give me an idea of the doctor's work so I feel the need for them to be available. Kelly was replaced by April she brought with her garments I was to change into. A robe that I could leave open either front or back, a flimsy panty, gripper socks, and a hair net. I asked about what to do with my hair and was told to just get it up inside the bonnet and they would do something with it in the OR. Since my hairline was changing they needed to maneuver my hair across my head. So now I sit, on the center stage chair sporting the garments for the OR and Cathy is stationed nearby in the support chair. We have both been in this theater before, on the boards of the stage of medical drama, but with reversing roles each time. I follow my eyes as they caress the room inch by inch in search of something that might give a hint to the personality of the ultimate director Dr. Geoffrey Stiller of this medical drama of change. There is a little poster on the wall giving a cartoon outline of his medical journey of training to starting this practice. April has changed the music back to seventies stuff at my request. Outside there is shuffling of papers and the door opens a second after a knock. A middle-aged lady comes in and introduces herself as Maria, "I will be your anesthesia nurse (CRNAs)." She sits down next to me on a wheelie chair with clipboard in hand. She is wearing black-rimmed glasses, has dark hair, and a pleasant smile. Just as with the other ladies there I say to her, even though I have just met you I love you. She laughs and tells us, "You can remember my name by the Sound of Music's piece *How Do You Solve a Problem Like Maria!*" Works for me! She goes over all the business of the anesthesia she will be using, something about a cocktail, and is careful to include Cathy in the conversation. We also get to laugh about the joke going on involving the staff. Maria tells us since she is the oldest here and has been with Dr. Stiller for sixteen years she kind of moms the rest of the young staff. It keeps me young she winks. What a wonderful bedside matter she has. She also has no problem with me keeping my aligner in during surgery. So far Cathy and I have been treated very well and have been made to feel very comfortable almost like we were part of the family too. Another knock at the door and in comes Dr. Stiller and his PA Riley. Maria smiles and slips out the door. Riley stands over against the wall near the door and Dr. Stiller takes Maria's chair next to me. Both Riley and Dr. Stiller's arms are covered with tattoos; it is almost like there had been contest at some point to see who could get the most done. Dr. Stiller is wearing a rainbow surgical cap and black scrubs. This is it, the great theater of plastic surgery, here sitting directly across from me Dr. Stiller smiles and asks, "What are we doing for you today?" Poof! All the questions have faded from my memory; in fact, it doesn't dawn on me to reach for my memory at all. Instead, I began to simply tell the story of my face in regards to its male markers that shout so loud to me each day. I gesture to my eye orbits, brows, forehead, hairline and jaw-line. I mourn that my one eyebrow is lower than the other. All these places cause me pain and Dr. Stiller listens fully giving me the feeling of I understand and can help. He stood up with enthusiasm and told us all he was excited to get started and I said I was too. Dr. Stiller and Riley left the room leaving Cathy and me in April's care; she weighed me and most importantly told me I could use the restroom on the way into the OR. I followed April out of the exam room then tarried waiting for Cathy to walk out of the exam room into the hallway. April was beckoning to me to hurry up as I gave Cathy one last kiss, we parted me toward the OR with April, and Cathy out the door toward the office. After I got to use the restroom April opened up the door to the OR and Maria greeted me with, "Welcome to our chilly OR! Come here and sit yourself down on this table. Now scoot down a little more and lay back with your arms out on the rests. Great perfect!" I looked up at the light fixture above the table trying to remember it; I think the brand name was 'Bovie' then everything just disappeared...

***

Cathy journaling in my place:

I still felt Cady's last kiss as I walked through the reception office waiting room. I didn't even notice if anyone was in the waiting room or if the office ladies looked up as I opened the door to hallway and entered the outside hall. I bumped into Kelly in the hallway she smiled telling me Cady is going to do fine and couldn't be in better hands, she is going to be beautiful and text us anytime for an update. I set my feet to walk up to where our car was parked. The gloom of the morning was giving away slowly to warmer temperatures but it is still stocking-hat and gloves cold. I say a little prayer for Cady and shiver a little despite wearing my hat and gloves. So odd to be walking alone she should be here being zig to my zag. I unlocked the car and tossed Cady's camisole and the pile of paperwork into the backseat. Cady's purse, phone, and car keys are now in my safekeeping in my backpack and it stays with me. I lock up the car, check the time 8:30, and ask Google for walking direction to Huckleberry's Market. Google tells me it is a ten-minute walk, my eyes tell me it is a ten minute uphill walk. I call Corey as I walk. Corey is gentle with me trying to calm my apparent anxiety I promise to keep him posted as the day goes on and he promises to say a little prayer for both of us. My feet have brought me across the parking lot that serves both Huckleberry's Market and Ace Hardware Store. I bypassed Ace Hardware and enter Huckleberry's; warm air greets me along with a 'welcome in' from some unseen clerk. Huckleberry's has a dining area with chairs and tables placed in the café area of the store. Several of the tables are occupied with one or two people doing breakfast or tapping on a laptop. I walked up to a spacey super-soft-voiced clerk who in a barely audible voice accepted my order for an iced Chai. I claimed a table and began to read mail on my phone while waiting for my Chai to arrive. Ten minutes came and left without any Chai so I checked back with the clerk only to find I needed to have taken my receipt over to an order basket on the other side of the café. Okay nice to know, now that I am a season pro here I have my Chai after a two-minute wait. For forty-five minutes, I am distracted by texting Casey, reading mail, and sipping my drink.

After finishing my Chai, I walked around the store and picked up a couple of chocolate bars (Seattle Chocolate), some Katz donut holes, and a box of Chai tea (herbal) all things I know Cady will love (except the Chai tea Cady hasn't developed an appreciation for it yet). Left the market after another 30-45 minutes and walked to Ace Hardware and looked at housewares - didn't find anything so walked back to our

663

car. Our car felt like a little bit of home in this lonely place; I looked at Facebook, read news, etc. Our car was warm (sun heating up the insides) and comfortable, so much so that I ended up taking a nap waking up at 10:30 to the fact I hadn't called mom yet. I texted Stiller's office for an update on Cady, then placed my call to mom. We chatted with the standard, I should have called earlier, she had been clearing out a closet for Mark, and she was pondering what to do with Grandma Tuttle's Greek souvenirs, etc. A text from Dr. Stiller's office came in right after I ended my call with mom, "Cady's is doing fabulous all is going well!"

After this good news I floated back into the clinic, took an elevator down to the 5th floor, walked to another hospital elevator, went down to the 2nd floor, used the restroom, and then went back to the car, which was still warm and comfortable. I sent several texts after noon but didn't hear anything. I gathered my nervous self up and went to the waiting room around 1:00 to sit and wait and ask status. At 1:20, was told Cady should go to recovery in 10-15 minutes. At about 1:50, I finally was allowed to go into the recovery room with her. Riley took me in and said, "Cady is doing great and is going to be so beautiful after she heals up." There was my Cady with a mound of ace bandage wound on and around her head, a splint on her nose, and barely opened eyes that were bruised above and below them. At that moment my heart leapt for joy to see her, never mind her condition. She had accomplished a huge step; we had accomplished a huge step. I took pictures of her per Cady's instruction to do so, then time for me to get busy! April, with a little help from Kelly, was charged with getting Cady going. They had managed to get her pants on, but not her top. She had blankets to cover her but they kept slipping down. I pulled them up several times, but seeing the futility of this endless cycle, I decided to get her top on her. April came to my aid. Cady mumbled in a moaning fashion her need for water and April got a bottle. Straws didn't work since Cady couldn't close her lips together. April got a cup and gave it to me I filled it with water and put it to Cady's lips, she sipped and only spilled it once dripping down her top. Before we put her top on, Cady's BP was constantly in the 98/65 range. April said that was fine because of the anesthetic. Kelly came in several times to check on Cady and rub her feet as she promised Cady she would do. I showed Kelly and April a picture of her toenails, which I had painted. Had to show them a picture since Cady had slip-proof socks on. Cady wanted to sit up and when she did, she would slap her legs and say, "You gotta wake up. Wake up!"

Finally, around 3:10, April and I decided time's up, Cady was awake enough to get her into a wheelchair. I went and retrieved the car and brought it to the door closest to the recovery room. We maneuvered Cady into the car and strapped her in, and I carefully left the parking lot trying to avoid all the potholes of the back alley. We were on our way back to the Airbnb! Cady would moan if I needed to change lanes or stop suddenly; once we got stuck behind a bus that kept stopping at every bus stop. It was rush hour and sleepy Spokane wasn't sleepy any more, there was too much traffic for me to go around the pokey bus, but finally I was able to. The trip seemed so very long but in what seemed to be double the amount of time of our practice drives we were back at the house. Then the moment came that I had been dreading, I had to get Cady out of the car and into the house by myself. I opened the front door of the house and then helped Cady out of the car and into the house. In places I had to almost carry her. She would take a couple steps forward and then go limply backwards the same amount doing a dance of staying in place. We finally moved into the house and she dropped into the nearby recliner. I put blankets on her and then went out to the car, collected all our stuff, locked up the car, and came into the house. Just Wow! Cady is safe in her chair and I take the time to text Casey and Corey of this accomplishment. In my text to Corey, I tell of having to almost carry Cady into the house and he returns, "You are stronger than you thought and what a surprise Cady will have to wake up back at the Airbnb after going to sleep in the OR!" Time for Nurse Cathy to get to work...

***

Back to me journaling:

I did wake up in the recliner at the Airbnb after surgery and had a cloudy memory of the trip from the OR. I didn't hurt, could hardly open my eyes, and just wanted to sleep. The dressing on my head added weight stressing my neck. We did check Facebook and welcomed all the positive comments and well wishes. It made me feel like I had done the right thing by sharing with family and friends so openly. This would continue as we shared my recovery day by day. There were no negative comments or reactions but there was a surprising silence from some family members. This did bother me a bit but the whole concept of transition is a very big thing for them to wrap their heads around. I understand this and accept silence as neither fair or foul recognizing it for whatever neutral position they are taking. I worry I have offended them (the silent ones) and long to explain in hopes of a change in heart on their part, but this is not for me to do. Our transition is for us, this is a paramount concept for me to get my head wrapped around.

The first night I slept in the recliner my sleep score was 98%, mostly because the anesthesia hadn't worn off yet, my nose was totally open, I could breathe freely, and I sure benefitted from the sleep. From here on things got worse, each night would bring the dread of sleeplessness and if I put together two to three hours in total I was lucky. Mostly I watched the clock move slowly as I hurt and prayed for the sun to come up. Clear breathing was over, my sinus passages swelled tight and at times felt like something foreign was blocking one or both so breathing was now a labor. Mouth breathing was awful and produced a dry hacking cough. During troubled sleep my fingers would claw at my nose in a vain effort to get air through in. I was so afraid I would undo the work done in first breaking and then resetting my nose into the beautiful shape I now had. My nose shape was held in place by an external splint across the bridge, a Band-Aid holding the tip up, internal sutures on either side of the tip, and the incision across the columella. By digging into my nose with a finger I could really disturb this. I was not to blow my nose but I longed for the open breathing I had right after surgery. I began to ice my face over and over again; sometimes this would open up my nose and reduce overall pain. Things happened as days passed. I sneezed one morning, something totally blocked my breathing afterward, I sneezed again this time something came out of my nose, it was big, black, and hard as a rock! I worried that it was something being used as a support holding my nose in its new shape. More time passed and more black rocks were forced out of my nose. I suddenly could breathe again! Then the cycle returned to swelling and a blocked nose, I continued with ice packs and steam from soup I would sip. Over the weekend I needed to talk to an afterhours doctor or PA but we never got the contact instructions so had to wait it out. What had come to trouble me further was that chewing was very painful so I mostly lived on bone broth. The only way pain control would work was to take pills spaced evenly over twenty-four hours. This meant waking up based on the clock and not the need for sleep. Cathy is right on top of this parceling out pills exactly on time in the face of broken sleep for her. With time my stomach became very irritated from the ibuprofen. I grow to hate bedtime and the struggle it had become. The dressing was irritating my skin and the smell was putrid. I would come to understand that my hair was full of a mix of dried and damp blood, just awful. I looked pretty scary, but we where determined to do anything to help healing and walking was at the top on the list to do. We did try to go for walks as the weather permitted and yes, we had several sunny days with light wind for good walking. The quiet little neighborhood we were staying in was made up of nice neat single-family houses. One day we came upon a yard full of little kids playing together. Play suddenly stopped as we walked by even their dog started toward us then cowered back again. One little boy after we had completely past their yard quickly ran to get ahead of us just to get a look at me again. I felt like Herman Munster from the old television show *The Munsters*. Tomorrow is the day we have been waiting all week to get to. The grand reveal comes tomorrow; I get the dressing off and I am so ready!

***

Thursday March 17, 2022. Today is one week since my surgery. We have learned that in addition to my brow lift Dr. Stiller did a brow shave to contour my forehead, removing the male lumps and bumps. This was so cool and was something I could only hope for. I had signed an image release of all of the surgery and Cathy was able to find a short video of my brow shave being done, so we shared it with our doctor. She really appreciated it but not as much as I do having it done! So my FFS included: brow shave, brow lift, hairline advancement, rhinoplasty, liposuction, neck lift, and facelift.

The Airbnb has been our recovery oasis and time has passed very slowly. We returned to Dr. Stiller's office without incident. Riley unwrapped the smelly mess and started to remove staples from across my forehead then stopped. She called Dr. Stiller to come see what was going on. The two of them decided to leave the staples in for another week, but Dr. Stiller did hand me a mirror so I could see myself. And yes, there I was and I cried; there in the mirror was the me I had never seen before. Dr. Stiller even told me, "You're beautiful Cadance." Truth was I was a total mess but that didn't seem to matter as I gazed at my new face, so hard to describe my cascading river of emotions at that moment. Cathy was given a tool and instructed on how to remove staples in ten days from now. Riley had her practice on two select staples Cathy tried very hard to be steady but it is a bridge we will have to cross on our own. Cathy drove us back to the Airbnb and the shower I have longed ten days for. Dr. Stiller told me that I would lose some of my hair but it is just temporary so I wasn't going to let shower stream hit my head directly. When Cathy had her stay in the ER her hair had become so matted that it looks impossible to untangle and the answer was going to have to be cutting that beautiful work of art. I refused to cut it and spent hours pulling one hair at a time from the tangle and yes in the end she got to keep all of her hair! My hair was as tangled as much as hers had been with the addition of being full of dried blood and metal staples. What we came up with was for me to sit in the tub while Cathy gently poured a bowl full of water over my mess, then shampoo a little and repeat. It took an entire tank of hot water and well over an hour to complete, but I was free of that awful dirty brown putrid blood and my hair was mine again; not some evil plaything with a mind of its own. What an experience to go through! No one shared this FFS experience on the net. In the end, it was the most relief I have ever had from a shower/bath in my life. We took pictures and we marveled on how different I looked what a wonderful afternoon. I now wear a tie-dye stocking cap to cover my staples and the many scabs that still cling to my scalp. To celebrate we drove to Cole's Gluten-Free Bakery and Café for dinner. I had pancakes (soft and easy to chew) for the third time this trip and Cathy had their enchiladas. She had fish-and-chips when we first arrived and an omelet the next day. Casey was flying in to drive us home tomorrow. He would Uber from the airport over to the Airbnb and should arrive sometime after eleven o'clock tonight. We had taken pictures of the Airbnb from the road showing the address and our car in the driveway then sent them to his phone. Everything worked, Casey arrived in good spirits and snacked on some of our treats that I couldn't eat because of my sore jaw. Casey had been making a point that we needed to get up early so he could be back home again by two o'clock but right now he seemed relaxed. He told us he could sleep in any bed and checked them all out. I still didn't sleep much and the lack of sleep was really telling on me. I had trouble thinking straight and was sure glad Casey was here to drive us home. I gave up trying to sleep at four o'clock in the morning, it was still dark but the struggle wasn't worth it anymore. We were going home in just over an hour so I got up. Cathy had pre-packed all of our stuff and all we had to do was load the car and go. Casey was up by five o'clock and we were on the road after a quick breakfast. It was a nice drive; Casey set his speed in the low seventies and was quick to find a stopping place as my need arose. It quickly became apparent that I couldn't have driven Cathy and myself home but I didn't need to Casey was here for us. It really was a once in a lifetime experience to be driving along with our first born enjoying conversation and, in effect, getting to know each other at this point in our lives. Our talk didn't center on people external to the three of us but did include them as we learned more about each other. The countryside flowing past our car's windows was our classroom and the curriculum was us. Casey did want to be home at his house by two

669

o'clock when school was to let out and at our pace this was going to be no problem to achieve. We would stop at the same two Starbucks as we had coming to Spokane for a restroom break then continue on; finally, we came to the point where I-90 can be exited for I-405 our normal route to our house. Casey asked if we would like to go over the I-90 floating Bridge instead just for the fun of it. We quickly agreed to add a little more joy to our trip. Our trip ended at SeaTac airport parking garage where Casey had parked his car. We said our goodbyes and I drove us home what a wonderful treat to be home!

***

Thursday March 24, 2022. Cathy and I have to drive back to Spokane on Monday the 28th at 11:45 am. After all the dressings were removed I developed a lump on the left side of my face. It was hot and sore and made chewing food a very painful experience. I figured it was something that was just going to go away with time so during recovery week I only ate very soft foods and iced many times of the day. The ice took the bite out of the soreness but didn't seem to reduce the lump much. My only hope was time passing but on day thirteen (we were at home now) I suddenly decided to take a picture and send to it Riley and Kelly via email. I thought this would be a good benchmark for our next appointment on April seventh. I was expecting to get a return text saying it will be something they will check on that day, but instead I got a request to come sooner. Wow! I have no idea what to think about it now. Our guess was it had been an area of fat transfer not taking root. So, our plan is to get up early on Monday and drive to be in Spokane at our 11:45 appointment then leave to get home on the same day. Sleeping is very hard for me I can't sleep on my sides at all because of pain from the staples around my ears; the only saving grace is the natural comfort of our home bed. I never sleep through the night in any motel bed, all I can expect is a night of tortured sleeplessness. This leaves us with the risk of same day travel for the benefit of sleeping at home.

***

Forever and Two Days More

Tuesday March 29, 2022. Let us begin two days ago on Sunday March 27, 2022 the day before our return trip to Spokane on Monday. Cathy and I have pitched back and forth about whether a one-day trip was a wise idea, it was me really doing all pitching back and forth. I was nervous, leading to fear, moving to panic then repeating the cycle. Some of it was legitimate, such as I do have trouble seeing at night, and in order to make the appointment time we have to start at four-thirty in the dark of the morning. Staying overnight lets us travel during full daylight, but there would be no sleep at all for me in any motel in the shape I am in right now. Other things only boarded on legitimacy such as Dr. Stiller doing something surgical to my lump that would negate me being able to drive back home. I had searched Facebook groups about lumps after FFS and found ugly images of drains poking out of dressing wound around heads. Gotta love Facebook groups. The truth of the matter was the lump had continued to shrink in size, not to the point of it being gone but to the point that my chewing was much less painful. So I fought the battle of the one-day trip vs. two-day with a motel stay. Poor Cathy receiving collateral damage with each volley I threw at myself until I finally asked her to see if any motels had a room for Sunday night. The battle ended with the fact that there were not any rooms open because of a function going on in Spokane.

So with that decision final, I moved on to how do I get the folks at Dr. Stiller's office to care about us? I mean more than the steady stream of patients who walk-into-the-office-get-treated-then-disappear without anything noticeable. Without leaving any mark that made their time there memorable for the staff. I want people to care about me because during our time together I cared about them. I think it is an Anderson kind of thing, I have watched my father do this and it made an impression on me. People would remember his parting gesture and I loved the idea of helping to make someone feel better. So, with the one-day trip settled I came up with the idea of baking cookies for all of the staff over at Dr. Stiller's. It was a nice idea and in this time that focuses on everyone being self-centered gives a push back to the darkness of our times. After all, with the truth being told, they had given me this enormously freeing gift, a gift that I only dreamed of ever having a chance of obtaining in my lifetime. Even in the sea of discomfort and slow moving healing, I now have a reflection that is me inside and out. There are issues with doing the cookies, what do we put them into for sharing? I want to make sure the office desk ladies feel as special as the medical staff. Sunday fools me into thinking I have plenty of time to get stuff ready since packing is light with no overnight stay. Evening comes along with the realization that mixing and baking cookies takes hours! We have just enough ingredients to produce one hundred and eight cookies. My downfall is I tend to sample during the process and if chocolate chips are open they are fair game. I finish up at eleven-thirty with an unhappy stomach and the shock that we will only be getting three hours of sleep before getting up to leave.

It is Monday morning and we rush to pack the car to be on our way by four-thirty. I had broken what little sleep I was going to get by waking up at two-thirty with a sad stomach and tried to go back to sleep without great success. All this didn't matter the house was locked up, the car packed, and we backed out onto the road in the dark of the morning. Cathy was being very careful to help me by being watchful of the traffic all around us. It was early morning light traffic on I-405 and tedious driving for me vision wise. I have adequate vision even at night but not the vision of a twenty year old so being alert is very important. We leave the audio book off until daylight comes and it does come as we exit I-405 to join I-90 east. Now tension drops and the lifelong song of I-90 awakens our souls. We had left off a 'Perry Mason' story right at the courtroom scene and quickly were immersed in Perry Mason, Della Street, and Paul Drake's world. Our consciousness was expanded to include this unfolding mystery world while our attention still rested on the song of I-90 east over Snoqualmie Pass to all points east within Washington State. Cathy is the planner/navigator of all our trips she is leading us to the Ellensburg College Starbucks as our first rest-stop. They display a transgender flag in one of their windows and always seem so cheerful to us when we come in, as if we are a treat to them. It is six-thirty as we park in their lot, daylight is increasing minute by minute to a very fair day. Cathy orders our drinks while I use the restroom and when I get out she takes her turn as I wait with the drinks. Cathy likes to chat with the baristas here. We have come to understand that one tank of gas will get us clear across the state without any problem; the distance is three hundred miles. Our joke is we fill up at our local Costco and refill at the Costco in Spokane. It is Cathy's plan to continue east on I-90 to the Starbucks in Ritzville. They have multi-stall restrooms but this no longer bothers me as much as before, the truth is this is the proper place for me. My greatest fear is if there is a line but so far so good. I do feel conspicuous wearing the compression garment around my face and a stocking cap pulled down low over my head but no one has even looked twice on this trip. Perry Mason solved the murder mystery and we began another one as we rolled closer and closer to Spokane. It is nine-thirty as we pull into Cole's Gluten Free Bakery and Café in Spokane. We will have our breakfast here before driving over to Huckleberry's Market near Dr. Stiller's office. Food at Cole's is very nice, we use the restrooms and it is very clear that my stomach is still very unhappy. I am nervous about our appointment and I guess I am still letting it get to me. We shop at Huckleberry's then motor over to Dr. Stiller's office, park and say a prayer, then head into the building. Cathy has a big bag full of four plastic containers of cookies, sort of like Mrs. Santa Claus. As soon as we enter the waiting room and sign in using the kiosk, I make a little speech to the ladies at the front desk. I tell them I had a surgery here that changed my life and I am so happy, so here you go cookies for you all! They all cheered as I handed them one container of the cookies marked for the front desk. Okay, that worked great! I had sent email to Kelly to make sure she would be around today and she said she would. Now Erica comes to get Cathy and me and deposit us in an exam room. This is the same exam room that Riley unwrapped me in to reveal the true me. Erica has a laptop and starts typing while asking us pertinent questions about our visit. Cathy mentions staple removal and Erica pulls out a tool from a drawer then leaves us to ourselves. We have a short wait before there is a knock at the door and Dr. Stiller and Riley come in. They start to greet us but I interrupt with, but first we have cookies to share! This gets a big cheerful response as Cathy hands out two containers to Riley. The two containers of cookies get set on a little table near Riley as I explain the cookies' attributes. Dr. Stiller beams about the cookies sounding great and returns with, "Let's get a look at that lump." Dr. Stiller palpates the area around my lump and explains that, "Sometimes in working around this area there is a gland that can develop a fistula, but you have no drainage and it seems to be reducing." He teases us with, "This is too bad as I am a needle guy and I like to poke around to reduce these things, but yours is looking good! Keep icing the area and we can check it again in two weeks. You do look beautiful Cady and as the swelling goes down things will just get better and better!" Dr. Stiller then turns to leave and at the same time intercepts the two containers of cookies with the tease, "I'll take care of those, thanks again!" Dr. Stiller scooped up the two containers of cookies and whisked them out of the exam room, leaving Riley giving him funny looks. Erica comes in as Dr. Stiller leaves to assist Riley in removing the remaining twenty-six of the original thirty steel staples. Riley is steady-handed and has the same caring attitude about hurting whomever she is working on as I encountered with Marsha. Kindhearted people both of them. I leaned back in the exam chair being as still and supportive of Riley's movements as I could. I also practiced not associating the sound the tool made pulling out each staple with the pain from the action. The pain is comparable to that of electrolysis of the upper lip in intensity, but there is a unique deep ache that lingers after the staple is removed that is totally new to me. The feeling of something that was embedded in bone being removed is totally memorable. I have never really thought about pain being anything but pain, I mean other than the intensity of it but I am coming to understand differently. There are sensations around pain that modulate the experience of it. Burning, tearing, pressure, panic, and more, I wish not to add more to this palette. Just as with pain, relief is unique, so I set my mind to remember this facet also. Back to the cookie story: I give Riley a hug telling her how much I appreciate this life giving surgery and that she has a following on one of FFS support groups on Facebook. We all leave the exam room and ask the front desk ladies if they would tell Kelly we are here. One of them peeks into a room then says to Kelly, "Our favorite couple is here!" Kelly pops out of her office with a bright smile and we get to give her a container of cookies we have earmarked just for her. She is so excited and promises to share with Maria, we say our goodbyes and exit out of the office. It was just the right thing to brighten the whole day for them and that was exactly what we hoped for...

The time was nearing one o'clock and the only thing in our mind was the song I-90 westbound sings. Perry Mason helped us along the way and a forced twenty-minute nap in a Starbuck's parking lot kept us safe. We were home by six o'clock very tired and very happy to arrive home safe.

***

Wednesday March 30, 2022. Tomorrow will be three weeks since my surgery; time for a status report. I no longer have to wear the compression garment around my head and neck twenty-four hours a day and all thirty staples have been removed to Cathy's relief. She was going to have to be the one to remove any leftover stables at home. Showering is returning to normal with the exception of me being very gentle with my scalp as I still have several large scabs right at the hairline. The lump on the left side of my face is almost as flat as the right side and as each day passes chewing gets easier but not back to normal yet. My earlobes are much less sore, at one point I gave up on wires to keep my holes open, even as small as they were, they still irritated the stitches behind the earlobes. I am down to taking ibuprofen only at bedtime or as needed because of allergies. I no longer ice my head or face. The top of my head is numb to the touch just like I am wearing a rigid hardhat; the numbness starts at the crown of my head and ends just at the hairline scar. I am massaging the scar just under my chin to break up this tissue as doctor instructed; the area under my jaw is also numb and very tight. I can tolerate wearing my glasses for only short times now before the bridge of my nose becomes very sore. Numbness still encircles both of my ears radiating down my jaw to my neck. The scars behind my earlobe and at the top of my ears are very sore to touch. I am now using saline spray behind my ears to keep the scars clean. I clear my nose with saline spray, the scar across the columella is very sore and the suture just inside each nostril has been cut off by me as my body spits it out. I am very careful not to touch my nose to the extent of wearing ski gloves to bed at night. My fear is stretching the shape of my nose and undoing the surgery. I have begun to use Rogaine 5% once a day on the scar over my forehead. The stuff really dissolves scabs but it was suggest to use to slow hair loss from the shock of having the scalp lifted up and reattached. Dr. Stiller informed me matter of factually that I would lose my hair but it would only be temporary and grow back. I need to remember to use lipstick.

***

Thursday March 31, 2022. Transgender Day of Visibility. Transgender has become a hate issue a sort of political bludgeon that the left and right both use to gain advantage over the other. To those two sides there are no people who embody being transgender just the issue, sort of like a victimless crime, it is a peopleless issue. So, as they hate back and forth there is no thought given to the humanity of the population just the faceless issue. You can't hurt an issue can you; issues don't bleed, they don't take their lives out of hopelessness, and they don't live in fear of violence, but the people at the discarded heart of an issue do.

We saw Dr. Eaman at her new offices and got to share our adventure with her and a med student. I baked new office cookies and in return got a very close going over of my surgery areas. She thought I was healing well and suggested to use Mupirocin behind my earlobes to prevent staph infections. I related to Dr. Eaman that Dr. Stiller told me flatly that I was going to lose my hair but it would be temporary. In my heart I hoped that it would only be slight, but in the shower it is just sad how much catches in the drain strainer. Today is three weeks and I do feel so much less pain now but six weeks will really tell the tail, at least I hope it will. Tomorrow is Colby's sixteenth birthday party. There will be cake and ice cream at two o'clock, the local group should be at Casey's house and perhaps Mark also. A week from tomorrow is Mark Brehm's Foster HS reunion at Azteca Cathy and I are leaning toward going to it.

***

Saturday April 2, 2022. I was told that I no longer had to wear the head/neck compression garment, but just like with the compression garment for my tummy tuck it is clear I can't go without it yet. After one full day without the headgear, I got a cramp along my upper trachea. It felt like the top of the thyroid cartilage right where I had my Adam's apple shaved was trying to push itself out over the trachea. It was horrible! I put pressure on the structure and it returned back into proper shape. From then on I have worn the garment to sleep each night and off and on during the day. I am going to have to wean myself off the need for this garment, just as I did for the tummy tuck garment. Right now, as I type, I have the part of the garment around my neck in place without the compression across the top of my head. I have been reading in Facebook support groups and Reddit about hair loss from surgery. So many bad experiences, taking years to regrow if at all; a very few with little to no loss at all and no one thing to use to treat it with. I decided to try Argon oil something we got years ago and see if it will soften the thick mean scabs. Colby's birthday was fine and it was so good to see him and his sister in person. We just don't feel part of this family anymore and mourn the loss just as we don't feel part of the Joyce, Mark, and Linda group either. Everyone has their closed worlds or at least it seems to feel that way.

***

Tuesday April 5, 2022. Health update. I still have scabbing at my hairline and rub Rogaine in the area once a day to help keep what hair I can and to break up the scabs little by little. Tricky this, because as they breakup they bleed. I had let go of regularly icing my face and the top of my head. What has happened this last week is the top of my head from front to the crown aches and gets burning hot to touch. My only recourse is to apply ice packs until the fire is tamed leaving it cool to my touch. At this point I have to chase the heat that has now moved down my forehead spreading to my cheeks, nose, and earlobes. Yes my earlobes ache all the time and are very sore to the touch. There are no scabs I can see around my ears, but little white sutures front and back poke out and are sore to the touch. This is why I wear ski gloves whenever I sleep as a barrier to me unthinkingly touching any area of scabbing or where sutures are exposed. This is the only way to keep me from poking into my nose during restless sleep. Each night I dawn a compression garment around my neck and up over the top of my head all secured with hair clips. Add to this a stretchy cap over my head leaving only my eyes, nose, and mouth uncovered. I also wear socks wow as I think about it! Half way through the night I finally warm up and have to pull off the socks but all the rest stay on. We had an appointment with Dr. Stiller's office on Thursday but decided to put it off for a week because of heavy snow at the Pass. Maureen a checker at PCC who we have told about my surgeries gets so excited whenever we see her at the store, she is so affirming, supportive, and just plain happy for us. I don't appreciate the changes to my face, as I just see me, but most of the folks at Starbucks, PCC, or Marlene's Market go out of their way to point out how well I am healing. I like to think of it as 'we' are healing Cathy and I. The informal 1973 reunion at Azteca is this Saturday and we are leaning on going to it despite what I look like. Cathy revision surgery with Dr. Megan is April eleventh at two o'clock in the afternoon. To top all this off we will travel to Spokane three days after Cathy's surgery, Cathy tells me she will be fully up for this... We will check Cathy's sodium levels several days before her revision surgery just to be on the safe side. Since my FFS I have notice that I don't think about gender as much as before. I used to think about it off and on everyday but somewhere a switch is being thrown. I wonder if this trend will continue to grow as I heal, right now there is the turmoil that recovery gives in the form of pain obscuring the changes to my image both real and self constructed. I mostly center on my hairline losing ground with each falling hair from my head. Most experiences that I have read about tell of a year or more before things calm down. This is so dour as in my mind a mere year is a huge percentage of what is left of my time on Earth. Mixed with the relief from a lifetime aliment is the tattered woeful cloak we wear made up of all the years passed in lament of inaction.

***

Monday April 11, 2022. Mark B organizes a yearly informal class of 1973 reunion at the Southcenter Azteca on the first Saturday of April. This tradition had been dropped for the last two springs but renewed this year. Many classmates were so eager to once again meet face to face but alas many were still in fear to do so. Cathy and I were on the list of being eager but we also had our own fear or I should say I had fear. My fear was not bounded by health concerns but since FFS I look different, I am different in name and frame. I had formally changed my name in October of 2019 and announced our transition on Facebook. There were alternating affirming surgeries for both of us during the years of shutdown also. This all has occurred after our last time at this informal reunion in spring of 2019 leading to my trepidation of reconnecting with classmates. Truth was some of those classmates had followed our progress in transition on Facebook, so no surprise except of what I looked like right now in person, while others will be blindsided. In the way of explanation for my uneasiness of the moment, I point to the issues around transgender becoming a political football of left vs. right. I also have the ingrained fear of not passing, but on the positive side, the more feminizing surgeries I complete the less dysphoria I have. I have moved from a place of being constantly mindful of gender to one of it not crossing my mind. I am just me an older female. Now on to what happened before, during, and after the reunion.

In the week before our Saturday night reunion, I had been looking forward to showing off the new me. As we drew closer this changed greatly. I messaged Barbara asking if she was going, this would be a great relief because she is an ally we can count on to smooth any bumps. I got a return message that she wasn't going because of the curtain of fear that is drawn closed about health concerns. I replied that I understood but was looking for support since I do now look

679

differently and answer to a new name. There is no way to know who is going to show up but Barbara did tell me that two others she spoke to might be attending. Only a little ray of hope but I wondered if Michael might entertain the idea of going? He had talked about it a few days ago with the idea of making a connection with anyone willing to jam with him. Things happened to derail Michael from coming, his car died a complete death putting him in a very bad place. Cathy and I decided we would go no matter what and if anything happened we only had to leave and return home, kicking off the dust of any bad experience. After all, it could be a very affirming experience too. Saturday we slept in, I showered after we got up being careful to be very gentle with my hair; even so, I had another glob of hair fall out to add to the growing pile of deserters. My hair volume is a very sad thing for me to bear. Dr. Tony during an FFS consultation had told me he wouldn't touch my hairline where Dr. Stiller had aggressively advanced it during my Browlift. The downside of facial surgery is hair loss; right now, I have a scabby forehead that is balding into my hairline in places. I suddenly realized I need to hide this and we needed to decide what to wear. With only an hour until the event Cathy and I were in our bedroom with me in a panic trying on different combinations of tie-dye tops and tights. Nothing looked good to me and I looked awful. What a pit I had fallen into then the storm cleared; we would match using navy blue and brick red spiral tees with brick red tights. I wore a hair band to hide my scabby hairline, which also gave me a very feminine look. Cathy was taken back by this telling me, "You look great!" I felt better so off to the Southcenter Azteca to face what we find. We find a nice park near the door say a little prayer, and leave the protection of our car to walk toward the restaurant entrance. Two ladies both dressed in black were eyeing the parking lot looking for husbands who presuming had gone to fetch the car. We walk up the steps hand in hand as they leave. I open the door to the clatter of a very busy and full waiting room for dinner. People sitting with placid waiting faces somehow knowing that they have no choice but to wait. The hostess at the desk smiles at this colorful couple coming toward her and her gaze follows us as we enter the bar. We had seen Mark B in the bar chatting with someone, so with this confidence of being in the right place we slowly walked into the noisy bar. The place wasn't as crowded as in past times and Mark had put together several tables in hopes of lots of classmates filling the place. We walk over to Mark who is as tall and thin as he was in school. He shakes our hands with a sort of a tolerance of formality lacking in welcoming chatter. In past years Cathy would have gotten a hug from Mark and I a pat on the back with warm smiles and welcoming chatter. Now we really feel the absence of Barbara she would have been at Mark's elbow welcoming people in, it would have changed the evening for us. This evening it is the two of us coming toward him and not vice versa, in fact he moves away from us as soon as possible. Cathy and I are left standing alone but undaunted, Cathy spies two classmates that we follow on Facebook, Dan and Teresa sitting near another friend Candy. We walk across the bar to the table they are sitting at and engage in friendly conversation revolving about Cathy's bout with complications from the vaccine. Dan gets up and heads across the room so Cathy sits down to chat with Teresa. I see Reggie another classmate that I have promised Michael to give his cell number to. I am fixated on keeping my promise to my friend and also totally oblivious to the fact that I am about to be schooled in standing up for my gender. I walk around the table to where Reggie is chatting with two other male classmates and as I come near they turn their attention to me. They are curious about this gal dressed in colorful standout clothes, if that is what she is. I am greeted with questions nothing more. "Were you in the 1973 class? This is what's going on here tonight." I assure them that yes, I was in the class of 1973. My assurance was met with, "You don't look familiar, well kind of." In my naivety I hadn't prepared myself for this situation. I never entertained notion of being completely unidentifiable. I figured anyone would see I was with Cathy, who they would quickly identify, and make the connection from there. Here I was away from Cathy at the moment facing three guys I had gone to school with, who didn't have a clue who I was. I reached for how to overcome this predicament without just outing myself but couldn't see how to do it. I told my little

681

audience that I had gone to school with them but I looked different now. This only brought on blank stares so I came out directly with I was C---- Anderson. In the same breath I firmly put in, I go by Cady now. This declaration cleared the question but cost me mentally. The conversation had now taken on a new turn. One of the guys had an aha moment and said, "Oh, C---- Anderson. I remember you! So, you're female now?" The question stung me because I had always been female internally even in childhood. What was there for it then, but to bury yourself and be something you're not for a lifetime of internal torment. After all that has happened, to show me I could leave this torment behind, and be who I have always been, my answer to this comment should have been; I have always been female, not just now!

With the big riddle solved for them, they wandered off without any more to say. Reggie stayed wanting to know more. He had a groomed mustache and was wearing a black biker jacket. Reggie was a character; he loved playing a pirate with a group of performing friends but was now resigned to just being his colorful self. He remembered me as a heavy kid and marveled how thin I was. I answered his questions, both thoughtful and otherwise, and then turned to listening to him tell of his adventures. In the end, he accepted Michael's phone number, and also gave me his phone number with the promise to come visit he and his wife sometime at his house in Tulalip. Reggie's was my nicest conversation with any of the guys at the reunion. Cathy and I would just sit by ourselves sipping our non-alcoholic drinks hoping for someone to wander over to speak to us. Two more Facebook friends both female came over to chat and compliment me on my face. Finally, we both decided to give it until 7:30 and then go home. That time came but I thought we should give one more try to connect, so Cathy and I got ourselves up and walked over to Karen O she was at the moment sitting by herself. We said "Hi" and ventured into conversation. Karen did chat with us and thanked us for coming over to her. Karen from being Cathy's Facebook friend knew from our post about our journey. She was in the process of retiring and interested in spending time crafting, perfect fodder for a Cathy/Karen chat! That was nice, so we walked more looking for opportunities to start up with someone else. Dan was nearby and seemed willing to chat with us. Dan didn't recognize Cathy how ironic! Next came Toni she is not a Facebook friend so our conversation just touched on the changes on my face and how she would love to have age spots removed. A conversation with Dave about Casey's old house and his time plumbing it was nice. Then it really was time to go (8:15) we make it over to Mark B for a short obligatory handshake goodbye. Mark B isn't a Facebook friend but somehow has some knowledge that leads him away from us. To be fair, with all we have been through as a group, everyone has turned inward, it will be a long time before people find it safe to open up to one another again... We really did miss Barbara, she still doesn't feel safe in close company, and I get the feeling that I have offended her in some way also...

***

Tuesday April 12, 2022. Cathy's revision surgery with Dr. Megan up north in Mountlake Terrace was yesterday. The office of Phase Plastic Surgery has less of Dr. Baxter's personal taste and more of a group-practice feel to it. Gone are the gaudy flower arrangements in the reception/waiting room and in their place are popup advertisements for Botox treatments. The feel of intimacy is also gone, but we do have an appointment giving us a legitimate place here. We meet Janet as the door opens and are brought into a treatment room. We have been in this room before. I ask if Janet is now Dr. Megan's PA? No Janet is an OR scrub nurse filling in. I guess the Dr. Megan's PA has moved on. Janet hands Cathy a gown to change into and I make sure her mask is put in a safe place. A knock and in comes both Janet and Dr. Megan. Dr. Megan is excited to see us and wants to see how my face is doing also. We chat and feel the love. Dr. Megan will do the revision here with the aid of Janet. I get to watch first hand and Janet teases me that she may put me to work. Dr. Megan marks up the area to be removed then injects local anesthetic along the mean eight-inch scar. The needle is a long one and reminds me of my experience during my Blepharoplasty. Cathy is stoic but I know just how much

683

this part hurts. After two big syringes of local Dr. Megan pokes around to test numbness, Cathy tells her she can still feel the pokes so Dr. Megan uses a little more than begins to cut along her marks. Janet leaves to fetch something and suddenly Cathy lets out a sharp scream! Dr. Megan said that she will stay away for that area and injects more local before continuing. Janet comes back asking if that scream came from in here. Yup. Janet also asks Cathy if she has any redheads in her family. Cathy returns with yes there are redheads on her dad's side of the family. Janet goes on to remind us that redheads have a higher pain threshold and require much more anesthetic to dull anything over that threshold. A new revelation! Cathy is a redhead! It kind of explains a lot… It takes twenty minutes to remove a wedge of scar eight inches long and a pad of fat half that length. After the scream, I go over to stand next to Cathy so she can squeeze my hand and she does. My hand will eventually heal. I also talk to keep her distracted and me too. Dr. Megan does the neatest stitching job, just amazing to watch. Dr. Megan finishes closing the wound, cleans the area and applies steri-strips and Janet covers these with a wide adhesive tape. Cathy is finished! Dr. Megan brings a little steel bowl containing the sharps she has used in suturing over to the sink area. Janet tells her in a very complimentary way, "Look at you taking care of your sharps!" Dr. Megan returns with, "I always do!" I think this is a scrub nurse training the surgeon sort of thing. We all chat and Dr. Megan tells us we are just the greatest couple and to come back on April twentieth to check progress. Cathy gets dressed and we receive hugs from both Janet and Dr. Megan. This is a very busy week and we just checked off another box now onto healing up for both Cathy and me.

***

Tuesday April 18, 2022. It has been one year since Dr. Ken has left us. We got a reminder of his time as our Dentist when Cathy needed to see Dr. Rapoport over at Pacific Northwest Periodontics about tooth #3. It had been hurting and a root canal had already begin done on it so it needed pulling… During the exam Dr. Rapoport made comment on the gold crown on that tooth. He told us, "You have a beautiful gold crown on that tooth; you don't see gold workmanship like this anymore. The dental schools don't even teach how to do gold. Gold is the only metal I trust in my mouth!" He asked us who did the crown and we answered Dr. Ken Nishimoto. Dr. Rapoport asked us, "How is he doing?" We shared about his death after just retiring and how sad it was to lose him. Dr. Rapoport joined in our sadness with, "It doesn't seem that long ago since I last spoke with him so sad…"

It has been a little while since I have reported on how my healing is going so here we go. It has been a little over five weeks since surgery. I have shared pictures from the day after surgery through to one month (before and after pictures) after surgery on a private Facebook group (FFS Facial Feminization Surgery/Transgender). I only shared day after surgery and seven days later when I got the bandages off on our family and friends Facebook group. I have been hesitant to share my one-month pictures in this group because of all the political battling between left and right over transgender issues right now. The rhetoric has been increasingly demeaning and debasing to real people, who through no fault of our own, happen to be transgender. A very broad brush is being used to seek out any instance of someone transgender who can be used and then painted in the worst way possible, to defame them thus feeding the fire of political expediency of either side. So, my fear is bringing this down on me, as tolerant family or friends who are mindfully subject to right side thinking, are now being pushed by a much stronger rhetoric than ever before. It is an extreme heartless rhetoric that traditionally has been used against them. I would like to share, so that people will understand Cathy and me; hopefully they will see that we are just an older couple trying to find our way to continue our lives in a loving way. And then there is the fact I am vulnerable, I don't look perfect. I have had most of my hair fall out above my forehead, I still have thick scabs in the balding areas on either side of my middle part, the tight skin of my face is loosening bringing back small wrinkles, and my perfect brows are once again settling back down. I feel like I'm walking backward. The top of my head is numb to my touch along with the areas around my ears traveling down to and across my neck. I still feel like I am

685

wearing a helmet with a chinstrap. Although numb I have pain behind my ears right down to the earlobe. On my recall last week, I got Riley Dr. Stiller's PA to remove as many visible sutures as she could find. I had sutures I could feel all around my ears and inside my nose. Riley told us that my body was busy trying to spit out stitches that were dissolving under the surface and it is okay to remove them as they surface but only if they come out without resistance. So, this is a battle my body has with a foreign object that has no place being there. I have pulled little strings out of my nose that come right out but are like an inch long. The stuff is strong outside of our body until it is attacked and weakened deep inside the tissue. In short, it is like having many painfully enflamed slivers poking deep into your skin. They hurt and bring swelling until they are removed one way or another. Keep in mind that they are doing a job holding tissue together in a desired shape until healing makes that shape permanent. So, it is a juggling act as to when to leave the painful strings alone and when to tug on them in hopes that like all slivers they will come out. I find that I need to ice once a day on the top crown, cheek sides, forehead, bridge of my nose, ears, and jaw line. It is like the whole area has a building fever that gets more painful until it is knocked down by an ice pack. The cycle then repeats itself. I can tolerate wearing my glasses longer but not all day, as this hurts the bridge of my nose and my ears.

Good things to remember: My ears are pinned back nicely. My nose is very nice with no bumps along the ridge; in fact, it is very much the shape of the nose I had as child as far as length goes. My skin is very smooth and soft. My brow bones are much reduced. The one central negative is my hair loss... The pain I have now I hope will reduce over time as well as swelling. This hope comes from the experience I have had with other surgeries, but I have no experience with hair coming back after falling out...

***

Thursday April 21, 2022. Cathy and I both share time each day icing our hurts. Yesterday Cathy had an appointment with Dr. Megan to remove the steri-strips from the scar revision on her breast. She sure did bruise was Dr. Megan's comment. Cathy also made a coffee mug thanking Dr. Megan for changing our lives. There has been so much transgender bashing back and forth in the media that I'm hesitant to post anymore on FB about my medical transition. I am miserable from the constant ache healing is giving me; if I don't ice well at least once a day I become even more miserable. Sharing my progress is cathartic, so I thought to only share with safe people in a limited way. Natalie got to see me yesterday and was supportive, it wasn't that I expected otherwise, but truthfully I thought our time together was drawing to an end. Her massage did wonders in reducing my overall discomfort, which was a real blessing.

In print I decided to share with Deb about my FFS outcome, she was our one safe person and had been very supportive all during transition. I sent a link of a short video Dr. Stiller posted on Instagram showing a portion of my facial surgery. She, in turn posted this to me in messenger, about when we first ran into each other in an eye doctor's waiting room back in 2019, and I hadn't come out yet. We also hadn't seen each other in person since 1973.

***

Deb:

I haven't seen that boy from high school for a very, very long time. When I saw you two at the doctor's office that day I saw a very different C----. A C---- that most definitely was feminine. I didn't know if you were a feminine gay man or a trans woman, but despite being born a man, I knew that man had been shed. In that office I met Cady, nothing was said between the three of us, I know it is not my place to "out" anyone and when they are comfortable they will say something. Seeing your new face, the YOU face is exciting, but seeing You in YOUR face is where the excitement lies for me. There is no way for me to even begin to understand how horrible it must be to have lived the biggest chunk of your life in a body that wasn't yours. I have watched this process and I have seen more and more light come into your face into your eyes. Each step has added a new light to your eyes and lightened your step a bit. Like a flower slowly opening. It is so beautiful. So, this facial feminization softens away that boy. I bet Cathy will be able to start plants with your glow as you stare at the 'YOU' you have waited over 50 years to see.

That night I responded to this and shared my one-month before and after pictures.

Cady:
Hi Deb, I just re-read this last message from you and loved it so much. I would like to share my one-month-after pictures as well as my before pictures. Cathy and I love seeing your FB posts thank you for doing them dear one. Yes, I guess that I have finally shed that out-facing shell or very close to it. It is my joy and I hope it brings you joy in my sharing it with you.

Deb:
Wow just plain wow! You are so beautiful. Ah Cady so refined I actually got goosebumps from the feeling WOW. So, what do you feel when you look in the mirror? Do you feel comfortable with the woman looking back at you? Do you believe the reflection? I do! Oh, my friend, your face is matching your spirit...

***

Thursday April 28, 2022. We are going to the Pennella/Ramuta wedding this Sunday. So tricky to figure out what to wear, it has to be something that reflects my transition gender of female but at the same time doesn't call attention to it. We have the constraints that we normally both wear matching tie-dye. I have to be comfortable in wearing whatever if I am to have any chance for holding myself together and not run back home. Lastly, is the pressure of not offending anyone, especially if such an offence might keep them away from the Anderson family picnic this summer...

Me stuff. I had a waking dream this morning that not only left me in tears but also left me grasping for what is real and now as opposed to dead and gone. The dream came over me at the time near the end of my sleep cycle, that twilight time just before waking. The setting was the ranch house just as it had been back in 1970. I saw Hazel as the dream enveloped me. I looked at her and thought it was so nice to see her again. I realized at that moment I hadn't pictured her in my mind for a long time in any detail; I really couldn't because of fading memories, so much gone forever. Suddenly there she is in perfect detail! I had forgotten the shape of her chin, the little mole on one side of it, her hairstyle, and her bifocal glasses. There she was standing right in front of me as clear as day. What joy then confusion as reality faltered; I drifted past the confusion into a reality of being in the front room of the ranch house with my grandfather full of expectation of my being there, my mother calm and serene, my father in the background on the couch that folds down to become a bed. They were all together visiting with each other and happy that I was there also as if after a long absence. We were to sleep in the back room a bed had been made for us, I say us because I never feel singular Cathy is always with me sort of a single unit we two, but I wondered about me was I the me of now or before it felt odd? A wonderful night sleep followed by my mother coming through our room on the way to the front room. We got up and I thought to make breakfast in the kitchen that is attached to the back room. I couldn't figure out how to turn on the gas burners and when they did light how to turn them off. I was stressing me the controls seem to be contrary to what they should be. Then suddenly the realization came that all I had to do was walk into the front room and ask my mother for help. I knew she would have the answer and this was so relieving to me. I walked out into the front room and all four adults were chatting about the coming day we would spend together. Mom was sitting calm and smiling, grandpa was eager to get going and Hazel and dad were in the background. I looked at them there in that place thinking I am here too then wondered if I had died. After all, here was my birth family except for David, all alive and very real how else could I be with them but to be dead too. Didn't my father, as he neared death see his deceased family? Have I just died? A huge wave of sadness smothers me followed by a battle for reality of self. Then the loss of all I had loved that death had taken away again. The twisting and tearing of what was and what is separated into an unstable return to now. I say unstable because the shadow of my own death seems to be nearer to me. I awake to a shaking return to our bedroom full of mourning all those I had just been with and fearful of losing my life. Thoughts of needing a will quickly just destroyed me as if I was laying on my deathbed already. I cried and Cathy soothed me. I know it was a dream but so real as to bring trauma into my life. As today brought more stress about transitioning and how it separates us from other family, last night's dream pokes at my heart bringing loss and hopelessness.

***

Friday April 29, 2022. Corey chaperoned Quince's Kindergarten class's field trip to the San Diego Zoo today. He had a lovely parenting experience and I am so happy for him. I know he will keep this memory in his heart all of his life. I don't have to relate what he told me because he journals daily.

We spent the day in a mad effort to find clothes to wear to the wedding. It was very hard on both of us because we had never had to come up with party clothes since my coming out. In fact, I wonder if I have been using tie-dye tees to hide from wearing female cloths in public? We have ordered all kind of stuff most of which we will return. Right now we have two matching tops that look tie-dyed that will work but what to wear on the bottom is up for grabs. Costco had skorts that fit us, but are too short on me but on Cathy they look great! We have more stuff coming tomorrow. Things that might help are knee boots for me or a longer knee length skirt. If all else fails we will just wear our daily black tights with the new tops but I hope something will come up.

Me stuff. I continue to use Rogaine once a day on my bare hairline; it leaves the area tight and itchy causing me to rub my forehead to reduce the pressure. I am still numb in all the areas I have listed but feeling is very slowly returning. This comes at the edges where feeling was still normal and slowly pushes into the numb areas. As I rub my cheek toward my ear I can tell the band of numbness is getting narrower. My earlobes still hurt and I still can't tolerate earrings in the holes. Cathy is still able to get the gold wires through the holes but they soon become so sore we remove them. I can sleep on my sides chiefly my right side but it brings soreness to my right ear. There are raised scars behind both ears that are sore to the touch much more on the right than the left. My glasses' arms rest on them making wearing my glasses hurtful at the nose and ears. I have read of other folks' experiences with pain all over the head from FFS and how long it has lasted. Each person's healing is unique some report that it has taken over a year to get relief others three months but in all it seems complete freedom of soreness does take years. It has been nearly four years for all the soreness to be gone from my scrotum. I wonder how long for my face?

***

Friday May 6, 2022. We visited Pierced Hearts yesterday to have my pierced earlobes reopened. Cathy and I have tried and tried to push my normal earrings back through my earlobe but it just hurt too much to get them all the way through. The place has changed some but for the most part it is still as we experienced it three years ago. Joey was our piercer then; he was so sweet to us but his home is now in California. Chuck (Charlene) was who helped us this time. She was sweet too; must be part of the Tattoo/piercing culture. Reopening my earlobes did hurt, even with Chuck's gentle touch mostly because both of my earlobes are sore all the time from the surgery. No, the hole wasn't closed up but all the pulling Dr. Stiller did to tighten my facial skin distorted the pierced canal from being straight through. Chuck stretched each canal back into a straight line and put my normal green jewel ear studs back where they belong. So nice to be back together again but if something brushes against an earring I get a shock of pain. The task for me now is to smile through the pain; a very female thing. I was dreading going to bed last night knowing that if either ear touched my pillow pain would come as an instant shock. I use my hand when sleeping on my side to cup my ear protecting the earring from pressing anything. I slept surprisingly well as the night marched on, the pain wasn't any more than with no earrings. The straight axle of the earring seems to soothe the overall earlobe just like a splint on a broken bone. I wish I had done this sooner!

Healing report after two months. The numbness is shrinking in area and feeling is returning like a slow wave pulling back from the shore. The overall feeling of wearing a tight skullcap hat with chinstrap bucketed under my chin is still present but the hat is smaller in diameter and the chinstrap is narrower. I have hair growing back right at the center of my forehead hairline. Growth is around two inches two months after the surgery. Yes, I have lost a bunch of hair and all along my central part little two-inch hairs are repopulating my head. I put Rogaine on the area of either side of my central part right at my forehead hairline. Cathy has pulled out several very long hairs that were trapped under my skin right at my left temple. There was a very sore bump with a little hair poking out and when pulled it turned out to be four inches long! We have to keep a lookout for trapped hairs. I still had an oval scab one half by three quarters inch in diameter on the left side of my forehead just down from my central part. The scab feels like it pokes down into my forehead like a growth. I massage the scar underneath my chin daily to break it up. I still wear gloves at night to keep from picking at it. The scab had been twice this size but as each shower comes I break off the overhanging pieces. Another unpleasant thing that come in waves, is the top of my head heating up just like it has a raging fever. The entire area that was lifted up off my skull feels like it is on fire quickly becoming unbearable in pain and heat. The only thing that stops it is an ice pack; I use a big flat ice pack that covers the top of my head and overlaps onto my forehead. I lay down on my back with my head up, at first the cold is too much this in itself hurts, but in just a little while I will fall asleep to awake relieved. Back to the scab, I do try very hard not to touch it with the idea it is doing some good. I will be very relieved when the thing is gone...

We attended a lovely wedding in a beautiful venue on May 1st. Kendra Ramuta and Tyeson Pennella have exchanged vows. All my fears just melted away. Our little back-story is the panic I/we had in properly kitting ourselves out to attend the event. Cathy and I face each day in matching Tie-dye art clothes, this doesn't mean we can't wear something else it really doesn't. We can quit at any time... But there is this commitment thing, a principle, a self-identification, an understated rebirth of being a rebel, and even a style needing a champion. Okay we admit it we are hooked and I think people enjoy seeing us acting oddly or at least looking that way. A wedding is a respectful time you dress to show honor. Suffice to say that Cathy and Cady have lots of garments to return unused tomorrow, at the last minute we did find something appropriate that had a touch of tie-dye flavor in a stately way.

The really big problem is makeup; we are both so deficient in this area. We spent all of our time in desperate search for clothing totally ignoring the female face needs. I made panic-toned calls to women seeking advice and watched too many YouTube tutorials on makeup for older women. Smokey eye shadow, brow bone color, hooded eyes, eyelid primer, blending brushes, tightline mascara, brow palettes, and on and on. A dear friend told me to just get some makeup and have fun with it. Suffice to say that Cathy and Cady have much unused makeup. One hour before it was time to go to the wedding we were both defeated by our age and lack of practice in the mystique of makeup. Cathy did a simple eye shadow, a little mascara, and I did her brows with an eye palette. I did the old trick of putting eyeliner on an eyelash curler to do my-oh-so short eyelashes and wore a nice color (blushing berry #590) on my lips. It's sad in a way; both of us have had surgery to open up the area around our eyes so we could use eye makeup. We have both made the promise to each other to gain the skills of makeup. There's fun to be had!!!

***

Friday May 20, 2022. A new forehead scab formed over the dent left by the old scab. It has also dropped off and now the area is nice smooth skin. I have had more hair growth right at the midline point of my hairline. The hairs are two inches long and are slowly filling in the empty space there. I have become so self-conscious of my now high forehead that I hide the whole area with stretchy caps. I think I call more attention to myself by doing so. Cathy has told me over and over that I have to get over it, quit hiding, and be the authentic me. On our walk today we saw Bonny, a high school classmate of ours, gardening in her yard. We stopped to say hello. The long and short of our conversation was she has been following us on Facebook and was excited to see how my surgery came out. She complimented me with, "You look so good now!" Bonny then told us about her two aunts who, in their seventies, transitioned, "They both always felt just as you did, now they are in their eighties and happy." She was very supportive. We chatted about waiting so long in life but the time past wasn't at all friendly to transgender folk, completely opposite of what it is today. Yes, even with the negative undercurrent of late, it is so much better. Bonny told us she was in Spokane when we were, she had to arrange care for her ninety-two year old mother who is unable to care for herself, she now is sixty-five pounds and in failing health. This time in life is such a hard time for both of them. Bonny was also interested in our little four-day vacation we had in Ellensburg. In our mini vacation in Ellensburg, we stayed in Cottonwood Cottage at the Brick House Resort. The place is still under construction up Manastash Road on the Kittitas Valley rim. Two of five cottages are done and in use. The place is very peaceful and, importantly, is in a wind shadow. We as tourists spent three days checking out Ellensburg and the Cashmere Antique Malls. We spent evenings reading; I read *Super Late Bloomer* by Julia Kate, *Found in Transition* by Paria Hassouri, and *This Time For Me A Memoir* by Alexandra Billings. All were hard reads for me as they kept my mind on each person's transgender journey but I appreciated their stories, especially Alexandra Billings. I am still lingering in transition even with all the progress made so far, this is a very hard place to be and Alexandra's journey personified this. My reading experience was somewhat cathartic and draining at the same time. Cathy read *Titus* by Christy Barritt, *Vanish* by Lynn Shannon, *Critical Error* by Lynn Shannon, and *Ranger Protection* by Lynn Shannon. Cathy's reading experience was escapism into a world of murder and romance where the good guys and gals always win. It was so nice to get away for a few days and be so distracted.

Bonny asked us to keep posting our travels as she is always looking for ideas for travel in retirement. We also happened by Eli and Anna's place while they were outside so we got to talk to them. I didn't have my glasses on because the pressure they put on the bridge f my nose both hurts and mis-shapes it back to the bump I had. The good news is, if I don't wear my glasses the bump goes back down, the bad news is of course I can't see very well… When we got back home I looked in the mirror to see my surgery-scarred face. I had that face fixed in my mind as something I had to hide as it outed me moment by moment all day long. Instead, I saw progress back toward the female image, especially because of the hair coming back. It was what Bonny's compliment had tickled into my mind so that now a veil was being opened. This afternoon has been hard; my head has hurt so much more than earlier, a deep aching pressure all around the surgery site. I rub my forehead in an attempt to soothe the pain and feel the heat inside the top of my head. I am not running a fever but my hands are cold and the top of my head hot. During our little trip, I noticed that for the most part I felt better. This awful ache had been with me for five weeks without letting up. It seems to be a mix of my allergy symptoms amplified many times over and centered in on my surgery site. While in Ellensburg, this faded and I carefully rejoiced, it was just like the way I had been before this all started. I had numbness in the sides of my neck, up my face, and at the top of my head, but none of the pressure/pain. These few days were wonderful. I spent the time speculating, was it because I had stopped Rogaine, if that was the case, I would never use it again! It seemed to be a good candidate since I had forgotten to use it for a few days. Now it doesn't seem to be the cause as the pain has completely returned in severity this evening. I slept so well last night, scoring a ninety-two, but I don't hold out much hope for tonight's score. During our vacation I took a bedtime cocktail of ibuprofen (400mg total), Chlorpheniramine Maleate (4mg), Methylfolate, Bromelain, and Melatonin and will continue to do this before bed. Just as a note, I have even tried anti-yeast pills and they

695

didn't help either. There is something very weird going on with my mast cells…

***

Saturday May 21, 2022. The pressure/pain comes and goes, today is a goes day. We worked outside doing gardening in our yard trimming bushes, weed whacking, and lawn mowing in certain areas. I didn't wear a mask but didn't seem to need one… It's nighttime now and there is an increase in pressure around my head anywhere that I am still numb but nothing like yesterday. Yellow pills give relief but it is the strangest allergy reaction I have ever had… Cathy and I are alone this Saturday the grandkids are busy. We have had so many nice visits as they have grown up and are thankful for them, knowing that teenage years are very lean for grandparents.

Me stuff. The bridge of my nose is too sore to wear my glasses. I discovered, to my chagrin, that wearing my glasses was reshaping my nose bridge back to having a bump right between my eyes. I pushed on the lump/bump and, not unlike clay; it could be formed back into the smooth slope Dr. Stiller fashioned. It stays this way as long as I don't wear my glasses. I don't know how long before my nose bridge hardens up enough to accept the pressure of wearing glasses without deforming… I will try to go without glasses as much as possible.

***

Sunday May 22, 2022. I had another bout of pressure/pain in the face and top of my head that left me holding my head with my hands. So far yellow pills with ibuprofen or Tylenol slowly calm it down. My neck is so tight and I am beginning to get zingers as nerves begin to reattach, recovery is a long slow uncomfortable process… These last two days have been so sunny with temperatures reaching into the lower seventies that called for clothes to both protect and still be cool. We chose our pink cotton peasant shirts, they are tie-dye and long sleeved yet breathable. The necklines are a deep v-neck loosely laced at the bottom. The chest reveal shows the top of my camisole, it is so feminine. We walked our neighborhood in them and drove to the Starbucks on Ambaum for drinks. This Starbucks is the most welcoming and energetic of all our favorites. When we walked up to the counter the barista did a double take and shouted, "Ladies you look great!" It felt so nice to be a little more fem than our normal tie-dye tees give us.

***

Monday May 23, 2022. Today was clean all of the old shoes out of our house day. We tackled our bedroom shoe pile and sorted good give away shoes out from the trash shoes. Long haul all day cleaning out stuff that expanded into old clothes in overfilled drawers. One of the bottom drawers was home to my almost forgotten stash of crossdressing clothes. So long ago when I was very flat in my chest and narrow in my hips. Trying on an old garment sure points out the success of HRT! With a lot of old clothes from both of us purged we gain two empty drawers!

***

Tuesday May 31, 2022. We had a wonderful visit at our house with Quince and Corey! Casey and his family spent five hours on Sunday at our house visiting and playing games with us as one big happy family. Colby is blooming at sixteen he's tall, dark, and handsome, and I so miss my little partner in play. Now he is talking about Running Start next year. He asked if we were planning to take Quince to the Taneum Creek Cabin like we did them. No, things have changed but you're so sweet to remember our time there and to ask. He also reminded me that playing farm on our stairs is the most fun. A short time ago I had bought a vintage tin toy farm barn and silo along some more plastic farm animals to play with Q but we never got around to doing it this visit. Colby I love you and really feel the passage of time for us... B---- played cards with us and remained engaged in our visiting. She is blooming too. Q filled our house for four nights and four days with six-year-old magic of his own special making. It was an amazing magic allowing him to read vintage comic book after comic book at lighting speed just as if he was years older than his mark at six. His observations of our daily time together were rich, clean, and startlingly accurate. He and I sang silly songs, did magic tricks, and explored each other's worlds. With this joy also comes sorrow. Corey is uncomfortable giving me tight hugs now. I miss his full embrace, now what is left is a loose hug at an angle so that chests don't touch. It is a lost connection from my fathering days with my son, one, which can't be reclaimed in the physical form, I am in now. This is heartache, a soul crushing pain, I have not lost him but a physical barrier now exists where none was before. There is much loss in being transgender I am very grateful for the few things I haven't lost. Being transgender for me is a daily battle within myself and without myself. I have great compassion for anyone who is trans and especially those who battle later in life. You lose so much and there is no way around it. God leads us on paths of sorrow but we will walk where God has set us.

***

Wednesday June 1, 2022. June is Pride Month and this weekend Burien will have stuff going on Friday night and Saturday. My hair is slowly returning and I have noticed much less hair left in the shower drain screen. I am washing my hair as gently as possible to keep what is left on my head. The intense pressure ache all around my head is still in effect, it seems to follow allergy flair-ups. My left earlobe is far less sensitive now and okay to sleep on, but my right ear is still on fire. It is hard to judge if it is improving or not. My hair only lasts two days before it is just a stringy mess. I don't feel presentable most of the time; this is the part of FFS recovery that they don't tell you about. We will see Debbie Caddell on the tenth and I must remember to ask if her earlobes have stopped hurting yet also what face cream does she use? I wonder if a wig would help until my hair returns?

Cathy and I are digging through the computer room to gather up stuff to take to Value Village. We need to do this to our whole house but baby steps with a reachable goal each day is best for us right now. The new yard service we are using mowed our lawn yesterday. Another note, Facebook is very quiet seems as if many people have sort of given up on it. Grandma Dixon and Linda had a successful twelve-day vacation.

Forever and Two Days More

***

Thursday June 2, 2022. Cleaning and clearing out our overstuffed rooms goes on, our focus in the computer room. I am so tired of the fiery pins and needles all around my face, neck, and ears. Yellow pills seem to reduce the intensity but not to the point of being pain free. It is almost three months since the surgery and I wonder just how long this will go on? How long before the lumps of scars across my forehead smooth down, or my hairline returns, or my earlobes don't ache to the touch? I now have a high female forehead hairline that can be hidden with a stretch hairband and as I look at other folks' FFS post-op pictures I see that this is a common strategy. My hair loss is slowing and new hair is coming in… The Ambaum Starbucks baristas come close to applauding as we enter with our rainbow pride clothes on, such fun!

***

Monday June 13, 2022. Cathy made me a loving gift of a thirty-ounce tumbler with my silhouette blowing butterflies up into the wind from my extended hand. The caption on the cup is, "I love the woman I've become because I fought to become her." She even wrote she was proud of me!

This June so far has been a wet and cool one. We have had the sump pump run several times and the furnace on several occasions. Graduation for Foster High School was outside on the open field on a wet evening the rain held off long enough for the ceremony to be over. Mindy has caught Covid as have several other people we know but it is no big deal now, it just hangs in the air like a Sword of Damocles waiting to strike everyone. Prices for everything are going up week by week. We get our gas exclusively at Costco because they have the best prices for their members; the downside is we have to wait in long lines at the pumps.

Me stuff: After talking with Debbie about healing times and reading other results real recovery isn't complete for a year. My numbness is reduced by forty percent. I still have burning pain centered behind my ears especially at the earlobes. If I brush against

699

my earrings I get a stab of pain. Sleeping on my left side isn't so uncomfortable but right-side sleeping is a tossup at best because of the pressure on that ear. Numbness across my neck makes the area feel tight; I find I stretch against this pressure throughout the day. I practice holding my larynx up as a normal position hoping muscle memory will take hold of it. If my larynx falls it tips forward giving me an Adam's apple look and lower my pitch. Depression has become a shadow following us around. What was that shirt B---- had? The saying on it was, "Sometimes I wrestle with my demons other times we just cuddle together."

***

Saturday June 18, 2022. Do you have valid claims to the life experiences of your past male self? Can Cadance interject herself into the past experiences of a teenage boy or a young adult? Are those experiences of life lived still hers to relate to someone else who was of the same age? I was visiting with Craig G over in Thorp about the times we both lived through there as young adults. As I told my tales of a past ranch life I realized they belonged to a young male and here he is accepting me as someone else. Not someone else per se but some other gender. As I spoke of the young life I had, I had to be careful to lay the plausible foundation of this life being one of a female. Now after over an hour of conversation where I was never anything but an older woman to he and his wife I feel as if I somehow mislead them, I felt dishonest. Why should I feel this way? Earlier we had visited the old Thorp Mill where Cathy and I were both taken as two women. I don't know if people are just being nice or jaded. Do I really pass? And if I do this means I have transitioned. It happened, now who am I, and back to the beginning of this journal page do I have valid claim to his early life experiences. It wasn't Cady who lived in Thorp but a male imaged construct by another first name but I was him then. Craig G's experiences of life as a young man have matches to mine as I too lived on a ranch near his parents' place. I knew of people he knew, we both had experiences in common, but as I relate them now as a female person do we still have that common bond? Does Cadance Alane

Anderson have any valid past before the here and now? As I speak what value judgments are people who listen to me making about my gender? Are they deciding whether or not to accept me as a woman even though they have come to a different conclusion? Am I like Blanche DuBois? As she tells us, "I have always depended on the kindness of strangers." There is a sadness to be at the mercy of anyone who I might speak to or even walk by. Will I ever be in a place where daily I will not be called upon to defend my gender?

***

Monday June 20, 2022. I received an email answer to my question I asked Dr. Stiller's transgender surgical coordinator Hailie. She told me at my three-month post-op appointment last Thursday the 16th, that she would check in with Alison about the cost of my next surgery. I have no quote or anything and it is like forty-five days away and I haven't put any deposit down. My email answer came in that same day. No I don't have to put down a deposit as my insurance is paying for the whole surgery less my deductible. Wow! What a wonderful shock! I have never had insurance pay for any of my other surgeries! It also brings to light the fact that this surgery is very real and coming fast to me. I put major things out of my mind using the buffer of time, so they can safely be ephemeral to me as is all of the future. Now it hangs as something real with insurance's backing and all. It is a gift really; an answer to a prayer I didn't pray for because I didn't think it was at all possible. I have been focused each day on recovery, holding myself together as the constant pain from my scalp fills every moment. Days pass, always there is itching, burning, and pressure. These receded so slowly that it is hard to judge the improvement in where I am today vs. last week vs. last month. Bottom line is I am slowly moving down the pain scale but I still have this pain trio and it is still hanging at seven out of ten. Good news is my hair is growing back in albeit very slowly. I now completely believe the narrations I have read of recovery from this surgery. I am looking at six months to over a year before these days are a vague memory. Now I have to come to terms that I will still be in pain from this surgery while I am having another surgery done to my body. This is so daunting so depressing to face the day after what bottom surgery will bring to add to the pain I will already have... All I can hope for is to look forward to a year from this August in hope a new me will be better off for what is left of life.

***

Tuesday June 21, 2022. The longest day of the year; it is 10:00 and there is still a little day light left. Corey has Covid, Mindy has had Covid; the whole family across the street from Casey's has Covid. Casey is thinking he has come down with it.

Allie over at Smart Orthodontics is so supportive of our transition that it is a gift to keep them appraised of surgeries I have had and those coming up. Tina has asked about us so I sent before-pictures and after-pictures to Allie to share next time Tina is in the office.

***

Wednesday June 22, 2022. I have five more months of ortho treatments to go, okay except our dentist wants to cap tooth number 18 as soon as possible and our orthodontist would like to wait until she is done.

I have been reading online about Dr. Stiller and zero depth Vaginoplasty (Vulvoplasty). The write-up on his site sounds so perfect. I have been in dread of another surgery then cycled to being neutral about it. At this moment I am at peace with the coming surgery. It is beginning to dawn on me that transition is coming to a natural close. Not like tomorrow or next month but something like a year from now. I wonder what this will be like or how will this be defined. My ortho will be done, hair grown back, and all male plumbing reshaped. Surgical recovery near complete and constant pain only a memory.

***

Tuesday July 12, 2022. If my surgery date remains stable I have approximately twelve showers left before we leave to drive to Spokane. Five weeks is all that is left to me before I lose my unicorn status. I am not making light of what's to come in any way. I gave myself a dose of the seriousness of what we will be facing by going over the pre-surgical and post-surgical instructions from my packet from Hailie the care coordinator for transgender patients at Dr. Stiller's practice. I have all the paperwork needed because I just had FFS four months ago and everything should still be valid. The amazing thing is Medicare is going to pay for this surgery! Every other affirming surgery I have had was completely out of pocket, a big burden, but Cathy and I figured it was the price we had to pay. Back to the serious side of the surgery and recovery: We decided on zero depth or what is called vulvoplasty over full depth vaginoplasty. Our reasoning was recovery time was said to be shorter and there wasn't the need for lifetime dilation. Yes the recovery is shorter but both require drains, catheters, and surgical packing. Both relocate the urethra, dissect the penis to form a vulva, and split the scrotum to form labia. Both require the same pre-opt cleaning out of rectum. The difference is vaginoplasty cuts into the pelvic floor muscles where the vulvoplasty does not. So, when I wake up from surgery things will be different. I will be swollen and without lifelong body parts. There will be a tube sticking into me where my penis had been and packing glued, stitched, and taped all around it. It will take months for the swelling to go down and for urination not to spray all over (welcome to womanhood it says in the docs). What will I feel in the place where my penis had been, anything or nothing? Some days I feel like I don't have a penis perhaps it is my mind getting ready for what is to come. I look at the pictures of the completed surgery and all that is needed to get ready and recover then a shudder runs through me followed by an odd sense of looking forward to it. I go from wondering what the heck am I doing to bring it on. I have had these same feelings with each affirming surgery I have had. Each time before a surgery I doubt myself and my authenticity as to who and what I am; this is followed by absolute clarification afterward. I don't know why I doubt because we have come so far now this is just one last step to take, one more hill to climb, and one more travail to live through. This will be the most intense challenge for Cathy to take care of me and she isn't even blinking at it, love will do that it sure does for me when I take care of her.

Corey, Melinda, and Quince will be here from Monday the 18th night until Monday the 25th. They will visit with us, attend the Anderson family picnic at Seahurst Park (Casey and Mindy are hosting it), and visit with some of their friends who live in and around Seattle. I sure hope that we picked out the right venue for the picnic fingers crossed. We have so much to do to our house to get ready for their staying with us. Also, we have the Taneum Creek Cabin from the 26th until the 28th. Hopefully Colby will get to come see us and with luck maybe Casey will drive over for day trip.

***

Friday July 15, 2022. The oddest thing has been happening to me. I have been looking forward to my coming bottom surgery. It crosses my mind off and on about how nice it will be afterward. I notice when I happen not to have any feeling from my genitals and ponder how this will be my new normal. I go to the bathroom and ponder how I will not have to hold anything down anymore. Sure, it will be messy after surgery but at some time in the coming future it will calm down to a manageable normal action. I hope and dream that this surgery will have the shortest recovery of all I have had so far. It would be such a blessing if I just flew through the whole process with little pain and super-fast healing. Everything would function just as it is supposed to and I will be complete. This all started after Cathy and I attended Michael's family picnic. Michael invited us to come, especially to see his mom. I was female to all these nice older people at this picnic no having to correct anyone it just happened naturally. My voice worked better than I can remember it ever doing at staying in the female range. Greg came and our conversations fell to everyday things carefully avoiding anything personal about me. This does not mean any acceptance on his part but does the lay ground work for some kind of relationship sometime in the future. It was so nice; I think that is when I began to not fear the coming surgery with all its possible complications but embrace all it could do for me.

We drove to the Sequim Lavender Festival this morning to meet up with Cathy's mom and sister Linda. Marcus has a booth full of tie-

704

dye shirts for sale and we are excited to shop. The drive was easy, we listened to Perry Mason solve another murder as the miles passed by. Marcus at his tie-dye booth was sweet to us and the weather was tolerable. It almost had the feeling of old times, but too much has happen to everyone. We all are changed in some fundamental way, not for better but for the worse. Cathy's mom now has a wheel walker that she is getting used to; works well on cement but not so much on grass. Corey, Melinda, and Quince will be here Monday night for a week's stay. We will spend the weekend getting ready for them.

***

Tuesday July 26, 2022. We did get the house all straightened up, matter of fact parts of it haven't been this clean and tidy for a long time… I worried so much about the reunion picnic venue but in the end it was just perfect. It was an amazing family time, we had fifty Anderson relations show up even folks from Minnesota and California came. The downside for me is no matter how I tried to contact Dianne and Audrey either by phone or email I never got a reply back. This broke my heart because Audrey was so upset that she couldn't come to the last picnic. I had promised myself to make sure she wouldn't miss this one. Dianne too. And still, they did… Empathy is so lost now; you would think that family would rally to help their mothers etc., to get to events. On the other hand, we did have Aunt Luella come as Carol took it on herself to drive her.

***

Wednesday July 27, 2022. This has been the hottest part of summer so far in the low nineties. We put our air conditioner into our window, should only need it the remainder of this week. I have a little over two weeks until surgery. I had several conversations during the picnic about my transition, one uniquely odd one with Trepp. He said something about being in a gay dorm during college and that one guy who came out as trans, would a year later lose his best friend because of it. His ex-friend told him that their relationship had been built on a lie. Trepp was passionate in telling me this story and I was careful to hear him but unsure what his reason was in telling it. Catrina is head of stable security at Emerald Downs and knows our neighbor Sylvia. Catrina also wanted to know all about me, kind of in the same way Tamara did: Rapid fire stuff, such as why did I wait so long etc., I always try to inject some humor into this direct fire at target 'me' questioning tool. I talked to Aunt Luella (the last surviving sister of my dad) about my name now being Cadance she told me she will always see me as C---- I told her I just wanted to make sure I had done my due diligence in telling her. I did finally get hold of Dianne she had gotten my messages but was out at the coast with her grandson that weekend. I still have no way to get hold of Audrey. I will call Jim and Arlene sometime this next week about it. Tony told us Tom, who didn't come was having health problems with his thyroid.

I have four or five showers left before we leave for Spokane. Surgery stuff: I am going to have surgery before I am healed from my last surgery. I still don't have feeling on the top of my head, the front of my neck is continuously sore and stiff, and the scars behind my ears still hurt to sleep on. What kind of shape will I be in after this coming surgery? It is a huge thing I am going to have done to me. Although it is not full vaginoplasty in that the surgeon doesn't cut into the pelvic floor muscles he does move my urethra and disassemble my penis and scrotum. Drains, catheters, blood, and pain… Cathy is level headed on this being done, she knows me and she knows us. She has said, "This is the time for this to be done, we don't know what the future will be like if we wait." The reality is the left and right both use the trans issue as a battlefield without any concern for the humanity of the issue. It is just another thing to beat each other up with just like abortion. There are no people associated, no struggling souls just faceless numbers. But the truth is, there are real human beings at risk just trying to make it through life having hope that they have a champion on one side or the other. They don't, and this is the harsh reality that many have yet to comprehend.

***

Saturday July 30, 2022. Another hot day (95 degrees) spent in our bedroom near the air conditioner. Family all around us is busy within themselves so Cathy and I have to be our own best company. Michael is hard put with this heat; he is now seeing a specialist about the swelling of both his legs. This swelling is serious; he had also developed an infection in the skin on his legs, which was now splitting open leaving open wounds. Those wounds were not responding to antibiotics. I would love to call him to talk about my upcoming surgery but there isn't room on his plate to do this. God has given me several other folks to chat with and this helps. When I told one nice lady about my journaling she responded that I should be doing that right now! "You're going to want to remember how you felt right before having surgery. A month from now the memory will have faded." She was right so here I go.

I have seventeen days until Dr. Stiller performs a surgery that no one will see but will affect me more than any other has. I have had parts of myself shaved, trimmed off, and my belly fat moved to my breasts; these are visible to myself and others. I did have my testes removed completely but they had become a constant source of physical pain, I had no use for the hormone they produced and being internal, they are not so very visible to me. The bottom surgery I am going to have removes my penis; it is both healthy and functional in urinating but not so much in anything else... I was thinking about my body this morning just before getting up from bed. I do stretches next to the bed before dressing and as I massaged my legs after a yoga stretch I thought, I appreciate my legs. Over the years they have given me pain for whatever reason but they have moved my body when I asked them to. Funny I thought, I appreciate all my body parts for the same reason, it was just the arrangement of those parts that was so dour to my psyche. Up until now the gender affirming surgeries kept my body parts intact just rearranged them into proper form and function. This excludes my testes but as I said they had become a source of pain and not so directly visible to me. Back to my penis, it in step with my testes has given us two wonderful sons, and a kind of release valve from the pressure of being male but it is wrong. I do not hate it or condemn it but it is wrong. What I am trying to say is it has never been a natural part of me but something that was unnatural to have. There was a release of that 'unnatural feeling' when my testes were removed and I expect this will occur when my penis is removed also. I will keep in mind that parts of my penis will be reformed into my new female genitalia so some of what is lost will live on.

Several people have asked me how I feel about my upcoming surgery (our surgery really as it affects both of us). My answer is I am both excited and terrified. Excited at the prospect of being complete in mind and body, terrified by all my body is going to be put through and the recovery afterward. Facing pre-op steps of enemas, blood tests (at the last minute that could derail things), then waking up with drains and a catheter in place where I used to have a penis. Followed by days and nights of post-op pain. All of this culminated into the single question of; how long will it take my slow to heal body to rally once again and to find a way to function?

***

Tuesday August 2, 2022. This is the birthday month of my birth family, all three the exception being me in May. Today we got up at ten o'clock and had a breakfast of an egg and toast, reverting back from our hot-weather breakfast of fruit smoothies and protein bars. It was much cooler so we shut off the air conditioner and opened the front door to welcome the cool morning air. This morning I yielded to the 'get everything done that I won't be able to do after surgery' bug. We got the big ladder up so I could climb onto the roof to put new plastic over our retired metal chimney. As is always the case when I was up there it became apparent that more needed doing. I saw a gutter full of debris and the carport roof had tons of dry moss that needed to be removed before the fall rains came. I also notice how fearful I have become in being up on the roof. My natural balance is gone and because of foot pain I move about in a very dangerous way. I used to be proud of my ability to maintain the roof, it was even fun to up there, but now my aging body forces me to trade this away for safety sake. Anyway, I did not fall and the chimney, gutters, and carport roof are all good until next summer. I can't move the ladder myself anymore so it is all about teamwork between Cathy and me. We both have

Forever and Two Days More

electrolysis appointments with Marsha over at Caddell's at 4:30. The realization that surgery is really going to happen is weighing down on me, especially since it is August and not back in safe July anymore. Caddell's has a new receptionist, she is older and kind of shuffles around doing stuff. She is a stranger to us but we see Hope over in her new office and marched in to say hello. We chat and she is impressed with my coming surgery and has a few suggestions to help out. Hope is in love with the idea of us remaining together; she and her partner haven't stayed together after bottom surgery. Cathy has electrolysis with Marsha first so I chat a little more with Hope. Debbie pops in and I get to talk about my surgery again with a very affirming caring lady. They are all so encouraging and loving; I feel part of this place after fifteen years. Debbie reassures me that several women who she knows have had surgery with Dr. Stiller and none of them have been disappointed with the surgery. She tells me she has only heard good things about him. Debbie also made me promise to have Cathy let her know how the surgery is going. Debbie tells me she would love for Dr. Stiller to know that it is Caddell's who is doing his patients' hair removal so that he might come to trust her work; I promise to name drop. I get the best hug from Debbie and it is my turn with Marsha. I leave Cathy in the reception lobby to chat with everyone and follow Marsha to her new treatment room. Marsha is eager to chat and asks, "What do you want done today." I tell her, I have only one hair that is laughing at me that needs to be taken care of. She replies, "Only one?" Yup just one, I mostly want to catch up with you and to talk about my bottom surgery. We have been together all through my transition and I appreciate you so much. You were so gentle with me when I came out to you as transgender all those years ago, so supportive I felt like the two of us were a team from then on. Along with Sandy you were just who I needed to help me. You two amazing ladies, both with such important experience ranging back to Marsha Botzer and the early years of folks transitioning in the Seattle area. I needed your wisdom and your care, thank you Marsha. We chatted on and on she did find the one dark hair on my chin but none other than that on my face. I had her do my arms and as she poked along we had the best time

709

talking as old friends. I fully explained the surgery to her in every detail and promised to have Cathy let her know on how I was doing as soon as it was over. I got the best hug yet as we parted. Every time I pull into a parking lot at some store I think of Marsha's trick of 'just knowing' there will be a spot open for her and sure enough one is waiting for her. It's a good philosophy; perhaps this surgery is my parking spot waiting for years for me to pull into it. So, we had lots of affirming affection from some very caring friends that consider Cathy and me as family. I was very tired as we got into the car; the weight of the coming surgery was upon me. It's coming at me; I am going to go through with it, while I never thought I would come to this place in my journey. It was out of my reach physically, financially, Biblically, and chronologically. And yet here I am so ecstatic and so frightened.

***

Wednesday August 3, 2022. Deaconess Hospital called me to get health information. The lady was no nonsense and very business-like. I sent an email to Hailie at Dr. Stiller's with some questions and got a response from April.

***

Saturday August 6, 2022. Here we are, with Casey's away at Long Beach and Corey's away in St. Louis. One week until we travel to Spokane to meet with fate. Speaking of fate, I was wondering what I would post on FB as a sort of conclusion to transitioning… I awoke to the question and had the wonderfully clear answer as I open my eyes but can't keep it for more than a few minutes. Here are scraps that did stick:

I have been public to family and friends on Facebook about me medically transitioning male to female. You have seen snips of my surgeries in step with Cathy's surgeries. We traded her breast reduction for my enhancement, body contouring to give us both waists, our faces were changed to smooth out wrinkles, open up eyes, and then my nose reshaped along with my forehead to feminize my face. Thousands of little red-hot laser and electrolysis burns all over my body and on parts of hers. My neck smoothed out by scraping my

710

Adam's apple flat and male organs cast away. Over six hundred hours in therapy with a truly great mental health counselor specializing in gender issues. All that is left is one final surgery to complete my (ours really) personal cycle of transition. In the beginning I didn't think it would be needed just as I didn't think any of them would be, but I didn't understand a lot of things about me. I only knew mental pain, discord, and uncontrollable hopelessness. In the end I chose life and God brought resource after resource to guide me along. I began to understand little by little and in doing so began to rebuild my path in life. Now here I am at the doorstep of my last surgery that no one will see but means so much. Everyone we have spoken to who has had gender surgery (bottom surgery is the slang term for it) reports the same outcome and that is the relief it gives. It is not about sex it is the relief of truly being part of self in mind and body. Cathy and I have chosen the least invasive form of it but still it will be the hardest recovery so far but if successful comes with the great reward of inner peace. And with this surgery comes the end of transition, oh there will be revisions here and there as healing continues for years really, but the medical part will be over. Learning and growing as female, in the last years of my life, is not transition but more of a settling down result, just as ongoing aging is. I have tried to make sense of life from the moment I became sentient. As a child I came to know Jesus Christ's gift to us of pure love and forgiveness of our base sins allowing us a path to pray to the Almighty perfect God of all creation. This beautiful perfect equation rested in my heart all of my life but no other experience in childhood or adulthood for that matter made sense no matter how my mind tried to order them. I chose the female name 'Cadance' because the rhythm and dance of life was impossible to follow all through my life as male imaged. It's only now possible in the smallest of ways, as Cadance grows stronger little by little. If you doubt the reality of being transgender just look at all the pain and loss we go through to complete our journeys. So here you go, I have shared all that Cathy and I journeyed to get to truly being us. In less than one week we will face the biggest change and the greatest challenge to any couple. The journey that started in 1973 with two young adults sitting on a front porch in the cool evening air of summer holding hands, they had been baking chocolate chip cookies; one turned to the other and said, "I have something to tell you about me." They stayed together after that for the journey had started with consent and is now near a new milestone...

***

Friday September 2, 2022. My second life-giving surgery (this time SRS) occurred seventeen days ago and here I sit with the most profound sense of peace I have ever known. Of the two surgeries (FFS and SRS), FFS was harder to recover from. I don't feel a loss of any part of my body; instead, I have a new feeling of restored balance. This time my surgery was at Deaconess Hospital in place of Dr. Stiller's office. Our biggest fear was me being trapped in the hospital overnight and separated from Cathy. This fear comes from our time of Covid. Deaconess Hospital has a waiting room with a reader board showing patient progress from pre-op, surgery, post-op, and recovery. Cathy was allowed to be with me in recovery where our fear almost became real as I was slow to wake up and couldn't feel my feet. The nurse told us they were waiting for a room to be available for an overnight, which panicked both of us. Cathy was insistent that I be released; she was with me and fully capable of caring for me (you go girl). In the end and after all the aftercare instructions were drilled into my nurse-to-be Cathy, I was wheeled out and put into our car. There wasn't a moment of regret, only of accomplishment. Of course, I had a catheter for a week but no great discomfort. I had always had great fear of all things medical but here I am having overcome them. We had several checkups with Doctor Stiller and staff, each one a step toward removing layers of dressings separating me from the new me. Now to recount the last appointment before our final release into the wild...

We overcame the barrier left by the shadow of Covid by pulling on our green tie-dyed masks as we entered the door proclaiming Stiller Aesthetics. We are old timers here greeted warmly by the ladies sitting at the reception desk who now joyfully peek over their screens at us. There is a sign-in screen on a freestanding pad for Cathy to poke at, even here we have learned the trick of just touching the menu button

712

marked 'no cards' as a shortcut in the process. Plastic surgeon's offices are a pass-thru affair; one patient after another checking in for a surgery then checking out after the completion of that surgery. All drift away and become a forgotten accomplishment of the practice joining the constant flow of anonymous people through the office. Of course, there are always a few who stand out in one way or another. Cathy and I are one of the few; everyone in the office-side and the medical-side of this practice has told us this. It could have been the gluten-free chocolate chip cookies I baked (twelve dozen total) to give to everyone, or the fact we always wear matching tie-dye shirts, or that we gave Dr. Stiller a shirt to match ours (we gave Kelly one too; she was very special to us), or that I cried with joy when my FFS dressing came off and again when my vaginoplasty dressing came off (I was overcome in both cases), or was it the nice email I wrote to Dr. Stiller and sent through Kelly articulating the life-changing and life-giving he had just granted me with these surgeries. In the end I think it was the fact that Cathy and I were so outwardly and inwardly in love with each other, we had together overcome so much and in the end never faltered in that love. We were cute as a couple but more importantly we belonged together; our love was apparent this set us apart.

So, after we checked in, Shelly the receptionist wanted to know how far in our list of things to do in Spokane we had gotten through. I had previously explained to her that after I was free of my catheter I realized this was as much of a vacation as a surgery stay and we needed to treat it this way. She energetically offered up a verbal list of places to see and do that she loved about Spokane while Cathy quickly took note. Our promise was to report back to her and the other office ladies of our adventures at each place. We recounted each of our adventures to her and those around her: River Front Park and its sky ride, the shops nearby reflecting the book *To Kill a Mocking Bird* by Harper Lee, the parks and gardens all around the city, and in each place someone local after being told we were visiting their city would add more places and things to our list. They both were excited by our adventure and loved that they had started us off on it. Cathy sat down and I stood (more comfortable now than sitting for me) to wait for someone to come get us. The door leading to the inner sanctum of exam rooms and operating suite opened and out rushed an excited Kelly arms open to give us a hug. We had met Kelly when we first came to Dr. Stiller's for a consultation for an FFS procedure; she was the surgical consultant and scheduler for facial procedures. She was full of energy and compassion and we hit it off at her first smile. She loved our story of how we faced transition together and she loved my name 'Cadance'. We would trade emails back and forth sharing pictures of us in our many tie-dye shirts. It was Kelly who asked us to go along with a joke the staff was playing on Dr. Stiller one day. Now she hugged us on this, our last appointment, telling us that we would always be her favorite patients. She added, "You two will always be stand-outs here with us above all the rest, just remember this and if I can do anything for you I am just an email away, oh and keep sending pictures to share, you just don't realize how special you two are to us here."

After Kelly left we were led to exam room two, I was given a gown, and told to undress. We had been in all three exam rooms; one and two were simple affairs of a central chair, wheeled stool, and a single visitor chair. Exam room three (or treatment room) was at least twice as big with many cabinets and medical paraphernalia; this room sported a plaque outlining Dr. Stiller's medical career to the present. Each room has a warning sign not to smoke or vape in this room. Anyway, I stood and pondered the chair, which was covered with paper and an absorbent pad. It is a padded exam chair and I have faced it before when I had my catheter out a week ago. I am sore in sitting and it takes a bit to work myself to face sitting down. I take off my shoes, cutoffs, and leak proof undies (I used Depends), leaving my shirt and socks on. I carefully try to position my sore bottom gently down on the chair then drape the gown over my bare legs in a modest fashion. Done! I'm okay for the moment if I sit still. I look around the room taking familiar note of the picture (nude woman sitting with her back to the viewer) stuck to the wall at a slight angle, the small sink, counter, and cabinets, and Cathy sitting watching me. We chat and tease each other; this is the appointment that will give us clearance to

714

travel home tomorrow. Casey is flying in tonight and will be our driver to take the pressure off of Cathy and me. It will be a long trip and I hope a somewhat comfortable one for me, but I am realistic also. Very soon Dr. Stiller will come in, greet us, and pull the two sliding footrests out from their hidden pockets on either side of the chair, then ask me to scoot forward and put my feet in the stirrups.

This isn't the first time recalling the week prior; then it was to remove my catheter and pass judgment on the work he had done the week before. Dr. Stiller had been chatty, catching up on how I had been feeling over that week, then he told me in a gentle voice, "Now is the time to remove the catheter, it will be over in just a minute take a breath and try not to tense up." I watch as he used a syringe to deflate the catheter's balloon in my bladder holding the catheter in place. With his next movement my breath was taken away completely leaving me struggling in vain to gain control of my body. In just a few seconds it was over and I was told to start breathing again. I needed the reminder as it felt as if my urethra had been pulled inside out but the sudden pain gave way for relief to come in as soon as I let it in. He examined his work and asked if I would like to see it. Yes! He handed me a mirror and then lifted each new structure for me to see, mons pubis, labia majora, labia minora, clitoris hood, clitoris, urethra, and opening where my vagina would be. My expectations were never so high as this; to actually have all these female structures were just too much to hope for. I became overwhelmed and tears came, then elation, then joy, all cycled over and over. It is indescribable to anyone who is not transgender the relief/joy of that moment; as close as I can match it to is like being told that the war (pick a war) is over. Everyone is coming home, no more fear, no struggle to exist, no more shortages or blackouts, your life is yours once again to live. Dr. Stiller was even moved by my reaction.

Now back to the present, here we are again at the end of this journey, the four of us: doctor, his very quiet PA taking notes in the corner, Cathy, and me. Dr. Stiller examines my new structures as I ask questions about the flow of pink tinged liquid on my pad. We want to know if it is normal and when it might either stop or be a sign of trouble. He tells us that it is normal and then finds that I have burst a stitch. My heart sinks. Without comment, he pulls out a piece of four by four gauze from a drawer, wraps it around his finger, and guides it into the pocket that would hold the vaginal opening. "This will heal it up by drawing fluids to the wound; it should change back to a beefy red over time. Change the gauze as needed. Other than that, you are free to travel but every hour or so stop and walk around, promise me you'll do this." Yes, we promise... Exam is over hugs to everyone, we have a telehealth appointment in two weeks. With this both sweet and somewhat sour outcome, because of the burst stitch, our adventure is ended... We did make the acquaintance of Cassie (Cassandra) and Henry. She was my surgery sister; she had the same surgery but four days after me. We messaged each other during our time together. Since I was ahead of her I could answer many questions about each day of recovery that she would be facing. On the last day of our stay, I asked if she would like a dozen eggs we had left over and she responded, "Yes, I love eggs!" Cathy and I drove to the trailer park where she and her partner were staying. Cassie is fifty and Henry is forty-seven both are lovely people. Cathy loved talking with Henry sharing what it is like to be a spouse to a trans partner and I with Cassie on our mutual experiences. They live in Puyallup! I hope that the future will allow us to meet again... We are now friends on Facebook.

Casey did arrive the night before we were to drive home. It was a truly unique experience to once again spend the night under the same roof with our son, just Casey and us. As promised Casey was happy to stop every hour or two as I felt the need to stiffly walk around. I have come to know every bump on I-90 personally. The air-inflated donut worked best for me but it was a job keeping a position that was tolerable. I did use the proper restrooms without fear this time; the sound of me urinating was just the same as every other female in the stalls near me. I have been fearfully nervous about this surgery for the last five months. It is over now; I have no feeling of loss of any body part at all just, a feeling of normalcy of my new but mentally old to me structures. I asked Dr. Stiller to reuse (repurpose) as much tissue as possible from my old genitals and he did as I asked. Much of the tissues between male and female are the same just repurposed. Cathy and I now have all of what is left of our lives. There is healing to wait for and recovery to work on, there may be revisions needed to surgical sites or complications to be faced, but in any case our medical transition is done and guess what? We still love each other!

***

Friday December 2, 2022. I got my braces removed today, marking the end of my orthodontics treatments. Ali is such a wonderful person; she is stanchly supportive of people living their authentic selves. She told me it was an honor and a joy to have watched me as I transitioned. You never know whose life you touch as yours is made right…

Our grandteen has come out as nonbinary and is using the pronouns they and them. This has given us pause, or should I say given Cathy pause to understand that nonbinary describes how she has always felt but had no words to use. Cathy has been reflecting on how she has drifted between the two shores of the binary all her life never fully comfortable on the female shore. Here at long last is a moniker she can use to purvey the structure of the feeling that kept her out of place and lost all of her youth. Cady had words for her torment of being male-imaged on that night so long ago but Cathy didn't; her torment remained undefined in her mind. That torment of being female with all it entails but dysphoric in actualizing that binary state of being physically and mentally female especially in intimacy. Moment by moment Cathy is female but mentally isolated within that gender binary, both to herself and from other binary females. To an observer of the two of us, her sexual attraction on the surface would appear to be to other females, but she is not gay in the traditional sense; neither is she straight in the traditional sense, the result is a mixture of both. What Cathy is attracted to is an all-encompassing intimate friendship holding heartfelt love for each other and breaching the boundary of any gender restriction. In better words, Cady being transgender brings a newfound freedom to their relationship for both of them. Cathy says there was something she saw in Cady on that summer night so long

717

ago that touched a hidden place in her heart and now there is nothing to hide anymore.

***

In the end, after all was said and done, I realized that both of us were continually searching for a path to stay together as a couple. We wanted this feeling we had for each other to grow and not ever be lost, right from the start of our lives together and right through transition. We both truly loved each other; that never wavered but it wasn't until I was forced to face transition that the continual search became a desperate one for both of us. I shuddered and Cathy quaked; we became ourselves, our love for one another became this wonderful deep experience that we had been searching for. In the truest sense, our life-long fear of losing each other every step of the way led to the most fulfilling love we now have forever and two days more.

About the Authors

We walk in our neighborhood daily, always wearing matching tie-dye shirts and black tights. Our neighbors have all been told our story and accept us as Cathy and Cady. I always wave at passing cars on our quiet side street and, after a while, now get friendly waves in return. We walk or perhaps parade each day as our unique selves through our little loop walk, two older ladies always matching right down to our tennis shoes. We say hello to strangers, people walking dogs, and our neighbors. Nick and Kim, who live next to the house our son used to live in, are always a joy to stop and talk too. They have turned their house into a little farm, complete with a few chickens; so cool! When Colby was little, he would peek through their shared fence looking for Kim to talk too. Sheila (our first reader) and Kevin walking their dogs, John and Donna busy with their little grandkids, Katrina (who is never still), Verna (who is so publicly minded), Dave and Bonnie with their lovely roses, John and Margaret with their very friendly big dogs always aching to get Cathy's attention, and Bob with the best kept motor home around. All these folks are the heart of our little world and all just see us and accept us as we are. Our very close next-door neighbors Sylvia and Arlene who we have known for most of our married life are our now supportive friends to us. There are exceptions, couples that no longer speak to us, as well as some family members, but overall, we find so much joy in all who are accepting and encouraging to us. Life is good and we're happy together.

Made in the USA
Middletown, DE
10 September 2024

60133756R00432